HANDBOOK OF DEVELOPMENTAL FAMILY PSYCHOLOGY AND PSYCHOPATHOLOGY

Recent titles in the

Wiley Series on Personality Processes

Irving B. Weiner, *Editor*

University of South Florida

Handbook of Developmental Family Psychology and Psychopathology

Luciano L'Abate, Editor

A WILEY-INTERSCIENCE PUBLICATION

JOHN WILEY & SONS, INC.

New York • Chichester • Brisbane • Toronto • Singapore

Library of Congress Cataloging-in-Publication Data:

Handbook of developmental family psychology and psychopathology/
   edited by Luciano L'Abate.
      p.   cm.—(Wiley series on personality processes)
   Includes index.
   ISBN 0-471-53527-3 (cloth : alk. paper)
   1. Family—Mental health.   2. Family—Psychological aspects.
   3. Problem Families.   I. L'Abate, Luciano, 1928-   .   II. Series.
      [DNLM: 1. Family—psychology.   2. Family Therapy—methods.
   3. Psychopathology.   WM 430.5F2 H23546 1994]
RC455.4.F3M35   1994
306.85—dc20
DNLM/DLC
For Library of Congress   93-17725

Contributors

James F. Alexander, Ph.D.
Professor of Psychology
University of Utah
Salt Lake City, Utah

Ileana Arias, Ph.D.
Associate Professor of Psychology
University of Georgia
Athens, Georgia

Lynn Barnett-Morris, Ph.D.
Associate Professor
Department of Leisure Studies
University of Illinois
Champaign, Illinois

Victor G. Cicirelli, Ph.D.
Professor of Developmental and
    Aging Psychology
Purdue University
West Lafayette, Indiana

Andrew Christensen, Ph.D.
Professor of Psychology
University of California, Los Angeles
Los Angeles, California

C. Ewing Cooley, Ed.D.
President
Fourth Street Foundation
Arlington, Texas

Ann C. Crouter, Ph.D.
Associate Professor of Human
    Development
Department of Human Development
    and Family Studies
The Pennsylvania State University
University Park, Pennsylvania

Mario Cusinato, Ph.D.
Dipartimento di Psicologia Generale
Universitá degli Studi
Padova, Italy

W. Hobart Davies, Ph.D.
Research Associate
Department of Psychology
Michigan State University
East Lansing, Michigan

Doris R. Entwisle, Ph.D.
Professor of Sociology
The Johns Hopkins University
Baltimore, Maryland

Frank D. Fincham, Ph.D.
Professor of Psychology
University of Illinois
Champaign, Illinois

Hiram E. Fitzgerald, Ph.D.
Professor of Psychology
Michigan State University
East Lansing, Michigan

Tamara L. Fuller, M.S.
Department of Psychology
University of Illinois
Champaign, Illinois

Ian H. Gotlib, Ph.D.
Professor of Psychology
Northwestern University
Evanston, Illinois

David A. Gray, Ph.D.
Associate Professor and Chairman
Department of Management
University of Texas at Arlington
Arlington, Texas

Jeffrey J. Haugaard, Ph.D.
Assistant Professor
Department of Human Development
    and Family Studies
Cornell University
Ithaca, New York

Christopher L. Heavey, Ph.D.
Assistant Professor of Psychology
University of Nevada
Las Vegas, Nevada

Anita Landau Hurtig, Ph.D.
Clinical Associate Professor
Department of Pediatrics
University of Illinois at Chicago
Chicago, Illinois

Penny B. Jameson, Ph.D.
Department of Psychology
University of Utah
Salt Lake, City, Utah

Janice R. Joplin, M.A.
Graduate Research Associate
Department of Management
University of Texas at Arlington
Arlington, Texas

Ernest N. Jouriles, Ph.D.
Assistant Professor of Psychology
University of Houston
Houston, Texas

Michael T. Klinger, Ph.D.
Research Associate
Department of Psychology
Michigan State University
East Lasing, Michigan

Luciano L'Abate, Ph.D.
Professor Emeritus of Psychology
Georgia State University
Atlanta, Georgia

Catherine M. Lee, Ph.D.
Associate Professor
Child Study Center
University of Ottawa
Ottawa, Ontario, Canada

Jay A. Mancini, Ph.D.
Professor and Department Head
Department of Family and Child
    Development
Virginia Polytechnic Institute and
    State University
Blacksburg, Virginia

Cathleen Erin McGreal, Ph.D.
Assistant Professor of Psychology
Michigan State University
East Lansing, Michigan

Elizabeth G. Menaghan, Ph.D.
Professor of Sociology
Ohio State University
Columbus, Ohio

K. Daniel O'Leary, Ph.D.
Distinguished Professor of
    Psychology
State University of New York at
    Stony Brook
Stony Brook, New York

Dennis K. Orthner, Ph.D.
Professor of Families and Children
School of Social Work
The University of North Carolina
Chapel Hill, North Carolina

Karen Taylor Pape, B.S.
Research Assistant
Department of Psychology
University of Georgia
Athens, Georgia

James Campbell Quick, Ph.D.
Professor of Management
University of Texas at Arlington
Arlington, Texas

Brenda Seery, M.A.
Doctoral Candidate
Department of Human Development
    and Family Studies
The Pennsylvania State University
University Park, Pennsylvania

James L. Shenk, Ph.D.
Cognitive Therapy Institute
San Diego, California

Clifford H. Swensen, Jr., Ph.D.
Professor of Psychological Sciences
Purdue University
West Lafayette, Indiana

Robert A. Zucker, Ph.D.
Professor of Psychology
Michigan State University
East Lansing, Michigan

Series Preface

This series of books is addressed to behavioral scientists interested in the nature of human personality. Its scope should prove pertinent to personality theorists and researchers as well as to clinicians concerned with applying an understanding of personality processes to the amelioration of emotional difficulties in living. To this end, the series provides a scholarly integration of theoretical formulations, empirical data, and practical recommendations.

Six major aspects of studying and learning about human personality can be designated: personality theory, personality structure and dynamics, personality development, personality assessment, personality change, and personality adjustment. In exploring these aspects of personality, the books in the series discuss a number of distinct but related subject areas: the nature and implications of various theories of personality; personality characteristics that account for consistencies and variations in human behavior; the emergence of personality processes in children and adolescents; the use of interviewing and testing procedures to evaluate individual differences in personality; efforts to modify personality styles through psychotherapy, counseling, behavior therapy, and other methods of influence; and patterns of abnormal personality functioning that impair individual competence.

IRVING B. WEINER

University of South Florida
Tampa, Florida

Preface

This book was edited to follow up on and bring up to date a previous publication dealing with the then new field of family psychology (L'Abate, 1985). The previous publication was a cross-sectional view of family psychology, devoid of developmental and psychopathological perspectives. Both perspectives are the major focus of this book. Despite the fact that there is no acknowledged discipline of family psychology, various strands indicate continuous growth in this field. This book, as did the previous one, wants to capture under one cover all the existing strands that have come to the fore in multifarious fashion in the last decade. It affirms that all these strands, when put together, indeed form a substantive body of knowledge that makes up the discipline of family psychology.

As the previous publication did, this one came about as a result of the coercion and exhortation of psychology editor Herb Reich, whom I have known as a friend for more years than I care to remember. He prevailed up on me to undertake this book, knowing full well that this was the kind of project I would find very difficult, if not impossible, to refuse. Family psychology has been my major interest in the last quarter century, and the possibility of giving it a developmental, as well as a psychopathological, slant was too enticing to turn down.

Some contributors to the previous volume have also contributed to this publication, providing a valuable and necessary sense of continuity. Many contributors, of course, are new. Although I expected some objections to the title for this volume, none was raised. Every contributor seemed to understand what I meant when I mentioned this title, although no formal or substantive discipline of family psychology with its subordinate discipline of developmental family psychology as yet exists. I am grateful to all of the contributors for their gracious and collegiate collaboration.

The book is divided into three major parts. After a historical introduction, the major and more substantive part, Part 1, discusses most components of what represents an individual's family life cycle in its various manifestations. Part 2 deals with developmental psychopathology within the context of the family. Rather than repeat traditional nosological categories, it seemed more important to get to the roots of most psychopathology—physical illness and physical, emotional, and sexual abuse. What most authors found, however, was a paucity of developmental data, strengthening the possibility that various forms of abuse lie at the roots of much psychopathology, which then develops on its own. The abuse may disappear with time, but its costly and numerous effects may persist for the rest of a person's life and beyond, to second and third generations.

Part 3 has two chapters that examine the clinical and theoretical implications of the previous chapters, an effort well worth the extra time it took to complete this volume. Finally, it was important to prognosticate about the future of a field that still lacks academic recognition (world wide, few academic courses on family psychology exist). If it were not for family therapy, would the field of family psychology ever have emerged?

This volume should appeal to developmental, personality, and social psychologists, who talk in general about context, culture, ecology, environment, or "situation," but are not sure and cannot specify what this context is. It should appeal to students in training, who want a substantive preparation for a contextual approach to personality development, and to clinicians, who may want to find substance for what, up to now, may have seemed to be an ill-defined discipline. Family therapists, of course, should find this volume a background for strengthening their practice.

LUCIANO L'ABATE

Atlanta, Georgia
November 1993

Contents

Introduction

CHAPTER 1

What Is Developmental Family Psychology?

LUCIANO L'ABATE

Developmental family psychology concerns itself with the life cycles (most of them different) of various members of the same family as a unit. Emphasis on "various members of the same family" is not a trivial differentiation. Family psychology differs from family sociology and family therapy in stressing the relationship of each individual member to the other members of the same family. Family sociology and therapy, on the other hand, stress the importance of the family as a unit, as a system at a supraordinate level from the individual (L'Abate, 1992). The terms *span, course,* or *cycle* are used here interchangeably. A substantive body of knowledge and applications attests to and supports the emergence and existence of this field of study (Elder, 1984; Elder & Caspi, 1988; Hartup & Rubin, 1986; Kreppner & Lerner, 1989). Consequently, the purpose of this book is to put together some, if not most, of the literature on the developmental life span from the context of the family life cycle (Aldous, 1978; Baltes, Featherman, & Lerner, 1990; Baltes, Reese, & Nesselroade, 1988; Clausen, 1986; Goldberg & Deutsch, 1977; L'Abate, 1983, 1985, 1987; L'Abate & Thaxton, 1983; Steinberg, 1981; Sze, 1975), normal as well as abnormal (Allman & Jaffe, 1975; Hersen & Last, 1990), also including personality development (Lefrancois, 1990; Litz, 1976; Turner & Helms, 1986) and the social psychology of family development. This book should bridge the gaps among these psychological disciplines, integrating them into one framework.

V. C. Cicirelli (personal communication, November 14, 1990) noted that the foregoing nondefinition of family "still leaves open the meaning of family." What makes individuals members of the same family—blood relations; sharing the same household; meeting certain legal requirements; interacting in some fashion; or maintaining certain types of relationships? These questions in themselves can be used as criteria for a definition of what the family is. These criteria do not encompass the phenomenological definition of family as perceived by its members, who assert that they are family members as *they* understand it. This may not be an improvement over past definitions; however, it will have to suffice for the moment.

Various strands resulted in the genesis and production of this book. First, developmental psychology has expanded from a traditionally monadic, *behavior-*

in-a-vacuum view to a relational, transactional viewpoint that stresses the importance of family variables. This expansion included the realization that development takes place first in the context of marriage and the family, progressing from childhood friends, to school influences, peer pressure in adolescence, occupation, and leisure activities (Bowlby, 1969, 1973, 1980).

Second, development occurs along a variety of routes. Here, a *delta* model, much like the estuary of a large river, seems to embody the view that most individuals in most families go straight ahead, normatively following the mainstream, major flow of the river; whereas some go sideways and get lost in the marshes of life; others who go sideways come back to the mainstream; some stop altogether; some recoup; and some never recover along the path from birth to death (Caspi, Elder, & Herbener, 1990; White, 1991).

Third, no trajectory is like another trajectory. Yet, in the midst of all this variety, some similarities can be found. One can safely predict that most members of the same family will follow different life cycle patterns (Kreppner & Lerner, 1989; Rossi & Rossi, 1990). What similarities, if any, can we find among these differences?

Fourth, the transition to a transactional, multirelational, and multidirectional paradigm allowed us to see that development takes place within a context, and that the most immediate, influential context throughout the life span, *is* the family (Bell & Harper, 1977; Lerner & Spanier, 1978). Attachment and object relations theories (Bowlby, 1969, 1973, 1980) were helped in this regard by Ainsworth's operationalization of stranger's anxiety (Bretherton & Waters, 1985; Parkes & Stevenson-Hinde, 1982).

Fifth, in the field of interpersonal relationships, the interdependence of intimate relationships has emerged independently of developmental life span psychology or family therapy (Burgess & Huston, 1979; Duck, 1973, 1982, 1988; Gilmour & Duck, 1986; Hinde, 1979). This field assumes that behavior and personality develop in continuous and prolonged contact and exchange with important others.

Relationships, especially intimate relationships, are not only in vogue but de rigueur. Swensen's seminal work (1973) was followed by Burgess and Huston's (1979) work, wherein *exchange* and *interdependence* became the new "buzz" words. Kelley (1979), Kelley and Thibaut's (1978), and Murstein (1978) went more in the direction of close dyadic relationships, including marriage. Hinde (1979), to this day, has given the best summary of how social psychological concepts apply to intimate (close and prolonged) relationships. Eventually, this trend culminated with increased interest in the nature of love and intimacy (Cusinato & L'Abate, 1994; Derlega, 1984; Dion & Dion, 1985; Duck & Gilmour, 1981; Kelley et al., 1983; Perlman & Duck, 1987; Sternberg, 1987). As a result of this trend, social exchange theory became one of the more influential theories in family relationships (Nye, 1982). When applied to close, prolonged, *and committed* relationships, all the references above and many others not cited here, would form part—if not the bulk—of a new discipline of family psychology (L'Abate, 1983, 1985, 1987, 1992). To date, however, there is no formal field of family psychology as an academic discipline. In fact this term is often used synonymously with *family therapy* (Kaslow, 1990).

DEVELOPMENT OR SOCIALIZATION?

The term *development* implies to some the notion of growth from *inside* the individual, whereas the term *socialization* implies to others growth from *outside* the individual (Clausen, 1968; Danziger, 1971; Hoppe, Milton, & Simmel, 1970; McNeil, 1969; Zigler & Child, 1973). For instance, an early summary about theories of development had no reference to family or any other external socialization agents (Langer, 1969), supporting the conclusion that, at least in the past, developmental and personality psychology have viewed behavior as taking place in a *vacuum* (L'Abate, 1985). Fortunately, this view was corrected by other theoretical summaries (Baldwin, 1980; Maier, 1969). Rather than consider these terms as mutually exclusive, they could be viewed as two railroad tracks joined by ties or two sides of the same coin. One cannot exist without the other.

Socialization implies the influence of external agents, whereas development may imply, to some theorists, internal growth almost *despite* external agents (Clausen, 1968; Goslin, 1969; McNeil, 1969; Zigler & Child, 1973). In these early references, external agents, more often than not, were identified by distal and vague references such as *culture* or *society*, rather than by proximal factors, such as the parents or caretakers. Although more than 15 years ago references to the influence of the family on development were few and far between in most psychology textbooks, at least 15% of the pages in child development textbooks did refer to family-related variables as socialization agents (Dunne & L'Abate, 1977).

What percentage of developmental or socialization textbooks is presently devoted to family variables such as parents, siblings, family of origin, or marriage (L'Abate, 1985; Dunne & L'Abate, 1977)? There are still many textbooks on this topic, especially in the field of personality (Pervin, 1990), that contain either no references or a very few, almost trivial, number of references to family variables (Ault, 1980; Brodzinsky, Gormly, & Ambron, 1986; Eisenberg, 1987; Endler, Boulter, & Osser, 1968; LaBarba, 1981), perpetuating the myth of development in vacuum. A representative sample of most developmental life span psychology texts (Baltes & Brim, 1979; Baltes et al., 1990; Baltes & Schaie, 1973; Datan & Ginsberg, 1975; Goulet & Baltes, 1970; Nesselroade & Reese, 1973) yielded 7 chapters devoted to family-related topics out of 86 chapters, a percentage that approximates one found in an earlier analysis (Dunne & L'Abate, 1977). This percentage suggests that a relational; that is, contextual, perspective is not yet as influential as some would like to believe. The monadic paradigm is still stoutly entrenched in psychology, and it will take more than this or other works to change it. In a recent handbook of personality theory and research (Pervin, 1990), for instance, in 727 pages of text, there were no references to marriage and/or parents. Three pages were devoted to assortative mating, and nine passing references were made to families in general, families and anxiety states, families and influence on self-construction, families and personality disorder, families and siblings, twins, and variations in mental states related to families. Two chapters were devoted to person–situation interaction (Higgins, 1990; Magnusson, 1990) and one chapter to personality continuity and change across the life course (Caspi & Bem, 1990).

A related question is: With which parts of personal and personality development should we be concerned? Should we look at the development of affects over the life cycle and their relationship to the family? Should we look at cognitive development, as Rebok (1987) has done, and consider it separate and independent from affective, intellectual, and interpersonal development? Should we conclude from the above considerations that developmental psychology is as difficult to describe as the proverbial elephant? Is this field going around its subject matter blindly probing its different parts, each with different meanings and functions? A family perspective may allow a more integrated approach. A developmental family perspective may add the life span approach, in addition to integration.

On the basis of the foregoing remarks, it is now possible to define what is meant by developmental family psychology by summarizing and expanding its subject matter in Tables 1.1, 1.2, and 1.3. The contents of Table 1.1 are based on the work of early developmental theorists (Buhler, Erikson, Havinghurst, & Sheely), as already done by Aldous (1978) and Eklund (1980). This framework does not include the life cycle of in-laws and friends, as well as leisure activities. These topics are considered separately in appropriate chapters. However, this limitation does not preclude their eventual and inevitable inclusion in a future "grand" perspective. Aspects of the marital life cycle are summarized in Table 1.2 and the family life cycle is summarized in Table 1.3. Admittedly, these summaries are relevant to a normative, traditional view (White, 1991). This view could be considered almost irrelevant, considering that nowadays most life sequences do not follow many normative paths. An adolescent may become a mother before becoming a self-sustaining individual, or even less probable, a partner in a lasting, committed relationship. Consequently, these summaries serve as idealized guidelines that are still followed by the majority (White, 1991).

THE IMPORTANCE OF THEORY

A major task of researchers in this emerging field is to consider which theory or theories are most helpful to understand and predict life span development of the family (Miller, 1989). In addition to traditional theorists, such as Bandura, Bowlby, Erikson, Freud, and Piaget, researchers in this field will need to attend to new integrative approaches that may supersede these theorists and advance theory along relational *as well as* intrapsychic lines. For instance, most traditional theories considered in developmental psychology emphasize hypothetical or inferred internal factors (Levinson, Darrow, Klein, Levinson, & McKee, 1978;

TABLE 1.1 Normative Individual Life Cycle—An Outline

A. Infancy: years 1–4—overcoming dependency and establishing self-awareness
B. Childhood: years 5–8—physical independence—emotional dependence
C. Latency: years 9–12—learning to give and to receive
D. Adolescence: years 13–19—developing individuality
E. Early adulthood: years 23–30
    1. Intimacy—isolation: years 18–30
        a. Pulling up roots: years 17–20
        b. Leaving the family: years 17–24
        c. Trying out various life courses: years 20–28
    2. Marriage—the trying twenties
        a. Childbearing
        b. Work
        c. Choosing and establishing a life cycle
        d. Involvement into adulthood
F. Middle adulthood: years 31–50
    1. Generativity vs. stagnation: years 30–55
        a. Deciding about life goals in personal and in work relationships: years 28–43
        b. Management of household tasks
        c. Management of a career
        d. Transition: around age 30
        e. Settling down: years 32–38
    2. Late adulthood: years 43–48
        a. Evaluation of past achievement and/or failures
        b. Becoming one's own person: years 35–39
        c. Catch thirties: years 30–40
        d. Midlife transition: years 40–45
        e. Entering late adulthood, building a new life structure: years 45–50
        f. Midlife crisis: years 40–50
G. Integrity vs. despair: years 55–death
    1. Late adulthood: years 51–
        a. Redirection of energy
        b. Acceptance of one's life
        c. Developing a point of view
    2. Age 50 transition: years 50–55
    3. Second middle-age structure: years 55–60
    4. Late adulthood transition
    5. Late adulthood and retirement
        a. Activity versus passivity
        b. Involvement vs. isolation
        c. Getting on vs. giving up
    6. Death

TABLE 1.2 Normative Stages of the Marital Life Cycle

Stages	Issues
1. Courtship and marriage	Isolation vs. intimacy Freedom vs. commitment Individuality vs. merging Family loyalties vs. old and new
2. Childbearing and early parenting	From dyad to tryad Shifting generations—realignment of loyalties Nurturance: giving vs. receiving Symbiosis: health vs. pathology Possession vs. sharing Cooperation vs. competition Conductivity vs. reactivity

3. Childbearing socialization	Parenting as singles or as partners
	  (separateness vs. integration)
	Patterns of parenting
	  Authoritarian vs. laissez-faire
	  Authoritative vs. democratic
	  Rigid vs. flexible
	  Abusive/reactive vs. conductive/
	  creative
	Permeability of boundaries
	  Individuals vs. dyads
	  Family vs. society

4. Middle age and adolescence	Separation vs. symbiosis Crisis and menopause Intimacy—individuality renegotiated Facing nonbeing

5. Old age	Retirement: fulfillment vs. emptiness
	  Generativity vs. despair
	  Coping with increased dependence
	Physical impairment, illness, death

Miller, 1989). Should we not look for theories that allow linkage of internal states or traits with external, interpersonal behavior, especially within the family? The relevance of *internal* and *external* theories, however, may need to be considered within a historical perspective (Grinder, 1967), as well as within one important issue of life cycle theories and research—that is, the issue of stability versus change, an issue that is considered after a bird's-eye view of the course of development from a theoretical perspective.

THE STATUS OF THEORY IN FAMILY FUNCTIONING AND DYSFUNCTIONING: A BRIEF HISTORICAL PERSPECTIVE

Theory has been an important aspect of family studies from their inception. In their pioneering work, Nye and Berardo (1966) considered the following theories

TABLE 1.3 Aspects of the Normative Family Life Cycle

Years	Marital	Parental	Sibling	Educational	Occupational
1–16			Competition vs. collaboration between and within generations with role models of other siblings	Finished–unfinished	
17–25	Marriage role differentiation	Child bearing and rearing	Voluntary–involuntary competition with other priorities	Continuation–discontinuation: College Professional school	Labor–blue collar
26–35	Lessening of satisfaction	1. Birth of last child. 2. Greatest feelings of inadequacy in parental role 3. Increasing demands		Decreasing job satisfaction	White collar
36–45	Lowest point of satisfaction	Beginning of empty nest	Declining contacts	Peaking	Blue and white collar income
46–59	Return to couple relations, increase in satisfaction, greater need for companionship	1. Empty nest completed 2. Marriage of children 3. Grandparenthood	Reinstatement of contacts	Peaking of professional income	
60+	Death of one spouse	Parents return to their children for advice and help—children become parents to their parents		Retirement	

to be relevant to our understanding of the family: anthropologic, structural–functional, institutional, interactional, situational, psychoanalytic, social–psychological, developmental, economic, legal, and religious. Burr (1973), in a classic review of theory construction, concentrated on substantive topics where social exchange, balance, role, and sociological variables were reviewed. In a more detailed follow-up, Burr, Hill, Nye, and Reiss (1979a, 1979b) included the following viewpoints: choice and exchange, symbolic interactional, general systems, conflict, and phenomenologic. More recently, Sprey (1990) included the economic, political, sociological, feminist–interpretive, postpositivist, and process viewpoints.

Although family studies did include social psychological viewpoints, the reverse was not true (Deutsch & Krauss, 1965; Shaw & Costanzo, 1970). Originally, most social psychologists did not concern themselves with enduring, intimate matters. The pioneering contributions of Byrne (1971) about attraction and Swensen's early review (1973) were indications of future trends in the field. Swensen summarized various approaches to the study of interpersonal relations (Sullivanian; verbal and nonverbal communication; transactional analysis; existential phenomenology; empirical; social exchange; attitudes and attraction; needs; games; role; and encounter). Later, Talmadge and Ruback (1985) included attribution, social exchange, equity, and power theories. Other relevant topics were interpersonal attraction, the confluence model, and self-esteem mainte-nance. Talmadge and Ruback concluded their review with the note that:

> Thus, research with families is likely to promote the development of theory that has both greater breadth and depth than is now possible . . . since social psychology as a discipline is becoming more and more of an applied science, research on the family and interactions with family therapists could help maintain its viability and expand its realm of influence. . . . (p. 129)

From this cursory survey, we can see that practically any viewpoint has been used to understand families. Consequently, what criteria are used for inclusion of a theory to understand personality development in the family? Because practically everything can be included, where practically any selection of a particular theory can be justified, we would need to show how a theoretical concept can be applied and eventually evaluated in its seeming relevance to personality development in the family. In addition to being relational, any concept selected for application to developmental family psychology would need to be relevant from the viewpoint of the life cycle. If it is not applicable throughout the life cycle, its applicability possibly would become limited to its stages.

Another important trend that cannot be reviewed, even cursorily, here is the whole field of parent–child relationships and parenting skills (Gross, 1989), which historically could be considered the forerunner of family psychology (Sears, Rau, & Alpert, 1965; Whiting & Child, 1953; Yarrow, Campbell, & Burton, 1968). In addition to the foregoing theories included in order to understand personality development and socialization within the context of the family life cycle, in his monumental and influential handbook, Goslin (1969) included social learning, internalization, cognition, cognitive-developmental (moral), psychoanalysis, cultural viewpoints, and interpersonal interaction. Baldwin (1980) included Freud, Heider, Lewin, Piaget, and Werner, as well as social learning and the sociological viewpoint. Muus (1975), in his review of theories of adolescence, included Barker, Erikson, Freud, Gesell, Havighurst, Hollingsworth, Kohlberg, Lewin, social learning theory in general, and European theorists such as Kretschmer, Kroh, Piaget, Remplein, and Zeller.

A case can be made, therefore, for finding theories common to both child and adult development as well as to family functioning and dysfunctioning. However, is commonality of influence the only criterion for choice of a theory? If we were to argue that social psychological concepts are useful to understand development over the family life cycle, we could simply list them, as above. However, simple listing would not be sufficient. We would need to evaluate how the concepts are valid and relevant and how they relate to each other in a more or less meaningful way, in a nomological network. Consequently, we would need to find which concepts are more relevant to which part of development in the family and how they fit, or fail to fit, together.

WHAT COURSE FAMILY DEVELOPMENT?

Developmental psychology can learn from social psychology by applying some of its concepts and findings to the family life cycle. It has been found increasingly useful (L'Abate, 1994) to conceptualize development across the family life cycle according to at least six important social psychological concepts: (1) space and social settings from ecological psychology (Barker, 1968); (2) time and negotiation (L'Abate, 1994); (3) impression formation and management (Schlenker, 1980, 1984); (4) attribution theory (Jones, Kanouse, Kelley, Nisbett, Valins, & Weiner, 1971); (5) resource exchange theory (Foa & Foa, 1974); and social comparison theory (Festinger, 1954). The rest of this section elaborates how each of these theories may help integrate developmental family psychology with social psychology.

Space and Social Settings

Space is what we live in, from the cradle to the grave (Altman, 1975; L'Abate, 1964, 1976, 1983, 1985, 1994; Linder, 1976). Living in space means having to modulate, modify, and moderate our approach–avoidance tendencies into workable, functional choices of who, what, when, how, and why we approach and who, what, when, how, and why we avoid at the same time. Any act of approach toward somebody or something is a choice and possibly an act of avoidance of someone or something else. These acts transform themselves over time, going toward a functional, selective, careful balance of these tendencies in most cases, and toward a dysfunctional amplification of one at the expense of the other. From these tendencies attachments are developed, with successive stages of dependence, denial of dependence, and, in mature adulthood, acceptance of interdependence.

The challenge to developmental family psychology will be to tease out how space is used from the very outset of conception and how it will influence development throughout the life span. For instance, what will happen to the child who was conceived in and continued to live in a cramped, dingy, little room in contrast to a child who was conceived in and continued to live in spacious, warm, light rooms, with a minimum of interference from other children or neighbors and pleasant music rather than continuous noise, shouting, fighting, and uproars? How do space and spatial factors affect conceptions of time and temporal perspective?

Time and Negotiation

In addition to space and spatial concepts such as dependence and intimacy, developmental family psychology must pay attention to time and temporal concepts such as temporal perspective, and speed of reaction such as reactivity in intimate, interdependent relationships. Problem solving, bargaining, negotiation, and decision making are all similar processes (L'Abate, 1994). Will a family in its beginning stages of development be able to reach consensus? What about the same family toward the final stages of its life cycle? What factors determine the ability to negotiate and solve problems in a family? What changes in problem solving will occur as a function of time?

Impression Formation and Management

The issue of impression formation and management is relevant to an understanding of development within the family according to levels of description and explanation (Altman & Taylor, 1973; Schlenker, 1980, 1984; Snyder, 1987). We may put our best foot forward socially to make a good impression, but we may differ in how we impress others in our families. We may be nasty inside the home and nice outside it, or vice versa. The discrepancy or consistency between these two levels of public and private description, which have been called *presentational* and *phenotypical,* respectively (L'Abate, 1964, 1976, 1994), are important to an understanding of family functioning/dysfunctioning. Some families stress external appearance at the expense of internal substance; some reverse this trend. Most families balance both levels appropriately. Consequently, we must distinguish between levels of description and levels of explanation; how families want to appear externally from how they behave inside their homes.

However, as soon as we accept the importance and validity of these two levels, we need to determine how we can explain them, their consistencies, inconsistencies, and contradictions (Wakefield, 1989). At an internal, often "unconscious," level, we may use intrapsychic concepts such as self-esteem, self-perception, and the like to "explain" why members of a family present themselves in one way publicly and behave in another way in the privacy of their homes. Once we accept such a structural or situational explanation, we would have to introduce a historical developmental view to "explain" the internal constructs we have used to "explain" discrepancies or consistencies between public and private behaviors (L'Abate, 1976, 1994). One level of explanation is incomplete without the other.

The challenge for developmental family psychologists would be to find out how children develop self-presentational images consistent or inconsistent with how they behave in the home. For instance, some children are problematic at home but are not problematic in school. Some children do not seem problematic at home (at least the parents deny it), but are problematic in school. There are, of course, children who are not problematic in either setting and those who are. What makes them behave so differently from one setting to another? Will these children grow up to be nasty at work and nice at home or nice at work and nasty at home (Higgins, Snyder, & Berglas, 1990)?

Attribution

The attribution of attributions, the fact that much of our reality is of our making, is not too different from early views of general semantics about the relativity of our perceptions (Jones et al., 1971). Nonetheless, the importance of subjective perceptions is especially relevant to how and what family members do and say about each other. Attributions reflect the importance of the phenomenological reality of individual perceptions, especially in close relationships where distortions, deletions, and generalizations are most apt to become exaggerated and amplified, or denied and suppressed. The importance of attributions is especially relevant to how family members see themselves and each other and how they exchange these attributions. The most important attribution, fundamental to how families are formed and maintained, is the attribution of love.

The challenge to developmental family psychology here lies in ascertaining how these attributions are developed and maintained in the home and how they are transferred to other settings (school, work) later. For instance, if children learn to attribute responsibility to their siblings without learning to acknowledge their own part in what happens among them, will those children learn to maintain these denials and externalizations later in life, claiming others to be responsible for their own behaviors? In other words, what are the antecedents—social, familial, and personal—of how a child is learning to assume responsibility? Provided we may already have information on this subject, what will happen to a child's attributions later in life?

Resource Exchange

Resource exchange theory (Foa & Foa, 1974) has greatly influenced thinking about personality development within family relationships (L'Abate, 1994). Foa and Foa argued that six resource classes are continuously exchanged (given and taken) between and among us: status, love, information, services, goods, and money. These six classes can be reduced to three modalities: (1) being or presence by combining status and love; (2) doing or performance, by combining services and information; and (3) having or production by combining money and goods. Status was changed to the attribution of importance and love was changed to intimacy (L'Abate, 1994). Both are two sides of the same coin of the ability to love. The first modality of *being* is nonnegotiable. The other two, *doing* and *having* are negotiable. Together *doing* and *having* define *power.*

The first and major attribution that occurs in the formation of a family, either between partners from the outset of their relationship or between parent and child from conception and before, is the attribution of *importance.* Singer (1987), in his encyclopedic and historical treatise on love, arrived at the conclusion that, ultimately, love is the *bestowal of value.* This process of bestowal of value does not seem too different from the attribution of importance. Love is modulated and expressed through approach–avoidance tendencies on the basis of both importance and intimacy. Whereas love is not negotiable, doing and having are negotiable in functional families but are confused with love and negotiated poorly or not at all in dysfunctional families. In dysfunctionality, power is confused, diffused, and fused with presence. Neither presence nor power is expressed properly and positively (Jacob, 1987). The ability to negotiate derives from temporal discharge–delay, control tendencies detailed elsewhere (L'Abate, 1964, 1976, 1983, 1986, 1994).

How are spatial and temporal tendencies transformed later in life and how do they operate within the context of the family? For instance, will a child who is well balanced in his or her approach–avoidance tendencies in kindergarten be able to achieve a greater degree of intimacy in his or her marriage? Can a hyperactive child eventually learn to become intimate in his or her marriage and learn to negotiate issues successfully in an intimate relationship?

In conclusion, this section argues that development through the family life cycle takes place in a world of space, which leads to intimacy and closeness in intimate relationships. The world of time leads toward either negotiation or failure to negotiate among family members.

Social Comparison

According to social comparison theory (Festinger, 1954; Wood, 1989), self-definition throughout the life cycle takes place through a continuum of likeness that underlies the processes of symbiosis–autism, sameness–oppositeness, and similarity–differentness (L'Abate, 1976). From this internal, hypothetical continuum of likeness and its dialectical processes, three different styles in intimate relationships can be derived (L'Abate, 1986): (1) the apathetic–abusive style derives from symbiotic–autistic self-definition; (2) the reactive–repetitive style derives from digital, either-or, sameness–oppositeness self-definition; and (3) the conductive–creative style derives from similarity–differentness in self-definition.

The first two styles are dysfunctional, whereas the third style is functional. In the conductive style, attribution and affirmation of importance are reciprocal (selfulness). In reactive–repetitive relationships there is either denial of self-importance and affirmation of the other's importance (selflessness) or there is denial of the other's importance and affirmation of self-importance (selfishness). In abusive–apathetic relationships there is denial of both self-importance and importance of the other (no-self). Resources exchanged relate to a continuum of likeness to the extent that the apathetic–abusive and reactive–repetitive styles are based on denial of importance to self or other (loved ones) or both, whereas the conductive–creative style is based on the affirmation of importance of self and other.

By listening to children and adults carefully, we discover that they make continuous comparisons to loved, trivial, and disliked others. What do these attributions of likeness mean in the way we learn to define ourselves over the life cycle? Will a child defined by oppositeness or noncompliance persist to be oppositional later in life—in the marriage, for instance? If the answer is yes, will oppositeness continue into old age? How many oppositional children become conforming adults? The challenge of the future lies in seeing how these views, most of them derived from laboratory work, apply to real-life development within families, both at work and in leisure-time activities.

STABILITY OR CHANGE?

A crucial issue in life cycle development refers to the controversy concerning whether behavior does or does not change, especially during the adult years (Caspi & Bem, 1990). The controversy has been fueled by researchers who are adamant in their denial of changes (McCrae & Costa, 1990) on empirical grounds, and by clinicians who are just as adamant in supporting the opposite position (Nemiroff & Colarusso, 1990).

This controversy is similar to the controversy over adolescence as a sturm und drang stage, as seen by clinicians, versus adolescence as a normal transition with minimal upsets in a normal population, as seen by researchers (Offer, Ostrov, & Howard, 1981). When we sample "normally" functioning subjects, we may find very little, if any, change. When we sample people in crisis or in conflict, we will find a great deal of change *if* they undergo some kind of psychotherapeutic experience. Here is where the delta model, alluded to in the beginning of this chapter, may become useful. Within the mainstream of the river there are predictable continuity and stability of flow. Rivulets, sidestreams, creeks, and sideway extensions may meander along a variety of unpredictable pathways, some of them deviating and distancing themselves from the main-stream, some returning to it, and some disappearing, never to return.

Within this controversy there are a variety of related issues such as the following. If there were to be change, would it occur at the core or at the periphery of personality? What is the core and what is the periphery? If we cannot find consensus on what constitutes either aspect, how can we resolve the issue? The same questions could be raised about dealing with internal versus external or proximal–distal aspects of change, if there are any. Another way to look at this controversy would be to differentiate between measurable or unmeasurable dimensions, as in subjective versus objective. By the same token, if there were to be changes, would they be fast or slow, short-lived or permanent, limited to specific areas of functioning or pervasive and extensive to the whole personality?

One way to solve some of these issues would involve looking at personality along a continuum of experiencing on the receptive input side of behavior and of expressing on the output side (L'Abate, 1994). The controversy may be understood as representing an emphasis on different extremes of the same continuum. For example, researchers such as McCrae and Costa (1990), who stress stability and deny any evidence or possibility of measurable changes in adult development, base their conclusions on the "objective evidence" of paper-and-pencil, self-report tests—that is, the expressive side. They are willing to admit to changes in behaviors and habits, attitudes and opinions, social roles, and interpersonal relationships, and even such "receptive" dimensions as identity and self-concept. However, they are not willing to admit to changes in what they conceive as the five important dimensions of personality: extraversion, neuroticism, openness to experience, agreeableness, and conscientiousness. Hence, one issue in this controversy is whether personality should be defined in a *narrow* sense, as represented by "objective" expressive dimensions, or in a *wide* sense, including not only paper-and-pencil expressive measures but other measures as well, some of them receptive—aspects not considered by McCrae and Costa—and some of them expressive, such as habits, attitudes and opinions, social roles, and interpersonal relationships.

Hence, whether there is stability or change depends a great deal on how we define personality. A narrow view might predict stability, whereas a wide view would predict change (Nemiroff & Colarusso, 1990). A narrow view would limit its consideration mainly to the expressive side of personality strictly defined by paper-and-pencil measures, whereas a wide view would also include the receptive side of personality as well as other aspects not included in self-report questionnaires.

INDIVIDUAL, DYADIC, AND MULTIRELATIONAL LIFE CYCLES

Although most life span developmental psychology originally concerned itself with individuals, a survey of these textbooks shows an increasing frequency of contributions and citations to family variables. Once we begin to look at life span development/socialization from a contextual or person × situation viewpoint, it follows that a variety of life courses need consideration. For instance, most individuals would follow four stages of development, going from personhood to partnership to parenthood and then back to personhood (Lowenthal, Thurner, & Chiriboga, 1976; White, 1991). After the loss of a spouse, the individual life course must be considered *in relationship* to other related life courses, such as those of parents, siblings, mate(s), and children, as well as one's occupational career, friends, and leisure. These are the life priorities that must be considered in a developmental view of the life cycle, unless we stay fixed or regress to a monadic, behavior-in-a-vacuum view.

GENDER DIFFERENCES IN FAMILY LIFE CYCLE

We should have three different models for development of individuals in the family. One model would apply to women and the other would apply to men. The third would apply to their interaction (Baker, 1987; Barnett, Biener, & Baruch, 1987; Carter, 1987; Fausto-Sterling, 1985; Hess & Ferree, 1987; Lee & Stewart, 1976; Lips & Colwill, 1978; Maccoby, 1966; Pleck, 1981; Shaver & Hendrick, 1987; Sonderegger, 1984; Spence & Helmreich, 1978; Stoller, 1968). For instance, women outlive men by at least 7 years in the United States. This difference would suggest that different life course processes have taken place within each gender, producing different outcomes.

FUNCTIONALITIES AND DYSFUNCTIONALITIES
IN LIFE-COURSE DEVELOPMENT

The same point could be made about psychopathology, where gender differences may become even more pronounced (Al-Issa, 1980). A delta model of development would suggest that the life course is not free of stops, detours, jumps, and slow and fast advances (Caspi & Elder, 1988; Elder & Caspi, 1988). Can we predict functional as well as dysfunctional life span development? Functional behavior, as well as pathology, develops intergenerationally (Allman & Jaffe, 1975; Cicchetti, 1990; Hersen & Last, 1990; Keating & Rosen, 1990; Lewis & Miller, 1990; Roff & Ricks, 1970). What factors make for the repetition of continuous or discontinuous, functional or dysfunctional behavior?

Once we acknowledge the presence of a developmental field of study within the context of the family, we must concern ourselves with how to deal with the many dysfunctionalities, temporary or permanent, that emerge over the family life cycle (Carter & McGoldrick, 1988; Falicov, 1988; Liddle, 1983; Thomas, 1990).

CONCLUSION

This brief, introductory survey attempts to show how various strands support the view that a new field of specialization called, for lack of a better term, developmental family psychology is emerging. Advocates of this view theorize that most development and socialization take place within the context of the family life span.

REFERENCES

Aldous, J. (1978). *Family careers: Developmental change in families.* New York: Wiley.

Al-Issa, I. (1980). *The psychopathology of women.* Englewood Cliffs, NJ: Prentice-Hall.

Allman, L. R., & Jaffe, D. T. (1975). *Abnormal psychology of the life cycle.* New York: Harper & Row.

Altman, I. (1975). *The environment and social behavior: Privacy-personal space-territory-crowding.* Pacific Grove, CA: Brooks/Cole.

Altman, I., & Taylor, D. A. (1973). *Social penetration: The development of interpersonal relationships.* New York: Holt, Rinehart & Winston.

Ault, R. L. (Ed.). (1980). *Developmental perspectives.* Santa Monica, CA: Goodyear.

Baker, M. A. (1987). *Sex differences in human performance.* New York: Wiley.

Baldwin, A. L. (1980). *Theories of child development.* New York: Wiley.

Baltes, P. B., & Brim, O. G., Jr. (Eds.). (1979). *Life-span development and behavior (Vol. 2).* New York: Academic Press.

Baltes, P. B., Featherman, D. L., & Lerner, R. M. (Eds.). (1990). *Life-span development and behavior. (Vol. 10).* Hillsdale, NJ: Erlbaum.

Baltes, P. B., Reese, H. W., & Nesselroade, J. R. (1988). *Life-span developmental psychology: Introduction to research methods.* Hillsdale, NJ: Erlbaum.

Baltes, P. B., & Schaie, K. W. (Eds.). (1973). *Life-span developmental psychology: Personality and socialization.* New York: Academic Press.

Barker, R. G. (1968). *Ecological psychology.* Stanford, CA: Stanford University Press.

Barnett, R. C., Biener, L., & Baruch, G. K. (Eds.). (1987). *Gender and stress.* New York: Free Press.

Bell, R. Q., & Harper, L. V. (1977). *Child effects on adults.* Lincoln: University of Nebraska Press.

Bowlby, J. (1969). *Attachment and loss. Vol. I: Attachment.* New York: Basic Books.

Bowlby, J. (1973). *Attachment and loss. Vol. II: Separation, anxiety and anger.* New York: Basic Books.

Bowlby, J. (1980). *Attachment and loss. Vol. III: Loss, sadness and depression.* New York: Basic Books.

Bretherton, I., & Waters, E. (Eds.). (1985). Growing points of attachment theory and research. *Monographs of the Society for Research in Child Development, 50,* Serial No. 209.

Brodzinsky, D. M., Gormly, A. V., & Ambron, S. R. (1986). *Lifespan human development.* New York: Holt, Rinehart & Winston.

Burgess, R. L., & Huston, T. L. (Eds.). (1979). *Social exchange in developing relationships.* New York: Academic Press.

Burr, W. R. (1973). *Theory construction and the sociology of the family.* New York: Wiley.

Burr, W. R., Hill, R., Nye, F. I., & Reiss, I. L. (Eds.). (1979a). *Contemporary theories about the family. Vol. I. Research-based theories.* New York: Free Press.

Burr, W. R., Hill, R., Nye, F. I., & Reiss, I. L. (Eds.). (1979b). *Contemporary theories about the family, Vol. 2. General theories/theoretical orientations.* New York: Free Press.

Byrne, D. (1971). *The attraction paradigm.* New York: Academic Press.

Carter, B., & McGoldrick, M. (1988). *The changing family life cycle: A framework for family therapy.* New York: Gardner.

Carter, D. B. (1987). *Current conceptions of sex roles and sex typing: Theory and research.* New York: Praeger.

Caspi, A., & Bem, D. J. (1990). Personality continuity and change across the life course. In L. A. Pervin (Ed.), *Handbook of personality theory and research* (pp. 549–575). New York: Guilford.

Caspi, A., & Elder, G. H., Jr. (1988). Emergent family patterns: The intergenerational construction of problem behavior and relationships. In R. Hinde & J. Stevenson-Hinde (Eds.), *Relationships between families* (pp. 218–240). Oxford, UK: Oxford University Press.

Caspi, A., Elder, G. H., Jr., & Herbener, E. S. (1990). Childhood personality and the prediction of life-course patterns. In L. N. Robbins & M. Rutter (Eds.), *Straight and devious pathways from childhood to adulthood* (pp. 13–33). Cambridge, UK: Cambridge University Press.

Cicchetti, D. (1990). *The emergence of a discipline: Rochester symposium on developmental psychopathology.* Hillsdale, NJ: Erlbaum.

Clausen, J. A. (Ed.). (1968). *Socialization and society.* Boston: Little, Brown.

Clausen, J. A. (1986). *The life course: A sociological perspective.* Englewood Cliffs, NJ: Prentice-Hall.

Cusinato, M., & L'Abate, L. (1994). A spiral model of intimacy. In S. Johnson & L. Greenberg, (Eds.), *Intimacy and marital relationships.* New York: Brunner/Mazel.

Danziger, K. (1971). *Socialization.* Middlesex, UK: Penguin.

Datan, N., & Ginsberg, L. H. (Eds). (1975). *Life-span developmental psychology: Normative life crises.* New York: Academic Press.

Derlega, V. J., (1984). *Communication, intimacy, and close relationships.* New York: Academic Press.

Deutsch, M., & Krauss, R. M. (1965). *Theories in social psychology.* New York: Basic Books.

Dion, K. K., & Dion, K. L. (1985). Personality, gender, and the phenomenology of romantic love. In P. Shaver (Ed.), *Self, situations, and social behavior* (pp. 209–239). Newbury Park, CA: Sage.

Duck, S. W. (1973). *Personal relationships and personal constructs: A study of friendship formation.* New York: Wiley.

Duck, S. W. (1982). *Personal relationships. 4: Dissolving personal relationships.* New York: Academic Press.

Duck, S. W. (Ed.). (1988). *Handbook of interpersonal relationships.* London: Wiley.

Duck, S., & Gilmour, R. (Eds.). (1981). *Personal relationships.* New York: Academic Press.

Dunne, E. E., & L'Abate, L. (1977). The family taboo in psychology textbooks. *Teaching of Psychology, 5,* 115–117.

Eisenberg, N. (Ed.). (1987). *Contemporary topics in developmental psychology.* New York: Wiley-Interscience.

Eklund, S. J. (1980). Life span development and families. *Dimensions, 9,* 16–19.

Elder, G. H., Jr., (1984). Families, kin, and the life course: A sociological perspective. In R. D. Parke (Ed.), *Advances in child development research: The family* (pp. 80–136). Chicago: University of Chicago Press.

Elder, G. H., Jr., & Caspi, A. (1988). Human development and social change: An emerging perspective on the life course. In N. Bolger, A. Caspi, G. Downey, & M. Moorehouse (Eds.), *Persons in context: Developmental processes* (pp. 77–113). New York: Cambridge University Press.

Endler, N. S., Boulter, L. R., & Osser, H. (Eds.). (1968). *Contemporary issues in developmental psychology.* New York: Holt, Rinehart & Winston.

Falicov, C. J. (Ed.). (1988). *Family transitions: Continuity and change over the life-cycle.* New York: Guilford.

Fausto-Sterling, A. (1985). *Myths of gender: Biological theories about women and men.* New York: Basic Books.

Festinger, L. (1954). A theory of social comparison processes. *Human Relations, 7,* 117–140.

Foa, U. G., & Foa, E. B. (1974). *Societal structures of the mind.* Springfield, IL: Charles C. Thomas.

Gilmour, R., & Duck, S. (Eds.). (1986). *The emerging field of personal relationships.* Hillsdale, NJ: Erlbaum.

Goldberg, S. R., & Deutsch, F. (1977). *Life-span individual and family development.* Monterey, CA: Brooks/Cole.

Goslin, D. A. (Ed.). (1969). *Handbook of socialization theory and research.* Chicago: Rand McNally.

Goulet, L. R., & Baltes, P. B. (Eds.). (1970). *Life-span developmental psychology: Research and theory.* New York: Academic Press.

Grinder, R. E. (1967). *A history of genetic psychology: The first science of human development.* New York: Wiley.

Gross, J. (1989). *Psychology and parenthood.* Philadelphia: Open University Press.

Hartup, W. W., & Rubin, Z. (Eds.). (1986). *Relationships and development.* Hillsdale, NJ: Erlbaum.

Hersen, M., & Last, C. G. (1990). *Handbook of child and adult psychopathology: A longitudinal perspective:* New York: Pergamon.

Hess, B. B., & Ferree, M. M. (Eds.). (1987). *Analyzing gender: A handbook of social science research.* Newbury Park, CA: Sage.

Higgins, E. T. (1990). Personality, social psychology, and person-situation relations: Standards and knowledge activation as a common language. In L. A. Pervin (Ed.), *Handbook of personality theory and research* (pp. 301–338). New York: Guilford.

Higgins, R. L., Snyder, C. R., & Berglas, S. (Eds.). (1990). *Self-handicapping: The paradox that isn't.* New York: Plenum.

Hinde, R. A. (1979). *Towards understanding relationships.* New York: Academic Press.

Hoppe, R. A., Milton, G. A., & Simmel, E. C. (Eds.). (1970). *Early experiences and the processes of socialization.* New York: Academic Press.

Jacob, T. (Ed.). (1987). *Family interaction and psychopathology: Theories, methods, and findings.* New York: Plenum.

Jones, E. E., Kanouse, D. E., Kelley, H. H., Nisbett, R. E., Valins, S., & Weiner, B. (1971). *Attribution: Perceiving the causes of behavior.* Morristown, NJ: General Learning Press.

Kaslow, F. W. (1990). *Voices in family psychology.* Newbury Park, CA: Sage.

Keating, D. P., & Rosen, H. (1990). *Constructivist perspectives on developmental psychopathology and atypical development.* Hillsdale, NJ: Erlbaum.

Kelley, H. H. (1979). *Personal relationships: Their structures and processes.* Hillsdale, NJ: Erlbaum.

Kelley, H. H., Bersheid, E., Christensen, A., Harvey, J. H., Huston, T. L., Levinger, G., McClintock, E., Peplau, L. A., & Peterson, D. R. (1983). *Close relationships.* New York: W. H. Freeman.

Kelley, H. H., & Thibaut, J. W. (1978). *Interpersonal relations: A theory of interdependence.* New York: Wiley-Interscience.

Kreppner, K., & Lerner, R. M. (Eds.). (1989). *Family systems and life-span development.* Hillsdale, NJ: Erlbaum.

LaBarba, R. C. (1981). *Foundations of developmental psychology.* New York: Academic Press.

L'Abate, L. (1964). *Principles of clinical psychology.* New York: Grune & Stratton.

L'Abate, L. (1976). *Understanding and helping the individual in the family.* New York: Grune & Stratton.

L'Abate, L. (1983). *Family psychology: Theory, therapy, and training,* Washington, DC: University Press of America.

L'Abate, L. (Ed.). (1985). *Handbook of family psychology and therapy.* Pacific Grove, CA.: Brooks/Cole.

L'Abate, L. (1986). *Systematic family therapy.* New York: Brunner/Mazel.

L'Abate, L. (1987). *Family psychology II: Theory, therapy, prevention, and training.* Washington, DC: University Press of America.

L'Abate, L. (1992). Family psychology and family therapy: Comparisons and contrasts. *American Journal of Family Therapy, 20,* 3–12.

L'Abate, L. (1994). *A theory of personality development.* New York: Wiley.

L'Abate, L., & Thaxton, L. M. (1983). The family as a unit of psychological study and practice. *Academic Psychology Bulletin, 5,* 71–83.

Langer, J. (1969). *Theories of development.* New York: Holt, Rinehart & Winston.

Lee, P. C., & Stewart, R. S. (Eds.). (1976). *Sex differences: Cultural and developmental dimensions.* New York: Urizen.

Lefrancois, G. R. (1990). *The lifespan.* Belmont, CA: Wadsworth.

Lerner, R. M., & Spanier, G. B. (Eds.). (1978). *Child influences on marital and family interaction: A life-span perspective.* New York: Academic Press.

Levinson, D. J., Darrow, C. N., Klein, E. B., Levinson, M. L., & McKee, B. (1978). *The seasons of a man's life.* New York: Knopf.

Lewis, M., & Miller, S. M. (Eds.). (1990). *Handbook of developmental psychopathology.* New York: Plenum.

Liddle, H. A. (Ed.). (1983). *Clinical implications of the family life cycle.* Rockville, MD: Aspen.

Linder, D. E. (1976). Personal space. In J. W. Thibaut, J. T. Spence, & R. C. Carson (Eds.), *Contemporary topics in social psychology* (pp. 445–477). Morristown, NJ: General Learning Press.

Lips, H. M., & Colwill, N. L. (1978). *The psychology of sex differences.* Englewood Cliffs, NJ: Prentice-Hall.

Litz, T. (1976). *The person: His and her development throughout the life cycle.* New York: Basic Books.

Lowenthal, M. F., Thurner, M., & Chiriboga, D. (1976). *Four stages of life: A comparative study of women and men facing transitions.* San Francisco: Jossey-Bass.

Maccoby, E. E. (1966). *The development of sex differences.* Stanford, CA: Stanford University Press.

Magnusson, D. (1990). Personality development from an interactional perspective. In L. A. Pervin (Ed.), *Handbook of personality theory and research* (pp. 193–222). New York: Guilford.

Maier, H. W. (1969). *Three theories of child development.* New York: Harper & Row.

McCrae, R. R., & Costa, P. T., Jr. (1990). *Personality in adulthood.* New York: Guilford.

McNeil, E. B. (1969). *Human socialization.* Belmont, CA: Brooks/Cole.

Miller, P. H. (1989). *Theories of developmental psychology.* New York: W. H. Freeman & Co.

Murstein, B. I. (Ed.). (1978). *Exploring intimate life styles.* New York: Springer.

Muus, R. (1975). *Theories of adolescence.* New York: Random House.

Nemiroff, R. A., & Colarusso, C. A. (Eds.). (1990). *New dimensions in adult development.* New York: Basic Books.

Nesselroade, J. R., & Reese, H. W. (Eds.). (1973). *Life-span developmental psychology: Methodological issues.* New York: Academic Press.

Nye, F. I. (Ed.). (1982). *Family relationships: Rewards and costs.* Beverly Hills, CA: Sage.

Nye, F. I., & Berardo, F. M. (Eds.). (1966). *Emerging conceptual frameworks in family analysis.* New York: Macmillan.

Offer, D., Ostrov, E., & Howard, K. (1981). *The adolescent: A psychological self-portrait.* New York: Basic Books.

Parkes, C. M., & Stevenson-Hinde, J. (Eds.). (1982). *The place of attachment in human behavior.* New York: Basic Books.

Perlman, D., & Duck, S. W. (Eds.). (1987). *Intimate relationships: Development, dynamics, and deterioration.* Newbury Park, CA: Sage.

Pervin, L. A. (Ed.). (1990). *Handbook of personality theory and research.* New York: Guilford.

Pleck, J. H. (1981). *The myth of masculinity.* Boston: MIT Press.

Rebok, G. W. (1987). *Life-span cognitive development.* New York: Holt, Rinehart & Winston.

Roff, M., & Ricks, D. F. (Eds.). (1970). *Life history research in psychopathology.* Minneapolis: University of Minnesota Press.

Rossi, A. S., & Rossi, P. H. (1990). *Of human bonding: Parent-child relations across the life course.* Hawthorne, NY: Aldine de Gruyter.

Schlenker, B. R. (1980). *Impression management: The self-concept, social identity, and interpersonal relations.* Monterey, CA: Brooks/Cole.

Schlenker, B. R. (1984). Identities, identifications, and relationships. In V. J. Derlega (Ed.), *Communication intimacy, and close relationships* (pp. 71–104). Orlando, FL: Academic Press.

Sears, R. R., Rau, L., & Alpert, R. (1965). *Identification and child rearing.* Stanford, CA: Stanford University Press.

Shaver, P., & Hendrick, C. (Eds.). (1987). *Sex and gender.* Newbury Park, CA: Sage.

Shaw, M. E., & Costanzo, P. R. (1970). *Theories of social psychology.* New York: McGraw-Hill.

Singer, I. (1987). *The nature of love. 3: The modern world.* Chicago: University of Chicago Press.

Snyder, M. (1987). *Public appearances/private realities: The psychology of self-monitoring.* New York: W. H. Freeman.

Sonderegger, T. B. (Ed.). (1984). *Psychology and gender: Nebraska symposium on motivation.* Lincoln: University of Nebraska Press.

Spence, J. T., & Helmreich, R. L. (1978). *Masculinity and femininity: Their psychological dimensions, correlates, and antecedents.* Austin: University of Texas Press.

Sprey, J. (Ed.). (1990). *Fashioning family theory: New approaches.* Newbury Park, CA: Sage.

Steinberg, L. D. (Ed.). (1981). *The life cycle: Readings in human development.* New York: Columbia University Press.

Sternberg, R. J. (1987). *The triangle of love: Intimacy, passion, commitment.* New York: Basic Books.

Stoller, R. J. (1968). *Sex and gender.* New York: Science House.

Swensen, C. H., Jr. (1973). *Introduction to interpersonal relations.* Glenview, IL: Scott, Foresman.

Sze, W. C. (Ed.). (1975). *Human life cycle.* New York: Aronson.

Talmadge, L. D., & Ruback, R. B. (1985). Social and family psychology. In L. L'Abate (Ed.), *The handbook of family psychology and therapy* (pp. 102–139). Pacific Grove, CA: Brooks/Cole.

Thomas, R. M. (1990). *Counseling and life-span development.* Newbury Park, CA: Sage.

Turner, J. S., & Helms, D. B. (1986). *Contemporary adulthood.* New York: Holt, Rinehart & Winston.

Wakefield, J. C. (1989). Levels of explanation in personality theory. In D. M. Buss & N. Cantor (Eds.), *Personality psychology: Recent trends and emerging directions* (pp. 332–346). New York: Springer-Verlag.

White, J. M. (1991). *Dynamics of family development.* New York: Guilford.

Whiting, J. W. M., & Child, I. L. (1953). *Child training and personality.* New Haven, CT: Yale University Press.

Wood, J. V., (1989). Theory and research concerning social comparisons of personal attributes. *Psychological Bulletin, 106,* 231–248.

Wrightsman, L. S. (1988). *Personality development in adulthood.* Newbury Park, CA: Sage.

Yarrow, M. R., Campbell, J. D., & Burton, R. V. (1968). *Child rearing: An inquiry into research and methods.* San Francisco: Jossey-Bass.

Zigler, E. F., & Child, I. L. (Eds.). (1973). *Socialization and personality development.* Reading, MA: Addison-Wesley.

PART ONE

Life Cycle of the Functional Family

CHAPTER 2

The Individual in the Family Life Cycle

VICTOR G. CICIRELLI

To fully understand individuals in the family life cycle, we must collect additional data documenting individual and family development throughout the life span. We must also formulate theories more powerful than those that exist today; theories that can explain and predict both individual and family development and how they influence one another's development over the life cycle. However, with or without researcher awareness, such theories begin with or derive from metatheories, usually called *metamodels*.

This chapter presents an overview of the dominant metamodels in science today. Among other things, a metamodel helps to identify and also to limit the types of theories that can be formulated to explain phenomena (Sternberg, 1990). Basic assumptions of each metamodel are explicated, as well as the metamodel's implications for selecting different types of variables and specifying relationships between them. This is the starting point for deriving a specific theory or a more general school of thought. Clarifying the basic origins of theories in metatheory should help family researchers to interpret and apply existing theories and to construct better ones.

MEANING OF METAMODEL

A model is a representation of something; it does not describe but represents reality. Models can be specific or general. For example, a scale model represents a particular object. Thus, a blueprint of a house represents the basic parts of the house and how they relate to one another, but it does not describe the actual house in terms of all its attributes.

A theoretical model is more general in that it represents a theoretical concept. For example, intelligence may be represented by a geographical map of the mind (Sternberg, 1990). This approach has led to a school of thought that maps the mind, with various theorists postulating different numbers of intellectual abilities ranging from 1 to 120, measuring and collecting appropriate data regarding such abilities, and using different factor analysis methods to confirm or disconfirm their existence.

Another model represents intelligence as a computer (Sternberg, 1990). In this case, researchers have developed different theories of the process of intellectual functioning, written appropriate computer software to represent these processes, and then determined how well the results from running the software with specific parameters corresponded to actual data from the real world. In a similar fashion, intelligence can be represented by other models, with specific theories and schools of thought derived from such models.

At a more general level, models exist to represent whole fields or domains of knowledge. However, the broadest model possible is one that represents all existing phenomena; it represents the nature of both man and the world. Such world views are called metamodels. The nature of the person and the world are assumed to be represented by such models, and different meanings and explanations of development are derived accordingly (Salthouse, 1991).

TYPES OF METAMODELS

At present, three important metamodels exist: organicism (or organismic), mechanism, and contextualism, with contextualism subdivided into pure contextualism and quasi contextualism (Ford & Lerner, 1992). This chapter discusses these metamodels.

From the organicism metamodel, schools of thought have been formulated in the cognitive, moral, and personality areas. Examples of specific theories from each family are Piaget's (1954) cognitive development theory, Kohlberg's (1981) moral development theory, and Erikson's (Erikson, 1968; Erikson & Erikson, 1981) ego development theory.

From the mechanism metamodel, various schools of thought have been derived such as radical behaviorism, moderate behaviorism, and social learning theories. Examples of specific theories are Skinner's (1953) operant conditioning theory, Hull's (1942) hypothetical–deductive learning theory, and Bandura's (1986) observation learning theory.

Theories based on the contextualism metamodel are still being formulated and tested. Life span developmental psychology (Baltes, 1987) is not a theory but an influential perspective or set of beliefs that includes contextualism. Developmental systems theory (Ford & Lerner, 1992; Kreppner & Lerner, 1989) is a new formulation based on quasi contextualism, as is L'Abate's (1990, 1992a, 1992b) theory of family functioning. The latter is novel and is quite promising in the family area.

In the following sections, each of the three major metamodels is discussed in turn.

ORGANICISM

Basic Assumptions of the Organismic Metamodel

The metamodel of organicism assumes that the person is represented best by a biological organism. This means that the person is similar to a dynamic system in which all the components are continually interacting and interdependent (Langer, 1969; Laszlo, 1972). Three types of causality are predominant in a dynamic system. However, reciprocal causality is basic; that is, the components of the system are simultaneously causing each other to behave in a certain manner. They are interdependent, with each component influencing every other component. Without this concept of causality, the concept of a dynamic system would lose its meaning. Second, teleological causality exists, which means that the direction and end point of development of the system are predetermined by genetic and maturational factors. (It does not mean that the future determines the present.) In an organismic system, there is a weak interaction between heredity and environmental factors, so that heredity determines the direction and end point of development, whereas environment merely determines the rate and possibly the level of development attained.

The total system also involves many subsystems that are highly organized and coordinated to function as a total system. Development consists of the increasing complexity and efficiency of functioning of these subsystems, and concomitantly, of the total system. The direction of development is manifested by a fixed sequence of stages for various subsystems in which qualitative differences in organization emerge at each stage until an end point is attained. End points may differ for different subsystems. For example, in Piaget's (1954) theory, intellectual development begins at birth and goes through various qualitative changes or stages in the way the person reasons or thinks until the formal operational stage, usually in late adolescence. For Erickson (1968) and Erikson and Erikson (1981) qualitative changes in personality occur at various stages up to the stage of ego integrity, usually in late adulthood.

In short, teleological causality involves genetic and maturational changes in the person, leading to different stages and different end points for different subsystems.

Third, formal causality exists in an organismic system. That is, causal rules or patterns can be identified by which the system operates to maintain or restore equilibrium at each stage of development. Such a concept of causality leads to the formulation of explanatory principles by which the organism or system as a whole maintains or restores its existing organization at a particular stage. For example, concepts such as homeostasis, balance, equilibrium, and negative feedback (Ford & Lerner, 1992) are theoretical notions formulated to account for patterns of activity by which the total system maintains itself. Efficient and material causality do exist, but they are secondary because the focus in this approach is to understand systems and the reciprocal relations between components.

Explanation of Change

Change does not have to be explained; it is intrinsic to the organismic system (Langer, 1969; Laszlo, 1972). Because change is a given, the person is viewed as intrinsically active, developing his or her capacities in the predetermined direction. However, conflict between the existing organization of the system and the environment often provides an impetus for further development through resolution of conflict. For example, through consciousness, the person spontaneously attends to the environment, attempts to understand it, and constructs his or her own world in doing so. The person never knows the world as it really is; instead, behavior is guided by the individual's interpretation of it. When the individual fails to interpret incoming stimuli in terms of what he or she already knows, there is a feeling of conflict, contradiction, or inconsistency. The impetus to resolve the latter leads to new mental growth, either by revising the original interpretation of the stimuli or modifying existing capacities that allow for understanding such stimuli. Such mental growth or understanding leads to a new balance between the complexity of incoming stimuli and the capacity to understand them. In other words, there is a strong tendency to maintain or restore an existing balance or organization in the system, but when imbalance cannot be restored by existing mechanisms, then imbalance leads to growth to reach a new stage of development. Balance is then maintained at this new stage until the amount of inconsistency, contradiction, or conflict can no longer be ignored, and there is impetus for regaining balance but at a more complex stage of development.

Although there are self-construction and self-regulation, and the content of what one individual learns may be quite different from what others learn, the direction in which capacities develop follows a predetermined fixed sequence to an end point.

Role of Context

Although some may distinguish between context and environment, we consider the terms to be essentially synonymous. In this view, the boundary of the system is the person's skin. The context is separate from the individual; it is static and passive in its influence on the individual. The context provides resources; for example, raw materials such as food, sunlight, existence of symbol systems, and so on, which the individual uses in his or her own manner as he or she develops. The context can influence the rate of development, however, depending upon the quality and quantity of resources in the environment. Moreover, if the environment or context is extremely deficient in providing basic resources or raw materials, then the direction and level of development may be influenced negatively. For example, lack of vitamin D may lead to rickets, or extreme deprivation of love may lead to an insecure and anxious individual.

Implications for Individual Development
Within a Family Context

One implication of an organismic metamodel is that the individual's development follows a fixed sequence through various stages of development, and that development occurs primarily from within, so that the context has relatively little influence. By analogy, some family theorists have constructed family stage theories in which the family as a whole goes through certain stages that essentially follow a fixed sequence, such as marriage, birth of a child, child rearing, launching of children, and so on.

Of course, when generating theories based on a stage concept, we must avoid mistakes that past theorists have made to account for individual differences in family functioning. Stages should be defined that are qualitatively distinct according to theory-based logical criteria, that are applicable to cross-cultural situations and other historical periods, and that include nontraditional forms of families, such as single-parent families (White, 1991).

However, because the direction and end point of development come from within individual family members or from tasks intrinsic to family stages, the linkage between individual and family development is limited and primarily concerned with the resources that family members provide for each other. These resources may influence the rate or level of both individual and family development. The linkage here is the supportive context provided to the person by family members so that the person is able to feel loved and accepted; to become less defensive; and to reflect, gain insight, and make intelligent choices that contribute to development.

Also, we must regard the family as a system including the target individual and other family members. In such an organismic system, there is a need for family members to maintain a balance between their cooperation or harmony and their competition or conflict in order to maintain the system. Theories formulated from this metamodel attempt to explain how the direction of individual and family development is facilitated or inhibited by the context, how linkage between them exists to maintain balance in the family system, how imbalance occurs, and how it is restored at a higher level of family development or functioning.

CONTEXTUALISM

Basic Assumptions of the Contextualism Metamodel

The basic unit of the contextualism metamodel is the event (Pepper, 1942). An event is a happening at a given moment in time as a result of the interaction of all the aspects of a system. The contextualism metamodel is based upon the following ideas.

The Person-Context

The person and the context cannot be separated as in organicism. Rather, the system includes both the person and the environment or context. One has no meaning without the other; the person's behavior can only be understood within the context wherein it occurs, and the context has no relevance if it is not occupied by someone. A person's smile may be indicative of happiness if the social context reveals that others are smiling with the person. On the other hand, the person's smile may indicate hostility if the social context reveals that others are dying and pleading for help.

Multilevel Context

The context consists of different levels of variables that are organized or coordinated in their activity (Riegel, 1976). The term *level* refers to variables of similar size units and common content. However, the individual's position as part of the total context can vary somewhat depending upon the way levels are identified.

One conceptualization views the context as consisting of the following level of variables: inner biological, individual-psychological, physical, and sociocultural (Riegel, 1976). Variables at the biological and psychological levels are within the individual, whereas variables at the physical and sociocultural levels are located in the environment surrounding the individual. However, to understand the individual's behavior and development, we must consider the reciprocal interactions, not only for levels *within* the individual and the environment, but *between* the individual and the environment. Thus, the individual and environment are viewed as one total context; that is, they must be considered together to understand any changes that occur.

Another conceptualization (Ford & Lerner, 1992) involves a large hierarchy of levels that cut across both the individual and the environment. In this case, levels may involve atomic, molecular, chemical, biological, physical, psychological, community, social, societal, cultural, and historical variables, and so on. The number of levels is arbitrary, depending upon the number that can be identified and is useful for understanding. Using appropriate instruments, one can identify variables both within and outside the individual at the levels appropriate to the phenomena to be studied.

The level of organized variables can also be viewed in another way. According to Baltes (1987), the individual's development is a product of the reciprocal interaction of history-graded, normative-graded, and nonnormative-graded factors. History-graded normative factors include variables within the individual and from the environment, such as the gene pool of a cohort, and an economic depression representing a historical time period. These are generational variables and have long-range effects. Age-graded normative variables include biological variables, such as the expected time of puberty, and environmental variables, such as the expected time of high school graduation, which are common to a particular culture. Nonnormative events are biological variables, such as occurrence of diabetes, and environmental variables, such as the death of a spouse, that are unique to the individual.

Context can also be conceptualized in terms of a set of concentric circles with the individual in the middle, with each circle representing a level of organized variables or factors. This view of context implies that different levels of variables may be more proximate and others more distal to the individual. Some levels of variables may exist in the present, whereas others exist in the past but have long-range effects; some levels of variables are common to everyone, whereas others are unique to an individual.

Regardless of variations in the conceptualization of context, it always involves levels of organized variables and reciprocal interaction within and between levels, and between such variables and the individual.

Reciprocal Causality

Although contextualism accepts several conceptions of causality, such as formal, efficient, material, and incidental causality (Lerner & Kauffman, 1985), the notion of reciprocal causality is predominant. The person–multilevel context is a dynamic system; that is, there is reciprocal interaction within each level of variables, between levels of variables, and between the person and the different levels of variables. Reciprocal causality is essential for contextualism, making the system dynamic, with interdependent, organized, and continually interacting components leading to continual change.

The total dynamic system may be too large for any one study. The researcher must focus on the outcome for a particular variable in the system, such as subjective experience or behavior of the person, and delineate the boundaries of a subsystem of variables involved in answering the research question.

Change and Development

As in the case of organicism, activity and change do not need to be explained; they are given as starting points of contextualism. Change occurs when a difference between points is detected over time. Development is a type of change by which the individual increases in complexity of organization, such as the coordination of new or more refined structures and functions, which further enhances survival and adaptation relative to existing conditions in the environment. Developmental change cannot be defined without a concomitant increase in adaptation.

In contrast to organicism, the direction of development in contextualism is not predetermined and does not have an end-point to development. This position involves a strong interaction between heredity and environment; there is no teleological causality based on a genetic–maturational blueprint that overrides the environment or context. The effect of genes depends upon the environment, and the effect of the environment depends upon the genes and previous development. The direction of change emerges from the ongoing reciprocal interaction among levels of variables, the person's development up to that point, and the person's self-construction of the future.

During the reciprocal interaction between the individual and the multilevel context, the timing at which certain aspects of the context interact with the individual can lead to different outcomes rather than the same outcome or a predetermined outcome (Ford & Lerner, 1992). Also, as reciprocal interaction occurs, function modifies structure and the latter modifies function (Baltes, 1987; Ford & Lerner, 1992). This is the basis for plasticity of the individual, increasing individual differences in old age, increasing multidirectionality (change or development occurring in different directions), and increasing multi-linearity (different characteristics of the individual simultaneously changing or developing in different directions).

Role of Context

In contextualism, the context is inseparable from the person. It is dynamic rather than static; that is, a reciprocal influence exists between the context and the person. It is organized at every level rather than being a mere collection or aggregate of variables. The individual can only be understood within a context.

Although the foregoing discussion characterizes contextualism in general, a distinction must be made between pure contextualism and quasi contextualism.

Pure Contextualism

Causality and the Direction of Development

In pure contextualism, not only is there is no end-point to development, but the direction of development is totally unpredictable. There is no necessary connection between the reciprocal interaction of person–multilevel context at a given moment in time and the next moment in time. What has happened previously does not necessarily determine or influence what development occurs at the next moment (Ford & Lerner, 1992). We might think of this as the ultimate in creativity as novel directions of development continue to emerge. Also, it follows that there are no limits to the increase in plasticity, individual differences, multidirectionality, and multilinearity. However, an issue might be raised in regard to pure contextualism. If everything is relative to the emerging context, then there is no possibility of building permanent knowledge. There is no basis for continuity, hence no possibility of building a cumulative body of scientific knowledge. Such a state of affairs would violate the basic notion of science, only if we assume that science must be concerned with building a stable and cumulative body of knowledge. If the person has the skills to deal with each novel situation as it emerges, then the focus of science would be on pragmatism; that is, identifying what works to deal with each unique situation. Only those skills would be cumulative that would help understand continual novelty.

In any case, if we take a long-term perspective, then an accumulated body of knowledge is an illusion because change is inevitable. The rate of change varies with different parts of the context, and in some cases, it may be so slow that it cannot be detected for quite some time. Yet, change is inevitable in the long term.

However, it may be possible to reconceptualize pure contextualism to include the idea that behind the appearance of total unpredictability there is predictability; that is, some sort of order may underlie apparent disorder. From such a meta-theoretical view, chaos theory (Gleick, 1987) would seem to apply as a possible derivation, so that ultimately predictability would be possible within the framework of pure contextualism.

Implications for Individual Development
Within the Family Context

At the present time, pure contextualism has not been applied to understanding individual development within the family. Obviously, it is difficult to think of individual and family development and the linkage between the two as being totally unpredictable.

However, it is possible to apply pure contextualism without describing or explaining the direction or end-point of development in advance. We could approach the change in the direction of development as a series of unique events in the present, with the researcher acting as a trouble shooter approaching each individual and family as unique to describe and understand for a short duration of time. Within that short time period, the trouble shooter could deal with any problems or decisions to be made. Eventually, skills in diagnosing a situation and helping to solve problems and make decisions in a present or contemporary situation could be transferred. Research would involve observation, sophisticated case studies, trouble-shooting skills, and the literary essay. Using this approach, the researcher might at least understand and appreciate the uniqueness of the person's development within the family context.

Quasi Contextualism

Causality and the Direction of Development

In one sense, pure contextualism might make total unpredictability a virtue, which it might be, if it represented emerging creativity. The quasi-contextualism position retains some degree of predictability.

Quasi contextualism is conceptualized as if total unpredictability of development were the ideal, with various strategies used to deal with total unpredictability. But in fact, strategies are used that can predict, to a certain degree, the direction of development, while, of course, retaining a degree of unpredictability. Laws of probability may be used to determine the degree to which the deviation in development from some normative direction of development can be predicted (Ford & Lerner, 1992). Such an approach is taken because it is assumed that some degree of organization, internal coherence, previous development, or early learning exists that ensures some degree of continuity or constraint within the individual from moment to moment (L'Abate, 1990, 1992a, 1992b; Cohen, Evans, Stokols, & Krantz, 1986; Ford & Lerner; Gollin, 1981; Stokols, 1987).

A further argument is that the direction of development is neither genetically predetermined nor totally unpredictable. The direction of development can be calculated as deviating from a normative standard of development with a certain degree of probability. There is a hereditary predisposition to develop in a certain direction, but there is also a reciprocal interaction with a multilevel context that permits various directions of development to emerge within a certain range (Scarr, 1982). Similarly, it follows that there are limits regarding the degree of plasticity, individual differences, multidirectionality, and multilinearity.

In carrying out research work, it would be overwhelming to include the total context if we were to attempt to collect data simultaneously on all the variables involved. There is a discrepancy between the conceptual notion of reciprocal interaction of variables within a multilevel context and the feasibility of considering them all within one study, especially as they are in dynamic interaction.

In practice, boundaries can be established to identify a subsystem of variables to be studied in relation to a particular problem. First, we can identify the target variable, and then theorize as to the contextual variables that are most important in the particular situation (Altman & Rogoff, 1987).

We can investigate such questions as the following: Does the individual's development vary in different settings? Is the development of individual *A* influenced by individual *B?* If so, does it depend upon the setting? Does the relationship between individuals *A* and *B* have a greater influence on the development of individual *B* than the relationship between individuals *C* and *B?* Does this vary with the setting? Do individuals *A* and *B* develop patterns of communication through their reciprocal interaction? Does their reciprocal interaction change *A* and *B,* which in turn changes their patterns of communication, and so on? Do these relationships vary in different settings? At what timing or stage of life do certain life events influence the relationship between other variables? However, all such studies must deal with reciprocal effects of variables, including any feedback loops and requiring such techniques as multivariate nonrecursive path analysis (Loehlin, 1992).

We can also carry out observational studies wherein the process patterns between individuals and the context are determined over time, as well as the reciprocal influence between process and structure (or characteristics) of the individuals and nonliving aspects of the context.

Implications for Individual Development Within the Family Context

The individual develops in relation to other individuals; that is, the individual develops in social interaction with others. In the quasi-contextualist position, the individual and family are part of the same context; they are all persons influencing each other in a reciprocal manner. To think in terms of individual development is simply to focus on one person among the family members (Ford & Lerner, 1992).

The individual is embedded in a multilevel context, with the proximal and important factor being the family. Although the focus of this chapter is the family context, quasi contextualism is also concerned with other levels of the context, such as the extrafamilial context of school, work, peers, and so on. However, within the family context, we would want to understand the processes by which family members interact with each other. Family members may interact in different ways to change each other; relationships between different family members may influence each other.

MECHANISM

Basic Assumptions of the Mechanistic Metamodel

The core of the mechanistic model is the machine; man and the world are considered to be similar to or analogous to a machine (Langer, 1969). Obviously, there are many kinds of machines, including the computer, but they all have certain elements in common.

A machine is basically passive or inactive. Initiation of activity or change comes from external forces or decay from within. Machines do not develop, but they do wear out. They are composed of parts that act independently of each other, and their total effect is the sum of the activities of the parts.

To state that man is similar to a machine is to assert that man is basically passive. The individual does not initiate activity, behavior, or change; these are induced from the outside. It may be that even physiological activity, such as the electrical activity in the brain, is not intrinsic to tissue or organs but is induced from the outside, although we cannot detect the induction process at present. The body may be like a transformer where weak currents are induced from outside and are amplified to provide the internal activity that we ordinarily detect, thereby creating the illusion of intrinsic activity.

The individual perceives reality directly. There is a direct correspondence between what the individual perceives and the real world. The individual may construct his or her perceptions, but they correspond to the real world. The fact that the external environment can be perceived directly allows for the influence of external forces.

Consciousness exists but is an epiphenomenon; that is, it does not cause anything, but is merely a by-product of causal chains of events initiated from external or internal forces. The individual may observe ongoing events and have the illusion of causing them, but they are beyond that person's control. The passivity of the individual, direct perception of reality, and consciousness as an epiphenomenon all serve to limit any possibility of the individual's acting as a cause of his or her own activity, behavior, or development.

Two types of forces or causes operate here. *Efficient cause* is an application of an external force on the individual. It is the immediate antecedent factor that initiates activity, behavior change, or development. *Material cause* is an internal cause in the sense of a deficiency or defect in the material of an object, such as a defect in the brain that leads to erratic behavior.

Another aspect of the mechanistic approach is that the influences of heredity and environment are considered to be independent of each other, their combined effect being additive. This is important, because if one antecedent variable qualifies the effect of another on a dependent or consequent variable, the interaction effect of the two antecedent variables is not the additive effects of the individual variables. This meaning of interaction is quite different from the reciprocal interaction found in organicism and contextualism.

In the mechanistic framework, context is synonymous with the environment. It is static and separate or independent of the individual. However, context includes the external or efficient cause operating on the individual.

When this framework is applied to psychology, forces are translated into external stimuli leading to conditioning or learning (Langer, 1969). Internal forces may be normal or defective physiological functioning that influences behavior. Learning is the connection of external stimuli to overt behavior, regardless of all the intervening connections and activities that may occur in modern conceptions of this viewpoint. Individual change and development over time take place as a result of learning or conditioning. Thus, development becomes synonymous with sustained learning or learning over long time periods. If we understand the principles of learning, we can program the environment to initiate activity, behavior, and the direction of change in the individual. This is the process approach to understanding development in the individual.

Some might argue that pure contextualism is a form of environmental determinism wherein the individual can be changed or molded into anything desired. Contextualism would then be the metamodel for operant behaviorism (Morris, 1988). But this does not follow. Although both mechanism and pure contextualism hold that the direction in which the individual develops is unlimited in its possibilities, the mechanist believes that such change or development is controlled by others shaping the individual from the outside. Hence, the direction of change is unlimited but predictable, based upon the schedules of reinforcement used with a particular individual. In contrast, the contextualist believes that the direction of change or development is unlimited and unpredictable, because the cause of development is the reciprocal interaction between a continually changing individual and a changing multilevel context.

Role of Context

In the mechanistic position, the individual is related to the context in one of two ways. First, the context is simplistic (Ford & Lerner, 1992), reduced to a unilevel where it has been translated into stimulus–response units. If certain parts of the context, such as social-cultural aspects, cannot be translated, they are simply ignored. Such an approach would be typical of behavior analysis or operant conditioning. Second, context is viewed as the statistical interaction between levels of antecedent variables. As such, contextual variables can be used in analysis of variance or multivariate statistical procedures (e.g., recursive path analysis) to help understand or qualify unidirectional causal theories.

The researcher may desire to understand the relationship of antecedent variables to outcome. In this case, context may be considered to be multilevel. Previous questions asked from a contextualistic viewpoint may also be considered here, if only unidirectional causality and statistical interaction are involved. For example, if a researcher is investigating the effect of one relationship upon another relationship (such as the effect of the quality of the spouses' relationship on the quality of sibling relationships), this type of question can be answered under a mechanistic approach, with the assumption that unidirectional causality is involved.

Implications of Mechanism for Individual Development Within the Family Context

The context in this case is limited to the family. However, the family as such is a collection of individuals, each having an independent effect on the target individual, with the total effect on the target individual being the sum of the individual effects. Informal conditioning or learning goes on between each family member and the target individual in the naturalistic family environment, leading to sustained learning or development over time. The researcher might want to carry out naturalistic studies to observe the informal processes of learning occurring. If the interest is only in input and output, we might carry out a regression analysis to determine whether family context variables, such as the number of siblings or parental warmth, account for most of the variance in the subject's behavior or learning, and also to determine to what extent these factors statistically interact as they influence the subject's behavior or learning.

From a mechanistic viewpoint, family members have certain values that are transmitted in the process of socializing children. Informally, family members condition children according to implicit reinforcement schedules to learn certain behaviors or roles. It is the parents or older siblings who mold or shape the younger children. Nutritional patterns, exercise patterns, learning experiences, and so on, can all be programmed with appropriate reinforcers, or schedules of reinforcement, to socialize individuals in the family. In summary, individual family members have individual impacts on the target individual, and they mold or shape the latter's direction of development according to their own values and norms. There is no end-point to development, but the direction of the target individual's development is related to antecedent family variables that operate in only one direction, from family member to the target individual. Family context, then, is a vehicle for molding or shaping the individual's development by other family members.

The linkage between individual and family development is difficult to ascertain because the concept of development has been reduced to sustained learning. However, it would seem to be the molding or shaping of the individual's development through informal conditioning or other learning techniques involving some schedule of rewards and punishments.

DISCUSSION

Individual and family development both take place over the life span. How the individual develops within the family context, and the linkage between individual and family development, are still somewhat of an open question.

Summary of Metamodels

This chapter does not attempt to document such development and linkage by reviewing and integrating empirical studies, or to explain them by any particular theory. Instead, it attempts to make explicit the assumptions of metamodels from which schools of thought or specific theories have been or can be generated to account for development.

Organicism

Organicism implies stage models of individual and family development, with the direction and end-point of individual development determined primarily from genetic or maturational factors. Family context is separate from the individual, and linkage to individual development is limited to providing a supportive and caring environment to facilitate the rate of development. The latter also includes the individual and family as part of a system in which a harmonious balance relative to conflict is maintained to facilitate the development for family members. Schools of thought and specific theories can be derived from this framework, identifying the kinds of stages involved, how balance or harmony is maintained or restored among family members, and how imbalance occurs leading to new levels of harmonious development for the family as a whole.

Contextualism

From a contextualism metamodel, there is reciprocal interaction between all family members; to discuss individual development is merely to focus on a particular individual in the larger family system. Such reciprocal interaction leads to development in different directions, with no end-point for the various family members. The linkage between the individual and family members is in the reciprocal interaction between them that simultaneously changes all of them. The direction and end-point of development depend upon the reciprocal interaction of different levels of variables, the timing of their interaction, and the previous organization or development of the individual. Schools of thought and specific theories can be derived from such a starting point, specifying how variables interact, what variables are involved from what levels, and the timing of their interaction.

Mechanism

From a mechanistic metamodel, the individual does develop in a context but it has a different meaning from context in a contextualism metamodel. For the mechanist, context can be a unilevel concept involving only stimulus–response units in which others relate to the individual in order to mold or shape him or her according to the norms of society. In some formulations of mechanistic theory, context can involve multilevels, but nevertheless, it represents antecedent variables having a unidirectional direct effect or a statistical interaction effect on the individual.

From a mechanistic metamodel, the individual is molded by the family, whereas both are shaped by the larger environment or context. Development becomes synonymous with sustained learning, especially conditioning. The family context is separate from the individual, and the latter is conditioned or socialized according to the family norms and values, which in turn represent the larger culture. As in contextualism, there is neither a predetermined direction nor an end-point to either individual or family development. However, development of the individual is determined by family values and norms, but not in reciprocal interaction with the latter. The linkage is the use of informal learning or conditioning by family members to socialize the individual.

On the Meaning of Context

The literature contains numerous papers in which authors use the term *context* in various ways without making explicit the underlying metamodel representing that context, thus confusing the reader trying to understand the role of context (Winegar & Valsiner, 1992a, 1992b). Sometimes the terms *context, contextual,* and *contextualizing* are confused with *contextualism* as a world view or metamodel. Different meanings of context lead to different views on family context and its relationship to the individual's development over the life cycle.

It is important to realize how different the meaning of context is within different metamodels. It is important because the label *context* is used with increasing frequency in the writings of different theorists and researchers, and the term is sometimes confused with *contextualism* as a metatheoretical viewpoint. Therefore, when discussing family context, it should be made clear whether the context referred to is that of organicism, mechanism, or contextualism, thus avoiding any confusion of the concept of context with contextualism. In short, for mechanism, the environment determines the direction and end-point of development; for organicism, the environment facilitates the rate of development and possibly the level of development attained; for quasi contextualism, the environment reciprocally interacts with the person so that they mutually determine the direction and end-point of development; and for pure contextualism, the environment and the individual also mutually influence each other but with unpredictability as to the direction and end-point of development.

Future Directions

More important, a comprehensive theory is needed to explain individual and family development and their linkage over the life span, a theory from which precise predictions can be made and confirmed. Because such a theory does not yet exist, and because such theories are based upon metamodels containing assumptions about the nature of man and the world, then it may be essential to: (a) explore the present metamodels in greater depth to generate new theories; (b) search for new metamodels; and (c) develop new hybrids of existing metamodels. Some researchers (Reese & Overton, 1970) feel that metamodels are mutually exclusive. However, some schools of thought and specific theories do not fit precisely into these categories. Some require a hybrid metamodel integrating organicism and contextualism, such as the humanistic theories of Maslow (1954) or Rogers (1969), or the developmental systems theory and living systems framework (Ford & Lerner, 1992), or life span development and aging theories (Cicirelli, in press). Certainly, the family of information theories and specific theories based on Freudianism are generated more from a hybrid mechanistic-organicistic metamodel than from either metamodel alone.

Contextualism is the present fad in metamodels. However, its potential for generating specific theories and schools of thought is only now being exploited. Instead of remaining a perspective or set of beliefs that includes contextualism, life span developmental psychology may eventually become a broad theory generated from quasi contextualism. The possibility of an integration of chaos theory with pure contextualism has yet to be explored.

In any event, explaining individual and family development and their linkage over the life span does involve understanding the basic underlying assumptions of the nature of man and the world; this is the starting point for generating theories. Many researchers still do not understand this thesis. They feel that a theory should be based on experience alone, divorced from any preconceived metatheories. But this position is a metatheory in itself; such empiricism can generate only certain kinds of theories that may fall short of explaining and predicting individual and family development over the life span.

REFERENCES

Altman, I., & Rogoff, B. (1987). World views in psychology: Trait, interactional, organismic, and transactional perspectives. In D. Stokols & I. Altman (Eds.), *Handbook of environmental psychology* (pp. 7–40). New York: Wiley.

Baltes, P. B. (1987). Theoretical propositions of life-span developmental psychology: On the dynamics between growth and decline. *Developmental Psychology, 23,* 611–626.

Bandura, A. (1986). *Social foundations of thought and action: A social cognitive theory.* Englewood Cliffs, NJ: Prentice-Hall.

Cicirelli, V. G. (in press). Intergenerational communication in the mother–daughter dyad regarding caregiving decisions. In N. Coupland & J. Nussbaum (Eds.), *Discourse in life-span development.* Newbury Park, CA: Sage.

Cohen, S., Evans, G. W., Stokols, D., & Krantz, D. S. (1986). *Behavior, health and environmental stress.* New York: Plenum.

Erikson, E. H. (1968). *Identity, youth, and crisis.* New York: Norton.

Erikson, E. H., & Erikson, J. M. (1981). On generativity and identity. *Harvard Educational Review, 51,* 249–269.

Ford, D. H., & Lerner, R. M. (1992). *Developmental systems theory.* Newbury Park, CA: Sage.

Gleick, J. (1987). *Chaos: Making a new science.* New York: Penguin.

Gollin, E. S. (1981). Development and plasticity. In E. S. Gollin (Ed.), *Developmental plasticity: Behavioral and biological aspects of variations in development* (pp. 231–331). New York: Academic Press.

Hull, C. (1942). Conditioning: Outline of a systematic theory of learning. *Yearbook of the National Society for the Study of Education, 42* (2), 61–97.

Kohlberg, L. (1981). *The philosophy of moral development.* New York: Harper & Row.

Kreppner, K., & Lerner, R. M. (Eds.). (1989). *Family systems and life-span development.* Hillsdale, NJ: Erlbaum.

L'Abate, L. (1990). A theory of competencies × settings interactions. *Marriage and Family Review, 15,* 253–269.

L'Abate, L. (1992a). *A resource exchange classification of settings.* Unpublished manuscript, Georgia State University, Atlanta.

L'Abate, L. (1992b). *A theory of personality development.* Manuscript submitted for publication.

Langer, J. (1969). *Theories of development.* New York: Holt, Rinehart & Winston.

Laszlo, E. (1972). *The systems view of the world: The natural philosophy of the new developments in the sciences.* New York: Braziller.

Lerner, R. M., & Kauffman, M. B. (1985). The concept of development in contextualism. *Developmental Review, 5,* 309–333.

Loehlin, J. C. (1992). *Latent variable models: An introduction to factor, path, and structural analysis* (2nd ed.). Hillsdale, NJ: Erlbaum.

Maslow, A. H. (1954). *Motivation and personality.* New York: Harper & Row.

Morris, E. K. (1988). Contextualism: The world view of behavior analysis. *Journal of Experimental Child Psychology, 46,* 289–323.

Pepper, S. C. (1942). *World hypotheses: A study in evidence.* Berkeley: University of California Press.

Piaget, J. (1954). *The construction of reality in the child.* New York: Basic Books.

Reese, H. W., & Overton, W. F. (1970). Models of development and theories of development. In L. R. Goulet & P. B. Baltes (Eds.), *Life-span developmental psychology: Research and theory* (pp. 115–145). New York: Academic Press.

Riegel, K. F. (1976). From traits and equilibrium toward developmental dialectics. In W. J. Arnold & J. K. Cole (Eds.), *Psychology and gender: Nebraska symposium on motivation* (pp. 349–408). Lincoln: University of Nebraska Press.

Rogers, C. R. (1969). *Freedom to learn.* Columbus, OH: Merrill.

Salthouse, T. A. (1991). *Theoretical perspectives on cognitive aging.* Hillsdale, NJ: Erlbaum.

Scarr, S. (1982). Development is internally guided, not determined. *Contemporary Psychology, 27,* 852–853.

Skinner, B. F. (1953). *Science and human behavior.* New York: Macmillan.

Sternberg, R. J. (1990). *Metaphors of mind: Conceptions of the nature of intelligence.* Cambridge, UK: Cambridge University Press.

Stokols, D. (1987). Conceptual strategies of environmental psychology. In D. Stokols, & I. Altman (Eds.), *Handbook of environmental psychology* (pp. 41–70). New York: Wiley.

White, J. M. (1991). *Dynamics of family development: A theoretical perspective.* New York: Guilford.

Winegar, L. T., & Valsiner, J. (Eds.). (1992a). *Children's development within social context, Vol. 1: Metatheory and theory.* Hillsdale, NJ: Erlbaum.

Winegar, L. T., & Valsiner, J. (Eds.). (1992b). *Children's development within social context. Vol. 2: Research and methodology.* Hillsdale, NJ: Erlbaum.

CHAPTER 3

The Longest Bond: The Sibling Life Cycle

VICTOR G. CICIRELLI

Most individuals' relationships with their siblings are likely to be the longest bonds they will have with anyone during their lives; therefore these relationships merit attention. This chapter presents new concepts, issues, areas of inquiry, and research findings about the sibling relationship over the life cycle, citing literature published since my earlier review in the first handbook of family psychology (Cicirelli, 1985b). Because the field is so broad, the approach taken in this chapter is topical.

MEANING OF THE SIBLING RELATIONSHIP

Meaning of a Relationship

The personal relationship perspective (Duck & Perlman, 1985; Hartup, 1975; Hinde, 1981; Huston & Robins, 1982; Kelley et al., 1983) provides the background for the definition of a relationship: the interdependency of two individuals as manifested in their interactions (actions, verbal and nonverbal communication), which influence their beliefs, knowledge, attitudes, and feelings toward each other and, which, in turn, influence their further interactions. The cognitive and affective dispositions are long lasting and relatively stable, and they account for the influence of individuals in their absence, for continuation of the relationship over periods when there is no behavioral interaction, and for the motivation to make contact after a separation. A relationship involves two individuals, with events and relationships with other individuals providing the context in which the original relationship is embedded.

Many types of relationships exist (marital, romantic, parent–child, work, friendship, etc.), defined by differences in attributes that characterize the interdependency or interconnectedness between individuals.

The Sibling Relationship

The distinguishing characteristic of a sibling relationship is that it is between two individuals who share common biologic origins from both parents. Because the relationship is ascribed rather than voluntary, most siblings have a commitment to maintain it. The sibling relationship lasts longer than most others with siblings typically sharing a long history of intimate family experiences. Moreover, the sibling relationship is more egalitarian than other relationships. (Half-siblings share biologic origins from only one parent, whereas stepsiblings and adoptive siblings have no common biologic origins. Depending upon family circumstances, they may or may not share other characteristics of a sibling relationship.)

Stability of the Sibling Relationship

An hourglass effect in sibling involvement—wherein sibling closeness and interaction gradually decrease in early adulthood, are low in the middle adult years, and rise again in late adulthood and old age—is well supported by research findings (Bedford, 1993). Apart from such a general trend, individual sibling relationships seem to wax and wane with life circumstances. In a 4-year longitudinal study (Bedford, in press) about two thirds of the respondents reported a change in feelings toward a sibling over time, related to life events. The direction of the change depended upon the interpretations and interactions of the siblings in reaction to the events, and it was likely to be positive rather than negative.

EXPLAINING SIBLING SIMILARITIES AND DIFFERENCES

The nature–nurture issue is one that is relevant to the study of sibling differences. Applying the methods of behavioral genetics (twin studies, adoption studies) to sibling differences (Scarr & Gracek, 1982), has helped to make it clear that not only does genetic similarity fail to explain sibling differences in personality, psychopathology, and cognition, but that the environment shared by siblings also provides little explanation for such phenomena. Authors of two excellent recent reviews of this literature (Dunn & Stocker, 1989; Hoffman, 1991) conclude that environmental influences not shared by siblings must, therefore, account for the differences. Siblings may not only experience different environments outside the home (different playmates, different teachers, etc.), but environments experienced by different siblings within the home may also differ as a result of differential parental treatment, sibling interactions themselves (including the children's perceptions and interpretations of each other's behaviors), and events experienced by one sibling but not the other (Dunn & Stocker, 1989).

Differences in mothers' behaviors toward young siblings have been observed (Brody, Stoneman, & Burke, 1987; Bryant & Crockenberg, 1980; Dunn & Munn, 1986; Dunn, Plomin, & Daniels, 1986; Stocker, Dunn, & Plomin, 1989). Older children (Furman & Buhrmester, 1985) and adolescents (Daniels, Dunn, Furstenberg, & Plomin, 1985) have reported differential parental treatment. Such differences were associated with sibling adjustment and relationship to each other, when one sibling perceived him- or herself as the deprived or unfavored child. In interactions with one another, older siblings tended to be initiators of behavior, and younger siblings were followers (Abramovich, Corter, Pepler, & Stanhope, 1986; Brody et al., 1987; Dunn & Munn, 1986; Rodgers & Rowe, 1988).

However, the situation may be somewhat more complex than presented above. Hoffman (1991) points out that the child is an active interpreter of his or her environment, as well as an elicitor of parent and sibling behaviors. As a result, the child's interpretation of parent and sibling influences determines whether the characteristics of the sibling or their opposite will appear in the child. Furthermore, the child's age, gender, and physical appearance (attractiveness, resemblance to a parent, and so on) at the time of a given event, also influence personality development. Finally, sibling similarity is greater in such things as attitudes and values than in personality traits.

DIMENSIONS AND TYPES OF RELATIONSHIPS WITH SIBLINGS

In Cicirelli (1985b), such basic dimensions of the sibling relationship as feelings of closeness, rivalry, and involvement were discussed. Findings of increased closeness between elderly sisters were reported in Bayen, Gruber-Baldini, and Schaie (1991). Sibling rivalry may be considerably greater in adulthood than was previously thought, decreasing little with advancing age, based on the use of projective techniques (Bedford, 1989) and extended interviews (Gold, 1989b).

Rather than using single dimensions or a profile of dimensions, Bank and Kahn (1982) identified several types or patterns of sibling relationships—fused, blurred, hero worship (idealization), mutual dependence (loyalty), dynamic independence, hostile dependence, rigid differentiation, and disownment. Gold (1989b) identified five types of sibling relationships—intimate, congenial, loyal, apathetic, and hostile. These typologies were upheld by data reanalysis using a "fuzzy set" clustering methodology (Gold, Woodbury, & George, 1990), in a study of African Americans (Gold, 1990), and in an independent replication (Scott, 1990). To the extent that the existence of such types can be generalized, they may prove useful for describing sibling relationships.

INFLUENCE OF SIBLINGS

Siblings as Models

As might be expected, older siblings can serve as models for their younger siblings in a variety of behaviors. Children as young as 6 months showed significant improvement on cognitive tasks after observing sibling modeling (Wishart, 1986). In adolescence, as well, older siblings have been found to have a "pioneering" influence on younger siblings' sexual behavior (Rodgers & Rowe, 1988).

Well-Being

As noted earlier, different parental treatment of siblings was associated with poorer adjustment in childhood and adolescence (Daniels et al., 1985; Furman & Buhrmester, 1985). The issue of whether sibling relationships influence well-being in adulthood and old age remained unresolved until recently. McGhee (1985) found that frequency of interaction with siblings was unrelated to the well-being of older people, but the existence and potential availability of a sister was related to greater life satisfaction for both men and women. O'Bryant (1988) found that interaction with married sisters predicted a higher positive affect among older widows. In my own work (Cicirelli, 1989), the perception of a close bond to sisters by either men or women was related to well-being, whereas a close bond to brothers seemed to have little relevance for well-being.

SIBLINGS AND PSYCHOTHERAPY

The sibling relationship can contribute to poor adjustment and psychopathology. However, despite Bank and Kahn's (1982) early work on sibling therapy, the literature on psychotherapy in childhood and adolescence tends to concentrate on family therapy more than sibling influence. In a recent volume on sibling therapy (Kahn & Lewis, 1988), Lewis (1988) recommended sibling group therapy in situations where specific problems exist between siblings, where there is a family crisis, or where the family structure is unstable. The goals of such therapy are to support and strengthen the natural sibling hierarchy, to enable the children to support and care for each other emotionally. Adolescent siblings can take a more active role in psychotherapy (Harris, 1988), helping siblings to understand their own roles and behaviors more clearly and to alter those roles in order to effect change in the family system.

Siblings, present or absent, continue to be important to adjustment in adult life. Bank (1988) states that sibling conflicts are the outgrowth of a disturbing family situation early in life and need to be resolved. He advocates helping the patient grow to see the problematic sibling relationship as part of the entire family pattern in childhood, and to reduce the idealization of parents. Sibling problems can reappear when adult siblings must care for an aged parent. Here, the goal of therapy is to help the group to work together to achieve an appropriate care plan for the parent (Tonti, 1988).

Sibling relationships can be important factors in mental health problems of elderly persons (Cicirelli, 1988). Early conflicts and estrangements persisting from childhood or from times of later critical incidents (Dunn, 1984), long-term sibling dependencies, or reactivated rivalries and aggressions can all necessitate therapy, but few guidelines exist for treatment. Close-knit siblings can be seen either as a group or individually for therapy (Church, 1986; Kahn, 1988; Toman, 1988). Approaches range from probing sibling relationships in the course of psychoanalysis (Rosner, 1985), to individual therapy, to inclusion of siblings in family therapy or family counseling (Palazzoli, 1985). Reminiscence used in the life review process has gained favor as an approach to therapy with older people (Butler, 1963; Gold, 1986; Molinari & Reichlin, 1985; Osgood, 1985).

COMMUNICATION WITH SIBLINGS

Communication between siblings is an important means of influence, however little research into sibling communication exists. Ervin-Tripp (1989) indicates that older siblings do much of the communication work within the family—communicating with the younger children, trying to understand their communications; accommodating to the younger children's low level of language competence; soliciting repetition; asking clarification questions; and offering expansions. Shared family history and common language experiences should enable older siblings to practice an intimate communication style, with many shortcuts and implied meanings (Cicirelli, 1985a); indeed, most communication between elderly siblings centered on discussions of family events and concerns, and on old times in general.

SIBLINGS AS FRIENDS

Many parallels between siblings and friends suggest that siblings may be viewed as friends (Connidis, 1989; Connidis & Davies, 1990). Both typically are age peers, play a broad range of roles, and have ready access to each other; the relationship is characterized by egalitarianism, equal power, sociability, and limited obligations. However, sibling relationships differ from friendships in that the sibling bond is ascribed, whereas the friendship bond is voluntary; moreover, siblings compete for parental attention, whereas friends do not. Although three fourths of Connidis's subjects considered at least one sibling to be a close friend, friends were more prominent in their *companion* network, whereas siblings were more prominent in their *confidant* network, suggesting that friends and siblings occupy subtly different roles in the support systems of older individuals.

SIBLINGS IN FAMILY BUSINESSES

For some siblings, interaction includes participation in a family-owned business. According to Carroll (1988), some 12 million businesses in the United States are family owned, although the number of these in which siblings are partners or co-workers is not known. Family issues and business issues are inextricably interwoven in such ventures. In sibling interactions on business matters, old themes of intimacy, dependency, rivalry, trust, and fairness in the sibling relationship reappear, with business themes of power, control, responsibility, and succession in the business depending upon harmonious sibling relationships for successful resolution.

DEVIANT SIBLING RELATIONSHIPS: INCEST, VIOLENCE, AND ABUSE

In Cicirelli (1985b), the existence of excessively aggressive sibling interactions and coercive sexual interactions was noted. Yet, relatively little research into these problems is available. Alpert (1991) suggests that although some sexual exploration between siblings may be normal, the age difference between the children; the presence of coercion; and the frequency, duration, and purpose of the sexual behavior are all factors that indicate sexual abuse. Victims of childhood sibling sexual abuse not only are more likely to be abused as adults, but their ability or desire to marry is impaired, with almost half never marrying. This is not surprising, given that continuing anger toward sibling abusers is found to persist well into adulthood (Wiehe, 1990). Heiman (1988) has suggested various therapeutic steps for such cases.

Sibling violence, perhaps even more than sibling sexual abuse, is a significant problem in many families. Alpert (1991) reported that up to 30% of children live in violent homes. Patterson (1986), who found that up to half of the children referred to clinicians for aggressive and antisocial behaviors at school also displayed such behaviors at home with their siblings, concluded that the deviant behavior was actually "trained" and practiced within the family environment.

SIBLING HELPING RELATIONSHIPS

Over the life span and in most cultures, siblings perform a variety of helping and supportive activities for each other (Weisner, 1989), ranging from sibling caregiving (Bryant, 1989; Dunn, 1989) and teaching (Ervin-Tripp, 1989) in childhood, to exchange of goods and services in adulthood, to social support and caregiving in old age.

Developmental tasks (Goetting, 1986) of siblings in early and middle adulthood include providing companionship and emotional support, cooperating in the care of elderly parents, and providing occasional aid and services; whereas tasks of siblings in old age include providing aid and direct services to other siblings, as well as increasing social support. Most adults have been socialized to accept norms of proper sibling behavior; those with stronger sibling responsibility expectations also reported more contact with siblings (Lee, Mancini, & Maxwell, 1990).

Sibling helping activities in old age have been more extensively studied than those in early and middle adulthood. Despite the fact that most older people regard their siblings as a resource to be called upon if needed (Cicirelli, 1989; Goetting, 1986), relatively few actually rely on a sibling for caregiving help. Only about 7% of impaired elderly persons received help from siblings (Cicirelli, Coward, & Dwyer, 1992); the need for help was associated with an elder sibling's impairments of instrumental functions and tended to go to those elderly siblings with neither spouse nor children. Among elderly African Americans and Anglos, Suggs (1989) found that siblings exchanged help in the areas of illness, housekeeping, and transportation. Gold (1986, 1989a), in a longitudinal study of sibling helping patterns, found that instrumental help went to older and widowed siblings. Although instrumental help declined over time, it was because the helpers' own needs or declining health prevented them from continuing to assist their sibling. Bedford (1989) reported that instances of sustained sibling help in old age were rare, although siblings did help in crisis situations. In interviews with recent widows, O'Bryant (1988) found that sibling help was greatest when the sibling lived nearby and there was no adult child in the vicinity; help tended to be gender-stereotypic. Cicirelli (1990) found that tangible support from siblings to hospitalized elders was second only to support from spouses; the most desired sibling help was psychological support, a type of help for which siblings may be uniquely suited by virtue of their common values and perceptions (Avioli, 1989; Dunn, 1985; Cicirelli, 1988).

Most sibling helping relationships tend to be characterized by balanced reciprocity in the exchange of help (Avioli, 1989; Bedford, 1989; Gold, 1989a; Johnson, 1988; Suggs, 1989). When reciprocity is not possible, an elderly person may extend help to a sibling based on a shared history of reciprocal aid, but such help is usually temporary unless some reciprocation occurs (Brady & Noberini, 1987; Stoller, 1985). Unilateral or unreciprocated help seems to distress both the sibling giver and the sibling receiver. However, reciprocity did not seem to be an issue for the majority of elderly persons, who indicated that they would or might consider living with a sibling (Borland, 1989).

ADULT SIBLINGS AS CAREGIVERS
TO ELDERLY PARENTS

If caring for aging parents is a developmental task of middle-aged adult siblings, it is of interest to know the extent to which each sibling in the family participates, particularly because it is generally assumed that one adult daughter assumes the principal caregiving role (Aldous, 1987; Brody, 1990). Matthews' studies (Matthews, 1987, 1988; Matthews, Delaney, & Adamek, 1989; Matthews & Rosner, 1988; Matthews & Sprey, 1989) have focused on the contributions of the entire middle-aged sibling subsystem to the care of elderly parents. In the two-child family, Matthews and Rosner found that pairs of adult sisters tended to share responsibility for help. In larger families, support was less likely to be shared by all, especially in those families with one or more brothers (Matthews & Rosner). For larger families, five types of sibling participation in parent care were identified: routine regular help, back-up help, circumscribed help limited by amount or type, sporadic help, and dissociation from any responsibility to help the parent. Sisters were more likely to use routine or back-up styles of participation, whereas brothers' help tended to be sporadic or circumscribed. Brothers spent fewer hours helping than did their sisters. Yet, brothers seemed willing to cooperate and to fulfill their filial obligations. Brody (Brody, Brody, Hoffman, Kleban, & Schoonover, 1989; Brody, Kleban, Hoffman, & Schoonover, 1988) found that daughters serving as principal caregivers provided three times as many hours of help weekly as did sisters who lived nearby and six times as many hours as their nearby brothers. However, recent work by Coward and Dwyer (1990) indicated that sons from sibling networks with no sisters available provided essentially as many hours of care as daughters from networks with no available brothers.

Adult children with intact marriages reported giving significantly more help to their elderly parents than their siblings, whereas those with disrupted marriages reported giving about the same amount of help as did their siblings (Cicirelli, 1984). In both cases, however, there were gender differences in the type of help provided.

In a more recent study (Cicirelli, 1992a), four patterns of sibling care sharing were identified: principal caregiver provides all care, while siblings provide none—5% of families; principal caregiver provides over half the caregiving load, while siblings share the remainder—55%; respondent provides more care than siblings, but no one provides more than half the caregiving load—19%; and approximately an equal division of caregiving between all siblings—21%. In most families, siblings coordinated their help to parents. Despite the apparent inequities in caregiving contributions, most respondents felt that the division of caregiving responsibilities with their siblings was fair.

Findings of various studies of siblings in the adult child generation show considerable convergence, despite the different methods used (Cicirelli, 1992b), indicating much more support from siblings than was previously recognized. It must be remembered, of course, that respondents' egocentric bias will lead them to overestimate their own contributions in relation to those of their siblings (Lerner, Somers, Reid, Chiriboga, & Tierney, 1991). Overall, sisters provide more and different types of help than brothers, and they tend to share help more equally. Some studies indicate that brothers abdicate caregiving roles sooner than sisters do (Brody, 1990; Montgomery & Kamo, 1989), although Stoller (1990) found no difference. A sex role taboo may prevent sons from giving more intimate types of care to their mothers (Coward & Dwyer, 1990; Matthews, 1988; Montgomery & Kamo), contributing further to the prevalence of women as caregivers.

Adult Siblings as Decision Makers

One important area of adult children's help to elderly parents is making decisions about the parent's care. Decisions about current care were made by all siblings in only one sixth of families, but about two thirds felt that siblings would make future decisions together, in the event of the parent's incapacity (Cicirelli, 1992a). Furthermore, daughters who assumed the principal caregiving load made more paternalistic decisions for the parent than those who shared caregiving with siblings; it seems that siblings making caregiving decisions as a group show more respect for the elderly parent's autonomy than a single adult child making decisions independently.

SIBLING DEATH AND GRIEVING

Death of a sibling, whenever it occurs, can have profound effects on an individual. The level of the child's understanding of death, the nature of the child's personality, and the circumstances of the death will interact to determine a child's reactions to sibling death (Bank & Kahn, 1982; Coleman & Coleman, 1984; Stephenson, 1986). Apparent lack of grief may reflect the inability to comprehend the loss. On the other hand, adolescents may suppress their grief in order to appear strong to their peers. Excessive guilt reactions, distorted concepts of illness and death, death phobias, disturbed attitudes toward doctors, hospitals, and religion, and disturbances in behavior and cognitive functioning can all accompany childhood grief over a sibling's death. When sibling death occurs in childhood (Bank & Kahn; Cain, Fast, & Erickson, 1964; Stephenson), the survivor may be regarded as a substitute expected to live up to an idealized image of the deceased sibling, whatever the cost to his or her own personality.

From a retrospective study of adults who had lost a sibling in childhood, Rosen (1984–85) concluded that significant prohibitions (denial of the death, lack of communication, and injunctions to be strong) exist against adequate mourning and working through the loss. In this study, more than two thirds lost a sibling with little or no advance knowledge. Only about three fourths attended the funeral services, approximately the same proportion as that in a study by McCown (McCown, 1984; McCown & Pratt, 1985). McCown found that about one fourth of bereaved children showed problem behaviors in the year following the sibling death. Loss of a sibling creates significant difficulty for a surprisingly large proportion of children.

Sibling death in childhood may be particularly traumatic because of its nonnormative nature and the child's lack of understanding. However, adjustment to sibling loss in adulthood and old age is not necessarily easier. Moss and Moss (1986, 1989) found a heightened sense of personal vulnerability to death when a sibling dies in adulthood, particularly if the sibling dies unexpectedly or "off-time" with unfinished developmental tasks to complete, leaving the surviving siblings with feelings of emptiness, helplessness, and hopelessness. There is a search for meaning in the sibling's death and a sense of existential incompleteness in the family; renegotiation of family relationships in such a circumstance can also present difficulties. Almost half of elderly siblings found the loss to be somewhat difficult. The same themes found in earlier adulthood were present in old age; however, the survivors had learned how to master losses and grief and most adjusted well to the sibling's death.

EXPLAINING SIBLING RELATIONSHIPS WITH THEADULT ATTACHMENT THEORY

Most research on sibling relationships has been atheoretical in nature, or one or another existing theory is cited in an ad hoc explanation. However, it is necessary to explain the origin of bonds between siblings and the persistence of such bonds over time and distance into old age. Although there has been some use of generational solidarity theory (e.g., Gold, 1987), using the notion of normative solidarity to account for the origin of the sibling bond tends to be descriptive rather than explanatory.

Life span attachment theory (Bowlby, 1979, 1980) provides an explanation of the origin and persistence of sibling relationships. (The interested reader is referred to Cicirelli [1983, 1985b, 1989] for a fuller explanation.) Briefly, attachment is an ethological–adaptational theory rooted in evolutionary biology, incorporating such concepts as biologically determined development of social attachments and the adaptational value for survival of family members sharing a common gene pool (Lamb, 1988; Nash, 1988; Scarr & Gracek, 1982). Attachment refers to an emotional or affectional bond between two people; essentially, it is being identified with, having love for, and desiring to be with the other person, and it represents an individual's internal state. Somewhat later than the development of the attachment bond itself, a protective aspect of attachment develops in which the attached person takes measures to prevent the loss of the attachment figure (e. g., preserving or restoring the attachment figure's health). Such attachment extends to siblings in childhood and continues into adulthood and old age. A recent study (Cicirelli, 1989) found that sibling psychological support is related to an indicator of the strength of the attachment bond, with a stronger relationship when attachment to a sister is involved.

CONCLUSION

This update of my earlier chapter (Cicirelli, 1985b) has identified new and diverse areas in sibling studies (e.g., siblings as caregivers and decision makers during caregiving) in addition to noting progress in continuing areas of investigation.

1. Considerable progress has been made uncovering the various influences that contribute to sibling personality similarities and differences, the main influences being differential parental treatment, sibling interactions themselves, and children's active interpretations of each other's behaviors.

2. Gender differences in sibling relationships and sibling influence continue to be important, with the special roles of females in relation to helping behaviors and feelings of well-being of particular importance.

3. New areas are being explored, such as death and grief following loss of a sibling, sibling communication, sibling business relationships, and sibling helping relationships.

4. Longitudinal studies that explore how sibling relationships develop and change are an important step to understanding the forces that influence such relationships at all stages of life.

5. There has been progress in understanding deviant and dysfunctional sibling relationships, with greater emphasis on sibling group therapy.

In future work, investigations of new phenomena regarding the sibling relationship should continue so the range of sibling activities throughout the life span can be uncovered fully and described in detail. In particular, we need further studies of early and middle adulthood. In addition, we need to continue investigations to expand our knowledge of siblings from various ethnic racial backgrounds, as well as half-, step-, or adoptive siblings.

The formulation of theories or perspectives that could organize findings of existing studies and guide the direction of future studies is still very limited. It may be fruitful to conceptualize sibling studies across the life span from the personal relationship perspective mentioned in the beginning of this chapter. Although a perspective is not a theory in itself, it is a broader framework within which theories and studies can be formulated and performed. If we think of sibling studies as representing various aspects of personal relationships between sibling dyads, then we can focus on the problems and issues common to the larger field of personal relationships.

First, we should focus on describing and explaining the ongoing process and content involved in the relationship of a sibling dyad, including the dynamics of sibling interactions. Second, the sibling subsystem in larger families usually involves more than one or two siblings and should be studied more thoroughly. Third, to study sibling relationships in context, we should determine how various life events influence sibling relationships, how sibling relationships, in turn, influence relationships involving other family members, and the reciprocal impact of the larger family system on sibling relationships. Fourth, from the developmental and aging viewpoints, more longitudinal studies must be performed to determine how sibling relationships develop, the factors related to maintaining the quality of sibling relationships, and the factors related to disrupting, reducing, or dissolving such personal relationships over time. Finally, theories must be formulated and tested to explain both sibling personal relationships and changes in these relationships over time. Moreover, attachment theory and empirical tests of its implications must be explored further.

In general, we need to gain a fuller understanding of the sibling relationship over the life span as it is influenced by life events, the sibling subsystem, the larger family system, and the cultural milieu. This is a very big order that, at present, can be approached only in a piecemeal fashion. However, there are promising beginnings, and we hope that such efforts will increase, leading to a mature theoretical understanding of siblings' personal relationships throughout the life cycle.

REFERENCES

Abramovitch, R., Corter, C., Pepler, D. J., & Stanhope, L. (1986). Sibling and peer interaction: A final follow-up and a comparison. *Child Development, 57,* 217–229.

Aldous, J. (1987). New views on the family life of the elderly and the near-elderly. *Journal of Marriage and the Family, 49,* 227–234.

Alpert, J. L. (1991, August). *Sibling, cousin, and peer child sexual abuse: Clinical implications.* Paper presented at the convention of the American Psychological Association, San Francisco.

Avioli, P. S. (1989). The social support functions of siblings in later life. *American Behavioral Scientist, 33,* 45–57.

Bank, S. P., (1988). The stolen birthright: The adult sibling in individual therapy. In M. D. Kahn & K. G. Lewis (Eds.), *Siblings in therapy: Life span and clinical issues* (pp. 341–355). New York: Norton.

Bank, S. P., & Kahn, M. D. (1982). *The sibling bond.* New York: Basic Books.

Bayen, U. J., Gruber-Baldini, A. L., & Schaie, K. W. (1991, November). *Parent–child and sibling relationships in later adulthood: Predictors of contact frequency and perceived closeness.* Paper presented at the annual meeting of the Gerontological Society of America, San Francisco.

Bedford, V. H. (1989). Understanding the value of siblings in old age. *American Behavioral Scientist, 33,* 33–44.

Bedford, V. H. (1993). Relationships between adult siblings. In A. E. Auhagen & M. von Salisch (Eds.), *Interpersonal relationships* (pp. 119–142). Gottingen, Germany: Hogrefe.

Bedford, V. H. (in press). Changing affect toward siblings and the transition to old age. *Proceedings of the Second International Conference on the Future of Adult Life.* Leeuwenhorst, The Netherlands.

Borland, D. C. (1989). The sibling relationship as a housing alternative to institutionalization in later life. In L. Ade-Ridder & C. B. Hennon (Eds.), *Lifestyles of the elderly* (pp. 205–219). New York: Human Sciences Press.

Bowlby, J. (1979). *The making and breaking of affectional bonds.* London: Tavistock.

Bowlby, J. (1980). *Attachment and loss: Vol. III. Loss, stress, and depression.* New York: Basic Books.

Brady, E. M., & Noberini, M. R. (1987, August). *Sibling support in the context of a model of sibling solidarity.* Paper presented at the 95th Annual Meeting of the American Psychological Association, New York.

Brody, E. M. (1990). *Women in the middle: Their parent care years.* New York: Springer.

Brody, E. M., Hoffman, C., Kleban, M. H., & Schoonover, C. B. (1989). Caregiving daughters and their local siblings: Perceptions, strains, and interactions. *Gerontologist, 29,* 529–538.

Brody, E. M., Kleban, M. H., Hoffman, C., & Schoonover, C. B. (1988). Adult daughters and parent care: A comparison of one-, two-, and three-generation households. *Home Health Care Services Quarterly, 9,* 19–45.

Brody, G. H., Stoneman, Z., & Burke, M. (1987). Child temperaments, maternal differential behavior, and sibling relationships. *Developmental Psychology, 23,* 354–362.

Bryant, B. K. (1989). The child's perspective of sibling caretaking and its relevance to understanding social–emotional functioning and development. In P. G. Zukow (Ed.), *Sibling interaction across cultures: Theoretical and methodological issues* (pp. 143–164). New York: Springer-Verlag.

Bryant, B., & Crockenberg, S. (1980). Correlates and dimensions of prosocial behavior: A study of female siblings with their mothers. *Child Development, 51,* 529–544.

Butler, R. N. (1963). The life review: An interpretation of reminiscence in the aged. *Psychiatry, 26,* 65–76.

Cain, A. C., Fast, I., & Erickson, M. E. (1964). Children's disturbed reactions to the death of a sibling. *American Journal of Orthopsychiatry, 34,* 741–745.

Carroll, R. (1988). Siblings and the family business. In M. D. Kahn & K. G. Lewis (Eds.), *Siblings in therapy: Life span and clinical issues* (pp. 379–398). New York: Norton.

Church, M. (1986). Issues in psychological therapy with elderly people. In I. Hanley & M. Gilhooly (Eds.), *Psychological therapies for the elderly* (pp. 1–21). London: Croom Helm.

Cicirelli, V. G. (1983). Adult children's attachment and helping behavior to elderly parents: A path model. *Journal of Marriage and the Family, 45,* 815–822.

Cicirelli, V. G. (1984). Marital disruption and adult children's perception of their siblings' help to elderly parents. *Family Relations, 33,* 613–621.

Cicirelli, V. G. (1985a). The role of siblings as family caregivers. In W. J. Sauer & R. T. Coward (Eds.), *Social support networks and the care of the elderly: Theory, research, and practice* (pp. 93–107). New York: Springer.

Cicirelli, V. G. (1985b). Sibling relationships throughout the life cycle. In L. L'Abate (Ed.), *The handbook of family psychology and therapy* (pp. 177–214). Homewood, IL: Dorsey.

Cicirelli, V. G. (1988). Interpersonal relationships among elderly siblings. In M. D. Kahn & K. G. Lewis (Eds.), *Siblings in therapy: Life span and clinical issues* (pp. 435–456). New York: Norton.

Cicirelli, V. G. (1989). Feelings of attachment to siblings and well-being in later life. *Psychology and Aging, 4,* 211–216.

Cicirelli, V. G. (1990). Family support in relation to health problems of the elderly. In T. H. Brubaker (Ed.), *Family relationships in later life* (2nd ed., pp. 212–228). Newbury Park, CA: Sage.

Cicirelli, V. G. (1992a). *Family caregiving: Autonomous and paternalistic decision-making.* Newbury Park, CA: Sage.

Cicirelli, V. G. (1992b). Siblings as caregivers in middle and old age. In J. W. Dwyer & R. T. Coward (Eds.), *Gender, families, and elder care* (pp. 84–101). Newbury Park, CA: Sage.

Cicirelli, V. G., Coward, R. T., & Dwyer, J. W. (1992). Siblings as caregivers for impaired elders. *Research on Aging, 14,* 331–350.

Coleman, F. W., & Coleman, W. S. (1984). Helping siblings and other peers cope with dying. In H. Wass & C. A. Corr (Eds.), *Childhood and death* (pp. 129–150). Bristol, PA: Hemisphere.

Connidis, I. A. (1989). Siblings as friends in later life. *American Behavioral Scientist, 33,* 81–93.

Connidis, I. A., & Davies, L. (1990). Confidants and companions in later life: The place of family and friends. *Journal of Gerontology Social Sciences, 45,* S141–149.

Coward, R. T., & Dwyer, J. W. (1990). The association of gender, sibling network composition, and patterns of parent care by adult children. *Research on Aging, 12,* 158–181.

Daniels, D., Dunn, J., Furstenberg, F. F., & Plomin, R. (1985). Environmental differences within the family and adjustment differences within pairs of adolescent siblings. *Child Development, 56,* 764–774.

Duck, S., & Perlman, D. (1985). *Understanding personal relationships: An interdisciplinary approach.* London: Sage.

Dunn, J. (1984). Sibling studies and the developmental impact of critical incidents. In P. B. Baltes & O. G. Brim (Eds.), *Life span development and behavior* (Vol. 6, pp. 335–353). Orlando: Academic.

Dunn, J. (1985). *Sisters and brothers.* Cambridge, MA: Harvard University Press.

Dunn, J. (1989). Siblings and early social understanding. In P. G. Zukow (Ed.), *Sibling interaction across cultures: Theoretical and methodological issues* (pp. 106–116). New York: Springer-Verlag.

Dunn, J., & Munn, P. (1986). Sibling quarrels and maternal intervention: Individual differences in understanding and aggression. *Journal of Child Psychology & Psychiatry & Allied Disciplines, 27,* 583–595.

Dunn, J., Plomin, R., & Daniels, D. (1986). Consistency and change in mothers' behavior towards young siblings. *Child Development, 57,* 348–356.

Dunn, J., & Stocker, C. (1989). The significance of differences in siblings' experiences within the family. In K. Kreppner & R. M. Lerner (Eds.), *Family systems and life-span development* (pp. 289–301). Hillsdale, NJ: Erlbaum.

Ervin-Tripp, S. (1989). Sisters and brothers. In P. G. Zukow (Ed.), *Sibling interaction across cultures: Theoretical and methodological issues* (pp. 184–195). New York: Springer-Verlag.

Furman, W., & Buhrmester, D. (1985). Children's perceptions of the qualities of sibling relationships. *Child Development, 56,* 448–461.

Goetting, A. (1986). The developmental tasks of siblingship over the life cycle. *Journal of Marriage and the Family, 48,* 703–714.

Gold, D. T. (1986). Sibling relationships in retrospect: A study of reminiscence in old age (Doctoral dissertation, Northwestern University, Evanston, IL). *Dissertation Abstracts International, 47,* 2274A.

Gold, D. T. (1987, August). *Generational solidarity: Sibling ties in late life.* Paper presented at the meeting of the American Psychological Association, New York.

Gold, D. T. (1989a). Generational solidarity. *American Behavioral Scientist, 33,* 19–32.

Gold, D. T. (1989b). Sibling relationships: A typology. *International Journal of Aging and Human Development, 28* (1), 37–51.

Gold, D. T. (1990). Late-life sibling relationships: Does race affect typological distribution? *Gerontologist, 30,* 741–748.

Gold, D. T., Woodbury, M. A., & George, L. K. (1990). Relationship classification using grade of membership analysis: A typology of sibling relationships in later life. *Journals of Gerontology, 45,* S43–51.

Harris, E. G. (1988). My brother's keeper: Siblings of chronic patients as allies in family treatment. In M. D. Kahn & K. G. Lewis (Eds.), *Siblings in therapy: Life span and clinical issues* (pp. 314–337). New York: Norton.

Hartup, W. W. (1975). The origins of friendships. In M. Lewis & L. A. Rosenblum (Eds.), *The origins of behavior. Vol. 4. Friendship and peer relations* (pp. 11–26). New York: Wiley.

Heiman, M. L. (1988). Untangling incestuous bonds: The treatment of sibling incest. In M. D. Kahn & K. G. Lewis (Eds.), *Siblings in therapy: Life span and clinical issues* (pp. 135–166). New York: Norton.

Hinde, R. A. (1981). The bases of a science of interpersonal relationships. In S. Duck & R. Gilmore (Eds.), *Personal relationships (Vol. 1): Studying personal relationships* (pp. 1–22). New York: Academic Press.

Hoffman, L. W. (1991). The influence of the family environment on personality: Accounting for sibling differences. *Psychological Bulletin, 110,* 187–203.

Huston, T. L., & Robins, E. (1982). Conceptual and methodological issues in studying close relationships. *Journal of Marriage and the Family, 44,* 902–925.

Johnson, C. L. (1988). Relationships among family members and friends in later life. In R. Milardo (Ed.), *Families and social networks* (pp. 168–189). Newbury Park, CA: Sage.

Kahn, M. D. (1988). Intense sibling relationships: A self psychological view. In M. D. Kahn & K. G. Lewis (Eds.), *Siblings in therapy: Life span and clinical issues* (pp. 3–24). New York: W. W. Norton.

Kahn, M. D., & Lewis, K. G. (Eds.). (1988). *Siblings in therapy: Life span and clinical issues.* New York: Norton.

Kelley, H. H., Berscheid, E., Christensen, A., Harvey, J. H., Huston, T. L., Levinger, G., McClintock, E., Peplau, L. A., & Peterson, D. R. (1983). Analyzing close relationships. In H. H. Kelley, E. Berscheid, A. Christensen, J. H. Harvey, T. L. Huston, G. Levinger, E. McClintock, L. A. Peplau, & D. R. Peterson (Eds.), *Close relationships* (pp. 20–67). New York: W. H. Freeman.

Lamb, M. E. (1988). Social and emotional development in infancy. In M. H. Bornstein & M. E. Lamb (Eds.), *Developmental psychology: An advanced textbook* (2nd ed., pp. 359–410). Hillsdale, NJ: Erlbaum.

Lee, T. R., Mancini, J. A., & Maxwell, J. W. (1990). Sibling relationships in adulthood: Contact patterns and motivations. *Journal of Marriage and the Family, 52,* 431–440.

Lerner, M. J., Somers, D. G., Reid, D., Chiriboga, D., & Tierney, M. (1991). Adult children as caregivers: Egocentric biases in judgments of sibling contributions. *Gerontologist, 31,* 746–755.

Lewis, K. G. (1988). Young siblings in brief therapy. In M. D. Kahn & K. G. Lewis (Eds.), *Siblings in therapy: Life span and clinical issues* (pp. 93–114). New York: Norton.

Matthews, S. H. (1987). Provision of care to old parents: Division of care among adult children. *Research on Aging, 9,* 45–60.

Matthews, S. H. (1988, October). *Gender and the division of filial responsibility.* Paper presented at the conference on Gender Roles through the Life Course, Ball State University, Muncie, Indiana.

Matthews, S. H., Delaney, P. J., & Adamek, M. E. (1989). Male kinship ties: Bonds between adult brothers. *American Behavioral Scientist, 33,* 58–69.

Matthews, S. H., & Rosner, T. T. (1988). Shared filial responsibility: The family as primary caregiver. *Journal of Marriage and the Family, 50,* 185–195.

Matthews, S. H., & Sprey, J. (1989). Older family systems: Intra- and intergenerational relations. In J. A. Mancini (Ed.), *Aging parents and adult children* (pp. 63–77). New York: Heath.

McCown, D. E. (1984). Funeral attendance, cremation, and young siblings. *Series in Death Education, Aging, and Health, 8,* 349–363.

McCown, D. E., & Pratt, C. (1985). Impact of sibling death on children's behavior. *Death Studies, 9,* 323–335.

McGhee, J. L. (1985). The effects of siblings on the life satisfaction of the rural elderly. *Journal of Marriage and the Family, 47,* 85–91.

Molinari, V., & Reichlin, R. E. (1985). Life review reminiscence in the elderly: A review of the literature. *International Journal of Aging and Human Development, 20,* (1) 81–92.

Montgomery, R. J. V., & Kamo, Y. (1989). Parent care by sons and daughters. In J. A. Mancini (Ed.), *Aging parents and adult children* (pp. 213–230). New York: Lexington Books.

Moss, M. S., & Moss, S. Z. (1986). Death of an adult sibling. *International Journal of Family Psychiatry, 7,* 397–418.

Moss, S. Z., & Moss, M. S. (1989). Death of an elderly sibling. *American Behavioral Scientist, 33,* 94–106.

Nash, A. (1988). Ontogeny, phylogeny, and relationships. In S. W. Duck (Ed.), *Handbook of personal relationships* (pp. 121–141). New York: Wiley.

O'Bryant, S. L. (1988). Sibling support and older widows' well-being. *Journal of Marriage and the Family, 50,* 173–183.

Osgood, N. J. (1985). *Suicide in the elderly: A practitioner's guide to diagnosis and mental health intervention.* Rockville, MD: Aspen.

Palazzoli, M. S. (1985). The problem of the sibling as the referring person. *Journal of Marital and Family Therapy, 11,* 21–34.

Patterson, G. R. (1986). The contribution of siblings to training for fighting: A microsocial analysis. In D. Olweus, J. Block, & M. Radke-Yarrow (Eds.), *Development of antisocial and prosocial behavior: Research, theories, and issues* (pp. 235–261). Orlando: Academic.

Rosen, H. (1984–85). Prohibitions against mourning in childhood sibling loss. *Omega (Amityville), 14,* 307–316.

Rosner, S. (1985). On the place of siblings in psychoanalysis. *Psychoanalytic Review, 72,* 457–477.

Rodgers, J. L., & Rowe, D. C. (1988). Influence of siblings on adolescent sexual behavior. *Developmental Psychology, 24,* 722–728.

Scarr, S., & Gracek, S. (1982). Similarities and differences among siblings. In M. E. Lamb & B. Sutton-Smith (Eds.), *Sibling relationships: Their nature and significance across the life span* (pp. 357–381). Hillsdale, NJ: Erlbaum.

Scott, J. P. (1990). Sibling interaction in later life. In T. H. Brubaker (Ed.), *Family relationships in later life* (2nd ed., pp. 86–99). Newbury Park, CA: Sage.

Stephenson, J. (1986). Grief of siblings. In T. A. Rando (Ed.), *Parental loss of a child* (pp. 321–338). Champaign, IL: Research Press.

Stocker, C., Dunn, J., & Plomin, R. (1989). Sibling relationships: Links with child temperament, maternal behavior, and family structure. *Child Development, 60,* 715–727.

Stoller, E. P. (1985). Exchange patterns in the informal support networks of the elderly: The impact of reciprocity on morale. *Journal of Marriage and the Family, 47,* 335–348.

Stoller, E. P. (1990). Males as helpers: The role of sons, relatives, and friends. *Gerontologist, 30,* 228–235.

Suggs, P. K. (1989). Predictors of association among older siblings: A black/white comparison. *American Behavioral Scientist, 33,* 70–80.

Toman, W. (1988). Basics of family structure and sibling position. In M. D. Kahn & K. G. Lewis (Eds.), *Siblings in therapy: Life span and clinical issues* (pp. 45–65). New York: Norton.

Tonti, M. (1988). Relationships among adult siblings who care for their aged parents. In M. D. Kahn & K. G. Lewis (Eds.), *Siblings in therapy: Life span and clinical issues* (pp. 417–434). New York: Norton.

Weisner, T. S. (1989). Comparing sibling relationships across cultures. In. P. G. Zukow (Ed.), *Sibling interaction across cultures: Theoretical and methodological issues* (pp. 11–25). New York: Springer.

Wiehe, V. R. (1990). *Sibling abuse: Hidden physical, emotional, and sexual trauma.* New York: Lexington Books.

Wishart, J. G. (1986). Siblings as models in early infant learning. *Child Development, 57,* 1232–1240.

CHAPTER 4

The Marital Life Cycle

A Developmental Approach to the Study of Marital Change

TAMARA L. FULLER and FRANK D. FINCHAM

How do marriages develop and change over time? Researchers have attempted to answer this fundamental question for several decades, and, as a result, marital quality has become the most widely investigated construct in the marital literature (Glenn, 1990). Extensive reviews document an association between marital satisfaction and numerous variables (e.g., demographic and individual difference characteristics, spouse behaviors, and attributions for marital events, see Fincham & Bradbury, 1990). Although empirical inquiry has provided an impressive array of ways in which satisfied and dissatisfied married couples differ, it has added little to our understanding of the *dynamics* of marital change.

Recognizing the need to focus on *change* processes in close relationships, marital researchers have recently increased their efforts to identify variables that predict changes in marital satisfaction. However, most of this longitudinal research has developed independently of the preexisting family development perspective. Although not intended as a theory of marital development, the family development perspective has contributed several concepts to the study of marital dynamics in an attempt to delineate the normative processes of transformation through which most families progress (Mattessich & Hill, 1987; White, 1991). One of the most influential is the notion of the family life cycle, which refers to a series of stages families typically experience as they develop. Several researchers have applied the concept of life cycle analysis to the study of marital functioning over time (e.g. Rollins & Cannon, 1974; Rollins & Feldman, 1970; Spanier, Lewis, & Cole, 1975). The concept of a "marital life cycle" is appealing, and the applicability of this perspective to marital research deserves closer scrutiny.

This chapter presents an analysis of the marital life cycle perspective and examines the ways in which it can help to answer the fundamental question of how marriages change over time. The chapter begins with a brief review of recent longitudinal research on marriage. Our critique of this research leads to an examination of the family development perspective and its associated concepts and assumptions. Following a synopsis of this perspective, we examine the ways in which marital researchers have used the framework to study marital functioning over time, and we discuss the problems associated with this research. In response to these shortcomings, a broader developmental framework for the study of marital dynamics is described, and the potential utility of the framework to guide future research is illustrated.

LONGITUDINAL RESEARCH ON MARRIAGE

Overview of Recent Longitudinal Research

Although numerous correlates of marital satisfaction have been identified, marital researchers are interested ultimately in their causal antecedents. Because both practical and ethical restraints make experiments in this domain extremely difficult, researchers have conducted longitudinal studies to address questions concerning the antecedents of marital change. We offer a brief overview and critique of such longitudinal research.

Communication and Socioemotional Behaviors

Markman (1979, 1981, 1984) conducted a 5 1/2-year investigation to test the hypothesis that negative communication patterns lead to marital distress. Twenty-six premarital couples participated in an initial laboratory session during which they engaged in several problem-solving discussions. During these discussions, each spouse rated the intent of the messages they sent, as well as the impact of the partners' messages they received. Measures of relationship satisfaction were then obtained at one year (Time 2), 2 1/2 years (Time 3), and 5 1/2 years (Time 4). Initial results indicated that neither impact nor intent ratings correlated with premarital relationship satisfaction. A similar pattern of results was found at the Time 2 follow-up. However, a different picture emerged at Times 3 and 4. The more positively couples rated their premarital communication exchanges, the more satisfied they were with their relationship both 2 1/2 and 5 1/2 years later. These results were interpreted as providing evidence that communication deficits precede the development of marital distress (Markman, 1981, 1984), and they have been corroborated by more recent findings (Markman, Floyd, Stanley, & Storaasli, 1988).

In a similar vein, Filsinger and Thoma (1988) examined the association between premarital communication behaviors and relationship satisfaction over a 5-year period. Only 1 of 10 aspects of premarital communication—female interruptions—was found to predict later marital adjustment. Those couples in which wives tended to interrupt husbands were characterized by lower levels of adjustment for both spouses at the 5-year assessment. Interestingly, female interruptions were not related to relationship satisfaction at the premarital stage, again suggesting that longitudinal predictors of marital change may differ from the cross-sectional correlates of satisfaction.

Gottman and Krokoff (1989) similarly found a difference in the communication behaviors that predict concurrent and future marital satisfaction. Wives' positive verbal behavior strongly predicted concurrent marital satisfaction for both spouses, but it predicted *deterioration* in marital satisfaction over a 3-year period. Conversely, for both partners, conflict engagement was associated with concurrent marital dissatisfaction but predicted improvement in marital satisfaction over time. Other communication behaviors, such as defensiveness, stubbornness, and withdrawal from interaction were predictive of both concurrent distress and deterioration of marital satisfaction over time. Although the findings of this study have been strongly challenged on methodological grounds (Woody & Costanzo, 1990), it seems that conflict engagement of a specific kind may be functional for a marriage longitudinally, but conflict that involves defensiveness, stubbornness, and withdrawal may be dysfunctional over the longer term.

Using self-reports of partner behavior, Huston and Vangelisti (1991) found that negative behaviors (e.g., wife failed to do something husband asked, wife dominated conversation) two months after the wedding predicted changes in wives', but not husbands', satisfaction two years later. In contrast, affectional expression and sexual interest did not predict later satisfaction for either spouse. Although the importance accorded husbands' negativity in determining future relational outcomes is consistent with the results of Gottman and Krokoff (1989), direct comparison of these two studies is not possible in view of the different behaviors examined and methodologies employed. In fact, proper interpretation of spouse reports of partner behavior is dubious because the findings of several studies question the objectivity and reliability of spouses as observers of partner behavior (e.g., Christensen, Sullaway, & King, 1983).

Affective and Physiological Variables

Levenson and Gottman (1983, 1985) conducted a 3-year longitudinal study to examine the relationship between affective and physiologic variables and marital satisfaction. Couples engaged in a low-conflict and a high-conflict discussion while physiologic data were obtained continuously. In a separate session, each spouse provided a continuous self-report of affect while viewing a videotape of the interaction. The findings revealed that general physiologic linkage (mutually escalating arousal patterns) accounted for 60% of the variance in concurrent marital satisfaction, but was unrelated to satisfaction three years later. Conversely, a broad-based pattern of physiologic arousal was unrelated to marital adjustment at the initial assessment, but it was found to predict declines in satisfaction in such a way that the more aroused the couple was *both before and during* the initial conversation, the more their marital satisfaction declined over the ensuing three years. Levenson and Gottman interpreted these findings in terms of *expectations* couples have concerning their interactions. Based on past interactive experiences, happily married couples may develop expectations of pleasure and optimism concerning upcoming interactions, whereas for unhappy couples, these expectations may be dreadful and pessimistic. These pleasurable or unpleasurable expectations may, therefore, account for the arousal differences observed during baseline periods before the interaction, when couples face each other for five minutes in silence, knowing they will soon be engaged in interaction. This arousal is carried over into the interaction itself.

The affective data revealed that the only significant concurrent correlate of marital adjustment, wives' negative affect, did not predict later adjustment. Affective variables predictive of change in satisfaction were those involving negative affect reciprocity. Marital satisfaction declined when husbands did not reciprocate their wives' negative affect and when wives did reciprocate their husbands' negative affect. Using a different affect coding scheme, Smith, Vivian, and O'Leary (1991) found that although negative affect expressions (e.g., dissatisfaction, upset, distress) exhibited premarriage were associated with relationship dissatisfaction cross-sectionally, they were not predictive of declines in marital satisfaction over time. On the other hand, affective disengagement (e.g., quietness, sluggishness, silence) during the premarital discussion was not related to concurrent satisfaction, but it was a significant predictor of decreased marital adjustment at both the 18 and 30-month follow-up points.

Cognitive Variables

Fincham and Bradbury (1987) examined the association between attributions or explanations for marital events and later marital satisfaction. Spouses completed measures of marital satisfaction and provided attributions for marital difficulties and negative partner behaviors at two points in time, approximately 12 months apart. Attributions were associated with satisfaction at both assessment points. More importantly, wives' attributions predicted their later marital satisfaction, even after the effects of earlier satisfaction had been statistically removed. Specifically, a rating of the cause of negative partner behavior and marital difficulties as located in the husband, and as global and stable, was related to declines in marital satisfaction a year later. In a similar manner, attributing blame to the husband and inferring his behavior to be intentional and reflective of selfish motivation predicted declines in wives' satisfaction. For husbands, attributions at Time 1 were unrelated to marital satisfaction at Time 2. However, in a more recent study, causal attributions predicted satisfaction 12 months later for both husbands and wives (Fincham & Bradbury, 1991).

To explore whether the prediction of later satisfaction from earlier attributions reflects a more general association between cognitive variables in marriage and marital satisfaction, Fincham and Bradbury (1987) also assessed the longitudinal impact of unrealistic relationship beliefs. Despite a concurrent association, unrealistic relationship beliefs did not predict later satisfaction, after the variance due to earlier satisfaction had been removed. Moreover, the longitudinal association between attributions and satisfaction is not an artifact of their joint relation with depression or self-esteem because statistically controlling these latter variables has no impact on the longitudinal association (Fincham & Bradbury, 1991). Thus, the predictive and potentially causal relationship between attributions and marital satisfaction does not seem to extend to cognitive variables more generally, or to be an artifact.

Personality Variables

Following Terman, Buttenweiser, Ferguson, Johnson, & Wilson's (1938) observation that "unhappy temperament" may play a causal role in marital success, several early, large-scale surveys examined the association between personal characteristics and marital adjustment. For example, Terman and Oden (1947) found that a self-report measure of emotional stability administered to their subjects at 7 to 14 years of age was related to marital happiness 18 years later. Similarly, Uhr (1957) revealed that neuroticism scores on the Bernreuter Personality Inventory taken before marriage were related to men's, but not women's, marital satisfaction 18 years after marriage.

More recently, Bentler and Newcomb (1978) followed 77 newlywed couples for a period of 4 years and found that the emotional stability and objectivity of the wives and the deliberateness and introversion of the husbands were predictive of later marital adjustment. Finally, Kelley and Conley (1987) reported on the antecedents of marital stability and satisfaction for a group of 300 couples followed over a period of 45 years. Three aspects of personality—wives' neuroticism, husbands' neuroticism, and husbands' impulse control—were strongly related to long-term marital outcomes.

Summary and Critique

To summarize, marital researchers have attempted to delineate the factors that influence marital change through the use of longitudinal studies. The majority of these investigations have explored the determinants of change in marital satisfaction and have linked changes to a number of different antecedents, such as communication deficits, negative affect reciprocity, negative attributions for partner behaviors, and emotional instability or neuroticism. When viewed as a whole, a consistent pattern emerges from the results of these studies, because the correlates of concurrent marital satisfaction often differ from variables that predict later marital functioning.

At a practical level, these findings call into question the validity of extrapolating cross-sectional findings for understanding marital dynamics. At a theoretical level, they highlight the need for marital researchers to move beyond identification of empirical relationships and begin to develop models or frameworks to explain these longitudinal findings. Although a few marital researchers have made initial progress into this domain (e.g., Bradbury & Fincham, 1989, 1991; Gottman, 1990), a truly *developmental* model of marital change has not emerged. Not surprisingly, recent longitudinal research fails to address questions concerning the developmental pattern of marital change, and we lack basic understanding of the processes that are critical at different points along the marital career. Although it does not focus exclusively on the marital dyad, the family development perspective may provide additional insight into the processes involved in marital change.

FAMILY DEVELOPMENT PERSPECTIVE

The family development perspective originated in Duvall and Hill's (1948) landmark report to the Committee on the Dynamics of Family Interaction at the National Conference on Family Life. Although several researchers have made additional contributions to this framework during the ensuing forty years (e.g. Mattessich & Hill, 1987; White, 1991), many of the basic concepts have remained essentially unchanged since the theory's original formulation. The most basic assumption of the family development perspective is that the family, as a social group, is shaped by developmental processes similar to those experienced by individuals. Thus, families are "born," they "mature" through different stages of development, and ultimately they "die." More formally, "family development is the process whereby stages of family life are sequenced so that the probability of any stage is determined by the duration of time in a specific previous stage" (White, 1991, p. 42).

Family Development Theory

The Family as a System

Implicit in this definition are assumptions about the family as a structured system (Mattessich & Hill, 1987). *Each* person within the family occupies a specific position, attached to which are roles (e.g., "wife" and "mother"), each with its own set of associated norms specifying appropriate or required behaviors for that position. Another systemic feature implicit in this definition is that of interdependence among family members. Thus, the actions or behaviors of one family member have consequences for all other members, so that a change in any part of the family system will affect each of the other parts.

Family Development as a Process

Another important element of the definition stated earlier is its specification of family development as a *process* rather than a static description of family organization at different time points. The emphasis on family dynamics raises several important issues concerning the nature of change within the family. One such issue concerns whether developmental processes consist primarily of discrete or continuous changes. Most family development theorists view stages as discontinuous or disjunctive, marking qualitatively distinct periods in the life course of the family (White, 1991). Although the concept of stages is central to the family development perspective, disagreement exists as to the critical elements that distinguish one stage from another. Criteria that have been used to differentiate among family stages include: family size and structure, role of relationships among family members, age composition of family members, developmental stage of the oldest child, and occupational status of the family breadwinner (Mattessich & Hill, 1987; White, 1991). Various combinations of these criteria have led to family stage formulations consisting of as few as 2 stages to as many as 24 (Mattessich & Hill, 1987). Lack of consensus on the precise definition of a family stage is a major weakness in this area of research.

Another important issue relating to stages is the process that precipitates a move from one family stage to the next. Although most family development theorists agree that movement from one family stage to the next is precipitated by some type of transitional *event,* disagreement exists over the essential characteristics of the event. Some researchers believe that family developmental changes depend on the developmental tasks and challenges encountered by individual family members (White, 1991). Following from the systemic concept of interdependence, transitions or changes in one family member brought about by maturation or societal expectations are thought to lead to changes in the behaviors of each other family member. In response to this temporary period of destabilization, family members experiment with different patterns of interaction until a new, satisfactory family structure is adopted. The adoption of this new pattern of interaction, which typically contains elements from the previous structure, ushers in a new period of behavioral stability among the family members.

In contrast to this is the view in which family transitions are precipitated by critical life events. Rapoport (1963) suggested that families experience "normative crises of transition," which propel them into the next stage of development. As the term "normative crisis" implies, this theory of family development focuses on transitional events that almost all families encounter, identified in sequence as the crisis of marriage, the crisis of parenthood, the crisis of deparentalization, the crisis of leavetaking or launching, and the crisis of family dissolution (Rapoport, 1963). Hill and Joy (1981) expanded on the notion of critical transitions by introducing concepts from family stress theory to the study of family development. Families are thought to maintain a relatively stable pattern of organization as long as no major role changes are provoked. However, the occurrence of several significant stressor events within a short period of time forces the family into major reorganization. Thus, movement from one family stage to another is the result of a "pile-up" of both normative and nonnormative critical events.

Family Developmental Tasks

Central to most definitions of family development is the notion of developmental tasks. Borrowing from theories of individual development, some family theorists have proposed that each stage within the family life cycle is associated with particular tasks or challenges that must be accomplished or mastered (e.g., Carter & McGoldrick, 1980). Successful negotiation of the tasks in one stage is thought to ease the family's transition into the next, whereas failure to accomplish these tasks handicaps the family and increases the risk of failure in future stages of development. Several researchers have attempted to delineate tasks that couples and families encounter as they pass through life cycle stages (Carter & McGoldrick, 1980; Markman, 1989; Storaasli & Markman, 1990). However, as White (1991) notes, failure to specify a common set of family developmental stages suggests that developmental tasks associated with the various stage formulations are descriptive at best.

Summary

Family development theory suggests that families, like individuals, engage in a process of regular and orderly change over time, labeled the *family life cycle*. This life cycle is composed of discrete stages characterized by interaction patterns qualitatively distinct from previous and subsequent interaction patterns. Each stage presents the family with unique developmental tasks that must be mastered successfully to ensure continued healthy development. Movement from one family stage to the next is precipitated by a transitional event, which may be a normative crisis event, a nonnormative, stressful life event, or a combination, or "pile-up," of the two. Finally, family development occurs at a systemic level, so that changes that occur in one family member have repercussions for the entire family system. It is this notion of systemic interdependence that prompted marital researchers to examine the influence of family life cycle stages on marital functioning.

Research on the Family Life Cycle and Marital Satisfaction

In their decade-long review of marital quality research, Spanier and Lewis (1980) cited the impact of children and the effects of the family life cycle as the two topics that had received the greatest attention. The rationale for this interest was derived from family development theory. That is, the age-linked changes that occur during family development, such as changes in family size and composition and changes in children's activities (e.g., entering school, reaching adolescence), are thought to constitute important role transitions for the entire family system, including the marital dyad (e.g., the birth of the first child is likely to bring about many changes in the roles and interaction patterns within the family system in such a way that the activities and demands of the marital role are temporarily overshadowed by those of the parental role). Such changes in established role relationships are likely to have implications for marital functioning across the family life cycle.

Cross-Sectional Research

To investigate this possibility, a number of studies have examined the relationship between family stages and marital quality by conducting large-scale, cross-sectional analyses (e.g., Rollins & Cannon, 1974; Rollins & Feldman, 1970; Spanier, Lewis, & Cole, 1975). The results of most of these studies indicate a U-shape in the level of marital quality over the family career, with satisfaction highest among preparental couples, lowest among couples with elementary school-age and teenage children, and high once again among couples with grown children who no longer live at home. However, overgeneralizations of these results have occurred within the literature, and they are often stated in causal language (Menaghan, 1982).

In response to such misleading interpretations, a number of researchers have outlined problems associated with these studies, including the failure to control for economic resources, social class, family size, or occupational status (Anderson, Russell, & Schumm, 1983; Menaghan, 1982, 1983; Spanier & Lewis, 1980). Because of their cross-sectional nature, these studies also confound cohort effects and selective survival effects with differences that may exist (Spanier & Lewis). Finally, the absolute size of the differences in marital satisfaction between couples occupying different family stages is not particularly impressive (Anderson et al.; Menaghan; Spanier & Lewis). In fact, only about 4% to 8% of the variance in marital satisfaction can be explained by the family life cycle, which is "in a practical sense a relatively minor and unimportant trend in terms of its predictive value" (Rollins & Cannon, 1974, p. 277).

Longitudinal Research

The weak and inconsistent results of these cross-sectional studies may be a reflection of the inadequacy of their design, rather than the absence of a link between family life cycle stage and marital quality (Menaghan, 1983). In response to these criticisms, Klein and Aldous (1979) suggested that researchers use short-term longitudinal designs to examine the impact of family life cycle transitions on marital functioning. Such designs involve following couples across a transition period to permit comparison of marital functioning before and after roles have changed. Transitional couples may also be compared to similar couples who did not make a transition.

Several short-term longitudinal studies have examined the impact of life cycle transitions on various aspects of marital quality, the majority of which have investigated the effects of transitions involving children. In their review of research on the transition to parenthood, Belsky and Pensky (1988) found that both the interactions and activities of married couples and their feelings about the marriage changed following the birth of the first child. Expressions of positive affect significantly declined from the last trimester of pregnancy through the ninth month postpartum, while conflicts between spouses increased during the same time period. Given these changes, it is not surprising that the majority of studies reveal a decline in marital satisfaction after the birth of the first child (e.g., Cowan et al., 1985; Moss, Bolland, Foxman, & Owen, 1986; Ruble, Fleming, Hackel, & Stangor, 1988). In general, wives seem to be more susceptible than husbands to the negative changes in satisfaction associated with the transition to parenthood (see Belsky & Pensky, 1988).

Children's transition to adolescence is another critical event thought to affect the marital relationship. Cross-sectional data reviewed earlier suggest that couples with adolescent children may represent the low point in marital satisfaction across the family life cycle. In addition, pubertal maturation is associated with increases in parent–child distance, adolescent autonomy, and parent–child conflict (Steinberg, 1987), all of which may influence the functioning of the marital dyad. Therefore, it is surprising that the two investigations of marital quality across this developmental period found no significant changes in marital satisfaction (Menaghan, 1983; Steinberg & Silverberg, 1987). Steinberg and Silverberg did reveal, however, that a lack of closeness in the same-sex parent–child relationship (i.e., father–son, mother–daughter) predicted decreased marital satisfaction. This suggests that it is not the presence of adolescents per se that causes marital satisfaction to decline during this period, but some as yet unspecified process through which adolescents influence the spousal relationship.

Many of the cross-sectional studies of family life cycle stage and marital satisfaction have reported marital adjustment levels to be higher among couples in the later stages of marriage than among those in the middle stages (e.g., Anderson et al., 1983; Rollins & Cannon, 1974; Rollins & Feldman, 1970). Unfortunately, only one longitudinal study has examined changes in marital quality occurring in the later stages of the family life cycle. Menaghan (1983) compared the marital functioning of transitional couples whose youngest child left home (thus ushering in the "empty nest" stage) to a similar group of couples whose child left home, but the child was not the last to leave. Transition to the "empty nest" was associated with increased feelings of equity in the marriage, but such changes were not accompanied by increased feelings of affection or fulfillment in the marriage. Thus, although departure of the children from home does seem to increase some aspects of marital functioning, these changes are not uniform across different domains of experience.

Summary and Critique

Dissatisfaction with the methodological weaknesses inherent in cross-sectional research prompted researchers to employ short-term longitudinal studies to examine family stages and marital functioning. With the possible exception of the transition to parenthood, this research does not show the consistent effects on marital functioning predicted by family development theory. As noted by Menaghan (1983, p. 383), "Clearly, family transitions do bring some changes to parents' daily lives; but these findings suggest that those changes, and their impact on marriage, may not be nearly so uniform as the notion of role transitions and family stages connote." The weak explanatory power of family life cycle stages has led some researchers (e.g., Anderson et al., 1983; Nock, 1979) to question their predictive utility and to propose the use of such alternative predictor variables as spouse age or length of marriage. In contrast, others have suggested that "more is to be gained from future research that seeks to evaluate why and how the family life cycle operates than from research that stops at showing its relatively weak effect on marital adjustment over time" (Schumm & Bugaighis, 1986, p. 167).

In line with such a recommendation, several researchers have begun to examine variables that may moderate or influence the effects of family stage transition on marital functioning. For example, Belsky and Rovine (1990) found that certain demographic, personality, marital, infant, and life-event variables predicted which couples increased and which couples decreased in marital satisfaction across the transition to parenthood. Similarly, Schumm and Bugaighis (1986) reanalyzed data from a previous study (Anderson et al., 1983) and showed that much of the observed decline in marital satisfaction for parents with preschool children could be attributed to a specific group of low-income mothers with full-time employment. These wives felt that they had too little time to discuss daily matters with their husbands, although they perceived their husbands to be as caring and understanding as did other, less distressed wives. Finally, Lee (1988) found that participation in nonmarital activities and roles, such as friendships, work, and church, influenced the amount of marital satisfaction experienced by couples as their children left home.

What can we conclude about the usefulness of "marital life cycle" for understanding changes in marital quality? The perspective is compelling and, with more precise specification, has the potential to increase our understanding of marital quality. For example, the recent trend toward investigating variables that may moderate the effects of family life cycle transitions on the marital relationship seems promising; however, a word of caution is appropriate. The few studies that have examined the impact of moderating variables seem to have chosen these variables in an arbitrary manner. In addition to decreasing the likelihood that these variables will be *meaningful* moderators, this undirected choice of variables makes it difficult to interpret significant findings that may occur. To increase our understanding of the marital relationship, an organizing framework is needed to guide future research.

A PROCESS–PERSON–CONTEXT MODEL
OF MARITAL DEVELOPMENT

Models of Development

Knowledge of developmental models and their limitations can guide marital researchers as they attempt to use findings from longitudinal research on marriage and the family development perspective to construct a developmental model of marital change. Bronfenbrenner (1988) has outlined four models that have been used to study human development and each is considered here briefly.

The social address model compares the developmental outcomes of individuals growing up in different social or environmental settings. Although frequently employed, social address models focus on only one set of variables that may influence development (i.e., those in the environment) to the exclusion of other possible relevant factors. Moreover, a given social address is presumed to be the same for all persons "living" at that address, regardless of their biologic or psychologic characteristics. Not only are social address models limited by their exclusive focus on the environment, but the *process* through which these environmental variables exert their influence is left unspecified.

In contrast, the personal attributes model attempts to account for variations in developmental outcomes by examining psychological differences among individuals at an earlier time point. This model assumes that personal characteristics present early in life will have the same consequences for later development regardless of the environment in which later development occurs. Also, like the social address model, the personal attributes model does not specify or investigate the processes through which characteristics observed early in life affect the course of later development.

Some of the problems associated with the social address and personal attributes models are eliminated in the person–context model, which examines the joint effects of both environmental and personal characteristics on development. Thus, it allows for the possibility that various combinations of environmental and personal attributes can produce developmental effects that cannot be predicted from independent assessment of either domain. Although person-context models represent an improvement over the more simplistic models described earlier, this type of model is not without problems. Specifically, the person–context model also fails to specify the process through which properties of the person and properties of the environment combine to produce a particular developmental outcome. Thus, marital development researchers may choose to use more comprehensive models that attempt to describe the processes through which marital changes occur.

An example of such a model is the process–person–context model. Studies using such a model must provide information on at least three separate domains: the personal characteristics of the developing individuals, the context in which the development is taking place, and the process through which their development is brought about. These models allow for the possibility that the potency, and even the direction, of the process may vary as a joint function of both the properties of the context and the properties of the developing person. The processes specified by such models may exert their influence on development through either proximal mechanisms, in which the features of the immediate context (both psychologic and environmental) bring about developmental change, or through more distal mechanisms, in which features of the environment beyond the immediate context influence the power and the direction of the proximal processes. The potential of the process–person–context model to increase our understanding of marital development is great, and the next section illustrates this potential by providing a hypothetical example of how the course of marriage may be influenced by such factors.

A Process–Person–Context Understanding of Marital Development

Let us consider a segment of the marital development of two couples: John and Jane Johnson, and Stan and Sally Stanley. Both couples entered marriage with a high level of relationship satisfaction, and they maintained this level of satisfaction for approximately the first two years of marriage. At this point in their marriages, both couples experienced a normative transitional event, the birth of their first child. Research has shown that marital satisfaction tends to decline following the birth of the first child, but that this effect is not invariant across couples (Belsky & Pensky 1988; Belsky & Rovine, 1990); and indeed, the marital satisfaction of one couple, Stan and Sue, remained high, but the satisfaction of the other couple, John and Jane, declined. Why did these differences occur? The process–person–context model of marital development proposes that a consideration of person and context variables may enhance our understanding of the process of marital change. Therefore, we consider each of these components in turn.

The Processes of Marital Development

Differences in marital functioning between the Johnsons and the Stanleys across the transition to parenthood are likely to result, in part, from differences in the coping and adaptational skills of the spouses. Coping and adaptational processes have long been recognized as important determinants of an individual's response to stress (e.g., Lazarus & Folkman, 1984). Family development researchers have also realized that adaptive processes play an important role in the *family's* ability to cope with stressful events. Hill (1949) provided the original conceptualization of the process of family adaptation to stressful events in his *ABCX* model.

> A (the stressor event)—interacting with B (the family's crisis meeting resources)—interacting with C (the definition the family makes of the event)—produce X (the crisis).

Since this original formulation, researchers have attempted to elaborate further on the way couples adapt to both normative and nonnormative stressful life events. Hansen and Johnson (1979) suggested that transition events produce a feeling of *heightened ambiguity* concerning roles and rules of interaction. During this period, the couple or the family experiments with new patterns of interaction, but do not necessarily abandon their established patterns immediately. Interaction is restructured through a *process* of experimentation with new patterns of feeling and behaving, while holding onto the safety of more familiar patterns. Such experimentation continues until a new pattern of interaction is achieved that is acceptable to each of the individuals involved. Successful negotiation of this process leads to a new stage of equilibrium and continued high levels of relationship satisfaction, whereas failure to achieve a consensus about new roles and interactions may lead to decreased levels of satisfaction and possible relationship dissolution. Thus, it may be that Stan and Sue were able to experiment with new patterns of interaction following the birth of their child until a satisfactory new pattern was found, whereas John and Jane failed to do so. However, the ability of the couples to engage in these adaptive processes is influenced by both personal and contextual variables.

Person Variables

Researchers examining the effects of minor daily stress on health and mood have revealed the importance of psychologic factors in the coping process. For example, DeLongis, Folkman, and Lazarus (1988) found that persons with low self-esteem were more likely to experience an increase in psychologic and somatic problems following stressful days than were persons with high self-esteem. The finding that the effects of daily stressors are not uniform across individuals has led researchers to propose that certain psychologic and environmental characteristics may function as vulnerability factors, in such a way that individuals possessing these factors may be more susceptible to the effects of stressful events than persons lacking these factors (Caspi, Bolger, & Eckenrode, 1987; DeLongis et al.).

It is a commonly held belief in psychology that an individual's early relationships with his or her parents will influence relationship functioning in later life. In addition, there is evidence to suggest that marital instability is frequently transmitted across generations (McLanahan & Bumpass, 1988). These considerations have led family development researchers to examine early family relationships as possible vulnerability factors for later marital and family instability (e.g., Carter & McGoldrick, 1980). Although not originally derived as an explanation of marital development, attachment theory (see Bowlby, 1988) has recently been adapted to the study of adult romantic relationships (Hazan & Shaver, 1987) and has the potential to increase our understanding of the process of marital change.

Building on the research of Ainsworth and her colleagues (Ainsworth, Blehar, Waters, & Wall, 1978), Hazan and Shaver (1987) proposed that an individual's early relationship with his or her primary caregiver leads to the development of one of three distinct attachment styles that endure throughout childhood and into adulthood, where they become powerful influences on the ways that adults experience romantic love and behave in close relationships. *Securely* attached adults are comfortable with intimacy, are able to trust and depend on their partner, and are not worried about being abandoned or unloved. *Avoidantly* attached individuals are uncomfortable with intimacy and closeness, have difficulty depending on others, have little confidence in their partner's availability, and do not worry about being abandoned. Individuals identified as *anxiously* attached seek extreme closeness in a relationship and are often worried about being abandoned and unloved. The processes through which attachment styles influence relationship quality are likely to be complex, but it is likely that part of this influence will occur via coping and adaptation to normative and nonnormative crises and developmental tasks.

Returning to our two hypothetical couples, attachment issues seem particularly salient to the successful resolution of marital tasks that occur with the birth of the first child. Specifically, the birth of a child often requires that a couple decrease the amount of intimacy and leisure activity that they shared before the child's arrival, and this process may be facilitated or hindered by the spouses' attachment styles. Stan and Sue both exhibit a secure attachment style, meaning that they are comfortable with intimacy and trust and do not fear being abandoned. This style of attachment enables them to tolerate the decreased level of activity and intimacy that often accompanies the birth of a child, without fearing that they are being abandoned by their spouse. This, in turn, contributes to the high level of marital satisfaction they enjoyed following the birth of their child. Jane, on the other hand, exhibits an anxious attachment style, and she often worries about being abandoned by John. Her fear of abandonment prevents the couple from developing alternative interaction patterns following the birth of their child, forcing them to use a pattern of interaction that is no longer adaptive. The strain caused by outdated modes of relating may be a contributing factor to the Johnson's decrease in marital satisfaction.

Context Variables

Factors that decrease a couple's ability to cope with normative and nonnormative events may be located in the environment as well as within the individual. Evidence from the stress and coping literature points to the importance of socioenvironmental factors such as chronic ecological stress, availability of social support, and presence of major life events as moderators of the impact of stress on health and mood (e.g., Caspi et al., 1987; DeLongis et al., 1988). Family development researchers have also recognized that the presence of environmental stressors will influence the family's ability to adapt to developmental events and tasks (Hill & Joy, 1981; McCubbin & Patterson, 1982), and stressful circumstances such as unemployment (Moen, 1982), poverty (Colon, 1980), and chronic illness (McCubbin, Nevin, Cauble, Larsen, Comeau, & Patterson, 1982) have been identified as vulnerability factors to decreased marital stability.

The context of marital development is likely to be influenced by social as well as environmental factors. Society creates norms surrounding marital and family development concerning the timing and sequence of transitional events as well as appropriate behaviors associated with different family roles. Failure to comply with these norms may place the family at increased risk for instability or dissolution. Neugarten (1976) proposes that family developmental events are much more likely to be traumatic if they occur off-time than if they occur according to society's expected sequence. Events that upset the sequence of the life cycle, such as the birth of a child before marriage or late in the marriage or the death of a child, may function as vulnerability factors in marital development by decreasing the couple's available coping resources and leaving them susceptible to the deleterious effects of other marital stressors.

Returning again to our two couples, we now consider the environmental factors that contributed to their different patterns of marital development. Stan and Sue are both college educated and have jobs that are intrinsically and financially rewarding. The economic security provided by their dual careers enables them to afford adequate child care and to plan for their child's future. This security undoubtedly facilitates their ability to cope with the stressors normally associated with the birth of a child, and therefore contributes to the stability of their marriage. Neither John nor Jane are college educated. John has recently been laid off, and Jane is employed full-time outside the home. The financial strain caused by John's unemployment has forced them to move in with his parents, which also enables his mother to provide child care while Jane works and John looks for employment. The strain caused by these circumstances, in addition to the burdens normally associated with the birth of a child, must be viewed as factors influencing this couple's decline in marital satisfaction.

Summary

We used the process–person–context model to examine some factors that influenced the marital development of two hypothetical couples at a specific point in their marital careers. For the purpose of clarity, these factors were dichotomized and labeled *person* and *context* variables. In reality, these two sets of variables are *not* independent, and do exert their influence on the process of marital development in an interactive manner. For example, the financial burden caused by John's unemployment forced Jane to work extra hours, leaving them with less time to spend together. Additionally, the living arrangement with John's parents afforded them very little privacy, hence very little possibility for intimacy. Although these contextual factors exerted an independent effect on John and Jane's marital development, the negative effects were exacerbated by personal variables. Jane's anxious attachment style sensitized her to feelings of abandonment, which were heightened by their living arrangement, in addition to those caused by the birth of their child. Thus, although both person and context variables exert independent effects on the process of marital development, it is *only* through their *joint* consideration that we can understand their complex and interactive effects on marital change.

It should be noted that, for the sake of brevity, our hypothetical example examined only one small segment of marital development. In addition, we highlighted only a few of the possible variables likely to influence this process. A process–person–context model of marital development demands that researchers examine the processes and variables that influence different stages of development. Although some of these variables will be important throughout the marital life cycle, others may exert an influence at only certain points along the marital career. Therefore, this model highlights the need for marital researchers to use longitudinal designs that follow couples as they experience critical transition events.

Evaluation of the Process–Person–Context Model

We proposed that the use of the process–person–context model can enhance our understanding of marital change, and we provided an illustrative example of its potential utility. In this section we evaluate the model, first comparing it to other models of marital change, and then highlighting its strengths and limitations.

Comparison with Other Models

Although application of process–person–context models to the study of marital development seems promising, it is possible that the concepts described are merely new terms for components of comparable frameworks. Therefore, we contrast this model with three existing models in the marital domain.

Kelley et al. (1983) provide the most comprehensive model of close relationships. Formulated as a description of relationships in general, this model does not focus specifically on the marital dyad. Instead, it outlines a general framework for understanding dyadic interaction. According to this framework, each participant in the interaction experiences a chain of events, including affective, cognitive, and behavioral events. The events *within* each person's chain are causally connected (e.g., a cognitive event may produce an affective event), and the events between the two person's chains are causally interconnected. Interaction is influenced, however, by relatively stable causal conditions that exist both in the environment and within the interacting individuals. Changes in the interaction are produced by changes in the causal conditions surrounding the interaction. Thus, according to Kelley et al., the study of personal relationships consists of the assessment and specification of the interdependence between the chain of events as well as identification of the causal conditions that affect the interaction.

Thus, the Kelley et al. (1983) model is similar to the process–person–context model in that they both offer an organizing framework consisting of several broad classes of variables that may influence dyadic interaction. They are also alike in that their application is not limited to the study of the marital relationship, but may be used to analyze close dyadic relationships of many forms (e.g., friendships, co-workers, spouses, parents and children). However, the two models differ in the purposes for which they were formulated. The Kelley et al. model "spells out, in what are intended to be descriptive, nontheoretical terms, what investigators of close relationships will inevitably study and, in general, how such phenomena must be studied" (1983, p. xiv). The model seeks to describe the processes involved in moment-to-moment dyadic interaction. In contrast, the process–person–context model attempts to delineate the process of relationship development, which includes, but is not limited to, an analysis of dyadic interaction. The model draws on concepts derived from developmental theory, such as transitional events, stages, and developmental tasks, to add to our understanding of marital development. Thus, the two models, although similar in scope, differ in the degree to which developmental changes are emphasized.

Other models focus exclusively on the marital relationship. Bradbury and Fincham's (1989, 1991) contextual model builds on the findings of observational research and identifies five components necessary for understanding marital interaction. According to this framework, a *behavior* is enacted by a spouse, which is perceived by the partner, who then engages in a series of processing events that serve to impart meaning to the behavior. On the basis of this processing, the partner will enact a behavior of his or her own, which will serve as a stimulus that the spouse will process, which will lead, in turn, to him or her enacting a behavior, which the partner will process, and so on. The *processing stage* is influenced by transient thoughts and feelings that compromise the *proximal context* of the interaction. This context is updated frequently throughout the course of the interaction and provides an immediate setting within which each new partner behavior is processed. A second component influencing the processing stage is the *distal context,* which is composed of the relatively stable psychologic characteristics of the spouse. The proximal and distal contexts influence each other, in such a way that the stable characteristics of the spouse will influence his or her transient thoughts and feelings during an interaction, which, over time, will modify the stable characteristics, and so on. Finally, the *appraisals,* or thoughts and feelings that a spouse has outside of interaction with his or her partner, may influence the course of future interaction, and be influenced by such interaction.

Finally, Gottman (1990) has proposed a model of marital change based on interaction patterns shown by couples in response to transient drops in marital satisfaction. According to this model, couples may respond in one of two ways—they may engage in activities that bring them closer together, or they may engage in conflict and disagreement. The marital satisfaction of couples who engage in positive activities together will remain stable or even increase over time. The satisfaction of those couples who engage in conflict may increase or decrease over time, depending on the type of conflict enacted. If the individuals feel loved and respected during the disagreement, they will feel closer to one another following the conflict and marital satisfaction will improve. If the conflict engenders feelings of perceived threat, however, the physiologic arousal of the spouses will increase, the interactions will become more negative and stereotyped, and marital satisfaction will decrease.

The models offered by Bradbury and Fincham (1989, 1991) and Gottman (1990) provide an explanation of changes in marital satisfaction based on a microanalytic analysis of the behaviors and intrapersonal responses that occur during and after marital interaction. This approach to understanding marital change differs from that offered by the process–person–context model in a number of ways. The most obvious difference between the approaches is the level at which they seek to describe marital change. The Bradbury and Fincham (1989, 1991) and Gottman (1990) models describe marital dynamics at a microinteraction level, with fluctuations in marital satisfaction proposed to result from the shifting thoughts, feelings and behaviors generated by ongoing marital interaction. Process–person–context models, in contrast, seek to describe marital change at a broader level by examining the ways in which personal and environmental factors influence developmental processes.

A related difference is that the approaches seek to understand different *types* of marital change. The Bradbury and Fincham (1989, 1991) and Gottman (1990) models analyze changes in marriage that result from continuous marital interaction, whereas process–person–context models are more developmental in nature and, thus, attempt to explain changes in marriage resulting from normative developmental events. Thus, the two approaches do *not* seem to be redundant, but instead seek to describe and explain different aspects of marital change. As such, they are not incompatible, and it is quite possible that both should be considered in order to provide a comprehensive understanding of the dynamics of marriage.

Strengths and Limitations of the Model

The process–person–context model of marital development capitalizes on the strengths of both the longitudinal research on marriage and the family development perspective, and, thus, provides a more complete understanding of marital development than those offered by either approach in isolation. It emphasizes the longitudinal perspective now favored by marital researchers, but also moves us beyond the empirical relationships established by the longitudinal research to consider the specific conditions under which such associations occur. Most longitudinal research on marriage fails to discriminate among couples at different developmental stages. As a result, the relationships revealed by such research are assumed to hold true for couples at very different points along the marital career, while in reality, the results may be an accurate reflection of only a subsample of couples at a specific stage of development. For example, recent data show that the duration of a marriage influences the association between marital unhappiness and the dissolution of the marriage (White & Booth, 1991). The process–person–context model sensitizes researchers to the developmental nature of marital change, and the use of such a model may, therefore, reveal associations that would otherwise remain obscure.

Thus, the process–person–context model capitalizes on the strengths of the longitudinal research and enriches it by considering developmental aspects of marital change. In this respect, the model bears a strong resemblance to the ideas offered by the family development perspective. Family development research, however, has been criticized for its failure to produce consistent effects and its lack of predictive utility (e.g., Menaghan, 1983). In response to these shortcomings, researchers have begun to use short-term longitudinal designs to examine variables that may moderate the effects of family stage transitions on marital functioning (e.g., Belsky & Rovine, 1990; Schumm & Bugaighis, 1986). The process–person–context model formalizes this trend by specifying two broad classes of variables likely to influence the process of marital change and highlighting the fact that *both* are necessary to provide a comprehensive understanding of marital change.

A final strength of the model is its inclusiveness. By specifying broad sets of variables that deserve consideration in an account of marital development, the process–person–context model may be adapted to the needs of researchers studying many different aspects of marital dynamics. Thus, rather than providing a precise delineation of a limited domain of marital development, the process–person–context model provides a general paradigm from which to examine many aspects of development. This decision represents a trade-off between specificity in explanation versus inclusiveness of the domain explained and, as such, may also be regarded as a limitation of the model. Because it is general enough to include most variables examined by marital researchers, we could argue that the process–person–context model lacks the specificity to be labeled a model of marital development. Although it is true that the model does not propose a specific group of variables to completely explain marital development, it delineates two broad domains of variables, both of which will be necessary to describe marital change adequately. Therefore, it should be viewed as a general framework for approaching the study of marital development, rather than a precise specification of marital dynamics.

CONCLUSION

This chapter opened with the question of how marriages develop and change over time. In their attempts to answer this, psychologists have used increasingly sophisticated longitudinal designs and developed several models of marital change, but have ignored theory and research provided by family development research. This chapter illustrated the usefulness of a developmental approach to the study of marriage, and it introduced a developmental framework with the potential to enhance our understanding of marital change. Although no attempt was made to outline specific topics for future research, it is our hope that researchers will use the ideas presented here as an impetus to think about and incorporate developmental issues into their research, so that we may generate a more complete understanding of the marital life cycle.

REFERENCES

Ainsworth, M. D. S., Blehar, M. C., Waters, E., & Wall, S. (1978). *Patterns of attachment: A psychological study of the strange situation.* Hillsdale, NJ: Erlbaum.

Anderson, S. A., Russell, C. S., & Schumm, W. R. (1983). Perceived marital quality and family life cycle categories: A further analysis. *Journal of Marriage and the Family, 45,* 127–139.

Belsky, J., & Pensky, E. (1988). Marital change across the transition to parenthood. *Marriage and Family Review, 12,* 133–156.

Belsky, J., & Rovine, M. (1990). Patterns of marital change across the transition to parenthood. *Journal of Marriage and the Family, 52,* 109–123.

Bentler, P. M., & Newcomb, M. D. (1978). Longitudinal study of marital success and failure. *Journal of Consulting and Clinical Psychology, 46,* 1053–1070.

Bowlby, J. (1988). *A secure base: Parent child attachment and healthy human development.* New York: Basic Books.

Bradbury, T. N., & Fincham, F. D. (1989). Behavior and satisfaction in marriage: Prospective mediating processes. *Review of Personality and Social Psychology, 10,* 119–143.

Bradbury, T. N., & Fincham, F. D. (1991). A contextual model for advancing the study of marital interaction. In G. J. O. Fletcher & F. D. Fincham (Eds.), *Cognition in close relationships* (pp. 127–147). Hillsdale, NJ: Erlbaum.

Bronfenbrenner, U. (1988). Interacting systems in human development. In N. Bolger, A. Caspi, G. Downey, & M. Moorehouse (Eds.), *Persons in context: Problem behavior and normal youth development.* New York: Cambridge University Press.

Carter, E. A., & McGoldrick, M. (1980). The family life cycle and family therapy. In E. A. Carter & M. McGoldrick (Eds.), *The family life cycle: A framework for family therapy* (pp. 3–20). New York: Gardner Press.

Caspi, A., Bolger, N., & Eckenrode, J. (1987). Linking person and context in daily stress process. *Journal of Personality and Social Psychology, 52,* 184–195.

Christensen, A., Sullaway, M., & King, C. E. (1983). Systematic error in behavioral reports of dyadic interaction: Egocentric bias and content effects. *Behavioral Assessment, 5,* 129–140.

Colon, F. (1980). The family life cycle of the multiproblem poor family. In E. A. Carter & M. McGoldrick (Eds.), *The family life cycle: A framework for family therapy* (pp. 343–382). New York: Gardner.

Cowan, C., Cowan, P., Heming, G., Garrett, B., Coysh, W., Curtis-Boles, H., & Boles, A. (1985). Transitions to parenthood: His, hers, and theirs. *Journal of Family Issues, 6,* 451–482.

DeLongis, A., Folkman, S., & Lazarus, R. S. (1988). The impact of daily stress on health and mood: Psychological and social resources as mediators. *Journal of Personality and Social Psychology, 54,* 486–495.

Duvall, E. M., & Hill, R. (1948). *Report to the Committee of the Dynamics of Family Interaction.* Washington, DC: National Conference on Family Life.

Filsinger, E. E., & Thoma, S. J. (1988). Behavioral antecedents of relationship stability and adjustment: A five-year longitudinal study. *Journal of Marriage and the Family, 50,* 785–795.

Fincham, F. D., & Bradbury, T. N. (1987). The impact of attributions in marriage: A longitudinal analysis. *Journal of Personality and Social Psychology, 53,* 510–517.

Fincham, F. D., & Bradbury, T. N. (1990). *The psychology of marriage: Basic issues and applications.* New York: Guilford.

Fincham, F. D., & Bradbury, T. N. (1991). Marital satisfaction, depression, and attributions: A longitudinal analysis. *Journal of Personality and Social Psychology, 64,* 442–452.

Glenn, N. D. (1990). Quantitative research on marital quality in the 1980s: A critical review. *Journal of Marriage and the Family, 52,* 818–831.

Gottman, J. M. (1990). How marriages change. In G. R. Patterson (Ed.), *Depression and aggression in family interaction* (pp. 75–101). Hillsdale, NJ: Erlbaum.

Gottman, J. M., & Krokoff, L. J. (1989). Marital interaction and satisfaction: A longitudinal view. *Journal of Consulting and Clinical Psychology, 57,* 47–52.

Hansen, D., & Johnson, V. (1979). Rethinking family stress theory: Definitional aspects. In W. Burr, R. Hill, F. Nye, & I. Reiss (Eds.), *Contemporary theories about the family: Vol. I. Research-based theories* (pp. 26–44). New York: Free Press.

Hazan, C., & Shaver, P. (1987). Romantic love conceptualized as an attachment process. *Journal of Personality and Social Psychology, 52,* 511–524.

Hill, R. (1949). *Families under stress.* New York: Harper & Row.

Hill, R., & Joy, C. (1981). *Operationalizing the concept of critical transition to generate phases of family development.* Unpublished manuscript.

Huston, T. L., & Vangelisti, A. L. (1991). Socioemotional behavior and satisfaction in marital relationships: A longitudinal study. *Journal of Personality and Social Psychology, 61,* 721–733.

Kelley, H. H., Berscheid, E., Christensen, A., Harvey, J. H., Huston, T. L., Levinger, G., McClintock, E., Peplau, L. A., & Peterson, D. R. (1983). *Close relationships.* New York: Freeman.

Kelley, E. L., & Conley, J. J. (1987). Personality and compatibility: A prospective analysis of marital stability and marital satisfaction. *Journal of Personality and Social Psychology, 52,* 27–40.

Klein, D. M., & Aldous, J. (1979). Three blind mice: Misleading criticisms of the "family life cycle" concept. *Journal of Marriage and the Family, 41,* 689–691.

Lazarus, R. S., & Folkman, S. (1984). *Stress, appraisal, and coping.* New York: Springer.

Lee, G. R. (1988). Marital satisfaction in later life: The effects of nonmarital roles. *Journal of Marriage and the Family, 50,* 775–783.

Levenson, R. W., & Gottman, J. M. (1983). Marital interaction: Physiological linkage and affective exchange. *Journal of Personality and Social Psychology, 45,* 587–597.

Levenson, R. W., & Gottman, J. M. (1985). Physiological and affective predictors of change in relationship satisfaction. *Journal of Personality and Social Psychology, 49,* 85–94.

Markman, H. J. (1979). Application of a behavioral model of marriage in predicting relationship satisfaction for couples planning marriage. *Journal of Consulting and Clinical Psychology, 47,* 743–749.

Markman, H. J. (1981). Prediction of marital distress: A 5-year follow-up. *Journal of Consulting and Clinical Psychology, 49,* 760–762.

Markman, H. J. (1984). The longitudinal study of couples' interactions: Implications for understanding and predicting the development of marital distress. In K. Hahlweg & N. S. Jacobson (Eds.), *Marital interactions: Analysis and modification* (pp. 253–281). New York: Guilford.

Markman, H. J. (1989). *The long-term effects of premarital intervention.* Unpublished manuscript.

Markman, H. J., Floyd, F. J., Stanley, S. M., & Storaasli, R. D. (1988). Prevention of marital distress: A longitudinal investigation. *Journal of Consulting and Clinical Psychology, 56,* 210–217.

Mattessich, P., & Hill, R. (1987). Life cycle and family development. In M. B. Sussman & S. K. Steinmetz (Eds.), *Handbook of marriage and the family* (pp. 437–469). New York: Plenum.

McCubbin, H. I., Nevin, R. S., Cauble, A. E., Larsen, A., Comeau, J. K., & Patterson, J. M. (1982). Families coping with chronic illness: The case of cerebral palsy. In H. I. McCubbin, A. E. Cauble, & J. M. Patterson (Eds.), *Family stress, coping, and social support* (pp. 169–188). Springfield, IL: Thomas.

McCubbin, H. I., & Patterson, J. M. (1982). Family adaptation to crises. In H. I. McCubbin, A. E. Cauble, & J. M. Patterson (Eds.), *Family stress, coping, and social support* (pp. 26–47). Springfield: Thomas.

McLanahan, S., & Bumpass, L. (1988). Intergenerational consequences of family disruption. *American Journal of Sociology, 94,* 130–152.

Menaghan, E. (1982). Assessing the impact of family transitions on the marital experience. In H. I. McCubbin, A. E. Cauble, & J. M. Patterson (Eds.), *Family stress, coping, and social support* (pp. 90–108). Springfield: Thomas.

Menaghan, E. (1983). Marital stress and family transitions: A panel analysis. *Journal of Marriage and the Family, 45,* 371–386.

Moen, P. (1982). Preventing financial hardship: Coping strategies of families of the unemployed. In H. I. McCubbin, A. E. Cauble, & J. M. Patterson (Eds.), *Family stress, coping, and social support* (pp. 151–168). Springfield: Thomas.

Moss, P., Bolland, G., Foxman, R., & Owen, C. (1986). Marital relations during the transition to parenthood. *Journal of Reproductive and Infant Development, 4,* 57–67.

Nock, S. L. (1979). The family life cycle: Empirical or conceptual tool? *Journal of Marriage and the Family, 41,* 15–26.

Neugarten, B. (1976). Adaptation and the life cycle. *Counseling Psychologist, 6,* 45–67.

Rapoport, R. H. (1963). Normal crises, family structure, and mental health. *Family Process, 2,* 68–80.

Rollins, B. C., & Cannon, K. C. (1974). Marital satisfaction over the life cycle: A reevaluation. *Journal of Marriage and the Family, 36,* 271–282.

Rollins, B. C., & Feldman, H. (1970). Marital satisfaction over the family life cycle. *Journal of Marriage and the Family, 32,* 20–28.

Ruble, D., Fleming, A., Hackel, L., & Stangor, L. (1988). Changes in the marital relationship during the transition to first-time motherhood: Effects of violated expectations concerning division of household labor. *Journal of Personality and Social Psychology, 55,* 78–87.

Schumm, W. R., & Bugaighis, M. A. (1986). Marital quality over the marital career: Alternative explanations. *Journal of Marriage and the Family, 48,* 165–168.

Smith, D. A., Vivian, D., & O'Leary, K. D. (1991). The misnomer proposition: A critical reappraisal of the longitudinal status of "negativity" in marital communication. *Behavioral Assessment, 13,* 113–124.

Spanier, G. B., & Lewis, R. A. (1980). Marital quality: A review of the seventies. *Journal of Marriage and the Family, 42,* 825–839.

Spanier, G. B., Lewis, R. A., & Cole, C. C. (1975). Marital adjustment over the family life cycle: The issue of curvilinearity. *Journal of Marriage and the Family, 37,* 263–275.

Steinberg, L. (1987). The impact of puberty on family relations. *Developmental Psychology, 23,* 451–460.

Steinberg, L., & Silverberg, S. (1987). Influences on marital satisfaction during the middle stages of the family life cycle. *Journal of Marriage and the Family, 49,* 751–760.

Storaasli, R. D., & Markman, H. J. (1990). Relationship problems in the early stages of marriage: A longitudinal investigation. *Journal of Family Psychology, 4,* 80–98.

Terman, L. W., Buttenweiser, P., Ferguson, L. W., Johnson, W. B., & Wilson, D. (1938). *Psychological factors in marital happiness.* New York: McGraw Hill.

Terman, L. M., & Oden, M. H. (1947). *The gifted child grows up: Twenty-five year follow-up of a superior group.* Stanford, CA: Stanford University Press.

Uhr, L. M. (1957). *Personality changes during marriage.* Unpublished doctoral dissertation, University of Michigan, Ann Arbor.

White, L. K., & Booth, A. (1991). Divorce over the life course: The role of marital happiness. *Journal of Family Issues, 12,* 5–21.

White, J. M. (1991). *Dynamics of family development: A theoretical perspective.* New York: Guilford.

Woody, E. Z., & Costanzo, P. R. (1990). Does marital agony precede marital ecstasy? A comment on Gottman and Krokoff's "Marital interaction and satisfaction: A longitudinal view." *Journal of Consulting and Clinical Psychology, 58,* 499–501.

CHAPTER 5

Parenting Over the Family Life Cycle

MARIO CUSINATO

PARENTING AND FAMILY LIFE CYCLE STUDIES

It is universally known that parental experience evolves as years go by, as children grow up, and parents grow old; however, adequate theoretic and methodologic approaches in a developmental perspective to parental tasks remain to be established and accepted. As already underlined by L'Abate in his introduction, the reasons are several. Parent–child relationships across the life course have often been examined within the developmental perspective on the family, taking advantage of theoretical and empirical investigations, but, simultaneously, such examinations have often faced the repercussions of the criticism of this perspective.

Mattessich & Hill (1987) open the review of the literature on the family developmental perspective with some challenging questions.

> Has this perspective resulted in an intelligible and useful rendering of the phenomenon of family organizational change? Has the notion of family stage increased our understanding of how families change from marriage to dissolution? Has the stage notion contributed significant, independent explanatory power, beyond much less complex notions, in research applications where the "Family life cycle" is an antecedent to some dependent variable(s) of primary interest? Has the developmental perspective, either alone or in tandem with life course analysis, adequately established a theory of how families develop over time? (p. 437)

In their review, they look for adequate answers, but their concluding remarks pose further questions. Differences in family development are established for families who vary by race, marital status, and marriage order. However, some of the data can be only speculative until longitudinal research follows cohorts to determine the precise timing of marriage, divorce, remarriage, first and later births, movement in and out of the labor force, and so on. Such longitudinal research is difficult; therefore, this perspective cannot be validated completely from the empirical viewpoint. Nevertheless, some studies seem to have provided us with remarkable pointers.

The present perspective, focusing on position and roles and their dynamic counterparts, leaves open a discussion on the issue of variability in role performance by incumbents of family positions; namely, individual family members. It is necessary to explain how personality types and competence levels of family members interact with the developmental process. In the last decade, some studies on parent–child relationships have made considerable steps in this direction.

The concept of *critical transition* requires improved operationalization, despite the fact that some critical moments in a family—for example, the child in adolescence—have been closely examined, allowing some clarity from the conceptual point of view. Mattessich and Hill (1988) reiterate how much of the imagery of the family cycle is carried over from the individual's life cycle. It is important to point out the main variables that, in interaction, explain the rise, inflection point, and decline typical of life span family development. Further investigation of parenting is very useful in combining research on the individual's life cycle with that on the parent–child relationship in its developmental stages.

From the methodologic viewpoint, some research must be considered. Moreover, studies of the family development phenomenon must be considered. Family development must be distinguished in its use as either a dependent or independent variable. In research projects on parenting over the family life cycle, such methodologic distinctions can be made. Last, Mattessich and Hill (1988) recognize the need for further research on the last stage of the family career, often called the *empty nest,* especially considering the remarkable increase in average life expectancy (Norton, 1983).

Problems concerning the family developmental perspective belong only partially in the parenting experience; indeed, from a review of the literature I believe that assurances in the parent–child subsystem can spur more convincing answers to those problems. In fact, the breakup of a marriage and/or the establishment of new family ties does not destroy the parent–child relationship, although they can make it more complex. Difficulty conceptualizing the childless couple from a developmental viewpoint is somewhat unrelated to the parenting developmental perspective. Parenthood implies continual adaptation to physiologic and psychologic changes within the self, parallel to and in conjunction with changes in the child and the child's expanding world (Benedek, 1970).

PARENTING EXPERIENCE

It is not enough to say that parenthood is defined as identifying who cares for the child; in this sense, we could understand it as opposite that of the developmental concept of parenting experience, which moves step by step, coping with critical transition moments and developmental tasks as they occur. Parenthood can be understood as the result of the developmental experience both subjectively (the sense of parenthood as acquired through the daily experience of having children), culturally (sociohistorical forces have shaped the meaning of parenthood), and socially (the parenting task is influenced by the social background). The relation between parenthood and parenting is dialectic: the meaning of parenthood anticipates, accompanies, and condenses the parenting experience over the life cycle. Therefore, it is useful to consider this point further.

First, let us define parenthood. "The images of motherhood and fatherhood reveal our shared ideals, standards, beliefs, and expectations regarding men and women as parents" (Thompson & Walker, 1989, p. 859). Both *enduring* and *emerging* images exist, much to the confusion of mothers and fathers. Several authors have described the enduring image of motherhood (Boulton, 1983; Chodorow & Contratto, 1982; Daniels & Weingarten, 1988; Glenn, 1987): motherhood is inevitable; every woman will or should be a mother. A woman's identity is tenuous and trivial without motherhood. A woman enjoys and intuitively knows what to do for her child; she cares for her child without ambivalence or awkwardness. Motherhood is a constant and exclusive responsibility. A mother is all-giving and all-powerful. The mother devotes herself to her child's needs and holds her child's fate in her hands. Amid idealization and blame, the enduring image of motherhood is incompatible with the facts of women's sexuality and occupations outside the home.

The enduring image of fatherhood has been studied by some researchers (Daniels & Weingarten, 1988; Pleck, 1987): father is the breadwinner who lacks the ability or desire to nurture his child day-to-day—he funds the family but keeps his distance. Our images of motherhood and fatherhood in African American and Hispanic American families are exaggerated in such a way that ideals become flaws. African American mothers are imagined to be all-powerful matriarchs (McCray, 1980). African American fathers are deemed, at best, aloof and, at worst, absent (McAdoo, 1988). Hispanic American fathers are imagined to be standoffish, swaggering authoritarians (Mirandé, 1988). These are myths: African American couples share child rearing no less, and perhaps more, than do anglo* couples, and African American husbands are as intimately involved with their children as are anglo husbands, although it may be more difficult for them to provide for and protect their children (Allen, 1981; McAdoo; Peters, 1985).

The emerging "new fatherhood" or "new parenthood," however, is the image of mothers and fathers sharing the full weight of raising their children (Bronstein, 1988; LaRossa, 1988; Pleck, 1985). "New" fathers are intimately, actively involved with their children; they are responsible and care for their children day-to-day. Prime time television bolsters this image; indeed television fathers often are portrayed as more active parents than are television mothers (Dail & Way, 1985). With juggled schedules and good day care in the early years, "new" mothers and fathers can have fulfilling working lives and rich and rewarding family lives. Both "new" parents can have it all, including a sense of fairness, respect, and cooperation with each other (Bronstein, 1988).

These new and traditional images form the background for the active and personal parenting experience: they are either validated or denied by parenting activities and the experience that develops and evolves along the parental life cycle.

---

* Note: Throughout this book the term *anglo* is used to refer to Caucasians in general, not merely those of Anglo-Saxon descent.

TIME MARKS THE PARENTING EXPERIENCE

The developmental perspective of parental experience places the variable *time* at the center of attention. A first aspect is obvious: time marks the parent–child relationship from the time of conception. Over the years, parents mature in age, experience, and knowledge of their child. With time, the child matures biologically and psychologically, maintains relationships with his or her parents, finds his or her own identity, increases his or her autonomy, and cares for the elderly parent. The same life cycle unites parental experience and filial experience. It is interesting to note how the life cycle implies a kind of equilibrium between the two experiences.

During the early part of the life span, parents provide food, clothing, shelter, love, and guidance for the child. These things are essential for the child's survival, development, and eventual independence in young adulthood. During child rearing, there is an imbalance in the exchange of help in favor of the child. If parents care sufficiently for the child, they meet whatever obstacles occur and make whatever sacrifices are needed to carry out the responsibilities of child rearing. Through all this, the child develops the basic attachment bond that provides a foundation for all later relationships. Filial idealization is present at this life stage, when children tend to perceive their parents as more idealized beings than they do at any other stage of life.

When the child is in young adulthood and the parent is in middle age, there is more balance in the exchange of help. Middle-aged parents may babysit the grandchildren (Kivnick, 1982; Rossi & Rossi, 1990), help with finances (Troll, Miller, & Atchley, 1979), and so on, while the young adult may assist the parent with house maintenance, occasional transportation, and the like. There is a greater mutual exchange of help—but not necessarily an equal exchange—as well as a relative measure of independence of child and parent from each other. Filial idealization leads to filial disenchantment. In the later part of the parent's life span, when the child has grown to middle age, exchange of help may shift more in favor of the elderly parent. The process becomes reversed. Child rearing was essential for the survival, maintenance, development, and eventual independence of the child. At this stage of life, parent care is essential for the maintenance and continued survival of the elderly parent. Filial disenchantment gives way to filial maturity.

If we conceive of this sequential shift in the exchange of helping behaviors throughout the life span as a necessity, both for species survival of the young and for fulfillment of the elderly's potential life span before death, then parent care and child rearing become intrinsically related. Keeping these aspects of mutual help in a finely tuned balance over the life span would seem to be an aim in itself for the species, although the degree to which such an aim has been attained has varied over the centuries, depending upon the social forces at play.

This global equilibrium of the life span is not outside the parent–child relationship, but inside the organizational intervention that gives structure to the parent–child relationship. This parental timing "has its foundation neither in Newton's absolute time, nor in Kant's a priori construction, but rather in Einstein's pluralities of relative times, in Bergson's relational approach, in Husserl's interior times" (Strati, 1984, p. 9). The temporalities of a complex organization, marked by irreversibility and made up of a "plurality of times," are each connected to the other through multiple and subtle articulations (Zanarini, 1985). From the same perspective, LaRossa (1983) distinguishes physical time and social time; the latter is subjective and phenomenological, according to previous investigations on subjective time as temporal trajectories (Glase & Strauss, 1968) and time tracks (Lyman & Scott, 1970). *Physical* time and *subjective* time stand in complex relation: often we hear people say that physical time is scarce, a 24-hour day is not enough, and they cannot cram all their engagements into their schedule. In fact, tracks or trajectories can be experienced as episodic or continuous, humanistic or fatalistic, surprising or gradual. Contrary to what might be expected, the more intricate a schedule is, the more likely the people conforming to that schedule will feel that time is in short supply (Lewis & Weingart, 1981). In this way, the intricacy of a schedule affects the way physical time is perceived; an advance in synchronization represents a step in synchronization efforts. In a general sense, we can say that the time tracks of parents are different from their children's and that the synchronization task engages and worries the protagonists.

The schedule that characterizes families with infants is, in part, a function of the fact that babies are ignorant of the social clock (LaRossa, 1983). Nevertheless, research on early social interactions (Bell & Harper, 1977; Kaye, 1980a, 1980b; Richards, 1974; Schaffer, 1977) confirms that the adult and the child constitute, as early as the first months of life, a system open to mutual feedback, characterized by bidirectionality and organizational interactions. The parent–child relationships during the school years often are characterized by common satisfaction and their phenomenological *time* synchronization is fairly easy to achieve. Time tracks of parents and adolescents are lived in a rather difficult way—the latter want to *run,* whereas the former want to *walk.* In the launch family, subjective times are different, but the common task is to accept differences rather than to force synchronization. Elderly parents and adult children have different time tracks; if they live under the same roof, synchronization may be an effort.

Synchronization is further favored by the awareness of transition periods, which helps to avoid ambiguous positions such as "advance too quickly" or "backward flight." For this reason, it is preferable to focus on transition moments, rather than on developmental stages that cover a long period. Furthermore, transition moment rites are considered to be culturally determined modalities capable of defining the transition, almost as if the protagonists' watches had to be "culturally synchronized"; therefore, the child's transition rites from adolescence to youth have been investigated, as well as the transition rites of children who are leaving home (Quinn, Newfield, & Protinsky, 1985). Rites are cultural opportunities to synchronize the protagonists' times; however, much is left to personal commitment, which requires ability and patience. LaRossa (1983) aptly defined patience as "a socially constructed sense of time" (p. 586).

PARENTING STAGES OF LIFE

We have noted that temporality is marked by a "plurality of times." The stage distinction is by now considered classic (Aldous, 1978; Duvall, 1977; Mattessich & Hill, 1988). Various stages of the life cycle explain both functional and dysfunctional parent–child relationships. The functional pattern is typical of the situation in which usual and optimal conditions occur; the dysfunctional pattern underlines the problems that must be faced and solved, although these patterns do not necessarily have pathologic implications. The functional and dysfunctional patterns of parent–child relationships in life cycle perspectives are summarized in Table 5.1.

THEORETICAL FRAMES OF THE PARENTING LIFE CYCLE

Several theoretical approaches have been used to study parent–child relationships over the various stages of the life cycle. The initial phases of the cycle have been researched more thoroughly than the final phases. The symbolic interaction framework is meaningful. It was developed from the seminal scholarship of William James, John Dewey, Charles Horton Cooley, W. I. Thomas, and George Herbert Mead (Blumer, 1969; Manis & Meltzer, 1978; Meltzer, Petras, & Reynolds, 1975). The basic idea of this framework is that humans lead their lives both in a symbolic and physical environment: this influences their interactions within social groups.

In family interactions, family members communicate through complex sets of meanings; these allow family members to share experiences and to involve two or more people in a very meaningful social process (Burr, Leigh, Day, & Constantine, 1979). Parents and children are aware of their significance to each other: they are tied by an affectionate bond and know full well how socially important their expectations are. From a young child's perspective, parents reach this status because they can control a large spectrum of resources, which include the ability to nurture, to look after their child's physical well-being, and to provide answers in many areas. For their part, parents know their children's significance—their presence alters many of the parents' life experiences and adds entirely new dimensions to their self-concepts (LaRossa & LaRossa, 1981; LeMasters, 1970).

For many years, the parent–child relationship has been under the influence of unidirectional conceptualizations mainly involving the influence of parent characteristics on the social characteristics of children and their personalities. Typical research areas are: parental behavior and parental child-rearing typologies (Rollins & Thomas, 1975; Steinmetz, 1979); observational learning (Bandura, 1976); and generational transmission (Acock & Bengton, 1980). This tradition focused on the larger social contexts that influence parent–child relationships: culture (Mindel & Habenstein, 1975; Staples & Mirandé, 1980; Tseng & Hsu,

TABLE 5.1   Parenting Life Stages

A. Infant and parents' stage	
—Parents' functional patterns	Nurturing, protecting, and caring for infant
Infant's functional patterns	Total dependency on parents
—Parents' dysfunctional patterns	Child rejection, negligence, or abuse
Infant's dysfunctional patterns	Regression and withdrawal from forming relationships with parents
B. Younger child and parents' stage	
—Parents' functional patterns	Adjustment of triadic relation to child
	Provision of behavior model for child to imitate
	Provision of appropriate restrictions and limitations
Child's functional patterns	Achieving psychological separation from parents
	Achieving autonomy
	Mirroring and imitating parents' behavior
	Mastering omnipotent wish
—Parents' dysfunctional patterns	Inability to let child gradually separate from parents
Child's dysfunctional patterns	Prolonged symbiotic relation with parents
C. Older child and parents' stage	
—Parents' functional patterns	Sensitivity to child's growth needs
	Provision of opportunities for child to do things for self within child's abilities
	Letting child go and grow
	Enjoying life through child's experience
Child's functional patterns	Search for individuality
—Parents' dysfunctional patterns	Insensitive to child's growth needs
	Inhibition or limitation of child's individuality
Child's dysfunctional patterns	Failure to seek individuality
D. Adolescent and parents' stage	
—Parents' functional patterns	Provision of assistance in establishment of role and identity
	Toleration and compromise of the cultural gap that may exist between generations
Adolescent's functional patterns	Development of self-image and identity
—Parents' dysfunctional patterns	Parents feel their child undervalues them
	Unwilling to negotiate cultural gap with adolescent
Adolescent's dysfunctional patterns	Adolescent believes that parents depreciate him or her
	Adolescent rebels against parents

Continued

TABLE 5.1   Parenting Life Stages (con't)

E. Adult child and parents' stage	
—Parents' functional patterns	Letting grown-up child go and be independent
	Accepting adult-to-adult relationships with grown-up-child
	Standing by with encouragement, reassurance, and appreciation
Child's functional patterns	Relative independence from parents
	Develop adult-to-adult relationship with parents
	Seek guidance and support from parents whenever they are needed
—Parents' dysfunctional patterns	Unable to let grown-up child go and be independent
Child's dysfunctional patterns	Fail to develop adult-to-adult relationships with parents
F. Adult child and aged parents' stage	
—Parents' functional patterns	Reverse role to be taken care of by child
Child's functional patterns	Reverse role to take care of aged and incapacitated parents
—Parents' dysfunctional patterns	Resistance to giving up authoritative role toward grown-up child
	Refusal of help from adult child when needed
Child's dysfunctional patterns	Inability to take the reversed role, still expecting parents to be omnipotent
	Rejection and negligence of incapacitated aged parents when they need help

Adapted from Tseng & Hsu, 1991.

1991); social class (Bernstein, 1971, 1973; Gecas, 1979); history (Elder, 1981); family structure (Schooler, 1972); and gender (Baumrind, 1980). An approach opposite to these has been used to investigate how children influence the attitudes, behaviors, and identities of parents (Bell & Harper, 1977; Lerner & Spanier, 1978). The bidirectional–systemic perspective tries to overcome the unidirectional one, starting from the premise that infants and children are active agents as much as their parents. From this perspective parent–child interaction is investigated as a dynamic process of closely woven sequences of interaction (Osofsky & Connors, 1979; Parke, 1979). Within this bidirectional approach, is the approach focusing on the mutual attachment processes (Ainsworth, 1979; Bowlby, 1973), as well as the complex transactions within the parent–child dyad and the surrounding social environment (Belsky, 1981; Garbarino, 1982).

Family scholars have been baffled by the fact that some families can cope easily with—and occasionally even thrive on—life's hardships, whereas other families under similar stressors or during family transitions seem to buckle under seemingly unimportant life changes. We refer in particular to the Hill

ABCX crisis model (Hill, 1949, 1958). Originating in the field of sociology, this model adopted concepts from system theory, family developmental theory, and Erikson's (1959, 1968) psychosocial theory of individual development. Physiologists (Selye, 1974) in the field of medicine and psychologists (Lazarus, 1966; Mikhail, 1981) have also focused on stress and coping. Stressors, family transitions, resources, family tensions, and crises are the basic concepts. Intending to integrate these lines of research, McCubbin, Couble, and Patterson (1982) defined a stressor as *a life event impacting upon the family unit which produces, or has the potential of producing, change in the family social system.* The specific event recognition is not agreed upon by everyone. For example, Hill (1949) classified stressors in terms of their impact upon the family unit and identified: (1) accession (changed family structure by adding a member); (2) dismemberment (changed family structure by losing a member); (3) loss of family morale and unity; and (4) changed structure and morale. In contrast, Lipman-Blumen (1975) advanced diverse criteria for the assessment of family crises such as origin, onset, degree of severity, length of adjustment to the stressor, and so on. Some family researchers have investigated the links between stress and physical illness (Dorenwend & Dorenwend, 1974; Holmes & Rahe, 1967); others have classified stressor events according to their desiderability, frequency, and intensity (Pearlin & Schooler, 1978). In the Family Stress and Coping Project of the University of Minnesota, researchers developed standardized scores for family life transitions (McCubbin, Patterson, Bauman, & Harris, 1981; McCubbin, Patterson, & Wilson, 1981).

Regarding family life transitions, it is important to distinguish between normative and nonnormative events. Events are viewed as normative by family scholars because they are ubiquitous (they occur in most families), expectable (families could anticipate their occurrence at certain scheduled points in the family life cycle), and short-term (nonchronic) (McCubbin & Figley, 1983). By and large, investigators found that strain scores related to the experience of normative events were lower than scores for nonnormative events (Pearlin & Schooler, 1978). Family sociologists in the area of family development have focused on *critical role transitions,* which occur in most families and serve as demarcation points for stages in the family life cycle. In this manner, the normative term is associated with major developmental role changes and task assignment changes that occur in families with children. These normative stressor events are viewed as short-term experiences, accompanied by changes in role expectations and rules for interacting that occur during each transition period; the amount of stress is related to the number or degree of role behavior changes for the whole family unit, independently of any family perception of stress (George, 1980; McCubbin & Figley, 1983).

Family resources for meeting the demands of stressor events and hardship are the family members' abilities to prevent an event or a transition from creating a crisis or disruption (Burr, 1973); in this way, resources become part of the family's capabilities for resisting crises. When the family compares demands and resources and perceives an imbalance, there emerges a family stress that varies in intensity depending on the situation, the characteristics of the family unit, and the psychological and physical well-being of its members. Different from stress, which is characterized by an imbalance between demand and capability, crisis is represented by the family's inability to regain stability and the constant pressure to allow changes in the family structure, as well as patterns of interaction. Crisis, therefore, requires restructuring of the system by a new focus on the terms and a search for new resources to cope with the situation. This process can lead to a positive or negative adjustment. The recurrent process is read in the light of a double ABCX model to interpret two distinct phases: the adjustment phase in response to a stressor and the adaptation phase that occurs following a family crisis (McCubbin & Patterson, 1981).

TRANSITION TO PARENTHOOD

Researchers interested in family development have often focused on transition to parenthood (Hobbs & Wimbish, 1977; Belsky, 1981). Those researchers who see the family as a complex and integrated system of roles and statutes have focused their studies on whether the arrival of a first child provokes a crisis in the married couple's relationship, changing from a dyadic to a triadic system. According to some, the transition to parenthood is, indeed, a period of crisis (Dyer, 1963; LaRossa & LaRossa, 1981; Wainwright, 1966); others have challenged this conclusion (Hobbs, 1965; Hobbs & Wimbish, 1977; Hobbs & Cole, 1976) and have underlined the satisfactory and positive consequences of having a child (Russell, 1974).

This body of research has some methodological problems (i.e., many retrospective assessments, nonrepresentative groups of the total population, data from different subjects, insufficient longitudinal studies) and conceptual deficiencies. To solve the latter point, Umberson and Gove (1989) suggest estimating the effects of parenting on three general dimensions of psychological well-being: affect, satisfaction level, and life meaning. Measures of affect "seek to represent the positive and negative feelings which are associated with everyday experiences" (Campbell, 1981, p. 22). Measures of satisfaction can be viewed as quality-of-life indicators. The dimension of life-meaning focuses on "the degree to which one feels that one's life has meaning and experiences oneself as a person of value" (Umberson & Gove, 1989, p. 44).

The arrival of a child causes "emotional benefits" (Miller & Sollie, 1980). The child is perceived to be a source of feelings that are constructive and gratifying for parents: they enjoy watching him or her, playing with him or her, and participating in his or her conquest of the world. The emotional benefits are conceived of differently by mothers and fathers: mothers have a special attachment to their child, whereas fathers underline their closeness to the partner and a general feeling of positive emotion in the family rather than a particular relationship with their child. A child, however, leads to enrichment and development of the self; parents are spurred to be more responsible and to think of the future: in other words, the life-meaning dimensions widen. At the same time, family cohesion increases. Children are seen as a bond between the parents, who must face a common and interdependent task, as well as show mutual consent for the well-being of their child (Olson & McCubbin, 1983). Last, parents identify themselves, to a certain extent, with their child: they relive memories, needs, and wishes of their own infant days and of their past while their child is growing up. Parents derive great pleasure seeing their child grow and develop.

These gratifying aspects coexist with some negative aspects that have emerged from studies on the transition to parenthood. Parents are tired, their sleep is inadequate, and housework increases. Women, especially, lament the situation because it is generally up to them to care for the baby (Entwisle & Doering, 1981). Understandably, husband–wife relationships are strained. The new parents need time to adjust to their new roles and to find new operation modalities; this may occasionally lead to conflicts (La Rossa & LaRossa, 1981). They feel they are not doing what they want to do, but rather what another person wants them to do. Moreover, several studies have revealed a decrease in couples' sexual satisfaction. The two partners need an adjustment period following the changes caused by pregnancy and childbirth.

The emotional costs faced by the new parents are many. The most evident is the total responsibility for another being, who depends completely and continually on the adult and will do so for years. It is also difficult for new parents to accept their own uncertainty and ambiguity about their abilities to look after the child (Pincus & Dare, 1978). Not to be underestimated are the costs and restrictions imposed on social life, amusement, relaxation, friends, money availability, and career. The child's continuous need for adult caregiving is a recurrent reason for the diminished time available for relationships outside the family and is in conflict with the parents' wishes (Hobbs, 1965; Hobbs & Cole, 1976). Likewise, there is less opportunity for employment outside the home, especially for women (Rapaport & Rapaport, 1976). Baruch, Barnett, and Rivers (1987) argued that parenting is particularly stressful for women, and that parental stress undermines women's well-being more than men's. In parenthood, mothers face greater change, both positive and negative, in themselves and in their lives than fathers do; mothers experience more change in daily routines, moods, sense of themselves as parents, feelings of autonomy and competence, and sexuality (Cowan et al., 1985; Harriman, 1983; Weiss, 1985). Mothers with a chronically mentally ill child report more distress than fathers (Cook, 1988), and mothers grieve more than fathers when a child dies (Littlefield & Rushton, 1986).

Only a few days after the birth of their first child, parents find themselves alone, facing a situation requiring drastic readjustment; infant care experience is often nonexistent. In any case, the presence of a newborn can be a moment of growth for the new parents, both as individuals and as a couple. They are called upon to face specific developmental tasks, which can be distinguished within a relational approach and an organizational approach (Table 5.2).

TABLE 5.2 Developmental Tasks

Relational Tasks	Organizational Tasks
Accept the child into the family system	Adjust life to child's presence
Adjust relationships with family of origin	Organize models of shared responsibility
Adjust communication ways within the couple	Organize sharing of housework
Adjust relationships with the environment (friends, work, services, etc.)	Organize free time
	Organize relations with own job
	Organize relations with social environment (social services, etc.)

The future atmosphere of the family, as well as the individual and relational welfare of its members, is affected by the way parents can and do face these tasks. They are faced better by couples who have established a high level of marital competence before their child's birth (Lewis, 1988). There seems to be a continuity between the previous stage and the following.

We now introduce two topics that can be placed at the beginning and at the end of what we have just considered: parenthood as a point of arrival after a transitional period (transition timing to parenthood); and the changes occurring in a family when a second child is born (second child family transition).

Timing in Transition to Parenthood

Over the past fifty years, there have been remarkable changes in women's fertility patterns in both Europe and in the United States (Eggenbeen & Uhlenberg, 1989; Saporiti, 1989). In this connection, two aspects are particularly important: (1) the average age of mothers and fathers has decreased across cohorts of children (few children have parents more than 35 years older than themselves); and (2) a rather swift decline in fertility. Since the early 1960s, the trend has been to delay first births; now, about one baby in three is born to a mother 25 years old or older (Wilkie, 1981). Contraception and planned parenthood have made it easier for couples to delay birth of a first child. The timing of first births affects fertility rates, family economics, and relationships among generations. In recent years, career women, especially those with higher educations, have adopted a delayed parenthood strategy. This same strategy has been followed by couples who prefer to remain childless (Rindfuss, Bumpass, & John, 1980; Roosa, 1988).

Within this sociohistorical frame, we can ask about relational and individual well-being. Is it better to have children when still young or later on in life? Do childless couples fare better or worse than couples with children? Research has highlighted several aspects, not easily linked one to another. The belief still lingers that childless women have forgone meaning in life; however research has shown that women who are childless, either by choice or infertility, enjoy the same level of personal welfare as mothers (Baruch, Barnett, & Rivers, 1983; Callan, 1987). Various studies suggest that couples who delay having children may have more problems in their children's adolescence (Baldwin & Nord, 1984; Rossi, 1980a). This stage of a child's development is very delicate and a large age gap between parents and children may be deleterious if the older parent cannot relate to or remember his or her own adolescence as well as a younger parent. It has been suggested (Rossi, 1980b) that the older mother feels her adolescent child to be more critical of her and not emotionally close. Furthermore, although she may try to overcome her aging phase, the older mother may turn inward and be less accessible emotionally. Rossi (1980a) found that the older the woman at first birth, the greater her difficulties in raising her children.

Other authors only partially replicated these results (Daniels & Weingarten, 1988). The older the parents, the more tired they seem to become discharging their roles as guardians; nevertheless, difficulties experienced during children's adolescence cannot be used as parameters to distinguish the older from the younger parent. Heuvel (1987) proposes that the older parent's increased maturity and competence can represent an advantage in rearing children, especially when the sex variable is taken into account both in the parent and in the child. Mother–daughter and father–son pairs were shown to fare better because of the parent's later age at first birth.

Studies on the basis of empirical approaches and longitudinal designs have not found any evidence about older mothers in terms of personal and relational variables (MacDermid, Huston, & McHale, 1990; Roosa, 1988). Compared to childless couples, couples with children show a decline in participating in companionable activities together over time. Still, parents did not differ from nonparents in love feelings and marital satisfaction, even more than a year after the birth of their first child. The child's physical health and the social support enjoyed by the parents are also extremely important.

Parenting Transition with Second Child

The pivotal nature of the transition to parenthood is generally recognized. It is also widely known that the first and second births may have different effects on husbands and wives. The "parental imperatives" (Gutman, 1975) experienced by mothers and fathers at each birth may explain these effects. The birth of a first child logically is assumed to have a more marked effect on women, as they acquire their parenthood responsibilities, are directly involved with labor and delivery, and must immediately take on the following child-care responsibilities. Furthermore, maternal parental roles are more explicitly set out than paternal roles in our society (Hobbs & Cole, 1976; Russell, 1978). First-time fathers can probably adapt to fatherhood by taking on traditionally oriented role differentiations; they would be under less related stress in adjusting to their new role as providers for mother and child and would focus more on job security. The birth of a second child is an event that potentially affects fathers and mothers differently. The event may be especially salient for men, because they are compelled to take on concrete parental activities. Mothers, too, must face some changes, and they experience high levels of stress. A certain degree of separation is involved between the mother and her first child when a second child is born. The separation, which is very stressful both for mother and child, is especially felt by the father, who is required, perhaps for the first time, to assume a more direct and active role in child rearing. Furthermore, he must serve as a link between the child at home and the mother in the hospital. Between the birth of his first and second child, the father is training for the job, so to speak, of caring for his child, and he gradually achieves some definition of parental role. When the second pregnancy is confirmed, the time up to the delivery may be used by the father to train for his future increase in child-care responsibilities (Entwisle & Doering, 1981).

When the second child is born, both mother and father must face the developmental transition from a triadic to a tetradic system. At this particular point in time, the father plays a crucial role—he must take on his share of child care to relieve the mother from being forced to "double" her existence for each child (Krepper, Paulsen, & Schuetze, 1982). The potential increase in the father's participation in the family after the second child's birth is, therefore, an important topic for research (Belsky, Gilstrap, & Rovine, 1984; Grossman, 1987; Stewart, 1990).

PARENTING CARE WITH PRESCHOOL CHILDREN

Special attention has been focused on the first two years of the child's life within the study of parent–child relationships. Most important is the role of the traditional psychoanalytic theory (Cath, Gurwitt & Gunsberg, 1989; Stern, 1985), as well as the more recent ethological attachment theory (Ainsworth, 1979; Schaffer, 1977). It has been assumed that the first years of life determine, or at least outline, future development. Nevertheless, without taking anything away from those assumptions, they have been reviewed partly based on the belief that humans are open to developmental change throughout the life cycle. It is a well-known fact that active parental presence during infancy is extremely important. The years devoted to rearing the growing child are also essential to parents' maturation and to the validation of their parental abilities (Bradley, 1985; Giveans & Robinson, 1985).

Parenting Activities

Women and men as parents relate to their children in different ways and tend to do different things with and for their children. Several aspects underlined by researchers as peculiar to parenting with preschool children may overlap into later stages of parenting, but they are uppermost in the child's first and second year of life and in his or her nursery school years. Ruddick (1982) defined mothers' attentive love and care as preserving life, fostering growth, and shaping an acceptable person. Constant, careful, assiduous, and loving parenting is seen as essential in mothers, but not in fathers (Boulton, 1983; Daniels & Weingarten, 1988). Researchers have focused on the circumstances and personal characteristics that foster fathers' involvement in parenting (Barnet & Baruch, 1987; Crouter, Perry-Jenkins, Huston, & McHale, 1987), but mothers' involvement has not received similar consideration. Fathers' contribution continues to be seen in this way by most mothers, fathers, and researchers (LaRossa & LaRossa, 1981; Ross, Mirowsky, & Huber, 1983). Kranichkfeld (1987) argues that the bonds between mothers and children are disregarded and invisible sources of women's family power.

Mothers, not fathers, provide the "continuous coverage" babies require, and their free time is sacrificed in order to do so. Unless fathers lend a hand, mothers always must be on call to satisfy their children's needs. Mothers tend to be the continual presence in young children's lives—more so than fathers, they nurse, assist, respond, and soothe. Fathers are not an abiding presence; they come and go, they are different, changeable, physical, exciting, agreeable, and loved playmates for young children. Playing is a less demanding activity than caregiving, but fathers do other things when spending time with their children (LaRossa & LaRossa, 1981).

Children are seldom alone with their fathers, and their time together typically is monitored by mothers checking what goes on between father and child (Bronstein, 1988; Clarke-Stewart, 1978). The roles of mothers as comfort givers and of fathers as playmates are quite distinct and pronounced when both parents are with the child, but when fathers become accustomed to sharing the daily care of the child, the distinction disappears and mothering and fathering seem to be much the same (Daniels & Weingarten, 1988).

Most fathers are breadwinners as well as playmates. They believe they are providers first and foremost and it follows that they consider themselves to be good fathers when they are good providers. Fathers are concerned about the responsibility of providing for their children's welfare (Clarke-Stewart, 1978; LaRossa & LaRossa, 1981). McKee (1982) encouraged a study of fathers in their own right—and not only in comparison with mothers—for a greater appreciation of fathering. The role of fathers as providers should perhaps receive more attention and further study should be devoted to the nature of fathers' interest and investment in their children, to their sensitivity to their children, and to their concerns about the educational, moral, decision-making and disciplinary aspects of rearing children.

Parenting Experience

Researchers tend to consider parenting activities in the light of who does what and how often only and to reduce the experience of parenting to general satisfaction with the parent–child relationships (Boulton, 1983; LaRossa & LaRossa, 1981; McKee, 1982). The inquiry needs to be widened—in the light of both enduring and emerging images of motherhood and fatherhood and the differing activities of mothers and fathers, what are the implications of men's and women's experiences as parents? The experience acquired in parenting preschool children is, therefore, paradigmatic.

Mothering is a contradictory as well as a complex experience: it is frustrating, irritating, and overwhelming, but it is also fulfilling and rewarding. After interviewing 50 married mothers of small children, Boulton (1983) described how mothers feel constant and exclusive responsibility for their children. Two modes of experiences emerged: an immediate response to the day-by-day routine occupations of child care, and a wider sense of purpose in child rearing. Looking after small children is quite unsettling and irritating for mothers. The need for constant vigilance and the continual task of finding something to do for unreasonable and self-centered children can often become too much for mothers. Children often do not allow mothers to get on with other activities (such as housework): because of the children, mothers are confined to the home, and they require routines to help them feel less overwhelmed. On the other hand, children bring more meaning, purpose, fulfillment, commitment, and value to mothers' lives. Mothers' hopes, dreams, and ambitions typically are focused on their children, and they want to give their children what they missed when they were young. But, mostly, mothers' sense of purpose is founded on feeling needed by and essential to their children. It is important to mothers' sense of personal worth that children want and depend upon them, in particular. About one third of mothers enjoy mothering and appreciate its fuller meaning; another third have mixed experiences and feelings; and the remaining third neither enjoy nor find meaning in mothering. Boulton (1983) found that enjoyment or sense of purpose, usually accompanying the image of motherhood, was not necessarily brought about by children. Nevertheless, mothering is shaped by the enduring image of motherhood as a continual and total responsibility. Frustration and meaning are words associated by mothers to the responsibility for their children. Middle-class, more than working-class, mothers seem to be trapped between the enduring and emerging images of motherhood. As mothers, they experience loss of freedom and identity, although they look for meaning in their children's dependency. Baruch, Barnett, & Rivers (1983) in their research on midlife women, studied two similar experiences of mothering. They concluded that mothers who like and enjoy their children feel a greater sense of mastery and pleasure in life, whereas less mastery was reported by mothers who think they are needed, special, and irreplaceable to their children. Ambivalence is provoked in mothers by the tension between the continuous and total responsibility and the enduring image of motherhood. Hock, Guezda, & McBride (1984) found that the majority of new mothers are convinced of the importance of maternal care. Although two thirds of mothers are prepared to return to work before their baby's first birthday, about three quarters would prefer to stay at home with the baby.

LaRossa & LaRossa (1981) found that fathers, too, experience the routine day-to-day activities and the wider social value of parenting. Nevertheless, mothers are more sensitive to their babies' interpersonal abilities and derive more satisfaction from the time they spend with their babies. Fathers treasure their children, but do not consider looking after them a very pleasurable experience. They are dedicated to child care and rearing; and they derive status from being fathers, but they feel "imprisoned" when they have to look after their children. Heath (1976) found that most men grew out of patience and irritable with their children and considered themselves to be inadequate fathers. Child-rearing involvement left them dissatisfied and confused (Heath; Weiss, 1985).

Greater involvement with their children makes men feel more adequate as fathers (Barnett & Baruch, 1987). The few men who are constantly involved with their children's daily routine experience the same ambivalence about parenthood that mothers have always felt: their relationships with their children are close and rewarding, but frustration, worry, boredom, testiness, and tiredness take their toll on fathers, too (Berheide, 1984; Lamb, Pleck, & Levine, 1986). When fathers are active and constant participants in their children's lives, they become sensitive to their children's cues and aware of the changes in their children (Daniels & Weingarten, 1988). Although fathers generally believe that their involvement in their children's lives should be direct, most do not participate directly in their children's care (LaRossa, 1988). Cohen (1987) discovered that most men are involved emotionally in fatherhood, although their activities may not display this involvement. It is typical for fathers to feel alternatively good and bad about direct involvement, as well as to take pride in their fathering as compared to their own fathers and to feel guilt about their fathering as compared to the new image of fatherhood (LaRossa, 1988).

PARENTING SCHOOLCHILDREN

Formal entry into elementary school makes the child face and compare him or herself to many external and internal changes. The child must master more and more complex academic subjects, learn to get on with peers, and learn to cooperate with adults in authoritative positions.

The quality of the mother–child relationship seems to affect differentially the intellectual development of boys and girls (Brody & Stoneman, 1982; Golinkoff & Ames, 1979). Boys' intellectually superior performance seems to be encouraged by a close and continuous relationship with their mothers, whereas daughters seem to be more intellectually stimulated when the relationship with their mothers is progressively more distant. This does not mean that a distant mother–daughter relationship promotes intellectual development, but that an active life on the part of a mother who does not confine herself to domestic chores, is stimulating for the daughter.

A high level of fathers' involvement, together with an accepting and caring inclination and time spent in active teaching, promotes children's intellectual ability. Boys are oriented toward achievement in school by their fathers' own success and achievement orientation; girls are motivated to achievement by their fathers' friendliness to his wife and daughter (Clarke-Stewart, 1977). Children's orientation toward achievement may be greatly affected by their mothers; mothers' demands for achievement seem particularly important from a developmental viewpoint. High and explicit achievement standards seem to motivate a positive orientation toward performance. Parents who promote achievement during the school years, give a high value to education and always reward school success. Achievement is encouraged by parents' interest in the child's day-to-day school activities and by their praise of positive performance. It is also helped by an intellectual atmosphere at home, by modeling structured work habits, and by the parents being the child's teachers when needed (Crondall, Dewey, Katovsky, & Preston, 1964; Kagan & Moss, 1962). Children's success in school and their general intellectual development are facilitated by parenting that is caring but not restrictive, responsive but not controlling, and stimulating but not directive. An inclination to independence and a family structure that encourages and benefits such behaviors, are ideal for the developmental needs of a child (Belsky & Vondra, 1985; Clarke-Stewart, 1978). The child's development is remarkably affected by the understanding between parents and the quality of their marital relationship (Brody & Pilligrini, 1986; Goldberg & Easterbrooks, 1984).

Unless some nonnormative, stressing events occur, the child's elementary school period is demanding but it also represents a time of well-being and satisfaction for parents. The child still requires parental physical presence, but beyond that, he or she needs a significant relationship; nevertheless, the necessary cares are not so totally absorbing. Children's relationships with their teachers and peers encourage independence and discovery of the surrounding world (MacDonald & Parke, 1984). If parents manage to achieve an authoritative relationship, which avoids both an authoritarian and a permissive position, they do a lot for their children's socioemotional competence (Baumrind, 1968; Mussen, Harris, Rutherford, & Keasey, 1970). During this period, parents can devote time and energy toward their realization, both personal and as a couple; they can institute and nurture relationships outside the family; and they can enjoy significant and gratifying experiences with their children (Rapaport & Rapaport, 1975).

PARENTING ADOLESCENTS

Many researchers, as well as clinical reporters and the popular literature, have underlined, especially in the 1960s and 1970s, stress from parenting adolescent children (Steinberg, 1981; Walters & Walters, 1980). It is suggested that marital relationships suffer most when the couple's children are adolescents (Rollins & Feldman, 1970). In the 1980s, research challenged this image of adolescence as a period of *Sturm und Drang* (Dusek & Flaherty, 1981; O'Malley & Bachman, 1983; Steinberg & Silverberg, 1986). Adolescence does not seem to be an excessively turbulent time; adolescents experience harmony rather than conflict with their parents and they generally identify themselves with and like their parents. However, we must not exaggerate the level of harmony during adolescence in the way that past research overestimated the conflicts linked with this period.

Looking at adolescence in contextual and developmental terms, much emphasis has been given to social context and intercontext connections: among family, school, and work; among generations; and among historical periods (Elder, 1981; Furstenberg, Brooks-Gumm, & Morgan, 1987; Small & Eastman, 1991). Thus, the unsettling qualities of adolescence and the resultant problematic parent–adolescent relationship have been emphasized. Some meaningful elements have been pointed to by researchers' heightened interest in the interactions of physiologic, cognitive, and social processes in adolescence.

Pubertal maturation seems to have an impact on the family structure, independent of changes that may be due to adolescents' chronological age (Savin-Williams & Small, 1986). Greater distance, dissatisfaction, and conflict in the parent–child relationship are generally associated with pubertal maturation (Papini & Sebby, 1987; Steinberg, 1987; Steinberg & Hill, 1978). The phenomenon is more remarkable between adolescents and mothers, and it is most noticeable midway through the pubertal cycle. There are, nevertheless, some contradictory indications in the literature (Steinberg, 1981). Physical and biologic maturation are connected to other critical developmental changes, such as cognitive development (Dornbusch, 1989) and identity formation (Kroger, 1989). These developmental changes are affected by the school, work and other contexts outside the family. The comprehensive research of Simmons and her colleagues (Simmons & Blyth, 1987) on transition to adolescence has demonstrated how rate of maturation interacts with social context to influence adolescents' self-image and other psychologic and behavior outcomes. For many middle and late adolescents, the workplace (usually part-time employment) stands as an important context, affecting both school and family life (Greenberger & Steinberg, 1986). The transition from adolescence has its assorted problems and troubles; for example, occupational concerns, engagement and marriage, on-going education, and so forth (Mortimer, Lorence, & Kumka, 1986).

Within this developmental trend, linked to historic and social connections, parenting looks complex, although not always dramatic and/or with pathologic outcomes. Parental support is one of the strongest variables in the literature focusing on adolescent socialization. It has a positive correlation with cognitive development, conforming to adult standards, moral behavior, internal locus of control, self-esteem, instrumental competence, and academic achievement of children and adolescents. We can, therefore, say that greater parental support leads to greater social competence in children (Rollins & Thomas, 1979). We must conclude that lack of parental support is linked to negative socialization outcomes for children and adolescents, such as low self-esteem, delinquency, deviance, drug abuse, and other disturbing behaviors. Some authors (Peterson & Rollins, 1987; Simons & Miller, 1987) have distinguished several components in the support variable: general support, physical affection, companionship, and prolonged contact. The components seem to vary according to the sex of parent and child: parents were shown to have greater companionship with the child of their same sex; physical attachment, continuous contact, and general support had different effects on sons' and daughters' self-esteem, according to the parent's sex.

Control is a second important variable. Because it is rather complex, we must distinguish among diverse styles of control in view of their potential socialization consequences: authoritarian versus authoritative control and coercion versus induction (Baumrind, 1978). "Failure to distinguish between the qualitative different styles of control has contributed to much of the inconsistency and confusion in the research on the effects of parental control" (Gecas & Seff, 1991, p. 214). Other components of parental control are considered important, such as a certain amount of protectiveness, guidance, supervision and checking, firmness, clear definition of rules, and basis of power assertion (McDonald, 1982; Peterson & Rollins, 1987). The issue of parental control seems to be the focal point of many conflicts and much of the stress of parent–adolescent interaction; adolescence is, in fact, a period when children look for greater freedom from parental constraint and parents try to retain some control over their children. Evidence seems to point to the importance of parent's and adolescent's sex in the parent–adolescent relationship; there is a wider responsibility for socialization along same-sex lines (Hill & Atkinson, 1988; Steinberg, Elmen, & Mounts, 1989).

In any consideration of parent–adolescent relationship, it is essential to contemplate a perspective on the developmental stages of the parents. Thirty years ago, McArthur (1962) argued impressively that many parent–adolescent conflicts could be explained by the opposition existing among the individual developmental tasks of the middle-aged parents. Relationships between generations should run more smoothly when parents feel they are productive, centered, and masters of their own lives. Adolescents who question parental values and abilities in the parents' home may exacerbate the parents' own internal turmoil (Kidwell, Fischer, Dunham, & Baranowski, 1983).

RELATIONSHIPS OF ADULT CHILDREN AND THEIR PARENTS

Family problems in middle-aged couples have only recently been investigated. Focus had been mainly on infancy and adolescence, and only lately, especially in Erikson (1976), a developmental outline of the individual has been traced that included the last years of life. Whether parents have young adult children, or whether they are older parents with fully matured children, Erikson stresses that their task is not negative, seen only in the light of resignation and self-sacrifice; indeed, their task is further reflection on their own adult identity, which implies overcoming their narcissism. This is not easy, but it is fruitful.

Parenting During the Launching Stage

Parents find themselves caught between their children, who are about to leave the family unit, and their own, older parents. They are personally involved in the developmental task of separating from their children and in the renegotiation of their relationship as a couple. While the young adult child is required to follow a clear progression in his or her separation from the family unit and to define individual, professional, and social identities, parents are, at the same time, in the midst of facing the complementary task of separating from their children (Salomon, 1973), as well as accepting their children's increasing independence, and changing their relationship with their offspring by taking on a less gratifying but more proper role, in their children's quest for autonomy. These tasks are closely woven together to form a single process of family distance regulation, which requires ever increasing differentiation, more and more involved individualization, and greater flexibility. Independence often characterizes relationships between small children and adults; counterdependence is the frequent style of adolescence; interdependence is the most appropriate style between adult children and parents. The small and gradual adjustments made both by parents and children in order to adapt to the increasing differentiation, particularly evident in late adolescence, affect the crucial event of children's leaving home. The distance regulation between children and parents before this event may affect the way in which the event takes place, either by increasing or decreasing its dramatic meaning; it can even prevent departure from the home (Haley, 1980; Stierlin, 1978).

We must emphasize that the home-leaving process is long and complex and it may not finish entirely until the child is age 30 (Williamson, 1981). The fundamental stages of this process are: (1) achievement of complete autonomy through the establishment of an adult professional status, possibly an affective one; and (2) the children have matured enough to feel compassion for the man and the woman who cared for them as parents. This feeling springs from direct knowledge of the inner feeling of their personal experiences and on the growing acceptance of the later stages of life. Transition for the parents is represented by parental power loss and the need to "give way" to the next generation.

After the home-leaving event, both parents and children are called upon to renegotiate the child–parent relationship in the light of the adult status they both now have. In general, a temporary distance between children and parents allows the establishment of new boundaries; once these are clearly defined, a rapprochement can take place. If it is successful, parents find it easier to overcome the inevitable feeling of loss left in the wake of the home-leaving event. Furthermore, the child–family reunion "according to ways consistent with the adult status" may add a sense of wholeness and continuity to the parents' lives (Rhodes, 1977). Terkelsen (1980) maintains that the young adult who keeps in touch with his or her family of origin has a more favorable developmental process, compared to the adult who ceases all parental contact.

Currently a contradiction is emerging between the social stereotype underlining the independent and autonomous aspects of adulthood and family relationships that are characterized over many years by reciprocal dependence and generational alliance (Cohler & Geyer, 1982). This social stereotype seems to correspond to the requirements of counterdependence, rather than interdependence. There is, in fact, a new phenomenon called "prolonged families" in Europe, as well as in the United States (Clemens & Axelsen, 1985; Scabini & Donati, 1988). A number of young adults above the average marrying age of the reference population still live with the family of origin; this phenomenon is more widespread in lower classes, but it is more striking in the upper classes. The reasons for and the functions of this prolonged stay in the family are complex, and they differ among different social strata. In the upper classes, children stay in order to improve their means of living in terms of the quality and choice of life. In lower classes, it is a way to avoid potentially dismal living conditions, unemployment, or enforced inactivity, as well as to guard against marginalization and/or poverty. The prolonged family is, therefore, a product of both necessity and choice, the combination of which varies according to sex, social stratum, geographic area, and family subculture. The prolonged family can require new relational interactions. These can be characterized by a desire for closeness, material support, care, reciprocal help, affection, and communication that can sometimes be conflictual and other times narcissistic, but otherwise more psychologically mature and oriented to a new family network. There is a new element in the prolonged family as compared to the enlarged family of the past: the elderly parent does not live with the married child, but the child lives with the parent. Moreover, for both generations, the situation is not so strictly defined; there are more opportunities to come and go, and a wider range of opportunities exists for attachment and distancing in more uncertain, temporary, and contingent ways. This new phenomenon deserves further attention and study.

Parenting During the Empty Nest Phase

This phase is the outcome of the complex separation process. The parental couple must continue to be flexible: parents must adapt to the children's leave-taking, they must create new interests for themselves and accept and cultivate new relationships that will be, in the future, psychologically familial. This parenting phase is, in fact, characterized by remarkable changes, by a variety of "exits" and "entries," requiring many "active" and "competent" adjustment abilities, highlighted by Olson & McCubbin (1983). Favorable outcome of this task leads to greater experience and to the possibility of experiencing new roles in relationships; sometimes a parent whose children are all of the same sex may acquire a "child" of the other sex to satisfy a long-standing wish. Failure to achieve the task, however, brings a deep sense of frustration. In this case, the most frequent sensation is that of having been robbed of one's own children; the older parental couple may either withdraw into a sad isolation or, more often, tend to aggravate the conflictual elements being elaborated by the young couple.

Parents must revise their relationship as a couple after the young adult children's leave-taking. Lowenthal & Chiriboga (1972) report that most middle-aged couples they interviewed considered that time of life as the best in the family life cycle. It is seen as a period of greater freedom (Deutscher, 1964): the man is freed from financial worries and the woman has greater freedom from housework. This allows parents to tend to themselves more and to pursue different activities, as well as to enjoy a better and more relaxed relationship together. Deutscher identifies a third form of freedom, which he defines "freedom to be oneself;" that is, the relaxation from having to be abiding life models for their children. This revision of the couple's relationship is defined as a "new discovery" (Rhodes, 1977; Stinnet, Carter, & Montgomery, 1972), because their shared interests are rediscovered and their truest feelings can be expressed again.

Possible sources of disagreement may originate from a lack of shared interests and values; that is, difficulties felt at this time of life may derive from previously unresolved problems that naggingly resurface as the partners come face-to-face with each other with no possibility of escape. On the psychorelational plane, parents are living a composite experience, both in the dynamic and sequential sense. The loss of a parental relationship with their children may lead to depression, which can be replaced by a restructuring task, involving other personal and family areas, and by an active adjustment, combined with "exits" and "entries" of new family members. This composite experience is revealed in the couple satisfaction index (Rollins & Feldman, 1970; Olson & McCubbin, 1983): it is at its lowest when the children leave home, but it tends to increase rapidly during the following years.

Both parents must face another series of phenomena during this phase. The first symptoms of aging now emerge, both physiologic and psychologic. Menopause and the male climacteric are the most obvious physiologic changes, and these have complex implications for the person and for the couple. Frequently, some health problems emerge that can set limitations and cause worry (Engel, 1987).

CHILDREN HELPING ELDERLY PARENTS

Adult children helping elderly parents may be able to appreciate and comprehend better the life span perspective and complex relation between child rearing and parent caring. Nevertheless, today's social forces may disturb the child-rearing and parent-caring mechanisms to a greater extent than in previous decades or centuries.

Two conditions are peculiar to our time. First, in the early decades of this century, most parents died in their sixties and seventies. Nowadays, an increasing number of people live well into their eighties or nineties (Riley & Riley, 1986; Siegel & Taeuber, 1986). This increases the need for parental care because it is quite likely that very elderly parents will have chronic poor health, and they may depend more and more on their children for longer than ever before. Caring for their parents helps parents complete the full potential of the life span. Naturally, the best possible thing would be to improve both the length and the quality of life (Mutran & Reitzes, 1984). Second, alternative family forms have developed throughout society and will continue to do so (Cicirelli, 1983). Without passing moral judgment on alternative family forms, it is possible that they may have disrupted the helping relationship between adult child and elderly parent. Family was considered a lifetime arrangement before the advent of these alternative family forms, and family members were committed to each other. The alternative family forms do not seem to generate such a degree of commitment, because people can easily divorce or move in and out of a relationship that has no legal or other formal obligation. An effect of such events may be a dramatic interruption of the child-rearing and parent-caring system through the life span.

The reluctance and/or absence of commitment of adult children to care for their elderly parents as previous generations of adult children did might be linked to greater filial anxiety. Filial anxiety may become the uppermost theme of middle-aged children, replacing filial maturity. These two concepts are not necessarily mutually exclusive, but considering one's parents as people in their own right may become secondary to the anxiety of anticipating the care of that parent. Filial anxiety and diminished commitment to helping parents on the part of adult children may prevent parents, living longer than in the past, from reaching the full potential of their life span or from enhancing the quality of their lives. Of course, most elderly people would rather be independent and look after themselves for as long as possible, but the very elderly have little choice but to live in an old people's home or their children's home.

Adult children were once the most important support system for their elderly parents, and, to some extent, they still are. Blieszner & Mancini (1987) in their study of well-educated, healthy, resourceful elderly parents found them to be happy about routine interactions with their children. Moreover, they only relied on direct assistance in the most exceptional circumstances. Such beliefs are not an exception and not the monopoly of a single social status group. Several recent studies have shown that many older parents have face-to-face contact with their children on a weekly basis and, when face-to-face contact is impossible, they use other methods to keep in touch (Troll, Miller, & Atcheley, 1979). The psychologic meaning of such closeness is clear: the greater the amount of contact and interaction, the greater the sense of welfare felt by the older parent.

One aspect related to spending time together is the nature of support in a relationship; that is, the nature of instrumental and emotional exchange and reciprocity. Studies on exchange, assistance, and support performed over the past 25 years have shown a large measure of intergenerational involvement, both instrumental and affective. Older parents are shown to continue to provide their adult children with varying support; they are not only at the receiving end of support. Parents' support seems to be a lasting aspect of the parenting role. Typically, elderly parents are more likely to assist their children, rather than to receive assistance from them (Riley & Foner, 1968). Moreover, inability to reciprocate, rather than the need for assistance, weakens the morale of older parents (Stoller, 1985). Neither the parental nor the child generations, however, should be considered only to be givers or receivers of help when all types of support are considered. Relationships, on the whole, are important for the personal welfare of elderly parents. It is not always possible to realize such a reciprocity of contact, communication, and support. Things are more difficult when the elderly parents become chronically ill and the adult children must assume the burdens of presence, financial commitment, affective willingness, while at the same time, they are occupied with the care and upbringing of their own children. Adult children abruptly come face-to-face with their personal and interpersonal limitations. Economic, demographic, and social trends in our modern world seem to decrease the amount and kinds of aid they can give. The cost of institutionalization is becoming beyond the reach of the average family. Many elderly parents may have to live with their middle-aged children, and such living arrangements are not certain to be satisfactory for them (Camdessus, 1989).

Adult children with alternative family lives may provide inadequate child care to their children, thus decreasing children's survival rate or providing inadequate development. One aspect of this has been the increase in child abuse. Young children, in turn, may provide less parent care in their adult years. It is hypothesized that parent care is part of the intergenerational life span sequence reciprocally related to child rearing. Child care and parent care can affect each other for better or worse, for the individual and, by extension, for society—ultimately, even for the species. If parent care is perceived in this way, it must be evaluated from a life span perspective, and the quality of both child care and parent care must be reassessed, as well as their relationship to each other within a culture.

REFERENCES

Acock, A. C., & Bengton, V. L. (1980). Socialization and attribution processes: Actual versus perceived similarity among parents and youth. *Journal of Marriage and the Family, 42,* 501–515.

Aldous, J. (1978). *Family careers: Developmental change in families.* New York: Wiley.

Ainsworth, M. S. D. (1979). Attachment as related to mother–infant interaction. *Advances in the Study of Behavior, 9,* 2–52.

Allen, W. R. (1981). Moms, dads, and boys: Race and sex differences in the socialization of male children. In L. E. Gary (Ed.), *Black men* (pp. 99–114). Newbury Park, CA: Sage.

Baldwin, W. H., & Nord, C. W. (1984). Delayed childbearing in the U.S.: Facts and fiction. *Population Bulletin, 39,* 1–43.

Bandura, A. (1976). *Social learning theory.* Englewood Cliffs, NJ: Prentice Hall.

Barnett, R. C., & Baruch, G. K. (1987). Determinants of fathers' participation in family work. *Journal of Marriage and the Family, 49,* 29–40.

Baruch, G. K., Barnett, R., & Rivers, C. (1983). *Lifeprints: New patterns of love and work for today's women.* New York: New American Library.

Baumrind, D. (1968). Authoritarian versus authoritative parental control. *Adolescence, 3,* 255–272.

Baumrind, D. (1978). Parental disciplinary patterns and social competence in children. *Youth & Society, 9,* 239–276.

Baumrind, D. (1980). New directions in socialization research. *American Psychologist, 35,* 639–652.

Bell, R. Q., & Harper, L. V. (1977). *Child effects on adults.* Hillsdale, NJ: Erlbaum.

Belsky, J. (1981). Early human experiences: A family perspective. *Developmental Psychology, 17,* 3–23.

Belsky, J., Gilstrap, B., & Rovine, M. (1984). The Pennsylvania infant and family development project, I: Stability and change in mother–infant and father–infant interactions in a family setting at one, three, and nine months. *Child Development, 55,* 692–705.

Belsky, J., Vondra, J. (1985). Characteristics, consequences, and determinants of parenting. In L. L'Abate (Ed.), *The handbook of family psychology and therapy* (Vol. 1, pp. 523–556). Pacific Grove, CA: Brooks/Cole.

Benedek, T. (1970). Parenthood during the life cycle. In E. J. Anthony & T. Benedek (Eds.), *Parenthood* (pp. 185–206). Boston: Little, Brown.

Berheide, C. W. (1984). Women's work in the home: Seems like old times. In B. B. Hess & M. B. Sussman (Eds.), *Women and the family: Two decades of change* (pp. 34–55). Binghamton, NY: Haworth.

Bernstein, B. (1971). *Class, codes, and control: Theoretical studies toward a sociology of language* (Vol. 1). London, UK: Routledge & Kegan.

Bernstein, B. (1973). *Class, codes, and control: Applied studies toward a sociology of language* (Vol. 2). London, UK: Routledge & Kegan.

Blieszner, R., & Mancini, J. A. (1987). Enduring ties: Older adults' parental role and responsibilities. *Family Relations, 36,* 176–180.

Blumer, H. (1969). *Symbolic interactionism.* Englewood Cliffs: Prentice Hall.

Boulton, M. G. (1983). *On being a mother. A study of women with pre-school children.* London, UK: Tavistock.

Bowlby, J. (1973). *Attachment and loss: Separation anxiety and anger* (Vol. 2). London, UK: Hogarth.

Bradley, R. H. (1985). Fathers and the school-age child. In S. M. H. Hansen & T. W. Bozett (Eds.), *Dimensions of fatherhood* (pp. 141–169). Newbury Park, CA: Sage.

Brody, G. H., & Pilligrini, A. D. (1986). Marital quality and mother–child and father–child interaction with school-age children. *Developmental Psychology, 22,* 291–296.

Brody, G. H., & Stoneman, Z. (1982). Family influences on language and cognitive development. In J. Worell (Ed.), *Psychological development in the elementary years* (pp. 321–358). New York: Academic.

Bronstein, P. (1988). Father–child interaction: Implications for gender role socialization. In P. Bronstein & C. P. Cowan (Eds.), *Fatherhood today: Men's changing role in the family* (pp. 107–124). New York: Wiley.

Burr, W. R. (1973). *Theory construction and the sociology of the family.* New York: Wiley.

Burr, W. R., Leigh, G. K., Day, R., & Constantine, J. (1979). Symbolic interaction and the family. In W. R. Burr, R. Hill, F. I. Nye, & I. L. Reiss (Eds.), *Contemporary theories about the family* (Vol. 2, pp. 42–111). New York: Free Press.

Callan, V. J. (1987). The personal and marital adjustment of mothers and of voluntarily and involuntarily childless wives. *Journal of Marriage and the Family, 49,* 847–856.

Camdessus, B. (1989). *Les crises familiales du grand âge* (Family crises in old age). Paris, France: ESF.

Campbell, A. (1981). *The sense of well-being in America: Recent patterns and trends.* New York: McGraw-Hill.

Cath, S. H., Gurwitt, A., & Gusberg, L. (1989). *Fathers and their families.* Hillsdale, NJ: Analytic.

Chodorow, N., & Contratto, S. (1982). The fantasy of the perfect mother. In B. Thorne & M. Yoalom (Eds.), *Rethinking the family: Some feminist questions* (pp. 54–75). New York: Longman.

Cicirelli, V. G. (1983). A comparison of helping behavior to elderly parents of adult children with intact and disrupted marriages. *Gerontologist, 23,* 619–625.

Clarke-Stewart, K. A. (1977). *Child care in the family: A review of research and some propositions for policy.* New York: Academic.

Clarke-Stewart, K. A. (1978). And daddy makes three: The father's impact on mother and young child. *Child Development, 49,* 466–478.

Clemens, A. W., & Axelsen, L. J. (1985). The not-so-empty-nest. The return of the fledgling adult. *Family Relations, 34,* 259–264.

Cohen, T. F. (1987). Remaking men: Men's experiences becoming and being husbands and fathers and their implications for reconceptualizing men's lives. *Journal of Family Issues, 8,* 57–77.

Cohler, B. J., & Geyer, S. (1982). Psychological autonomy and interdependence within the family. In F. Welsh (Ed.), *Normal family processes* (pp. 196–228). New York: Guilford Press.

Cook, J. A. (1988). Who "mothers" the chronically mentally ill? *Family Relations, 37,* 42–49.

Cowan, C. P., Cowan, P. A., Cole, L., & Cole, J. P. (1978). The impact of a first child's birth on the couple's relationship. In W. P. Miller, L. F. Newman (Eds.), *The first child and family formulation* (pp. 296–324). Chapel Hill, NC: Carolina Population Center.

Cowan, C. P., Cowan, P. A., Heming, G., Garrett, E., Coysh, W. S., Curtis-Boles, H., & Boles, A. J. (1985). Transitions to parenthood: His, hers, and theirs. *Journal of Family Issues, 6,* 451–481.

Crondall, V. J., Dewey, R., Katovsky, W., & Preston, A. (1964). Parents' attitudes and behaviors and grade school children's academic achievements. *Journal of Genetic Psychology, 104,* 53–66.

Crouter, A. C., Perry-Jenkins, M., Huston, T. L., & McHale, S. M. (1987). Processes underlying father involvement in dual-earner and single-earner families. *Developmental Psychology, 23,* 431–444.

Dail, P. W., & Way, W. L. (1985). What do parents observe about parenting from prime time television?. *Family Relations, 34,* 491–499.

Daniels, P., & Weingarten, K. (1988). The fatherhood click: The timing of parenthood in men's lives. In P. Brostein & C. P. Cowan (Eds.), *Fatherhood today: Men's changing role in the family* (pp. 36–52). New York: Wiley.

Deutscher, J. (1964). The quality of post parental life. *Journal of Marriage and the Family, 26,* 52–60.

Dorenwend, B. S., & Dorenwend, P. P. (1974). *Stressful life events.* New York: Wiley.

Dornbusch, S. (1989). The sociology of adolescence. *Annual Review of Sociology, 15,* 233–259.

Dusek, J. B., & Flaherty, J. F. (1981). The development of the self-concept during the adolescence years. *Child Development, 46,* 1–67.

Duvall, E. M. (1975). *Family development* (5th ed.). Philadelphia: Lippincott.

Dyer, E. D. (1963). Parenthood as crisis: A re-study. *Marriage and Family Living, 25,* 196–201.

Eggenbeen, D. J., & Uhlenberg, P. (1989). Changes in the age distribution of parents, 1940–1980. *Journal of Family Issues, 10,* 169–188.

Elder, G. H. (1981). History and the family: The discovery of complexity. *Journal of Marriage and the Family, 43,* 489–519.

Engel, N. S. (1987). Menopausal stage, current life change, attitude toward women's roles, and perceived health status. *Nursing Research, 36,* 353–357.

Entwisle, D., & Doering, S. (1981). *The first birth: A family turning point.* Baltimore, MD: Johns Hopkins.

Erikson, E. H. (1959). Identity and life cycle. *Psychological Issues, 1,* 18–164.

Erikson, E. H. (1968). *Identity, youth, and crisis.* New York: Norton.

Erikson, E. H. (1976). *Adulthood.* New York: Norton.

Furstenberg, F. F., Brooks-Gumm, J., & Morgan, S. P. (1987). *Adolescent mothers in later life.* New York: Cambridge.

Garbarino, J. (1982). *Children and families in the social environment.* Hawthorne, NY: Aldine de Gruyter.

Gecas, V. (1979). The influence of social class on socialization. In W. R. Burr, R. Hill, F. I. Nye, & I. L. Reiss (Eds.), *Contemporary theories about the family* (Vol. 1, pp. 365–404). New York: Free Press.

Gecas, V., & Seff, M. A. (1991). Families and adolescents: A review of the 1980s. In A. Booth (Ed.), *Contemporary families. Looking forward, looking back* (pp. 208–225). Minneapolis: National Council on Family Relations.

George, L. (1980). *Role transitions in later life.* Pacific Grove, CA: Brooks/Cole.

Giveans, D. L., & Robinson, M. K. (1985). Fathers and the preschool age child. In S. M. H. Hansen & F. W. Bozett (Eds.) *Dimensions of fatherhood* (pp. 115–140). Newbury Park, CA: Sage.

Glase, B., & Strauss, A. (1968). *Time for dying.* Hawthorne, NY: Aldine de Gruyter.

Glenn, E. N. (1987). Gender on the family. In B. B. Hess & M. M. Ferree (Eds.), *Analyzing gender: A handbook of social science research.* Newbury Park, CA: Sage.

Goldberg, W. A., & Easterbrooks, M. A. (1984). Role of marital quality in toddler development. *Developmental Psychology, 20,* 504–514.

Golinkoff, R. M., & Ames, G. J. (1979). A comparison of fathers' and mothers' speech with their young children. *Child Development, 50,* 28–32.

Greenberger, E., & Steinberg, L. (1986). *When teenagers work: The psychological and social cohorts of adolescent employment.* New York: Basic Books.

Grossman, F. (1987). Separate and together: Men's autonomy and affiliation in the transition to parenthood. In P. Bernman & F. Pedersen (Eds.), *Men's transitions to parenthood* (pp. 89–112). Hillsdale, NJ: Erlbaum.

Gutman, D. (1975). Parenthood: A key to the comparative study of the life cycle. In N. Datan & L. Glinsberg (Eds.), *Life span developmental psychology: Normative life crises* (pp. 167–184). New York: Academic.

Haley, J. (1980). *Leaving home. The therapy of disturbed young people.* New York: McGraw-Hill.

Harriman, L. C. (1983). Personal and marital changes accompanying parenthood. *Family Relations, 32,* 387–394.

Heath, D. (1976). Competent fathers: Their personalities and marriages. *Human Development, 19,* 26–39.

Heuvel, A. V. (1987). The timing of parenthood and intergenerational relations. *Journal of Marriage and the Family, 49,* 483–491.

Hill, G. D., & Atkinson, M. P. (1988). Gender, familial control, and delinquency. *Criminology, 26,* 127–149.

Hill, R. (1949). *Families under stress.* New York: Harper & Row.

Hill, R. (1958). Generic features of families under stress. *Social Casework, 49,* 139–150.

Hobbs, D. F. (1965). Parenthood as crisis: A third study. *Journal of Marriage and the Family, 27,* 367–372.

Hobbs, D. F., & Cole, S. P. (1976). Transition to parenthood: A decade replication. *Journal of Marriage and the Family, 38,* 723–731.

Hobbs, D. F., & Wimbish, J. (1977). Transition to parenthood by black couples. *Journal of Marriage and the Family, 39,* 677–689.

Hock, E., Guezda, M. T., & McBride, S. L. (1984). Mothers of infants: Attitudes toward employment and motherhood following birth of the first child. *Journal of Marriage and the Family, 46,* 423–431.

Holmes, T., & Rahe, R. (1967). The social readjustment rating scale. *Journal of Psychosomatic Research, 11,* 213–218.

Kagan, J., & Moss, H. A. (1962). *Birth to maturity: A study in psychological development.* New York: Wiley.

Kaye, K. (1980a). Why don't we talk "baby talk" to babies? *Journal of Child Language, 7,* 489–507.

Kaye, K. (1980b). The infant as a projective stimulus. *American Journal of Orthopsychiatry, 50,* 732–736.

Kidwell, J., Fischer, J. L., Dunham, R. M., & Baranowski, M. (1983). Parent and adolescent: Push and pull of change. In H. I. McCubbin & C. R. Figley (Eds.), *Stress in the family: Coping with normative transitions* (pp. 74–89). New York: Brunner/Mazel.

Kivnick, H. Q. (1982). *The meaning of grandparenthood.* Ann Arbor: University of Michigan.

Kranichfeld, M. L. (1987). Rethinking family power. *Journal of Family Issues, 8,* 42–56.

Krepper, K., Paulsen, S., & Schuetze, Y. (1982). Infant and family development: From triads to tetrads. *Human Development (Basel, SZ), 25,* 373–391.

Kroger, J. (1989). *Identity in adolescence. The balance between self and other.* London, UK: Routledge.

Lamb, M. E., Pleck, J. H., & Levine, J. A. (1986). Effects of paternal involvement on fathers and mothers. In R. Lewis & M. Sussman (Eds.), *Men's changing roles in the family* (pp. 67–83). Binghamton, NY: Haworth.

LaRossa, R. (1983). The transition to parenthood and the social reality of time. *Journal of Marriage and the Family, 45,* 579–589.

LaRossa, R. (1988). Fatherhood and social change. *Family Relations, 34,* 451–457.

LaRossa, R., & LaRossa, M. M. (1981). *Transition to parenthood: How infants change families.* Newbury Park, CA: Sage.

Lazarus, R. (1966). *Psychological stress and coping process.* New York, NY: McGraw-Hill.

LeMasters, E. E. (1970). *Parents in modern America.* Homewood, IL: Dorsey.

Lerner, R. M., & Spanier, G. B. (1978). *Child influences on marital and family interaction: A life-span perspective.* New York: Academic Press.

Lewis, J. D., & Weingart, A. J. (1981). The structures and meanings of social time. *Social Forces, 60,* 432–462.

Lewis, J. M. (1988). The transition to parenthood, II: Stability and change in marital structure. *Family Process, 27,* 273–283.

Lipman-Blumen, J. (1975). A crisis framework applied to macrosociological family changes: Marriage, divorce, and occupational trends associated with World War II. *Journal of Marriage and the Family, 37,* 889–902.

Littlefield, C. H., & Rushton, J. P. (1986). When a child dies: The sociobiology of bereavement. *Journal of Personality and Social Psychology, 51,* 797–802.

Lowenthal, M. F., & Chiriboga, H. (1972). Transition to the empty nest: Crisis, challenge or relief? *Archives of General Psychiatry, 29,* 8–14.

Lyman, S., & Scott, M. (1970). *A sociology of the absurd.* Pacific Palisades, CA: Goodyear.

MacDermid, S. M., Huston, T. L., & McHale, S. M. (1990). Changes in marriage associated with the transition to parenthood: Individual differences as a function of sex-role attitudes and changes in the division of household labour. *Journal of Marriage and the Family, 52,* 475–484.

MacDonald, K., & Parke, R. (1984). Bridging the gap: Parent–child play interaction and peer interactive competence. *Child Development, 55,* 1265–1277.

Manis, J. G., & Meltzer, B. N. (1978). *Symbolic interaction.* Newton, MA: Allyn & Bacon.

Mattessich, P., & Hill, R. (1987). Life cycle and family development. In M. B. Sussman & S. K. Steinmetz (Eds.), *Handbook of marriage and the family* (pp. 437–469). New York: Plenum.

McAdoo, J. (1988). Changing perspectives on the role of the black fathers. In P. Bronstein & C. P. Cowan (Eds.), *Fatherhood today: Men's changing role in the family* (pp. 79–92). New York: Wiley.

McArthur, A. (1962). Developmental tasks and parent–adolescent conflict. *Marriage and Family Living, 26,* 189–191.

McCray, C. A. (1980). The black woman and family roles. In R. LaFrances (Ed.), *The black woman* (pp. 67–78). Newbury Park, CA: Sage.

McCubbin, H. I., & Figley, C. R. (Eds.). (1983). *Stress and the family, I: Coping with normative transitions.* New York: Brunner/Mazel.

McCubbin, H. I., Cauble, E., & Patterson J. (Eds.). (1982). *Family stress, coping, and social support.* Springfield, IL: Thomas.

McCubbin, H. I., Patterson J., Bauman, E., & Harris, L. H. (1981). *Adolescent–family inventory of life events and changes (A-FILE).* St. Paul, MN: Family Social Science.

McCubbin, H. I., & Patterson J. (1981). *Systematic assessment of family stress, resources and coping: Tools for research, education, and clinical intervention.* St. Paul, MN: Family Social Science.

McCubbin, H. I., Patterson J., & Wilson, L. (1981). *Family inventory of life events and changes (FILE), Form C.* St. Paul, MN: Family Social Science.

McDonald, G. W. (1982). Parental power perceptions in the family: The influence of adolescent characteristics. *Youth & Society, 14,* 3–32.

McKee, L. (1982). Fathers' participation in infant care. A critique. In L. McKee & M. O'Brien (Eds.), *The father figure* (pp. 120–138). London, UK: Tavistock.

Meltzer, B. N., Petras, J. W., & Reynolds, L. T. (1975). *Symbolic interaction: Genesis, varieties, and criticism.* London, UK: Routledge & Kegan.

Mikhail, A. (1981). Stress: A psychophysiological conception. *Behavioral Medicine, 7,* 9–15.

Miller, B. C., & Sollie, D. L. (1980). Normal stress during the transition to parenthood. *Family Relations, 25,* 459–465.

Mindel, C. H., & Habenstein, R. W. (1975). *Ethnic families in America: Patterns and variations.* New York: Elsevier Scientific.

Mirandé, A. (1988). Chicano fathers: Traditional perceptions and current realities. In P. Bronstein & C. P. Cowan (Eds.), *Fatherhood today: Men's changing role in the family* (pp. 93–106). New York: Wiley.

Mortimer, J. T., Lorence, J., & Kumka, D. S. (1986). *Work, family, and personality: Transitions to adulthood.* Norwood, NJ: Ablex.

Mussen, P. H., Harris, S., Rutherford, E., & Keasey, C. B. (1970). Honesty and altruism among preadolescents. *Developmental Psychology, 3,* 169–194.

Mutran, E., & Reitzes, D. C. (1984). Intergenerational support activities and well-being among the elderly: A convergence of exchange and symbolic interaction perspectives. *American Sociological Review, 49,* 117–130.

Norton, A. J. (1983). Family life cycle: 1980. *Journal of Marriage and the Family, 45,* 267–275.

Olson, D. H., & McCubbin, H. J. (1983). *Families: What makes them work?* Newbury Park, CA: Sage.

O'Malley, P., & Bachman, J. (1983). Self-esteem: Change and stability between age 13 and 23. *Developmental Psychology, 19,* 257–268.

Osofsky, J. D., & Connors, K. (1979). Mother-infant interaction: An integrative view of a complex system. In J. D. Osofsky (Ed.), *The handbook of infant development* (pp. 519–548). New York: Wiley.

Papini, D., & Sebby, R. (1987). Adolescent pubertal status and affective family relationships: A multivariate assessment. *Journal of Youth and Adolescence, 16,* 1–5.

Parke, R. D. (1979). Perspective on father–infant interaction. In J. D. Osofsky (Ed.), *The handbook of infant development* (pp. 449–590). New York: Wiley.

Pearlin, L. I., & Schooler, C. (1978). The structure of coping. *Journal of Health and Social Behavior, 19,* 2–21.

Peters, M. F. (1985). Racial socialization of young black children. In H. P. McAdoo & J. L. McAdoo (Eds.), *Black children* (pp. 159–173). Newbury Park, CA: Sage.

Peterson, G. W., & Rollins, B. C. (1987). Parent–child socialization: A review of research and applications of symbolic interaction concepts. In N. B. Sussman & S. K. Steinmetz (Eds.), *Handbook of marriage and the family* (pp. 471–507). New York: Plenum.

Pincus, L., & Dare, C. (1978). *Secrets in the family.* London, UK: Faber & Faber.

Pleck, K. H. (1985). *Working wives/working husbands.* Newbury Park, CA: Sage.

Pleck, J. (1987). American fathering in historical perspective. In M. S. Kimmel (Ed.), *Changing men: New directions in research on men and masculinity* (pp. 83–97). Newbury Park, CA: Sage.

Quinn, W. H., Newfield, M. A., & Protinsky, H. O. (1985). Rites of passages in families with adolescents. *Family Process, 24,* 101–111.

Rapaport, R., & Rapaport, R. N., (1976). *Dual career families reexamined.* New York: Harper & Row.

Rhodes, L. S. (1977). A developmental approach to the life cycle of the family. *Social Casework, 58,* 301–311.

Richards, M. P. M. (1974). The development of psychological communication in the first year of life. In K. J. Connolly & J. S. Bruner (Eds.), *The growth of competence.* London, UK: Academic.

Riley, M. W., & Foner, A. (1968). *Aging and society: Vol. 1. An inventory of research findings.* New York: Russell Sage Foundation.

Riley, M. W., & Riley, J. W. (1986). Longevity and social structure: The potential of the added years. In A. Pifer & L. Bronte (Eds.), *Our aging society: Paradox and promise* (pp. 53–77). New York: Norton.

Rindfuss, R. R., Bumpass, L., & John, C. S. (1980). Education and fertility: Implications for the roles women occupy. *American Sociological Review, 45,* 431–447.

Rollins, B. C., & Feldman, H. (1970). Marital satisfaction over the family life cycle. *Journal of Marriage and the Family, 32,* 20–28.

Rollins, B. C., & Thomas, D. L. (1975). A theory of parental power and child compliance. In R. Cromwell & D. Olson (Eds.), *Power in families* (pp. 38–60). Newbury Park, CA: Sage.

Rollins, B. C., & Thomas, D. L. (1979). Parental support, power, and control techniques in the socialization of children. In W. R. Burr, R. Hill, F. I. Nye, & I. L. Reiss (Eds.), *Contemporary theory about the family* (Vol. 1, pp. 317–364). New York: Free Press.

Roosa, M. W. (1988). The effect of age in the transition to parenthood: Are delayed childbearers a unique group?. *Family Relations, 37,* 322–327.

Ross, C. E., Mirowsky, J., & Huber, J. (1983). Dividing work, sharing work, and in between: Marriage patterns and depression. *American Sociological Review, 48,* 809–823.

Rossi, A. S. (1980a). Aging and parenthood in the middle years. In P. B. Balter & O. G. Brim (Eds.), *Life span development and behavior* (pp. 138–205). New York: Academic.

Rossi, A. S. (1980b). Life span theories and women's lives. *Signs. Journal of Women in Culture and Society, 6,* 4–32.

Rossi, A. S., & Rossi, P. H. (1990). *Of human bonding: Parent–child relations across the life course.* Hawthone, NY: Aldine de Gruyter.

Ruddick, S. (1982). Maternal thinking. In B. Thorne & M. Yalon (Eds.), *Rethinking the family: Some feminist questions* (pp. 76–94). New York: Longman.

Russell, C. S. (1974). Transition to parenthood: Problems and gratification. *Journal of Marriage and the Family, 36,* 294–302.

Russell, G. (1978). The father role and its relation to masculinity, femininity, and androgyny, *Child Development, 49,* 1174–1181.

Salomon, M. A. (1973). A developmental conceptual premise for family therapy, *Family Process, 12,* 179–188.

Saporiti, A. (1989). Historical changes in the family's reproductive, patterns. In K. Boh, M. Bak, C. Clason, M. Pankratova, J. Ovortrup, G. B. Sgritta, & K. Waerness (Eds.), *Changing patterns of European family life. A comparative analysis of 14 European countries* (pp. 191–216). London, UK: Routledge.

Savin-Williams, R. C., & Small, S. A. (1986). The timing of puberty and its relationship to adolescent and parent perceptions of family interactions. *Developmental Psychology, 22,* 342–347.

Scabini, E., & Donati, P. (1988). *La famiglia "lunga" del giovane adulto. Verso nuovi compiti evolutivi* (The "long" family of the adult child. Toward new developmental tasks). Milan, Italy: Vita e Pensiero.

Schaffer, H. R. (Ed.). (1977). *Studies in mother-infant interaction.* New York: Academic Press.

Schooler, C. (1972). Birth order studies: Not here, not now! *Psychological Bulletin, 78,* 161–175.

Selye, H. (1974). *Stress without distress.* Philadelphia: Lippincott.

Siegel, J. S., & Taeuber, C. M. (1986). Demographic dimensions of an aging population. In A. Pifer & L. Bronte (Eds.), *Our aging society* (pp. 79–110). New York: Norton.

Simons, R. L., & Miller, M. G. (1987). Adolescent depression: Assessing the impact of negative cognitions and socioenvironmental problems. *Social Work, 32,* 326–330.

Simmons, R. G., & Blyth, D. A. (1987). *Moving into adolescence: The impact of pubertal change and school context.* Hawthorne, NY: Aldine DeGruyter.

Small, S. A., & Eastman, G. (1991). Rearing adolescents in contemporary society: A conceptual framework for understanding the responsibilities and needs of parents. *Family Relations, 40,* 455–462.

Staples, R., & Mirandé, A. (1980). Racial and cultural variations among American families. A decade review of the literature on minority families. *Journal of Marriage and the Family, 42,* 887–903.

Steinberg, L. (1981). Transformations in family relations at puberty. *Developmental Psychology, 17,* 833–840.

Steinberg, L. (1987). Impact of puberty on family relations: Effects of pubertal status and pubertal timing. *Developmental Psychology, 23,* 451–460.

Steinberg, L., Elmen, J. D., & Mounts, N. (1989). Authoritative parenting, psychosocial maturity, and academic success among adolescents. *Child Development, 60,* 1424–1436.

Steinberg, L., & Hill, J. (1978). Patterns of family interaction as a function of age, the onset of puberty, and formal thinking. *Developmental Psychology, 14,* 683–684.

Steinberg, L., & Silverberg, S. (1986). The vicissitudes of autonomy in early adolescence. *Child Development, 57,* 841–851.

Steinmetz, S. K. (1979). Disciplinary techniques and their relationship to aggressiveness, dependency, and conscience. In W. R. Burr, R. Hill, F. I. Nye, & I. L. Reiss (Eds.), *Contemporary theories about the family* (Vol. 1, pp. 405–438). New York: Free Press.

Stern, D. N. (1985). *The interpersonal world of the infant.* New York: Basic Books.

Stewart, R. B. (1990). *The second child. Family transition and adjustment.* Newbury Park, CA: Sage.

Stierlin, H. (1978). *Delegation und Familie* (Delegation and family). Frankfurt, Germany: Suhrkamp.

Stinnet, H., Carter, L., & Montgomery, J. (1972). Marital needs satisfaction of older husbands and wives. *Journal of Marriage and the Family, 34,* 665–670.

Stoller, E. D. (1985). Exchange patterns in the informal support networks of the elderly: The impact of reciprocity on morale. *Journal of Marriage and the Family, 47,* 335–342.

Strati, A. (1984). L'introduzione dei confini temporali nello studio delle scelte organizzative (Introduction of time boundaries in organizational choices). In S. Gherardi & A. Strati (Eds.), *Sviluppo e declino: la dimensione temporale nello studio delle organizzazioni* (Development and decay: Time dimension in organization study) (pp. 7–12). Trento, Italy: Department of Political Sciences.

Terkelsen, G. K. (1980). Toward a theory of family life cycle. In M. McGoldrick & E. A. Carter (Eds.), *The family life cycle: A framework for family therapy* (pp. 21–51). New York: Gardner.

Thompson, L., & Walker, A. J. (1989). Gender in families: Women and men in marriage, work, and parenthood. *Journal of Marriage and the Family, 51,* 845–871.

Troll, L. E., Miller, S. J., & Atchley, R. C. (1979). *Families in later life.* Belmont, CA: Wadsworth.

Tseng, W., & Hsu, J. (1991). *Culture and family. Problems and therapy.* Binghamton, NY: Haworth.

Umberson, D., & Gove, W. R. (1989). Parenthood and psychological well-being. Theory, measurement, and stage in the family life course. *Journal of Family Issues, 10,* 440–462.

Wainwright, W. H. (1966). Fatherhood as a precipitant of mental illness. *American Journal of Psychiatry, 123,* 40–44.

Walters, J., & Walters, L. H. (1980). Parent-child relationships. *Journal of Marriage and the Family, 42,* 807–824.

Weiss, R. (1985). Men and the family. *Family Process, 24,* 49–58.

Wilkie, J. R. (1981). The trend toward delayed parenthood. *Journal of Marriage and the Family, 43,* 583–591.

Williamson, D. S. (1981). Personal authority via termination of the intergenerational hierarchical boundary. A "new" stage in the family life cycle. *Journal of Marital and Family Therapy, 7,* 441–450.

Zanarini, G. (1985). *L'emozione del pensare* (Thought emotion). Bologna, Italy: Clup-Cleub.

CHAPTER 6

The Family Across Generations: Grandparenthood

CATHLEEN ERIN MCGREAL

THE GRANDPARENTAL ROLE

Of Silver Hair and the Rocking Chair

> A kindergarten teacher was singing a song to her little charges about dear grandma, and how we like to bring her a shawl as she sits by the fire. Suddenly, she noticed the pert, fortyish grandmother of one of her pupils standing in the doorway. "Of course, boys and girls, you understand this song is about great-grandmothers," she added hastily. Shawls and fireplaces are scarcely characteristic of either the equipment or the habitat of grandmothers or of mothers-in-law today. This notion is thoroughly out of date.

> (Neisser, 1951, p. 1)

The kindergartners in this anecdote are now in their mid-forties; many will soon become grandmothers and grandfathers, if they are not already. Has the stereotype of grandparents as elderly persons been dispelled? How will the transition to grandparenthood affect their lives? How do grandfathers and grandmothers differ in their grandparenting experiences? Does ethnicity influence their roles? Can changes be predicted based upon the developmental needs of grandchildren? How are intergenerational relationships affected by divorce? Are there rights inherent to grandparenthood? This chapter addresses these questions.

Generally, grandparenthood occurs in middle age. Current descriptions of grandparents note that the elderly image no longer applies: "Today's grandparents are doing a lot to dispel the stereotypical image of silver-haired, cuddly individuals who are content baking cookies, digging gardens or crocheting baby booties from a rocking chair. . . . they have thriving careers and active social lives, . . . they take a more youthful approach to grandparenting" (Turner, 1989, p. 36). The fact that we have been trying to shed this stereotype since the 1950s confirms the strength of the "aged grandparent" myth in American culture. The best age to become a grandparent, according to middle-aged individuals, would be from

45 to 50 years-of-age (Neugarten, Moore, & Lowe, 1965). Grandparenthood may be a transitional point used to define age categories (young, middle-aged, old) in American society. However, the age category defined by this transition seems to be that from youth to middle-age, rather than from middle to old age, as the stereotype would suggest.

Roles and Styles of Grandparents

Just what is expected of grandmother in American families? How widespread is the emotional isolation of grandparents from the larger family? What roles may grandmothers play in the rearing of their grandchildren? Which are mutually satisfying and why? Which are stressful and how may they be avoided?

(Duvall, 1954, pp. 158–159)

Many of these questions have been answered in Neugarten & Weinstein (1964). They reported five grandparenting styles (formal, fun seeking, parent surrogates, reservoirs of family wisdom, and distant figures) that have become classic descriptions of variations in the grandparental role. The significance of grandparenthood has been described further by role type (apportioned, symbolic, individualized, remote) determined through factor analyses and predicted by life-style variables (Robertson, 1977). Researchers using these five grandparenting types with "expectant" grandparents confirmed them, but the role types were not found to be related to life-style variables (McGreal, 1986). Kivnick (1982) defined five dimensions in the grandparenting role: 1) the role is central to the person's life; 2) the grandparent is a valued elder in the family; 3) feelings of immortality exist through the clan; 4) the grandparents become reinvolved with their personal pasts and relive earlier life experiences, remembering their own grandparents; and 5) the grandparents indulge their grandchildren. Cherlin and Furstenberg (1986, p. 70) reported that classifying roles can lead to a static view, "as if we could pin a label on a grandmother shortly after her first grandchild was born ('funseeker' or 'distant figure') and be sure that the label would remain accurate for all her grandchildren for the rest of her life." Therefore, they described grandparenthood not only in terms of styles (remote, companionate, involved) but also in terms of careers, based on the age of the grandchild. Because the ages of grandchildren vary, these career stages overlap. Age of the grandparent is also an important variable (Baranowski, 1990).

The role of the grandparent in the United States is defined primarily by grandparents and their extended families. A behavior considered to be supportive in one family may be deemed annoying in another. In general, grandparents are expected to encourage independence in their adult children and to refrain from interfering in childrearing (Cherlin & Furstenberg, 1986). Grandparents may find themselves in a double bind. Thomas (1990, p. 175) cites mothers' descriptions of supportive grandparental behavior (e.g., "helps out when asked and gives constructive criticism") and of interfering behavior (e.g., "they try to tell you how to raise your child"). A fine line exists between constructive criticism and interference.

Ethnic and Cultural Variations

Over the past decade, we have increased our awareness of the importance of considering ethnicity and culture in discussions of grandparenting; however, few empirical investigations have included these considerations. Research on the grandparent–grandchild relationship within African American families has focused primarily on multigenerational families in the same household and/or on adolescent African American mothers' relationships with the maternal grandmother. African American children are more likely to live with a grandparent than are their counterparts. In 1989, The Commerce Department's Census Bureau reported the residence patterns of children under the age of 18 years: 13% of African American children, 5% of Hispanic American children, and 3% of Caucasian children lived in their grandparent's home ("Black children", March/April 1991). Jackson (1986) reported similar patterns in African American and Caucasian grandparent–grandchild relationships. For example, African American grandparents wanted to live near their grandchildren, although not in the same household; such grandparents served as anchor points for grandchildren. Jackson concluded that many families probably followed "familial norms characteristic of the larger culture" (p. 194). However, Wilson (1984) noted the importance of considering the cultural context of the African American family. He investigated single-mother and married-mother families with grandmothers living with the family, living next door, or living in the local community. Unique to this study is the inclusion of a residential grandmother in a dual-parent family. When grandmothers lived in a single-parent household, they perceived themselves to be more demanding, controlling, and punishing toward their grandchildren than did grandmothers in other family structures. Differences in the perception of the family climate were found among four different family structures; comparisons with other samples "provided convergent validity for the thesis that black Americans have distinct differences from majority white families (Tolson & Wilson, 1990, p. 424). In poor African American families, accelerated family timetables are normative, with transition to grandparenthood expected to occur in the mid-30s (Burton, 1990). Several studies have focused on adolescent mothers and their own mothers (Flaherty, 1988) and on the modeling of parenting methods by grandmothers (Stevens, 1984). Few investigations have considered paternal grandparents. Kennedy (1991) described racial differences in patterns of closeness and shared activities between college students and their grandparents. Further investigation of middle-class and intact families will provide a more comprehensive view of grandparenthood within the African American community.

Empirical investigations show strong intergenerational relationships in Mexican American families (Markides & Martin, 1990). Despite high levels of solidarity, expectations of the older generation were not met by their children

(Markides, Boldt, & Ray, 1986). The middle generation and their adult children had the highest levels of association, followed by middle-generation activities with parents. The lowest levels of association were found between the older generation and their adult grandchildren. However, there were few differences in regard to the sentiment expressed by each generation. A small exploratory study investigated Hispanic American grandparents from countries of origin other than Mexico (Raphael, 1988). The majority were involved in their grandchildren's daily lives, and all stressed biological continuity. Comparisons of Hispanic American populations in this study and that of Markides are not possible because of the differences in data collection modes. The impressive work of Markides should stimulate comparable empirical investigations.

Few systemic investigations of grandparenthood have been conducted in other ethnic groups. These are cited briefly in discussions of Native American and Amish family life (Gelfand & Barresi, 1987). Diversity among Caucasian ethnic groups and Judaic and Christian religious traditions also have been described (see Bengtson & Robertson, 1985). Cross-cultural research shows contrasting norms between countries. For example, Hurme (1988) found differences in regard to filial responsibilities when comparing intergenerational relationships in Finland with those in the United States. Cross-cultural research on grandparenting reveals issues that are of primary importance at a particular point in a country's history. For example, current research on Chinese grandparents explores the notion of a "4–2–1" problem engendered by the government's one-child policy: Do four grandparents and two parents produce one spoiled child (Falbo, 1991)?

Gender and Grandparenting: Noticing the Forgotten Man!

In 1981, Hagestad and Speicher pointed out that grandfathers were "forgotten men" in investigations of family relationships. Several reasons have been suggested for this: the greater longevity of women means that more elderly grandparents are likely to be women; women maintain relationships with their kin; and women may be more willing to serve as research subjects (Baranowski & Schilmoeller, 1991). Also, a historical overview of developmental psychology shows that research into the role of men in family relationships has been neglected in favor of an emphasis on the mother–child relationship (Tinsley & Parke, 1988).

Retrospective accounts suggest that maternal grandmothers and grandfathers see grandchildren equally often; however, the women interact with their grandchildren more during these visits than do the men (Eisenberg, 1988). Tinsley and Parke (1987) observed parents and grandparents in brief periods of dyadic play with their infant child/grandchild. Infants with high scores in cognitive, social, and motor development had grandfathers who were playful and responsive; moreover, their grandmothers were affectionate, highly verbal, and used teaching interactions. This association shows an intergenerational pattern of differential interaction by gender, both styles of which are related to infant development. Gender differences showed patterns similar to those found for parent–infant play—grandfathers were less likely to demonstrate caregiving behaviors or to laugh, smile, or kiss the baby. Similarly, grandfathers of preschoolers reported playing rough-and-tumble games, whereas grandmothers read books and played indoors with conventional toys (Russell, 1986).

Sex of the grandchild is described as an influential factor in grandfatherhood (Tinsley & Parke, 1988), although the evidence is conflicting. Grandfathers have remarked that adult children encourage them to avoid sexism in relationships with grandchildren, and they report few interactional differences based on sex (Baranowski & Schilmoeller, 1991). However, the importance of this variable remains unclear; sex and lineage patterns may interact. Baranowski (1990) contacted 106 grandfathers through a modified random-dialing screening procedure. The men provided descriptive information regarding all their grandchildren and then selected as a target the grandchild they had seen most frequently during the past year. Altogether there were 115 maternal grandsons, 111 maternal granddaughters, 117 paternal grandsons, and 114 paternal granddaughters. Despite this even distribution of grandchildren, fewer paternal granddaughters were chosen (n = 17) than paternal grandsons (n = 30), maternal granddaughters (n = 30) and maternal grandsons (n = 29). Why did this pattern of contact develop? These findings merit further attention.

Age-related factors in regard to grandfatherhood have been confounded with cohort. Thirty years ago, men over 65 tended toward formal relationships with grandchildren, whereas men under 65 either sought fun or felt distant (Neugarten & Weinstein, 1964). Recent research suggests interactional differences based on age: men between 50 and 56 years of age were more playful and affectionate in play with grandbabies than were older or younger grandfathers (Tinsley & Parke, 1988). The meaning of grandfatherhood seems to vary with age; older men attribute greater meaning to reinvolvement with their personal pasts and the centrality of their roles and attitudes of indulgence toward their grandchildren than do younger grandfathers (Baranowski, 1990).

Is the symbolic importance of grandchildren as biological renewal (bloodline carried on; continuity of family line) influenced by gender? The primary significance of grandparenthood was reported to be biological renewal by 42% of grandmothers and 23% of grandfathers (Neugarten & Weinstein, 1964). Because more maternal than paternal grandparents were studied, the sex differences may occur because women perceive biological continuity through daughters and men through sons. Intergenerational research suggested closer bonds between paternal grandfathers and grandsons and between maternal grandmothers and granddaughters (Hagestad & Speicher, 1981). Thomas (1989) found that grandfathers emphasized generational immortality more than grandmothers did. Further empirical research is necessary given our cultural acceptance of this concept. For example, the birth of a handicapped grandchild is described as difficult because it introduces unpredictability into the extension of the family (Vadasy, Fewell, & Meyer, 1986), and arguments for visitation rights stress the importance of bloodline: "It is a biological fact that grandparents are bound to their grandchildren by the unbreakable links of heredity" (New Jersey Supreme Court, cited in George, 1988, p. 14). Perhaps the importance of having someone to carry on the family line emerges toward the end of the life cycle. Men in poor health, when compared to healthy men, attributed more meaning to grandparenthood in terms of achieving immortality through one's descendants (Baranowski, 1990). This has implications for studies of the effect of age on perceptions of grandfatherhood. The perception of the time remaining in one's life may prove to be a more significant variable than actual chronologic age. The symbolic significance of grandchildren may be determined by comparing "grandchildless" individuals to their peers with grandchildren; men and women may attach different symbolic meanings to grandchildren (or lack thereof).

Changing Roles in Family Crisis

Family needs change during stressful times, and grandparents often become more involved. For example, the discovery that a child has a handicapping condition has been described as a crisis that reverberates throughout the extended family (Gabel & Kotsch, 1981). Expectations become ambiguous and grandparents may lack access to professional consultations concerning the disability. Participants in programs developed for such grandparents had many questions concerning appropriate methods of support. Typical questions were: "What is the current research on her handicap?"; "What can we do to develop his talents?"; "What will help his parents most?" (Vadasy et al., 1986). Even families with effective intergenerational communication systems in place prior to the crisis may have difficulty adjusting to role changes. A more thorough consideration of these issues by professionals would be beneficial.

DEVELOPMENTAL ASPECTS OF THE GRANDPARENT–GRANDCHILD RELATIONSHIP

Infancy and Childhood

The initial organization of the grandparent–grandchild relationship is influenced by the grandparents' perceptions of grandparenthood occurring "on-time" or "off-time" (Hagestad & Burton, 1986). Expectant grandparents in Scotland took a "wait and see" attitude before the birth of the grandchild, not wanting to make plans until they could see how things might develop (Cunningham-Burley, 1984). Grandparents observed in play sessions in the home of 7-month-old grandchildren were gentler with the babies than were the parents (who were more competent and flexible) (Tinsley & Parke, 1987). The Bailey Scales of Infant Development showed higher developmental scores for babies whose grandparents had frequent contact with the family (Tinsley & Parke, 1987). In a laboratory playroom, toddlers (aged 12–24 months) were placed in a situation designed to study attachment behaviors (Myers, Jarvis, & Creasey, 1987). The toddlers showed similar behaviors toward mothers and maternal grandmothers, indicating that both provided security; strangers did not function in this way. The grandmothers in this study had close mother–daughter relationships and lived near to each other. Research on the development of attachment between grandparents and their infant/toddler grandchildren who do not live nearby is necessary. Tomlin and Passman (1989) found that toddlers' bonds to grandmothers were influenced by the physical and emotional responsibilities the grandmother assumed in providing care.

Children's abilities to participate actively in interpersonal relationships increase throughout childhood. Perceptions of grandparenthood are linked to levels of cognitive development in such a way that 4- and 5-year-olds emphasized concrete interactions, such as receiving love and presents (Kahana & Kahana, 1970). Eight- and 9-year-olds stressed mutuality and fun as important, whereas preadolescents (ages 11–12) once again preferred indulgent grandparents. Content analysis of children's essays on grandparents (written for a contest sponsored by a grandparent's advocacy group) revealed that most children describe what the grandparents do for them (Ponzetti & Folkrod, 1989). First and second graders emphasized nurturance and gifts more often than older children; fourth and fifth graders mentioned the sense of connectedness and pride in family history more than the younger children. These results indicate the need for research on the change in particular grandparent–grandchild relationships over time. Grandchildren may elicit certain grandparental behaviors at particular developmental levels. A grandmother who longs to reminisce about the years of raising her own children is likely to find a receptive audience in an older child rather than a younger one. A grandfather who takes pride in family rituals may find that younger grandchildren emphasize the importance of the concrete symbols used in the ritual, whereas older children perceive the connectedness between generations and the historical continuity. Beyond direct grandparent–grandchild interactions, significant indirect influences may be exerted through the parents. For example, the advice given by maternal grandmothers influenced the disciplinary decisions of mothers regarding their 10-year-olds under laboratory conditions (Tomlin & Passman, 1991).

Adolescence and Young Adult Years

For teenagers, grandparents can be a sensitive sounding board for life plans, a nonjudgmental listener to their fears of personal inadequacy or failure, and a wonderfully appreciative audience for their performances and achievements.

(Elkind, 1990a, p. 169)

Is the meaningful relationship described above typical of many relationships, or do most teenagers and their grandparents have symbolic relationships with little attachment? Adolescents, referring to a target grandparent, reported frequent discussions of personal issues (Dellmann-Jenkins, Papalia, & Lopez, 1987). Companionship with grandparents (e.g., playing cards, shopping) occurred at least on a monthly basis for most of the teenagers. Subjects were not asked which grandparent they had selected, so patterns of sex and lineage in the dyads cannot be examined. Given the existence of a meaningful relationship, what aspects of self-disclosure contribute to intimacy? *Honesty* and *depth* of the disclosures were related to solidarity for both grandparents and grandchildren (Downs, 1988). Grandchildren perceived the *amount* of disclosure as related to the closeness in the dyad, and grandparents emphasized the *intent* of disclosure. Intimacy within this relationship has theoretical implications for psychological well-being. Close relationships between adolescents and their grandparents may be beneficial to the successful resolution of adolescents' identity issues (Baranowski, 1982) and to the grandparents' mental health (Kivnick, 1982) within an Eriksonian theoretical framework.

Matthews and Sprey (1985) investigated the relationships of 132 adolescents (17 to 20 years), obtaining specific information about living and deceased grandparents. Relationships with particular grandparents were described in terms of current and retrospective closeness. Determination of the availability of grandparents has implications for the study of lineage patterns. For example, by late adolescence, only 25% reported a living paternal grandfather, whereas 40% of the maternal grandfathers were living. Grandmothers (paternal = 58%; maternal = 59%) were more likely to be alive than were grandfathers. Maternal relationships were closer than relationships with paternal grandparents. This pattern was established before adolescence, with most of the grandchildren indicating consistency in closeness since childhood. Grandchildren's perceptions of mother's and father's attitudes toward each grandparent showed a complex intergenerational pattern of influence. The lack of a close relationship between a father and his mother-in-law did not influence the grandchild's closeness to the maternal grandmother; however, the perceived relationship between a mother and her mother-in-law was a factor in the grandchild's feelings toward the paternal grandmother. Close attachment to paternal grandmothers was more likely if she had been seen often during childhood. This variable was less influential for maternal grandmothers. Empirical findings regarding geographic proximity are provocative, especially considering the mobility of many families in the United States. Geographic distance between grandparents and grandchildren has been strongly criticized (Kornhaber & Woodward, 1981), and it has been suggested that retirement programs explain the impact of geographic moves on intergenerational relationships (Ramirez Barranti, 1985). Research is imperative to determine the extent of this impact.

Grandchildren feel a sense of obligation toward their grandparents; however, they keep in touch because they enjoy them (Kennedy, 1989). Kennedy (1991) provides characteristic reasons for feeling close to grandparents: perception of similarity to the grandparents and enjoyment of their company; perception of a special expression of interest toward oneself by the grandparent; and admiration of, yet relaxation with, the grandparent. Kennedy's findings regarding differences in regard to family form, gender, birth order, and race suggest several avenues for further research.

Langer (1990) studied the social support system between older grandparents (65 to 91 years) and their ongoing relationships with at least one adult grandchild. The grandparents had greater expectations for emotional than instrumental support, and grandchildren met these needs. The interactional patterns of middle-aged grandchildren and their grandparents must be directly investigated. Is this a time when the middle-aged individuals reassess their relationships with grandparents, while they prepare to become grandparents? The period of middle age has not received as much attention by researchers as have the beginning and ends of the life cycle, and it requires further study.

MARITAL CHANGES IN THE MIDDLE GENERATION: REDEFINING THE GRANDPARENT–GRANDCHILD RELATIONSHIP

Reorganization of Intergenerational Relationships

At the turn of the century, President Roosevelt strongly denounced the appalling divorce rates (McGreal, 1988); today divorce has become commonplace. Adult children often do not reveal marital problems to their parents before the breakup of a marriage (Cherlin & Furstenberg, 1986). Therefore, despite its prevalence, divorce in many extended families is an unexpected stressor. As Margaret Mead noted:

> In human societies, we almost always find a contrast between life as people believe it to be, and life as it is lived by some, if not all, members of that society.... People often cling in their minds to a pattern far removed from the realities of everyday life; the more remote their ideal is from reality, the more the conflicts that arise.

> (Mead, 1971, pp. 107–108)

Ahrons and Bowman (1982) reported that, in general, contact between grandmothers and their adult children followed a curvilinear pattern. For a year after divorce, there was an increase in contact, but following that year, contact returned to predivorce levels. Based upon this pattern, one might hypothesize a healthy intergenerational response to divorce: turning to one's parents at a time of crisis for consolation and support, and then, returning to more independence after the initial stresses are reduced. Gladstone (1988) found that grandmothers increased personal advice to young grandchildren following divorce. Grandparent–grandchild contact usually remained the same or increased. Factors associated with increased visits between grandmothers and grandchildren included: 1) geographic mobility, in which generations resided in closer proximity after the divorce, allowing for greater intergenerational support; 2) use of grandmother's home for visitation rights by the noncustodial parent; 3) assumption of child-care responsibilities by grandmothers when custodial daughters were at work; and 4) departure of the child-in-law from the grandchild's home so that the grandmother felt more comfortable in regard to frequent visits (Gladstone, 1987).

In an intensive study of intergenerational adaptation to divorce, Johnson (1988) found that most grandparents gave a significant amount of help to divorcing adult children. Over a 40-month period postdivorce, the number of services received from parents declined, although the quality of the relationship improved. Johnson identified three types of reorganization in postdivorce families: *generational, nucleated,* and *network.* The *generational* reorganization most frequently occurred among women who were in need of financial help. These individuals had high expectations for support from relatives; in general, their mothers lived up to expectations. Eventually, most of these women became less dependent, intentionally distancing themselves from direct bonds of dependency. In this method of reorganization, we might hypothesize the greatest difficulty in terms of grandparents assuming a long-term surrogate parenting function. It may be difficult for some adult children to intentionally break from parental bonds; some grandparents may have difficulty "allowing" their adult children to risk independence once again. Grandparents may be tempted to pursue custodial rights as their adult child attempts to break away. This reorganizational style also risks conflict with in-laws, because both the divorcing individuals and their families blame the former spouse for the dissolution of the marriage. Therefore, grandparents who feel cut off from their grandchildren because of intergenerational solidarity in the family of the custodial parent (the former child-in-law) may seek visitation rights in order to maintain their own relationships with grandchildren.

The *nucleated* reorganizational style tended to be shown in individuals with few economic problems and with friendly, although distant, family relationships (Johnson, 1988). The grandparental and parental generations stressed the importance of independence; expectations between the generations were low. Relationships were neutral, with little warmth or animosity expressed. From this description, difficulties with surrogate parenthood would seem unlikely. Rather, intergenerational conflict may occur if the grandparents (especially in-laws who may place familial values above independence) have greater expectations for interaction with the grandchildren than the privacy of this nuclear unit allows. Pursuit of greater levels of contact may be perceived to be a threat by nuclear families who maintain strict boundaries around their immediate family unit. Thus, this style could lead grandparents to seek visitation rights, although from a different perspective than grandparents in a generational family system.

The third reorganizational style identified by Johnson (1988) involves the formation of a loosely-knit social *network.* Relationships are voluntary associations based on interpersonal attraction, rather than familial obligation. There is little interference between generations, and both generations remain friendly with the former child-in-law and the other set of grandparents. Upon remarriage, the new in-laws were incorporated into the network.

Step-Grandparents

Step-grandparenthood occurs as a result of the remarriage of either a grandparent or a parent. Two important factors in the negotiation of step-grandparent–step-grandchild relationships are the age of the child at the time of remarriage and whether the child lives with the step-grandparent's adult child (Cherlin & Furstenberg, 1986). When young adults described the relationship with the step-grandparent seen most often, 48% reported that the relationship was important to them, and 63% desired more contact (Trygstad & Sanders, 1989). Elkind (1990b) noted that parents often are on the lookout for signs of favoritism when the grandchildren are from different marriages. Contact may be reduced if parents perceive differential treatment. Step-grandchildren are less likely to use kinship terms than are grandchildren (Cherlin & Furstenberg, 1986). Given the lack of societal norms regarding step-grandparenthood and the wide latitude in negotiating the relationship, terms of address range from formal titles (Mr. Inglot), to informal use of first names (Mark); from familiar kinship names (Grandpa Kuchar), to idiosyncratic terms (Grandfriends). It would be interesting to investigate forms of address in regard to step-grandparenthood in order to determine whether the form adopted by a particular family is associated with the significance of the role across generations.

Conflict Across the Generations—Legal Issues and Visitation Rights

A reorganizational style considered transitory by one generation because of the circumstances of divorce may be considered permanent by another generation. Renegotiation of the relationship may become emotionally charged. Gladstone (1987) found two factors associated with a decrease in grandparent–grandchild visits after divorce: difficulty redefining the relationship and unresolved familial conflicts. Without clear communication regarding new expectations, contact may be diminished. Intergenerational relationships after divorce highlight a concept stressed by Matthews and Sprey (1984)—grandparenthood is a relationship between individuals embedded within a family system, rather than an attribute solely of the grandparents. In fact, high levels of contact between grandparents and grandchildren do not, in and of themselves, mean a healthy communication pattern within the family. For example, after remarriage a new child-in-law may be supportive of the grandparent by providing access to the grandchildren. On the other hand, it may indicate an effort to decrease the amount of time spent in the role of step-parent.

Recently, intergenerational conflicts have become legal and political issues; the psychological effects of court-ordered intergenerational visitation remain unknown. Visitation issues primarily affect families experiencing parental death or divorce. However, in 1991, the New York Court of Appeals awarded visitation rights to a grandfather whose grandson lived in an intact family home (*Vital Connections,* 1991). This is a drastic change from common-law tradition. In the past, parents not deemed unfit determined levels of visitation (Wilson & DeShane, 1982). It was thought that parental authority would be undermined if grandparents were given rights over objections of the parents (Thompson, Scalora, Castrianno, & Limber, 1991). A 1947 decision in a California case illustrates this view of parental rights.

> There is nothing in the record which would indicate that the association of the plaintiff and her grandchild would be anything other than beneficial to the child. However, the court does not have the power to compel the parents to allow the grandmother the right of visitation merely because the relationship is that of grandparent.
>
> (Odell v. Lutz, cited in Foster & Freed, 1982, p. 85)

In contrast to the *Odell* v. *Lutz* decision, grandparents in all fifty states now have the legal right to petition for visitation with their grandchildren (Thompson et al.). Circumstances for the right to petition court vary from state to state. Passage of a uniform visitation law is a high priority among grandparental rights activists.

A key aspect of visitation statutes is based on the premise that it is in the "best interests of the child" to develop and maintain a relationship with the grandparents. "Grandparents seeking standing under these statutes are not doing so on the basis of *their* rights but in the interest of their grandchildren" (Wilson & DeShane, 1982, p. 70). Determining a child's best interests is a difficult judgment (Thompson et al., 1991). It has been suggested that individuals may be "good" grandparents and yet have negative parent–child interactions (Foster & Freed, 1981). From this point of view, disrupting an ongoing relationship with a grand-child because of hostility between parents and grandparents is not necessary. Other views suggest that children suffer when placed in the center of intergenera-tional conflict. For example, Thompson et al. (1991, p. 299) reported a case in which a deputy sheriff, by court order, forcibly brought a grandson to his grandparents. The value of this visit to the child's emotional well-being is indeed questionable. Although consideration of visitation rights has centered on the child, it is evident that there is an agendum for the "best interests of the grandparent." In a 1983 congressional hearing, Kornhaber stated that "[g]rand-parenting gives elders a role for old age, in a society that does not have a role for old age" (cited in Shandling, 1986, p. 121). Undeniably, it is in the best interests of all generations to develop strong kinship networks. It seems difficult, however, to develop positive family relationships through court-ordered contact. Another difficulty lies in the number of petitioners who desire greater contact with the child. Six states included great-grandparents as individuals with the right to petition for visitation (George, 1988). Bean (1985/86, p. 441) suggested that intervention, when harm to the child is not involved, "is an unconstitutional infringement upon and deprivation of the right of parents to raise their child in accord with their own values".

This discussion of the effects of marital stability was simplified by considering only the divorce of the middle generation. Unfortunately, many grandparents must renegotiate kinship relationships based upon their own divorces. At the birth of our children, my husband and I received baby books, which included a family-tree page. Ever optimistic, the books contained illustrations based on marital stability across the generations. It was startling to note that despite an age difference of less than a decade, the family trees of our older daughters differed from those of our younger children. As Korenblum pointed out (1980, p. 44), "It is becoming increasingly difficult to recognize the new species of family tree. With changing intergenerational relationships, it's being whittled down; branches are pruned with divorce, new buds are spliced on with remarriage."

CONCLUSIONS

The stereotype of grandparents as elderly persons remains strong, despite evidence to the contrary. The transition to grandparenthood is significant; grandparents have not disengaged from intergenerational relationships. Rather than assuming a particular role, families negotiate interactional patterns between the generations based upon a number of factors, including developmental level of the grandchild, gender, marital situation of the family, and the age/health of the grandparent. Ethnic and cultural variations exist. The unique needs of family systems under crisis require effective systems of communication involving extended family members. Conflict across generations has led to legislative and political action. Grandparental rights activists have supported laws encouraging court-ordered intergenerational visitation, although the psychological ramifications have yet to be determined. Although the beginning and the ends of the individual life cycle have been studied comprehensively, the decades of middle age remain to be researched. Transition to grandparenthood and the changing intergenerational relationships negotiated over time merit further attention.

REFERENCES

Ahrons, C. R., & Bowman, M. E. (1982). Changes in family relationships following divorce of adult child: Grandmother's perceptions. In E. O. Fisher (Ed.), *Impact of divorce on the extended family* (pp. 49–68). Binghamton, NY: Haworth.

Baranowski, M. D. (1982). Grandparent–adolescent relations: Beyond the nuclear family. *Adolescence, 17,* 575–584.

Baranowski, M. D. (1990). The grandfather–grandchild relationship: Meaning and exchange. *Family Perspective, 24,* 201–215.

Baranowski, M. D., & Schilmoeller, G. L. (1991, November). Grandfather–grandchild interaction: Does grandchild gender make a difference? Paper presented at the 53rd Annual Conference of the National Council on Family Relations, Denver, CO.

Bean, K. S. (1985/86). Grandparent visitation: Can the parent refuse? *Journal of Family Law, 24,* 393–449.

Bengtson, V. L., & Robertson, J. F. (Eds.). (1985). *Grandparenthood.* Beverly Hills, CA: Sage.

"Black children likely to live with grandparents." (1991, March/April). *Society, 28,* 2.

Burton, L. M. (1990). Teenage childbearing as an alternative life-course strategy in multigeneration black families. *Human Nature, 1,* 123–143.

Cherlin, A., & Furstenberg, F. F., Jr. (1986). *The new American grandparent: A place in the family, a life apart.* New York: Basic Books.

Cunningham-Burley, S. (1984). On telling the news: Grandparenthood as an announceable event. *International Journal of Sociology and Social Policy, 4,* 52–69.

Dellmann-Jenkins, M., Papalia, D., & Lopez, M. (1987). Teenagers' reported interaction with grandparents: Exploring the extent of alienation. *Lifestyles: A Journal of Changing Patterns, 3/4,* 35–46.

Downs, V. C. (1988). Grandparents and grandchildren: The relationship between self-disclosure and solidarity in an intergenerational relationship. *Communication Research Reports, 5,* 173–179.

Duvall, E. M. (1954). *In-laws pro and con: An original study of interpersonal relations.* New York: Association Press.

Eisenberg, A. R. (1988). Grandchildren's perspectives on relationships with grandparents: The influence of gender across generations. *Sex Roles: A Journal of Research, 19,* 205–217.

Elkind, D. (1990a). The joys that grandparents bring. *Parents' Magazine, 65,* p. 169.

Elkind, D. (1990b). *Grandparenting: Understanding today's children.* Glenview, IL: Scott, Foresman.

Falbo, T. (1991). The impact of grandparents on children's outcomes in China. *Marriage and Family Review, 16,* 369–376.

Flaherty, M. J. (1988). Seven caring functions of Black grandmothers in adolescent mothering. *Maternal–Child Nursing Journal, 17,* 191–207.

Foster, H. H., Jr., & Freed, D. J. (1982). Grandparent visitation: Vagaries and vicissitudes. In E. O. Fisher (Ed.), *Impact of divorce on the extended family* (pp. 79–100). Binghamton, NY: Haworth.

Gabel, H., & Kotsch, L. S. (1981). Extended families and young handicapped children. *Topics in Early Childhood Special Education, 1,* 29–35.

Gelfand, D. E., & Barresi, C. M. (Eds.). (1987). *Ethnic dimensions of aging.* New York: Springer.

George, J. (1988). Children and grandparents: The right to visit. *Children Today, 17,* 14–18.

Gladstone, J. W. (1987). Factors associated with changes in visiting between grandmothers and grandchildren following an adult child's marriage breakdown. *Canadian Journal on Aging, 6,* 117–127.

Gladstone, J. W. (1988). Perceived changes in grandmother–grandchild relations following a child's separation or divorce. *Gerontologist, 28,* 66–72.

Hagestad, G. O., & Burton, L. M. (1986). Grandparenthood, life context, and family development. *American Behavioral Scientist, 29,* 471–484.

Hagestad, G. O., & Speicher, J. L. (1981). Grandparents and family influence: Views of three generations. Paper presented at the meeting of the Society for Research in Child Development, Boston, MA.

Hurme, H. (1988). Child, mother, and grandmother: Intergenerational interaction in Finnish families. *Jyvaskyla Studies in Education, Psychology, and Social Research,* No. 64. Jyvaskyla, Finland: University of Jyvaskyla.

Jackson, J. (1986). The extended family—Black grandparents: Who needs them? In R. Staples (Ed.), *The black family: Essays and studies* (pp. 186–194). Belmont, CA: Wadsworth.

Johnson, C. L. (1988). Postdivorce reorganization of relationships between divorcing children and their parents. *Journal of Marriage and the Family, 50,* 221–231.

Kahana, B., & Kahana, E. (1970). Grandparenthood from the perspective of the developing grandchild. *Developmental Psychology, 3*, 98–105.

Kennedy, G. E. (1989). College students' relationships with grandparents. *Psychological Reports, 64*, 477–478.

Kennedy, G. E. (1991). Grandchildren's reasons for closeness with grandparents. *Journal of Social Behavior and Personality, 6*, 697–712.

Kivnick, H. Q. (1982). *The meaning of grandparenthood.* Ann Arbor: University of Michigan Press.

Korenblum, T. (1980, June). Divorced from a generation. *Maclean's, 93*, 44.

Kornhaber, A., & Woodward, K. L. (1981). *Grandparents/grandchildren: The vital connection.* Garden City, NY: Anchor/Doubleday.

Langer, N. (1990). Grandparents and adult grandchildren: What do they do for one another? *International Journal of Aging and Human Development, 31*, 101–110.

Markides, K. S., Boldt, J. S., & Ray, L. A. (1986). Sources of helping and intergenerational solidarity: A three-generations study of Mexican Americans. *Journal of Gerontology, 41*, 506–511.

Markides, K. S., & Martin, H. W. (1990). *Older Mexican Americans.* San Antonio: The Tomas Rivera Center.

Matthews, S. H., & Sprey, J. (1984). The impact of divorce on grandparenthood: An exploratory study. *Gerontologist, 24*, 40–47.

Matthews, S. H., & Sprey, J. (1985). Adolescents' relationships with grandparents: An empirical contribution to conceptual clarification. *Journal of Gerontology, 40*, 621–626.

McGreal, C. E. (1986). Grandparental typologies: A critical evaluation. *Infant Mental Health Journal, 7*, 235–241.

McGreal, C. E. (1988). In great-grandma's nursery. *Infant Mental Health Journal, 9*, 305–318.

Mead, M. (1971). Anomalies in American postdivorce relationships. In P. Bohannan (Ed.), *Divorce and after* (pp. 107–125). Garden City, NY: Anchor.

Myers, B. J., Jarvis, P. A., & Creasey, G. L. (1987). Infants' behavior with their mothers and grandmothers. *Infant Behavior and Development, 10*, 245–259.

Neisser, E. G. (1951). *How to be a good mother-in-law and grandmother.* New York: Public Affairs Committee.

Neugarten, B. L., Moore, J. W., & Lowe, J. C. (1965). Age norms, age constraints, and adult socialization. *American Journal of Sociology, 70*, 710–717.

Neugarten, B. L., & Weinstein, K. K. (1964). The changing American grandparent. *Journal of Marriage and the Family, 26*, 199–204.

Ponzetti, J. J., Jr., & Folkrod, A. W. (1989). Grandchildren's perceptions of their relationships with their grandparents. *Child Study Journal, 19*, 41–50.

Ramirez Barranti, C. C. (1985). The grandparent/grandchild relationship: Family resource in an era of voluntary bonds. *Family Relations, 34*, 343–352.

Raphael, E. I. (1988). Grandparents: A study of their role in Hispanic families. *Physical & Occupational Therapy in Geriatrics, 6*, 31–62.

Robertson, J. F. (1977). Grandmotherhood: A study of role conceptions. *Journal of Marriage and the Family, 39*, 165–174.

Russell, G. (1986). Grandfathers: Making up for lost opportunities. In R. A. Lewis & R. E. Salt (Eds.), *Men in families* (pp. 233–259). Newbury Park, CA: Sage.

Shandling, J. L. (1986). The constitutional constraints on grandparents' visitation statutes. *Columbia Law Review, 86*, 118–138.

Stevens, J. H. (1984). Black grandmothers' and black adolescent mothers' knowledge about parenting. *Developmental Psychology, 20*, 1017–1025.

Thomas, J. L. (1989). Gender and perceptions of grandparenthood. *International Journal of Aging & Human Development, 29,* 269–282.

Thomas, J. L. (1990). The grandparent role: A double bind. *International Journal of Aging & Human Development, 31,* 169–177.

Thompson, R. A., Scalora, M. J., Castrianno, L., & Limber, S. P. (1991). Grandparent visitation rights: Emergent psychological and psycholegal issues. In D. K. Kagehiro & W. S. Laufer (Eds.), *Handbook of psychology and law* (pp. 292–317). New York: Springer.

Tinsley, B. J., & Parke, R. D. (1987). Grandparents as interactive and social support agents for families with young infants. *International Journal of Aging & Human Development, 25,* 259–277.

Tinsley, B. J., & Parke, R. D. (1988). The role of grandfathers in the context of the family. In P. Bronstein & C. P. Cowan (Eds.), *Fatherhood today: Men's changing role in the family* (pp. 236–250). New York: Wiley.

Tolson, T. F. J., & Wilson, M. N. (1990). The impact of two- and three-generational Black family structure on perceived family climate. *Child Development, 61,* 416–428.

Tomlin, A. M., & Passman, R. H. (1989). Grandmothers' responsibility in raising two-year-olds facilitates their grandchildren's adaptive behavior: A preliminary intrafamilial investigation of mothers' and maternal grandmothers' effects. *Psychology and Aging, 4,* 119–121.

Tomlin, A. M., & Passman, R. H. (1991). Grandmothers' advice about disciplining grandchildren: Is it accepted by mothers, and does its rejection influence grandmothers' subsequent guidance? *Psychology and Aging, 6,* 182–189.

Trygstad, D. W., & Sanders, G. F. (1989). The significance of stepgrandparents. *International Journal of Aging and Human Development, 29,* 119–134.

Turner, R. D. (1989, March). Grandparents aren't what they used to be. *Ebony, 44,* 36, 38, 40, 44.

Vadasy, P. F., Fewell, R. R., & Meyer, D. J. (1986). Grandparents of children with special needs: Insights into their experiences and concerns. *Journal of the Division for Early Childhood, 10,* 36–44.

Vital Connections: The Grandparenting Newsletter. (Fall, 1991). Vol. VIII. Lake Placid, NY: Foundation for Grandparenting.

Wilson, K. B., & DeShane, M. R. (1982). The legal rights of grandparents: A preliminary discussion. *Gerontologist, 22,* 67–71.

Wilson, M. N. (1984). Mothers' and grandmothers' perceptions of parental behavior in three-generational black families. *Child Development, 55,* 1333–1339.

CHAPTER 7

Subcultural Diversity in American Families

DORIS R. ENTWISLE

Between 1981 and 1989 almost 6 million citizens from Asia, Africa, Europe, and Latin America added to the already huge ethnic diversity of American families. Over the same period, strong economic and social pressures within the United States led to increases in the *structural* diversity of these families. In some ethnic groups, however, such as Chinese Americans, the rate of structural change has been slower than it has been for others, such as African Americans. The net result is that structural variations magnify subcultural differences even more.

American families, although already changing in the immediate post-World War II era, at midcentury were conceptualized as static social groups. Mainly nuclear in form, they allowed for 1) sexual access between some adult members; 2) legitimate reproduction to occur; 3) child care and upbringing to be carried out; and 4) economic goods to be produced or at least consumed (Zelditch, 1964). In recent decades, however, because the prevalence of nuclear families has declined, the *majority* of U. S. families has become *non*nuclear. This demographic shift, along with numerous economic and social changes, has altered fundamentally the way families are viewed. In fact, *life course* research now occupies much of the family research domain. The family unit is now thought of as having a life course of its own, wherein structure can metamorphose at any time. Because family structure changes in response to economic and social forces, the family can have distinctive patterns from one historical period to the next.

This chapter reflects the life course approach and its emphasis on fluid family structure. First, we describe *structural* differences among families that belong to different subcultural groups, emphasizing how these families change in response to social and historical pressures. Second, we discuss variation in family *process or function* across subcultural groups, in light of both structural and ethnic variation. Interpretation of differences in how African American and anglo American parents socialize children, for example, requires that we take

---

Preparation of this chapter was supported by NICHD Grant No. 23943 "Black and white families and children's development."

into account differences in the family's structural form—whether the parent lives with a spouse, lives in an extended family, or lives alone governs how much social and economic capital is available for childrearing.

According to the definition of the Bureau of the Census, in use since 1947, a family consists of two or more people, living in the same household, who are related by blood, marriage, or adoption. We, likewise, mean by "family" two or more persons occupying the same household who are linked by marriage (a married couple), or a blood relation (parent and child). At times, however, we also refer to the wider circle of kin who do not necessarily share a residence, such as grandparents or other relatives. We also are interested in single parents with children, who share a household with unrelated adults—perhaps a live-in girlfriend/boyfriend or another single parent with children. Economic and social resources are likely to be more plentiful when more adults are in the household, so aggregated households of nonkin tend to spring up in groups where economic resources are scarce.

Over the last half century, as a life course approach has persuaded family researchers to adopt a dialectic and dynamic perspective, the family has assumed a new identity. It is now seen as a fluid unit that changes structure and adapts its functions as social institutions and economic conditions around it change. A major difference in families across subcultures is in their *degree of fluidity.* African Americans, for example, live in a wide variety of family forms—Kellam, Branck, Agrawal, and Ensminger (1975) estimate that at least 84 different family configurations existed in one poor African American community in Chicago in the late 1960s. Highly fluid families also tend to expand and contract within relatively short periods. The pregnant African American teenager is likely to remain with her family, and her male partner may or may not move in with her. If he does, however, he may soon leave (Furstenberg, 1976). If she has another child, she may be forced to go it alone.

Economic forces dictate some family arrangements; for example, extended family arrangements offer a means to buffer economic stress. Poor families are more likely to share residences than other groups (Cutright, 1978). At the same time, cultural customs and outlooks influence family function. Even middle-class African American families are more likely to contribute financially to extended family support networks than are similarly situated families of other ethnic groups (Hofferth, 1984).

Fewer and fewer children are raised in families where both parents have been married only once. Ethnic groups differ greatly, however, in the prevalence of divorce and remarriage. Divorced African American parents are about one tenth as likely to remarry as anglos and are somewhat less likely to produce a child in the new marriage (Bumpass, 1984). However, over half of African American children have half-siblings (including those born in nonmarital interludes), as compared to 14% of whites.

Ethnic groups also differ in how many women are in the labor force. The traditional male instrumental role is shared increasingly by wives and mothers in all groups. Among African Americans, however, the breadwinner role, now

mainly filled by women, has been more common for women all along. Employment rates of African American women have consistently exceeded those of
anglos, but the margin is diminishing. About 50% of African American and
43% of anglo women were in the labor force in 1970, for example; by 1989,
these figures had risen to 59% and 57%, respectively (United States, Department
of Commerce, 1991).

Hispanic Americans (Puerto Rican Americans, Cuban Americans, Mexican
Americans, and others), or Asian Americans (Chinese Americans, Japanese
Americans, Filipino Americans, and others) are often lumped together. Aggregat-
ing these groups under a common rubric can be highly misleading, however.
Mexican Americans divorce at about the same rate as nonHispanic Americans,
but Puerto Rican Americans divorce at much higher rates (Bean & Tienda,
1987), for example. In a similar vein, 75% of Cuban Americans, but only 50%
of Mexican Americans report help from relatives in the early years of their U.S.
residence (Portes & Bach, 1985). Therefore, we preserve subgroup distinctions
whenever possible.

STRUCTURE

The present subcultural differences in family structure reflect powerful demographic trends. Family patterns have been changing for *all* groups over the past
three decades in response to these trends (Jaynes & Williams, 1989). Generally,
we see lower marriage rates, higher divorce rates, lower birth rates, earlier and
more frequent sexual activity during adolescence, a higher proportion of births
to unwed mothers, a higher proportion of children in female-headed households,
a higher proportion of women working outside the home, and a higher percentage
of children living in poverty. Overall, ages at marriage are higher and family
formation is being delayed compared to earlier decades; half of those who do
marry will probably experience a disruption (Furstenberg, 1990). The *rate* at
which these many changes are occurring varies widely across subcultures, however. The National Committee for Research on the 1980 Census commissioned
a number of monographs to analyze and summarize major changes and trends
in American life. *American Families and Households* by James A. Sweet and
Larry L. Bumpass (1987), based on the 1980 Census data, offers the most
comprehensive picture yet available of subcultural and racial/ethnic variations
in family structure. Several years will pass before a parallel volume on family
structure based on the 1990 Census can be prepared. The summary of family
structure presented in this chapter draws heavily on the data presented by Sweet
and Bumpass, but when possible adds later data available from other sources.

Marriage

Marriage rates are on the decline for all women, but especially for African
Americans. In 1940, two-parent families made up about 76% of African Ameri-

can families, as compared to 85% of anglo families, and from 1940 to the late 1950s, the proportion of female-headed, African American families rose only slightly (Jaynes & Williams, 1989, p. 519). However, by 1980, almost 79% of anglo women age 35 to 39 were married, as compared to only 49% of African American women (Sweet & Bumpass, 1987, Table 4.2), and by 1989, 62% of anglo women were married, as compared to 44% of African American women (United States Department of Commerce, 1991). The proportion of married African Americans has been lower than the proportion of married people in the general population all along, and by 1988, it dropped to well below one half. In a complementary fashion, the proportion of never-married African American women rose sharply between 1970 and 1980 (those not married by age 29 rose from 17% to 29%) (Sweet & Bumpass, 1987, Table 3.5), and it rose again to 32% by 1988 (United States Department of Commerce, 1990).

The low marriage rate of African American women has been explained on the basis of imbalanced sex ratios and the deprived economic situation of African American men. Jaynes and Williams (1989, p. 539) note that, at age 26, African American women with less than a high school education are in a marriage pool of 651 men per 1000 women, and those with some college are in a pool with 772 men per 1000 women. They believe that the differences in the number of available partners may explain differences in family patterns between African Americans and anglos, but not the growing racial divergence. Other trends also would be consistent with a tight marriage market. For example, African American women, as compared to anglo women, are more likely to marry previously divorced, relatively older, and less educated men (Spanier & Glick, 1980).

The continuing and worsening employment problems of African American men over the past two decades have left African American women with little to gain economically from marriage. Cherlin (1992), however, believes that trends in employment and income cannot explain all of the decline in the African American marriage rate. He notes that flight from marriage has occurred among employed and better educated African American men, as well as among those who are less fortunate. Other data are consistent with Cherlin's hypothesis. For example, among men who fathered a child outside wedlock, when employment and education were controlled, anglos were four times as likely, and Mexican Americans more than twice as likely as African Americans to have married the mother of their child (Testa, Astone, Krogh, & Neckerman, 1989).

Other cultural differences affecting the likelihood of marriage also remain unexplained. For example, Mexican American women are somewhat more likely to marry than anglos, whereas Chinese American and Japanese American women are less likely to marry than anglos (Sweet & Bumpass, 1987, Table 3.2).

Interracial marriage is rare. In 1980, only 1/2 of 1% of all first marriages were between an African American and an anglo (Sweet & Bumpass, Table 2.9). Interracial marriages, nevertheless, increased somewhat between 1980 and 1988, especially in the West (Taylor, Chatters, Tucker, & Lewis, 1991), and especially for more highly educated men (Schoen & Wooldredge, 1989).

As the number of single women has risen so has the number of never-married adults with children. There were 1.4 million never-married persons with children in 1980, of whom 90% were women. The majority of these women (60%) were African American (Sweet & Bumpass, 1987, pp. 94–95). One explanation for the racial difference in the number of single mothers is that the age at which women marry has risen more among African Americans, exposing these women to nonmarital pregnancies over a longer period. Consistent with the general rise in age at marriage, out-of-wedlock births in anglos have increased, too. In 1970, 5.7% of such births were among unmarried women; by 1987 this rate had tripled (to 16.7%). The African American rate also rose over the same period (from 37.6% to 62.2%), but the *proportional* increase is smaller for African Americans; therefore, it draws less attention (United States Department of Commerce, 1990, Table 90). Paradoxically, the recent percentage of increase in births to anglo adolescents has triggered much of the social concern about teen and/or out-of-wedlock births, although the prevalence of out-of-wedlock births is much higher in the African American community (Nathanson, 1991).

Mothers without spouses often share households. Whether anglo, African American, or Mexican American, about one quarter of never-married women with children lived with their parents in 1980. Another 8% of never-married women were cohabiting (Sweet & Bumpass, 1987, Table 3.26). However, cohabitation was more frequent for anglos (over 13%) than for either African Americans (6%) or Mexican Americans (8%).

Divorce

The rate of divorce in the United States has increased by a factor of ten over this century (Furstenberg, 1990). Part of this family instability reflects a change in the economic basis of marriage. Lower fertility and the decreased value of domestic labor have made participation in the labor force more attractive to women, which in turn has increased women's relative power in the family and their independence. At the same time, the contractual basis of marriage has shifted. Emotional gratification, companionship, and intimacy are now the criteria by which the quality of marriages is judged, rather than the adequacy with which men fulfill the breadwinner role and women fulfill the housekeeper/ parent role.

The increased propensity to divorce, although it probably stems from the same general sources, plays out differently across subcultural groups (Sweet & Bumpass, 1987, Table 5.3). For instance, in 1980 over half (53%) of the first marriages of African American women disrupted within the first ten years. Native Americans (48%), Puerto Rican Americans (46%), and Hawaiian Americans (39%) also had high disruption rates. The lowest disruption rates were for Chinese Americans (14%), Japanese Americans (22%), Korean Americans (22%), and East Asian Indian Americans (7%). The rate in anglo women fell in the middle of this distribution, at 37%.

Whether partners who separate proceed to divorce also varies across subcultures. Divorce within a year follows three fifths of all separations. However, within 2 years after separation, only 42% of African Americans have legally divorced, as compared to 84% of anglos (Sweet & Bumpass, 1987, p. 205). Education is positively related to the probability of divorce after separation in all groups.

Rates of remarriage declined in all groups between 1970 and 1980, although with large ethnic differentials (Sweet & Bumpass, 1987, p. 196). Within 10 years of separation, 72% of anglo women remarried, as compared to 53% of Mexican Americans and 32% of African Americans. Corresponding figures are 82% for anglo men and 55% for African American men. Not remarrying is the modal pattern for separated African American women.

Children

Prior to this century, the United States was largely agrarian, and children were viewed economic assets who could help maintain the family farm and who could provide a form of old-age insurance for parents. In this century, children have become economic liabilities, valued mainly as sources of emotional gratification. Both the labor market changes and the increased survival rate of children over this century would predict a decrease in family size. However, only in the latter half of this century, as fertility control has become more efficient and more available, have all segments of the population begun to limit family size severely.

The decline in children's economic value that has prompted a decrease in family size over this century has produced some subtle ripple effects. As Blake (1989) points out, variance in family size has also begun to fall. This "sibsize transition" has profound implications for children's well-being. For example, if 80% of families in a society have one child, and only 20% of families have 6 children, average family size would be 2, but 60% of the children in this society would come from the large 6-child families. The paradox is that even a small percentage of large families in a society leads to a majority of individuals coming from large families.

Large family size tends to dilute socialization resources, whereas small size tends to concentrate resources. Children raised in smaller families are more likely to stay in school and do well in school, as compared to their counterparts from large families (Blake, 1989). Therefore, the availability of improved contraceptive procedures to *all* segments of the population has a net positive effect on upward mobility.

In 1980, Mexican American and African American families had relatively high fertility rates (4.5 and 3.8, respectively). Asian Americans, except for Vietnamese Americans, typically had the lowest rate (see Table 7.1). Because African Americans and Hispanic Americans form the largest percentages of the total nonanglo population—now about 15% and 12%—their relatively large

TABLE 7.1. Fertility Measures for Racial and Hispanic Groups, 1980

Group	Children Ever Born per Woman, Age 40–49*
NonHispanic anglo American	3.01
African American	3.83
Native American	4.13
Japanese American	2.20
Chinese American	2.82
Filipino American	3.03
Korean American	2.42
East Asian Indian American	2.72
Vietnamese American	4.62
Hawaiian American	4.09
Mexican American	4.46
Puerto Rican American	3.59
Cuban American	2.18

* First married by age 40.
Source: American Families and Households, by James A. Sweet and Larry A. Bumpass, © 1987, The Russell Sage Foundation. Used with permission of the Russell Sage Foundation.

family sizes will lead to a *majority* of the total population in the middle of the next century being persons who are now members of minority groups.

Birth data for 1985 and 1987 (Table 7.2) document the severity of risk factors present at birth for African Americans and Puerto Rican Americans. Low birth weight (LBW) is more common in African Americans (13%) and Puerto Rican Americans (9%) than in anglo Americans (under 6%). African Americans and Puerto Rican Americans also have the highest rates of births to unmarried and/ or teenaged girls, who in turn, are the mothers least likely to seek adequate prenatal care.

Maternal Employment

Labor force participation of mothers also varies by ethnicity. In 1980, employ-ment rates of African American mothers were higher than those of anglo mothers (Sweet & Bumpass, 1987, p.151), with the largest differential for mothers with preschool children. Considering only the mothers of children under age 3 in 1980, 53% of African Americans were employed, as compared to 35% of anglos and 34% of Mexican Americans (Sweet & Bumpass, Table 4.12). These differentials in maternal employment persist. In 1989, even for women with husbands present, almost 72% of African American mothers of children under age 6 were in the labor force, as compared to about 58% of anglo mothers (United States Department of Commerce, 1991, Table 643).

The African American versus the anglo American differential in maternal employment rates persists, even when allowing for the effects of education and husband's income (Sweet & Bumpass, 1987, p. 155). It could be related to

TABLE 7.2.   Live Births—Selected Characteristics: 1985 and 1988

Race and Hispanic origin	Births to Teenage Mothers (Percentage of Total)		Births to Unmarried Mothers (Percentage of Total)		Percentage of Births with Low Birth Weight (LBW)	
	1985	1988	1985	1988	1985	1988
Total	12.7	12.5	22.0	25.7	6.8	6.9
Anglo American	10.8	10.5	14.5	17.7	5.6	5.6
African American	23.0	22.7	60.1	63.5	12.4	13.0
Native American, Eskimo American, Aleutian American	19.1	18.4	40.7	(NA)	5.9	6.1
Asian and Pacific Islander	5.5	5.7	10.1	(NA)	6.1	6.3
Filipino American	5.8	6.2	12.1	(NA)	6.9	7.1
Chinese American	1.1	1.1	3.7	(NA)	5.0	4.7
Japanese American	2.9	2.8	7.9	(NA)	5.9	6.2
Hawaiian American	15.9	15.4	(NA)	(NA)	6.4	6.8
Hispanic origin	16.5	16.4	29.5	34.0	6.2	6.2
Mexican American	17.5	17.3	25.7	30.6	5.8	5.6
Puerto Rican American	20.9	21.4	51.1	53.3	8.7	9.4
Cuban American	7.1	6.1	16.1	16.3	6.0	5.9
Central and South American	8.2	8.1	34.9	36.4	5.7	5.7

Source: Adapted from Table 89, *Statistical Abstract of the United States,* United States Department of Commerce, 1991. (Represents registered births. Excludes births to nonresidents of the United States. Data are available on race of mother from all states, but data on Hispanic origin of mother are available from only 23 states and the District of Columbia. However, approximately 90% of all births to Hispanic American mothers occur to residents of these 23 states.)

family structure and child-rearing customs in the African American community. Among African American poor persons, for example, extended families are common and child-care tasks are often shared (Stack, 1974). The mother's ability to procure adequate child care could encourage her participation in the labor force. The breakup rate in African American marriages is also higher than that for anglos, and the possibility of marital breakup could persuade women not to relinquish employment. Overall, the high employment rate for African American mothers of young children is probably a consequence of the persistent low economic standing of African Americans, cultural customs, and perhaps the less pronounced gender distinctions between the provider and homemaker roles in African American families.

Single Parenting

Similar percentages of anglo American (3.0%), Hispanic American (2.9%) and African American (3.5%) children in single-parent families lived with their fathers in 1990 (See Table 7.3). The proportion of children living with single fathers almost doubled between 1980 and 1990 (United States Bureau of the Census, 1991, p. 4), but most children in a one-parent situation in 1990 still lived with their mothers. About 8% of all father–child families involved a never-married father in 1980, primarily children living with a cohabiting partner, who often is the mother of the child (Sweet & Bumpass, 1987, p. 271). Generally, fathers who are solo parents are more involved with older children. Over 17% of anglo children in one-parent families who lived with their fathers in 1980 were age 15 to 17 years, as compared to about 9% of those age 1 to 2 years (Sweet & Bumpass, Table 7.4).

A major racial/ethnic variation in one-parent families involves persons who never married. About one third of mothers among African Americans are single, as compared to 6% among anglos, and 16% among Mexican Americans (Sweet & Bumpass, 1987, p. 270).

Data for various ethnic groups on the distribution of children across family types (in 1980) show that for most Asian American children, living with two parents was more common than for anglos (Table 7.4). African Americans (46%), Puerto Rican Americans (59%), and Native Americans (63%) had the lowest rates of children living with two parents. For African Americans, Vietnamese Americans, and Native Americans, as many as 10% of children lived with neither parent in 1980. According to Stack (1974), in African American commu-

TABLE 7.3. **Distribution of Children by Parental Status and Race/Ethnicity of Child, 1960–1990**

		One Parent			
	Two Parents	Mother Only	Father Only	Other Relatives	Nonrelatives
Anglo American					
1990	79.0	16.2	3.0	1.4	0.4
1980	82.7	13.5	1.6	1.7	0.5
1970	89.5	7.8	0.9	1.2	0.6
1960	90.9	6.1	1.0	1.4	0.5
African American					
1990	37.7	51.2	3.5	6.5	1.0
1980	42.2	43.9	1.9	10.7	1.3
1970	58.5	29.5	2.3	8.7	1.0
1960	67.0	19.9	2.0	9.6	1.5
Hispanic American					
1990	66.8	27.1	2.9	2.5	0.8
1980	75.4	19.6	1.5	3.4	0.1
1970	77.7	(NA)	(NA)	(NA)	(NA)
1960	(NA)	(NA)	(NA)	(NA)	(NA)

Source: United States Bureau of the Census, Current Population Reports, Series P–20, No. 450, *Marital Status and Living Arrangements:* March 1990, U.S. Government Printing Office, Washington, DC, 1991.

TABLE 7.4.   Percent Distribution of Children by Family Status, 1980 and 1990

	Two Parents	Cohabiting Parent	Single Parent		Neither Parent
			Mother	Father	
1980					
NonHispanic Anglo	83.8	1.3	10.8	1.5	2.5
African American	46.0	2.9	39.0	2.2	9.9
Japanese American	87.6	0.9	7.6	1.3	2.6
Chinese American	88.6	0.3	6.0	1.5	3.6
Filipino American	84.9	0.9	8.8	1.6	3.8
Native American	63.4	3.1	20.8	2.6	10.0
Korean American	90.4	0.6	5.7	1.3	2.0
Vietnamese				2.8	
American	74.3	1.1	9.6		12.2
Asian Indian				1.0	
American	93.4	0.3	3.0		2.4
Hawaiian American	68.1	3.8	19.0	2.1	7.0
Mexican American	77.5	1.4	14.6	1.8	4.6
Puerto Rican				1.7	
American	59.4	2.6	31.8		4.4
Cuban American	81.4	0.9	12.6	1.2	3.9
1990					
African American	37.7	(NA)	51.2	3.5	7.5
Hispanic American	66.8	(NA)	27.1	2.9	3.3
Anglo American	79.0	(NA)	16.2	3.0	1.8

Source: Data for 1990 are from United States Bureau of the Census, *Marital Status and Living Arrangements, March 1990*, Current population reports, Population characteristics series P–20, No.450, U.S. Government Printing Office, Washington, DC, 1991. Data for 1980 are taken from *American Families and Households*, by James A. Sweet and Larry L. Bumpass, © 1987, The Russell Sage Foundation. Used with permission of the Russell Sage Foundation.

nities, the grandmother or another relative will assume permanent responsibility for rearing a child if the mother is deemed to be inadequate. However, African American children are three times as likely as anglo children to be in foster care because of neglect, and are more likely to remain in foster care for long periods (Taylor et al., 1991).

What about "extended" family patterns? Overall, in 1980, relatives in households other than parents were relatively few (12%). A major exception is in one-parent families, where the number was substantial (40%), if there was a child under 3 years (Sweet & Bumpass, 1987, p. 280). Grandparents were in the household in about half the families that included relatives other than parents. African American children were more likely to live in a household with other relatives than were anglos (27% compared to 8%) or Mexican Americans (19%) (Sweet & Bumpass, p. 280). Even when income is controlled, extended family arrangements are twice as common among African Americans as among anglos (Farley & Allen, 1987).

Three-generation families decreased a little over the past decade—6% of all children lived in a household with a grandparent in 1980, as compared to 5%

in 1990 (United States Bureau of the Census, 1991, p. 9). Often only the mother is present when children live with grandparents (50% in 1990 versus 40% in 1980), but extended family patterns differ by subculture. For children living in grandparents' homes in 1990, 21% of anglos, 3% of African Americans, and 18% of Hispanic Americans had two parents also present; whereas 38% of African Americans, 25% of anglos, and 21% of Hispanic Americans had *neither* parent present.

Single-parent families seem to carry over from one generation to the next (McLanahan & Booth, 1991)—women who spend part of their childhoods in one-parent families are more likely to marry and bear children early, experience a premarital birth, and to have a marriage disrupt. African Americans are an exception to this pattern because early marriage is independent of family background. Parental role models and parental monitoring of adolescent behavior seem to be the primary causes of these intergenerational patterns, not the economic deficit or the added stress associated with living in single-parent families.

Socioeconomic Status

The *1990 March Supplement to the Current Population Survey* shows that children's poverty is getting worse and that ethnic disparities in poverty are becoming more pronounced. The number of poor children under age 6 has risen dramatically since 1980, from about 4 to 5.1 million, over 25%. In 1989, rates for children under age 6 in poverty were highest for African Americans (50%), next highest for Hispanic Americans (40%), and other minorities (24%), all much higher than for anglos (14%). (See Figure 7.1).

Women's earning power is increasing, but it still is only about two thirds that of men's (Sorenson, 1991). Sex differences in wages produce some of the economic disadvantage for children living with their mothers only. Moreover, patterns of fertility, divorce, and remarriage generate a concentration of one-parent families with low education levels. In African American families, for example, almost 48% of single mothers are high school drop-outs, as compared to 34% of mothers in two-parent families (Sweet & Bumpass, 1987, Table 7.14). Most disturbing is the incidence of *persistent* poverty among African American children. Almost 90% of children who were consistently poor in 10 years of a 15-year period were African American (see Taylor et al., 1991 for citations).

Family type, ethnicity, and poverty definitely cluster together (see Table 7.5). Jaynes and Williams (1989) point to the substantial regularities between familial behaviors and socioeconomic conditions. For example, birth rates for unmarried mothers are higher for those of low socioeconomic status (SES). African Americans consistently lag behind other groups in terms of income and job security, and Jaynes and Williams attribute many of the differences in African American/ anglo American family structure to the precarious economic state of African Americans. This causal link is suggested more by income comparisons than by educational background comparisons, because income differences explain much of the African American versus anglo American differences in men's marital

Figure 7.1. Poverty rates for children under six, by race/ethnicity, 1989. (Adapted from National Center on Poverty, Figure 5, *Five Million Children: 1991 Update*. New York: Columbia University.)

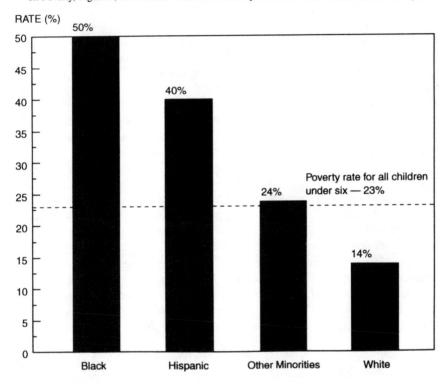

TABLE 7.5. **Poverty Status of Children by Family Status and Race/Ethnicity, 1980**

	Total		NonHispanic Anglo		African American		Mexican American	
	Poor	Adequate*	Poor	Adequate*	Poor	Adequate*	Poor	Adequate*
Two-parent	9.0	70.1	6.7	74.8	18.4	51.2	20.5	46.8
Cohabiting parent	17.9	53.3	12.4	62.1	27.2	40.4	19.8	44.8
Mother only	46.8	24.9	33.9	34.5	59.1	14.8	53.8	18.5
Father only	17.7	59.8	10.9	70.2	32.6	37.3	27.4	41.6
Neither	27.9	43.3	15.6	58.0	41.5	27.6	27.9	38.1
Total	20.7	61.5	10.0	69.8	37.1	34.1	25.9	42.2

* Adequate = family income at least twice the poverty standard.
Source: From *American Families and Households,* by James A. Sweet and Larry L. Bumpass, © 1987, The Russell Sage Foundation. Used with permission of the Russell Sage Foundation.

status, whereas years of schooling do not (see Jaynes and Williams, p. 529). This difference in explanatory power may stem from the fact that *years* of schooling fails to capture the profound differences in *quality* of schooling historically available to African Americans and anglos.

Eggebeen and Lichter (1991) estimate that child poverty rates would have been about one third less in 1988 if family structure had not changed since 1960. They note that in 1980, 10% of anglo children lived in poverty, as compared to 37% of African Americans and 26% of Mexican Americans. These percentages varied widely by family type, because almost 47% of all children in mother-only families were poor, as compared to only 9% of children in two-parent families. Even so, the poverty rate for African Americans and Mexican Americans was about triple the rate for anglos. By 1988, two thirds of African American one-parent families fell below official poverty thresholds, a rate 300% higher than that for African American two-parent families (67.6% vs. 17.0%). Eggebeen and Lichter found little evidence that racial differences in child poverty rates are linked to parental labor force participation. Rather, wage differences and other factors play a larger role in the relative economic well-being of African American children than that of anglo children.

Laosa (1988) also points to the sizeable income differences across ethnic groups when family type is held constant. Among Asian American single mothers with children *or* married couple families, annual incomes in 1979 were generally almost twice those for Puerto Rican Americans. He notes that neither the size of the sex differential in earning capacity nor the ability of single mothers to cope is the same across subcultural groups.

Irrespective of ethnicity, however, children who live with only one parent are comparatively disadvantaged. The National Commission on Children's (1991) national sample of African American, Hispanic American, and non-African American, non-Hispanic American families found the financial and emotional aspects of daily life were more difficult for single parents than for parents in intact families: ". . . 23% of single-parent households reported [incomes] under $10,000 a year compared to 2% in intact families and 6% in stepfamilies . . ." (p. 20). Single parents were also less likely "to consider their neighborhoods excellent or good places to raise children. . . .", and were generally two or three times as likely "to worry that their teenage children will be physically attacked, will become involved in selling drugs, will become pregnant or get a girl pregnant, will drop out of school, or will not be able to find a good job upon completing school" (p. 21).

Family Structure Change

Moynihan's (1965) hypothesis that slavery is a root cause of the flux in family structure of African Americans has faded from view. For one thing, it is difficult to reconcile Moynihan's hypothesis with the fact that single parenting among contemporary African Americans is not much higher than it is among groups who did not experience slavery, such as the Irish Americans of an earlier era, or the Puerto Rican Americans of today (Laosa, 1988). Also, the length of time elapsed between slavery, which ended in the 19th century, and the rise of single parenting in the latter half of the 20th century makes it hard to connect slavery with single parenting.

Social demographers are now explaining changes in family structure in several different ways. Some see the family as "here to stay" (Bane, 1976). The loss of a parent through death, common early in this century and in prior centuries, parallels the loss of a parent by divorce that is so common now. According to this view, divorce has replaced death as a mechanism for changing family structure and, in that sense, the family as an institution is no more unstable now than it was in earlier times.

Other demographers emphasize the changing economic trends that have prompted women to seek paid employment, which in turn makes them more independent and less content with traditional gender roles (Cherlin, 1992). Women with independent means are free to exit an unsatisfactory marriage. From this perspective, it is not that marriage itself is losing its attractiveness, but that economic resources enable people to move more readily from one marriage into another.

In a somewhat different vein, Sweet and Bumpass (1987) suggest that the institution of the family is not as sturdy as it was formerly, because family roles are increasingly less attractive when compared with other roles. Individuals now put self-fulfillment and emotional satisfaction first on their lists of values. Sweet and Bumpass believe family relationships will continue to be important for all Americans, but they think that family roles will compete less successfully with other adult roles in the foreseeable future.

Subcultural patterns also provide some insight into reasons for changes in family structure, because cultural traditions contribute to the imperfect correlation between marital stability and income across ethnic groups (Laosa, 1988). (See Table 7.6.) Chinese Americans have high incomes and a low incidence of single parenting; Japanese Americans have even higher incomes than Chinese Americans; however, single parenting is about twice as common in Japanese Americans as it is in Chinese Americans. Chinese Americans consider divorce a great shame and a family tragedy, and this may explain their lower divorce rate. Similarly, African American rates of single parenting are higher than Puerto Rican American rates, although Puerto Rican Americans are poorer. Puerto Rican Americans are likely to trace their heritage to Roman Catholic traditions, however, which militate against both divorce and out-of-wedlock births.

Religious differences in marital disruption often are not examined, although differences in divorce rates across religious groups in the United States are huge. Rates for Protestants are two to three times those for Jews, with Roman Catholics being intermediate (Cherlin & Celebuski, 1983). Differences in the likelihood of divorce by religious affiliation oppose strong trends in other characteristics positively associated with divorce, such as levels of income or education. Even after controlling for education and other critical variables, Cherlin and

TABLE 7.6.   Relationship Between Incidence of Single Parenting and Economic
Well-Being of Selected U.S. Ethnic and Racial Groups: 1980

Group	Percentage A*	Percentage B**	Per Capita Income† ($)	Median Income of All Families† ($)
Chinese American	6.5	8.2	7,476	22,559
Korean American	9.7	11.2	5,544	20,459
Filipino American	10.0	11.9	6,915	23,687
Japanese American	12.0	13.6	9,068	27,354
Total Anglo American	12.2	14.4	7,808	20,835
Irish American	12.2	14.6	8,534	20,719
Vietnamese American	13.8	18.5	3,382	12,840
Puerto Rican American‡	39.3	42.6	3,905	10,734
Total African American	41.8	45.8	4,545	12,598

* Percentage of families with own children under 18 years, headed by a woman with no
husband present.
** Percentage of families with own children under 18 years, headed by either a man or a
woman with no spouse present.
† Annual income 1979.
‡ Mainland.
Source: U.S. Bureau of the Census (1983). *1980 Census of the Population. General social
and economic characteristics: United States Summary* (PC 80-1-C1). Washington, DC:
U.S. Government Printing Office.

Celebuski reported that much of the Jewish/Protestant difference in divorce
rates remains.

These subcultural values and customs, which seem to be such strong determinants of family stability, merit further investigation. Because the United States
Bureau of the Census cannot elicit data on religious affiliation, other data must
be found to evaluate this important source of structural variation in families. More
generally, comparative research on subcultural differences in family structure is
needed that controls for socioeconomic status and related factors.

FUNCTIONING

Family differences across boundaries of national origin and social class seem
to be smaller now than in the past, but cultural traditions continue to affect
family life (Cherlin & Furstenberg, 1986). Undoubtedly, the greatest differences
in how U.S. families function are those produced by the kinds of structural
variation reviewed earlier in this chapter; however, single parenting is associated
with poor outcomes for children across all racial and ethnic groups. These
outcomes include lower educational attainment, greater numbers of drop-outs,
more adult poverty, more welfare dependence as adults, a greater likelihood of

out-of-wedlock births, a higher propensity to divorce, a higher delinquency rate, and more drug and alcohol use (McLanahan & Booth, 1991). Drop-out rates for youngsters from one-parent families are about 6% higher than those from two-parent families in the High School and Beyond (HSB) data used by Coleman (1989). Using the same HSB data, Mulkey, Crain, and Harrington (1992) find that achievement differences between one- and two-parent families are explained by child behaviors—absenteeism, neglecting homework, and frequent dating.

There is evidence that parenting problems start early. Adolescent mothers provide low levels of verbal stimulation for their infants, and the youngest teens underestimate infant needs and abilities (Lamb & Ketterlinus, 1990). Adolescents do not differ from older mothers in the depth of their feelings about and their love of their infants, but they may not react to the stresses of parenthood as capably as do older mothers, especially as their offspring continue to develop (Bolton & Belsky, 1986). At the same time, there is no evidence that adolescent mothers are more likely to abuse or neglect their babies.

Expectations children have for the future could explain some ethnic differences in family structures. Among girls who later become single mothers, more African Americans than anglo youngsters expect to become parents before marriage (Wilson & Neckerman, 1989). Along similar lines, McLanahan and Booth (1991) report that African American adolescents from mother-only families and African American, anglo American, and Hispanic American adolescents from remarried families are more likely to consider having a child out of wedlock than are adolescents from two-parent families.

Recently, the long-term picture for single mothers has come under closer scrutiny. In part, this effort springs from our desire to discover why some single mothers do so much better than others. There actually is enormous variation in how women who bear children out of wedlock fare over the long run, even within a single ethnic group. Of African American adolescents who became teen-aged mothers, for example, Furstenberg, Brooks-Gunn, and Morgan (1987) found that about 25% were financially secure within 20 years, with better outcomes related to stable marriages and postponing the births of additional children. Also, many of those mothers who were successful returned to school after dropping out. Others who were less successful and had long spells on welfare had additional children soon after the first and did not return to school.

In respect to single parenting, the image of African American families as having strong supportive kinship networks is strong. Stack (1974) and Kellam et al. (1975), who studied poor African American families in and around Chicago, found extensive resource and child-care responsibility sharing. Stack states: "Within a network of cooperating kinsmen, there may be three or more adults with whom, in turn, a child resides. . . . From the point of view of the children, there may be a number of women who act as 'mothers' toward them" (p. 63). Mexican Americans also tend to have large kinship networks, with much visiting and exchange (Keefe, 1984), but for them, such networks seem to meet social/emotional needs more than instrumental needs (Mindel, 1980).

However, extensive kinship networks may not be as universal or as supportive as was formerly believed. Even by 1980, African American household size was declining, and young women bearing children out of wedlock were increasingly forming their own households (Staples & Mirande, 1989). Gauden and Davis (1985) report that rural African American family networks included *fewer* persons to call upon for help in times of need than did the networks of rural anglos. Likewise, Cross (1990) found the social networks of African American families, defined as people who "really make a difference" in terms of daily activities, parenting needs, practical exchanges, and emotional support, were smaller than those of anglos, for both one- and two-parent families. These more recent studies take a comparative cross-group perspective, which often was lacking in earlier research.

The stereotypic image of Hispanic American families as extended and more stable than non-Hispanic American families is also being challenged (Bean & Tienda, 1987). Just as in other groups, differences in Hispanic American family structure are linked to economic conditions. Gender roles in Hispanic American families are often characterized as having a "machismo" cultural motif, with a lower rate of women's employment outside the home (Vega, 1991). Yet whether or not women work outside the home seems to be determined primarily by availability of employment, rather than by gender role standards. Immigration matters, too. For example, migrants from Puerto Rico are more likely to experience marital disruption than nonmigrants (Muschken & Myers, 1989). Mexican Americans who are legal residents tend to live in households with a parent, whereas illegal residents are likely to reside with brothers, sisters, and/or cousins (Chavez, 1985, 1988).

Several recent studies suggest that gender distinctions in the provider and homemaker roles are not as rigid in African American families as they are in anglo families (see Taylor et al., 1991, for citations). African Americans have more egalitarian roles in household labor even when the wife's employment status and relative earning power are taken into account. Nevertheless, as in other groups, African American women still perform the majority of household chores.

Marital disruption tends to strengthen maternal family ties all along the line (Cherlin & Furstenberg, 1986). Because disruption is higher and remarriage is less likely among African Americans than anglos, we could expect stronger matriarchal patterns in African American families, apart from any differences in culture or values. Unwed motherhood also tends to reinforce matriarchal patterns in African American families because African American adolescent mothers are younger and poorer than anglo adolescent mothers. For these reasons, they are more likely to continue to live with their families of origin.

With the exception of African Americans, there seems to be little difference according to religion or national origin in the behavior of grandparents. Judging from their national sample, Cherlin and Furstenberg (1986) say about grandparents: "Neither the Poles nor the Jews could violate the norm of noninterference except under special circumstances, such as a divorce. . . . The ritual occasions in which their families gathered varied . . . but on a day-to-day level, their relationships with their grandchildren seemed similar" (p. 135). In contrast, African American grandparents seemed much more heavily involved in day-to-day activities and much more likely to take a parenting role with their grandchildren. Cherlin and Furstenberg report that a large majority (87%) of African American grandparents said they corrected their grandchildren's behavior "often" or "sometimes," as compared to only 43% of anglos. Similarly, 71% of African Americans, as compared to 38% of anglos, had disciplined their grandchild in the past year. This kind of involvement, according to Cherlin and Furstenberg, is born of distress. It reflects the facts of African American family life, from a high incidence of unwed parenthood through higher mortality and incarceration rates in African American males. One indicator of the severity of these family stresses is that 44% of the surveyed African American grandparents had lived with their grandchildren for at least 3 months, as compared to 18% of the anglo grandparents.

The limited research on the effects of African American extended families on child development has focused mainly on the grandmother's presence for children of adolescent mothers (Wilson, 1989), but some work has emerged on African American family types in relation to schooling. Thompson, Entwisle, Alexander, and Sundius (1992) found that children from two-parent African American or anglo families improved their school conduct over the course of the first grade more than did children in single-parent families. African American children who lived with their mothers and extended family also improved more than their counterparts living with their mothers only.

Family Formation

The earlier literature on the transition to parenthood focused on married pairs, and dealt mainly with anglo families (See Entwisle & Doering, 1981, for a review). Recent research on family formation focuses more on single mothers and their children.

In 1987, over 62% of African American births, 33% of Hispanic American births, and close to 17% of anglo American births were to unmarried women. Out-of-wedlock births are now the modal pattern for both African American and Puerto Rican American (51%) mothers (United States Department of Commerce, 1990, Table 87). Little is known about fathers of out-of-wedlock children, but in families with teenage mothers, African American fathers are more likely to be involved in parenting than are anglo fathers (Danziger & Radin, 1990), although they are less likely to live with the child (Marsiglio, 1987).

African American children are said to be less likely than anglos to experience the detrimental effects of being raised by a single parent (Hetherington, Camara, & Featherman, 1983). Part of this advantage may come from the more effective coping mechanisms of African American, as compared to anglo teenage mothers (Thompson, 1986). Another part may also be that the children share living quarters with extended kin, as suggested above. Furstenberg and Crawford (1978) found that never-married women who lived with their parents were more likely to return to school and graduate, more likely to be employed, and less likely to be on welfare than were those who left their parents' homes. The present day pattern among many single women who choose to become a parent, not to marry the father, and to remain in the community during pregnancy, is well institutionalized among poor African Americans. There is not the demand for abortion or adoption found in more privileged groups, perhaps because opportunities for upward mobility among African Americans are very limited, in any case.

Exactly how a male partner affects the emotional climate of the family is not clear. Some studies (Colletta, 1981; Crockenberg, 1987; Unger & Wandersman, 1988) suggest that teen mothers with good male partner support are less rejecting and punitive with their children. Other studies find husbands and boyfriends to be a primary source of stress for teenage mothers (Garcia-Coll, Hoffman, & Oh, 1987), whereas others show the presence of the child's father in the home makes little difference for the mother's adaptation to parenthood (Furstenberg, 1976). For married, anglo working-class mothers, husband involvement in child care did not affect the woman's role evaluation of herself as a mother in the first few weeks after delivery. One year later, however, it had a negative effect: the more the husband participated in child care, the lower the woman's sense of maternal competence (Reilly, Entwisle, & Doering, 1987).

There is "color-blindness" in research on how fathers interact with young children, and little is known about how the transition to parenthood varies across subcultures (Berman & Pedersen, 1987). Research on adolescent fathers is especially limited because most teen programs are geared toward pregnant females or mothers. There is some suggestion that the African American community expects teenage fathers to help care for children, even if they remain single. Research on anglo teenage fathers is almost nonexistent.

Child Socialization

Decade by decade, the focus of research on how families of different subcultural groups socialize their children has changed. In the 1950's, the "culture and personality" approach to child socialization emphasized personality and value differences across ethnic groups. Beginning in the 1960s, the relatively poor school performance of working-class anglo children or African American children was attributed to lower-class language codes or to ethnic (black) dialects that, supposedly, did not provide adequate stimulation for children's cognitive growth. Another prominent theme of the 1960s was the "world view" of African Americans or other minority groups—trusting to luck or fate—thought to undermine a child's sense of personal control.

In the 1970s, the notion of "deficits" in school performance of minority group children fell into disfavor because it became increasingly clear that social structure, not language structure, could explain deficits in school performance. To cite a compelling example, Lambert and Tucker (1972) tracked the performance of middle-class English-speaking Montreal children enrolled in schools where instruction was conducted entirely in French, from kindergarten on up. By the fourth grade, French language competence, listening comprehension, and vocabulary of these English background Montreal children equaled that of monolingually instructed French children in similar schools. Only the French speaking skills of the English children were somewhat less. In addition, the arithmetic and English language competence of these English-speaking children, as measured on standardized tests, equaled that of other Anglophone children who had been schooled entirely in English. If receiving all instruction in a "foreign language" does not depress children's academic progress, as the Montreal experiments suggest, it is hard to see how dialect differences or other relatively minor structural language differences such as those among U.S. black dialects could explain the shortfalls in the school achievement of minority group children.

Recent research on cultural differences and children's schooling has taken off in a new direction. One study (Lee, Ichikawa, & Stevenson, 1987), which documents the superior school performance of Japanese and Chinese children in reading and math, as compared to U. S. children, attributes much of the advantage to Asian parents' beliefs that effort, not ability, produces superior school achievement. American parents tend to believe that ability, which is assumed to be fixed, is the main cause of good achievement.

Implicit developmental theories that parents hold vary somewhat across national boundaries. In Japan and the United States, when mothers of various socioeconomic levels reported on their "developmental timetables," Japanese mothers expected children to control their emotional behavior (crying, temper tantrums) and to be polite and obedient earlier in life than American mothers (Hess, Kashigawa, Azuma, Price, & Dickson, 1980). In both countries, higher SES mothers expected earlier development of cognitive skills than did lower SES mothers. Similar studies compared Australian mothers with Lebanese mothers (Goodnow, Cashmore, Cotton, & Knight, 1984) and Israeli mothers of European and Asian-African origin (Ninio, 1979).

Whether there are reliable differences in child-rearing patterns across subcultural groups *within* the United States when socioeconomic or family structure differences are controlled is still an open question. Non-Hispanic anglo mothers have been found to read more to their children and to have higher aspirations for their children than Hispanic American mothers, but these differences can be explained by the higher levels of schooling among the anglos (Jaramillo & Zapata, 1987; Laosa, 1982).

Values

The socialization messages that parents give their children reflect ethnic values and goals, as well as social status of the family. About two thirds of African American families convey explicit racial messages to their children (Taylor et al., 1991). These messages, which are more likely to be forthcoming if families live in mixed-race areas, caution male adolescents about racial barriers, whereas the emphasis for females is on racial pride. Harrison, Serafica, and McAdoo (1984) also see bicultural adaptation as the central and overriding goal of African American families, both urban and rural. They note that African American parent–child interactions involve contests between mother and child that teach children how authority figures set limits. This framework can also explain why low SES African American families apply strict, arbitrary rules; demand mature, independent behavior; and choose the most intense punishments for their children.

Status is strictly observed within Japanese American families. Children are expected to obey and respect their parents, and to have a deferential manner. Recent generations of Japanese Americans are less bound by custom than their forbears, but they continue to raise children according to traditional Japanese values that reflect the Confucian concepts of collectivity, order, and hierarchy (Harrison et al., 1984). These families begin by indulging the child; infants are carried and cuddled a great deal. Once children pass a certain age, however, immature behaviors are swiftly punished, usually by the father. The Chinese also indulge their young children, but they expect their older children to assume household duties and behave well because their actions reflect on the entire family.

Traditional Asian cultures generally stress the importance of the family at the expense of the individual (Staples & Mirande, 1989). The traditional value placed on the social collectivity leads parents to punish children for boastful, aggressive, or selfish behaviors (Harrison et al., 1984). Both Chinese and Japanese families frown upon overt expressions of affection, aggression, or assertion, probably because such restraint helps to maintain group organization and cohesion. Achievement is highly valued because it brings honor to the clan.

As noted earlier, religion is a strong determinant of subculture values, but rarely is it taken into account in family research. Cherlin and Celebuski (1983) point out that Jewish parents have fewer children than other parents, which allows these parents to invest heavily in their children's education. Moreover, because Jewish parents encourage autonomy and self-direction for their children, Cherlin and Celebuski believe that Jewish children are prepared for the more prestigious occupations in our society. Earlier studies (Rosen, 1959; Strodtbeck, 1958) comparing Italian American and Jewish American families in New Haven are consistent with these ideas, because Jewish parents were observed to encourage independence in their 6- to 8-year-old sons more than Italian (Roman Catholic) parents did.

Future Trends

Much more research is needed on how subculture differences in family structure and family functioning affect child outcomes. At present, descriptive information on family structure far exceeds the number of rigorous studies required to explain family structural changes fully.

We especially need broad-based studies that examine subculture differences in family structure, with SES taken into account. Family structure helps shape family values and world views, but the structure also responds to social perceptions and ethnic beliefs within the family. The increasing collaboration among family research specialists, spanning the fields of psychology, sociology, demography, and economics is encouraging (see *Developmental Psychology*, 1991, Vol. 27, No. 26). Furthermore, the life course perspective, which emphasizes the dialectic between the structure and function of the family as well as effects on the family of the society in which it is embedded, is opening up new avenues of research. Comparative research across subcultures offers an additional strategy that should lead to a deeper understanding of family change.

REFERENCES

Bane, M. J. (1976). *Here to stay: American families in the twentieth century.* New York: Basic Books.

Bean, F., & Tienda, M. (1987). *The Hispanic population of the United States.* New York: Russell Sage.

Berman, P. W., & Pedersen, F. A. (1987). *Men's transition to parenthood.* Hillsdale, NJ: Erlbaum.

Blake, J. (1989). *Family size and achievement.* Berkeley: University of California Press.

Bolton, F. G., & Belsky, J. (1986). The adolescent father and child maltreatment. In A. B. Elster & M. E. Lamb (Eds.), *Adolescent fatherhood* (pp. 122–140). Hillsdale, NJ: Erlbaum.

Bumpass, L. (1984). Some characteristics of children's second families. *American Journal of Sociology, 90,* 608–623.

Chavez, L. (1985). Households, migration, and labor market participation: The adaptation of Mexicans to life in the U.S. *Urban Anthropology, 14,* 301–346.

Chavez, L. (1988). Settlers and sojourners: The case of Mexicans in the U.S. *Human Organization, 47,* 95–108.

Cherlin, A. J. (1992). *Marriage, divorce, remarriage: Revised and enlarged edition.* Cambridge, MA: Harvard University Press.

Cherlin, A. J., & Celebuski, C. (1983). *Are Jewish families different?* New York: American Jewish Committee.

Cherlin, A. J., & Furstenberg, F. F., Jr. (1986). *The new American grandparent: A place in the family, a life apart.* New York: Basic Books.

Coleman, J. S. (1989). Social capital in the creation of human capital. *American Journal of Sociology, 94,* S95–S120.

Colletta, N. O. (1981). Social support and the risk of maternal rejection by adolescent mothers. *Journal of Psychology, 109,* 191–197.

Crockenberg, S. (1987). Predictors and correlates of anger toward and punitive control of toddlers by adolescent mothers. *Child Development, 58,* 964–975.

Cross, W. E. (1990). Race and ethnicity: Effects on social networks. In M. Cochran, M. Larner, D. Riley, L. Gunnarson, & C. R. Henderson (Eds.), *Extending families: The social networks of parents and their children* (pp. 67–85). New York: Cambridge University Press.

Cutright, P. (1978). Income and family events: Family income, family size, and family consumption. *Journal of Marriage and the Family, 33,* 161–173.

Danziger, S. K., & Radin, N. (1990). Absent does not equal uninvolved: Predictors of fathering in teen mother families. *Journal of Marriage and the Family, 52,* 636–642.

Eggebeen, D. J., & Lichter, D. T. (1991). Race, family structure, and changing poverty among American children. *American Sociological Review, 56,* 801–817.

Entwisle, D. R., & Doering, S. G. (1981). *The first birth.* Baltimore: The Johns Hopkins University Press.

Farley, R., & Allen, W. R. (1987). *The color line and the quality of life in America.* New York: Russell Sage.

Furstenberg, F. F. (1990). Divorce and the American family. In W. R. Scott & J. Blake (Eds.), *Annual review of sociology* (pp. 379–403). Stanford, CA: Annual Reviews.

Furstenberg, F. F., Jr. (1976). *Unplanned parenthood.* New York: Free Press.

Furstenberg, F. F., Brooks-Gunn, J., & Morgan, S. P. (1987). *Adolescent mothers in later life.* New York: Cambridge University Press.

Furstenberg, F. F., & Crawford, A. G. (1978). Family support: Helping teenage mothers to cope. *Family Planning Perspectives, 10,* 322–333.

Garcia-Coll, C. T., Hoffman, J., & Oh, W. (1987). The social ecology and early parenting of Caucasian adolescent mothers. *Child Development, 58,* 955–963.

Gaudin, J. M., & Davis, K. B. (1985). Social networks of black and white rural families: A research report. *Journal of Marriage and the Family, 47,* 1015–1021.

Goodnow, J. J., Cashmore, J., Cotton, S., & Knight, R. (1984). Mothers' developmental timetables in two cultural groups. *International Journal of Psychology (Journal International de Psychologie), 19,* 193–205.

Harrison, A., Serafica, F., & McAdoo, H. (1984). Ethnic families of color. In R. D. Parke (Ed.), *Review of child development research, Vol. 7: The family.* Chicago: University of Chicago Press.

Hess, R., Kashigawa, K., Azuma, H., Price, G. G., & Dickson, W. (1980). Maternal expectations for early mastery of developmental tasks and cognitive and social competence of preschool children in Japan and the United States. *International Journal of Psychology (Journal International de Psychologie), 15,* 259–271.

Hetherington, E. M., Camara, K. A., & Featherman, D. L. (1983). Achievement and intellectual functioning of children in one-parent households. In J. Spence (Ed.), *Achievement and achievement motives.* San Francisco: Freeman.

Hofferth, S. L. (1984). Kin network, race, and family structure. *Journal of Marriage and the Family, 46,* 791–806.

Jaramillo, P., & Zapata, J. T. (1987). Roles and alliances within Mexican American and Anglo families. *Journal of Marriage and the Family, 49,* 727–735.

Jaynes, G. D., & Williams, R. M. (1989). *A common destiny: Blacks and American society.* Washington, DC: National Academy Press.

Keefe, S. (1984). Real and ideal extended familism among Mexican Americans and anglo Americans: On the meaning of 'close' family ties. *Human Organization, 43,* 65–70.

Kellam, S. G., Branck, J. D., Agrawal, K. C., & Ensminger, M. (1975). *Mental health and going to school: The Woodlawn program of assessment, early intervention, and evaluation.* Chicago: University of Chicago Press.

Lamb, M. E., & Ketterlinus, R. D. (1990). Adolescent parental behavior. In R. M. Lerner, A. C. Peterson, & J. Brooks-Gunn (Eds.), *The encyclopedia of adolescence* (Vol. 2, pp. 735–738). New York: Garland.

Lambert, E. E., & Tucker, G. R. (1972). *Bilingual education of children: The St. Lambert experiment.* Rowley, MA: Newbury.

Laosa, L. M. (1982). School, occupation, culture, and family: The impact of parental schooling on the parent–child relationship. *Journal of Educational Psychology, 74,* 791–827.

Laosa, L. M. (1988). Ethnicity and single parenting in the United States. In E. M. Hetherington & J. D. Arasteh (Eds.), *Impact of divorce, single parenting, and stepparenting on children* (pp. 23–49). Hillsdale, NJ: Erlbaum.

Lee, S., Ichikawa, V., & Stevenson, H. W. (1987). Beliefs and achievement in mathematics and reading: A cross-national study of Chinese, Japanese, and American children and their mothers. In D. A. Kleiber & M. L. Maher (Eds.), *Advances in motivation and achievement: Enhancing motivation* (Vol. 5, pp. 149–179). Greenwich, CT: JAI.

Marsiglio, W. (1987). Adolescent fathers in the United States: Their initial living arrangements, marital experience, and educational outcomes. *Family Planning Perspectives, 19,* 240–251.

McLanahan, S. S., & Booth, K. (1991). Mother-only families. In A. Booth (Ed.), *Contemporary families: Looking forward, looking back* (pp. 405–428). Minneapolis: National Council on Family Relations.

Mindel, C. H. (1980). Extended familism among urban Mexican-Americans, anglos, and blacks. *Hispanic Journal of Behavioral Sciences, 2,* 21–34.

Moynihan, D. P. (1965). *The Negro family: The case for national action.* Washington, DC: United States Department of Labor.

Mulkey, L. M., Crain, R. L., & Harrington, A. J. C. (1992). One-parent households and achievement: Economic and behavioral explanations of a small effect. *Sociology of Education, 64,* 48–65.

Muschkin, C., & Myers, G. C. (1989). Migration and household family structure: Puerto Ricans in the U.S. *International Migration Review, 23,* 495–501.

Nathanson, C. A. (1991). *Dangerous passage.* Philadelphia: Temple University Press.

National Commission on Children. (1991). *Speaking of kids.* Washington, DC: Author.

Ninio, A. (1979). The naive theory of the infant and other maternal studies in two subgroups in Israel. *Child Development, 50,* 976–980.

Portes, A., & Bach, R. L. (1985). *Latin journey.* Berkeley: University of California Press.

Reilly, T. W., Entwisle, D. R., & Doering, S. G. (1987). Socialization into parenthood: A longitudinal study of the development of self-evaluations. *Journal of Marriage and the Family, 49,* 295–308.

Schoen, R., & Wooldredge, J. (1989). Marriage choices in North Carolina and Virginia, 1969–71 and 1979–81. *Journal of Marriage and the Family, 51,* 465–481.

Sorenson, E. (1991). *Exploring the reasons behind the narrowing gender gap in earnings.* Washington, DC: Urban Institute.

Spanier, G. B., & Glick, P. C. (1980). Mate selection differentials between whites and blacks in the United States. *Social Forces, 58,* 707–725.

Stack, C. B. (1974). *All our kin.* New York: Harper & Row.

Staples, R., & Mirande, A. (1989). Variation in family experience: Racial and cultural variations among American families: A decennial review of the literature on minority families. In A. S. Skolnick & J. H. Skolnick (Eds.), *Family in transition: Rethinking marriage, sexuality, child rearing, and family organization* (6th ed., pp. 480–503). Glenview, IL: Scott, Foresman.

Sweet, J. A., & Bumpass, L. L. (1987). *American families and households.* New York: Russell Sage.

Taylor, R. J., Chatters, L. M., Tucker, M. B., & Lewis, E. (1991). Developments in research of black families: A decade review. In A. Booth (Ed.), *Contemporary families: Looking forward, looking back* (pp. 275–296). Minneapolis: National Council on Family Relations.

Testa, M., Astone, A. M., Krogh, M., & Neckerman, K. M. (1989). Employment and marriage among inner-city fathers. *Annals of the American Academy of Political and Social Science, 501,* 79–91.

Thompson, M. S. (1986). The influence of supportive relations on the psychological well-being of teenage mothers. *Social Forces, 64,* 1006–1024.

Thompson, M. S., Entwisle, D. R., Alexander, K. A., & Sundius, M. J. (1992). The influence of family composition on children's conformity to the student role. *American Educational Research Journal, 29,* 405–424.

Unger, D. G., & Wandersman, L. P. (1988). The relation of family and partner support to the adjustment of adolescent mothers. *Child Development, 59,* 1056–1060.

United States Bureau of the Census. (1990). Current population reports, Population characteristics series P–20, No. 447, *Household and family characteristics: March 1990 and 1989.* Washington DC: U.S. Government Printing Office.

United States Bureau of the Census. (1991). Current population reports, Population characteristics series P–20, No. 450, *Marital status and living arrangements: March 1990.* Washington, DC: U.S. Government Printing Office.

United States Department of Commerce. (1990). *Statistical abstract of the United States.* Washington, DC: Bureau of the Census.

United States Department of Commerce. (1991). *Statistical abstract of the United States.* Washington, DC: Bureau of the Census.

Vega, W. A. (1991). Hispanic families in the 1980s: A decade of research. In A. Booth (Ed.), *Contemporary families: Looking forward, looking back* (pp. 297–306). Minneapolis: National Council on Family Relations.

Wilson, M. N. (1989). Child development in the context of the black extended family. *American Psychologist, 44,* 380–385.

Wilson, W. J., & Neckerman, K. (1989). Poverty and family structure: The widening gap between evidence and public policy issues. In A. S. Skolnick & J. H. Skolnick (Eds.), *Family in transition* (pp. 504–521). Glenview, IL: Scott, Foresman.

Zelditch, M. (1964). Family, marriage, and kinship. In R. E. L. Faris (Ed.), *Handbook of modern sociology* (pp. 680–733). Chicago:Rand McNally.

CHAPTER 8

Occupational Life Cycle and the Family

JAMES CAMPBELL QUICK, JANICE R. JOPLIN, DAVID A. GRAY, and C. EWING COOLEY

Love and work are central themes in some of the most influential theories of psychological well-being. Freud was among the first to argue that healthy psychological functioning required that a person develop the capacity to love and to work (Erikson, 1963). Erikson's own theory of the eight ages of man addresses the themes of love (intimacy versus isolation) and work (industry versus inferiority) as well. Although love and work may be, to some degree, intractable, both aspects of human development seem to be essential. Further- more, theoretical arguments by Maslow (1954) and Rogers (1961), as well as research by Vaillant (1977), support Freud's proposition that both work and love are essential to healthy psychological functioning.

The difficulties in achieving balance and integration between our needs for love and work may well have been exacerbated by the Industrial Revolution. Scott (1967) has argued that a bifurcation developed in our social identities with the advent of the Industrial Revolution, when it became necessary to leave home to "go to work," resulting in a split role identity between the organization and the family environments. Prior to that, especially in agrarian settings, work and home environments were inextricably intertwined. Thus, the natural, yet intractable, competing human needs for work and love create a situation of allocating scarce resources in families in capitalist economies. Piotrkowski's (1979) classic, naturalistic study examines the dilemmas families must resolve to achieve a balance between the need to work for the economic benefit of the family and the need to love and care for the emotional and developmental needs of family members.

The central thesis of this chapter is that balance and integration of the needs for work and love must be achieved. As Lobel states (1991), work and family investments need not necessarily compete with each other. Implicit in this thesis is the notion that the occupational life cycle must be viewed within the larger context of the overall life development, even where the career may be unusually long and gratifying, as was the case with Dr. Otto A. Faust, on whom we

Partial support for development of this chapter comes from a grant to the Center for Research on Managerial and Organization Excellence (CROME) from the Society for Human Resource Management. The authors thank Sharon A. Lobel for her helpful comments on an earlier draft of this chapter.

reported previously (Quick & Quick, 1990). In that case, his occupational career cycle lasted 64 years, from his preparation in medical school through his transitional years of retirement. Moreover, Dr. Faust's complete life cycle spanned nearly 102 years.

If we focus too closely on the occupation or career as a source of need gratification, we risk loosing both perspective and balance with regard to the complementary needs for family and loved ones, which may result in devastating consequences. Moreover, significant health risks are associated with social isolation and loneliness (House, Landis, & Umberson, 1988). We suggest that such risks are especially acute within an industrially and demographically complex, unstable environment, such as ours today. These complexities and dilemmas are illustrated in the case study of the Carry family. (All case studies are based on real cases, although names and specific features have been edited to ensure confidentiality.)

THE CARRY FAMILY

Both Mr. and Mrs. Carry were successful professionals who married after both were well established in their jobs and were ready to begin a family. After their twins were born, Mrs. Carry was required to spend more time on the job because of a reduction in personnel in her office. At first, Mr. Carry was able to take responsibility for many chores at home; however, he was also expected to carry a greater load at work. The conflicts between personal, work, and social demands grew to near crisis proportions.

Mrs. Carry was unable to maintain contact with friends who were important to her before marriage. She had little chance to interact with other women who also were attempting to combine their professional careers with raising a family. No family is close enough to provide sufficient and consistent support. Mrs. Carry began to feel exhausted and increasingly needed medical attention for numerous problems.

Mr. Carry was excited about his new family initially and enjoyed being active in parenting. He was willing to increase his share of responsibility at home when his wife's job began to demand more of her time. When he, too, was expected to spend extra time at his work, problems with time management began. It was very difficult to coordinate schedules. Both Mr. and Mrs. Carry felt unable to commit to a definite schedule. It was often uncertain if either would be available to pick up the twins. The baby-sitter was unable to accept this state of uncertainty because of her own familial commitments.

This couple experienced uncertainty about their priorities both as individuals and as a couple. They were unable to find sufficient time to discuss their problems. More and more of their time was absorbed with coping with the immediate needs of their jobs and the twins. Both were frustrated because they did not have the degree of professional achievement they formerly enjoyed. They were unable to maintain their social and professional networks and had not replaced those contacts with family-centered support systems. Their sense of hopelessness increased when they could not see an end to or a resolution of their problems.

The Carry family experienced a form of family system overload that caused an imbalance in their attempts to meet occupational and family needs.

Throughout this chapter we draw from eight family cases, such as that of the Carry family, to illustrate points and to examine dilemmas. The chapter contains four major sections. The first examines normal human development and intrapersonal needs throughout the life cycle. The second examines a set of contemporary industrial and labor market forces that place demands on the individual, as well as the family. The third section examines the unique stresses and strains faced by blended families and those of single working parents, both women and men. Finally, we address guidelines for action, both from the perspective of the occupation and the family.

SEASONS OF ADULT DEVELOPMENT—HUMAN GROWTH AND INTRAPERSONAL NEEDS

Foundation in the Early Years

Hazan and Shaver (1990) propose a functional parallel between *love* and *work* in adulthood to *attachment* and *exploration* in infancy and early childhood. In the early years, the two competing intrapersonal needs first emerge, and attachment and exploration are as intractable in the early years as are love and work in the adult years.

Bowlby (1982, 1988) and Ainsworth, Blehar, Waters, and Wall (1978) state that the presence of secure bases of attachment is essential to normal human development. They propose that attachment behavior is an instinctual form of behavior exhibited by the young when they are threatened by a predator. This is generalized to other situations of threat, danger, or notable uncertainty. If the attachment figure does not function as a secure base in these stressful times because of absence or unpredictability, then the young person experiences separation anxiety, which may interfere with his or her ability to establish and maintain healthy relationships.

Although this is an essential aspect of normal human development, more is required. The need to explore in the early years enables children to engage the environment, examine its many facets, and acquire information about the world. Gratification of this need is essential to normal development, enabling the child to become autonomous and to develop independent psychological functioning.

When these potentially competing needs are balanced, the person can experience psychological growth and become a self-reliant adult. Such people are able to work alone or with others, appropriately to the task and the situation (Quick, Nelson, & Quick, 1991). Their behavior is flexible and responsive to their own needs, as well as to the demands of the situation. They avoid counterdependence and overdependence, and they exhibit a healthy form of interdependent behavior (Quick, Joplin, Nelson, & Quick, 1992).

The Life Cycle

Levinson (1986) offers one of the most widely known and used models of the developmental periods in adulthood. Levinson's early work was based on male adult development; however, this model is intended to apply to both men and women. He views the life course as a sequence of alternating structure-building and structure-changing periods (a transitional period that eliminates the existing life structure and allows the building of a new one). His work, based on empirical findings, suggests that each period begins and ends at a well-defined average age; a variation of plus or minus two years around the mean was found to exist. The periods are:

1. Early adult transition (17–22 years)
2. Entry life structure for early adulthood (22–28 years)
3. Age 30 transition (28–33 years)
4. Culminating life structure for early adulthood (33–40 years)
5. Midlife transition (40–45 years)
6. Entry life structure for middle adulthood (45–50 years)
7. Age 50 transition (50–55 years)
8. Culminating life structure for middle adulthood (55–60 years)
9. Late adult transition (60–65 years)

Dacey (1989) indicates peak life periods when creativity may be most readily cultivated.

Males	Females
0–5 years	0–5 years
11–14 years	10–13 years
18–20 years	18–20 years
29–31 years	29–31 years
40–45 years	37–45 years
60–65 years	60–65 years

In addition, scholars, scientists, and artists whose peak productivity is between their 40s and 60s, produce almost as much in their 70s as earlier (Dacey, 1989). Tamir (1989a) outlines two healthy patterns of midlife transition among men: one is a striving pattern of upward achievement; and the other is a more generative pattern of investing in younger men. These healthy, alternative patterns of transition challenge myths about men at midlife, such as *midlife crisis.* (Tamir, 1989b).

Adult years found to be the most creative also overlap with Levinson's (1978) transition periods. Perhaps the personal uncertainty experienced by many in transition years is channeled into creative work experiences to fulfill the need for direction and focus. Work may provide the one stable place in which efforts are productive during the transition periods. Dacey (1989) also noted that the 40–45-years period marks a new separateness and is often a midcourse correction in both the career and family arenas. During the age period of 60–65-years, many individuals retire, and find themselves with free time and abundant remaining energy and the desire to be productive and useful. As a result, many elderly individuals become creative in different ways.

Men traditionally have had a stable career/work orientation across their life courses. Greater variation in focus of energies seems to occur over women's life courses, because family demands intervene and require occasional reallocations of energies between work and family. Hoffman (1989) states that the rates of participation in the labor force for married women with children under 6 years had risen to 57.4% in 1988 (United States Bureau of the Census, 1991). Women are now more attached to the labor market; they have reduced turnover rates, and higher proportions of women work full time and year around. Temporal patterns of women's employment still differ from that of men; women work somewhat more on a part-time and/or part-year basis. Their work is more often interrupted by demands to care for ill, aged, or young family members, and women have traditionally been expected to exhibit more flexibility between the work and family arenas. Therefore, although the amount of home labor performed by men has increased, women still do the greater amount.

The life-cycle stage of the family plays an important role in the work–family allocations. Families with young children must support these dependents. Hayghe (1986) found that families with older children are more likely to have a mother and/or adolescent siblings working to supplement family income.

Perhaps, because of increasing career interests among women, family unit structures in the life cycle have changed. Teachman and Schollaert (1989) note the increasing trend for women to marry and bear children at later ages. Among men, high current wages and high projected earnings are associated with being married and early first birth timing. Later family formation is associated with high wages among women.

Voydanoff (1990) presented the concept of a life-cycle squeeze. This is the period when a family's economic needs and aspirations are relatively greater than its resources. She delineates two primary times when a life-cycle squeeze may occur because the husbands' earnings are likely to fall short: in early adulthood and again in later adulthood when expenses for adolescents are greatest. For women who opt for a more traditional family–marriage arrangement, the life-cycle squeeze period is the prime time for women to work. For dual career couples, the economic strains of the life-cycle squeeze may be more severely felt because they lack disposable resources. Moreover, various needs remain unmet if financial planning was inadequate.

Occupational choices have an impact on the career–family interface. Henry Cisneros (Joplin, 1992) spoke about career choice and changes in his life. Family factors influenced his decision not to seek reelection to a fifth term as mayor of San Antonio in 1989; he was chairman and CEO of Cisneros Asset Management at the time of this interview. "My son was born in 1987 with serious health problems. A decision had to be made as to whether I would run for reelection in 1989. Given that the Mayor's office paid as little as it did, but yet demanded immense effort and energy, I, for the first time, began to think I had crossed the line from public service to self-sacrifice beyond the call. I have a series of obligations right now which involve getting my daughters through college and getting my son well, that probably keep me from doing exactly what I'd like to do because I have to keep one eye on the remuneration, the building of a financial base, so that's a practical reality of life."

The life course concept (Levinson, 1986), with its alternating periods of stability and transition, along with the peak periods of creativity outlined by Dacey (1989), has significant implications for both career and family decisions. Not only may they provide strong retrospective explanations, but they may be used prospectively in career guidance and decision making.

Risky Shifts in Adulthood Transitions

Men in their 30s often pour much of their energy into work, regarding it as more important than other aspects of their lives (Levinson, 1978). Although they may feel this to be true at that stage of their adult development, a transitional period often begins around age 40 in which love-related concerns, such as family relationships, feelings, and nurturing, may come to the fore, after having been relegated to a lower priority during the previous decade. The man who turns to his wife and family to gratify these love-related needs may find that his family has invested their energies elsewhere, while he was busy with work. Collins (1983) suggests that such circumstances frequently may underlie the circumstance of men and women in the workplace becoming lovers, thus creating organizational and personal dilemmas, if not downright tragedies.

THE EMMIT FAMILY

Mrs. Emmit decided several years ago to quit her job for full-time motherhood. She felt deprived, having grown up as the only child of a single, working mother, and she did not want her children to grow up the same way she had. Stability was also important to Mrs. Emmit because she and her mother moved often, forcing Mrs. Emmit to adapt to many new schools and to make new friends too often.

Mr. Emmit was the second of six children in a family that he considered "too stable." Although he accepted the value of a supportive family, he also wanted more freedom and the opportunity to do things for himself. Resentment grew as he had to provide for his family. He often felt as if he were competing with those families with two earners. He refused to take a second job to supplement the family income and gradually developed interests that kept him away from home.

Gradually, Mrs. Emmit focused more of her attention on the children and the marriage tended to become a partnership to provide for the children. She reacted to the children's being in school with feelings of loneliness and isolation. She rejected the idea of returning to work because she feared her previous training would no longer suffice in her field. Instead, she became involved with school activities and found that she disapproved of how and what her children were being taught. To combat this and the sense that she was losing contact with her children, she attempted to provide them with home schooling.

The Emmit family was in crisis. Mrs. Emmit was too absorbed with her children, who were not developing the independence to enable them to compete as adults. Mr. Emmit did not share in his wife's involvement with the children, and he became more resentful. Moreover, he began to seek personal fulfillment outside the family.

Although the Emmit family has not yet broken apart, balance and integration, which would provide stability, are lacking within the parental subsystem of the family. Without refocusing energies, the Emmits are likely to disintegrate as a family.

Part of the problem may be the somewhat artificial bifurcation that has occurred between the office and the home. Thus, the stereotypical domain of love is the family context and the stereotypical domain of work is the occupational context. The problem may be compounded by our false understanding of love and love relationships. As shown in Collins (1983), love relationships are often associated with romantic, sexual liaisons. This stereotypic, cultural set of associations persists despite the eloquent distinction made between love and sexual desire in Fromm's *The Art of Loving* (1956).

If love is concerned with intimacy and connection in human relationships, then love does not require physical union. Psychological union and bonding in work relationships may have the same traces of love that permeate relationships in a healthy family system. It could be argued that psychologically intimate, opposite sex relationships in the workplace are viable and do not carry with them the necessity of physical or sexual intimacy. In the case of the Emmits, is it possible that Mrs. Emmit should be allowing her children to do more "work;" that is, effortful growth to learn to be self-reliant? Furthermore, should Mr. Emmit cultivate psychologically, emotionally gratifying occupational relationships that are noncompetitive with his family relationship, in order to reduce his resentment?

SITUATIONAL AND LABOR FORCE CONTEXT

We have shown the importance of a healthy balance and integration of work and family relationships for the psychological well-being of the employee, the spouse, and the children. Clearly, characteristics of one's job and work situation can either frustrate or encourage development of the work and family situation (Friedman, 1991). Recently, four significant developments in the workplace have emerged that can have a significant impact on both work and the family: 1) the increasing fragility of the employment relationship; 2) corporate restructuring; 3) the changing occupational face of unemployment; and 4) changing workforce demographics. For purposes of our discussion, these developments are treated separately; however, they are related, and they may have similar impacts on, or they may provide similar opportunities for, the family. As the number of corporate career opportunities in middle management shrinks, increasing numbers of couples attempt small businesses of their own. These attempts offer unique opportunities and risks, as illustrated in the case of the Bobbitts.

THE BOBBITT FAMILY

Mr. and Mrs. Bobbitt owned a small successful business that had grown to a staff of over 20 individuals. The business was based on Mr. Bobbitt's technical expertise and his ability to market himself and his technical services. In the beginning, Mrs. Bobbitt quit her job to perform the record keeping and office management of the business. At that time, the business operated out of their home and a small shop.

The business was very successful, but problems in management increased greatly. Mr. Bobbitt maintained his personal style, but he had problems delegating responsibility and maintaining records. Initially, his wife was able to organize things and give her attention to details. Eventually, she became unable to control all the details of both the home and the business.

When the family business began, the Bobbitt's children were preschoolers. Mrs. Bobbitt was comfortable with the babysitting arrangements and was available in a crisis. She was also able to attend to the medical and social needs of the children. With the children in school and the business having grown, Mrs. Bobbitt became unable to spend as much time with the children as she would have liked. She became very dissatisfied with the family life style.

Both Mr. and Mrs. Bobbitt considered themselves successful in their business, but they were very unhappy. Mr. Bobbitt found it pleasant to spend more time away from home on business trips. Mrs. Bobbitt became very suspicious because she knew that their marriage relationship was poor. She also knew that her husband was drinking heavily and she feared that he was unfaithful.

This couple considered many solutions to their problems. They thought of selling the business. Mrs. Bobbitt wanted to quit working, but was afraid that they could not afford to replace her with someone who could do an adequate job. She also did not trust her husband to be responsible without her help to keep him organized. Mr. Bobbitt suggested that they should either hire a business consultant or begin therapy with a marriage counselor. Mrs. Bobbitt was reluctant to expose herself to the scrutiny of someone outside the family.

Changing Nature of the Employment Relationship

The employment relationship and one's attachment to work and the organization have evolved from the situation of job, work, and family being indistinguishable with respect to time and location, as was the case during colonial times, to an almost total separation of work from family. Emergence of the worker–manager relationship in large-scale, unionized manufacturing operations dates from the 1930s. The labor–management, adversarial relationship relegated the family to the role of victim in times of industrial conflict. Despite strikes and other forms of industrial conflict in the 1940s, 1950s, and 1960s, union and nonunion firms gradually drew the worker into an increasingly dependent relationship through continuous improvements in fringe benefits and in pension and retirement programs. The organization became head of the household. While the employee became more dependent on the organization, the firm did not necessarily reciprocate, as the concept and practice of employment at will remained strong. By the late 1970s, through the 1980s, and into the 1990s, the employment relationship became increasingly fragile and tenuous, despite the protections extended through numerous employment nondiscrimination laws. Global product and labor markets, deregulation, and the burdens of credit have fostered an employment relationship that can be characterized as short-term, devoid of loyalty, and even unpredictable (Atchison, 1991). Do these three characteristics also describe contemporary attitudes toward the marital relationship, as illustrated in rising divorce rates and declines in traditional and dual career families?

Corporate Restructuring

For more than a decade, corporate restructuring has been a significant, contributing factor to change in the employment relationship. Corporate restructuring has taken numerous forms—mergers, acquisitions, plant closures, bankruptcies, and relocations. A common thread running through these situations is workforce change, frequently resulting in employee reduction. Even the language and vocabulary of corporate restructuring strongly suggest negative consequences for the employee. Retrenchment, downsizing, delayering, demassing, outplacement, redundancy, free agent and disposable managers, and golden parachutes are all colorful terms (Hirsch, 1987) associated with corporate restructuring. In many situations, retrenchment, downsizing, or rightsizing are corporate attempts toward greater efficiency. This frequently results in severance of the employment relationship or the threat of a severed relationship, as in the case of the Allson family.

The Allson Family

Mr. Allson worked in midmanagement for a national company. At forty-two, he was in his fifth assignment with the company. He and his family lived far from their extended families. His wife returned to work in order to supplement the family income. Mr. Allson was discouraged because the economy slowed the growth of his company and his career seemed to be peaking. His chances for advancement were slim. The possibility of his being laid off was very real.

Mr. Allson experienced his midlife crisis about eighteen months previously. He had a brief affair with a younger woman, and he tried to plan a new life for himself. He found that he was unable to leave his family, and he returned to his former life style; however, he became depressed, although he did not describe himself as such. He was chronically tired and bored.

Mrs. Allson enjoyed her work and became successful. She was promoted and thought of continuing her education in order to be in line for further promotions. Her new success created problems within the family. The children missed the attention of their mother, and Mr. Allson had mixed feelings about his wife's success.

The oldest daughter was a high school senior. She was a slow-to-adapt child, who was unable to make new friends when the family moved. She became committed to her studies and withdrew from others. She had an avoidant personality and became obsessive.

The 14-year-old daughter had an outgoing personality and was able to make friends. She became dependent on friends during the period when her mother was absorbed with her new job and her father was distracted with his own needs. She was vulnerable to peer pressures because her parents, who always trusted her, were not observant and provided limited supervision.

The 9-year-old son discovered a peer group outside the family. He was overactive and had trouble with his school work. He was inattentive in class and did not complete his homework.

While not having successfully worked through the risky transition to his midlife yet, Mr. Allson was now confronted with the new risk of a layoff. In some families, layoff and subsequent unemployment may lead to role reversals in the family, with the wife becoming the primary provider. Such role reversals create internal family problems and conflicts related to social status, self-esteem, and sense of worth, which may, in turn, precipitate changes in family structure (May, Brown-Standridge, & Jorgensen, 1989).

Data from a study by Gray, Giacobbe, Quick, and Wheeler (1989) support the relationship between corporate restructuring and workforce reduction. In the 604 corporate restructuring situations reported by human resource professionals in a national survey funded by the Society for Human Resource Management, slightly more than two thirds of the situations involved reducing the workforce. As shown in Table 8.1, workforce reduction was far more common in retrenchment/downsizing and divestiture/closure situations than in corporate acquisitions and mergers. Furthermore, of those respondents indicating employee decreases, 82% specified that these reductions in force were clearly permanent. Although workforce increases occurred in about 23% of the acquisitions, the message of corporate restructuring to households dependent upon jobs and work is clear—plan for, prepare for, and expect job loss.

TABLE 8.1.   Restructuring and Workforce Reduction

Restructuring	Workforce Increase	Workforce Decrease	No Change
Acquisition	53	112	63
Merger	6	17	17
Retrenchment/downsizing	2	186	4
Divestiture/closure and other	16	91	37
Total	77	406	121
	(12.75%)	(67.23%)	(20.02%)

Data were obtained from the Fourth Annual (1989) Society for Human Resource Management—Commerce Clearing House (SHRM—CCH) Survey as conducted by the Center for Research on Organizational and Managerial Excellence (CROME) of the Department of Management, University of Texas at Arlington.

Changing Occupational Face of the Unemployed

For decades, businesses have adjusted their workforces through hiring and layoffs in response to changing economic conditions. Certainly, much corporate restructuring of recent years has been a response to (but, in a few cases, in anticipation of) economic change. Until recently, employee furloughs were concentrated in the nonsupervisory occupations found in construction, retail, and manufacturing industries. In the late 1980s and early 1990s, temporary and permanent layoffs associated with corporate restructuring and economy-driven workforce adjustments have had significant impact on managerial, professional, and technical occupations. In fact, from August 1989 to August 1990, nearly 75% of the newly unemployed were) managerial, professional, and technical employees (see Table 8.2). College educated and knowledge workers are no longer immune to unemployment. The unemployment lines have been filled with accountants, engineers, stockbrokers, executives, bank loan officers, and midlevel managers. Individual and family shock for the first-time unemployed has undoubtedly been difficult—possibly devastating for some. According to the national job search and outplacement firm of Drake, Beam, & Morin, Inc., many unemployed managerial and professional workers have faced job searches of months rather than weeks (O'Boyle & Hymowitz, 1990). Unfortunately, long job searches deplete severance payments and other family financial resources rapidly, thus exposing the family to further risk.

Changing Composition of America's Labor Force

Labor force and family unit characteristics have changed considerably over the past 20 years. Clearly, the most noticeable changes have been the relative decline of the traditional work/family unit (husband only working), the emergence of the dual career family, and the significant increase of single, working parent

TABLE 8.2.   The New Unemployed

Number of Unemployed by Occupation	August 1989	August 1990	Change (N)
Managerial, professional, technical, administrative, and clerical	1,478,000	1,842,000	364,000
Sales	658,000	646,000	−12,000
Service	1,104,000	1,105,000	1,000
Construction	317,000	377,000	60,000
Mechanics and repairers	343,000	395,000	52,000
Machine operators, laborers, and fabricators	1,490,000	1,467,000	−23,000
Farming, fishing, and forestry	218,000	223,000	5,000
Other	744,000	782,000	38,000
Total unemployed	6,352,000	6,837,000	485,000

Data assembled by the Bureau of Labor Statistics and reported in Thomas F. O'Boyle and Carol Hymowitz, "Layoffs This Time Hit Professional Ranks with Unusual Force," *The Wall Street Journal,* October 4, 1990, p. A15. Reprinted by permission of *The Wall Street Journal,* © 1990 Dow Jones & Company, Inc. All Rights Reserved Worldwide.

headed by males is increasing markedly. Several labor force and work/family unit changes are shown in Table 8.3.

The labor force grew considerably from 1970 to 1990 and underwent several significant compositional changes. Although the male labor force participation rate and segment of the labor force changed somewhat, the female segment adjusted dramatically. The number of women in the labor force increased from 29.7 million in 1970, to 56.7 million in 1990; this increase accounted for nearly 60% of the overall expansion of the labor force for this 20-year period. By

TABLE 8.3.   Changing Workforce Demographics

	1970	1990
Civilian labor force (in millions)	82.8	126.4
Male labor force participation rate	79.7	76.5
Female labor force participation rate	42.6	57.5
White males as percentage of labor force	49.5	43.1
Traditional work/family unit as a percentage of all families	41.9	20.0
Married, percentage with wife working	40.8	54.9
Female single parent as percentage of all families	6.2	10.8

These data all from the U.S. Bureau of the Census, the U.S. Department of Commerce, *Statistical Abstract of the United States: 1990;* the U.S. Bureau of the Census, the U.S. Department of Labor, "Employment and Earnings Characteristics of Families: First Quarter, 1991;" the U.S. Bureau of Labor Statistics, the U.S. Department of Labor, *Employment and Earnings* (January 1991); and U.S. Merit Systems Protection Board, *Balancing Work Responsibilities and Family Needs: The Federal Civil Service Response,* 1991.

29.7 million in 1970, to 56.7 million in 1990; this increase accounted for nearly 60% of the overall expansion of the labor force for this 20-year period. By 1990, women represented about 45% of the labor force and showed a labor force participation rate of nearly 58%. From the formation of the United States as a country until about 1970, white males were the majority in the labor force. As Table 8.3 indicates, white men rapidly are becoming the largest minority group.

The labor force patterns of work/family units have shown even more dramatic changes during this 20-year period. The traditional work/family unit continued its downward trend, while women as wives and single parents increased their attachment to the world of work. When the 20-year time frame is expanded to 50 years, these trends become even more pronounced. From 1940 to 1990, the traditional unit as a percentage of all families dropped from about 67% to 20%. Dual career units increased dramatically over this same period, from slightly less than 10% to about 43% (Hayghe, 1990; U.S. Merit Systems Protection Board, 1991).

The increase in the number of upwardly mobile women in dual career families has increased the complexity and nature of career decisions that couples—and families—must confront. The Dillons were a dual career family confronting a difficult and complex decision in their family life and the occupational life cycle of Mrs. Dillon. The complexities of the dilemmas and decisions confronting families such as the Dillons cannot be underestimated.

THE DILLON FAMILY

Mrs. Dillon was very successful in her career and planned to achieve periodic promotions within her company. It became apparent that the promotions she anticipated would require relocation and would involve life style adaptations. Mrs. Dillon had been married for five years to a man who had stabilized his position in a company. He felt secure in his position and was very happy settling into a comfortable routine. Although chances for his advancement were limited, he was appreciated at work and there were many benefits associated with it.

Mrs. Dillon had recently been offered the first major promotion that required relocation. Mr. Dillon was reluctant to leave his job and attempt to find another in a new community. Mrs. Dillon was accustomed to the support that her husband was able to provide. He enjoyed accepting responsibility for the many tasks required to maintain their home. Although Mrs. Dillon was happy in her marriage, she was committed to advancing her career.

After much discussion, Mr. and Mrs. Dillon were unable to resolve their dilemma. Mr. Dillon did not want to prevent his wife from getting her promotion; however, he did not believe that he would be able to make the adaptation that would be required of him. Mrs. Dillon did not want to force her husband, but it was clear that she would be upset if they could not make the move.

These situational and labor force developments suggest negative values in the employment equation; however, there are at least three positive and interesting developments as well. First, for many who work in information- and service-based occupations, the location of work is shifting back to the home and family setting. This shift is creating the potential for family and work integration similar to that which the colonists experienced. Second, there is an encouraging trend found in the increased interest in career planning. This is happening in both the individual and organizational domains. Clearly, careful and effortful planning can lead to better integration and balance of work and family needs. Third, the notion that big is better is giving way to a renewed emphasis on quality, core business, and entrepreneurial efforts through employee participation and empowerment. This shrinking of the business "scope" carries with it a greater potential for individual responsiveness and for integration of work and family needs.

BLENDED FAMILIES AND SINGLE, WORKING PARENT FAMILIES

Although the vast majority of families continue to be traditional or dual career families (63% in 1990 versus 76% in 1940), there has been a decline in these two major family categories (Hayghe, 1990). The increase in single, working female heads of households has been more than matched by the increase in single, working male heads of households. A major shift has been in the number of blended families in the culture, a circumstance sometimes masked by the way statistics are recorded. Blended families may be able to achieve integration and a healthy structure; however, occupational pressures on both parents and other internal tensions are more likely to lead to the kind of fragmentation experienced by the Hayworths.

THE HAYWORTH FAMILY

Mr. and Mrs. Hayworth had been married for six months. It was the second marriage for each of them. Mr. Hayworth's first wife had died two years earlier and he depended on his in-laws to take care of his 11-year-old daughter. Mrs. Hayworth had been divorced for five years and had custody of her 14-year-old son and 10-year-old daughter. Their father lived in another state, and he saw them two or three times a year for extended visits.

Mr. Hayworth worked in mid management and had been successful before his wife's death. It was difficult for him to concentrate on his work following her death. His in-laws did most of the parenting of his daughter, until his mother-in-law became too ill to assist. Mr. Hayworth became very dependent on his new wife and expected her to manage the home. Mr. Hayworth would have preferred to ignore the children and let Mrs. Hayworth do the parenting. Mr. Hayworth had depended on his first wife to take care of their daughter and the house.

The Hayworths tried to stay in his three-bedroom house. It was assumed that the girls could share a bedroom, but that arrangement was not successful. Mr. Hayworth was reluctant to get another house and tended to become impatient with the girls when they did not get along. Mr. Hayworth tended to vacillate between spending long hours at work, ignoring his problems at home or becoming so obsessed with home problems that he did not complete his work assignments.

Mrs. Hayworth had always worked long hours. She was prone to take responsibility for others, she would allow her husband to escape family problems. However, the added work of a new husband and preadolescent step-daughter had stretched her to the limit. When she worked late, she often came home to a household in turmoil. Mr. and Mrs. Hayworth had worked for the same company, but she had to find a new job after they married. The stress of adjusting to the new job added to her frustration.

Both Mr. and Mrs. Hayworth had expected to build close family ties. However, all members of the family began to avoid coming home because of the tension that they expected to find there. Their son wanted to spend all of his time with friends and their families. The girls had each wanted a sister, but they didn't know how to share or resolve their conflicts. They were not able to share friends or have friendships in different peer groups. Instead of becoming close, the Hayworth family was now fragmented.

Although single, working mothers have been a small portion of families over the decades, their numbers are growing. Mrs. Goodman's struggles with her work and finances, former husband, and her sons are not entirely atypical of the challenges these women face. Moreover, her avoidant behavior, confusion, uncertainty, and depression are not atypical.

THE GOODMAN FAMILY

Mrs. Goodman and her husband separated for the first time over five years ago. Since then, she has had continuing battles about property settlement, visitation with the children, and child support. Mr. Goodman has been inconsistent in his approach to his family. At times he was very interested in the children, and it has been impossible for Mrs. Goodman to develop a consistent family life. Several times she has moved in with her parents, and at other times, she has tried to make it on her own. She has tried having roommates to share expenses, but she has constantly had to fight an unbalanced budget. Once she tried to live with a man, but he could not get along with her boys. She has twice tried to work things out with her former husband.

Mrs. Goodman's oldest son was in junior high, and he was impossible to discipline. She wanted to believe that he was merely going through a stage and was really a good boy. However, she was afraid of the risks he took and often thought that she should be in better control of his behavior. She did not know what to do with him, but she did not like the advice she got from others. She sensed that his grandparents did not really understand his needs, but she doubted that she was capable of being an adequate parent. His father was often critical and threatening, but he was inconsistent and was seldom available for discipline.

Doubts about her parenting spread to other areas of Mrs. Goodman's life. She doubted that a man would want to be involved with a woman with three children and a former mate drifting in and out of her life. Uncertainty also restricted her work. She would have liked to increase her skills, and she tried to further her education. In the middle of one semester, her daughter suffered a lengthy illness and she was not able to complete her school work. She was not willing to risk more money on education.

Mrs. Goodman developed avoidant behaviors and became depressed. She felt hopeless about the needs of her children and her own future. She did not feel capable of solving her problems and did not know how to get help that she could trust and accept.

Along with single, working mothers, there has been a surprising growth in single, working fathers over the past decade. While not experiencing the sense of depression and hopelessness that Mrs. Goodman feels, Mr. Frankson has a different set of challenges and seems to be stuck in indecision. His sense of aloneness and lack of integration are not atypical.

THE FRANKSON FAMILY

Mr. Frankson attempted to rear his two children alone since his wife left him four years earlier. His 10-year-old daughter and 5-year-old son presented him with many parenting and homemaking problems for which he was ill-prepared. Mr. Frankson was the middle child of five children. He had an older and younger brother and sister. Because he was very active in school and athletics, Mr. Frankson had few responsibilities at home. His family encouraged him to be a single parent. They were able to help with extreme emergencies, but they were not available for the day-to-day work of keeping a family together. Mr. Frankson mastered many parenting skills.

As a single, working parent, Mr. Frankson was able to master the tasks of providing for the physical needs of his children. His son was an even-tempered child who did not require much special attention. His daughter spent much of her time caring for her brother after their mother left; however, it became difficult for her to "mother" her brother as he grew older. She was a serious child, who began to ask questions that Mr. Frankson could not answer.

In addition to his daughter's questions, Mr. Frankson had to deal with his own difficult questions. Mr. Frankson had not dated and had pushed away women he felt were too available. He was aware of his mixed feelings about dating and remarriage. He felt the pressure of this uncertainty, but he lacked sufficient time to work through his confusion. Mr. Frankson also knew that he did not have enough time to deal with the demands of his job. He was able to hold on at work, but he did not have the time and energy to provide the extra push that seemed to be required for promotion.

The problems that he faced regarding his work and his lack of a relationship constantly got pushed to the background while Mr. Frankson tried to cope with his daughter. As she approached puberty, Mr. Frankson worried about what to tell her about her mother. He doubted his ability to help a young girl make the transition into womanhood. Mr. Frankson became unable to decide what to pursue next. He decided that he should work toward a promotion, so that he could afford more help for his children. Then he thought that it might be best to remarry and provide his daughter with a mother. Later, he decided that he should spend more time with his daughter, but he did not know how to relate to her. Mr. Frankson began to feel that control of his life was slipping away as he tried to decide what to do.

Although the increased mobility of American families during the mid-1900s led to much fragmentation in the extended family structure, we may now be witnessing an increased fragmentation of nuclear family units. Such fragmentation leads to the blended family and single, working parent dilemmas as illustrated above.

CONCLUDING CONSIDERATIONS AND GUIDELINES

Four conclusions and guidelines can be drawn from our review of the literature and the family cases included in this chapter. First, it is important to increase awareness, both in individuals and families, of the needs for love and work. The absence of self-awareness concerning these two intractable drives, as in Mr. Allson's case, exposes people to the risks of internal and external conflict. The dilemmas created by these needs often defy simple solutions. Rather, there are often complex and apparently insoluble situations created within families that require patience, time, and help to work through. For example, the drifting of Mr. Emmit away from home can be neither easily nor quickly reversed; and, Mr. and Mrs. Dillon's dual career decisions demand patient problem solving.

Second, proactive or preventive strategies and planning in the formation of families may help to achieve greater balance and integration. Although it is not possible to anticipate all eventualities, premarital counseling and family planning activities are a step in that direction. These should also address individual developmental and life-cycle issues. Even as families find themselves enmeshed in an overload of work and family demands—such as in the case of Mr. and Mrs. Carry—it is beneficial to have a plan formulated to help a family work through the difficulties. Moreover, some plan is better than no plan at all.

Third, corporations must continue their responsiveness to family issues. Two examples of current responses concern maternity leave and child-care resources. Although family issues are not a formal concern of work organizations, they are an indirect concern, given the extraorganizational demands families place upon the employee. As a result, the formulation of corporate policies that are responsive to the needs of the workforce, without violating corporate values, will enhance the integration of the occupation and family needs.

Fourth, especially given the health risks associated with social isolation (House, Landis, & Umberson, 1988), attention must be given to the role of the family in the society and the need for supportive opportunities for those in the postwork years. This becomes a societal issue, given the potential longevity of individuals beyond their working years and the burden of health costs for society. The case of Dr. Faust, whose life extended 14 years beyond retirement, is a good illustration (Quick & Quick, 1990). The period beyond the working years would have been significantly longer (37 years versus 14 years) had he chosen the traditional retirement age of 65 years, rather than retiring at 88 years. In addition to his strong family support system, he built additional social supports among friends and former colleagues. Few individuals so single-mindedly pursue healthy self-care. Society must attend to providing opportunities for individuals in their postemployment years.

REFERENCES

Ainsworth, M. D. S., Blehar, M. C., Waters, E., & Wall, S. (1978). *Patterns of attachment: A psychological analysis of the strange situation.* Hillsdale, NJ: Erlbaum.

Atchison, T. J. (1991). The employment relationship: un-tied or re-tied? *Academy of Management Executive, 5,* 52–62.

Bowlby, J. (1982). *Attachment and loss, Vol. I: Attachment* (rev. ed.). New York: Basic Books.

Bowlby, J. (1988). *A secure base.* New York: Basic Books.

Collins, E. C. G. (1983). Managers and lovers. *Harvard Business Review, 83,* 142–153.

Dacey, J. S. (1989). Peak periods of creative growth across the lifespan. *Journal of Creative Behavior, 23,* 224–247.

Erikson, E. H. (1963). *Childhood and society* (2nd ed.). New York: Norton.

Friedman, D. E. (1991). *Linking work–family issues to the bottom line. Report 962.* New York: Conference Board.

Fromm, E. (1956). *The art of loving.* New York: Harper & Row.

Gray, D. A., Giacobbe, J., Quick, J. C., & Wheeler, K. G. (1989). *Corporate Restructuring: HR involvement crucial to success of mergers, acquisitions, and downsizing.* Chicago: Commerce Clearing House.

Hayghe, H. V. (1990). Family members in the work force. United States Bureau of Labor Statistics. *Monthly Labor Review, 113,* 10–19.

Hazan, C., & Shaver, P. R. (1990). Love and work: An attachment–theoretical perspective. *Journal of Personality and Social Psychology, 39,* 270–280.

Hirsch, P. (1987). *Pack your own parachute.* Reading, MA: Addison-Wesley.

Hoffman, L. W. (1989). Effects of maternal employment in the two-parent family. *American Psychologist, 44,* 283–292.

House, J., Landis, K., & Umberson, D. (1988). Social relationships and health. *Science, 241,* 540–545.

Joplin, J. R. (1992, April). Unpublished interview with Dr. Henry Cisneros, Dallas, TX.

Levinson, D. J. (1978). *The seasons of a man's life.* New York: Knopf.

Levinson, D. J. (1986). A conception of adult development. *American Psychologist, 41* (1), 3–13.

Lobel, S. A. (1991). Allocation of investment in work and family roles: Alternative theories and implications for research. *Academy of Management Review, 16,* 507–521.

Maslow, A. (1954). *Motivation and personality.* New York: Harper & Row.

May, J. L., Brown-Standridge, M., & Jorgensen, S. R. (1989). Unemployed and underemployed professional males: Stress and sexual difficulties. Paper presented at the Annual Meeting of the National Council on Family Relations, New Orleans.

O'Boyle, T. F., & Hymowitz, C. (1990, October 4). Layoffs this time hit professional ranks with unusual force. *Wall Street Journal,* pp. A1 and A15.

Piotrkowski, C. S. (1979). *Work and the family system.* New York: Free Press.

Quick, J. C., Joplin, J. R., Nelson, D. L., & Quick, J. D. (1992). Behavioral responses to anxiety: Self-reliance, counterdependence, and overdependence. *Anxiety, Stress, and Coping, 5,* 41–54.

Quick, J. C., Nelson, D. L., & Quick, J. D. (1991). The self-reliance inventory. In J. W. Pfeiffer (Ed.), *The 1991 annual: Developing human resources* (pp. 149–161). San Diego, CA: University Associates.

Quick, J. C., & Quick, J. D. (1990). The changing times of life: Career in context. In J.C. Quick, R.E. Hess, J. Hermalin, & J.D. Quick (Eds.), *Career stress in changing times* (pp. 1–24). Binghamton, NY: Haworth.

Rogers, C. R. (1961). *On becoming a person.* Boston: Houghton Mifflin.

Scott, M. (1967). The bifurcation of work and family life. Seminar on the church and the world of work. Chicago: Presbyterian Institute of Labor and Industrial Relations at McCormick Seminary.

Tamir, L. M. (1989a August). Team behavior and participant age: An exploratory analysis. Paper presented at the 97th Annual Convention of the American Psychological Association, New Orleans.

Tamir, L. M. (1989b). Modern myths about men at midlife. In S. Hunter & M. Sundel (Eds.), *Midlife myths: Issues, findings, and practice implications.* Newbury Park, CA: Sage.

Teachman, J. D., & Schollaert, P. T. (1989). Economic conditions, marital status, and the timing of first births. *Sociological Forum, 4,* 27–45.

The United States Bureau of the Census, United States Department of Commerce. (1987). *Statistical abstract of the United States: 1986 (107th ed.).* Washington DC: United States Government Printing Office.

The United States Bureau of the Census, United States Department of Commerce. (1991). *Statistical abstract of the United States: 1990.* Washington, DC: United States Government Printing Office.

The United States Bureau of the Census, United States Department of Labor. (1991). Employment and earnings characteristics of families: First quarter 1991. Washington, DC: United States Department of Labor. 10 pages.

United States Bureau of Labor Statistics. United States Department of Labor. (1991, January). *Employment and earnings.* Washington, DC: United States Government Printing Office.

United States Merit Systems Protection Board. (1991). *Balancing work responsibilities and family needs: The federal civil service response.* Washington, DC: United States Government Printing Office.

Vaillant, G. E. (1977). *Adaptation to life.* Boston: Little, Brown.

Voydanoff, P. (1990). Economic distress and family relations: A review of the eighties. *Journal of Marriage and the Family, 52,* 1099–1115.

CHAPTER 9

Leisure and Family over the Life Cycle

DENNIS K. ORTHNER, LYNN BARNETT-MORRIS, and JAY A. MANCINI

Leisure behaviors and experiences are critical to the development of individuals and families. The discretionary time shared between parents and children, husbands and wives, siblings and other close relations often defines the nature of those relationships and influences personal and social development. During leisure individuals are able to step out of their assigned roles, capture the essence of a relationship, and share an experience that can help mold their personalities, personal and family role expectations, and patterns of relationship interaction. Although family development is also influenced by time spent in task obligations, such as work, household tasks, and community responsibilities, leisure experiences are particularly valuable for children and adults because they offer opportunities less constrained by predefined roles that may limit interaction, learning, and relationship development.

Recognition of leisure as an organizing principle for individual and family development is comparatively new (Orthner & Mancini, 1991). Before the twentieth century, roles of family members were much more circumscribed by work and household responsibilities. Attachments and bonds between family members were formed by strong social constraints and complementary gender ascribed roles (Levinger, 1965). Males and females in the family were socialized differently. Family leisure activities were heavily gender differentiated and complemented the respective work roles of men and women in society. With urbanization and industrialization, however, family roles changed and leisure experiences became more important in conditioning the relationships between family members. Burgess characterized this change as a shift from the *institutional family* to the contemporary *companionship family,* in which family success depends more on the ability of family members to reconcile their divergent needs and interests successfully through shared experiences, rather than on their abilities to submerge individual needs and interests in favor of larger family goals (Burgess & Locke, 1945). This transformation was noted in the now classic "Middletown" study of American families. Compared to the families of that town in the 1920s, the Middletown families of the 1970s (Caplow, 1982) were found to spend much more time in leisure experiences together and to value that time as important to their relationships.

The value now placed on companionship between family members has reached nearly universal proportions. A national sample of adults listed "spending time with your family" and "companionship" as the two most common objectives in life (United Media, 1982). A recent national survey of time use found that home-based activities are by far the most common leisure activities among American adults (Decision Research, 1987). When time diary data were analyzed, family activities were found to be the most frequently engaged in by family members (Juster & Stafford, 1985). This emerging, but strong, tie between leisure experiences and family development led Bellah, Madsen, Sullivan, Swidler, & Tipton (1985) to conclude that the emerging "therapeutic" ideology of the family has now become the predominant perspective in Western society. This ideology views the family primarily in terms of psychological gratification, focusing primary importance on shared time and interaction between family members.

LEISURE AND THE FAMILY

This chapter examines the role that leisure experiences play in the development of individuals and families over the life cycle. Previous reviews of this research and literature have focused primarily on specific stages of the family life cycle, without considering the patterns and changes that evolve over the life course. Thus, the research upon which this review is based tends to reflect the interests of child psychology and development in the childhood years, family psychology and development in the early to midadult years, and family and social gerontology in the later years of life.

It is important to understand that leisure is not a concept upon which there is total consensus regarding its meaning or parameters. The term *leisure* is often differentially applied to free time, particular kinds of experiences, or a mental attitude. For purposes of this chapter, leisure is defined largely in its social/psychological sense of an experience and attitude associated with discretionary time. Thus, recreational experiences are deemed to be leisure to the extent that they are engaged in freely by participants. In addition, the portion of the chapter that focuses on childhood uses the term *play* rather than *leisure*. This is reflective of the terminology used in the literature; however, we contend that it is more in the nature of a semantic justification than of a substantive one. *Leisure* applies equally as well to much of children's activities.

Recent theories stress the defining conditions of leisure to be: the individual's perception of freedom of choice, activities chosen for reasons intrinsic to the anticipated experience, and the accompanying and/or resulting sensations of positive affect. Children's play can be viewed as incorporating these dimensions: children play because they are motivated intrinsically to do so, they also perceive freedom in their choices, and they similarly experience intrinsic satisfaction. In addition, family leisure most often involves children as participants. Thus, the term *play* is used throughout the section on childhood to be consistent with the literature, but the leisure phenomenon under study throughout this chapter is consistent.

From the perspective of the family, there are several key needs that leisure experiences support over the life cycle. The most critical personal and relational needs include attachment and bonding, relational identification, interaction, stress management, and social support. Each of these complex needs reflects the concerns of individuals and families, and their importance is maintained throughout the life course. Clearly, attachment and bonding are extremely important during infancy, but they are no less important among older adults. Similarly, identification with intimate relationships, interpersonal interaction, and stress management continue to be important from childhood through adulthood. Each of these needs is facilitated through experiences in shared leisure.

Today, leisure experiences are often the context within which these personal developmental needs are met. We contend that the context within which most family members develop their attachments to one another, their sense of cohesion to their relationships, and the communication and problem solving that make family relationships successful occur during leisure experiences. The quality of family life and the adequacy of personality development are increasingly defined in terms of the ability of family members to develop and periodically revise the basis of their attachments. Negotiation and customization of relationships has replaced the wholesale adoption of traditional patterns of relating to one another. Leisure experiences foster these new family processes and provide the context within which healthy personality development is encouraged.

LEISURE AND FAMILY IN CHILDHOOD

Troll (1972) asked 100 people to describe any person they currently knew or had known, and the overwhelming majority, with an age range of 10 to 91, named one of their parents. It is fascinating to realize the extent of parental influence on children's lives, even years after the parents have died. Current literature supports this view, with the vast majority of authors agreeing on the importance of interactive play between father, mother, and child. This section describes reciprocal play interactions between family members from a developmental perspective. It has been well documented that children pass through stages in their cognitive, social, emotional, and physical development. Not only do their characteristics, needs, preferences, and interactional patterns differ at each stage, but their interactions with family members and the play responses which they in turn elicit differ also. Because the dynamic interplay between the child and his or her family members is in a continual state of change, it can be viewed most effectively from a developmental perspective.

Infants and Toddlers

New parents often report one of their most exhilarating experiences is when their infants begin to play with them. Most parents enjoy playing with their babies, but what they may not realize is that their play, besides bringing such joy, is extremely beneficial to infants. As parents initiate and structure their play with their infants, the child is offered a richer and more varied experience than he or she could ever possibly obtain if left alone to play. Escalona (1968) conducted what has come to be recognized as a classic study of mother–infant play. Her major finding was that infant play is facilitated and encouraged by the parent's structuring role and that the play that results is more sophisticated and sustained than that found in infants with limited access to parental play partners. Much research has been conducted since this study to investigate further the value of parent–infant play. Results of these studies indicate five major benefits of parent–infant play: 1) it keeps the infant at an optimal level of arousal so the infant is neither bored nor overly excited (Power & Parke, 1982); 2) parent–child play provides the infant with a feeling of control over its environment, thereby fostering self-confidence and promoting intellectual growth (Watson & Ramey, 1972); 3) play exposes the infant to intense social interaction with its parents, thus facilitating the process of parent–infant attachment (Stern, 1977); 4) parent–child play encourages the infant to explore its surroundings; and 5) parent–child play causes the infant to attend more closely to the social aspects of language (Ratner & Bruner, 1978).

Play has been shown to facilitate the bonding between parent and child during the first year of life. Infants with a secure attachment to their mothers are more likely to discover the appropriate uses of objects—as, for instance, when they realize that a ball is to be rolled or a toy truck can be pushed across the floor. Parents of closely attached infants have a high degree of self-esteem, are confident about their abilities to be good parents, show interest in their baby, make frequent eye contact, smile at their baby a good deal, and are emotionally expressive with their baby in play. In marked contrast, parents of insecurely attached children tend to be irritable and anxious, lacking self-confidence and not seeming to enjoy parenthood.

Parents also play a significant role in facilitating the infant's social development through interactive social games and role structuring (Barnett, 1991). Social play is a cooperative interchange in which infants learn to influence others. In social play, infants' gestures and actions are responded to, thereby acquiring meaning. Repetition, a salient feature of infant social play, also allows the infant to participate, thereby gaining control over the parents' behavior. Parents play a significant role in facilitating the socialization process through early social games with their infants. There is repetition of roles at the end of each understood sequence of activity. Awareness of others is reinforced in such games because careful attention to a play partner's actions is required. Parent–infant play is also such a happy experience for both individuals that the process of attachment between parent and child is facilitated. Finally, because these early social games involve much verbalization, it has been suggested that such play encourages the development of language in children (Bruner, 1983).

Recent emphasis has shifted away from the mother–child dyad to acknowledge the roles that fathers play in their child's social development. There is evidence that infants form their own independent relationships with their mother and father, and that each relationship contributes to the child's later social adaptation (Main & Weston, 1981). From infancy onward, observations in the home and in the laboratory reveal that mothers' play interactions are substantially different from fathers'—mother–child play is characterized as smooth, less arousing, more verbal, didactic, and more often toy-mediated. In contrast, father–child play is more arousing, unpredictable, and physical (Lamb, 1977; MacDonald & Parke, 1984). There is also evidence that boys and girls differentially model their parents' leisure preferences and patterns in their own play choices and interactions (Barnett & Chick, 1986).

Not only mothers and fathers are involved in young children's play; siblings are extremely important play partners. There is evidence that the nature of play between siblings differs markedly from that of the mother or father and child. Moreover, research has shown that children as young as 24 months can take part in joint role enactment in sibling play interactions. They can make explicit a transformation of their own identity and can share a framework of pretend play with a brother or sister. This is considered remarkably mature behavior for such young children, and it has not been observed with mothers or fathers in play. There are also important differences in the themes of imaginative play shared with the mother and with the sibling. Children with highly participant mothers and those with highly participant siblings have quite different play experiences. There is data to suggest that growing up in a family with a mother who is disinterested in and unsupportive of pretend play will not necessarily be a disadvantage if the family includes a friendly and affectionate sibling.

The importance of parents and the family network can also be illustrated by research with maltreated children. Research with maltreated infants at high risk indicates that they have relatively consistent negative affective patterns in communications with their caregiver (Gaensbauer, Mrazek, & Harmon, 1980). Very different parental play styles and patterns of interaction have been observed with these infants, consisting of an aimless quality in their play interactions, sad and depressed facial expressions, active disorganized play with frequent shifts from engagement and pleasure to withdrawal and anger, and low frustration tolerance with frequent angry outbursts. Frodi and Lamb (1980) found that maltreating parents have different psychophysiological responses to the cries of their infant, thus suggesting that these parents are less effective than nonmaltreating parents in responding to the affective expressions of their infants.

Preschoolers

Play has been found to facilitate attachment between parent and child, and attachment predicts the quality of play throughout the preschool years. Preschoolers who are the most closely attached to their parents are the most likely to engage in fantasy play with objects, and their make-believe play is more sustained and more complex than that of insecure children (Slade, 1987). At the age of 2 years, they are more likely to function independently, and by the age of 5 years, they have a greater degree of curiosity and behavioral flexibility, and they are more environmentally oriented in their free play (Belsky, Garduque, & Hrncir, 1984).

A large research project more specifically examined the influence of the mother's interactive play behavior with the child and that child's later educational achievement, social/emotional competence, and intelligence (Levenstein, 1985). The project was conducted with 2- to 4-year-old children from lower income families; the data indicated that the mother's general verbal responsiveness in reply to the child during play predicted the child's level of self-confidence, social responsibility, and math skills in kindergarten. These same quality play interactions also reliably predicted reading scores two years later and IQ scores, as well as social responsibility and self-confidence. Smiles as positive gestures demonstrated by the child in play were also predictors; lack of smiling and negative gestures were similarly predictors of negative outcomes. Significantly, a mother's general responsiveness and warmth are much more important to the child's school success than are attempts to teach the child specific information.

These different styles of parent–child play also relate strongly to social development. MacDonald and Parke (1984) found that 3- to 5-year-old popular boys had mothers and fathers who were more engaging and elicited positive affect during play, mothers who were verbally stimulating, and fathers with low directiveness but physical playfulness. Girls whose teachers rated them as popular had physically playful, affect-eliciting, but nondirective fathers, and directive mothers. Boys showed a consistent profile of positive characteristics associated with paternal engagement and physical and maternal verbal characteristics associated with paternal engagement and physical and maternal verbal play. The most robust finding concerned the ability of the parent and child to maintain physical play interactions. For both boys and girls, physical play (especially with the father) was positively related to ratings of the child's popularity. For boys, the extent to which the mother verbally engaged her son was a significant correlate of peer popularity. Maternal directiveness was positively associated with popularity for girls, but paternal directiveness for boys was negatively linked with popularity ratings.

In their roles as managers, parents can directly and indirectly influence their children's social lives by engaging in activities, providing opportunities, or making choices that may purposefully or inadvertently alter both qualitative and quantitative aspects of children's relationships with peers. Two types of parental managerial roles suggest that parents can be seen both as educators and as facilitators of social contact. Parents may explicitly set out to facilitate their child's interactions with other children by acting in a variety of roles. They may serve as coaches as they give advice, support, and directions about the most helpful and successful strategies for managing peer relationships. They may act as supervisors of peer–peer play in which their child participates; they may directly assist the children in initiating and maintaining play with other children. Parents can also influence their children's social relationships by providing opportunities for social contacts. This can occur in a variety of ways, including the choice of a residential neighborhood, the opportunity to participate in activities involving other children (e.g., preschool, clubs, sports), or as social arranger (e.g., scheduling and chauffeuring to facilitate social contacts).

Middle Childhood

Dramatic cognitive, social, emotional, and physical changes occur in the period when the child's world expands to include school and considerable organized activity; play and games in this context mirror these changes. The emerging awareness of truly interactive peer play experiences and the potential to assume other roles and negotiate social contracts leads the child to seek age-mates for play and to minimize play interactions within the family. During this period, the child is increasingly concerned with demonstrating competence, and the need to avoid feelings of inadequacy and inferiority is paramount. With these changes come new abilities, interests, and potentials that, in turn, lead the child naturally into participation in games and sports and more structured, rule-governed play activities. There is also expansion into other play forms, such as expressive, creative, and constructive activities. As might be expected, the play of girls and boys differs significantly in all aspects: choice of playmates, activity preference, activity level, affectivity, play style, and manner of interaction. In middle childhood, peer relationships engender activities no longer completely under parental control. On the other hand, the child is still living in the family and depends on parental provision and support. This situation of the child interacting daily in two different social systems makes it necessary to analyze the relationship between the child's earlier and enduring socialization within and through the family and the quality of his or her integration into the social peers network.

Kleiber and Kelly (1980) argued that leisure choices become significantly limited by this increased preoccupation with socialization. An overemphasis on one type of activity, such as can be seen with an athletic father pushing skill development in his son, may ultimately result in the child having a less playful attitude in general (Kleiber, 1978). Thus, parents who allow the child considerable initiative and choice in play may see the benefits through the development of later play behavior and attitudes toward play and leisure in general.

Although parents undeniably have the greatest influence on children within this age range, siblings serve as a play resource for other children in the family as well. For example, research has shown that children with older siblings are more likely than firstborn or only children to take risks and to engage in sports, especially dangerous ones (Yiannakis, 1976). Research that attempts to describe the play between siblings within this age period is still largely lacking.

Adolescence

The majority of adolescents consider their relationship with their parents as positive and name their parents as their relevant persons of confidence (the mother more frequently than the father). Lerner and Knapp (1975) compared the actual and perceived attitudes of late adolescents and their parents. They concluded that "both adolescents and parents misperceived the extensiveness of the divisions between them. Adolescents significantly overestimated the number of major differences between themselves and their mothers and fathers, while these two parental groups significantly underestimated such divisions" (p. 17). The relationship between the adolescent and his or her family in leisure is a combination, almost simultaneously, of pleasure, amusement, trust, conflict, control, anxiety, and tension.

The major developmental task of adolescence is ego identity, or autonomy. In theories of adolescence, the family is given a major role in grounding the ego identity through an early parent–child (or mother–child) relationship. According to Erikson (1959), a basic catalyst in the process of developing ego identity is the adolescent's separation from the parents and the construction of a self-image independent from the family ties. Small children idealize their parents and accept them without reservation. In early adolescence, this idealized image of the parents crumbles and as a result, parents tend to be highly criticized. Only during late adolescence does the child gain a more realistic perception of his or her parents. The basic premise is that a close emotional parent–child relationship during the early years supplies the underpinning the adolescent needs to sever infantile ties. From this assumption, it follows that lack of emotional closeness in the early parent–child relationship leads the young adult to attempt to make up for the emotional attachment he or she did not experience in his or her early childhood. This prevents or renders healthy separation more difficult in adolescence.

There is empirical evidence that illustrates the role of the family in shaping adolescent development and styles of interaction. Several authors (e.g., Niemi, 1988) have found that richness in the family's communication together, a positive home atmosphere, and open expression and discussion of conflicts, correlate strongly with 15-year-olds' thoughts about their family, themselves, and life in general. Hauser, Powers, and Noam (1984) proposed a model that illustrates how the adolescent ego develops through family transactions, and it contrasts enabling and constraining interaction styles. In later adolescence (18–21 years), security in familial relationships provided the support for meaningful exploration and experimentation, and it enhanced the adolescent's sociability, facilitating identity formation processes (Kamptner, 1988).

The search for personal identification so characteristic of this period and the threat of being "lost in the crowd" can be mediated partially by leisure. Leisure, a setting in which the adolescent can either exercise individual choices or respond to group pressure, can be a significant context in which identity crises can become resolved. Involvement in sports and social clubs still depends on the varying influences of modeling and social reinforcement provided by parents, peers, teachers, the media, and on cultural values. Although same-status peers are highly influential in the choice of leisure activities and associations, parents and family members continue to exert some influence. Noe and Elifson (1975) investigated the role of peers and parents as influential agents in the leisure orientations of middle-class suburban youth. An "egalitarian rebellious" orientation to leisure was associated with independence from parents and peers in both males and females. An additional finding was that parents did not seem to share an influence on leisure behavior, and the father had more overall influence. These "rebellious" patterns were also observed by Rapoport and Rapoport (1975), who noted that many adolescents go through a "hedonistic phase" where the pursuit of immediate, sensual pleasures is in direct contrast to the more puritanic work ethic and deferred gratification patterns of their parents. This seeking of immediate pleasures through leisure experiences is a departure from the prevailing influence of schools that, as parents do, tend to emphasize achievement through effort and tolerance of delayed rewards. The importance of leisure in adolescence, it has been argued, is that "it is a primary context for self-expression and social integration. It is, thus, critical in obtaining feedback relative to role learning and individual identity. It provides an optimum setting for experimenting with social relationships and individual potentials" (Kleiber & Kelly, 1980, p. 109).

The potential for leisure experiences to enhance the development of new relationships is particularly evident in dating and courtship. The formation of intimate relationships in adolescence and young adulthood tends to occur during recreational events in which "going out together" is associated with a mutually pleasurable experience, whether going to a party, seeing a movie, or playing tennis. Over the course of adolescence, there is a dramatic decline in parent-planned activities and a shift from activities dominated by persons of the same sex toward more time being spent with persons of the opposite sex (Orthner, Giddings, & Quinn, 1987). Many of the cross-sexual activity patterns that begin in adolescence serve as the basis for relational development in early marriage (Crawford, Godbey, & Crouter, 1986). Thus, the closing years of adolescence create the seeds for personal relational development in adulthood. By establishing leisure and relationship patterns that provide a basis for intimacy and satisfaction in adulthood, what started in infancy through active play with parents reaches the point, in adolescence, of generating new relationships through the use of play and an effective means of turning strangers into friends, companions, and even lovers.

LEISURE AND FAMILY IN YOUNG AND MIDDLE ADULTHOOD

Leisure experiences of most adults are dominated by marriage and family. As noted earlier, most young and middle adults today spend a majority of their discretionary time with other family members, and they place the highest value on that time. Leisure experiences, therefore, play a major role in how family relationships are formed and maintained in adulthood. Unfortunately, research on adult relationships has been dominated by investigations of work, parent, and household tasks with little attention being given to leisure behavior. This situation is now being corrected, as the role of leisure and recreation is better understood in terms of family development.

Leisure and Family Adjustment

With rates of divorce and marital conflict at an all time high, it is critically important to identify factors that promote personal and family adjustments and adaptation. One of the critical developmental tasks of adulthood is that of establishing and maintaining meaningful relationships that promote personal well-being and psychological health. Clearly, the quality of marriage and family relationships is one of the most significant factors in supporting psychological well-being. Leisure behavior and experiences may play a very significant role in promoting positive personal and family outcomes.

Interpersonal Attachments

Most research on family behavior has examined its consequences for the attachments between family members, including the level of affect associated with adult marital relationships. One of the most consistent findings in this research is that husbands and wives who share leisure time together in joint activities tend to be much more satisfied with their marriages than those who do not (Hawks, 1991). This finding holds whether the data are derived from attitudes regarding the sharing of family activities (Holman & Jacquart, 1988), or from records of actual leisure activity participation rates (Orthner, 1975). This relationship is so consistent that there does not seem to be any recent study that fails to find an association between the sharing of joint leisure activities and the level of positive affect among married men and women.

Shared leisure activities have been found to be particularly important to the satisfaction of wives, especially early in the marriage (Orthner, 1975; Smith, Snyder, & Morisma, 1988). During these years, relational attachments can be fragile because other reciprocal obligations, such as parenthood, voluntary associations, and friendship networks, are not as well established, and the marriage may be destabilized by more frequent moves and competing career demands. During this time, shared leisure experiences provide an important basis for relationship identity and attachments to the other. The more time allocated to joint participation in leisure activities that are mutually preferred, the more special the relationship becomes, and the greater the attachment associated with that relationship (Crawford, 1988).

A related, but consistent finding in the literature is the negative impact on marital attachments of each spouse's spending time alone in activities. Investigations of family time have found that higher than normal levels of time spent alone in leisure tends to be associated with lower levels of marital adjustment and attachment to the married partner (Hawks, 1991). Consistently, this finding is more true for wives than husbands, suggesting that women may be more likely to interpret higher levels of time spent alone as rejection or lack of concern on the part of their husbands. Individual activities, in and of themselves, are not deemed to influence family bonds negatively. Instead, it seems that when these activities become the dominant pattern in the family, this indicates lower levels of regard for the marital relationship.

A third type of family leisure behavior that has been examined in terms of family attachments are parallel leisure activities. These activities involve a shared setting, but typically do not promote participant interaction. The most common form of this is television watching. Orthner (1975) found that parallel activities are less likely to influence the marital attachments of husbands and wives positively. Palisi (1984) found similar results in a three-nation study, with positive but lower associations between marital adjustment and parallel leisure activities when compared to joint activities more likely to engage couples in interaction. More recently, Holman and Jacquart (1988) found that "low-joint," parallel activities were negatively associated with marital satisfaction for both husbands and wives. They concluded that leisure activities that require little or no communication provide little benefit to families and may actually reduce the interaction skills necessary to facilitate relational adaptation.

Relational Interaction

Shared leisure experiences offer the potential benefit of increasing interaction among participants and opening avenues for communication that can carry over to other aspects of the relationship. The relationship between shared leisure activities and marital communication is most commonly reported in the research literature. For example, Orthner (1976) found a very strong relationship between participation by husbands and wives in joint leisure activities and the level of their communication, as well as a strong negative relationship between participation in individual activities and marital communication. A study of marital adjustment in Belgium supported this finding, indicating that the frequency of joint leisure activities was positively related to marital communication, especially the nonverbal communication of caring (Presvelou, 1971).

It is interesting to note that higher levels of family interaction tend to be associated most with shared leisure participation in outdoor recreation activities. When different types of family activities are examined, there is a consistent pattern in the data indicating that family members who participate in outdoor recreation together tend to have higher levels of relationship communication and positive relational affect (cf. West & Merriam, 1970; Hill, 1988). It has been suggested that outdoor recreation may be associated with positive family attributes because it stimulates interaction among family members. Activities such as camping and hiking tend to break down traditional family roles, stimulate new patterns of communication, and concentrate attention on the relationships between family members. Thus, the benefits of outdoor recreation may not be tied to the actual activity itself, but to the interactional benefits associated with activities engaged in outdoors.

Conflict Management

Leisure roles and activities can also exert an impact on relational conflict. A national survey of American adults found that one third of American families experience stress from leisure conflicts (Straus, Gelles, & Steinmetz, 1980). In that survey, only household roles and sexual intimacy were more likely to cause family conflicts. Similar results were found in a worldwide study of military families (Orthner, 1980). In that study, conflicts over the use of leisure time and opportunities for companionship were found to be more stressful than child-rearing or family finances.

Among newly married husbands and wives, Holman (1981) found a positive relationship between the amount of shared leisure activities and verbal aggression. These findings were interpreted as an indication of increased overall interaction among couples who shared common activities, although, as part of that interaction, increased conflicts also occurred. Orthner and Mancini (1980) suggested that shared activities are likely to increase both positive and negative communication, and they serve as a healthy mechanism for reducing family tension and disagreements.

Parallel activities, such as television watching, have been hypothesized to reduce overt family tension by reducing negative interactions and minimizing communication that might lead to conflict (Orthner & Mancini, 1980). This hypothesis was confirmed by Rosenblatt and Cunningham (1976) in their study of television watching and family tension. These researchers found that levels of interpersonal tension were higher in families who lived in higher density household settings. However, if television watching increased with higher levels of density, there was less direct family conflict in these families. Thus, the parallel leisure activity (television watching) diminished family communication and reduced overt conflict, although interpersonal tension levels remained relatively high.

Leisure Socialization

The passing on from one generation to the next of leisure interests and competencies is a major activity of adulthood. It is common for husbands and wives to develop common leisure interests during courtship and to continue those interests in the early years of marriage. In addition, parents often use family time and rituals to initiate children into activities that they enjoy. Kelly (1974) found that about half the activities of the adults in his study had begun in childhood, and among those begun in adulthood, family members were the primary source of learning 63% of their current activities. Yoshioka (1981) found that parents or other family members were involved in the initial introduction of 83% of the recreational activities engaged in by children. Family recreational activities were much more likely to have been introduced during childhood than during adulthood.

Benefits for children of recreation with parents have been described in several key studies. Hume, O'Connor, and Lowrey (1977) examined boys who were either well adjusted or poorly adjusted and their parents. They found that among the boys, those who were poorly adjusted tended to watch more television, to spend less recreational time with their parents (especially their fathers), and to have fewer social contacts overall, especially with their fathers and other siblings. The fathers of the less well-adjusted boys also watched more television, engaged less in family recreation, and had fewer social contacts within the home.

The effects of parental involvement on adolescent development may be particularly important. Harris and Associates (1981) found that teenagers, especially girls, felt that their fathers did not spend enough time with them. In addition, they wanted to spend more time with their parents in various recreational activities, including going on vacation, talking together, and going to movies. This study revealed little difference between dual-earner and single-earner families in the amount of time that teenagers spent with their parents or in their desire for more family time. These concerns of adolescence were also reflected in a study of a national sample of adolescents (Orthner, Giddings, & Quinn, 1987). This study found that participation with parents in joint leisure activities was strongly associated with willingness to confide in parents, especially fathers, and with the psychological well-being of youth, especially daughters. Activity patterns were separated into instrumental activities designed to meet specific objectives and more informal expressive activities, including leisure activities. The data indicate that shared participation in leisure activities were associated more with adolescent–parent communication, adolescents' willingness to confide in parents, and the psychological well-being of adolescents.

Leisure and Marital Stability

Leisure experiences also are often hypothesized as promoting family stability. In this sense, stability implies relational continuity and lower probabilities for marital separation and divorce. As important as adjustment is to families, the bases for relational continuity are not necessarily the same as those for relational attachments and interaction. Attachments can be temporary, whereas stability is affected by a longer term process.

Very little attention has been given to relational stability and the use of leisure time and activities. One study examined differential divorce rates among persons from countries participating in a multinational study of leisure time use (Varga, 1972). That study found that countries with higher rates of marital and family shared leisure also tended to have higher divorce rates. Unfortunately, the same countries in that study that reported higher levels of shared family leisure also had divorce laws that were more likely to permit unhappy marriages to terminate. Thus, the relationship between marital stability and shared leisure was probably spurious.

More recently, Hill (1988) examined the data from the 1975–1981 Time Use Longitudinal Panel Study in order to test the association between shared leisure time among spouses and divorce probability. Her findings indicate that the amount of time shared between husbands and wives during the baseline period was significantly associated with marital stability five years later. In particular, the more time spent in shared leisure, the lower the probability of divorce, even when controlling for the presence and age of children. Of all the factors examined in the study, participation in recreational activities was the strongest contributor to marital stability. Even participation in activities such as watching television together was related to higher levels of stability, although the greatest associations were between shared outdoor recreation and lower divorce rates.

Leisure and Family Transitions

Over the family life cycle, families make a number of normative transitions associated with personal and family development. During times of transition, family members often have to develop new roles, communicate their intentions, resolve conflicts, and reestablish normative patterns of mutually acceptable behavior and affect. Typically, these periods are also times when leisure activities can change, or new barriers can arise that limit opportunities to continue traditional leisure patterns.

Transition to Marriage

Studies of early marriage generally confirm the importance of leisure activities to marital quality at that time. Unless children are also present, the number of barriers to shared leisure activities are comparatively low, and resources available to families often permit a wide choice of commercial and social activities (Witt & Goodale, 1982). Activity levels themselves change very little from the latter stages of courtship through the first few years of marriage, continuing the premarital contribution of leisure experiences to personal well-being and relational identity.

The employment pattern in the new family does not seem to affect the contribution of leisure activities to marital interaction and quality. Orthner and Axelson (1980) found that the wife's employment actually increased shared leisure participation among husbands and wives in early marriage. Schramm (1985) found a significant positive relationship between intimacy and shared leisure time among dual-career couples. At this stage of the family life cycle, employment is not a barrier to the amount of leisure time available to the couple, and it may increase the resources they have for recreation together.

Transition to Parenthood

The presence of children significantly changes the way husbands and wives relate to each other. The amount of time available for marital leisure activities declines, although the sum total of family recreation time may not change significantly. Recreation and play with children tends to increase, resulting in an overall balance of recreation not substantially different from the period before children appeared in the relationship. Men report a substantial increase in the amount of time they spend in activities alone or with nonfamily members, whereas women are much more likely to be engaged in activities with their children (Orthner, 1975).

The major life cycle transition during parenthood is a substantial change in the barriers to leisure enjoyment among family members (Witt & Goodale, 1981). Perceptions that one does "not have enough free time" increase markedly during the entire childbearing period, and they decrease only after the children are gone. Similarly, family obligations are perceived to increase significantly, diminishing flexibility, especially to mothers, and creating increased activity centered on the children, rather than on the adults, in the household. As a consequence, this research found that over the course of child-rearing, adult leisure experiences tended to suffer, and both husbands and wives tended to report higher levels of daily stress and less ability to meet family and friends' expectations for companionship and mutual enjoyment.

Transition to the Empty Nest

There is a tendency for the leisure interests of husbands and wives to diverge over the course of marriage, particularly during the middle years of the family life cycle (Mancini & Orthner, 1978). After children are launched, however, interests in companionship tend to increase substantially, and the level of companionship tends to be significantly related to the quality of the marital adjustment (Orthner, 1975). Both joint and parallel activities shared by husbands and wives contribute to readjustments in the marriage as children leave home. Only a predominance of activities engaged in alone tends to diminish satisfaction with leisure and attachments to the marriage.

Barriers to shared leisure activities also diminish significantly in the middle years of marriage. Employment becomes less inhibiting to family leisure and resources for shared leisure increase. Both women and men perceive a reduction in family obligations and fewer claim that they do not have enough free time. On the negative side, however, both husbands and wives tend to report less motivation for shared leisure after the child-rearing stage (Witt & Goodale, 1981). It has been suggested that leisure may become a less important basis for family attachments among some couples because of increased investments in work obligations and children during the primary parenting years (Rapoport & Rapoport, 1975). On a more positive note, among husbands and wives who are personally committed to constructive adjustments to their new life stage, barriers to shared leisure were significantly lower. Witt and Goodale note that "these individuals may feel less constrained by family obligations and freer to lead their own lives" (p. 43). Thus, in the middle years of marriage, some families reconceptualize their relationships, focusing them on shared time and leisure, whereas others continue in the pattern of relational divergence begun during parenthood and focus on personal interests and minimal shared leisure time.

LEISURE AND FAMILY IN OLDER ADULTHOOD

Spending time with family and actively engaging in leisure pursuits are said to provide numerous benefits to people in the later years of the life cycle. Kantor and Lehr (1975) contend, "One's satisfaction with existence is closely dependent on whether he feels he is getting what he wants out of life, a goal irrevocably connected with the utilization of time" (p. 89). Rapoport and Rapoport (1975) note, "The meaning of leisure in later life is complex and variable" (p. 312). Brubaker (1990) states, "For many older persons, family relationships are key to receiving support and negotiating everyday demands," but "the dynamics of later-life family relationships are not fully understood, nor is the complexity of these relationships fully described" (p. 13). These comments serve as a guideline for what follows in this chapter. The goal is to elaborate the relationships between leisure and family life for older adults. This nexus has rarely been studied by either family psychologists or by gerontologists (Mancini & Blieszner, 1989).

Transitions in Later Life

Relationships with family members are pivotal for older adults. These relationships may exist with siblings, spouses, children, and grandchildren. Not only does the family represent a potential support mechanism for older people, but younger generations often receive support from their elders. Involvement with the family provides opportunities for the older person to influence the lives of significant others in meaningful ways. Studies of the help exchange patterns between older and younger generations shows that mutual support is both expressive and instrumental (Lewis, 1990). Instrumental activities include anything involving goods and services (child care, housekeeping, and sick care) and expressive activities include showing affection, listening to problems, and providing encouragement.

The significant family relationship issues for older adults are best represented by the term *transitions,* occurring at several generational levels: the oldest, the middle, and the youngest generation; and at several family composition levels: the marital dyad, and the parent–child dyads. From a developmental perspective, there is movement within each generation and between the generations. For example, the older person may be experiencing the transition that accompanies a change in employment status, the death of a spouse, or a change in health. The mid-life adult in the family may be experiencing the loss of one parent, the launching of her or his own children, or the leveling-out of his or her career development. Young adult family members may be coping with educational and early career choices, establishing their own nuclear family, or becoming more independent from their parents. In all, any number of events that require a transition may be occurring. The transitions that individuals make always involve others in the family, so that an event that originates in one generational cohort of the family migrates to the others.

Leisure, Relationship Patterns, and Change

Leisure is the principal context in which relationships among older adults develop their character. Within the parameter of time, family members act, react, interact, debate, negotiate, support, show affection, teach, and disclose. Leisure provides a unique way for family members to develop their relationship because, by definition and by expectation, leisure time is less constrained and more pleasurable. This is not to say that expectations are necessarily met, because both cohesion and dissonance can occur (Orthner & Mancini, 1980). However, fewer family rules exist to govern leisure time.

Reorganization of Family Time

Many events require a reorganization of time for older adults, including changes in health or the loss of someone close. One transition that is normative in later adulthood occurs when people retire from full-time work. At that point, the amount of discretionary time changes, so that more choices of time use are available. Because time is no longer structured by employment, the retired person must make more decisions about time use. How time is reorganized can have dramatic outcomes for many people in the family. At the least, their expectations change. A retired man may expect that he and his wife will now do everything together. A wife who has not worked outside the home may expect that she and her husband will travel extensively. The retired older adult may expect to spend more time with his or her offspring and to do more with the grandchildren. It is unlikely that any of the above expectations will have been discussed among the various family members.

Activity Pattern Changes

Research has shown that leisure and recreation participation tend to decline with advancing age (Cutler & Hendricks, 1990). However, the amount and rate of decline is influenced by many factors, including individual health, economic resources, activity type, and family life cycle. Kelly (1987) has reported that activity declines pertain to outdoor and physically active pursuits, rather than to family and social activities. Time may be used in certain ways, such as participation in organizations, because of the developmental stage of younger family members (Cutler, 1976).

A key dimension as to why activity patterns may change involves activity preferences. Mancini and Orthner (1978) examined the leisure and recreational preferences of wives and husbands across the family life cycle. Overall, husbands' preferences for collaborative leisure pursuits (those requiring interaction with others) were higher as cohorts aged, and wives' preferences for independent activities were higher as cohorts aged. Dorfman and Heckert (1988) found that often in retirement, household roles were more likely to be shared, joint decision making increased significantly, and couples were much more likely to participate together in joint leisure activities.

Patterns of Intimacy and Friendship

An often unrecognized component of the "family" of older adults is their friendship network. Studies of psychological well-being and social support suggest that interaction and intimacy with friends is significant (Adams & Blieszner, 1989; Crohan & Antonucci, 1989). Close friendships function in the lives of older adults in several ways; they provide opportunities for attachment, social integration, assistance, guidance, competence, and nurturance (Weiss, 1969). Research on the above shows that shared leisure participation in friendships is associated with less loneliness, more positive feelings about aging, and less personal agitation (Mancini & Blieszner, 1992).

Relationships with Adult Children

There is substantial research on the nature of parent–child relationships when both parent and child are mature adults (Mancini & Blieszner, 1989; Mancini, 1989). The parent–child dyad remains prominent as people age and is the primary link between the older adult and the rest of the family. Much of the exchange between older people and others in the family occurs with their adult children. The nature of the parent–child relationship changes and transitions are required if the dyad is to remain viable. This is seen clearly in the area of decision making. The mature child does not expect that her or his parent will be involved in her or his decisions without express invitation. Nor is the older parent anxious to cede their personal decision-making rights to their adult child. This area is ripe for conflict because of what one generation does not understand about the individual needs and expectations of the other. One common basis for relationships between older adults and their adult children is shared leisure interests. Weiss and Bailey (1985) found that elderly parents often continue to maintain many of the leisure patterns they established earlier in life, which they used in socializing their children. Thus, middle-aged children were likely to have the same leisure interests as their parents, particularly those of the same sex.

Grandparenting

About 94% of older adults with adult children are grandparents (Roberto, 1990). Although there is relatively little research concerning grandparent–grandchild relationships, what is known suggests considerable variability in the grandparent role. Many years ago Neugarten and Weinstein (1964) identified several types of grandparenting, one of which they labeled *fun seeker*; that is, the relationship with the grandchild is mainly informal and playful. More recent research by Cherlin and Furstenberg (1986) identified a similar style of grandparenting as *companionate*; that is, typified by an easygoing and friendly style of interaction.

The grandparent experience is said to contribute to both the psychological well-being (Kivnick, 1982) and psychosocial development (Kivnick, 1985) of the older adult. The sense that life is good and positive may be enhanced by the bond that develops between a young person, who looks up to an elder and who is treated in a special way by that elder, and the older adult, who takes joy in the vitality of the young and in having a unique relationship with the young person. From an individual developmental perspective, the grandparent role may give the older adult an opportunity to develop new ways of caring and showing affection toward another, and an opportunity to demonstrate wisdom.

Close Relationship Loss

Loss is both a pivotal event and a significant emotion. Although loss occurs for many different reasons (moving away, separation, divorce, retirement) we focus here on loss caused by death of a family member or of a friend. Close relationship loss is a change not easily mitigated, because that which we experience with people with whom we are close is unique and cannot be repeated with others in the same way. What we experience with family and friends is often tied to a developmental period or circumstance, so the experience has special meaning (Blieszner & Mancini, 1992).

Loss of Friends

Because of the intensity of friendship ties between older adults, loss through death has great significance. As with kin, friends exchange emotional and practical support. Activities are shared and a history of intimacy is established. Consequently, when that bond is severed, personal disorganization occurs and there is a need for recovery and adjustment. At some point, emotional acceptance must occur (Weiss, 1988).

Loss of Spouse

As with the loss of a friend, when a spouse dies there is a disruption in attachment. Losing a spouse is especially common for older adult women. Almost 40% of women 65 to 74 years are widowed, whereas 80% of men in that age group are married and living with their wives. When a spouse dies, the stress is usually substantial because of the changes required in lifestyle; therefore, many transitions must occur for recovery to be complete. Research shows that the most effective coping strategies used by widows and widowers are often tied to rebuilding leisure experiences, including keeping active, learning new skills, doing things with family, and maintaining active friendships (Heinemann & Evans, 1990).

Interplay of Interpersonal Development and Leisure

The interplay between what happens in families and how time is used is constant and significant. Older adults with active leisure lifestyles experience many therapeutic outcomes (Mancini, 1984). When people experience a change, they often ask, "What am I going to do?" Satisfactory adaptation to life course transitions has much to do with what they do with their time. Leisure experiences continue to be important to the establishment and maintenance of relationships and for coping with the loss of those relationships. There is always a context within which things happen. For both intragenerational and intergenerational relationships, leisure serves as a primary vehicle to support relationship development. Doing things with others fosters relationships; not doing things with others diminishes them.

Part and parcel of relating to one's adult children and grandchildren and one's intimate friends is spending time with them in activities that are largely by choice and less due to obligation. Time spent in leisure provides experiences that become important parts of the history of a relationship or of a family. This history, created through the shared leisure experiences, is what can help people through a loss. Moreover, enjoyable activities aid in the transitions forced by loss, benefiting the individuals and the relationships. Personal and relational freedom occurs during leisure moments; for adults it may be the only time that they can permit themselves to play. For younger family members, it is part of their socialization experience.

CONCLUSION AND DISCUSSION

As this chapter indicates, leisure experiences vary in their contribution to family members over the family life cycle. The symbolic meaning and value of play for children is somewhat similar to its value for adults, but its relative contribution to the developmental needs of each person in the family is not necessarily uniform. Children, young adults, and older adults place different values on family relationships at different points of their lives, but leisure experiences retain their importance in defining personal and relational satisfaction. Kelly (1991) notes that the personal benefits of leisure are clearly developmental.

> Through the life course, the play of leisure is a crucial context in which individuals take action that contributes to their development. Not only the play of children, but the relatively open action of adults in every life period provides for both the continuity and change of self-definitions and lines of action. Leisure and recreation provide opportunities for self-creation and expression that may be limited in other roles and contexts. (p. 420)

Erikson's (1959) stages of child and adult development reflect the changing contributions that leisure makes to personal development over the family life cycle. Initially, gentle and supportive play between parents and children conditions the level of trust that the child needs in its environment. As children develop into adolescence, recreation and leisure roles provide opportunities to test new skills and capabilities for independence and interpersonal competence. In young adulthood, needs for intimacy are expressed in play and contribute to interpersonal attachment and commitments. In middle adulthood, family leisure experiences encourage generativity, the passing on of the self through socialization of others, including children, friends, and colleagues. In later adulthood, personal and relational integrity are affirmed through memories of contributions that have been made to others and the value that comes from contributing to others through shared intimacy among contemporaries and shared experiences with those they have influenced over their lifetimes.

Over the family life cycle, the patterns of leisure can vary in terms of activity patterns, settings, and constraints. Research has consistently confirmed that leisure activities vary according to the age of the person and the stage of the family life cycle. The importance of play cannot be underestimated for children, but the types of activities engaged in by children vary significantly as they mature. Likewise, childless adults have more discretionary time and engage in a wider range of leisure activities than do adults who are parents (Holman & Epperson, 1984). This differentiation of activities continues into middle age and older adulthood (Mancini & Orthner, 1978).

The importance of activity differentiation comes from the ways through which leisure activities promote relationship interaction and cohesion. Shared leisure activities promote opportunities for communication, the exchange of new ideas, and the development of new roles that may challenge traditional patterns of interaction in the family. Playing together offers new opportunities for seeing one another in a new light and developing new rules for relating to one another. Likewise, shared leisure experiences promote relational cohesion through the common satisfactions gained in special activities that are associated with the family. Family satisfaction is often tied to special experiences that occur during leisure and recollections of favorite family occasions such as vacations, special trips, or times spent together in unique family activities.

Settings for leisure activities can also characterize the family and can change over the family life cycle. The leisure experiences of children are often spatially limited, and child development is often characterized by the boundaries parents set for their children's explorations. Adult leisure settings are substantially larger and often characterized by special places or islands within which leisure activities are engaged, such as the TV room, basement, or the health club (L'Abate, 1990). Settings for adult leisure often define the nature of leisure experiences, as well as its personal or social outcomes. Clearly, watching television dominates family leisure today, but this often stifles communication, whereas increasingly rare activities such as family game playing stimulate interaction.

Significant constraints have been identified that serve as barriers to leisure experiences and can limit the opportunity for leisure activities to make a positive impact on personal and family development. Perhaps the most common barrier is that of leisure time itself. Time for leisure experiences is often given lower priority than time for other obligations. The value of leisure may be verbally affirmed, but it is not always sufficiently powerful to generate the substantial time needed to reify its meaning. Work hours are no longer diminishing, as was once predicted. The majority of wives and mothers are now in the labor force, and children's time is often consumed by preprogrammed events. Each of these forces restricts access to discretionary time and the experience of leisure in families, limiting opportunities to share play recreation and mutual enjoyment.

Implications for Research and Practice

Research on the role of leisure for personality development in the family needs further development. The major problem in the current research is the conflicting conceptualizations of leisure, with researchers defining leisure behavior and experiences in different ways. More consistent operational definitions are needed, and a strong theoretical foundation is needed in order to achieve this. Much of the current research is sociologic and descriptive. More effort must be given to identifying the social psychological outcomes of leisure experiences, particularly as they relate to family processes. Very few studies have examined the consequences of leisure experiences for family members in relation to one another. Research methodologies and measurement systems other than surveys must be employed in order to explore the causal relationship between leisure activities and the outcomes hypothesized in this chapter.

Family intervention and therapy also must give greater attention to the role of leisure in healthy family and personality development. All too often, leisure experiences are reviewed anecdotally, without substantial grounding in practice theory. Studies of leisure behavior or interventions among clinical samples are very rare, although more attention has recently been given to this issue in family psychology (L'Abate, 1990). It is also important to understand how different leisure experiences contribute to cohesion in families with different patterns of interaction. Not all families are organized in the same way, and leisure experiences may contribute very differently to the cohesion of some families than that of others.

In conclusion, it is clear that leisure experiences have potential value to families and to those assisting families to make more effective personal and relational adjustments. Family stress is enormous today, and leisure experiences are frequently used to ameliorate that stress. Research confirms that "the family that plays together often stays together," but we need much more information than we now have to assist family members in making good choices about how to use their time together in a way that effectively builds relational quality. The ambivalence that many families have about leisure is also reflected in the social and behavioral sciences. The research and practice professions must give more attention to this important concept so the complexity of family relationships today and their impacts on personal development and well-being can be more fully understood.

REFERENCES

Adams, R. G., & Blieszner, R. (Eds.). (1989). *Older adult friendship: Structure and process.* Newbury Park, CA: Sage.

Barnett, L. A. (1991). Developmental benefits of play for children. In B. L. Driver, P. J. Brown, & G. L. Peterson (Eds.), *Benefits of leisure.* State College, PA: Venture.

Barnett, L. A., & Chick, G. E. (1986). Chips off the ol'block: Parents' leisure and their children's play. *Journal of Leisure Research, 18,* 266–283.

Belsky, J., Garduque, L., & Hrncir, E. (1984). Assessing performance, competence, and executive capacity in infant play: Relations to home environment and the security of attachment. *Developmental Psychology, 20,* 406–417.

Bellah, R. N., Madsen, R., Sullivan, W. M., Swidler, A., & Tipton, S. M. (1985). *Habits of the heart: Individualism and commitment in American life.* Berkeley: University of California Press.

Blieszner, R., & Mancini, J. A. (1992). Developmental perspectives on relationship loss. In T. L. Orbuch (Ed.), *Close relationship loss: Theoretical perspectives* (pp. 142–154). New York: Springer.

Brubaker, T. H. (Ed.). (1990). *Family Relationships in Later Life* (2nd ed.). Newbury Park, CA: Sage.

Bruner, J. S. (1983). *Child's talk.* New York: Norton.

Burgess, E. W., & Locke, H. J. (1945). *The family: From institution to companionship.* New York: American Book.

Caplow, T., Bahr, H. M., Chadwick, B. A., Hill, R., & Williamson, M. H. (1982). *Middletown families.* Minneapolis: University of Minnesota Press.

Cherlin, A., & Furstenberg, F. (1986). *The new American grandparent.* New York: Basic Books.

Crawford, D. W., Jr. (1988). The patterns of leisure companionship during the early marital relationship. Unpublished doctoral dissertation, The Pennsylvania State University.

Crawford, D. W., Godbey, G. G., & Crouter, A. C. (1986). The stability of leisure preferences. *Journal of Leisure Research, 18,* 96–115.

Crohan, S. E., & Antonucci, T. C. (1989). Friends as a source of social support in old age. In R. G. Adams & R. Blieszner (Eds.), *Older adult friendship: Structure and process* (pp. 129–146). Newbury Park, CA: Sage.

Cutler, S. J. (1976). Age profiles of membership in sixteen types of voluntary associations. *Journal of Gerontology, 31,* 462–470.

Cutler, S. J., & Hendricks, J. (1990). Leisure time use across the life cycle. In R. H. Binstock & L. K. George (Eds.), *Handbook of aging and the social sciences* (3rd ed., pp. 169–185). New York: Academic.

Decision Research. (1987). *1987 Leisure study.* Lexington, MA: Author.

Dorfman, L. T., & Heckert, D. A. (1988). Egalitarianism in retired rural couples: Household tasks, decision making, and leisure activities. *Family Relations, 37* (1), 73–78.

Erikson, E. (1959). *Identity and the life cycle.* Madison, CT: International Universities Press.

Escalona, S. (1968). *The roots of individuality.* Chicago: Aldine.

Frodi, A., & Lamb, M. E. (1980). Child abusers' responses to infant smiles and cries. *Child Development, 51,* 238–241.

Gaensbauer, T., Mrazek, D., & Harmon, R. (1980). Affective behavior patterns in abused and/or neglected infants. In N. Frude (Ed.), *The understanding and prevention of child abuse: Psychological approaches.* London, UK: Concord Press.

Harris, L. and Associates. (1981). *Families at work: The General Mills American family report.* Minneapolis, MN: General Mills.

Hauser, S. T., Powers, S. I., & Noam, G. G. (1984). Familial contexts of adolescent ego development. *Child Development, 55,* 195–213.

Hawks, S. R. (1991). Recreation in the family. In S. J. Bahr (Ed.), *Family research: A sixty-year review, 1930–1990,* (Vol. 1, pp. 387–433). Toronto: Lexington Books.

Heinemann, G. D., & Evans, P. L. (1990). Widowhood: Loss, change, and adaptation. In T. H. Brubaker (Ed.), *Family relationships in later life* (2nd ed. pp. 142–168). Newbury Park, CA: Sage.

Hill, M. S. (1988). Marital stability and spouses' shared time. *Journal of Family Issues, 9*, 427–451.

Holman, T. B. (1981). *A path analytic test of a model of early marital quality: The direct and indirect effects of premarital and marital factors.* Unpublished doctoral dissertation, Brigham Young University, Provo, UT.

Holman, T. B., & Epperson, A. (1984). Family and leisure: A review of the literature with research recommendations. *Journal of Leisure Research, 16,* 277–294.

Holman, T. B., & Jacquart, M. (1988). Leisure-activity patterns and marital satisfaction: A further test. *Journal of Marriage and the Family, 50,* 69–77.

Hume, N., O'Connor, W. A., & Lowery, C. R. (1977). Family, adjustment, and the psychosocial ecosystem. *Psychiatric Annals, 7,* 345–355.

Juster, F. T., & Stafford, F. P. (1985). *Time, goods, and well-being.* Ann Arbor: Survey Research Center, Institute for Social Research, University of Michigan.

Kamptner, N. L. (1988). Identity development in late adolescence: Causal modeling of social and familial influences. *Journal of Youth and Adolescence, 17,* 493–514.

Kantor, D., & Lehr, W. (1975). *Inside the family: Toward a theory of family process.* New York: Harper Collins.

Kelly, J. R. (1974). Socialization toward leisure: A developmental approach. *Journal of Leisure Research, 6,* 181–193.

Kelly, J. R. (1987). *Peoria winter: Styles and resources in later life.* Lexington, MA: Lexington Books.

Kelly, J. R. (1991). Sociological perspectives on recreation benefits. In B. L. Driver, P. J. Brown, & G. L. Peterson (Eds.), *Benefits of leisure* (pp. 419–422). State College, PA: Venture Publishing.

Kivnick, H. (1982). *The meaning of grandparenthood.* Ann Arbor, MI: The University of Michigan.

Kivnick, H. (1985). Grandparenthood and mental health: Meaning, behavior, and satisfaction. In V. Bengtson & J. Robertson (Eds.), *Grandparenthood* (pp. 151–158). Newbury Park, CA: Sage.

Kleiber, D. A. (1978). Games and sport in personality and social development. Unpublished manuscript, University of Illinois, Champaign.

Kleiber, D. A., & Kelly, J. R. (1980). Leisure, socialization, and the life cycle. In S. Iso-Ahola (Ed.), *Social psychological perspectives on leisure and recreation* (pp. 91–137). Springfield, IL: Thomas.

L'Abate, L. L. (1990). A theory of competencies × settings interations. In D. G. Unger (Ed.), *Families in community settings: Interdisciplinary perspectives.* Binghamton, NY: Haworth.

Lamb, M. E. (1977). Father–infant and mother–infant interaction in the first year of life. *Child Development, 48,* 167–181.

Lerner, R. M., & Knapp, J. R. (1975). Actual and perceived intrafamilial attitudes of late adolescents and their parents. *Journal of Youth and Adolescence, 4,* 17–36.

Levenstein, P. (1985). Mothers' interactive behavior in play sessions and children's educational achievement. In C. C. Brown & A. W. Gottfried (Eds.), *Play interactions: The role of toys in parental involvement in children's development* (pp. 160–167). Skillman, NJ: Johnson & Johnson.

Levinger, G. (1965). Marital cohesiveness and dissolution: An integrated review. *Journal of Marriage and the Family, 27,* 19–28.

Lewis, R. A. (1990). The adult child and older parents. In T. H. Brubaker (Ed.), *Family relationships in later life* (2nd ed., pp. 68–85). Newbury Park, CA: Sage.

MacDonald, K., & Parke, R. D. (1984). Parent–child physical play: The effects of sex and age on children and parents. *Sex Roles: A Journal of Research, 15,* 367–378.

Main, M., & Weston, D. R. (1981). The quality of the toddler's relationship to mother and father: Related to conflict behavior and the readiness to establish new relationships. *Child Development, 52,* 932–940.

Mancini, J. A. (1984). Leisure lifestyles and family dynamics in old age. In W. H. Quinn & G. A. Hughston (Eds.), *Independent aging: Family and social systems perspectives* (pp. 58–71). Rockville, MD: Aspen.

Mancini, J. A. (Ed.). (1989). *Aging parents and adult children.* Lexington, MA: Lexington Books.

Mancini, J. A., & Blieszner, R. (1989). Aging parents and adult children: Research themes in intergenerational relationships. *Journal of Marriage and the Family, 51,* 275–290.

Mancini, J. A., & Blieszner, R. (1992). Social provisions in adulthood: Concept and measurement in close relationships. *Journal of Gerontology: Psychological Sciences, 47,* 14–20.

Mancini, J. A., & Orthner, D. K. (1978). Recreational sexuality preferences among middle-class husbands and wives. *Journal of Sex Research, 14,* 96–106.

Neugarten, B. L., & Weinstein, K. (1964). The changing American grandparent. *Journal of Marriage and the Family, 26,* 199–204.

Niemi, P. M. (1988). Family interaction patterns and the development of social conceptions in the adolescent. *Journal of Youth and Adolescence, 17,* 429–444.

Noe, F. P., & Elifson, K. W. (1975). The pleasures of youth: Parent and peer compliance toward discretionary time. Paper presented at the American Sociological Association Convention, Chicago.

Orthner, D. K. (1975). Leisure activity patterns and marital satisfaction over the marital career. *Journal of Marriage and the Family, 37,* 91–102.

Orthner, D. K. (1976). Patterns of leisure and marital interaction. *Journal of Leisure Research, 8,* 98–111.

Orthner, D. K. (1980). *Families in blue: A study of U.S. Air Force married and single parent families.* Washington, DC: Department of the Air Force.

Orthner, D. K., & Axelson, L. J. (1980). The effects of wife employment on marital sociability. *Journal of Comparative Family Studies, 11,* 531–543.

Orthner, D. K., Giddings, M. M., & Quinn, W. H. (1987). *Youth in transition: A study of adolescents from Air Force and civilian families.* Athens: University of Georgia Press.

Orthner, D. K., & Mancini, J. A. (1980). Leisure behavior and group dynamics: The case of the family. In Seppo E. Iso-Ahola (Ed.), *Social psychological perspectives on leisure and recreation* (pp. 307–328). Springfield, IL: Thomas.

Orthner, D. K., & Mancini, J. A. (1991). Benefits of leisure for family bonding. In B. L. Driver, P. J. Brown, & G. L. Peterson (Eds.), *Benefits of leisure* (pp. 419–422), State College, PA: Venture.

Palisi, B. J. (1984). Marriage companionship and marriage well-being: A comparison of metropolitan areas in three countries. *Journal of Comparative Family Studies, 15,* 43–56.

Power, T. G., & Parke, R. D. (1982). Play as a context for early learning: Lab and home analyses. In I. E. Sigel & L. M. Laosa (Eds.), *The family as a learning environment* (pp. 223–241). New York: Plenum.

Presvelou, C. (1971). Impact of differential leisure activities on intraspousal dynamics. *Human Relations, 24,* 565–574.

Rapoport, R., & Rapoport, R. N. (1975). *Leisure and the family life cycle.* London: Routledge & Kegan Paul.

Ratner, N., & Bruner, J. (1978). Games, social exchange, and the acquisition of language. *Journal of Child Language, 5,* 391–401.

Roberto, K. A. (1990). Grandparent and grandchild relationships. In T. H. Brubaker (Ed.), *Family relationships in later life* (2nd ed., pp. 100–112). Newbury Park, CA: Sage.

Rosenblatt, P. C., & Cunningham, M. R. (1976). Television watching and family tension. *Journal of Marriage and the Family, 38,* 103–111.

Schramm, M. L. (1985). *The relationship of intimacy to use of leisure time in dual-career couples.* Unpublished doctoral dissertation, Texas A & M University.

Slade, A. (1987). Quality of attachment and early symbolic play. *Developmental Psychology, 23,* 78–85.

Smith, G. T., Snyder, T. J., & Morisma, B. R. (1988). Predicting relationship satisfaction from couples' use of leisure time. *American Journal of Family Therapy, 16,* 107–109.

Stern, D. N. (1977). *The first relationship.* Cambridge, MA: Harvard University Press.

Straus, M., Gelles, R., & Steinmetz, S. (1980). *Behind closed doors.* New York: Doubleday.

Troll, L. E. (1972). The salience of members of three-generation families for one another. Paper presented at the American Psychological Association Annual Meeting, Honolulu.

United Media Enterprises Report on Leisure in America. (1982). *Where does the time go?* New York: Author.

Varga, K. (1972). Marital cohesion as reflected in time budgets. In A. Szalai (Ed.), *The use of time.* pp. 357–375. The Hague: Mouton.

Watson, J. S., & Ramey, C. T. (1972). Reactions to response contingent stimulation in early infancy. *Merrill-Palmer Quarterly, 18,* 219–227.

Weiss, R. S. (1969). The fund of sociability. *TransAction, 6,* 36–43.

Weiss, R. S. (1988). Loss and recovery. *Journal of Social Issues, 44,* 37–52.

Weiss, C. R., & Bailey, B. B. (1985). The influence of older adults' activity selection on their progeny's expectations for their own future. *Activities, Adaptation, & Aging, 6,* 103–114.

West, P. C., & Merriam, L. C., Jr. (1970). Outdoor recreation and family cohesion: A research approach. *Journal of Leisure Research, 2,* 251–259.

Witt, P. A., & Goodale, T. L. (1981). The relationships between barriers to leisure enjoyment and family stages. *Leisure Sciences, 4,* 29–49.

Yiannakis, A. (1976). Birth order and preference for dangerous sports among males. *Research Quarterly for Exercise and Sport, 47,* 62–67.

Yoshioka, C. F. (1981). Leisure socialization and adult and child related decision-making interactions in family recreational activities. Unpublished doctoral dissertation, University of Oregon, Eugene.

CHAPTER 10

Older Individuals in the Family

CLIFFORD H. SWENSEN

People over 65 years are in the last stage of family life (Duvall, 1971). They have a life expectancy of 15 to 20 years or more (U.S. Bureau of the Census, 1990; TIAA-CREF, 1991), and this life expectancy is increasing. Most are married and have children, grandchildren, and living siblings (U.S. Bureau of the Census, 1988).

This increasing life expectancy has produced an overlap in the lives of parents and children above 50 years, and an overlap in the lives of grandparents and grandchildren of more than 20 years (Uhlenberg, 1980). Most families have four or five generations living at the same time. The extended time of life overlap produces greater family intimacy between generations. Four or five living generations create greater complexity in family relationships (Bengtson, Rosenthal, & Burton, 1990; Hagestad, 1986, 1988).

People in the last stage of life must cope with three main transitions: retirement, physical decline and disability, and death (Bishop & Shoemaker, 1987). Each of these transitions imposes tasks that must be accomplished (Giordano & Beckham, 1985) and that affect relationships within the family.

Most older people live within families with spouses, children, grandchildren, and living siblings. In this stage of life, they must cope with retirement, physical decline, and death. In this chapter, we discuss these relationships and the problems older people must cope with within these relationships.

MARRIAGE

Marital Satisfaction

Most couples report the postretirement stage as the most satisfying stage of marriage (Ade-Ridder, 1985, 1990; Bengtson, et al., 1990; Sporakowski & Hughston, 1978; Swensen, 1987). These marriages are particularly satisfying in the 63 to 69 year period (Gilford, 1986). Satisfied couples have the following characteristics (Brubaker & Ade-Ridder, 1987; Ferraro & Wan, 1986; MacKinnon, MacKinnon, & Franken, 1984):

1. They reserve time for themselves.

2. They control their time so they can engage in rewarding activities.

3. They maintain open communication in their relationship.

4. They have greater involvement in church.

5. They are confident of resolving conflicts.

6. They are satisfied with their health.

7. They have a healthy sexual relationship and a satisfactory expression of affection.

8. They are satisfied with their finances.

9. They perceive their mates as not being moody, stubborn, jealous, or possessive.

10. They have relationships with friends.

11. The husband has a positive attitude toward retirement.

The husband's morale is most affected by health concerns, whereas the wife's morale is most affected by concerns about family well-being (Bishop, Epstein, Baldwin, Miller, & Keitner, 1988; Sporakowski & Axelson, 1984).

Although most postretirement couples report that the last stage of marriage is the best, some studies report that the longer a couple is married, the less satisfied they are (Blood & Wolf, 1960; Cuber & Harroff, 1965; Pineo, 1961). Other studies found that marriage satisfaction is curvilinear—declining in the childrearing years, then improving after the children leave home (Rollins & Cannon, 1974).

Perhaps the solution to this disagreement can be found by investigating which aspects of marriage change over the life cycle and for whom they change. Studies have shown that the expressions of love, marriage problems, and commitment to the spouse as a person all decline over the course of marriage (Swensen, Eskew, & Kohlhepp, 1981; Swensen & Trahaug, 1985). Expressions of love can decline when couples talk to each other less. Marriage problems can decline when couples sever relationships with others who cause problems in the marriage. Commitment can shift from that to the spouse as a person to commitment to the marriage as a social compact.

However, these declines do not exist in all couples. Those with a more complex ego development and who maintain or increase their commitment to their spouse as a person can increase their expressions of love and can have fewer marriage problems. Older couples evaluate their marriages more highly than young married couples (Ade-Ridder, 1990). Finally, studies consistently show that older, married people are more satisfied with their lives than single, divorced, or widowed older people (Gilford, 1986). Therefore, older, married couples may rate their marriages as very satisfactory because they perceive themselves to be significantly more satisfied with their lives than their unmarried peers.

Marital Transitions

Older couples must cope with three main transitions in their postretirement marriage relationship. The first transition is retirement. The other transitions are physical decline and disability, and, finally, death.

Retirement

At retirement the husband and wife usually begin to spend more time together. Most report being happy after retirement (Johnston, 1990; Keating & Cole, 1980; Tryban, 1985), but there can be problems. For many spouses, this increased time together can result in finding their spouse's heretofore mildly annoying habits to be almost intolerable. (Johnston, 1990).

When a husband retires, he spends more time at home, shifts his main focus from work to his wife (Keating & Cole, 1980; Tryban, 1985), and the relationship becomes more equal in power (Hesse-Biber & Williamson, 1984; Sporakowski & Axelson, 1984). With the husband spending more time at home, the wife loses both her autonomy in running the household and the privacy she may have enjoyed during work hours when she was home alone.

Furthermore, with the husband becoming more involved in his relationship to his wife, she has less time to devote to other activities, or to relationships with friends outside the marriage. There is evidence that men become more affiliative and concerned with interpersonal relationships, whereas women become more instrumental and assertive as they age (Giordano & Beckham, 1985; Long & Mancini, 1990). Moreover, wives who have worked miss contact with work colleagues (Keating & Cole, 1980).

These changes change the nature of the marriage relationship and can create conflict or exacerbate previous conflicts between husband and wife. If the changes lead to deeper sharing and a more intimate marriage relationship, the change is a welcome one to the wife. If the change reduces the wife's privacy, autonomy, and intimacy with friends without compensatory improved intimacy with the husband, she is less satisfied.

Sickness and Caregiving

When one spouse suffers a potentially fatal or dementing illness, it produces tension in the relationship. Part of the tension is a function of having to adapt to change in the relationship (Swensen, 1985). Some tension may come from the strain of caring for the spouse (Wright, 1991) and some from fear of the spouse's death (Johnson, 1985).

Both husbands and wives get sick and provide care for their spouses, but because of the difference in life expectancy, the most common pattern is for the husband to be the sick spouse and the wife to be the caregiver. Regardless of which spouse becomes ill, the primary caregiver is the well spouse (Brubaker, 1985).

When one spouse becomes sick, the couple become more isolated from others, with the sick spouse becoming preoccupied with coping with the illness and the well spouse preoccupied with caring for the sick spouse. The sick spouse loses power, and the caregiving spouse gains power (Johnson, 1985).

Caregiving produces a role overload, which puts greater stress on the caregiving spouse (Brubaker, 1985). Time spent caring for a spouse suffering from some disorders, such as brain impairment, may be almost total (Enright, 1991). Most frequently, wives bear the caregiver burden alone. Husbands as caregivers are more likely to elicit outside help (Johnson, 1985), and they generally receive more help from the family network (Enright).

Those who care for an afflicted spouse are more likely to become depressed and anxious (Vitaliano, Russo, Young, Teri, & Maiuro, 1991). Caregiving spouses with health problems, who lack social support from friends and family, and who have a negative outlook on life are especially at risk for developing psychological symptoms.

Couples with one spouse dying of cancer increase their overt expressions of affection to each other, but they withdraw their commitment to each other as persons (Swensen & Fuller, 1992). The quality of life of sick spouses is most related to the quality of their marriage relationship, whereas the quality of life of caregiving spouses is most highly related to how well they are coping with the practical problems they must face (Fuller & Swensen, 1992).

Death and Widowhood

The inevitable end of the last stage of the family life cycle comes with the death of one of the marital partners. With the children raised and retirement from outside work, the couple tend to focus their lives more on each other and their relationship. This situation has led to the observation that, "It is paradoxic that when the marital relationship may assume a new importance, older couples are faced with the task of anticipating and preparing for eventual widowhood for one of the spouses." (Bishop & Shoemaker, 1987, p. 28).

Couples' anticipation of death is reflected in wives' increased concern with the health of their husbands (Heinemann & Evans, 1990; Swensen & Fuller, 1992). Anticipation of death is also reflected in the increased expression of overt affection combined with an intrapsychic withdrawal of commitment to the other person. Anticipation of death does not reduce the intensity of grief following death, but it does help foster long-term adaptation to the loss (Heinemann & Evans). Evidence suggests that widows adjust better to grief if they have discussed these matters with their spouses before death (Hansson & Remondet, 1987).

The initial response to death is numbness. Overt symptoms begin 1 to 4 months after death and last from 1 to 3 years. These symptoms may include sadness, crying, anxiety, depression, loss of appetite, weight loss, sleep disturbances, tiredness, and a decline in general health. Research comparing widows with married women of the same age and life situation reports that it takes from 2 to 11 years for the difference in the psychological status of the two groups to disappear (Heinemann & Evans, 1990). Grief over the loss of a mate to whom one has been married for many years may never be totally resolved

(Thompson, Gallagher-Thompson, Futterman, Gilewski, & Peterson, 1991). Moreover, if the caretaking role was arduous, the caretaking spouse tends to avoid dwelling on the marriage after the death (Vinick, 1984). Husbands who nursed their wives do not think of remarriage. Evidence suggests that individuals who contemplate remarriage after widowhood will be successful if their children and friends approve, if the marrying couple have known each other for a long time, and if they move into a house that has belonged to neither of them before their remarriage (Brubaker, 1985; McKain, 1972).

CHILDREN

Nature of the Elderly Parent and Adult Child Relationship

Increased life expectancy has created closer and more complex relationships within the family of the older person (Hagestad, 1986, 1990; Uhlenberg, 1980). The likelihood of a parent with three children having a child die in childhood declined from 0.50 in 1900 to 0.06 in 1976 (Uhlenberg), and the likelihood of a child losing a parent before age 15 declined from 0.24 to 0.05. The assumption is that, in the past, with the likelihood of losing any given child in childhood, parents remained relatively detached from their children. With the probability, today, that a child will outlive the parent, parents can risk forming more intimate relationships with their children.

Furthermore, with increased longevity, the lives of parents and children overlap by 50 or more years. With fewer children in each family, there are fewer children for parents to relate to and, therefore, a greater emotional investment in each child. Thus, with more time and less competition, the relationship between parents and children becomes more intense and intimate. There is often much affection and mutual activity between parents and children (Bengtson et al., 1990; Bromberg, 1983; Walker & Allen, 1991).

The large number of living generations adds to the complexity of the elderly parent–adult child relationship. The elderly parent relates to a child who is himself or herself also a parent, and probably also a grandparent. Thus, the adult child of the elderly parent may be playing the role of child, parent, and grandparent simultaneously.

Regular and frequent contact with their children is very important for older people (Giordano & Beckham, 1985). One study (Greenberg & Becker, 1988) of older parents reported that 97% had seen or talked to a child in the past week. Although reports indicate that contact with children is not related to the life satisfaction of the elderly (Giordano & Beckham), this may be a function of the kind of contact, and not of contact per se. The nature and length of children's visits contributes significantly to elderly parents' well-being (David-son & Cotter, 1982). Satisfaction with relationships with children is related to the adjustment and morale of the elderly (Hansson & Remondet, 1987).

Positive, helpful contact contributes significantly to the elderly parent's well-being; negative contact detracts from well-being. The right kind and amount of contact between parents and children includes living in separate households, which is true of most older people today (Brody, 1985; Sundström, Samuelsson, & Sjöberg, 1989).

Most adult children feel close to their parents and feel obliged to them (Brody, 1985; Brubaker 1985; Finley, Roberts, & Banahan, 1988). Brody states that because of increased life expectancy, children care for their parents more today than they ever did in the past, but the myth that children today do not care for their parents persists because there is some truth underlying it. That truth is that no matter how much children do for their parents, it cannot equal the total care the children received from their parents in the days of the children's infancy and childhood.

The obligation children feel toward their parents is a function of their relationship to the parents, sex of the child, and the distance the child lives from the parent (Finley, Roberts, & Banahan, 1988). The greater the distance from the parent, the less obligation children feel. Women feel more obligation to mothers the more affection they have for them. For men, distance from the mother is the only variable related to their maternal obligation. Women feel less obligation to their fathers if the woman's other roles conflict with her obligation to her father. The obligation men feel for their fathers is not affected by other role demands. The more education women have, the less obligation they feel for their fathers, but education does not reduce men's sense of obligation to their fathers. Affection is positively related to obligation women feel for mothers-in-law, but not for obligation to fathers-in-law. Affection is related to a sense of obligation to fathers-in-law for men (Finley, Roberts, & Banahan).

Because of the increased closeness between aged parents and children, death is distressing to both. However, loss of an aged parent is one of the least distressing losses to a child, whereas loss of an adult child is the most distressing loss for an aged parent (Parkes, 1972).

Evidence suggests that the loss of a child was regretted in the past, but it was not so devastating to parents as it is now. There seem to be two reasons for this. One is that, with the decline in the death rate for children and the increase in life expectancy, the death of a child is not expected (Hagestad, 1986, 1990; Parkes, 1972). A death that does not come when expected is "off-time," and its effects are more distressing than the death of an aged parent, which comes when expected; that is, "on-time." A second reason is that, with the decline in the birthrate, the loss of any given child is more devastating. Losing one child when you have ten children is not as distressing as losing one child when you have only two (Parkes, 1972).

The strongest aged parent–adult child relationship is usually between mothers and daughters. Mothers and daughters have more frequent interaction than do fathers or sons (Bengtson et al., 1990). The mother–daughter relationship is the main connecting link in most families (Hagestad, 1986).

Aged Parents and Adult Children Aid Each Other

Both parents and children aid each other; however, more aid generally flows from parents to children than from the children to the parents (Giordano & Beckham, 1985; Greenberg & Becker, 1988; Morgan, Schuster, & Butler, 1991). Parents provide financial help, housing, babysitting, practical advice, and emotional support. Children provide instrumental aid and emotional support to their parents. The aid flows to whomever needs help (Bromberg, 1983). Parents provide the most aid to children who are having problems, such as financial stress or divorce (Greenberg & Becker). Children provide more instrumental aid, such as transportation or doing chores around the house, as the parents become older and less physically able (Bromberg). The total number of supportive exchanges between parents and children decreases as the parents become older (Morgan et al., 1991), but the amount of aid parents provide children continues to be greater than the amount of aid children provide parents until very great age. Estimates are that for some kinds of aid, the aid provided by children does not exceed that provided by parents until parents are age 100 years or more.

It is unclear whether there is a difference between ethnic groups in the amount of parent–child support exchanged (Mitchell & Register, 1984; Mutran, 1985; Sokolovsky, 1985), but blacks are more likely to live with their children than are whites (Mitchell & Register), which creates the possibility of more frequent exchange of help.

Divorce disrupts the interchange between parents and children, especially between children and their fathers. Ninety percent of married fathers report frequent contact with at least one of their adult children, but only one half of divorced fathers communicate with one of their children on a weekly basis (Cooney & Uhlenberg, 1990). One third of divorced older fathers have lost contact with one or more of their adult children. This significantly reduces the likelihood of a divorced father receiving aid from adult children in old age. Divorce disrupts the family network of men, and many divorced men express the feeling they no longer have a family (Hagestad, 1986).

Problems of Adult Children Distress Aged Parents

The problems of adult children are especially distressing to aged parents. The most distressing problems among adult children for aged parents are emotional problems, physical illness, marital difficulty, and alcohol or drug abuse.

The divorce of adult children is especially distressing to aged parents (Greenberg & Becker, 1988; Hagestad, 1986; Swensen, 1983). It not only creates emotional distress in the divorcing child, for which the aged parent may be called on to provide emotional support, but it creates practical and emotional problems for the parent as well. If the divorcing child is a daughter, it may mean the daughter returns home, requiring financial support. If the daughter has children, the aged parents may find themselves again required to care for small children. If the divorcing child is a man, the aged parents often find themselves cut off from contact with their grandchildren.

The most distressing problem of adult children for aged mothers is an adult daughter who has cut off all contact with the family (Greenberg & Becker, 1988). For fathers, the most stressful problem among adult children is a son who continues to depend on the family for support, often because of drug or alcohol problems.

The more problems an adult child has, the more likely a parent is to express dissatisfaction with the relationship with the child, and the less positive affect the parents feel for the child (Greenberg & Becker, 1988).

Adult Children Provide Care for Aged Parents

Taking care of aged parents is becoming a normal experience for adult children (Brody, 1985; Greene, 1989; Myers, 1988). The need to care for elderly parents usually arises when the aged parent suffers a health or financial crisis (Lewis, 1990). Unfortunately, caring for aged parents is a stage of life for which few adult children prepare.

Children provide a variety of different kinds of care for parents (Dwyer & Coward, 1991; Morgan et al., 1991). These include household chores, negotiating with outside agencies, and providing social and emotional support (Cicirelli, 1990). For the more severely impaired parent, this might include helping them to eat, dress, bathe, or toilet.

The necessity of caring for aged parents upsets the family homeostasis and creates a strain for the adult children (Brody, 1985; Dura, Stukenberg, & Kiecolt-Glaser, 1991; Myers, 1988). This strain may be a consequence of practical problems, such as lack of preparation for caring for an aged parent, the conflict between taking care of the parent and earning a living or parenting dependent children, the strain of having to travel distances to be with the parent, the strain of having the parent move into the home, and loss of personal freedom.

Other factors can also contribute to the strain. When the child takes care of a parent, roles shift, and power within the relationship changes (Barusch, 1987; Hesse-Biber & Williamson, 1984; Shaw, 1987). Parents are used to taking care of children, and children are used to being cared for by their parents; not vice versa. For the child, caring for a parent means the parent is in confirmed decline and the child has lost life's most significant source of support. It is unsettling for both parties.

Caring for an aging parent may reactivate old dependency–independency conflicts or old sibling rivalries (Brody, 1985; Myers, 1988). Also, having to care for an aged parent is a reminder that life is not eternal, and produces the distress that accompanies anticipation of the death of the parent (Brody; Shaw, 1987).

Research suggests that the longer care goes on, and the more additional duties the caregiver has, the less satisfying the parent–child relationship becomes (Walker & Allen, 1991). The daughter usually shoulders the greatest part of the caregiving burden (Bengtson et al., 1990; Brody, 1985; Hansson & Remondet, 1987). Emotional support from other members of the family and counseling can alleviate the strain of caregiving (Brody; Greene, 1989; Myers).

GRANDPARENTS AND GRANDCHILDREN

Being a grandparent is a normal part of the last stage of the family life cycle for most people (Giordano & Beckham, 1985; Hagestad, 1988). Because most people become grandparents, it is an expected transition in life (Hagestad, 1986, 1988; Hagestad & Burton, 1986), coming usually in the empty nest stage of the family life cycle. People at this stage of life who have children but don't yet have grandchildren often express disappointment at not having made the expected transition to grandparenthood (Troll, 1985).

Because of increased longevity, most grandparents will live to see their grandchildren reach adulthood, thus they can expect a long relationship with them (Hagestad & Burton, 1986; Roberto, 1990; Uhlenberg, 1980).

Factors Affecting Grandparents' Relationship with Grandchildren

A variety of factors affect the closeness of grandparents' relationship with their grandchildren. The most important variable is how close the grandchild lives to the grandparent (Cherlin & Furstenberg, 1986; Kivett, 1985), accounting for 62% of the variance in the frequency of visits between grandparents and grandchildren. Feelings of closeness correlate highly with frequency of contact (Kivett, 1985).

Children of daughters tend to be closer to grandparents than children of sons (Brubaker, 1985; Fischer, 1983; Matthews & Sprey, 1984), with the maternal grandmother usually the closest grandparent to grandchildren. Closeness to grandchildren decreases as the grandchildren become older (Kivett, 1985; Roberto, 1990). Younger grandchildren report attachment, nurturance, and receiving gifts most often as important aspects of the relationship with their grandparents. Older children report pride in family history, companionship, and guidance (Ponzetti & Folkrod, 1989).

With the increasing divorce rate and subsequent remarriage of divorced spouses, the number of step-grandparents has increased. Most step-grandchildren rate their relationships with step-grandparents as neutral. Step-grandchildren who acquired the step-grandparents at an early age, live close to their step-grandparents, and were satisfied with the remarriage of their parent, had closer relationships with step-grandparents than step-grandchildren who were older, lived at a distance, and were unhappy with the remarriage (Trygstad & Sanders, 1989).

Although some research suggests that minority groups may have more involvement of grandparents with their families, and more support from their families (e.g., Raphael, 1988; Schmidt, 1982; Sokolovsky, 1985), evidence indicates that this support is declining.

Crisis and Divorce

In times of crisis in the family—such as divorce, immigration, financial difficulty, and illness—grandparents serve as a source of stability to the distressed family (Cherlin & Furstenberg, 1986; Raphael, 1988; Thomas, 1990).

The divorce of children may result in grandparents having more contact with their grandchildren if the grandchildren live nearby, the divorcing child is a daughter with custody of the children, and the children are young (Cherlin & Furstenberg, 1986; Gladstone, 1988; Hagestad, 1986; Johnson, 1988; Matthews & Sprey, 1984; Thomas, 1990). On the other hand, if the divorcing child is a son without custody of the children, and the daughter-in-law moves some distance away from the grandparents, the grandparents may lose contact with their grandchildren (Hagestad, 1988; Matthews & Sprey, 1984).

The divorce of children may create a "double bind" for the grandparents, because the divorcing child may want help and support for the grandchildren but may also complain about the grandparents interfering in childrearing (Thomas, 1990).

Sometimes grandparents are forced into the role of surrogate parents. Grandparents usually do not want to repeat the parent role with their grandchildren, so the relationship with their grandchildren becomes ambivalent (Johnson, 1988). Those grandparents forced into the parent role with their grandchildren fare best if they have the support of a spouse and have legal custody of the grandchildren (Kennedy & Kenney, 1988).

The Meaning of Grandparenthood

It has been suggested that, "A loving relationship with grandchildren can help to compensate for the losses of aging, particularly if grandparents feel they have something valuable to give their grandchildren," (Robinson, 1989). The meaning of grandparenthood is primarily emotional and symbolic (Cherlin & Furstenberg, 1986; Fischer, 1983). However, in times of crisis, the instrumental role becomes more important (Hagestad, 1986; Wilcoxon, 1987), when grandparents may be called upon to care for children or to provide financial support.

Factor analysis of grandparents' views of grandparenthood has revealed five main factors in grandparenthood: 1) centrality; 2) valued elder; 3) immortality through clan; 4) reinvolvement with personal past; and 5) indulgence (Kivnick, 1983).

Centrality is the degree to which grandparenthood is central to the grandparents' lives. Valued elders are concerned with being a resource person and with how the grandchildren will remember them. *Immortality through the clan* is the feeling of immortality achieved through descendants and continuity of the family. The idea of immortality through the continuity of the clan is particularly important to grandfathers (Thomas, 1989). *Reinvolvement with the personal past* is a sense of reliving events from the past and consciously thinking and wondering about one's own grandparents. *Indulgence* is lenience when catering to the wishes of the grandchildren. Indulgence is a more important aspect of grandparenthood for grandmothers than grandfathers (Thomas).

Satisfaction with Grandparenthood

Older women expressed greater satisfaction with grandparenthood. Moreover, their satisfaction was greater if their grandchildren were younger and if they had some responsibility, but not the primary responsibility, for helping the grandchildren (Thomas, 1989, 1990).

SIBLINGS

Most older people have siblings (Bengtson et al., 1990; Moss & Moss, 1989). Relationships to siblings are the longest lasting relationships in most peoples' lives (Brubaker, 1985; Cicirelli, 1988; Moss & Moss, 1986).

Siblings generally maintain relationships with each other. One study reports that 77% of a sample of older people with a mean age of 74 years reported at least one sibling was a close friend (Connidis, 1989). About one half of people over 65 years have at least weekly contact with one sibling (Brubaker, 1985; Cicirelli, 1988), and only 3% have lost touch with their siblings. The relationship with siblings improves with age, so that sibling relationships in old age are generally quite positive (Bedford, 1989; Cicirelli, 1988; Gold, 1989b) and important (Avioli, 1989; Gold, 1989a; Cicirelli).

Several variables contribute to the improvement in sibling relationships in old age. The first is that hostility, rivalry, resentment, and envy between siblings decreases with age (Bedford, 1989; Cicirelli, 1988; Gold, 1989b). With retirement, and children raised, elderly siblings have more time to spend with each other (Bedford). Generational solidarity may also play a part (Avioli, 1989; Gold). As we age, our relationships with those who have shared the same experiences and memories become more important, particularly as the number of people with whom we share common experiences diminishes. With increased age comes the perception of the possibility of needing support, and siblings are one source of support. Although siblings do provide some instrumental support, most support from siblings is psychological (Avioli; Cicirelli; Gold). Most instrumental care is provided by spouses first and then by children, with siblings serving as backup. The amount of support provided by siblings increases from the seventh to the ninth decade of life (Cicirelli). Finally, siblings are the last remaining tie of the older person to his or her family of origin (Bedford).

Variables that affect the closeness of siblings' relationships in old age are proximity, sex, marital status, and shared values. Siblings who live near each other generally have a closer relationship than siblings who live at a distance from each other (Connidis, 1989; Matthews, Delaney, & Adamek, 1989; Suggs, 1989). Sisters have closer relationships than brothers, and sibling pairs that include a sister are closer (Avioli, 1989; Cicirelli, 1988; Gold, 1989a; Gold, 1989b). Furthermore, relationships with sisters seem to become more important and more emotionally supportive in old age (Cicirelli; Scott, 1990). Sibling pairs in which at least one member is single have more frequent contact than sibling pairs in which both are married (Connidis). Siblings who share values have more frequent contact than those who don't (Suggs).

Positive relationships with siblings in old age promote well-being (Cicirelli, 1988, 1989). However, if contact with a sibling undermines the sense of independence or the equitable nature of the relationship, it can affect morale negatively (Avioli, 1989). There is little study of ethnic differences in sibling relationships in old age; however, one study reports similar relationships among blacks and whites (Suggs, 1989).

One would expect that, with the sibling relationship being the most long lasting, death of a sibling might be especially distressing. However, evidence indicates that most react to the death of a sibling with a sense of invulnerability, a renewed sense of resiliency, and a reaffirmation of life (Moss & Moss, 1989). However, it seems reasonable to conclude that the impact of death of a sibling would depend upon the nature of the relationship.

Evidence indicates that, for most older people, family relationships become more important than they were in the middle stages of life. This increase is partly for practical reasons and partly for psychological and symbolic reasons. With retirement, older people have more time to devote to family relationships, and fewer competing outside relationships. With sickness, there is a need for kin to provide care and emotional support. With death or the threat of death, there is a need for the psychological support of kin. With the approaching end of life, there is an increased need to affirm the value of one's life and to make sense of one's life. For most people, the greatest affirmation of self-value and sense of purpose is found in their families.

REFERENCES

Ade-Ridder, L. (1985). Quality of marriage: A comparison between golden wedding couples and couples married less than fifty years. *Lifestyles: A Journal of Changing Patterns, 7*, 224–237.

Ade-Ridder, L. (1990). Sexuality and marital quality among older married couples. In T. H. Brubaker (Ed.), *Family relationships in later life.* (2nd ed., pp. 48–67). Newbury Park, CA: Sage.

Avioli, P. S. (1989). The social support functions of siblings in later life. *American Behavioral Scientist, 33*, 45–57.

Barusch, A. S. (1987). Power dynamics in the aging family: A preliminary statement. *Journal of Gerontological Social Work, 11*, 43–56.

Bedford, V. H. (1989). Understanding the value of siblings in old age. *American Behavioral Scientist, 33*, 33–44.

Bengtson, V., Rosenthal, C., & Burton, L. (1990). Families and aging: Diversity and heterogeneity. In R. H. Binstock & L. K. George (Eds.), *Handbook of aging and the social sciences* (pp. 263–287). San Diego: Academic.

Bishop, D. S., Epstein, N. B., Baldwin, L. M., Miller, I. W., & Keitner, G. I. (1988). Older couples: The effect of health, retirement, and family functioning on morale. *Family Systems Medicine, 6,* 238–247.

Bishop, S. M., & Shoemaker, Y. B. (1987). Married couples in later life: The ecologic transition of retirement. *Family and Community Health, 9,* 22–33.

Blood, R. O., & Wolf, D. M. (1960). *Husbands and wives: The dynamics of married living,* New York: Free Press.

Brody, E. M. (1985). Parent care as a normative family stress. *Gerontologist, 25,* 19–29.

Bromberg, E. M. (1983). Mother–daughter relationships in later life: The effect of quality of relationship on mutual aid. *Journal of Gerontological Social Work, 6,* 75–92.

Brubaker, T. H. (1985). *Later life families.* Newbury Park, CA: Sage.

Brubaker, T. H., & Ade-Ridder, L. (1987). Relationships between marital quality, social, and familial interactions by residential location: Implications for human service professionals. *Lifestyles: A Journal of Changing Patterns, 8,* 137–145.

Cherlin, A., & Furstenberg, F. F. (1986). Grandparents and family crisis. *Generations, 10,* 26–28.

Cicirelli, V. G. (1988). Interpersonal relationships among elderly siblings. In M. D. Kahn & K. G. Lewis (Eds.), *Sibling therapy: Life span and clinical issues* (pp. 435–456). New York: Norton.

Cicirelli, V. G. (1989). Feelings of attachment to siblings and well-being in later life. *Psychology and Aging, 4,* 211–216.

Cicirelli, V. G. (1990). Family support in relation to health problems of the elderly. In T. H. Brubaker (Ed.), *Family relationships in later life* (2nd ed., pp. 212–228). Newbury Park, CA: Sage.

Connidis, I. A. (1989). Siblings as friends in later life. *American Behavioral Scientist, 33,* 81–93.

Cooney, T. M., & Uhlenberg, P. (1990). The role of divorce in men's relations with their adult children after midlife. *Journal of Marriage and the Family, 52,* 677–688.

Cuber, J. F., & Harroff, P. B. (1965). *The significant Americans.* New York: Appleton-Century.

Davidson, W. B., & Cotter, P. R. (1982). Adjustment to aging and relationships with offspring. *Psychological Reports, 50,* 731–738.

Dura, J. R., Stukenberg, K. W., & Kiecolt-Glaser, J. K. (1991). Anxiety and depressive disorders in adult children caring for demented parents. *Psychology and Aging, 6,* 467–473.

Duvall, E. (1971). *Family development* (4th ed.). Philadelphia: Lippincott.

Dwyer, J. W., & Coward, R. T. (1991). A multivariate comparison of the involvement of adult sons versus daughters in the care of impaired parents. *Journal of Gerontology, 46,* 259–269.

Enright, R. B. (1991). Time spent caregiving and help received by spouses and adult children of brain-impaired adults. *The Gerontologist, 31,* 375–383.

Ferraro, K. F., & Wan, T. (1986). Marital contributions to well-being in later life. *American Behavioral Scientist, 29,* 423–437.

Finley, N. J., Roberts, M. D., & Banahan, B. F. (1988). Motivators and inhibitors of attitudes of filial obligation toward aging parents. *Gerontologist, 28,* 73–83.

Fischer, L. R. (1983). Transition to grandmotherhood. *International Journal of Aging and Human Development, 16,* 67–78.

Fuller, S. R., & Swensen, C. H. (1992). Marital quality and quality of life among cancer patients and their spouses. *Journal of Psychosocial Oncology, 10,* 41–56.

Gilford, R. (1986). Marriages in later life. *Generations, 10,* 16–20.

Giordano, J. A., & Beckham, K. (1985). The aged within a family context: Relationships, roles, and events. In L. L'Abate (Ed.), *The handbook of family psychology and therapy* (pp. 284–320), Homewood, IL: Dorsey.

Gladstone, J. W. (1988). Perceived changes in grandmother–grandchild relations following a child's separation or divorce. *Gerontologist, 28,* 66–72.

Gold, D. T. (1989a). Sibling relationships in old age: A typology. *International Journal of Aging and Human Development, 28,* 37–51.

Gold, D. T. (1989b). Generational solidarity: Conceptual antecedents and consequences. *American Behavioral Scientist, 33,* 19–32.

Greenberg, J. S., & Becker, M. (1988). Aging parents as family resources. *Gerontologist, 28,* 786–791.

Greene, R. (1989). A life systems approach to understanding parent–child relationships in aging families. *Journal of Psychotherapy, 5,* 57–69.

Hagestad, G. O. (1986). The aging society as a context for family life. *Daedalus, 115,* 119–139.

Hagestad, G. O. (1988). Demographic change and the life course: Some emerging trends in the family realm. *Family Relations, 37,* 405–410.

Hagestad, G. O. (1990). Social perspectives on the life course. In R. H. Binstock & L. K. George (Eds.), *Handbook of aging and the social sciences,* (3rd ed., pp. 151–168). San Diego: Academic.

Hagestad, G. O., & Burton, L. M. (1986). Grandparenthood, life context, and family development. *American Behavioral Scientist, 29,* 471–484.

Hansson, R. O., & Remondet, J. H. (1987). Relationships and the aging family: A social psychological analysis. *Applied Social Psychology Annual, 7,* 262–283.

Heinemann, G. D., & Evans, P. L. (1990). Widowhood: Loss, change, and adaptation. In T. H. Brubaker (Ed.), *Family relationships in later life* (2nd ed., pp. 142–168). Newbury Park, CA: Sage.

Hesse-Biber, S., & Williamson, J. (1984). Resource theory and power in families: Life cycle considerations. *Family Process, 23,* 261–278.

Johnson, C. L. (1985). The impact of illness on late-life marriages. *Journal of Marriage and the Family, 47,* 165–172.

Johnson, C. L. (1988). Active and latent functions of grandparenting during the divorce process. *Gerontologist, 28,* 185–191.

Johnston, T. (1990). Retirement: What happens to the marriage. *Issues in Mental Health Nursing, 11,* 347–359.

Keating, N. C., & Cole, P. (1980). What do I do with him 24 hours a day? Changes in the housewife role after retirement. *Gerontologist, 20,* 84–89.

Kennedy, J. F., & Keeney, V. T. (1988). The extended family revisited: Grandparents rearing grandchildren. *Child Psychiatry and Human Development, 19,* 26–35.

Kivett, V. R. (1985). Grandfathers and grandchildren: Patterns of association, helping, and psychological closeness. *Family Relations, 34,* 565–571.

Kivnick, H. (1983). Dimensions of grandparenthood meaning: Deductive conceptualization and empirical derivation. *Journal of Personality and Social Psychology, 44,* 1056–1068.

Lewis, R. A. (1990). The adult child and older parents. In T. H. Brubaker (Ed.), *Family relationships in later life* (2nd ed., pp. 68–85). Newbury Park, CA: Sage.

Long, J. K., & Mancini, J. A. (1990). Aging couples and the family system. In T. H. Brubaker (Ed.), *Family relationships in later life* (2nd ed., pp. 29–47). Newbury Park, CA: Sage.

MacKinnon, R. F., MacKinnon, C. E., & Franken, M. L. (1984). Family strengths in long-term marriages. *Lifestyles: A Journal of Changing Patterns, 7,* 115–126.

Matthews, S. H., Delaney, P. J., & Adamek, M. E. (1989). Male kinship ties: Bonds between adult brothers. *American Behavioral Scientist, 33,* 58–69.

Matthews, S. H., & Sprey, J. (1984). The impact of divorce on grandparenthood: An exploratory study. *Gerontologist, 24,* 41–47.

McKain, W. C. (1972). A new look at older marriages. *Family Coordinator, 21,* 61–69.

Mitchell, J., & Register, J. C. (1984). An exploration of family interaction with the elderly by race, socioeconomic status, and residence. *Gerontologist, 24,* 48–54.

Morgan, D. L., Schuster, T. L., & Butler, E. W. (1991). Role reversals in the exchange of social support. *Journal of Gerontology, 46,* 278–287.

Moss, M. S., & Moss, S. Z. (1986). Death of a sibling. *International Journal of Family Psychiatry, 7,* 397–418.

Moss, S. Z., & Moss, M. S. (1989). The impact of the death of an elderly sibling. *American Behavioral Scientist, 33,* 94–106.

Mutran, E. (1985). Intergenerational family support among blacks and whites: Response to culture or to socioeconomic differences. *Journal of Gerontology, 40,* 382–389.

Myers, J. E. (1988). The mid/late life generation gap: Adult children with aging parents. *Journal of Counseling and Development, 66,* 331–335.

Parkes, C. M. (1972). *Bereavement: Studies of grief in adult life.* New York: International Universities Press.

Pineo, P. C. (1961). Disenchantment in the later years of marriage. *Marriage and Family Living, 23,* 3–11.

Ponzetti, J. J., & Folkrod, A. W. (1989). Grandchildren's perceptions of their relationships with their grandparents. *Child Study Journal, 19,* 41–50.

Raphael, E. I. (1988). Grandparents: A study of their role in Hispanic families. *Physical & Occupational Therapy in Geriatrics, 6,* 31–62.

Roberto K. A. (1990). Grandparent and grandchild relationships. In T. H. Brubaker (Ed.), *Family relationships in later life* (2nd ed., pp. 100–112). Newbury Park, CA: Sage.

Rollins, B. C., & Cannon, K. L. (1974). Marital satisfaction over the family life cycle: A reevaluation. *Journal of Marriage and the Family, 36,* 271–282.

Schmidt, A. (1982). *Grandparent–grandchild interaction in a Mexican-American group.* Los Angeles: Spanish Speaking Mental Health Research Center, Occasional Paper Number 16.

Scott, J. P. (1990). Sibling interaction in later life. In T. H. Brubaker (Ed.), *Family relationships in later life* (2nd ed., pp. 86–99). Newbury Park, CA: Sage.

Shaw, S. B. (1987). Parental aging: Clinical issues in adult psychotherapy. *Social Casework, 68,* 406–412.

Sokolovsky, J. (1985). Ethnicity, culture, and aging: Do differences really make a difference? *Journal of Applied Gerontology, 4,* 6–17.

Sporakowski, M. J., & Axelson, L. V. (1984). Long-term marriages: A critical review. *Lifestyles: A Journal of Changing Patterns, 7,* 76–93.

Sporakowski, M. J., & Hughston, G. A. (1978). Prescriptions for happy marriage: Adjustments and satisfactions of couples married for 50 or more years. *Family Coordinator, 27,* 321–327.

Suggs, P. K. (1989). Predictors of association among older siblings. *American Behavioral Scientist, 33,* 70–80.

Sundström, G., Samuelsson, G. & Sjöberg, I. (1989). Intergenerational transfers: Aging parents living with adult children and vice versa. *Zeitschrift für Gerontologie, 22,* 112–117.

Swensen, C. H. (1983). A respectable old age. *American Psychologist, 38,* 327–334.

Swensen, C. H. (1985). Personality development in the family. In L. L'Abate (Ed.), *The handbook of family psychology and therapy*, (vol. I, pp. 73–101). Homewood, IL: Dorsey.

Swensen, C. H. (1987). Long-term marriage in Norway and the U.S.A. In J. P. Myklebust & R. Ommundsen (Eds.), *Psykologprofesjonen mot å 2000* (pp. 239–250). Bergen, Norway: Universitetsforlaget AS.

Swensen, C. H., Eskew, R., & Kohlhepp, K. (1981). Stage of family life cycle, ego development, and the marriage relationship. *Journal of Marriage and the Family, 43,* 841–853.

Swensen, C. H., & Fuller, S. (1992). Expression of love, marriage problems, commitment, and anticipatory grief in the marriages of cancer patients. *Journal of Marriage and the Family, 54,* 191–196.

Swensen, C. H., & Trahaug, G. (1985). Commitment and the long-term marriage relationship. *Journal of Marriage and the Family, 47,* 939–945.

Thomas, J. L. (1989). Gender and perceptions of grandparenthood. *International Journal of Aging and Human Development, 29,* 269–282.

Thomas, J. L. (1990). The grandparent role: A double bind. *International Journal of Aging and Human Development, 31,* 169–177.

Thompson, L. W., Gallagher-Thompson, D., Futterman, A., Gilewski, M. J., & Peterson, J. (1991). The effects of late-life spousal bereavement over a 30-month interval. *Psychology and Aging, 6,* 434–441.

TIAA-CREF. (Teachers Insurance and Annuity Association-College Retirement Equities Fund). (1991). *Comparing TIAA-CREF income options.* New York: Author.

Troll, L. E. (1985). The contingencies of grandparenting. In V. L. Bengtson, & J. F. Robertson (Eds.), *Grandparenting,* (pp. 135–149). Newbury Park, CA: Sage.

Tryban, G. M. (1985). Effects of work and retirement within long-term marital relationships. *Lifestyles: A Journal of Changing Patterns, 7,* 207–223.

Trygstad, D. W., & Sanders, G. F. (1989). The significance of stepgrandparents. *International Journal of Aging and Human Development, 29,* 119–134.

Uhlenberg, P. (1980). Death and the family. *Journal of Family History, 5,* 313–320.

United States Bureau of the Census. (1988). Marital status and living arrangements: March 1988. *Current Population Reports.* Series P. 20, No. 433, p. 3.

United States Bureau of the Census. (1990). *Statistical abstract of the United States: 1990* (110th ed., p. 73, Table 104). Washington, DC: United States Government Printing Office.

Vinick, B. H. (1984). Elderly men as caretakers of wives. *Journal of Geriatric Psychiatry, 17,* 61–68.

Vitaliano, P. P., Russo, J., Young, H. M., Teri, L., & Maiuro, R. D. (1991). Predictors of burden in spouse caregivers of individuals with Alzheimer's disease. *Psychology and Aging, 6,* 392–402.

Walker, A. J., & Allen, K. R. (1991). Relationships between caregiving daughters and their elderly mothers. *Gerontologist, 31,* 389–396.

Wilcoxon, S. A. (1987). Grandparents and grandchildren: An often neglected relationship between significant others. *Journal of Counseling & Development, 65,* 289–290.

Wright, L. K. (1991). The impact of Alzheimer's disease on the marital relationship. *Gerontologist, 31,* 224–236.

PART TWO

Disruptions, Detours, and Dysfunctionalities in the Family Life Cycle

CHAPTER 11

Marital Conflict and Divorce

A Developmental Family Psychology Perspective

CHRISTOPHER L. HEAVEY, JAMES L. SHENK, and ANDREW CHRISTENSEN

It is abundantly clear that couples in distressed marriages experience more frequent and more negative conflicts than couples in satisfied relationships (e.g., Geiss & O'Leary, 1981). These findings, however, do not help to clarify either the developmental processes that lead couples to a point where they experience frequent conflicts, nor do they delineate the implications of these conflicts for the developmental course of the relationship. Marital conflict and divorce only can be understood fully from a developmental viewpoint. From this perspective, there are two critical issues involved in understanding conflict and divorce in marriage. First, it is necessary to examine the role that individual development and development of the relationship play in contributing to marital conflict. In other words, both the developmental history of each partner and inherent processes of relationship development contribute to the extent to which a couple experiences conflict in their relationship. Second, it is important to understand the role conflict plays in determining the course of relationship development. How conflicts are handled plays a critical role in determining whether a relationship will progress to stability and mutual satisfaction or will deteriorate to mutual distress and/or divorce (Peterson, 1979; Storaasli & Markman, 1990). Couples whose relationships move toward divorce face a new set of decision points and, should they divorce, a new set of developmental challenges. This chapter provides an overview of empirical research addressing how developmental processes affect marital conflict and divorce, as well as how marital conflict and divorce affect developmental processes. Due to space limitation, we do not discuss the important issue of how marital conflict and divorce affect the development of children. For a review and discussion of research concerning the impact of marital conflict on child functioning see Grych and Fincham (1990); for a review of the effects of divorce on children see Emery (1988).

The term *conflict* is used in literature on marriage to denote both latent conflicts of interest (Kelley & Thibaut, 1978) and open conflict between partners (Doherty, 1981). Peterson (1983) distinguishes between *structural* conflicts of interest and *open* conflicts. Structural conflicts are characterized by incompatibility in the goals of two people, whereas open conflicts are overt disagreements between two individuals. Unless otherwise stated, we use the term *conflict* to refer to open conflicts between spouses.

Kelley et al. (1983) define close relationships as characterized by high degrees of interdependence and lasting over long periods of time. Clearly, marriage is a prototype of close relationships. The high degree of interdependence character-istic of marriages makes structural conflicts of interest inevitable (Kelley, 1979). These structural conflicts serve as predisposing conditions to open conflicts (Peterson, 1983).

Neither structural conflicts nor open conflicts are inherently positive or nega-tive relationship events (Margolin, 1988). Rather, they are an inevitable and central aspect of close relationships. How these conflicts are handled, however, can be either functional or dysfunctional for the relationship. Thus, we begin by discussing how development affects conflict and follow with a discussion of how conflict affects the developmental course of marriages.

ROLE OF DEVELOPMENT IN CONFLICT

There are two primary avenues through which development affects marital conflict. First, the developmental history of each of the spouses and their develop-ment once in the relationship contribute to the extent to which the marriage will experience both structural conflicts and open conflicts. Second, natural developmental processes of romantic relationships also affect the extent to which a couple experiences conflicts.

Individual Development and Conflict

What an individual brings to a relationship plays a role in determining the extent to which the relationship will experience conflict. Christensen (1991) suggests four general explanations for marital distress: poor problem-solving skills, psy-chopathology, poor temperament, and incompatibility. Each of these possible causes of distress has its roots in the developmental history of the spouses.

It is a basic tenet of behavioral conceptions of marital distress that poor conflict resolution skills are a primary cause of marital difficulties (Christensen, 1983; Jacobson & Holtzworth-Munroe, 1986). When structural conflicts arise, some couples are unable to reach a mutually satisfying resolution because they lack effective problem-solving skills. Thus, the structural conflict remains and predisposes the couple to future open conflicts. Besides increasing the frequency of conflicts, it is implicit in this model that frustration over the lack of a mutually satisfying resolution also adds to the couple's dissatisfaction.

The best way to examine the relationship of problem-solving skills to conflict resolution and marital adjustment would be to assess the level of skills of each partner early in the relationship, and then follow the level of conflict and satisfaction over time. However, we are only able to assess skills through performance, and performance may vary due to an individual being either unwilling or unable to display a particular set of skills at a given time. It seems particularly likely that distressed spouses may choose not to display their most constructive problem-solving skills because of built-up anger and resentment. Nonetheless, many studies have shown that distressed couples display more destructive and less constructive problem-solving behaviors than do nondistressed couples (see Baucom & Adams, 1987; O'Leary & Smith, 1991; Schaap, 1984; Weiss & Heyman, 1990 for reviews). Distressed couples have also been found to display more negative problem-solving behavior when interacting with their partner than when interacting with strangers (e.g., Vincent, Weiss, & Birchler, 1975). Finally, several studies have examined the encoding and decoding skills of distressed and nondistressed couples. These studies have shown that distressed couples display more channel inconsistency than nondistressed couples (Noller, 1982), and that distressed couples are generally less effective at both encoding and decoding messages (Noller, 1987). These differences seem to be particularly pronounced among males (Gottman & Porterfield, 1981; Noller, 1987).

Thus, the bulk of the empirical evidence indicates that distressed partners display poorer problem-solving skills than nondistressed partners. Different theoretical models would suggest different roots for this skills deficit. However, all would generally agree that the source of the difficulties can be found in the developmental histories of the partners.

Researchers have also documented the relationships between psychopathology and marital conflict and distress. For example, depression has been consistently related to levels of marital distress (Coyne, Kahn, & Gotlib, 1987) and level of marital conflict (Schafer & Keith, 1983). Although, in many cases, marital distress may precede the onset of depression (e.g., Birtchnell & Kennard, 1983; Matussek & Wiegand, 1985), depression may also place considerable strain on a relationship, predisposing the couple to conflicts. Other psychiatric illnesses have also been shown to be related to marital distress and marital conflict (e.g., Hoover & Fitzgerald, 1981).

Personality factors that Christensen (1991) considers characteristics of poor temperament are also predictive of poor marital quality. The most studied of these temperament characteristics is neuroticism. For example, Kelly and Conley (1987) found that "husband's impulsiveness and the neuroticism of both spouses are potent predictors of negative marital outcome" (p. 34). Other studies have supported this conclusion with regard to neuroticism (e.g., Zaleski & Galkowska, 1978). O'Leary and Smith (1991) review longitudinal studies of various aspects of poor temperament and conclude that "neuroticism, impulsivity, emotional instability, irritability, psychopathology, fearfulness, poor social adjustment, and similar constructs are associated with poor marital adjustment" (p. 197).

Finally, marital researchers have found evidence supporting the assertion that couples who are more similar have happier and more stable relationships. For example, Bentler and Newcomb (1978) found that "correlational similarity between marital partners, based on personality traits measured at the beginning of the marriage, was substantially higher for couples who remained together after 4 years than for couples who decided to end their marriage within that period of time" (p. 1065) and that these divorcing couples experienced more problems than the happy couples. Similarly, Christensen and Shenk (1991) found that the discrepancy between spouses' level of desired intimacy was positively associated with the extent to which couples displayed destructive demand/withdraw behaviors during conflicts. Moreover, they found that both divorcing couples and couples seeking marital therapy displayed a higher degree of discrepancy in the desire for closeness than did happily married couples. There is now a considerable body of research that indicates that degree of similarity between spouses is positively associated with marital success (O'Leary & Smith, 1991). Although it has not been demonstrated, it seems reasonable to assume that similarity promotes marital success by minimizing the extent to which a couple experiences structural conflicts.

Thus, the developmental history of partners influence their problem-solving skills, their psychopathology, their temperament, and their similarity or incompatibility. These four factors influence the extent to which couples experience conflict and satisfaction in marriage. Additionally, conflicts and distress arising from any of these four areas increases the likelihood that the couple will experience conflict and distress in the other areas (Christensen, 1991). For example, couples with a high degree of incompatibility and subsequent serious structural conflicts are likely to find their conflict resolution skills tested to a greater extent than couples who are more compatible. Moreover, these conflicts, and the resulting marital distress, are likely to exacerbate any neurotic tendencies in spouses, and they may even induce psychopathology (Birtchnell & Kennard, 1983; Matussek & Wiegand, 1985). One can imagine many permutations of the interaction between these four sources of marital conflict and distress.

The individual development of spouses, once they are in a relationship, can also be a source of conflict, if this development makes it difficult for either spouse to fulfill their needs. For example, Vines (1979) notes that couples are particularly likely to suffer from high levels of conflict and distress around the ages of 27 to 32 years because this is when many individuals experience an identity crisis. These types of individual crises have also been documented by life-span researchers (e.g., Kegan, 1983; Levinson, 1978). Couples may also simply "grow apart," if they do not develop in similar directions or at a similar pace. This can interfere with couples coordinating their behaviors so that both partners achieve their goals.

Relationship Development and Conflict

The extent to which a couple experiences conflict is also affected by the developmental processes inherent in marriage. For heuristic purposes, we can divide developmental processes of close relationships into those associated with relatively focal transition points versus those that progress gradually over relatively long periods of time. Examples of focal transitions include engagement, marriage, birth of the first child, children leaving home, and retirement (Carter & McGoldrick, 1980; Nock, 1981). Examples of more gradual developmental processes include the movement from passionate love to contentment (Berscheid, 1983; Solomon & Corbit, 1974), the repetitiveness of communication over time (Zietlow & Sillars, 1988), and long-term mutual adaptation.

Processes that involve focal transition points, such as birth of a child, often necessitate a rapid realignment of the marital relationship to accommodate the changed circumstances. This realignment can lead to structural and open conflicts. Due to space limitations, we focus on the transition to parenthood to illustrate the potential impact of transitions on marital conflict. (See chapter 4, this volume, for an in-depth discussion of the various transition points in marriage.)

To understand the impact of the transition to parenthood, researchers have examined differences in various aspects of marriages shortly before and after the birth of the first child. For example, Ryder (1973) found that wives felt their husbands did not pay enough attention to them after the birth of their first child. Similarly, Waldron and Routh (1981) found that wives' happiness decreased after having their first child. Neither of these studies found changes in the husbands' level of marital satisfaction. Other studies have shown that couples experience more conflict, fewer companionate activities, and exchange fewer positive behaviors after the birth of their first child (Belsky, Spanier, & Rovine, 1983). Belsky, Lang, and Huston (1986) found that wives with nontraditional gender-roles, whose share of the household responsibilities increased the most across the transition to parenthood, experienced the greatest declines in marital satisfaction. See Belsky (1990) for a review and discussion of literature on the transition to parenthood. These data provide strong support for the notion that couples must realign important aspects of their relationship after major transition points, such as the birth of the first child. This realignment involves attempting to negotiate mutually satisfying solutions to new structural conflicts that have arisen from the couples' changed circumstances. This negotiation process often takes the form of open conflict which may, at least temporarily, be a source of discontent.

To understand the impact of more gradual developmental processes, several studies have compared couples across general relationship stages. Storaasli and Markman (1990) used a longitudinal design to follow couples through their first 5 years of marriage. They divided the 5-year period into three stages: premarriage, early marriage, and early parenting. They found that conflicts associated with religion, jealousy, and friends generally decreased over time, whereas conflicts associated with sex, communication, and recreation generally increased over time. Wives reported a more dramatic increase in conflicts concerning sex, communication, and recreation than did husbands. They interpret these findings as indicating that early in relationships, the primary task involves forming a couple identity. Later in the development of the relationship, unresolved problems and an awareness of differences begin to build, "signaling the need to improve communication and promote togetherness through intimacy-enhancing activities" (p. 93).

Zietlow and Sillars (1988) used a cross-sectional design to compare couples in five different relationship stages: couples with no children or young children, couples with teenage children, couples with children leaving home, couples whose children have left home, and retired couples. They found that the self-reported salience of eight typical conflict areas declined linearly from young couples to retired couples. They also found that retired couples made fewer conciliatory statements during discussion of salient problem areas than did younger couples. They interpret these findings as suggesting that older couples use communication less as a means of adjusting the relationship, than as a means of expressing their feelings. Young and middle-aged couples, on the other hand, use conflict as a means of negotiating needed role adjustments. They note, however, that caution is warranted in interpreting their findings because of the probable impact of cohort differences and the nonrepresentative nature of their sample. Together, these two studies demonstrate that developmental processes of relationships affect both the types of conflicts experienced and the ways in which couples manage these conflicts. Clearly, however, much more work must be done to gain a clear understanding of the role of developmental processes in marital conflict.

It is clear from the research discussed above that the developmental history of each spouse, as well as their development within the relationship and inherent developmental processes of relationships, affect both the extent to which a couple will experience conflict and the types of conflicts they will experience. In other words, to understand fully the roots of marital conflict, we must understand the developmental processes that give rise to marital conflict. In the next section we address how the management of marital conflict, once it has arisen, affects the continuing development of the relationship.

ROLE OF CONFLICT IN DEVELOPMENT

Early marital researchers assumed that the personalities of the partners were the primary determinants of marital success (Baucom & Adams, 1987; Snyder, 1989); therefore, they were less interested in how couples behaved than in their personalities. However, early work in Interdependence Theory (Thibaut & Kelley, 1959) and the rise of behaviorally oriented models of intervention increased interest in how couples behaved in their relationship (e.g., Robinson & Jacobson, 1987). Now many theorists and researchers believe that the way couples resolve their conflicts will determine, in large part, the success of their relationship (Markman, Floyd, Stanley, & Storaasli, 1988).

Conflict is the central means through which couples seek to negotiate their incompatibilities in search of long-term mutual adaptation (Braiker & Kelley, 1979). Thus, conflict is neither inherently good nor bad; rather, it is an inevitable and central aspect of close relationships. Negotiating a mutually satisfying resolution to a structural conflict leaves a relationship stronger and more satisfying (Margolin, 1988; Peterson, 1983). However, conflicts that are not effectively resolved, due to either avoidance or an unsuccessful attempt at resolution, will often linger and reappear, and they may become a source of frustration and hostility that may eventually sunder a relationship. Furthermore, these unresolved conflicts may erode the partners' positive feelings about the relationship and interfere with the couples' normally reinforcing shared activities (Peterson, 1983; Storaasli & Markman, 1990).

Two lines of research support this reasoning. First, a growing body of literature exists that examines differences in the problem-solving behavior of distressed and nondistressed couples and how conflict behavior relates to longitudinal change in satisfaction. Second, a variety of studies demonstrate that teaching couples effective problem-solving skills early in their relationship enhances the probability for a successful relationship.

Conflict Behavior and Satisfaction

Most studies of marital conflict behavior use cross-sectional designs to examine the differences between distressed and nondistressed couples in the base-rates of specific conflict behavior or in the degree to which these couples reciprocate positive and negative behaviors (Weiss & Heyman, 1990). Although these base-rate studies are important for developing a behavioral profile of distressed couples, they fail to distinguish between conflict behavior as a *cause* of marital distress and conflict behavior as a *reflection* of marital distress. In other words, these designs do not allow a determination of whether distressed couples are less happy because they behave destructively, or if they behave destructively because they are less happy.

Studies that focus on patterns of reciprocity of positive and negative behavior begin to address the developmental processes of conflict. These studies examine the sequences of positive and negative acts. Evidence of higher than expected degrees of reciprocity indicate that couples get locked into positive or negative sequences of responding. Distressed couples have repeatedly been shown to be more likely than nondistressed couples to become locked into sequences of negative behaviors (Schaap, 1984). Inasmuch as these chains of negative behaviors interfere with the couple reaching a satisfying solution to the problem, this can be considered a microlevel description of a downward spiral.

Researchers have investigated other patterns of conflictual interaction. For example, a pattern in which one partner responds to the other's negative behavior by withdrawal has also been shown to be characteristic of distressed relationships (Christensen & Heavey, 1990; Christensen & Shenk, 1991; Peterson, 1979). Several studies have identified a typical gender linkage in this pattern, with women more likely to demand and men to withdraw (Notarius & Pellegrini, 1987; Christensen & Heavey, 1990; Christensen & Shenk, 1991). Roberts & Krokoff (1990) found that husbands' withdrawal predicted wives' hostility, whereas the reverse was not true.

The assumption of the above studies is that negative problem-solving behaviors interfere with a couples' reaching mutually satisfying solutions to their problems, thereby causing marital distress. However, with rare exceptions (e.g., Heavey, Layne, & Christensen, 1993; Koren, Carlton, & Shaw, 1980), this assumption has not been tested. Typically, studies only assess the behavior of distressed and nondistressed couples; they do not assess the outcome of the problem-solving discussions (i.e., whether couples perceive their interaction as resolving the problem). At this point, therefore, we can only assume that conflict behaviors found to be more characteristic of distressed couples interfere with effective problem solving.

Recently investigators have begun to look at the longer-term consequences of conflict behaviors by examining how these behaviors are related to change in global relationship satisfaction over time. Their reasoning is that behaviors that are truly functional will help couples resolve their problems, thereby increasing their long-term satisfaction with their relationship by eliminating structural conflicts. This design helps address the difficult problem of separating conflict behaviors that are a reflection of marital distress from those that are a cause of marital distress.

Markman (1979, 1981) was the first to use this methodology. He found that ratings of the subjective impact of messages, although unrelated to satisfaction measured concurrently, predicted satisfaction up to 5 years later. These studies, however, suffered from small sample size and a lack of ability to specify the exact nature of the "communication difficulties" that were predicting later satisfaction. Several more recent studies have used more sophisticated assessments of problem-solving communication to examine those behaviors associated with changes in satisfaction.

Filsinger and Thoma (1988) found that high levels of positive reciprocity predicted couples becoming less stable over 5 years. They found some evidence that high levels of negative reciprocity predicted later relationship instability and that the wife interrupting the husband was strongly inversely related to the man's level of satisfaction with the relationship, and positively related to relationship instability.

Gottman and Krokoff (1989) demonstrated that the relationship of conflict behaviors to cross-sectional satisfaction is often different from the relationship of these behaviors to change in satisfaction over time. For example, husbands' negative conflict behavior was inversely associated with concurrent satisfaction, but it was positively associated with change in satisfaction over 3 years. Wives' negative conflict behavior was negatively associated with concurrent satisfaction, but it was not associated with longitudinal change in relationship satisfaction. Similarly, Heavey, Layne, and Christensen (1993) found that wives' demandingness and negativity predicted longitudinal decline in wives' satisfaction, whereas husbands' demandingness and negativity predicted longitudinal increase in wives' satisfaction. However, Huston and Vangelisti (1991) found husbands' negativity predicted longitudinal decline in wives' satisfaction. Finally, Smith, Vivian, and O'Leary (1991) found that negativity during problem solving was negatively associated with Time 1 satisfaction but unrelated to satisfaction later in the relationship. They also found that degree of engagement was positively associated with longitudinal change in satisfaction.

Murphy and O'Leary (1989) performed a similar type of longitudinal study in which they examined how conflict management early in relationships related to the use of violence later in the relationship. After following a sample of engaged couples for 30 months, they concluded that the way couples handled conflicts early in marriage was a better predictor of the likelihood that the couple would later experience violence, than the couples' early level of relationship satisfaction: "The results suggest that early in marriage, the general manner of reacting to conflicts, rather than general dissatisfaction with the relationship is critical in understanding the development of physical aggression" (p. 582). This underscores the importance of effective conflict resolution for long-term relationship adjustment.

These studies represent the most sophisticated attempts to date to understand the impact of marital conflict behavior on the developmental course of marriage. However, two things should be clear from this brief review. First, the relationship of conflict behavior to concurrent satisfaction may be very different from the relationship of the same behavior to longitudinal change in satisfaction. This difference exists because conflict behavior is a reflection of each spouse's current disposition toward the relationship and degree of problem-solving skills, as well as a determinant of the future of the relationship through either contributing to, or interfering with the resolution of relationship problems. Second, we are only at the beginning stages of developing a clear picture of which conflict behaviors are functional and which are dysfunctional for long-term adjustment. Even at this early stage there are contradictory findings that must be reconciled. Nonetheless, this strategy for determining the impact of conflict behavior holds considerably more promise for distinguishing between conflict behavior that is a reflection of marital distress and conflict behavior that is a cause of marital distress than simply trying to catalog the differences in the conflict behavior of distressed and nondistressed couples.

Problem-Solving Training Programs and Satisfaction

Perhaps the most convincing data concerning the importance of problem-solving behavior for long-term relationship adjustment comes from studies that demonstrate the benefits of teaching couples effective problem-solving skills. The most comprehensive work in this area is that of Markman and his colleagues (e.g., Markman, Floyd, Stanley, & Storaasli, 1988). This group has shown that their premarital intervention program can prevent the typical decline in marital satisfaction experienced by most couples (Spanier, Lewis, & Cole, 1975) over a 3-year period. Markman et. al found that the only difference between those who participated in the preventative intervention and the control group at the conclusion of the intervention was that the intervention group displayed better problem-solving skills. However, after 3 years, the intervention group reported significantly higher levels of relationship satisfaction. Based on these data, Markman et al. concluded that the improvement in communication skills attributable to their prevention program is the most probable cause of the better outcome of the intervention group. O'Leary and Smith (1991) reviewed other prevention programs and concluded that these programs can be effective in preventing distress and reducing divorce. However, more research on the various components of these programs must be done before we can conclude that teaching couples more effective ways to resolve their problems is a primary mechanism through which these programs influence the course of marriages.

Unfortunately, very few couples participate in these prevention programs or other interventions that might enhance their ability to handle conflict. In general, many couples find themselves unable to find mutually satisfying solutions to their structural and open conflicts. These unresolved conflicts often linger and interact with the concomitant frustration and anger to generate a downward spiral of increasing hostility and more frequent conflicts. At some point, most couples who are unable to break the cycle of increasingly painful and intractable conflicts begin to consider separation and divorce. Thus, conflict, instead of prompting the mutual adaptation necessary to sustain a satisfying close relationship, serves as the beginning of the end for some couples.

MARITAL SEPARATION AND DIVORCE

The process of marital separation and divorce brings a complex array of changes to the couple and the family unit, but it certainly cannot be considered as an endpoint in the family life cycle. Divorce is perhaps best understood as an "unscheduled life transition" (Ahrons, 1980, p. 534), rather than a point of termination. In the United States, this view of divorce as part of the ongoing family life cycle is especially appropriate because divorce and remarriage are so common, and because children typically are involved. Currently, almost half the marriages in our country are likely to end in divorce (Glick, 1984). From these divorces, five of six men and three of four women can be expected to remarry (Cherlin, 1981). Children are involved in approximately 60% of these divorces (Bumpass & Rindfuss, 1979).

The impact of divorce within the family life cycle can be conceptualized at individual, interpersonal, and structural levels. The individual experiences various stages of cognitive, emotional, and behavioral adjustment. The couple contends with erratic patterns of approach, interaction, and withdrawal, as well as possible remarriage. Their changing relationship necessitates negotiation of many challenges including financial, legal, custody, co-parenting, and other social issues. The family system undergoes an array of transitions that require reorganization in terms of roles, boundaries, and rules in the process of establishing a new equilibrium as a binuclear family (Ahrons, 1980, 1981). At each of these levels of change, the divorce process is affected by the surrounding networks of family, friends, religious affiliations, and culture (Donovan & Jackson, 1990; Gander, 1991; Kaslow & Schwartz, 1987).

The transition from marriage to divorce occurs in various forms and across varied time tables (Spanier, 1988). The divorce process has been conceptualized in terms of several stage models (see Black, Eastwood, Sprenkle, & Smith, 1991; Ponzetti & Cate, 1988). These range from the more simple model proposed by Brown (1976), consisting of a decision-making phase and a restructuring phase, to the tedious 33-stage model offered by Shapiro (1984). We have adopted a stage model similar to that proposed by Kaslow (1984; Kaslow & Schwartz, 1987) and others, consisting of 3 stages: 1) decision making; 2) uncoupling; and 3) postdivorce recovery. This model is simple and straightforward, yet it focuses on the essential tasks the couple must negotiate in the divorce process.

The Decision-Making Phase

The process of deciding to divorce has been identified as the most critical, and possibly the most stressful aspect of the divorce experience (Donovan & Jackson, 1990; Framo, 1985). Donovan and Jackson assert that the final divorce decision likely evolves from a previous series of smaller decisions made as the individual assesses costs and benefits associated with the marriage and attempts to resolve cognitive dissonance regarding the relationship. This process may take up to two or more years of deliberation (Perlman, 1982; Spanier, 1988), and it typically involves intense periods of conflict and ambivalence (Ponzetti & Cate, 1987; Wright, 1989).

Ponzetti and Cate (1987), examining the course of conflict in dissolution, found that conflict increased significantly from the period of "recognition" of serious dissatisfaction for the individual to the period of "discussion" with others, including the spouse. Christensen and Shenk (1991) found that couples in therapy and recently separated couples, as compared to nondistressed couples, had more conflict over psychological distance versus closeness, and they showed more communication avoidance and demand/withdraw interactions.

Ambivalence about the decision to divorce often perpetuates conflicts for couples in the process of separating. Weiss (1975) argues that the ambivalence results from the interplay between concurrent feelings of attachment and anger between spouses. Ponzetti and Cate (1987) found, for example, that ambivalence about divorce was associated with higher levels of conflict throughout the divorce process. Evidence for ambivalence can be seen in the fact that couples frequently experience "post decision regret," and up to 40% of those who petition for divorce retract their decision in any given year (Donovan & Jackson, 1990).

Numerous proximal or distal influences within and outside the marital relationship may contribute to divorce. Influences from outside the marriage may include extramarital sexual partners, children, or economic factors (Spanier, 1988). Influences within the marriage include length of marriage and age at marriage (Neff, Gilbert, & Hoppe, 1991), disillusionment related to unmet expectations (Wright, 1989), and a host of other factors, including alcoholism, unfaithfulness, abuse, mental cruelty, and "sexual incompatibility" (Levinger, 1976). Kaslow and Schwartz (1987) report that recent complaints related to the divorce decision concern factors such as personality, values, and lack of communication. Similarly, Spanier and Thompson (1984) found that the chief sources of disagreement include: 1) gender role performance (e.g., sharing in housekeeping tasks); 2) quality of sexual relationship; 3) poor communication; and 4) changes in involvement (e.g., values, time spent together).

Several theories have been used to explain the decision to end the marriage relationship, as well as the intense emotional reactions observed in this period. Social exchange theory, developed originally by Thibaut and Kelly (1959), is the most frequently cited model for explaining the causes of divorce (Black et al., 1991; Donovan & Jackson, 1990). Levinger (1979), using a social exchange theory framework, characterizes marital stability in terms of a balance between attractions within the marriage, external pressures to remain married, and alternative sources of gratification outside the marriage.

Attachment theory offers another theoretical framework for understanding the decision-making process for couples considering divorce. The attachment bond functions in providing a sense of psychological security, continuity, and personal identity: "Therefore, threats to disrupt the attachment bond precipitate distress and behaviors directed at preserving the bond . . . The feelings evoked during this time are confusing to the couple and the individuals may believe that they are still in love and that additional efforts to preserve the marriage are warranted" (Donovan & Jackson, 1990, p. 28). The attachment bond may help explain why couples often cling desperately to the marriage, and struggle through intense ambivalence and conflict, although they are dissatisfied or have attempted to separate on repeated occasions.

Although addressed little, the developmental stage of the spouses must influence processes and reactions during the decision-making phase of the marital dissolution. Facing divorce as a senior citizen must be very different from facing divorce as a young adult. We know little about these differences, except as they are reflected in demographic trends. Although divorce rates have leveled out in general during the past decade, rates among older persons have been increasing (see Gander, 1991; Weingarten, 1989). Weingarten notes that over the past decade, rates of divorce increased 50% among adults between the ages of 40 and 65, and 35% among persons 65 and older. Several social and demographic trends undoubtedly influence these changes. These trends include: 1) the decline in mortality rates, which leaves less chance of marital termination by death; 2) increases in social and legal acceptance of divorce; and 3) other social changes, such as greater economic independence for women. More information is needed to understand the causes of increasing divorce rates among older couples.

The Process of Uncoupling

The process of uncoupling refers to the cognitive, emotional, and physical aspects of moving from married to divorced status. The actual physical separation, and the legal event of divorce, have both been used as points of delineation between these stages (e.g., Kaslow & Schwartz, 1987). Patterns of conflict and interaction do not necessarily change significantly at these milestones, however. Thus, a more comprehensive developmental perspective on divorce in the life cycle may best be represented by the loosely defined term "uncoupling."

The continuity of spousal and family relationships even after the physical separation has been well documented and analyzed (e.g., Ahrons & Rogers, 1987; Bohannan, 1973; Wallerstein & Kelly, 1980; Weiss, 1975). Jacobson (1983) found that the relationship between former spouses continued even when there were no children involved for recently separated couples and those in the process of filing for divorce. Reliance on the former spouse for emotional support and assistance in child-care or home tasks, were characteristic of the continuing tie between the former spouses. With longer time periods since the separation, couples with children are more likely to remain in contact than couples without children.

Bohannan (1970) defined the term "coparental relationship" in recognition of the ongoing relationship necessary as former spouses relate regarding issues with their children. Similarly, Ahrons (1980, 1981) has described the concept of "binuclear families" to reflect the continuity of family ties, even long after divorce and remarriage. Even in cases of maternal custody, Ahrons (1981) found that 84–85% of divorced spouses with children continued to maintain some kind of direct contact with one another one year after the divorce. Sixty-six % of divorced families with children reported a high degree of coparental interaction even 3 years after divorce (Ahrons & Wallisch, 1987). Remarriage of the husband was associated with reduced interaction, but remarriage of the wife did not result in such a change.

The process of cognitive and emotional separation begins at different points prior to the actual physical separation. Divorce is rarely a mutually agreed upon goal (Kressel, Jaffee, Tuchman, Watson, & Deutsch, 1980; Wallerstein & Kelly, 1980). The passive agent, or the one who is "left," is most vulnerable in that he or she may have been partially or totally surprised by the spouse's announcement to seek separation, and may begin the acceptance and grieving process at a much later point than the spouse who had been contemplating the decision for some time (Crosby, Lybarger, & Mason, 1987).

Gender differences in the reactions to divorce have been described by numerous researchers (e.g., Jacobson, 1983; Kaslow & Schwartz, 1987). In general, researchers have reported either 1) few differences in adjustment on the basis of gender, or 2) a phenomenon in which the early postseparation period in particular is harder for men (e.g., Bloom & Hodges, 1981). Veevers (1991) elucidates some specific factors related to gender differences: women tend to respond more to a loss of instrumental functions usually provided by husbands, whereas men responded more to the loss of expressive functions usually provided by wives. Hetherington, Cox, & Cox, (1978) report that women tend to hold on to anger and resentment toward their spouse for longer periods than men do. Observations such as these, however, may be related to various other factors, such as culpability in the events leading up to the divorce, who was the "leaver" versus "the left," financial well-being of the spouses, and whether or not a new lover was or is in the picture after the separation.

Intense reactions ranging from rage, to anxiety, to depression and frequent suicidal ideation, to remorse and longing for the absent spouse are present in the period during and following the separation (Jacobson, 1983; Weiss, 1975). Some researchers have emphasized the process of grieving, similar to that observed in response to death, as central to the understanding of reactions after divorce (Crosby, Lybarger, & Mason, 1987). Thus, former spouses, and children also, must negotiate the stages leading to final acceptance of the loss in order to move forward freely with their own development. Excessive involvement with the former spouse may prevent working through the loss and associated grief, resulting in reactivation of earlier conflicts and an aggravation of the emotional suffering (Jacobson, 1983).

The majority of exchanges between divorced couples in the early divorce period involve conflicts (Goldsmith, 1981; Kurdek & Blisk, 1983). Wallerstein and Kelly (1980) found that four fifths of all the men, and an even higher number of women, expressed anger and bitterness toward their spouses in the months following marital separation. The most common forms of conflict involved verbal assaults on the integrity and behavior of the divorcing spouse. Ponzetti and Cate (1987) found that conflict decreased once action to secure a legal dissolution was initiated. Jacobson (1983) found that some aspects of hostility decrease after the separation discussion, however divorce-related conflicts tend to increase. Furthermore, among violent couples, physical attacks often continued, although with decreased frequency, even many months after the separation. A number of the respondents in his study reported that the spouse had even tried to kill them at one time.

A number of researchers have emphasized the balance of both positive and negative relating between spouses after divorce (Veevers, 1991). Over half the former spouses in one study reported their relationships to be supportive and satisfying, despite continuing conflicts (Ahrons & Rogers, 1987). Thus, the postdivorce relationships may satisfy some legitimate adult attachment needs in the form of friendship, shared history, and extended family.

Timing in the developmental life cycle for each individual is also important for adjustment during this second phase of the divorce process. As we noted earlier with regard to the decision to divorce, very little research has focused on the experience of elderly spouses with respect to divorce. Weingarten (1989) noted that remarriage rates decline with age, especially for women, and that persisting attachment feelings toward former spouses were frequent among their older respondents. She also found that issues of generativity, relevant in stages of psychosocial development for the older adult, were salient in the reports of older divorcees. The desire to be "needed" or "affirmed" was also quite signifi-cant in the adjustment to the divorced status. Thus, some participants in her research project coped by becoming increasingly involved with church or other volunteer organizations, whereas others focused more on their adult children and grandchildren.

Postdivorce Recovery: Establishing Separate Lives

A number of developmental tasks must be addressed in the process of reaching a new state of equilibrium in the postdivorce relationship. A new self-concept as a single person or divorcee must be adopted in order to continue individual development and find a sense of identification with others. A new or modified social life is required as friendships are realigned or replaced, and the prospect of dating and eventual remarriage is contemplated or pursued. Financial, legal, socioeconomic, and geographic changes must be negotiated in the process of completing the adjustment to the new life. Separating spouses with children must complete the grief process in order to regain emotional stability and accept new co-parental roles for themselves as they dissolve their spousal relationship.

In most cases, both conflict and attachment decrease during the first year or two after the separation, although former spouses typically retain varying levels of hostile feelings. In fact, a substantial proportion of families remain as turbulent and conflicted following the divorce as they had been during the marriage, and in some cases, the level of discord actually increases (Hetherington et al., 1978). Wallerstein and Kelly (1980) found that at 18 months after separation, only 45% of the men and only one third of the women were no longer experiencing intense levels of bitterness. Nelson (1990) found that increased contact between the former spouses caused by shared custody and access to the children was related to higher levels of conflict and hostility at 2 years postseparation. However, she also found that extreme levels of verbal and physical violence at 2 and 3 years postseparation were not attributable to custody or visitation arrangements. Rather, as was found by Jacobson (1983), the report of extreme abuse during the marital years was predictive of postseparation violence.

Remarriage poses yet a new stage in the family life process. The transition to remarriage, if children are involved, necessitates a complex sequence of structural changes in roles and relationships, financial and legal modifications, and clarification of boundaries and expectations (Ahrons & Rodgers, 1987; Hobart, 1991). The challenges facing families in this complex process may help explain why remarriages are quite susceptible to dissolution (Glick, 1984). According to McGoldrick and Carter (1980), the complexity of the remarriage process indicates a need to add an additional phase in conceptualizing the family life cycle. The various patterns of interaction and adjustment for the couple in response to remarriage are beginning to receive attention in research on families and divorce (Hobart, 1991; Kaslow & Schwartz, 1987).

Kvanli and Jennings (1987) discuss the specific developmental tasks that must be addressed in the remarriage process in order for stabilization to occur and development to continue. They note that the formation of a solid marital relationship is difficult for the remarried couple because of old attachments, increased pressure to succeed "this time," and fears about risking intimacy and attachment after the trauma of the preceding divorce. For the single, former spouse, the remarriage of a former mate may stimulate anger, hurt, and other feelings yet unresolved with respect to the emotional divorce (Bohannon, 1973). Changes in one parent's involvement with their children, and sharing of parenting responsibilities, may also occur with remarriage, especially if step-children are involved. This may reignite conflicts between the former spouses.

Two particularly important developmental tasks for adults, the formation of a clear sense of identity and the realization of intimacy, are both disrupted and challenged by the experience of divorce (Rice & Rice, 1986). At age 25 or at age 55, the individual identity often encompasses concepts and roles such as "spouse," "married person," "family member," or perhaps "parent." With age, birth of children, or number of years married, such aspects of one's identity may be increasingly solidified. Thus, divorce may bring greater degrees of developmental challenge, in terms of redefining one's identity, depending on where one is in their life stage. Similarly, one's ability to reach out or adapt socially in the process of fulfilling intimacy needs may be affected by their developmental stage at the time of divorce. The skills, confidence, or motivation necessary for dating or forming new relationships, may be hindered at either end of the developmental span. Younger individuals may have moved into marriage straight from their family of origin, thus lacking the opportunity to deal with singlehood or to develop social skills in relating to new people. At the other end, older persons, those married for longer periods, or those with children, may have become dependent on the family for meeting social needs. They may have lost the skills or confidence needed to meet new people. Thus, meeting the developmental challenge of finding intimacy may be affected by the age and developmental stage of the divorcee.

These three stages of separation and divorce—decision making, uncoupling, and recovery—represent sequential and overlapping phases in the termination of marriage. As we discovered with conflict in marriage, this termination process is influenced by both individual and relationship development. Spouses' life stage and personality affect their divorce. The development of their relationship, such as whether they have children or not, also affects their divorce. Finally, as with marital conflict, the way partners handle their divorce will probably affect the speed with which they conclude it and their satisfaction with it.

Conflict discussed earlier within the married couple seems particularly endemic to the divorce process. At each stage, partners mark their movement away from each other through conflict. According to the grief model of divorce, spouses need to reach a stage where they accept the loss of their marriage and their partner. The cessation of conflict may mark this stage, and thus the success-ful conclusion of the divorce.

CONCLUSION

Continuity and change characterize the development of conflict through marriage and divorce. Continuity in the individual development of each spouse determines, to some extent, the nature of their marital conflict. Spouses' social skills, their psychopathology, their personality temperament, and their needs and interests form the basis for potential conflicts of interest in the marriage, which in turn, give rise to open conflict. During separation and divorce, which should mark a major change in the marriage, spouses often show remarkable continuities in their conflict with each other. They continue to have contact, and much of the contact is conflictual, often a predictable continuation of their conflict during the marriage.

Despite these dramatic continuities, the development of conflict in couples is also marked by both gradual and dramatic change. Longitudinal data on marriage suggest that the way couples handle their conflicts in the present may change their satisfaction in the future. Data also suggest that psychological intervention with couples early in their relationship may affect future satisfaction by changing the way couples resolve their conflicts. More dramatic changes can be found in couples during transitional periods that may prompt precipitous increases or decreases in conflict. Initial consideration of the possibility of separation and divorce may lead to increased conflict in couples. The actual separation and divorce may create dramatic decreases in the frequency of conflict simply by virtue of the fact that couples are no longer in each other's daily presence. Even with continuing postdivorce conflict, the data suggest that time, the maker of all changes, eventually has its impact on divorcing couples. To establish separate lives, divorcing couples must detach from their spouses, and detachment brings an eventual easing of conflict.

When asked to describe life, a wise man reportedly said, "Things change and they remain the same." The task for developmental family psychologists is to describe the ways in which things change and the ways in which they remain the same. What makes this enormously complicated is that any continuity or any change at any particular time is both a reflection of previous causal factors and a causal factor for future continuities and changes. As we noted earlier in the chapter, conflict can be a result of developmental processes, and a causal factor influencing future developmental processes. Therefore, we may add to the wise man's statement that everything that changes and everything that stays the same reflects past changes and continuities and influences future changes and continuities. We have our work cut out for us.

REFERENCES

Ahrons, C. R. (1980). Divorce: A crisis of family transition and change. *Family Relations, 29*, 533–540.

Ahrons, C. R. (1981). The continuing coparental relationship between divorced spouses. *American Journal of Orthomolecular Psychiatry, 51*, 415–428.

Ahrons, C. R., & Rodgers, R. H. (1987). *Divorced families: A multidisciplinary developmental view.* New York: Norton.

Ahrons, C. R., & Wallisch, L. (1987). The relationship between former spouses. In S. Duck & D. Perlman (Eds.), *Intimate relationships: Development, dynamics, and deterioration* (pp. 269–296). Newbury Park, CA: Sage.

Baucom, D. H., & Adams, A. N. (1987). Assessing communication in marital interaction. In K. D. O'Leary (Ed.), *Assessment of marital discord* (pp. 139–181). Hillsdale, NJ: Erlbaum.

Belsky, J. (1990). Children and marriage. In F. Fincham & T. Bradbury (Eds.), *The psychology of marriage* (pp. 172–200). New York: Guilford.

Belsky, J., Lang, M., & Huston, T. L. (1986). Sex typing and division of labor as determinants of marital change across the transition to parenthood. *Journal of Personality and Social Psychology, 50,* 517–522.

Belsky, J., Spanier, G. B., & Rovine, M. (1983). Stability and change in marriage across the transition to parenthood. *Journal of Marriage and the Family, 45,* 553–556.

Bentler, P. M., & Newcomb, M. D. (1978). Longitudinal study of marital success and failure. *Journal of Consulting and Clinical Psychology, 46,* 1053–1070.

Berscheid, E. (1983). Emotion. In H. H. Kelley, E. Berscheid, A. Christensen, J. H. Harvey, T. L. Huston, G. Levinger, E. McClintock, L. A. Peplau, & D. Peterson (Eds.), *Close relationships* (pp. 110–168). New York: Freeman.

Birtchnell, J., & Kennard, J. (1983). Does marital maladjustment lead to mental illness? *Social Psychiatry and Psychiatric Epidemiology, 18,* 79–88.

Black, L. E., Eastwood, M. M., Sprenkle, D. H., & Smith, E. (1991). An exploratory analysis of leavers versus left as it relates to Levinger's social exchange theory of attractions barriers, and alternative attractions. *Journal of Divorce & Remarriage, 15,* 127–139.

Bloom, B. L., & Hodges, W. F. (1981). The predicament of the newly separated. *Community Mental Health Journal, 17,* 277–293.

Bohannon, P. (1970). The six stations of divorce. In P. Bohannon (Ed.), *Divorce and after: An analysis of the emotional and social problems of divorce* (pp. 29–55). New York: Doubleday.

Bohannon, P. (1973). The six stations of divorce. In M. E. Lasswell & T. E. Lasswell (Eds.), *Love, marriage, and family: A developmental approach* (pp. 475–489). Glenview, IL: Scott, Foresman.

Braiker, H. B., & Kelley, H. H. (1979). Conflict in the development of close relationships. In R. L. Burgess & T. L. Huston (Eds.), *Social exchange in developing relationships* (pp. 135–168). New York: Academic.

Brown, E. (1976). Divorce counseling. In D. Olson (Ed.), *Treating relationships* (pp. 399–429). Lake Mills, IA: Graphic Publishing.

Bumpass, L., & Rindfuss, R. R. (1979). Children's experience of marital disruption. *American Journal of Sociology, 85,* 49–65.

Carter, E. A., & McGoldrick, M. (1980). *The family life cycle: A framework for family therapy.* New York: Gardner.

Cherlin, A. J. (1981). *Marriage, divorce, remarriage.* Cambridge, MA: Harvard University Press.

Christensen, A. (1983). Intervention. In H. H. Kelley, E. Berscheid, A. Christensen, J. H. Harvey, T. L. Huston, G. Levinger, E. McClintok, L. A. Peplau, & D. Peterson. (Eds.). *Close relationships,* (pp. 397–448). New York: Freeman.

Christensen, A. (1991, November). *Conflicts over psychological distance in marriage: Assessment and treatment considerations.* Workshop presented at the Annual Association for the Advancement of Behavior Therapy Convention, New York.

Christensen, A., & Heavey, C. L (1990). Gender and social structure in the demand/withdraw pattern of marital interaction. *Journal of Personality and Social Psychology, 59,* 73–81.

Christensen, A., & Shenk, J. L. (1991). Communication, conflict, and psychological distance in nondistressed, clinic, and divorcing couples. *Journal of Consulting & Clinical Psychology, 59,* 458–463.

Coyne, J., Kahn, J., & Gotlib, I. (1987). Depression. In T. Jacob (Ed.), *Family interaction and psychopathology: Theories, methods, and findings* (pp. 509–534). New York: Plenum.

Crosby, J. F., Lybarger, S. K., & Mason, R. L. (1987). The grief resolution process in divorce: Phase II. *Journal of Divorce & Remarriage, 10,* 17–40.

Doherty, W. J. (1981). Cognitive processes in intimate conflict: 1. Extending attribution theory. *American Journal of Family Therapy, 9,* 3–13.

Donovan, R. L., & Jackson, B. L. (1990). Deciding to divorce: A process guided by social exchange, attachment, and cognitive dissonance theories. *Journal of Divorce & Remarriage, 13,* 23–35.

Emery, R. E. (1988). *Marriage, divorce, and children's adjustment.* Newbury Park, CA: Sage.

Filsinger, E. E., & Thoma, S. J. (1988). Behavioral antecedents of relationship stability and adjustment: A five-year longitudinal study. *Journal of Marriage and the Family, 50,* 785–795.

Framo, J. L. (1985). Breaking the ties that bind: Impending divorce and the process of alienation. *Family Therapy Networker, 9,* 51–56.

Gander, A. M. (1991). After the divorce: Familial factors that predict well-being for older and younger persons. *Journal of Divorce & Remarriage, 15,* 175–192.

Geiss, S. K., & O'Leary, K. D. (1981). Therapist ratings of frequency and severity of marital problems: Implications for research. *Journal of Marital and Family Therapy, 7,* 515–520.

Glick, P. C. (1984). How American families are changing. *American Demographics, 6,* 20–27.

Goldsmith, J. (1981). Relationships between former spouses: Descriptive findings. *Journal of Divorce & Remarriage, 4,* 1–20.

Gottman, J. M., & Krokoff, L. J. (1989). Marital interaction and satisfaction: A longitudinal view. *Journal of Consulting and Clinical Psychology, 57,* 47–52.

Gottman, J. M., & Porterfield, A. L. (1981). Communicative competence in the nonverbal behavior of married couples. *Journal of Marriage and the Family, 43,* 817–824.

Grych, J. H., & Fincham, F. D. (1990). Marital conflict and children's adjustment: A cognitive-contextual framework. *Psychological Bulletin, 108,* 267–290.

Heavey, C. L., Layne, C., & Christensen, A. (1993). Gender and conflict structure in marital interaction: A replication and extension. *Journal of Consulting and Clinical Psychology, 61,* 16–27.

Hetherington, E. M., Cox, M., & Cox, R. (1978). The aftermath of divorce. In J. H. Stevens & M. Matthews (Eds.), *Mother-child, father-child relationships* (pp. 110–155). Washington, DC: National Association for Education of Young Children.

Hobart, C. (1991). Relationships between the formerly married. *Journal of Divorce & Remarriage, 14,* 1–23.

Hoover, C. F., & Fitzgerald, R. (1981). Marital conflict and manic-depressive patients. *Archives of General Psychiatry, 38,* 65–67.

Huston, T. L., & Vangelisti, A. L. (1991). Socioemotional behavior and satisfaction in marital relationships: A longitudinal study. *Journal of Personality and Social Psychology, 61,* 721–733.

Jacobson, G. F. (1983). *The multiple crises of marital separation and divorce.* New York: Grune & Stratton.

Jacobson, N. S., & Holtzworth-Munroe, A. (1986). Marital therapy: A social-learning-cognitive perspective. In N. S. Jacobson & A. S. Gurman (Eds.), *Clinical handbook of marital therapy* (pp. 29–70). New York: Guilford.

Kaslow, F. W. (1984). Divorce: An evolutionary process of change in the family system. *Journal of Divorce & Remarriage, 7,* 21–39.

Kaslow, F. W., & Schwartz, L. L. (1987). *The dynamics of divorce: A family life cycle perspective.* New York: Brunner/Mazel.

Kegan, R. (1983). *The evolving self.* Cambridge, MA: Harvard University Press.

Kelley, H. H. (1979). *Personal relationships: Their structures and processes.* Hillsdale, NJ: Erlbaum.

Kelley, H. H., Berscheid, E., Christensen, A., Harvey, J. H., Huston, T. L., Levinger, G., McClintock, E., Peplau, L. A., & Peterson, D. (1983). *Close relationships.* New York: Freeman.

Kelley, H. H., & Thibaut, J. (1978). *Interpersonal relations.* New York: Wiley.

Kelly, E. L., & Conley, J. J. (1987). Personality and compatibility: A prospective analysis of marital stability and satisfaction. *Journal of Personality and Social Psychology, 52,* 27–40.

Koren, P., Carlton, K., & Shaw, D. (1980). Marital conflict: Relations among behaviors, outcomes, and distress. *Journal of Consulting and Clinical Psychology, 48,* 460–468.

Kressel, K., Jaffee, N., Tuchman, B., Watson, C., & Deutsch, M. (1980). A typology of divorcing couples: Implications for mediation and the divorce process. *Family Process, 19,* 101–116.

Kurdek, L. A., & Blisk, D. (1983). Dimensions and correlates of mothers' divorce experiences. *Journal of Divorce & Remarriage, 6,* 1–24.

Levinger, G. (1976). A social psychological perspective on marital dissolution. *Journal of Social Issues, 32,* 21–47.

Levinger, G. (1979). Marital cohesiveness at the brink: The fate of applications for divorce. In G. Levinger & O. C. Moles (Eds.), *Divorce and separation* (pp. 137–150), New York: Basic Books.

Levinson, D. J. (1978). *The seasons of a man's life.* New York: Ballantine.

McGoldrick, M., & Carter, E. (1980). Forming a remarried family. In E. Carter & M. McGoldrick (Eds.), *The family life cycle: A framework for family therapy.* New York: Gardner.

Margolin, G. (1988). Marital conflict is not marital conflict is not marital conflict. In R. DeV. Peters & R. McMahon (Eds.), *Marriage and families: Behavioral treatment and processes* (pp. 193–216). Champaign, IL: Research.

Markman, H. J. (1979). The application of a behavioral model of marriage in predicting relationship satisfaction of couples planning marriage. *Journal of Consulting and Clinical Psychology, 4,* 473–479.

Markman, H. J. (1981). The prediction of marital distress: A five-year follow-up. *Journal of Consulting and Clinical Psychology, 49,* 760–762.

Markman, H. J., Floyd, F. J., Stanley, S. M., & Storaasli, R. D. (1988). Prevention of marital distress: A longitudinal investigation. *Journal of Consulting and Clinical Psychology, 56,* 210–217.

Matussek, P., & Wiegand, M. (1985). Partnership problems as causes of endogenous and neurotic depressions. *Acta Psychiatrica Scandinavica, 71,* 95–104.

Murphy, C. M., & O'Leary, K. D. (1989). Psychological aggression predicts physical aggression in early marriage. *Journal of Consulting and Clinical Psychology, 57,* 579–582.

Neff, J. A., Gilbert, K. R., & Hoppe, S. K. (1991). Divorce likelihood among Anglos and Mexican Americans. *Journal of Divorce & Remarriage, 15,* 75–97.

Nelson, R. (1990). Parental hostility, conflict, and communication in joint and sole custody families. *Journal of Divorce & Remarriage, 13,* 145–157.

Nock, S. (1981). The family life cycle: Empirical or conceptual? *Journal of Marriage and the Family, 41,* 15–26.

Noller, P. (1982). Channel consistency and inconsistency in the communications of married couples. *Journal of Personality and Social Psychology, 43,* 732–741.

Noller, P. (1987). Nonverbal communication in marriage. In D. Perlman & S. Duck (Eds.), *Intimate relationships: Development, dynamics, and deterioration* (pp. 149–176). Newbury Park, CA: Sage.

Notarius, C. I., & Pellegrini, D. S. (1987). Differences between husbands and wives: Implications for understanding marital discord. In K. Hahlweg & M. J. Goldstein (Eds.), *Understanding major mental disorder: The contribution of family interaction research* (231–249). Waldwick, NJ: Family Process.

O'Leary, K. D., & Smith, D. A. (1991). Marital interaction. *Annual Review of Psychology, 42,* 191–212.

Perlman, J. L. (1982). Divorce: A psychological and legal process. *Journal of Divorce & Remarriage, 6,* 99–114.

Peterson, D. R. (1979). Assessing interpersonal relationships by means of interaction records. *Behavioral Assessment, 1,* 221–236.

Peterson, D. R. (1983). Conflict. In H. H. Kelley, E. Berscheid, A. Christensen, J. H. Harvey, T. L. Huston, G. Levinger, E. McClintok, L. A. Peplau, & D. Peterson (Eds.), *Close relationships* (pp. 360–396). New York: Freeman.

Ponzetti, J. J., Jr., & Cate, R. M. (1987). The developmental course of conflict in the marital dissolution process. *Journal of Divorce & Remarriage, 10,* 1–15.

Ponzetti, J. J., Jr., & Cate, R. M. (1988). The divorce process: Toward a typology of marital dissolution. *Journal of Divorce & Remarriage, 11,* 1–20.

Rice, J. K., & Rice, D. G. (1986). *Living through divorce: A developmental approach to divorce therapy.* New York: Guilford.

Roberts L. J., & Krokoff, L. J. (1990). A time-series analysis of withdrawal, hostility, and displeasure in satisfied and dissatisfied marriages. *Journal of Marriage and the Family, 52,* 95–105.

Robinson, E. A., & Jacobson, N. S. (1987). Social learning theory and family psychopathology: A Kantian model in behaviorism? In. T. Jacob (Ed.), *Family interaction and psychopathology: Theories, methods, and findings* (pp. 117–162). New York: Plenum.

Ryder, R. G. (1973). Longitudinal data relating marriage satisfaction and having a child. *Journal of Marriage and the Family, 35,* 604–607.

Schaap, C. (1984). A comparison of the interaction of distressed and nondistressed married couples in a laboratory situation: Literature survey, methodological issues, and an empirical investigation. In K. Hahlweg & N. S. Jacobson (Eds.), *Marital interaction: Analysis and modification* (pp. 133–158). New York: Guilford.

Schafer, R. B., & Keith, P. M. (1983). Marital interaction and depression. *Journal of Social Service Research, 6,* 89–101.

Shapiro, J. L. (1984). A brief outline of a chronological divorce sequence. *Family Therapy, 11,* 269–278.

Smith, D. A., Vivian, D., & O'Leary, K. D. (1990). Longitudinal prediction of marital discord from premarital expressions of affect. *Journal of Consulting and Clinical Psychology, 58,* 790–798.

Snyder, D. K. (1989). Introduction to special edition on marriage. *Journal of Consulting and Clinical Psychology, 57,* 3–4.

Solomon, R. L., & Corbit, J. D. (1974). An opponent–process theory of motivation: I. Temporal dynamics of affect. *Psychological Review, 81,* 119–145.

Spanier, G. B. (1988). Diversity in the transition to divorce. In R. DeV. Peters & R. J. McMahon (Eds.), *Social learning and systems approaches to marriage and the family,* (pp. 128–144). New York: Brunner/Mazel.

Spanier, G. B., Lewis, R. A., & Cole, C. L. (1975). Marital adjustment over the family cycle: The issue of curvilinearity. *Journal of Marriage and the Family, 37,* 263–275.

Spanier, G. B., & Thompson, L. (1984). *Parting: The aftermath of separation and divorce.* Newbury Park, CA: Sage.

Storaasli, R. D., & Markman, H. J. (1990). Relationship problems in the early stages of marriage. *Journal of Family Psychology, 4,* 80–98.

Thibaut, J. W., & Kelly, H. H. (1959). *The social psychology of groups.* New York: Wiley.

Veevers, J. E. (1991). Traumas versus strengths: A paradigm of positive versus negative divorce outcomes. *Journal of Divorce & Remarriage, 14,* 99–126.

Vincent, J. P., Weiss, R. L., & Birchler, G. R. (1975). A behavioral analysis of problem solving in distressed and nondistressed married and stranger dyads. *Behavior Therapy, 6,* 475–487.

Vines, N. (1979). Adult unfolding and marital conflict. *Journal of Marital and Family Therapy, 5,* 5–14.

Waldron, H., & Routh, D. K. (1981). The effect of the first child on the marital relationship. *Journal of Marriage and the Family, 43,* 785–788.

Wallerstein, J. S., & Kelly, J. B. (1980). *Surviving the breakup: How children and parents cope with divorce.* New York: Basic Books.

Weingarten, H. R. (1989). The impact of late life divorce: A conceptual and empirical study. *Journal of Divorce & Remarriage, 12,* 21–39.

Weiss, R. S. (1975). *Marital separation.* New York: Basic Books.

Weiss, R. L., & Heyman, R. E. (1990). Observation of marital interaction. In F. Fincham & T. Bradbury (Eds.), *The psychology of marriage* (pp. 87–117). New York: Guilford.

Wright, D. (1989). Revitalizing exchange models of divorce. *Journal of Divorce & Remarriage, 12,* 1–19.

Zaleski, Z., & Galkowska, M. (1978). Neuroticism and marital satisfaction. *Behaviour Research and Therapy, 16,* 285–286.

Zietlow, P. H., & Sillars, A. L. (1988). Life-stage differences in communication during marital conflicts. *Journal of Social and Personal Relationships, 5,* 223–245.

CHAPTER 12

Mental Illness and the Family

CATHERINE M. LEE and IAN H. GOTLIB

Over the past decade, we have witnessed a dramatic surge of interest in family factors involved in the etiology, maintenance, and treatment of emotional disorders. This increased attention to family issues in psychopathology is due to a number of different factors. First, the family has become a focus for the study of psychopathology as a result of researchers' interest in the possible burden that the patients' symptomatology places on the other family members (e.g., Coyne et al., 1987; Rabins, Fitting, Eastham, & Fetting, 1990). Not only have researchers been interested in the reactions of others to having a disturbed family member, but several investigators have examined diagnosable symptomatology in other family members (e.g., Gallagher, Rose, Rivera, Lovett, & Thompson, 1989). More recently, in addition to this focus on the adverse effects of patients on other family members, there has been an increased emphasis on positive adjustment and coping in family members (e.g., Bristol, 1987).

In a second major line of research, investigators have examined the possible role that family members might play both in the etiology of the patient's disturbance and in subsequent relapse of the disorder. For example, with respect to etiology, considerable research efforts have focused on the hypothesis that a patient's symptomatology is related to the disturbance or conflict inherent in a dysfunctional marriage (Gotlib & Hooley, 1988) or, in the case of a child, to receiving inadequate parenting (Lee & Gotlib, 1991b). Similarly, with respect to relapse, a number of investigations have demonstrated that the presence of hostile or critical attitudes in family members significantly increases the probability that a formerly depressed or schizophrenic patient will experience another episode within a relatively short period of time (e.g., Hooley & Teasdale, 1989; Vaughn & Leff, 1976).

Finally, although the role of family members as change agents who may support the therapeutic process has had a long history with respect to children's disorders (cf. Harris, 1984), it is now receiving greater recognition with respect to emotional disorders of adulthood. Indeed, there is a growing body of research documenting the efficacy of marital- or family-oriented interventions for the treatment of depression (e.g., Gotlib & Colby, 1987), agoraphobia (e.g., Barlow,

O'Brien, & Last, 1984), alcoholism (e.g., O'Farrell, 1986), and schizophrenia (e.g., Leff, Kuipers, Berkowitz, Eberlein-Fries, & Sturgeon, 1982).

It is clear, therefore, that greater attention is now being given to understanding the association between mental illness and family functioning. This chapter provides the reader with an overview of the findings of research on family functioning and mental disorder. In organizing our review, we have adopted a family life cycle perspective (cf. Carter & McGoldrick, 1988). In accord with this framework, we begin with an examination of the literature on mental disorder and marriage. In this section, we assess the literature examining the relations between emotional disturbance and marital discord. The next stage in the family cycle involves the addition of children to the marriage. Consequently, we then turn our attention to the literature that has examined families in which a child has been diagnosed with a mental disorder. The following section of our review focuses on research that has examined the functioning of families in which a parent is diagnosed as having a mental disorder. The final life cycle phase we address concerns families in which an elderly member is diagnosed with Alzheimer's disease. Given the space constraints of this chapter, we restrict our review to studies that focus on family members' adjustment and their role in treatment. Therefore, we exclude those studies that examine family members as informants in the process of assessment of symptomatology. Finally, we conclude by addressing common themes that emerge across the literature that we have examined, and by proposing avenues for future research.

MARRIAGE AND PSYCHOPATHOLOGY

The relation between marital distress and psychopathology has been the focus of considerable research in recent years, and a number of investigations implicate marital distress and dysfunction in both the etiology and course of emotional disorder (Gotlib & McCabe, 1990). A growing body of literature demonstrates both that treatment outcome is less favorable in couples who are experiencing marital distress, and that relapse is more likely for those patients who return to unsatisfying marriages (cf. Hooley, 1986). Furthermore, evidence from a variety of sources has long indicated that living with a psychiatrically disturbed person exerts a significant toll on the individual's spouse and family, financially, emotionally, and physically (e.g., Noh & Avison, 1988). Relatively few individuals who exhibit severe mental illness marry (Gove, Hughes, & Styles, 1983). Consequently, investigators examining the relation between marital functioning and psychopathology have focused, by necessity, on nonpsychotic disorders. In particular, the disorders of depression, agoraphobia, and alcoholism have received the greatest empirical attention.

Depression

The association between depression and marital quality has generated perhaps the greatest interest of any disorder, both because of the consistent epidemiological finding of a high rate of depression among married women (e.g., Weissman & Boyd, 1983), and because of interpersonal conceptualizations of depression that implicate the role of marital discord in the etiology and maintenance of this disorder (e.g., Coyne, 1976). Considerable and varied evidence attests to the relation between marital distress and depression. For example, Paykel et al. (1969) found that the most frequent life event preceding the onset of depression was an increase in arguments with the spouse. Similarly, Vaughn and Leff (1976) found that depressed individuals are more vulnerable than are those with schizophrenia to hostile statements made by family members. Furthermore, Schless, Schwartz, Goetz, and Mendels (1974) demonstrated that this vulnerability to marriage-related stresses persists after depressed patients recover. Consistent with these results, Merikangas (1984) found the divorce rate in depressed patients two years postdischarge to be nine times that of the general population. Finally, a number of investigators have reported that lack of an intimate relationship with a spouse or boyfriend increased women's vulnerability for depression (e.g., Brown & Harris, 1978; Costello, 1982).

A large body of empirical literature indicates that marriages of depressed persons are dysfunctional. The results of studies examining the marital interactions of depressed persons consistently demonstrate that these interactions are associated with negative verbal and nonverbal behaviors (e.g., Ruscher & Gotlib, 1988), and are characterized by intentionally negative communication (e.g., Kowalik & Gotlib, 1987) and aggressive interactions (e.g., Biglan et al., 1985). Moreover, *spouses* of depressed persons have been found to report negative mood and to exhibit behaviors that reflect rejection of their spouse. For example, following interactions with their depressed partners, spouses have been found to report feeling depressed, hostile, and critical (e.g., Gotlib & Whiffen, 1989). They have also been found to argue frequently with their depressed spouse (Hautzinger, Linden, & Hoffman, 1982), to be negative in their communications with their spouse (Kowalik & Gotlib), and to be explicitly critical of their spouse (e.g., Hooley, 1986; see Gotlib & Hooley, 1988, for a more detailed review of this literature). Interestingly, there is evidence to suggest that problematic marital interactions and low marital satisfaction may not be specific to depression; rather, they may be characteristic of couples in which one spouse is experiencing any form of disorder (cf. Feldman & Gotlib, in press); for example, marital dysfunction is also frequently associated with agoraphobia and alcoholism.

Agoraphobia

Because agoraphobia is most prevalent in married women (cf. Hafner, 1986), it is not surprising to find that most of the theory and research in this area has focused on women and their marital relations. The importance of the marital relationship in the etiology, maintenance, and recovery from agoraphobic conditions has been highlighted by a number of theorists and researchers. Goldstein (1970) and Chambless and Goldstein (1981), for example, posited that most agoraphobic women are in unsatisfying relationships from which they wish to flee, but they do not leave because they fear independence. Similarly, Fodor (1974) suggested that agoraphobic women have been reinforced for extreme stereotypic female behavior and, consequently, become especially helpless, fearful, and dependent. Consistent with these postulations, Hand, Lamontagne, and Marks (1974) estimated that as many as 67% of agoraphobic women experience significant marital distress. It is important to note, however, that these formulations and statistics are derived largely from case studies and uncontrolled investigations (e.g., Goldstein & Swift, 1977).

The results of better controlled empirical examinations of marital distress and agoraphobia are less consistent in implicating marital dissatisfaction in this disorder. Assessments of marital adjustment and intimacy in female agoraphobic patients and their spouses reveal that agoraphobic couples report levels of marital satisfaction equivalent to those reported by nonpsychiatric, nondistressed couples (e.g., Arrindell & Emmelkamp, 1986).

In evaluating this body of literature, it is important to realize that agoraphobic patients who also exhibited marked depressive mood were excluded from these studies. Given the high prevalence of depressive disorders among agoraphobic patients (e.g., Chambless & Goldstein, 1981), it is likely that the participants in these studies represent a select subsample of women with minimal levels of depression. Moreover, given the association described earlier between depression and marital distress, this exclusion criterion probably also eliminated maritally distressed agoraphobic women from the studies. Thus, the results of these studies should be interpreted with some caution. Finally, although a change in diagnostic criteria in DSM-III-R now permits a diagnosis of agoraphobia in the presence of a co-existing depressive disorder, to date there have been no studies of the marriages of agoraphobic patients using these criteria. It is clear, however, that future studies in this area have the potential to elucidate the nature of the associations among depression, anxiety, and marital dysfunction.

Alcoholism

Compared with depression and agoraphobia, the alcoholism literature is in a relatively early stage with respect to the study of marital interactions and adjustment. Despite its extensive effects on the family, alcoholism has been viewed traditionally as an individual problem. Early research that broadened the perspective in this field to a marital or family focus relied on retrospective reports of alcoholics concerning their marital or family functioning (e.g., Davis, 1976). Because the results of these investigations were often equivocal, researchers have more recently examined directly marital or family interactions of alcoholics. In three such studies, Steinglass, Davis, and Berenson (1977), Jacob, Dunn, and Leonard (1983), and Frankenstein, Hay, and Nathan (1985) found that marital functioning often improved under conditions of intoxication, and concluded that alcohol use may provide a temporary solution to a dysfunctional marital system (but, see also Jacob & Krahn, 1988).

The long-term outcome for marital satisfaction in relation to alcohol consumption must be examined to determine how these factors affect the marriages over time. In this regard, Moos, Finney, and Gamble (1982) compared remitted alcoholics and relapsed alcoholics to a group of matched community control subjects on a variety of sociodemographic, coping, social, health-related, and family and work environment measures. Moos et al. found few differences between spouses of recovered alcoholics and community control spouses. In contrast, compared to control spouses, spouses of relapsed or nonrecovered alcoholics functioned more poorly. It appears from this study, therefore, that marital adjustment improves over time for alcoholics who recover from the disorder and for their spouses.

Finally, we should note that there is also growing evidence that marital therapy or spouse involvement represents a promising direction in the treatment of mental illness. Although individual therapy has been found to be effective in reducing the level of symptomatology in a number of disorders, it is less effective in ameliorating difficulties in marital functioning. In both depression and anxiety, marital therapy has been demonstrated to achieve both symptom relief and a reduction in marital discord (cf. Beach, Sandeen, & O'Leary 1990; Dewey & Hunsley, 1990). As Jacobson, Holtzworth-Munroe, and Schmaling (1989) note, however, the literature in this area is still in its early stages and firm conclusions await further research.

CHILD PSYCHOPATHOLOGY

We have seen in the preceding section that there are strong associations between quality of marital functioning and mental illness. The next stage in the family life cycle involves the addition of children to the marital dyad to form a family. In the following section we discuss the role of family factors in the childhood disorders of autism, hyperactivity, and conduct disorder.

Autism

Autism is the most severe behavior disorder of childhood. Despite its relative rarity, it has received considerable research attention because of the associated profound disruption in the child's development. Historically, the autistic child's family has been studied to examine the parents' role in etiology of the disorder. The clinical observation that parents, particularly mothers, of autistic children were cold and aloof fueled speculation that lack of maternal warmth disrupted the attachment process and led to the child's primary dysfunction in relating to others. Although some efforts to identify the personality flaws of parents of autistic children continue (e.g., Narayan, Moyes, & Wolff, 1990), evidence for an organic foundation for autism is now widely accepted and the search for parental factors in the etiology of the disorder no longer dominates research in this area (Morgan, 1988).

Currently, however, there is continued concern about the family members of autistic children (e.g., Harris, 1984). Various authors have offered developmental systemic formulations to help understand the challenges faced by members of families with an autistic child (e.g., Konstantareas, 1991). It seems intuitively obvious that the presence of an autistic child poses a severe challenge for other family members. Interestingly, and contrary to expectations, the data with respect to marital adjustment indicate that parents of autistic children show levels of marital adjustment that are comparable to those demonstrated by happily married couples (e.g., Koegel, Schreibman, O'Neill, & Burke, 1983). Moreover, empirical studies examining parental stress have yielded results that seem to differ as a function of the age of the child, whereas parents of younger autistic children report levels of stress similar to those reported by control parents (Koegel et al.), parents of autistic adolescents report significantly higher stress levels (Bebko, Konstantareas, & Springer, 1987). Interpreting recent research, Morgan (1988) concluded that there is no evidence of elevated rates of psychological disturbance among parents of autistic children, although the cumulative effects of stressors associated with rearing an autistic child could render a parent vulnerable to burnout and depression.

Little empirical research has examined the functioning of the siblings of autistic children. Results of the few existing studies suggest that siblings may experience various stresses in terms of embarrassment, increased chores, and less parental availability. However, living with an impaired sibling is not necessarily a harmful experience; indeed, it may even be associated with such positive effects in the sibling as greater maturity, supportiveness, and tolerance (Howlin, 1988). In general, factors associated with positive adjustment in family members seem to be related more strongly to resources within the family, than to attributes of the autistic child's dysfunction. Thus, perceptions of the adequacy of social support, family cohesiveness and expressiveness all seem to be more promising predictors of favorable family functioning than is severity of the child's disorder (Morgan, 1988).

Hyperactivity

Like autism, hyperactivity also has its onset in infancy. In contrast to autism, however, hyperactivity affects a large number of children and accounts for a significant proportion of referrals for treatment. The family environments of hyperactive children have received considerable research attention. In a seminal study, Mash and Johnston (1983a) found that parents of hyperactive boys demonstrated lower parenting self-esteem than did parents of nondisordered children. Self-esteem related to parental knowledge and skill was also related to the child's age, with parents of younger hyperactive boys reporting the poorest self-esteem. Mothers of hyperactive boys reported higher levels of stress than did mothers of nondisordered boys, and this pattern was more pronounced in mothers of younger hyperactive boys. This pattern of results may be explained by findings from direct observation that the behavioral interactions of hyperactive boys tend to improve with age (Barkley, Karlsson, & Pollard, 1985).

Researchers have consistently found that parents of hyperactive children report higher depression scores than do parents of nondisordered children (e.g., Befera & Barkley, 1985; Brown & Pacini, 1989). Furthermore, Cunningham, Benness, and Siegel (1988) reported that parental depression scores were linked to parents' ratings of family functioning, with higher depression being associated with poorer general family functioning; for mothers, depression scores were also linked to ratings of child behavior. Interestingly, Johnston and Pelham (1990) found few associations between maternal characteristics and *observed* mother–child behavior in a sample of mothers and their 4- to 12-year-old children with externalizing problems.

It should be noted that, despite the frequently cited finding of higher depression scores in parents of hyperactive children, "depression" in virtually all the studies in this area is assessed by self-report measures. In fact, in no study reported here were diagnostic interviews conducted. If we consider established cut-off scores for mild depression of 10 on the Beck Depression Inventory (BDI) and 16 on the Center for Epidemiological Studies Depression scale (CESD), it is clear that parents' scores in all these investigations, with the exception of mothers in the Befera and Barkley (1985) study (mean BDI = 10.2), were in the nondepressed range. Thus, although parents of hyperactive children clearly report greater distress than do parents of nondisordered children, it is imperative that this distress be distinguished from the clinical syndrome of depression (cf. Gotlib & Cane, 1989).

In addition to the individual functioning of parents of hyperactive children, researchers have also examined interpersonal factors such as marital adjustment, mother–child interactions, sibling interactions, and family functioning. Investigators have consistently reported poor marital adjustment in parents of hyperactive children (e.g., Befera & Barkley, 1985); moreover, a greater proportion of parents of hyperactive boys than of control children are separated or divorced (Brown & Pacini, 1989). Observational studies confirm that, compared to nondisordered families, hyperactive boys are less compliant toward their mothers, and their mothers are less positive toward their hyperactive children (e.g., Tarver-Behring, Barkley, & Karlsson, 1985). Furthermore, compared with sibling interactions of nondisordered children, sibling interactions of hyperactive youngsters have been found to be characterized by highly negative behaviors (Mash & Johnston, 1983b). Consistent with these findings, family members with a hyperactive child rate their family environment as less supportive and more stressful than do family members without a hyperactive child (Campbell, Breaux, Ewing, & Szumowski, 1986).

It is clear, therefore, that childhood hyperactivity acts as a stressor for the other family members. It is also possible, of course, that an aversive family environment might contribute to the severity of a child's hyperactive behavior. The results of a double-blind study of the effects of methylphenidate on hyperactivity are instructive in this regard. Schachar, Taylor, Wieselberg, Thorley, and Rutter (1987) found that, for children who responded positively to the medication, there was a concomitant improvement in family functioning. In contrast, family functioning remained unchanged in families of nonresponders. Considered collectively, these findings suggest that the roots of disturbed family patterns seen in families with a hyperactive child lie in disturbed child behavior, rather than the reverse (Fischer, 1990). Nevertheless, various family factors, including parental cognitions, may mediate the negative effects of having a hyperactive child (cf. Mash & Johnston, 1990).

It is informative to note that the psychological literature on hyperactivity has recently been dominated by a debate over the diagnostic significance of aggression in this disorder (e.g., Schachar & Wachsmuth, 1990). A central hypothesis focuses on the differential family role in the development of childhood disorders with and without aggression. We now turn to this issue.

Conduct Disorder

There is considerable controversy over the relative influences of genetic factors, parenting behaviors, socioeconomic status, and child behavior on family functioning in families with a child diagnosed with a conduct disorder (Lytton, 1990a, 1990b; Wahler, 1990). Many authors recognize the futility of such a debate and argue for the adoption of a transactional perspective that examines the interactions between genetic and environmental factors (e.g., Dodge, 1990). Perhaps one of the best developed theories to account for the development of conduct disorder is that proposed by Patterson (1982, 1986). In this model, parents and children develop a series of coercive exchanges in which each inadvertently reinforces the other for negative behaviors. The role of parental psychopathology has also been incorporated into the model in that maternal depressive behavior may serve to suppress negative behavior in children (Dumas & Gibson, 1990).

Through an examination of treatment failures, researchers have come to recognize the importance of contextual factors in conduct disorder. Webster-Stratton and her colleagues (e.g., Webster-Stratton, 1988; Webster-Stratton & Hammond, 1990), for example, conducted a program of studies in which they examined the roles of parental depression, marital adjustment, single-parent status, and parental stress in the treatment of 3- to 8-year-old conduct-disordered children. In these studies, pretreatment maternal depression was found to be a significant predictor of maternal ratings of child behavior following treatment. In contrast, fathers' perceptions of the child and their behaviors toward the child were unaffected by their own personal adjustment. Consistent with these findings, Johnston (1991) reported that depressed mood contributed unique variance to mothers' ratings of their children's behavior; in contrast, fathers' rating were unaffected by their adjustment; marital adjustment did not contribute to the variance of either parent's rating of child behavior. It seems, therefore, that there are parental gender differences in the relation between parental adjustment and ratings of child disturbance.

Taken together, the findings from studies of families with autistic, hyperactive, and conduct disordered children suggest that child psychopathology poses a challenge for all family members. The disruption in the child's normal development may interfere with the well-being of all family members, which in turn may lead family members to respond to the disordered child in a suboptimal manner. It is clear, however, that child psychopathology is not inevitably associated with poor outcome for all family members. Even where research clearly demonstrates group differences between families with a disordered child and families with a nondisordered child, the average scores for parental adjustment remain in the nonclinical range. Moreover, there is also considerable variability among the families of disordered children. Interestingly, in some disorders, such as hyperactivity, there seems to be an improved adaptation to the child over time. In contrast, families with an autistic child seem more likely to suffer from an accumulation of stressors and to fare more poorly over time.

Finally, there is also likely to be considerable variability over time *within* families, because children differ from one another at different periods of development with respect to their behavioral, affective, and cognitive functioning (cf. Digdon & Gotlib, 1985; Kendall, Lerner, & Craighead, 1984). In the case of children suffering from some form of psychopathology, the course of their disorder is superimposed on their developmental trajectory. Thus, in addition to normal developmental factors, we must take into account the stage of the disorder and the way in which symptoms set the child apart from his or her peers. It is likely, therefore, that family functioning varies according to both the stage of child development and the stage of the disorder. In this context, it is important that researchers and clinicians alike consider how the child's symptomatology may affect the various developmental tasks the child faces in cognitive, affective, social, and physiological domains at different ages.

PARENTAL PSYCHOPATHOLOGY

In this section, we remain in the child-rearing stage of the life cycle, but now examine the effects of parental psychopathology on children. The initial impetus for studies of parental psychopathology and child adjustment was a desire to understand the etiology of schizophrenia (e.g., Neale & Weintraub, 1975). The field has since expanded considerably, however, and researchers have now begun to examine the impact on children of other forms of parental psychopathologies, such as depression (e.g., Beardslee, Bemporad, Keller, & Klerman, 1983) and alcoholism (e.g., West & Prinz, 1987).

We begin this section with a review of current evidence for a link between alcoholism and psychopathology. Next, we outline large-scale, high-risk studies of the offspring of schizophrenic parents. Finally, because depression has been identified as a disorder associated with particular risk to the child, we discuss studies examining the relationship between parental affective disorder and child adjustment.

Families with an Alcoholic Parent

Whether proposing that alcoholism is the source or the manifestation of disturbed family relations, extant models share the assumption that children raised in an alcoholic environment are at risk for developing subsequent difficulties. There is concern that children in alcoholic families may be neglected, that they may witness or be victims of violence, that they may have poor role models and consequent disturbances in gender identity, and that they may learn passive and avoidant coping strategies, predisposing them to future alcohol abuse (Sloboda, 1974).

Recent attempts have been made to separate clinical folklore in this area from empirically established findings. In this context, there has been a growing appreciation of the heterogeneity of the alcoholic population, of the significance of considering the various phases of the disorder, and perhaps most importantly, of the necessity of considering the interpersonal context in which the alcoholic parent functions. In a comprehensive review, West and Prinz (1987) concluded that, compared to children of nondisordered parents, children of alcoholics were at elevated risk for conduct problems, alcohol abuse, cognitive difficulties, health problems, and affective symptomatology. Indeed, two recent investigations reported that children of alcoholic parents demonstrated drug and alcohol problems themselves, elevated levels of behavioral undercontrol, neuroticism, and diagnosable psychiatric disorder (Chassin, Rogosch, & Barrera, 1991; Sher, Walitzer, Wood, & Brent, 1991). Despite these risks, however, it is important to remain cognizant of the fact that not all children of alcoholics experience difficulties. Parental alcoholism, therefore, should not be considered to be inevitably associated with poor child adjustment.

Just as the early marital studies focused on *individuals* in marriages, the early studies of children of alcoholics similarly adopted a linear perspective, seeking to identify characteristics of children with an alcoholic parent. In contrast, a number of recent studies have examined family interactions of alcoholics. Jacob and his colleagues (e.g., Jacob, Ritchey, Cvitkovic, & Blane, 1981) videotaped family interactions of alcoholic and nonalcoholic parents. Alcoholic fathers were observed to be less instrumental and directive than were nonalcoholic fathers; not surprisingly, the mothers in alcoholic families assumed more responsibility than did their counterparts with nonalcoholic husbands. Corroborating these findings, Steinglass (1979, 1981) reported that, whereas members in families in which the alcoholic parent was currently drinking tended to function independently of each other, members in families with a currently abstinent parent were highly coordinated. These studies underscore the importance of distinguishing between different phases of alcoholism when examining families with alcoholic members, and they also highlight the association between drinking and lack of family involvement.

In sum, the precise nature of the risks for social, emotional, or psychiatric problems in children in alcoholic families has not been clearly established. Although there may be distinct alcohol-related phases in the development and functioning of families with an alcoholic parent, there also seem to be considerable areas of overlap between the problematic alcoholic family and other types of disturbed families.

Families with a Schizophrenic Parent

A number of large-scale projects were designed to examine the adjustment of children of schizophrenic mothers. In the Stony Brook High Risk Project, school-aged children of schizophrenic mothers were compared on a number of indices with children of nonpsychiatric mothers. To assess the specificity of any deficits observed in the offspring of the schizophrenic mothers, this project also included a group of children of unipolar and bipolar depressed mothers. Findings suggest that children of schizophrenic parents are at risk for maladjustment, but contrary to expectations, children of depressed parents are at equal or even greater risk (Weintraub, Liebert, & Neale, 1978; Weintraub, Prinz, & Neale, 1975).

Emery and his colleagues (Emery, Weintraub, & Neale, 1982) examined the relations among teacher ratings and peer ratings of the project children and the marital discord of their parents. Reminiscent of the pattern of results of their previous reports, both schizophrenic and depressed individuals scored similarly on the measure of marital adjustment, and lower than the controls. Moreover, the relationship between marital discord and children's school behavior was more pronounced in the depressed group than in the schizophrenic or the normal groups. This finding underscores the importance of examining the marriages and family relationships of parents with emotional disorders, such as depression. Once again, the interrelatedness of parental adjustment and marital discord is evident. It is clear that there is considerable overlap between these two factors, and that they have a joint impact on child adjustment.

In the Massachussetts Mental Health Center Project, Cohler and his associates (e.g., Cohler, Gallant, & Grunebaum, 1977; Cohler, Gallant, Grunebaum, & Kaufman, 1983) examined the young children of schizophrenic, psychotically depressed, and normal mothers over a period of about ten years. Cohler et al. (1977) reported that both the schizophrenic and depressed mothers were less likely to develop an interactive relationship with their child and had greater difficulty separating their own needs from the needs of their children. In a subsequent report, Cohler et al. (1983) found that depressed mothers were rated as less socially adjusted overall than were either the schizophrenic or the well mothers. Furthermore, compared with the other mothers, the depressed mothers reported that their children were less cooperative at home, were more symptomatic, and were less involved with the family.

The high-risk schizophrenia studies identified adjustment problems not only in children of schizophrenic parents, but in offspring of depressed parents as well. From these studies, it seems that lack of parental availability is a critical mechanism contributing to the increased risk to the child (cf. Lee & Gotlib, 1991a). Because these projects reported considerable risk for the children of depressed parents, investigations have now been conducted in order to examine more explicitly the adjustment and functioning of children of depressed parents.

Families with a Depressed Parent

Studies demonstrate that with young infants, the interactions of mothers reporting elevated levels of depressive symptomatology are characterized by withdrawal and a lack of engagement with and responsiveness to their infants (Bettes, 1988). Moreover, infants of symptomatically depressed mothers themselves tend to be rated as more passive than are infants of nonsymptomatic mothers (Whiffen & Gotlib, 1989).

Studies conducted with the preschool children of depressed mothers similarly indicate that these children are characterized by deficits in their social and cognitive functioning (Radke-Yarrow, Cummings, Kuczynski, & Chapman, 1985). Moreover, in several investigations depressed and nondepressed mothers have been found to differ with respect to their parenting behaviors (e.g., Kochanska, Kuczynski, Radke-Yarrow, & Welsh, 1987).

A number of investigators have examined the effects of maternal depression on school-age children. Using both parental reports (e.g., Weissman et al., 1984) and direct assessment (e.g., Beardslee, Schultz, & Selman, 1987; Hammen et al., 1987), investigators have found that school-age children of depressed parents function more poorly than do children of nondepressed parents in terms of psychological symptoms, diagnosable disorders and requiring treatment. Hops, Biglan, and their colleagues (Hops et al. 1987) conducted home observations of clinically depressed mothers and their families. Compared to normal mothers, depressed mothers emitted higher rates of dysphoric affect and lower rates of happy affect than did nondepressed mothers. Interestingly, conditional probability analyses revealed that maternal dysphoric behavior was effective in suppressing aggressive behavior in both spouses and children.

Finally, in an investigation in our laboratory (Lee & Gotlib, 1989a, 1989b, 1991b), we examined adjustment in four groups of children: children of depressed psychiatric patient mothers, children of nondepressed psychiatric patient mothers, children of nondepressed medical patient mothers, and children of community mothers. Our results indicated that compared to children of community mothers and children of nondepressed medical patient mothers, the children of depressed psychiatric patient mothers evidenced a high number of internalizing and externalizing problems. Interestingly, these children did not differ from children of nondepressed psychiatric patient mothers. Moreover, children's problems persisted even when their mothers were symptomatically recovered.

Considered collectively, these investigations suggest that both the family relationships and the adjustment of the children of depressed patients are less favorable than are those of nonpsychiatric individuals. Depressed parents' accounts of their own parenting behavior suggest that they lack many of the resources to enable them to be warm and consistent parents, and they are more tense and less effective with their children. Indeed, these self-reports have been corroborated by the results of a small number of observational studies of the children of depressed parents. Interestingly, within the broader category of depression, despite the greater genetic loading involved in bipolar than in unipolar depression, some studies suggest that children of unipolar depressed parent depressives exhibit more psychologic disturbance than do children of bipolar depressed parents depressives (cf. Cytryn, McKnew, Bartko, Lamour, & Hamovitt, 1982).

In summary, the studies reviewed on the offspring of alcoholic, schizophrenic, and depressed parents suggest that these children are at risk for developing a variety of emotional problems. It is important to note that in both children of alcoholic and of depressed parents, marital discord is frequently cited as a mediator of child difficulties, and the affective tone of parent–child interactions is often negatively charged. Moreover, in all the forms of psychopathology discussed here, the emotional availability of the parent for the child seems to be critical in determining the level of adjustment demonstrated by the child.

FAMILIES AND ALZHEIMER'S DISEASE

The increase in the proportion of elderly people in the population, together with health-care policies that advocate home care, have contributed to the growing awareness of the problems faced by families who are providing care for an elderly member suffering from Alzheimer's disease. It is widely recognized that caregivers, who include both spouses and adult children, face numerous stresses in dealing with a family member suffering from this degenerative disorder (Famighetti, 1986). This awareness has led to the extensive development of psychoeducational and support groups (Gonyea, 1989).

An important issue faced by caregivers is the decision of whether to care for the patient in the community or to seek institutionalization. Caregiver characteristics and well-being may weigh more heavily in such decisions than do patient characteristics (Colerick & George, 1986). Contrary to predictions, Pratt, Wright, and Schmall (1987) found that ratings of caregiver burden were comparable in families who were caregivers to community-dwelling Alzheimer's patients and in family caregivers to Alzheimer's institutionalized patients. Thus, freedom from responsibility for daily routines did not seem to alleviate the stress felt by family members.

In a recent well-controlled study, Gallagher et al. (1989) found that 46% of family members seeking help in dealing with the burden of caring for a relative with Alzheimer's disease met Research Diagnostic Criteria (RDC) for depression, whereas among nonhelp-seeking caregivers, the proportion meeting diagnostic criteria was only 18%. These findings underscore the importance of examining sources of variability within the population of caregivers. In a recent examination of predictors of well-being among caregivers of Alzheimer's patients, George and Gwyther (1986) found that mental health problems and caregiver well-being were more closely associated with characteristics of the caregiving situation than they were with severity of impairment of the Alzheimer's patient. In a comparison of caregivers of persons with Alzheimer's disease and caregivers of persons with cancer, Rabins et al. (1990) found comparable levels of emotional distress in the two groups, with 39% of caregivers scoring in the "case" range on a screening measure. In this sample, positive adjustment was predicted by the extent of the caregiver's social contacts, the degree of family cohesiveness and a feeling of support from one's religious faith. Emotional distress was predicted by few social contacts, low cohesiveness, and absence of religious faith. Similarly, Killeen (1990) found that caregivers of Alzheimer's patients reporting higher levels of stress tended to use emotion-focused, as opposed to problem-focused, coping strategies.

Recently there have been attempts to extend our understanding beyond a focus on the caregiver, to include members of the extended family such as sons- and daughters-in-law and grandchildren. Interestingly, Creasey, Myers, Epperson, and Taylor (1990) found that only caregiving adult daughters reported disruptions in their marital relationships; adult sons did not report disruptions that extended beyond their relationship with their disordered parent. Furthermore, neither sons nor daughters reported any disruption in their relationships with their own children.

In sum, the studies reviewed here identified various stressors in family members dealing with a parent or spouse diagnosed as having Alzheimer's disease. Interestingly, the level of distress is not predicted either by the severity of the patient's symptomatology or by the extent of his or her responsibilities for daily routines, but seems to be more closely related to characteristics of the caregiving situation.

CONCLUSIONS

In our brief review of the literature on mental illness at various phases of the life cycle, we have seen that there is a strong association between quality of marital functioning and mental illness. It is also clear from our review that child psychopathology poses a challenge for all family members. The disruption in the child's normal development may interfere with the well-being of all family members, which in turn may lead family members to respond to the disordered child in a negative manner. Studies reviewed on the offspring of alcoholic, schizophrenic, and depressed parents suggest that these children are at risk for developing a variety of emotional problems. Mediators of child difficulties include marital discord, the affective tone of parent–child interactions, and the emotional availability of the parent. Family members caring for a parent or spouse with Alzheimer's disease face numerous stressors and a significant proportion demonstrate evidence of emotional distress. Thus, across all phases of the family life cycle, the presence of a family member with some form of mental disorder clearly poses a challenge for other family members.

Across the different disorders reviewed here there are common consequences for family members in terms of stress and distress. Although the bulk of the research to date has focused on marital and parental relationships, it seems that whether the identified patient is a child, sibling, spouse or parent, mental disorder in a family member has important consequences for other family members. Family members may experience stress as daily routines are rendered more difficult, they may feel isolated from others, frustrated at their additional burdens and may feel saddened at the loss of normal interactions.

The impact of the identified patient's symptoms may be understood in terms of the way they disrupt the normal developmental trajectory and disturb normal family relationships. For example, in a marital relationship, the presence of a disordered spouse may result in a lack of intimacy and warmth; parents of autistic children may find that the attachment process is made more difficult by a child who does not respond to social cues; parents of hyperactive children may find that, at a time when other parents' children are developing responsibility, their children continue to require intense supervision; parents suffering from psychopathology may be less available for the tasks of parenting (see Lee & Gotlib, 1991a); and finally, the care of a parent or spouse suffering from Alzheimer's disease may require constant vigilance and the assumption of decision-making responsibilities.

The course of the patient's disorder is also superimposed on the developmental path of the family, which must be considered in attempts to understand family functioning. There are identifiable phases in the course of the disorder—emerging symptoms, assessment and diagnosis, implementation of treatment programs, and finally, improvement, stabilization or deterioration—and it is reasonable to expect that family members may be affected differentially at various stages. It seems that, in disorders where there is gradual improvement over time (e.g., hyperactivity), family stress may also diminish somewhat over time, whereas in disorders in which improvement is less marked (e.g., autism), families may suffer the effects of cumulative stress and frustration.

It is evident, too, that mental disorder in a family member may change patterns of interaction within the family. As the family member experiences depressed feelings, his or her appraisals of the disordered person also may be affected. The way other family members react to symptoms may have a profound influence on the patient's subsequent adjustment. For example, positive marital functioning may be associated with recovery among depressed or anxious patients, and parents with low levels of depression may be more likely to implement behavioral programs to help their disordered children.

Having acknowledged that psychopathology poses a challenge for all family members, it is critical to note that mental disorder is not inevitably associated with poor outcome for all family members. Indeed, the experience of having a disturbed family member has also been associated with family resourcefulness and caring. Interestingly, adjustment of family members seems to be related not so much to the intensity of the identified patient's symptomatology or to the objective burden, but to family characteristics such as closeness, expressiveness, and warmth. Thus, in the future it will be important to develop models that account for functioning in terms of what happens in the family, not simply in terms of the impact of symptoms. Relatively little research attention has been directed toward identifying the ways in which family members cope effectively with mental disorder, and this is clearly an area that merits future investigation. Because the bulk of research is cross-sectional in nature, it is impossible to make causal inferences. Thus, the coping process is unclear.

Related to this, it is important to recognize that, although there are commonalities in the experience of family members faced by mental disorder in the family, the population of persons with a disordered family member is not homogeneous. Even within disorders, there is considerable variability in how family members react. This point has been well demonstrated when differences have been found between family groups recruited in different ways (e.g., those families using services and those who do not). To date, research has tended to focus on negative factors such as burden and distress. By identifying resilient families, researchers may develop a better appreciation of such positive factors as coping and adjustment.

It is clear from this discussion and from the research reviewed in this chapter that many questions remain. We believe that the greatest need in this field is for longitudinal, prospective studies of the family, psychopathology, and coping. Although such investigations will undoubtedly be difficult to design and execute, the rewards, in terms of furthering our understanding of the relationship between family adjustment and emotional disorder, will be considerable.

REFERENCES

Arrindell, W. A., & Emmelkamp, P. M. G. (1986). Marital adjustment, intimacy, and needs in female agoraphobics and their partners: A controlled study. *British Journal of Psychiatry, 149,* 592–602.

Barkley, R. A., Karlsson, J., & Pollard, S. (1985). Effects of age on the mother–child interactions of ADD-H and normal boys. *Journal of Abnormal Child Psychology, 13,* 631–637.

Barlow, D. H., O'Brien, G. T., & Last, C. G. (1984). Couples treatment of agoraphobia. *Behavior Therapy, 15,* 41–58.

Beach, S. R. H., Sandeen, E. E., & O'Leary, K. D. (1990). *Depression in marriage.* New York: Guilford

Beardslee, W. R., Bemporad, J., Keller, M. B., & Klerman, G. L. (1983). Children of parents with major affective disorder: A review. *American Journal of Psychiatry, 140,* 825–832.

Beardslee, W. R., Schultz, L. H., & Selman, R. L. (1987). Level of social–cognitive development, adaptive functioning, and DSM-III diagnoses in adolescent offspring of parents with affective disorders: Implications for the development of the capacity for mutuality. *Developmental Psychology, 23,* 807–815.

Bebko, J. M., Konstantareas, M. M., & Springer, J. (1987). Parent and professional evaluations of family stress associated with characteristics of autism. *Journal of Autism and Developmental Disorders, 17,* 565–576.

Befera, M. S., & Barkley, R. A. (1985). Hyperactive and normal girls and boys: Mother–child interaction, parent psychiatric status, and child psychopathology. *Journal of Child Psychology and Psychiatry, 16,* 439–452.

Bettes, B. A. (1988). Maternal depression and motherese: Temporal and intonational features. *Child Development, 59,* 1089–1096.

Biglan, A., Hops, H., Sherman, L., Friedman, L. S., Arthur, J., & Osteen, V. (1985). Problem-solving interactions of depressed women and their husbands. *Behavior Therapy, 16,* 431–451.

Bristol, M. M. (1987). Mothers of children with autism or communication disorders: Successful adaptation of the Double ABCX Model. *Journal of Autism and Developmental Disorders, 17,* 469–486.

Brown, G. W., & Harris, T. (1978). *Social origins of depression.* New York: Free Press.

Brown, R. T., & Pacini, J. N. (1989). Perceived family functioning, marital status, and depression in parents of boys with Attention Deficit Disorder. *Journal of Learning Disabilities, 22,* 581–587.

Campbell, S. B., Breaux, A. M., Ewing, L. J., & Szumowski, E. K. (1986). Correlates and predictors of hyperactivity and aggression: A longitudinal study of parent-referred problem preschoolers. *Journal of Abnormal Child Psychology, 14,* 217–234.

Carter, B., & McGoldrick, M. (1988). Overview: The changing family life cycle—A framework for family therapy. In B. Carter & M. McGoldrick (Eds.), *The changing family life cycle—A framework for family therapy* (2nd. ed., pp. 3–28). New York: Gardner.

Chambless, D. L., & Goldstein, A. J. (1981). Clinical treatment of agoraphobia. In M. Mavissakalian & D. H. Barlow (Eds.), *Phobia: Psychological and pharmacological treatment* (pp. 103–144). New York: Guilford.

Chassin, L., Rogosch, F., & Barrera, M. (1991). Substance use and symptomatology among adolescent children of alcoholics. *Journal of Abnormal Psychology, 100,* 449–463.

Cohler, B. J., Gallant, D. H., & Grunebaum, H. U. (1977). Disturbance of attention among schizophrenic, depressed, and well mothers and their five-year-old children. *Journal of Child Psychology and Psychiatry, 18,* 115–136.

Cohler, B. J., Gallant, D. H., Grunebaum, H. U., & Kaufman, C. (1983). Social adjustment among schizophrenic, depressed, and well mothers and their school-aged children. In H. L. Morrison (Ed.), *Children of depressed parents: Risk, identification, and intervention* (pp. 65–97). New York: Grune & Stratton.

Colerick E. J., & George, L. K. (1986). Predictors of institutionalization among caregivers of patients with Alzheimer's disease. *American Geriatrics Society Journal, 34,* 493–498.

Costello, C. G. (1982). Social factors associated with depression: A retrospective community study. *Psychological Medicine, 12,* 329–339.

Coyne, J. C. (1976). Toward an interactional description of depression. *Psychiatry, 39,* 28–40.

Coyne, J. C., Kessler, R. C., Tal, M., Turnbull, J., Wortman, C. B., & Greden, J. F. (1987). Living with a depressed person. *Journal of Consulting and Clinical Psychology, 55,* 347–352.

Creasey, G. L., Myers, B. J., Epperson, M. J., & Taylor, J. (1990). Couples with an elderly parent with Alzheimer's disease: Perceptions of familial relationships. *Psychiatry, 53,* 44–51.

Cunningham, C. E., Benness, B. B., & Siegel, L. S. (1988). Family functioning, time allocation, and parental depression in the families of normal and ADDH children. *Journal of Clinical Child Psychology, 17,* 169–177.

Cytryn, L., McKnew, D. H., Bartko, J. J., Lamour, M., & Hamovitt, J. (1982). Offspring of patients with affective disorders: II. *Journal of the American Academy of Child Psychiatry, 21,* 389–391.

Davis, D. I. (1976). Changing perception of self and spouse from sober to intoxicated state: Implications for research in family factors that maintain alcohol abuse. *New York Academy of Science. Annals., 273,* 497–506.

Dewey, D., & Hunsley, J. (1990). The effects of marital adjustment and spouse involvement on the behavioral treatment of agoraphobia: A meta-analytic review. *Anxiety Research, 2,* 69–83.

Digdon, N., & Gotlib, I. H. (1985). Developmental considerations in the study of childhood depression. *Developmental Review, 5,* 162–199.

Dodge, K. A. (1990). Nature versus nurture in childhood conduct disorder: Is it time to ask a different question? *Developmental Psychology, 26,* 698–701.

Dumas, J. E., & Gibson, J. A. (1990). Behavioral correlates of maternal depressive symptomatology in conduct disordered children: II. Systemic effects involving fathers and children. *Journal of Consulting and Clinical Psychology, 58,* 877–881.

Emery, R., Weintraub, S., & Neale, J. M. (1982). Effects of marital discord on the children of schizophrenic, affectively disordered, and normal parents. *Journal of Abnormal Child Psychology, 10,* 215–228.

Famighetti, R. A. (1986). Understanding the family coping with Alzheimer's disease. *Clinical Gerontologist, 5,* 363–384.

Feldman, L., & Gotlib, I. H. (1993). Social dysfunction. In C. G. Costello (Ed.), *Symptoms of depression* (pp. 85–112). New York: Wiley.

Fischer, M. (1990). Parenting stress and the child with Attention Deficit Hyperactivity Disorder. *Journal of Clinical Child Psychology, 19,* 337–346.

Fodor, I. (1974). The phobic syndrome in women. In V. Franks & V. Burtle (Eds.), *Women in therapy* (pp. 132–168). New York: Brunner/Mazel.

Frankenstein, W., Hay, W. M., & Nathan, P. E. (1985). Effect of intoxication on alcoholics' marital communication and problem solving. *Journal of Studies on Alcohol, 46,* 1–6.

Gallagher, D., Rose, J., Rivera, P., Lovett, S., & Thompson, L. W. (1989). Prevalence of depression in family caregivers. *Gerontologist, 29,* 449–456.

George, L. K., & Gwyther, L. P. (1986). Caregiver well-being: A multidimensional examination of family caregivers of demented adults. *Gerontologist, 26,* 253–259.

Goldstein, A. (1970). Case conference: Some aspects of agoraphobia. *Journal of Behavior Therapy and Experimental Psychiatry, 1,* 305–313.

Gonyea, J. G. (1989). Alzheimer's disease support groups: An analysis of their structure, format, and perceived benefits. *Social Work in Health Care, 14,* 61–72.

Goodstein, R., & Swift, K. (1977). Psychotherapy with phobic patients: The marriage relationship as the source of symptoms and focus of treatment. *American Journal of Psychotherapy, 31,* 285–292.

Gotlib, I. H., & Cane, D. B. (1989). Self-report assessment of depression and anxiety. In P. C. Kendall & D. Watson (Eds.), *Anxiety and depression: Distinctive and overlapping features* (pp. 131–169). Orlando, FL: Academic.

Gotlib, I. H., & Colby, C. A. (1987). *Treatment of depression: An interpersonal systems approach.* New York: Pergamon.

Gotlib, I. H., & Hooley, J. M. (1988). Depression and marital distress: Current status and future directions. In S. W. Duck (Ed.), *Handbook of personal relationships* (pp. 543–570). Chichester, UK: Wiley.

Gotlib, I. H., & McCabe, S. B. (1990). Marriage and psychopathology. In F. D. Fincham & T. N. Bradbury (Eds.), *The psychology of marriage* (pp. 226–257). New York: Guilford.

Gotlib, I. H., & Whiffen, V. E. (1989). Depression and marital functioning: An examination of specificity and gender differences. *Journal of Abnormal Psychology, 98,* 23–30.

Gove, W. R., Hughes, M., & Styles, C. B. (1983). Does marriage have positive effects on the psychological well-being of the individual? *Journal of Health and Social Behavior, 24,* 122–132.

Hafner, R. J. (1986). *Marriage and mental illness: A sex roles perspective.* New York: Guilford.

Hammen, C., Gordon, D., Burge, D., Adrian, C., Jaenicke, C., & Hiroto, D. (1987). Maternal affective disorders, illness, and stress: Risk for children's psychopathology. *American Journal of Psychiatry, 144,* 736–741.

Hand, I., Lamontagne, Y., & Marks, I. M. (1974). Group exposure (flooding) in vivo for agoraphobics. *British Journal of Psychiatry, 124,* 588–602.

Harris, S. L. (1984). The family and the autistic child: A behavioral perspective. *Family Relations, 33,* 127–134.

Hautzinger, M., Linden, M., & Hoffman, N. (1982). Distressed couples with and without a depressed partner: An analysis of their verbal interaction. *Journal of Behavior Therapy and Experimental Psychiatry, 13,* 307–314.

Hooley, J. M. (1986). Expressed emotion and depression: Interactions between patients and high-versus-low-expressed emotion spouses. *Journal of Abnormal Psychology, 95,* 237–246.

Hooley, J. M., & Teasdale, J. D. (1989). Predictors of relapse in unipolar depression: Expressed emotion, marital distress, and perceived criticism. *Journal of Abnormal Psychology, 98,* 229–235.

Hops, H., Biglan, A., Sherman, L., Arthur, J., Friedman, L., & Osteen, V. (1987). Home observations of family interactions of depressed women. *Journal of Consulting and Clinical Psychology, 55,* 341–346.

Howlin, P. (1988). Living with impairment: The effects on children of having an autistic sibling. *Child Care, Health and Development, 14,* 409–416.

Jacob, T., Dunn, N. J., & Leonard, K. (1983). Patterns of alcohol abuse and family stability. *Alcoholism: Clinical and Experimental Research, 7,* 382–385.

Jacob, T., & Krahn, G. L. (1988). Marital interactions of alcoholic couples: Comparison with depressed and nondistressed couples. *Journal of Consulting and Clinical Psychology, 56,* 73–79.

Jacob, T., Ritchey, D., Cvitkovic, J. F., & Blane, H. T. (1981). Communication styles of alcoholic and nonalcoholic families when drinking and not drinking. *Journal of Studies on Alcohol, 42,* 466–482.

Jacobson, N. S., Holtzworth-Munroe, A., & Schmaling, K. B. (1989). Marital therapy and spouse involvement in the treatment of depression, agoraphobia, and alcoholism. *Journal of Consulting and Clinical Psychology, 57,* 5–10.

Johnston, C. (1991). Predicting mothers' and fathers' perceptions of child behaviour problems. *Canadian Journal of Behavioural Science, 23,* 349–357.

Johnston, C., & Pelham, W. E. (1990). Maternal characteristics, ratings of child behavior, and mother–child interactions in families of children with externalizing disorders. *Journal of Abnormal Child Psychology, 18,* 407–416.

Kendall, P. C., Lerner, R. M., & Craighead, W. E. (1984). Human development and intervention in childhood psychopathology. *Child Development, 55,* 71–82.

Killeen, M. (1990). The influence of stress and coping on family caregivers' perceptions of health. *International Journal of Aging and Human Development, 30,* 197–211.

Kochanska, G., Kuczynski, L., Radke-Yarrow, M., & Welsh, J. D. (1987). Resolutions of conflict episodes between well and affectively ill mothers and their young children. *Journal of Abnormal Child Psychology, 15,* 441–456.

Koegel, R. L., Schreibman, L., O'Neill, R. E., & Burke, J. C. (1983). The personality and family-interaction characteristics of parents of autistic children. *Journal of Consulting and Clinical Psychology, 51,* 683–692.

Konstantareas, M. M. (1991). Autistic, learning disabled, and delayed children's impact on their parents. *Canadian Journal of Behavioural Science, 23,* 358–375.

Kowalik, D. L., & Gotlib, I. H. (1987). Depression and marital interaction: Concordance between intent and perception of communication. *Journal of Abnormal Psychology, 96,* 127–134.

Lee, C. M., & Gotlib, I. H. (1989a). Clinical status and emotional adjustment of children of depressed mothers. *American Journal of Psychiatry, 146,* 478–483.

Lee, C. M., & Gotlib, I. H. (1989b). Maternal depression and child adjustment: A longitudinal analysis. *Journal of Abnormal Psychology, 98,* 78–85.

Lee, C. M., & Gotlib, I. H. (1991a). Family disruption, parental availability, and child adjustment. In R. J. Prinz (Ed.), *Advances in behavioral assessment of children and families.* (Vol. 5. pp. 171–199). London: Jessica Kingsley.

Lee, C. M., & Gotlib, I. H. (1991b). Adjustment of children of depressed mothers: A 10-month follow-up. *Journal of Abnormal Psychology, 100,* 473–477.

Leff, J. P., Kuipers, L., Berkowitz, R., Eberlein-Fries, R., & Sturgeon, D. (1982). A controlled trial of social intervention in the families of schizophrenic patients. *British Journal of Psychiatry, 141,* 121–134.

Lytton, H. (1990a). Child and parent effects in boys' conduct disorder: A reinterpretation. *Developmental Psychology, 26,* 683–697.

Lytton, H. (1990b). Child effects—Still unwelcome? Response to Dodge and Wahler. *Developmental Psychology, 26,* 705–709.

Mash, E. J., & Johnston, C. (1983a). Parental perceptions of child behavior problems, parenting self-esteem, and mothers' reported stress in younger and older hyperactive and normal children. *Journal of Consulting and Clinical Psychology, 51,* 86–99.

Mash, E. J., & Johnston, C. (1983b). Sibling interactions of hyperactive and normal children and their relation to reports of maternal stress and self-esteem. *Journal of Clinical Child Psychology, 12,* 91–99.

Mash, E. J., & Johnston, C. (1990). Determinants of parenting stress: Illustrations from families of hyperactive children and families of physically abused children. *Journal of Clinical Child Psychology, 19,* 313–328.

Merikangas, K. R. (1984). Divorce and assortative mating among depressed patients. *American Journal of Psychiatry, 141,* 74–76.

Moos, R. H., Finney, J. W., & Gamble, W. (1982). The process of recovery from alcoholism: II. Comparing spouses of alcoholic patients and spouses of matched community controls. *Journal of Studies on Alcohol, 43,* 888–909.

Morgan, S. B. (1988). The autistic child and family functioning: A developmental–family systems perspective. *Journal of Autism and Developmental Disorders, 18,* 263–280.

Narayan, S., Moyes, B., & Wolff, S. (1990). Family characteristics of autistic children. *Journal of Autism and Developmental Disorders, 20,* 523–535.

Neale, J. M., & Weintraub, S. (1975). Children vulnerable to psychopathology: The Stony Brook high-risk project. *Journal of Abnormal Child Psychology, 3,* 95–113.

Noh, S., & Avison, W. R. (1988). Spouses of discharged psychiatric patients: Factors associated with their experience of burden. *Journal of Marriage and the Family, 50,* 377–389.

O'Farrell, T. J. (1986). Marital therapy in the treatment of alcoholism. In N. S. Jacobson, & H. S. Gurman (Eds.), *Clinical handbook of marital therapy* (pp. 513–536). New York: Guilford.

Patterson, G. R. (1982). *Coercive family process.* Eugene, OR: Castalia.

Patterson, G. R. (1986). Performance models for antisocial boys. *American Psychologist, 41,* 432–444.

Paykel, E. S., Myers, J. K., Dienelt, M. N., Klerman, G. L., Lindenthal, J. J., & Pepper, M. P. (1969). Life events and depression: A controlled study. *Archives of General Psychiatry, 21,* 753–760.

Pratt, C., Wright, S., & Schmall, V. (1987). Burden, coping, and health status: A comparison of family caregivers to community dwelling and institutionalized Alzheimer's patients. *Gerontological Social Work with Families,* 99–112.

Rabins, P. V., Fitting, M. D., Eastham, J. & Fetting, J. (1990). The emotional impact of caring for the chronically ill. *Psychosomatics, 31,* 331–336.

Radke-Yarrow, M., Cummings, E. M., Kuczynski, L., & Chapman, M. (1985). Patterns of attachment in two- and three-year olds in normal families and families with parental depression. *Child Development, 56,* 884–893.

Ruscher, S. M., & Gotlib, I. H. (1988). Marital interaction patterns of couples with and without a depressed partner. *Behavior Therapy, 19,* 455–470.

Schachar, R., Taylor, E., Wieselberg, M., Thorley, G., & Rutter, M. (1987). Changes in family function and relationships in children who respond to methylphenidate. *Journal of the American Academy of Child and Adolescent Psychiatry, 26,* 728–732.

Schachar, R. J., & Wachsmuth, R. (1990). Family dysfunction and psychosocial adversity: Comparison of Attention Deficit Disorder, Conduct Disorder, normal and clinical controls. *Canadian Journal of Behavioural Science, 23,* 332–348.

Schless, A. P., Schwartz, L., Goetz, C., & Mendels, J. (1974). How depressives view the significance of life events. *British Journal of Psychiatry, 125,* 406–410.

Sher, K. J., Walitzer, K. S., Wood, P. K., & Brent, E. E. (1991). Characteristics of children of alcoholics: Putative risk factors, substance use and abuse, and psychopathology. *Journal of Abnormal Psychology, 100,* 427–448.

Sloboda, S. B. (1974). The children of alcoholics: A neglected problem. *Hospital and Community Psychiatry, 25,* 605–606.

Steinglass, P. (1979). The alcoholic family in the interaction laboratory. *Journal of Nervous and Mental Disease, 167,* 428–436.

Steinglass, P. (1981). The alcoholic family at home: Patterns of interaction in dry, wet, and transitional stages of alcoholism. *Archives of General Psychiatry, 38,* 578–584.

Steinglass, P., Davis, D., & Berenson, D. (1977). Observations of conjointly hospitalized "alcoholic couples" during sobriety and intoxication: Implications for theory and therapy. *Family Process, 16,* 1–16.

Tarver-Behring, S., Barkley, R. A., & Karlsson, J. (1985). The mother–child interactions of hyperactive boys and their siblings. *American Journal of Orthopsychiatry, 55,* 202–209.

Vaughn, C. E., & Leff, J. P. (1976). The influence of family and social factors on the course of psychiatric illness: A comparison of schizophrenic and depressed neurotic patients. *British Journal of Psychiatry, 129,* 125–137.

Wahler, R. G. (1990). Who is driving the interactions? A commentary on "Child and parent effects in boys' conduct disorder." *Developmental Psychology, 26,* 702–704.

Webster-Stratton, C. (1988). Mothers' and fathers' perceptions of child deviance: Roles of parent and child behaviors and child adjustment. *Journal of Consulting and Clinical Psychology, 56,* 909–915.

Webster-Stratton, C., & Hammond, M. (1990). Predictors of treatment outcome in parent training for families of conduct problem children. *Behavior Therapy, 21,* 319–337.

Weintraub, S., Liebert, D., & Neale, J. M. (1978). Teacher ratings of children vulnerable to psychopathology. In E. J. Anthony (Ed.), *The child and his family (Vol. 4), Vulnerable children* (pp. 335–346). New York: Wiley.

Weintraub, S., Prinz, R., & Neale, J. M. (1975). Peer evaluations of the competence of children vulnerable to psychopathology. *Journal of Abnormal Child Psychology, 6,* 461–473.

Weissman, M. M., & Boyd, J. H. (1983). The epidemiology of affective disorders: Rates and risk factors. In L. Grinspoon (Ed.), *Psychiatry update,* Vol. II. Washington, DC: American Psychiatric Press.

Weissman, M. M., Prusoff, B. A., Gammon, G. D., Merikangas, K. R., Leckman, J. F., & Kidd, K. K. (1984). Psychopathology in the children (ages 6–18) of depressed and normal parents. *Journal of the American Academy of Child Psychiatry, 23,* 78–84.

West, O. M., & Prinz, R. J. (1987). Parental alcoholism and childhood psychopathology. *Psychological Bulletin, 102,* 204–218.

Whiffen, V. E., & Gotlib, I. H. (1989). Infants of postpartum depressed mothers: Temperament and cognitive status. *Journal of Abnormal Psychology, 98,* 274–279.

CHAPTER 13

Chronic Illness and Developmental Family Psychology

ANITA LANDAU HURTIG

In a sensitive and seminal paper George Engel (1977) criticized and redirected health professionals in their conceptualization of the nature and process of physical illness. He described the limitations of the traditional "medical model" with its simplistic linear approach that assumes that disease is ". . . fully accounted for by deviations from the norm of measurable biological [somatic] variables [demanding] that behavioral aberrations be explained on the basis of disordered somatic [biochemical or neurophysiological] processes" (p. 130). As presented visually below, the biomedical model would reduce the presence of illness and its manifestations to an organic etiology, the implication being that treatment must be focused on the organic abnormality, or what Kety called "rational and specific" treatment (Kety, 1974).

<u>Biomedical Model</u>
Organic (biological) abnormality → Disease Process

Engel stated what seems obvious to mental health workers and to many physicians whose clinical experience enters into their conceptualization of the illness process; that is, the human experience of illness cannot be reduced to a simple biologic formulation, but it must include psychosocial factors as well. Engel's paper specified only psychological, social, and cultural factors. His argument did not attempt to enter into the complex area of the multiple and interactive web of psychosocial variables. His biopsychosocial model moved from a linear to a multivariate, interactive construction, although essentially unidirectional, as represented below,

Organic Factors ⟍
Psychological Factors ——⟩ Symptomatic Patient
Cultural Factors ——
Social Factors ⟋

adding not only additional "causal" factors, but changing the product from disease to patient, thus emphasizing the human experience as crucial to the health/illness model.

In the 16 years since Engel's paper challenged the medical establishment, health psychologists have taken up the challenge and have, through clinical narrative and scientific research investigations, essentially fleshed out Engel's bare-bones model. Psychologists, often in collaboration with physicians, have become increasingly involved in health care. This involvement has led to a growing recognition of the importance of two key elements in the dynamics of health behavior: 1) the role of the family; and 2) the role of developmental forces. However, research and clinical investigations in these two areas have, until recently, considered them as separate and separable entities.

THE FAMILY AND PHYSICAL ILLNESS

The family and its relation to illness has been the focus of an extensive body of research, guided by two hypotheses: 1) illness has an impact on the family that is either positive or negative; and 2) the family has a significant impact on the individual's adaptation to his or her illness, and to the disease process itself. In her review of the literature on families and the physically ill child, Shapiro (1983) states, "It is by now clear that an undeniable relationship exists between family and illness and that a specific illness both affects and is affected by the family context" (p. 13). These effects and affects have been verified in large, all-encompassing epidemiological studies (Gortmaker, Walker, Weitzman, & Sobel, 1990; Pless, Roghmann, & Haggerty, 1972), in multidisease studies (Minuchin, et al., 1975; Wallender, Varni, et al., 1989), and single disease studies (Anderson & Auslander, 1980; Hanson et al., 1989; Lewis & Khaw, 1982; Varni, Wilcox, & Hanson, 1988). The preponderance of these studies show consistent findings. Family functioning as measured by such diverse variables as marital satisfaction, respondent–spouse communication, cohesion, conflict, and frequency of disagreements, has a significant correlation with coping and adjustment of the patient (Wallender, Varni, et al., 1987; Pless, Roghmann & Haggerty) and a positive correlation with symptom patterns in a range of physical illnesses (Chen & Cobb, 1960).

As research on the relationship between family variables and physical illness has become more sensitive to the multiple factors that potentially mediate this relationship, increasingly complex models are needed to analyze the interaction. One model that has been the source of extensive studies focuses on the function of family stress as it has an impact on the illness process, both in terms of etiology and maintenance, as well as how the illness process in turn has an impact on the family's capacity to cope and to maintain adaptive role definitions. The link between stressful life events in the family and psychological and physical morbidity has been consistently supported (Dohrenwend & Dohrenwend, 1981; Rabkin, 1980), as has the family as a potential contributor or mediator of this relationship (Masters, Ceneto, & Mendlowiz, 1983). Cronkite and Moos (1984) have presented a conceptual model of the stress process that attempts to link the multiple moderating factors (Figure 13.1). Factors contributing to stress include familial sociocultural variables, such as social status and social resources, and familial psychological variables, such as spousal coping, self-esteem, and mood. Physical illness as a potential stress factor appears in many of the "boxes" that define stress, such as prior functioning (physical symptoms), and undesirable life events and ongoing stress (spouse's physical symptoms). The outcome variable (later functioning) also includes a physical illness component ("physical symptoms").

Although multivariate models of this type help to illustrate the complexity of the interaction between the family and illness, there are methodologic problems that complicate drawing conclusions. Physical illness is, by definition, a potential stressor. It is also a potential response to stress. As a result, as McCubbin et al. (1980) point out in their review of the family stress and coping literature, it is difficult to separate to what degree family factors are a response to or a contributor to the illness experience. Interpretations of the relationship of stressor (illness) to family functioning tend to be tautological. In addition, the potential for mediators of stress to have a significant impact on the relationship has been increasingly recognized.

Among these mediators, social support has been actively studied as a protective force contributing to a family's regenerative power. In their review of the literature on social support and serious illness, DiMatteo and Hays (1981) note that the preponderance of studies on familial social support reveal a positive

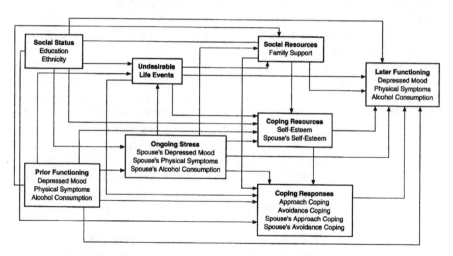

Figure 13.1. A Conceptual Model of the Stress Process. (From Cronkite, R.C., & Moos, R. H. [1984]. The role of predisposing and moderating factors in the stress-illness relationship. *Journal of Health & Social Behavior, 25,* 372–393.)

correlation between family support and improved prognosis, control, and compliance in such physical illnesses as cancer (Weisman & Worden, 1975), asthma (Berle, Pinsky, Wolf, & Wolff, 1952; DeAravjo, Van Arsdel, Holmes, & Dudley, 1973), and stroke (Robertson & Suinn, 1968). Berlemann & Syme's (1979) research revealed an inverse relationship between social support and host susceptibility and mortality. To analyze this social support model further, Holahan & Moos (1987) looked at gender differences in the relationship between social support and physical symptoms, and found that social support in both family and work environment was significantly related to physical symptom presentation in men, whereas for women, support in the family environment alone was significant. This research suggests that individual difference variables, such as gender, and more discrete variables such as role in the family, may define these relationships further.

In terms of illness in childhood and adolescence, literature on family factors has focused primarily on two areas: the impact of the child's illness on the family; and how family factors either contribute to or work against the child's capacity to cope with his or her illness. Generally, the research supports the conclusion that a physically and chronically ill child's adjustment is heavily dependent on the feelings and attitudes of his or her family, particularly the degree of conflict or cohesion in the family. Family characteristics which have been associated with a child's poor adjustment to his or her illness include: 1) fearful and overprotective parenting; 2) over-solicitous and guiltridden parenting; and 3) embarrassment or shame associated with the disease on the part of parents (Mattson, 1972). A number of studies of specific chronic illnesses have shown that aspects of family functioning are related to improved outcome. Reduced family conflict, emotional expressiveness, and family stability have been associated with better control of diabetes (Anderson, Miller, Auslander, & Santiago, 1981; Marteau, Block, & Baum, 1987; Tietz & Vidmar, 1972). Similar family characteristics have been associated with higher levels of adjustment in children dealing with the stresses of juvenile rheumatoid arthritis (Varni, Wilcox, & Hanson, 1988), cystic fibrosis (Lawlor, Nakielny, & Wright, 1966; Lewis & Khaw, 1982) leukemia (Kupst et al., 1982), and cancer (Spinetta & Maloney, 1978). A classic study of the impact of parental factors on chronically ill children and adolescents, which has resulted in extensive theorizing, conceptualizes a psychosomatic route for parental effects, specifically in the case of diabetes, but potentially in a wide range of chronic illness (Minuchin, Rosman, & Baker, 1978; Minuchin et al., 1975). The authors point to four defining characteristics of families that may exacerbate, or even produce, symptom patterns in a child: 1) enmeshment; 2) over-protectiveness; 3) rigidity; 4) and absence of conflict resolution.

The conclusions drawn from these studies clearly implicate the family in both positive and negative ways, with adjustment to and management of chronic illness. However, in the adult literature, and even more so in the child literature, the conceptualization of the patient, the family, and the illness relationship is flawed by the absence of longitudinal studies. Cross-sectional and correlational research is limited, because it cannot deal with the reality of the family, the child, and the illness as a process, all changing over time in response to the dynamic forces working within each component. While momentary relationships at any one point in time are analyzed, there is no way of separating cause and effect. Thus, poor adjustment of the chronically ill child may be a function of family disturbance (high conflict, low cohesion, etc.), or family disturbance may be a function of chronic illness. Most likely, the two are not separable outcome measures, but rather, they are interactive processes that depend, not only on multiple intervening mediators, but also on the time at which the process is stopped for measurement.

DEVELOPMENTAL CONSIDERATIONS AND PHYSICAL ILLNESS

There are three approaches to conceptualizing a developmental perspective in physical illness. The most common approach is that which considers how the patient is affected by illness at different points in the life cycle. The underlying assumption is that physical illness will have different implications at different stages of development. Erikson's model (1959) of psychosocial development across the life-span offers a template for considering how the essential tasks of normal development are influenced by external social and environmental events. Physical illness has the potential for disrupting this normal progression in specific and predictable ways.

For the infant, the sense of the world as a safe and stable place, with his or her own body and dependable others who serve to respond to it and protect it, is threatened by the presence of a chronic physical illness. For the ill infant, pain, hospitalization, failure of comforting response, as well as inconsistent or rejecting care are likely to result in a retreat from trust, with accompanying distrust, fear, and extended dependency.

For the toddler, the stage when autonomy is the major challenge, the child with physical illness is particularly vulnerable. This is the age of growing independence and self-control. The chronically ill child may be inhibited in these normal developmental thrusts by the real limitations of his or her illness, such as pain or immobility, or by the imposed limitations of fearful or overprotective parents, resulting in increased dependency, poor impulse control, and reduced self-esteem.

The preschooler's primary developmental task is mastery, or in Erikson's terms, initiative. This is a stage of progressive motor and social competence, with the acquisition of power and success in ever-broadening spheres of activity. For the physically ill child, restrictions associated with illness, both physical and social, serve to compromise this sense of mastery, resulting in excessive fearfulness and passivity. Again, parents may contribute to reduced initiative and productivity by restricting the activities and the independence of their ill child.

As the school-age child gradually widens his or her arena of activity, the focus is increasingly on the challenge of academic and social learning. This stage is described by Erikson as that of industry, with the goal of building a sense of competence. Illness may restrict this outcome through varied encumbrances, such as school absence due to hospitalization or doctor visits, or susceptibility to symptoms, necessitating isolation. Other restrictions may arise from physical limitations inhibiting activity, and the tendency for parents to overprotect and limit their chronically ill child.

The adolescent years are conceptualized in this life-span frame as particularly devoted to the attainment of a sense of personal identity. The classic struggle of this stage is between finding one's own selfhood through increasing independence and self-definition, while maintaining reliance on family that the early years foster and support. This struggle is most vulnerable to becoming confused, and its outcome, the attainment of a relatively cohesive sense of self, is most susceptible to regression and failure in chronically ill adolescents. The adolescent with a physical illness may have to confront alterations in body image that make the normal changes in appearance at this time even more difficult to accept. Secure sexual identity is heavily determined by being "just like" the other members of one's gender group in this stage. Physical illnesses, such as cystic fibrosis, diabetes, and sickle cell disease, with their tendency to cause thinness or weight gain and to inhibit sexual maturation, and cancer, with its treatment implications for cosmetic disfigurement, are examples of the challenges of disease to physical attractiveness and positive sexual identity at a stage when these qualities are primary issues. Body image is a crucial component of adolescent development, and when it is compromised, emotional disturbance may ensue (Hurtig & Rosenthal, 1987). The effects of physical illness often result in increased dependency on external authority figures—parents, nurses, and doctors, causing resentment and anger in adolescents, who are constantly having to face their ambivalence about growing up and striking out, often resulting in alternating aggressive and passive behaviors. Again, the adolescents' family and their extended support system may play a crucial role in fostering dependency through overcontrol and overprotectiveness.

If the challenge to the adolescent is to move through a difficult transition to selfhood, the challenge for the young adult is to strengthen that self to allow for investment in intimate relations. Forming close relationships is a gratifying but a dangerous project, with the possibilities of rejection, disappointment, and isolation. Physical illness may potentiate these dangers for the patient whose feelings of looking or being inadequate, different, or endangered may lead to withdrawal, anger, and defensive rejection. The illness, with its demands and dangers, may pose a threat to the other person in the dyad, leading to real, not imaginary, rejection. The role of being ill rather than the illness itself may set up the young adult's feelings of helplessness and loss of control, independent of the degree to which the illness actually has an impact on his or her life experiences.

Evidence from studies on illness severity and adjustment suggest that there is not a linear relationship between these two variables (Stein & Jessop, 1984), and that variables, such as family structure, social class and support, and previous personality, are major factors that may suppress the relationship (Hurtig, Koepke & Park, 1989). The individual's premorbid adjustment; that is, the degree to which he or she has navigated the earlier developmental shoals, is probably the most important factor in the ability to reach out and experience intimacy, an ability mediated by aspects of family functioning.

In the middle adult years, Erikson describes the stage of generativity, a term that encompasses investment in relationships—marital, parental, occupational, and/or community. The obverse is stagnation, the inability to feel productive and invested. Again, illness, whether chronic from childhood or emerging in this period, is potentially disruptive of generativity. Limitations in the physical realm may restrict occupational activity and challenge traditional social roles. Bodily impairments, either cosmetic or functional, are also challenges to comfort and security about one's place in the family and community. Illness at this stage may also lead to preoccupations with survival and one's bodily demands that preclude commitment to others.

Finally, the task of old age, integrity in the face of death, is particularly difficult for the physically disabled and ill, as it is mixed with intimations of mortality. The research on health and old age reflects growing awareness that older people are highly sensitive to the effects of illness, and their ability to cope with the challenges of aging are significantly compromised by illness.

Although Erikson's model is a valuable tool for anticipating the effects of physical illness at specific stages in the life cycle, there has been little empirical research to validate these assumptions. Most studies on developmental aspects of physical illness are cross-sectional, either investigating samples across a wide age range (Drotar, et al., 1981), or looking at selected age groups (adolescents, toddlers, and latency children) in isolation (Boyle, di Sant'Agnes, Sack, Milli-can, & Kulczycki, 1976; Czajkowski & Koocher, 1987; Hurtig & Park, 1989; Kellerman, Zeltzer, Ellenberg, Dash, & Rigler, 1980; Zeltzer, Kellerman, Ellenberg, Dash, & Rigler, 1980). A few studies have attempted to trace the progress of the illness/patient relationship over time. Following a group of chronically ill children into adolescence, Orr, Weller, Satterwhite, & Pless, (1984) reported that adjustment problems were most likely to occur when illness persisted into adolescence. Other studies have reported similar findings, suggesting that the results may be a function of the duration of the disease, as well as the age of the patient (Pless & Roghmann, 1971). The vulnerability of younger adolescents to reduced self-esteem and disturbances of self-image has been noted in the developmental literature (Simmons, Rosenberg, & Rosenberg, 1973), with the likelihood that this age group will be most susceptible to difficulties in coping with the added pressures of illness (Hurtig & Park, 1989).

A second approach to looking at physical illness from a developmental perspective changes the major focus from the patient to the family; that is, the development of the family over time and how the family is affected by physical illness at different points in the family cycle. The concept of a family life cycle is fairly new. A model of orderly changes in the family, based on previous stages and evolving in predictable ways, was initially developed by Haley (1973) and has been modified to cover an increasingly complex array of family dynamics. Combrinck-Graham (1983) describes the family life-cycle as a spiral (see Figure 13.2) in which there is an ongoing vacillation between relational styles labeled as *centripetal* (cohesive) or *centrifugal* (disengaged). Her model gives a dimensionality to the earlier, more simplistic description of psychosomatic (i.e., pathologic) families, by pointing to the appropriateness of *enmeshment* at certain stages of the family life cycle (for example, during the early child-bearing years) when closeness and cohesion are adaptive, in contrast to the family's middle years and the children's adolescence, when family relationships tend to be more outgoing and *disengagement* is more adaptive. As Combrinck-Graham points out, these terms are descriptions of relational styles, not

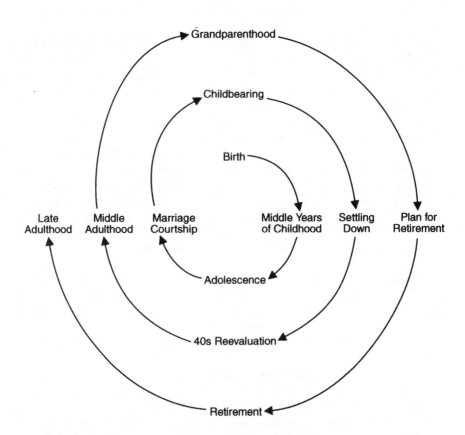

Figure 13-2. Family life spiral. (Reprinted from *Clinical Implications of the Family Life Cycle* by H. Liddle (Ed.), p. 38, with permission of Aspen Publishers, © 1992)

pathology. Pathology is predictable, however, when the stage in the family life cycle and the events in the family do not match that phase. It is predictable that chronic illness will represent a centripetal pull for the family, a demand situation for focus on the family and the familial socialization process. When the chronic illness occurs at a period where external orientation is developmentally appropriate, as in adolescence, or the young adult is leaving the family of origin, there is increased potential for derailment of the normal family life cycle. Beavers (1982) gives an example of the family of an anorectic adolescent in which control over eating, weight, and appearance was central, when disengagement and reduced control should have been the dynamic force in the family.

Another way of looking at the family life cycle has been offered by Brown (1980). He elaborated six major phases in the developmental cycles of families (see Table 13.1). As with other developmental models, this one implies that failures at any earlier phase will impede successful adaptation in subsequent phases. The potential for physical illness to disturb this adaptation is significant. For example, in Phase 1 the need for "relative disconnection" from family of origin in order to commit to the newly formed dyad is a well-recognized goal in order to achieve healthy marital relations. However, the young adult whose ties to the family of origin have been associated with survival, such as the cystic fibrosis patient whose life has depended on physical therapy, is likely to have difficulty in making the transition to a new "life-line" partner. The task of Phase IV, to "establish competence within the family system for helping each member to meet . . . adaptations that each must face in the world outside the family. . . ."—that is, to facilitate ego mastery for each family member—is a formidable challenge to a spouse or parent facing the possibility of disfigurement or even death from cancer and whose own adaptation is severely taxed.

Both models offer ways of understanding how the normal family life cycle may be rerouted in maladaptive ways by the presence of physical illness in the family. Research that merely *notes* the presence of disturbance in families secondary to physical illness does little to illuminate the process by which this occurs, or to offer approaches to ameliorating these consequences.

Finally, a third approach to understanding the relationship between physical illness and the developmental family is the recognition that the illness has its own characteristics and developmental trajectory, which interacts with the family and the patient's developmental status. One model for approaching this divides the illness process into *prediagnostic, diagnostic, pretreatment, treatment,* and *rehabilitation* or *resolution* phases (Leventhal, Leventhal, & Van Nguyen, 1985). In the prediagnostic phase of the illness, the anticipation of disease has the potential to disrupt family functioning in a number of ways, both functionally and emotionally. Parents who define themselves as genetically vulnerable, for real or imagined reasons, may decide not to have babies (Ben-Sira, 1977). This may cause tension between partners because of disagreement over the decision, or because of guilt or blame on the part of one or the other. In their studies of the attitudes toward cancer in families, Dent & Goulston (1982) note that attitudes toward the disease affect the move toward or away from preventive

TABLE 13.1   Developmental Cycle of Families

Phase I:	Establishing basic commitment to the marriage The developmental task is to manage successfully a relative disconnection from each of the families of origin and a restructuring of commitments to old friends, social activities, occupational and professional involvement, etc. A variety of transactional subsystems begin to function in this phase of development.
Phase II:	Creating sub-systems for mutual nurturance The developmental task is to establish a warm and empathic caregiving mutuality in the relationship, responsive to the arrival of a first child, who in turn, will reinforce the mutuality of positive feelings in the new family. A relatively successful evolution through Phase I and a further refinement of transactional subsystems facilitates the organization of this phase.
Phase III:	Defining effective interpersonal and intrapersonal mechanisms for encouragement of each person's individuality and autonomy The developmental task is to evolve a family system and subsystems through which spontaneous and warm encouragement of the individual development of each family member can occur in accordance with the levels of maturation and the adaptive tasks each may be confronting in any time period. Relative success in Phase I and II provides the fuel for this phase to evolve successfully.
Phase IV:	Facilitating ego mastery for each family member The developmental task is to establish competence within the family system for helping each member to meet the ever-proliferating adaptations that each must face in the world outside the family, even as each member is integrating inner psychic development and change. Effectively functioning subsystems in the family are essential if vital family experience is to occur in this phase.
Phase V:	Maintaining family integration during adolescence and young adulthood The developmental task is to sustain integrated family life even as the arrival of adolescence in the children, and middle age in the parents makes impacts on family value and belief systems, the marital commitment, the intergenerational boundaries, the communication patterns, the interpersonal alliances, the individual identities, the sexual adaptations, and the myriad changes that are inevitable for families in this phase of the family's cycle. Once again, effectively functioning transactional subsystems are essential for this to occur.
Phase VI:	Achieving mutual validation The developmental tasks of this phase are multiple, involving reworking but continuing integration of family relationships in order to preserve the capability of the family system to provide validation of each member as a lovable and valued person.

Source: Brown, S. L. The developmental cycle of families: Clinical impressions. *Psychiatric Clinics of North America 3* (3).

action. These behaviors may lead to exaggerated preventive approaches, such as total immersion in medication or doctoring, or unrealistic denial and avoidance. Either of these exaggerated responses can lead to anger, mistrust, and a breakdown of cohesion in the family, when it is most needed.

Periods of diagnoses and treatment of illness are inevitably traumatic and potentially highly disruptive to the developmental process, both for the individual and the family. The degree of disruption depends on a number of factors, including the family's and the individual's stage of development and the disease or illness diagnosed. Except in old age, illness is never experienced as a normative event, as "on-time" in terms of the expectable family life cycle (Neugarten, 1970). Events that are expectable or on-time are more readily integrated into the family's cycle, and they create less disruption. A diagnosis of osteosarcoma in a child or adolescent, or multiple sclerosis in a young adult is likely to have an impact on the family and individual in more disturbing ways than a diagnosis of pancreatic cancer in an aging parent. Diagnosis of cancer at any age, or of a fatal illness, such as cystic fibrosis or muscular dystrophy, will be experienced differently than a diagnosis of hypertension or asthma. Diagnosis of an illness in the family must challenge the balance of stability and change—that is, the homeostatic thrust of the family system (Minuchin, 1988). Although studies have shown that families in crisis tend toward greater cohesion (Kaplan, Smith, Grobstein, & Fishman, 1977), the ability of the family to integrate individual perceptions into a working and cohesive unit depends on where the family is in its own developmental stage, interacting with the nature and severity of the illness. There has been little research on the degree to which different types of illnesses alter the organization of relations between familial subsystems. Minuchin (1988) has pointed to the changing nature of subsystem boundaries in the face of parental illness, with increasing contact between generations, a pattern of increased involvement and concern in the younger adults and dependency in the older subsystem. These changes are more likely to occur when the illness is perceived as threatening or debilitating.

Rolland (1988) has noted the critical need to consider the time phases of an illness when attempting to understand the interaction between the illness, the individual, and the family. He identifies the major developmental time phases in the evolving illness process as *crisis, chronic,* and *terminal.* The crisis period includes Leventhal's prediagnostic and early diagnostic stages, when the demands on the family are to:

> (1) create a meaning for the illness event that maximizes a preservation of a sense of mastery and competency; (2) grieve for the loss of the pre-illness family identity; (3) move toward a position of acceptance of permanent change while maintaining a sense of continuity between their past and future; (4) pull together to undergo short-term crisis reorganization and; (5) in the face of uncertainty, develop a special system flexibility toward future goals. (pp. 155–156)

Each of these "key tasks" interacts with the individual and family developmental stage. For example, the need to preserve a sense of mastery and competence, although most clearly related to individual development, also applies to the family. The family is understood as made up not only of individuals, but functioning as a more or less cohesive system. The identification of a "pre-illness family identity" implies a shared identity, common to the unit, beyond the individual components. Such a family identity is more likely to be a characteristic of the more mature family. The potential for family disruption in the earlier stages of family development can be seen in the families of infants and young children diagnosed with Tay-Sachs, cystic fibrosis, muscular dystrophy, Wernig-Hoffman, or other chronic and fatal illnesses. These families are often unable to cope with the stresses of chronic and serious illness and various symptoms of systemic disintegration occur, including the breakup of the marriage (Hurtig & Medenis, 1990).

In addition to coping with the crisis stage of illness, the family must also move beyond it, into the chronic stage. This presupposes a flexibility that allows for increasing independence on the part of the identified patient and a reduction of what had been appropriate nurturance and protection in the earlier stages, but that becomes increasingly enmeshed and rigid in later phases. Rolland (1988) describes the crucial tasks of this period as the construction of normality in the face of uncertainty and disruption and the maintenance of maximal autonomy in the face of mutual dependency. The chronic stage is in many ways a greater challenge to families than the crisis stage. Both the illness and the family develop together, but the chronic stage may endure for extended periods, inhibiting the normal developmental thrust of the family. Brown (1980), in his description of Phase IV, refers to the task of facilitating ego mastery for each family member, which involves "effectively functioning subsystems." The normal parental subsystem, which has been undermined by illness in one of its members, as in the case of a mother of a teenage child stricken by multiple sclerosis, is no longer functional. At a time when children normally move increasingly out of the family orbit, one or more may be pulled in as replacements in the parental subsystem, thus creating role changes that subvert the developmental process for the individual children and the family as a unit.

The final, or terminal phase, occurs in those illnesses when death is anticipated and includes the period when the inevitability of death is recognized. The terminal phase may involve a gradual and subtle transition period for the family, as in childhood illnesses that evolve relatively slowly, such as muscular dystrophy or cystic fibrosis, or adult illnesses, such as metastatic cancer or AIDS. In such cases, the family may be held in a suspended state developmentally, once adaptive functions become obsolete and maladaptive. Cohesion and unity may represent the most effective coping in the crisis phase for the family facing a long-term illness, such as multiple sclerosis, but once the family has restructured to develop new roles for functioning, the challenge in the terminal phase is more on autonomous emotional coping and a resumption of autonomous as well as affiliate interactions. In contrast, a terminal phase that occurs suddenly, without extended preparatory transition, as in some forms of cancer, may be less likely to isolate the ill member from the family or to entrench an overprotective system.

However, the need to confront imminent death brings its own conflicts and crises. The family with a long history of a member's kidney dysfunction and dialysis, which has successfully restructured to deal with daily challenges around finances or clinic visits, may be unable to confront the affective demands that death and the grieving process imply.

As the various models and the multiple variables presented in this chapter suggest, the potential for understanding the complex dynamics that underlie the interaction of individual, family, and illness can only be realized using a developmental construct for all three entities. Empirical research on human functioning is limited, not so much by an inability to conceptualize the complexity of psychological, social, and biological forces, but by a tendency to stop the process; that is, to catch our variables at a moment in time, rather than to trace the process that emerges as we engage or observe. For this reason, until we develop the tools to multidimensionalize our observations, longitudinal case studies, sensitive to the life-span concept, are the most effective way to understand the interactional process.

It is difficult to conceptualize a visual analog that could capture the time dimension we have described for the three variables discussed. Leventhal, Leventhal, and Van Nguyen (1985) have attempted to do so in the form of a matrix, with systems (biological, psychological, and social) as the columns and illness phases as the rows. However, owing to the complexity of these "transactions" (a process linguistically evasive, given our unidimensional language limitations) the authors note that they:

> did not follow such a neat pattern as it is impossible to remain within the cells of such a matrix if one is discussing systems interactions. (p. 132)[1]

A 3-dimensional model that incorporates three developmental variables may challenge our temporal–interactional structuralization competency, but it is essential in order to render the microanalysis that will allow us to build the insights necessary to guide understanding and intervention.

The implications of this process-oriented transactional model can be illustrated best through a case study that represents how the developmental status of the patient and the family members interacts with the nature (chronicity and

---

[1]The role of sociocultural changes on the developmental process for families is dramatically illustrated by the increasing delay in childbearing that characterizes the 80s, resulting in new patterns and tasks. For example, adolescent conflicts over attachment and autonomy have traditionally occurred when the parent subsystem has matured, is cohesive and oriented toward mutual centrifugal and family-oriented activities. The older couple is, however, more likely to be invested in renegotiating intimacy and be absorbed in self and self–other activities, leaving little energy or patience for adolescent conflicts. The single-parent subsystem has received little investigation, and, as a characteristic constellation of our era, has enormous implications for the family life span and for the impact of illness.

severity) and status (diagnosis, crisis, termination) of the disease to complicate (or facilitate) adjustment and coping.

M. T., a beautiful 18-year-old, presented at the Pediatric Psychosocial Clinic, referred by her pediatrician, who had been treating her since the age of 6 months, when cystic fibrosis was diagnosed. At that time, her newly married mother and father had barely been able to move from self-discovery and mutual involvement before they were overwhelmed with the demands, both functional and emotional, of an infant with a major, chronic, and ultimately fatal illness.

The expectable and adaptive response to parenthood is a "mutuality of positive feelings." The potential for this to occur is dramatically challenged by the birth of a child with an eventually fatal illness. The first potential victim of this challenge is the parental subsystem. In this case, the baby's father became increasingly isolated, overwhelmed by the real and experienced distancing of his wife, whose energy was directed disproportionately to the physical needs of the baby, and by the narcissistic insult of fathering a baby whose genetic endowment, half his, was fatal. As the father pulled away, the mother turned increasingly to her extended family of origin, from whom she had only recently been able to separate. This mutual pulling away at a time when mutual nurturance was the primary task, served to intensify the mother/baby attachment, which became more and more enmeshed. M. T.'s father eventually abandoned the family, leaving the mother and child in a "mutually nurturant" relationship, as the infant (and later the child) replaced the father as mother's major attachment figure. To promote the distortion of roles further, the absence of a sibling subsystem, given the genetic nature of the disease and the decision not to have more children, heightened the imbalance, precluding the development of alternative subsystems, which are important for the facilitation of autonomous functions.

Although the earliest phase of the illness, with its initial shock, anger, denial, guilt, worry, and sadness caused a significant disruption of the family system, the reconstituted family was able to function relatively well, as the mother gained support from her family of origin and dealt with the financial strains by finding meaningful work. She reported that the ability to share the burden of the illness with her mother and sisters was the strategy that most facilitated her coping capacity during the early years of the child's illness. As Venters (1981) has noted in her discussion of family coping with cystic fibrosis, two strategies are reported by families as contributing most to their ability to maintain adaptive family functioning: 1) sharing the burden of the illness; and 2) endowing the illness with meaning. These coping strengths were maintained until the patient had to deal with a major developmental task that challenged both hers and the family's finely tuned balance. This task was separation, both emotional, and physical. As M. T. was age appropriately planning on going off to college, and as her mother became increasingly invested in developing a new relationship and relatively disconnecting from the mother/child dyad, the previously established balance became dramatically unbalanced, and M. T. began to fragment in a symptomatic representation of the breakdown of the system that had served to maintain her for so many years. The fragmentation took the form of panic attacks, leading her to leave college in her first semester and return home. The disruption had, however, created a fissure in the enmeshed and rigid system that had functioned adequately for years, and restructuring could only be accomplished through extended family and individual therapy.[2]

M. T. was able to work through her panic and later agoraphobia only by accomplishing the developmental tasks of identity formation and intimacy. To do this, she had to confront a number of terrifying issues: the relationship with a separate and independent adult who related on a mature and noninfantalizing level, the meaning and reality of her illness as only a piece of her identity rather than an external and hostile force, and her capacity to accept her "uniqueness" as a positive rather than negative element in a relationship. As these issues were confronted, M. T. entered a mutual relationship with a man whom she eventually married, and she began the tentative steps toward disconnecting from her family of origin, who had served literally as her life line. This challenge was the most difficult, as M. T. and her mother (who now lives one flight down in a two-flat building) struggle to achieve mutual validation in their own relatively independent domains.

It is crucial that families be helped to recognize not only how they are likely to be affected by the presence of a major illness, but also that their experience of the illness is a dynamic process that in many ways is predictable and potentially constructive. Researchers and clinicians in the field of health service have begun to recognize that dysfunctional reaction to primary illness is neither universal nor inevitable. The factors that serve to mediate between illness and adaptation have been conceptualized in a number of different ways—but one approach that has received little attention or exploration has been that of *active intervention.* When a family is helped to understand the complex dynamics underlying how and why they are experiencing the illness process in a particular way, they are better prepared to confront the trauma. These interventions are most effective when they are guided by knowledge of the potential of the family to either contain the trauma, or intensify it. This knowledge includes awareness, not only of the structure of the family, but also of its stage of development. Appropriate anticipatory guidance is often the most effective intervention health care workers can offer. In the case of M. T., sensitive attention to the marital dyad's conflicts over mutual dependency and isolation, and the difficult, but expectable, detour that a severely ill and abnormally demanding baby sets up might have served to prevent the breakdown of the family organization and the maladaptive replacement system. The family needs sensitive anticipatory guidance all along the

---

[2]The issues of separation need not be literal and physical. For children who have been protected in an enmeshed and rigidly protective dyad, particularly in single-parent families, a mother's adult romantic relationship or budding career may precipitate major anxiety or depression in one or both members of the dyad.

illness trajectory. This is true for children whose increased dependency demands are likely to exacerbate similar needs at different points in the marital dyad and in the sibling subsystem, as well as the extended generational families of origin, and also for adults.

The young adult who becomes ill and is forced to turn to the family of origin for disease-related caretaking, and who is prepared for feelings of outrage and of anger, is less likely to act out the hostility and conflict, which can often appear as withdrawal or noncompliance. The family of that young adult is normally, at this stage, moving into an increasingly externalized or centrifugal stage, with emphasis on developing their own lives, both together as a couple and individually in careers or nonfamily-related activities. The family may find itself fractious and conflictual when faced with the regressive pull. Preparation for that dystonic emotional response will deflect those responses, or at least the mystification and guilt that accompany them. The normal developmental dialectic of dependency and autonomy is particularly heightened by the appearance of serious illness in the young adult. This is nowhere more dramatic than in the occurrence of cancer, where recurrence and death are imminent threats. Although the young adult patient may sink into despondency exacerbated by the regressive pull toward dependency, individual family members' efforts to maintain their own integrity may stir feelings of abandonment in other family members. Sensitivity of the health provider to these family issues can serve to modify the intensity of conflict through explanation, understanding, and support.

Underlying the issues presented in this chapter is the concept of a dynamic process that defines the interaction among developing forces, specifically the family, the individual, and the illness. A developmental perspective accompanies a transactional orientation to illustrate the complex relationship between these domains. Once the developmental trajectory of each unit is grasped, the challenge is to recognize the ways in which they interact to create conflict and to construct adaptation. Although other forces, such as social and cultural systems, personality, and emotional characteristics, and the vagaries of human interactions, must also be recognized as contributors to this dynamic the expectable and predictable life course is a common denominator that offers a solid ground on which we can base certain expectancies that will guide our understanding and assistance to those families confronted with the trauma of chronic or debilitating illness.

REFERENCES

Anderson, B. J., & Auslander, W. F. (1980). Research on diabetes management and the family: A critique. *Diabetes Care, 3,* 696–702.

Anderson, B. J., Miller, J. P., Auslander, W. F., & Santiago, J. V. (1981). Family characteristics of diabetic adolescents: Relationship to metabolic control. *Diabetes Care, 4,* 586–599.

Beavers, W. R. (1982). Healthy, midrange and severely dysfunctional families. In F. Walsh (Ed.), *Normal Family Processes.* New York: Guilford.

Ben-Sira, Z. (1977). Involvement with a disease and health promoting behavior. *Social Science & Medicine, 11,* 167–173.

Berkman, L. F., & Syme, S. L. (1979). Social networks, host resistance, and mortality: A 9 year follow-up of Alameda County residents. *American Journal of Epidemiology, 109*(2), 186–204.

Berle, B. B., Pinsky, R. H., Wolf, S. O., & Wolff, H. G. (1952). A clinical guide to prognosis in stress disease. *Journal of American Medical Association, 149,* 1624–1628.

Boyle, I. R., Di Sant'Agnes, P. A., Sack, S., Millican, F., & Kulczycki, L. L. (1976). Emotional adjustment of adolescents and young adults with cystic fibrosis. *Journal of Pediatrics, 88*(2), 318–326.

Brown, S. L. (1980) The developmental cycle of families: Clinical impressions. *Psychiatric Clinics of North America, 3*(3), 369–381.

Chen, E., & Cobb, S. (1960). Family structure in relation to health and disease: A review of the literature. *Journal of Chronic Disease, 12*(5), 544–567.

Combrinck-Graham, L. (1983). The family life cycle and families with young children. In H. Liddle (Ed.), *Clinical implications of the family life cycle* (pp. 35–53). Rockville, MD: Aspen.

Cronkite, R. C., & Moos, R. H. (1984). The role of predisposing and moderating factors in the stress-illness relationship. *Journal of Health & Social Behavior, 25,* 372–393.

Czajkowski, D. R., & Koocher, G. P. (1987). Medical compliance and coping with cystic fibrosis. *Journal of Child Psychiatry and Psychology, 2,* 311–319.

De Araujo, G., Van Arsdel, P. P., Holmes, T. H., & Dudley, D. L. (1973). Life change, coping ability and chronic intrinsic asthma. *Journal of Psychosomatic Research, 17,* 359–363.

Dent, O., & Goulston, K. (1982). A short scale of cancer knowledge and some sociodemographic correlates. *Social Science & Medicine, 16,* 235–240.

Di Matteo, M. R., & Hays, R. (1981). Social support and serious illness. In B. Gottlieb (Ed.), *Social networks and social support.* Newbury Park, CA: Sage.

Dohrenwend, B. S., & Dohrenwend, B. P. (1981). Socioenvironmental factors, stress and psychopathology. *American Journal of Community Psychology, 9,* 128–164.

Drotar, D., Doershuk, C. F., Stern, R. C., Boat, T. F., Boyer, W., & Matthews, L. (1981). Psychosocial functioning of children with cystic fibrosis. *Pediatrics, 67*(3), 338–342.

Engel, G. (1977). The need for a new medical model: A challenge for biomedicine. *Science, 196,* 129–136.

Erikson, E. H. (1959). Identity and the life cycle: Selected papers. *Psychological Issues, 1*(1), 1–171.

Gortmaker, S. L., Walker, D. K., Weitzman, M., & Sobel, A. M. (1990). Chronic conditions, socioeconomic risks and behavioral problems in children and adolescents. *Pediatrics, 85*(3), 267–276.

Haley, J. (1973). *Uncommon therapy: The psychiatric techniques of Milton H. Erickson, M. D.* New York: Norton.

Hanson, C. L., Henggeler, S. W., Harris, M. A., Burghen, G. A., & Moore, M. (1989). Family system variables and the health status of adolescents with insulin dependent diabetes mellitus. *Health Psychology, 8*(2), 239–253.

Holahan, C. J., & Moos, R. H. (1987). Risk, resistance and psychological distress: A longitudinal analysis with adults and children. *Journal of Abnormal Psychology, 96*(1), 3–13.

Hurtig, A. L., Koepke, D., & Park, K. B. (1989). Relation between severity of chronic illness and adjustment in children and adolescents with sickle cell disease. *Journal of Pediatric Psychology, 14*(1), 117–132.

Hurtig, A. L., & Medenis, R. (1990, May). Cystic fibrosis: A comparative study of emotionally disturbed and well-adjusted adolescents. Poster presentation, *Society of Pediatric Psychology,* 3rd Regional Conference, Detroit, Michigan.

Hurtig, A. L., & Park, K. B. (1989). Adjustment and coping in adolescents with sickle cell disease. *Annals of the New York Academy of Sciences, 565,* 172–182.

Hurtig, A. L., & Rosenthal, I. M. (1987). Psychological findings in early treated cases of female pseudohermaphroditism caused by virilizing congenital adrenal hyperplasia. *Archives of Sexual Behavior, 16*(3), 209–223.

Kaplan, D. M., Smith, A., Grobstein, R., & Fischman, S. E. (1977). Family mediation of stress. In R. H. Moos (Ed.), *Coping with physical illness.* New York: Plenum.

Kellerman, J., Zeltzer, I., Ellenberg, L., et al. (1980). Psychosocial effects of illness in adolescents: I. Anxiety, self-esteem and perception of control. *Journal of Pediatrics, 97*(1), 126–131.

Kety, S. (1974). From rationalization to reason. *American Journal of Psychiatry, 131,* 957.

Kupst, M., Schulman, J., Honig, G., Maurer, H., Morgan, E., & Fochtman, D. (1982). Family coping with childhood leukemia: One year after diagnosis. *Journal of Pediatric Psychology, 7,* 157–174.

Lawler, R., Nakielny, W., & Wright, N. (1966). Psychological implications of cystic fibrosis. *Canadian Medical Association Journal, 94,* 1043–1046.

Leventhal, H., Leventhal, E. A., & Van Nguyen, T. (1985). Reactions of families to illness. Theoretical models and perspectives. In D. C. Turk & R. D. Kerns (Eds.), *Health, illness, and families.* New York: Wiley.

Lewis, B. L., & Khaw, K. (1982). Family functioning as a mediating variable affecting psychosocial adjustment of children with cystic fibrosis. *Journal of Pediatrics, 101*(4), 636–648.

Marteau, T. M., Block, S., & Baum, J. D. (1987). Family life and diabetic control. *Journal of Child Psychology & Psychiatry, 28,* 823–833.

Masters, J., Ceneto, M., & Mendlowiz, D. M. (1983). The role of the family in coping with childhood chronic illness. In T. Burish & L. Bradley (Eds.), *Coping with chronic illness: Research and applications.* New York: Academic.

Mattson, A. (1972). Long term physical illness in childhood: A challenge to psychosocial adaptation. *Journal of Pediatrics, 50,* 801–805.

McCubbin, H. I., Joy, C., Cauble, A. E., Comeau, J. K., Patterson, J. I., & Needle, R. H. (1980). Family stress and coping: A decade review. *Journal of Marriage and the Family, 42,* 855–871.

Minuchin, P. (1988). Relationships within the family: A systems perspective in development. In R. A. Hinde & J. Stevenson Hinde (Eds.), *Relationships within families: Mutual influences.* Oxford, England: Clarendon Press.

Minuchin, S., Baker, L., Rosman, B., Liebman, R., Milman, L., & Todd, T. (1975). A conceptual model of psychosomatic illness in children. *Archives of General Psychiatry, 32,* 1031–1038.

Minuchin, S., Rosman, B., & Baker, L. (1978). *Psychosomatic families.* Cambridge, MA: Harvard University Press.

Neugarten, B. (1970) Dynamics of transition of middle age to old age: Adaptation and the life cycle. *Journal of Genetic Psychiatry, 4,* 71–87.

Orr, D. P., Weller, S. C., Satterwhite, B., & Pless, I. B. (1984). Psychosocial implications of chronic illness in adolescence. *Journal of Pediatrics, 104,* 252–257.

Pless, I. B., & Roghmann, K. J. (1971). Chronic illness and its consequences: Observations based on an epidemiologic survey. *Journal of Pediatrics, 79*(3), 351–359.

Pless, I. B., Roghmann, K., Haggerty, R. J. (1972). Chronic illness, family functioning and psychological adjustment. *International Journal of Epidemiology, 1*(3), 271–277.

Rabkin, J. G. (1980). Stressful life events and schizophrenia: A review of the research literature. *Psychological Bulletin, 87,* 407–425.

Robertson, E. K., & Suinn, R. M. (1968). The determination of rate of progress of stroke patients through empathy measures of patient and family. *Journal of Psychosomatic Research, 12,* 189–191.

Rolland, J. S. (1988). Family systems and chronic illness: A topological model. In F. Walsh, & C. Anderson (Eds.), *Chronic disorders and the family.* New York: Haworth.

Shapiro, J. (1983). Family reactions and coping strategies in response to the physically ill or handicapped child: A review. *Social Science Medicine, 17*(14), 913–931.

Simmons, R., Rosenberg, F., & Rosenberg, M. (1973). Disturbance in the self-image at adolescence. *American Sociological Review, 38,* 553–568.

Spinetta, J., & Maloney, L. (1978), The child with cancer: Patterns of communication and denial. *Journal of Consulting and Clinical Psychology, 46,* 1540–1541.

Stein, R., & Jessop, D. (1984). Relationship between health status and psychological adjustment among children with chronic conditions. *Pediatrics, 73*(2), 169–174.

Tietz, W., & Vidmar, J. T. (1972). The impact of coping styles on the control of juvenile diabetes. *Psychiatry in Medicine, 3,* 67–75.

Varni, J. W., Wilcox, K. T., & Hanson, V. (1988). Mediating effects of family social support on child psychological adjustment in juvenile rheumatoid arthritis. *Health Psychology, 7*(5), 421–431.

Venters, M. (1981). Familial coping with chronic and severe childhood illness: The case of cystic fibrosis. *Social Science Medicine, 15A,* 289–297.

Wallender, J. L., Varni, J. W., Babani, L., Banis, H. T., & Wilcox, K. T. (1989). Family resources as resistance factors for psychological maladjustment in chronically ill and handicapped children. *Journal of Pediatric Psychology, 14*(2), 157–173.

Weisman, A. D., & Worden, J. W. (1975). Psychosocial analysis of cancer deaths. *Omega, 6*(1), 61–75.

Zeltzer, L., Kellerman, J., Ellenberg, L., Dash, J., & Rigler, D. (1980). Psychologic effects of illness in adolescence. II. Impact of illness in adolescents: Crucial issues and coping styles. *Journal of Pediatrics, 97*(1), 132–138.

CHAPTER 14

Physical Abuse

ILEANA ARIAS and KAREN TAYLOR PAPE

Medical and mental health professionals gave little empirical attention to intra-family violence until the 1960s. Publication of an article on the battered child syndrome by Kempe, Silverman, Steele, Droegmueller, and Silver in 1962 drew immediate interest and marked the beginning of empirical efforts to establish the prevalence and etiology of intrafamily violence in our society. During the 1960s, much of this work was limited to investigations of child abuse. In response to findings of widespread child abuse among American families, family researchers extended their focus and began to examine violence among other family units. An unprecedented level of attention to marital violence emerged during the 1970s, followed by examinations of dating or courtship violence and, most recently, elder abuse.

Although the empirical literature on intrafamily violence is relatively exten-sive, there is no unifying theory or theoretical framework to guide research activity or organize existing empirical findings. Lack of consensus on the defini-tions of intrafamily "violence," "abuse," or "aggression" is a major impediment to the theoretical consolidation of research findings. Typically, child abuse, spouse abuse, or elder abuse are defined as situations in which physically violent acts are committed by an individual against a family member (Gelles & Straus, 1979). In turn, violent acts are defined as those that are carried out with an actual or perceived intent of causing physical pain or injury to another. However, there is controversy among professionals regarding the severity of inflicted harm required to label violent behavior as abusive. Likewise, there is no consensus regarding whether or not negligence, psychological or verbal assaults, and vio-lence committed in self-defense are abusive.

For the present purposes, we have adopted the following definition of intra-family physical abuse: the commission of physically violent acts. Although not totally inclusive of potentially abusive situations in the family across the life cycle, this is the standard definition most frequently used in empirical research on intrafamily violence. In this chapter, we cover the research on prevalence and correlates of physical abuse, as defined above, during childhood, adolescence and young adulthood, adulthood, and late adulthood.

CHILD ABUSE

Prevalence

The use of physical force as child discipline is widely accepted in our society. Straus, Gelles, and Steinmetz (1980) found that 77% of parents felt that slapping and spanking are appropriate punishment for a 12-year-old, whereas 71% of parents thought it was, in fact, good to use these forms of discipline. Men were more likely to view slapping and spanking as appropriate than were women, and younger parents approved of this form of discipline more than older parents (Straus et al., 1980). Such acceptance should engender disinhibition among parents. Indeed, the most recent representative nationwide survey of violence in the family conducted by Straus and Gelles (1986) found that approximately 62% of parents reported at least one incidence of violence during the year preceding the survey. Although milder forms of violence, such as slapping, spanking, pushing, shoving, throwing an object at a child, or hitting the child with an object were most frequently reported, approximately 11% of parents reported committing more severe forms of violence, such as kicking, biting, punching, beating, threatening a child with a knife or gun, or using a knife or gun against a child. The prevalence of child abuse among ethnic minority families has been found to differ significantly from that of anglo, nonminority families. Although Hampton, Gelles, and Harrop (1989) found that the prevalence of overall parent-to-child violence among anglo families and African American families did not differ, significant differences were found in the prevalence rates of severe violence. Approximately 65% of parents in both groups reported engaging in some form of violence against a child during the year prior to the assessment, while approximately 10% of anglo parents and 22% of African American parents reported engaging in at least one act of severe violence. Similarly, although the prevalence rates of overall violence in anglo and Hispanic American families did not differ, Straus (1987) found a small but significant difference in the rates of severe violence. Approximately 10% of nonHispanic, anglo parents reported engaging in severe violence against a child, while 13% of Hispanic American parents reported using severe violence against a child. Although ethnic minority families seem to differ from anglo families on the prevalence of severe physical child abuse, they also differ on a number of socioeconomic factors found to be related to child abuse. However, studies examining ethnic differences in the occurrence of child abuse have not controlled for the potential influence of socioeconomic variation on variation in prevalence across ethnic groups.

With the exception of being threatened with or having a parent use a weapon, children seem to be victims of *repeated* violence during any given year (Straus et al., 1980). Although fathers seem more likely than mothers to report threats of using a weapon or the actual use of a knife or gun against a child, mothers seem more likely than fathers to employ other forms of violence. Sons have been found more likely to be victims of physical abuse than daughters (Straus et al., 1980), and younger children, particularly under the age of six, are more likely to be abused than older children (Gil, 1979; Straus et al., 1980). The gender differences in rates of victimization were found to increase as the severity of the violence increased.

Socioeconomic Factors

Although violence against children crosses all socioeconomic boundaries, child abuse seems to be more prevalent among families in lower socioeconomic strata. Families living below the poverty level have been found to employ twice as much violence toward their children as those who were the most "well-to-do" (Straus et al., 1980). Similarly, the rate of violence against children seems to be twice as high in blue collar than in white collar families (Straus et al., 1980), and the occupational status of abusive parents has been found to be lower than that of the general population (Gil, 1971).

Unemployed fathers and fathers employed part-time are more likely to abuse their children physically than fathers employed full time (Light, 1973; Straus et al., 1980). Mothers employed outside the home have been found less likely to be violent against their children than mothers not employed outside the home (Hargreaves, 1987). Thus, it seems that children may be at increased risk for abuse when parents are financially stressed, spend extended periods of time with them, and are deprived of opportunities for diversion and social support that may be provided by the work environment.

Violence against children is more common among young parents; that is, under 30 years (Straus et al., 1980), and it occurs more frequently among parents with nonmainstream religious affiliations. As mentioned above, although anglo and African American parents do not differ in their use of violence overall, African American parents are at higher risk for engaging in severe violence. Johnson and Showers (1985) found that African American children were more likely to have been struck with a belt, strap, or cord, and they were more likely to have been knifed or burned with an iron than anglo children. On the other hand, anglo children were more likely to have been struck with a board or paddle, or to have been hit with an open hand.

Family Composition and Structure

Single parenthood has been associated with abuse, and children are somewhat more likely to experience violence in homes where there is an unequal distribution of power between parents (Straus et al., 1980). Abuse may increase with the appearance of additional dependent children (Gelles & Straus, 1979; Straus et al.). This trend seems to hold true until the number of dependent children reaches about five. Thereafter, rates of violence begin to diminish, and they suddenly drop to no occurrence of violence in families with eight or more children (Straus et al.). However, Straus et al. found that, although the presence of each additional child increased the probability of abuse up to a point, this was true only for poor and disadvantaged families. Child abuse consistently has been associated with family isolation, and low rates of abuse have been associated with extensive social support networks (Disbrow, Doerr, & Caulfield, 1977; Garbarino & Sherman, 1980; Oates, Davis, Ryan, & Stewart, 1979).

Intrapersonal Characteristics of Abusers

Numerous intrapersonal characteristics of abusive parents have been examined. Various studies suggest that abusers are emotionally disturbed (Elmer, 1967), rigid and domineering (Johnson & Morse, 1968), angry, easily threatened, fearful of external control (Spinetta, 1978), and low in self-esteem (Anderson & Lauderdale, 1982; Spinetta & Rigler, 1972). Other studies have found child abuse to be associated with alcoholism (Blumberg, 1964), depression (Lahey, Conger, Atkeson, & Treiber, 1984), and a constant state of arousal in response to a variety of child behaviors (Wolfe, Fairbank, Kelly, & Bradlyn, 1983), particularly crying (Frodi & Lamb, 1980).

Earlier studies reported that only a small percentage of abusers were themselves abused in childhood (Gil, 1971; Silver, Dublin, & Lourie, 1969). However, Herrenkohl, Herrenkohl, and Toedter (1983) found that a larger percentage of abusers than nonabusers, 56% versus 38%, respectively, had been abused in childhood. In their nationally representative example, Straus et al. (1980) found a significant relationship between the experience of physical discipline in childhood and the use of ordinary and severe violence in adulthood. That is, the more parents had been physically punished in childhood, the more likely they were to engage in pushing, slapping, shoving, throwing objects at their child, beating, kicking, biting, and threatening with or using a knife or gun against their child.

Other intrapersonal variables have been studied but, in general, results have not been significant. Most studies have found no differences between abusers and nonabusers on psychoticism (cf. Spinetta & Rigler, 1972), IQ (Starr, 1982), negative perceptions about the child (Rosenberg & Reppucci, 1983; Starr, 1982), developmental expectations (Gaines, Sandgrund, Green, & Power, 1978; Spinetta, 1978; Starr, 1982), or attitudes towards discipline and childrearing (Rosenblatt, 1980).

Characteristics of Abused Children

Numerous child characteristics have been investigated as potential correlates of abuse. Characteristics include the child's age, gender, whether the child was wanted, prematurity, low birth weight, perinatal problems, general health status, birth defects, and temperament. Studies suggest that unwanted children (Berger, 1978; Weinstock, Tietze, Jaffe, & Dryfoos, 1976), younger, male children (Gil, 1979; Straus et al., 1980), and physically handicapped children (American Humane Association, 1985) are at higher risk for child abuse.

Concerning prematurity, perinatal problems, and general health status, research findings are equivocal. Some researchers have found prematurity to place a child at risk for abuse (Herrenkohl & Herrenkohl, 1979; Lynch & Roberts, 1977), whereas other researchers have found no association between prematurity and abuse (Corey, Miller, & Widlack, 1975; Holman & Kanwar, 1975; Starr, 1982). Assessing the relationship between low birth weight, a frequent correlate of prematurity, and abuse, Stern (1979) found that low birth weight infants were more than three times as likely to be battered than normal weight infants. Some investigators have found an association between perinatal problems and abuse (Holman & Kanwar, 1975; Lynch, 1975; Lynch & Roberts, 1977; Nakou, Adam, Stathacopoulou, & Agathonos, 1982) whereas others have failed to find such an association (Benedict, White, & Cornerly, 1985; Gaines et al., 1978; Starr, 1982). Lynch and Sherrod, O'Conner, Vietz, and Altemeier (1984) found evidence for an association between a child's general health status and abuse, but others have not (Starr et al., 1982). Finally, the empirical literature fails to support the notion that either birth defects (Herrenkohl & Herrenkohl, 1979; Starr) or child temperament (Starr) are significantly related to abuse.

Parent–Child Interaction

Abusive families have been characterized by more negative and less positive interactions among their members (Burgess & Conger, 1978). More specifically, abusive parents have been found to exhibit relational deficits (Dietrich, Starr, & Weisfeld, 1983; Herrenkohl, Herrenkohl, Toedter, & Yanushefiski, 1984) and to exhibit more aversive and fewer prosocial behaviors (cf. Wolfe, 1985). Abused children have been found to touch their parents less often than other family members touch them (Burgess & Conger) and to exhibit fewer positive and more aggressive behavior than nonabused children (Bousha & Twentyman, 1984). Abused children's aggressive behavior has been found to be directed toward other adults, as well as toward family members (Bousha & Twentyman; George & Main, 1979; Herrenkohl et al., 1984).

Effects

With the exception of physical injury, the effects of child abuse on children's development and functioning have not been firmly established. Nonetheless, numerous researchers have found a number of cognitive, socioemotional, and behavioral problems associated with abuse. Cognitive deficits include decreased scores on a variety of measures of intellectual functioning (Allen & Wasserman, 1985; Friedrich, Einbender, & Luecke, 1983; Koski & Ingram, 1977), retardation (Buchanan & Oliver, 1977; Sandgrund, Gaines, & Green, 1974), poor school performance (Kent, 1976), and deficiencies in language development and communication (Appelbaum, 1977; Friedrich et al.).

A wide variety of deficits in socioemotional behavior have also been found to be associated with abuse. Abused children have been found to be deficient in social cognition and social competency (Barahal, Waterman, & Martin, 1981; Camras, Grow, & Ribordy, 1983), to be immature and exhibit a decreased readiness to learn (Hoffman-Plotkin & Twentyman, 1984), to be sad, unhappy, and depressed (Green, 1978; Kinard, 1980), to be hyperactive and anxious (Wolfe & Mosk, 1983), and aggressive (George & Main, 1979; Green, 1978; Wolfe & Mosk, 1983). Abused elementary school children have been described as unpopular, poorly behaved, lacking a clear sense of identity, and having difficulty socializing with peers, establishing trust in others, and separating from their mothers (Kinard). Interpersonally, abused toddlers have been found to respond to the distress of peers with aggression, fear, and anger; whereas, nonabused toddlers responded to peers' distress with concern (Main & George, 1985). Furthermore, abused toddlers have been found to react to friendly overtures with avoidance and approach–avoidance responses (George & Main).

Individuals abused as children have often been involved in criminal behavior, violent relationships, and child abuse. In a 40-year longitudinal study, McCord (1983) found higher rates of juvenile delinquency and convictions for serious crime in abused boys than in nonabused boys. Upon closer examination, Smith, Bohnstedt, and Grove (1982) found that victims of abuse and controls were equally likely to be arrested, when both were of low socioeconomic status; however, victims of abuse were more likely than controls to be arrested when both were in the middle socioeconomic status.

SIBLING AND PARENTAL ABUSE

There is relatively little empirical work examining the prevalence, etiology, and consequences of sibling abuse and parental abuse. The available data indicate that both forms of intrafamily violence are fairly common. However, children's physical aggression typically is not expected to result in significant physical or psychological harm. Perhaps assumptions about the benign nature of children's violence have impeded further empirical scrutiny.

Sibling Abuse

The most comprehensive empirical account of sibling abuse resulted from the national survey conducted by Straus and his colleagues in 1975 (Straus et al., 1980). Approximately 82% of children between the ages of 3 and 17 were reported to have engaged in some form of violence against a sibling, while 16% were reported "beating up" a brother or sister during the year prior to the survey. According to these data, sibling abuse is the most frequent form of intrafamily violence in America. Compared to the 16% of children who beat up a sibling, only 1% of parents beat up their children, and only 1% of parents beat up a spouse (Straus et al.). Straus et al. found that older children engaged in less violence than younger ones. In all age groups, boys were more likely to abuse siblings physically than girls, and the highest levels of abuse occurred in families with male children only. Furthermore, there was a significant relationship between parental physical punishment and sibling abuse: the more violent parents are to a child, the more violent that child is to his or her siblings.

Parental Abuse

Eighteen percent of children between the ages of 3 and 17 have engaged in some form of violence against a parent (Straus et al., 1980). Gelles and Cornell (1987) confined their analyses of the national survey data to adolescents (age 10–17) and found that 9% engaged in some form of violence, while 3% engaged in severe violence, ranging from punching and kicking to the use of weapons. Although 11% of sons and 7% of daughters were violent with a parent, the gender difference was not statistically significant. Similarly, there was no association between age and violence among adolescents, perhaps because of the restricted age range. As previously reported with smaller samples (Warren, 1978), mothers were more likely to be the victims of overall and severe violence, and parental abuse was significantly related to child abuse and spouse abuse (Gelles & Cornell). That is, adolescents who were abused by their parents and/or had observed spouse abuse in the home were more likely to abuse their parents, than adolescents from nonviolent homes. Traditional correlates of child and spouse abuse, such as family socioeconomic status, stress, race, and family power structure were not found to be related to adolescent-to-parent violence.

DATING VIOLENCE

Prevalence

Violence has been found to occur in a substantial proportion of dating relationships, with estimates ranging from 20% to 50% (cf. Arias & Johnson, 1989). Although milder forms of violence, such as pushing and shoving, are the most common, extreme forms, such as choking and threats or assault with an object or weapon have been noted also (Cate, Henton, Koval, Christopher, & Lloyd, 1982; Henton, Cate, Koval, Lloyd, & Christopher, 1983). Violence has been shown to occur on multiple occasions in more than half the cases (Makepeace, 1981), and most forms of violence have occurred on at least two occasions for the majority of those involved (Henton et al.). Most studies indicate that violence is most likely to occur when relationships become more serious (Arias, Samios, & O'Leary, 1987; Cate et al.; Henton et al.), with *seriousness* variously defined in terms of relationship duration, frequency of contact, and degree of exclusivity, intimacy, and commitment.

Results of investigations of gender differences in dating violence are mixed. Three studies have found males more likely to be the perpetrators and females the recipients of violence (Makepeace, 1981, 1983; Yllo & Straus, 1981); however, numerous studies have found similar rates of perpetration and victimization for both genders (Arias et al., 1987; Bernard & Bernard, 1983; Cate et al., 1982; Henton et al., 1983). Comparisons of male and female perpetration and victimization, and the resulting findings, are highly debatable. The controversy centers on the operational definitions of the two constructs. Most researchers define perpetration according to either self- or other-reports of the number of violent acts an individual committed. This definition does not take into account the physical or psychological effects of the violence experienced or whether it occurred in self-defense. Thus, for example, a male who is hit or bitten by his girlfriend after he grabs her and proceeds to choke her may be classified as a "victim," while she may be classified as a "perpetrator" of dating violence.

Investigators in the field (Bograd, 1988) have argued that studies showing equal rates of perpetration and victimization are misleading. It has been suggested that dating partners be asked information other than frequency of behaviors enacted and received—such as severity of the behavior, injuries sustained or inflicted, and perceptions of their role in the altercation—in order to classify and describe dating violence accurately. Indeed, males have been found to use more severe levels of violence (Makepeace, 1983) than females, and females have sustained more severe levels of violence than males (Makepeace, 1986). Females were found to perceive their use of violence as *defense,* whereas males perceived their use of violence as *intimidation* (Makepeace, 1986). In addition, although males and females actually may be the recipients of violence as frequently, females reported sustaining physical injury and emotional trauma (Makepeace, 1986) and feelings of anger, hurt, and fear (Matthews, 1984) more often than males.

Characteristics of Dating Violence

Level of Involvement

Surprisingly, many of those experiencing dating relationship violence report increased involvement and relationship improvement following the occurrence of violence. Makepeace (1981) found that 15.8% of those involved in dating relationship violence remained involved to the same extent, whereas 28.9% reported becoming even more deeply involved. Matthews (1984) reported that 26% of both males and females reported no change in the relationship following violence, but 43% reported that the relationship had actually improved. Lo and Sporakowski (1989) found that among those experiencing abuse, 76.8% planned to continue the relationship, and 33.8% anticipated that the relationship would culminate in marriage.

Love

Not only is violence associated with deeper levels of involvement for some dating partners, violence has also been found to be associated with love. Matthews (1984) found that approximately 28% of both males and females interpreted violence as evidence of love. This lends support to an earlier report by Cate et al. (1982), who found that most individuals involved in dating relationship violence felt angry (73%) and confused (49%), but many also interpreted the violence as love (28.9%). In examining the meaning of relationship violence among high school students, Henton et al. (1983) found that, although anger and confusion were most often reported, love was reported by 26.5% of the victims and 31.3% of the aggressors.

Attributions of Blame and Responsibility

Although research shows that both males and females involved in dating relationship violence report feeling responsible, females may be particularly vulnerable to accepting responsibility for violent interaction. Supporting the notion of joint responsibility, Henton et al. (1983) found that 48.7% of high school students involved in relationship violence reported feeling equally responsible for the initiation of violence. A finer analysis conducted by Matthews (1984) utilizing a sample of college students, however, suggests that, although both males and females tended to view themselves as at least partially responsible for violence initiation, females were more likely to perceive themselves as solely responsible.

SPOUSE ABUSE

Prevalence

Results of the nationwide study of family violence conducted by Straus et al. in 1975 (Straus et al., 1980) shocked professional and lay circles by showing that approximately 28% of married couples experienced physical violence at sometime during the course of their marriage, and 16% experienced violence during the single year preceding the study. Mild forms of violence, such as pushing, grabbing, shoving, and slapping occurred more frequently than severe forms, such as kicking, choking, beating, and use of weapons (Straus et al.). Violence between spouses typically was not reported as an everyday occurrence but, having once occurred, it was often repeated and increased in intensity and frequency over time (Straus et al.).

In their second national survey 10 years later, Straus and Gelles (1986) found little change in the prevalence of violence among American couples. Approximately 15% of anglo respondents reported the occurrence of some form of violence during the year prior to the assessment, with 5% reporting severe violence. As previously found, there were elevated rates of violence among African American couples relative to anglo couples—25% of African Americans reported engaging in some form of violence, and 13% reported engaging in severe violence (Hampton et al., 1989). Hispanic American families, relative to anglo families, were characterized by higher levels of spouse abuse as well—23% and 11% of Hispanic American respondents reported engaging in some form of violence and in severe violence, respectively, during the year preceding the survey

(Straus, 1987). In all cases, throwing an object at the other, pushing, grabbing, shoving, and slapping were the most common forms of violence.

Rates of violence were comparable for men and women across subsamples, with the exception of the African American subsample. Among anglo families, 11% of male and 12% of female respondents reported engaging in some form of violence against their partners, and 3% and 4% of male and female respondents, respectively, reported engaging in severe violence (Hampton et al., 1989). Among Hispanic American families, 17% of male and female respondents and 7% of male and 8% of female respondents reported the use of violence overall and the use of severe violence, respectively (Straus, 1987). However, 17% of African American men and 20% of women reported engaging in some form of violence against their partners while 6% of men and 11% of women reported the use of severe violence (Hampton et al.).

Again, caution is recommended in comparing prevalence rates of violence among men and women. As is the case in research on dating violence, marital violence researchers often ignore factors such as initiation, frequency, inflicted harm, and intent to harm. Hence, although comparable percentages of anglo and Hispanic American men and women are physically aggressive toward their partners, it is not clear that anglo and Hispanic American men and women are equally "abusive." Similarly, although slightly greater percentages of African American women relative to men are physically aggressive toward their partners, it is not clear that they are more "abusive."

Sociocultural Factors

Spouse abuse has been found to occur in all ages, races, religions, and income and educational levels, but it seems more likely to occur in some groups than others. Violence has been shown to be more common among young spouses (Pagelow, 1981; Straus et al., 1980) and among those with low occupational status and income (Gelles & Cornell, 1985; Straus, et al.). Wife battering is likely when husbands are unemployed or dissatisfied with their jobs (Straus et al.). Higher rates of violence have also been shown to be associated with education—the most educated are the least likely to be involved in violent marital relationships (Straus et al., 1980). Rates of violence are highest for men and women who report no religious affiliation and lowest in families where the husband is Jewish (Straus et al., 1980). High rates of violence have also been found when husbands are members of nonmainstream religious groups (Straus et al.).

Intrapersonal Correlates of Marital Violence

In addition to demographic variables such as age, race, religion, income, and educational level, researchers have found contextual, intrapersonal, and interpersonal correlates. Spouse abuse has been found to be related to alcohol and drug use and abuse (Fagan, Stewart, & Hansen, 1983; Fitch & Papantonio, 1983), social isolation (Pagelow, 1981), violence in the family of origin (Kalmuss, 1984; Malone, Tyree, & O'Leary, 1989), number of dependent children, and stressful events (Straus et al.). More specifically, violence increases relative to increases in life stressors. Such life stressors include work, sexual problems, death, pregnancy, and increase in the number of dependent children (Straus et al., 1980). However, as is the case in child abuse, the relationship between violence and number of dependent children holds only to a point. With six or more children, reports of violence suddenly become nonexistent (Straus et al.). Pregnancy was thought to increase the risk for wife battering significantly (Helton, 1986; Sammons, 1981). However, Gelles (1988) recently reported that, although pregnant women, in fact, experienced greater rates of minor, severe, and overall violence, the relationship between pregnancy and violence disappeared after controlling for age. Gelles concluded that women under 25 years are more likely to be pregnant *and* to be abused by their partners.

Intrapersonal variables have been noted for both abusers and abused. In general, abusive men have been found to have low self-esteem (Goldstein & Rosenbaum, 1985), to be unassertive with their spouses (Rosenbaum & O'Leary, 1981), to be low in masculinity (La Violette, Barnett, & Miller, 1984), to blame others for their actions, to be pathologically jealous, to use sex as an act of aggression (Walker, 1979), and to be violent with others as well as with their partners (Fagan et al., 1983). Committing violence has also been found to be associated with abusers' beliefs and attitudes. Abusers have been found to have rigid, traditional sex role attitudes (Rosenbaum & O'Leary; Telch & Lindquist, 1984), and to believe that their behavior should not be viewed negatively (Walker, 1979). Violent husbands have also been found to express greater approval of violence than do nonviolent husbands (Straus, 1980).

Specific intrapersonal variables have been associated with being the victim of violence. For instance, abused women have been shown to hold traditional beliefs about sex roles (Dobash & Dobash, 1979), to accept responsibility for their abusers' actions (Andrews & Brewin, 1990), to feel helpless and hopeless (Walker, 1979), and to express more approval of violence than nonabused wives (Straus, 1980; Straus et al., 1980). Furthermore, abused women have been found to rely on sex as a way to establish intimacy (Walker, 1979), to be low in self-esteem (Star, Clark, Goetz, & O'Malia, 1979; Walker, 1979), high in depression and anxiety, and to have elevated MMPI profiles (Hughes & Rau, 1984; Telch & Lindquist, 1984). It is not clear, however, whether these characteristics are antecedents or consequences of abuse.

Interpersonal Correlates of Spouse Abuse

Interpersonal variables associated with spouse abuse include poor communication, interpersonal conflict, psychological aggression, and allocation of couple decision-making responsibilities. Walker (1979) found that communication between partners involved in violence was characterized by distortion, misinterpretation, and indirect expression of feelings. Margolin, John, and Gleberman

(1988) found that violent spouses, especially violent husbands, show greater negative affect and arousal, and greater reciprocity of negative affect during conflictual discussions than nonviolent spouses. Rates of violence have been shown to increase with increased levels of interpersonal conflict and decreased relationship satisfaction (O'Leary & Curley, 1986). Conflict over child-related issues seems to be particularly important (Straus et al., 1980). Violence is also more likely when decision-making power is solely in the hands of the husband, and it is least likely in democratic homes (Straus et al.). However, violence is more likely among couples where decisions are made jointly by husbands and wives, thus increasing the likelihood of conflictual interactions, rather than when husbands make some of the decisions and wives make other decisions independently (Straus et al.).

Consequences

Although both husbands and wives commit and receive violence, research on the consequences of abuse has been limited to the consequences to victims, and consequences to abusers have been largely ignored. Furthermore, research has consistently focused on the consequences to female victims because it is expected that they would experience more severe consequences than male victims. Men, relative to women, have the potential to cause more damage, to protect themselves more effectively from harm, and to escape an abusive attack more easily because of their size and strength advantages (Straus et al., 1980). Negative consequences of spouse abuse to women include physical injury (Fagan et al., 1983; Goldberg & Tomlanovich, 1984; Straus, 1986), divorce (Levinger, 1966), increased risk for suicide (Carmen, Reiker, & Mills, 1984; Stark, Flitcraft, & Frazier, 1983), and homicide (Federal Bureau of Investigation, 1982). Various symptoms of psychological distress have also been associated with victimization: such symptoms include fear, terror, nightmares (Hilberman & Munson, 1977–1978), inability to trust (Carmen et al.), low self-esteem (Carmen et al.; Walker, 1979), anxiety (Hilberman & Munson, 1977–1978; Walker, 1979), depression (Carmen et al.; Hilberman & Munson; Rounsaville & Lifton, 1983), helplessness (Walker, 1984), guilt (Ferraro & Johnson, 1983; Walker, 1979), shame, feelings of inferiority, loneliness, pessimism (Ferraro & Johnson), low ego strength, shyness, introversion, tension (Star et al., 1979), suspiciousness (Walker, 1979), and psychophysiological complaints, such as fatigue, backache, headache, general restlessness (Walker, 1979), and insomnia (Hilberman & Munson; Walker, 1979).

The effects of spouse abuse on the psychological and social adjustment of children have been examined. Children in families characterized by spouse abuse are likely to be abused themselves (Straus et al., 1980). Thus, it is often difficult to separate the effects of witnessing spouse abuse from those of being abused. However, samples of children of battered women residing in shelters, who have witnessed spouse abuse but have not been abused by a parent themselves, indicate that they exhibit higher levels of conduct and emotional difficulties than children from nonviolent homes (Hughes & Barad, 1983; Wolfe, Jaffe, Wilson, & Zak, 1985). However, children who have witnessed spouse abuse and are victims of child abuse are characterized by the greatest levels of maladjustment (Kalmuss, 1984). In addition, men and women who witnessed spouse abuse, but did not necessarily experience child abuse, in their families of origin are at risk for physically abusing a spouse (Kalmuss).

ELDER ABUSE

Prevalence

Estimates of the prevalence of elder abuse range from 1% to 10% (cf. Steinmetz, 1981). Elder abuse has been found to occur in all racial, ethnic, and socioeconomic groups (Steuer & Austin, 1980); to occur in rural, urban, and suburban communities (Walker, 1983); and to be recurrent (Boydston & McNairn, 1981). Anglo, middle-aged males suffering from emotional distress, mental illness, or substance abuse have been found to be at highest risk for abusing elders (Anetzberger, 1987).

Both men and women abuse their elderly relatives, with some studies finding women more likely to abuse than men (Lau & Kosberg, 1979), and other studies finding men more likely to abuse than women (Boydston & McNairn, 1981; Wolf, Strugnell, & Godkin, 1982). However, after correcting for time spent with the victim, it has been suggested that males may be more likely to mistreat elders than females (Finkelhor, 1983). Elder abusers are most likely to be relatives (Miller & Dodder, 1989; Pillemer, 1985b), and they may be more likely to be spouses than children of elderly parents (Pillemer & Finkelhor, 1988). Although spouse abuse may be more common than parent abuse among elderly persons, Wolf and Pillemer (1989) found that more cases of parent abuse than spouse abuse were considered life-threatening by case workers. Most studies found women to be victimized more often than men (cf. Johnson, O'Brien, & Hudson, 1985; Miller & Dodder), although Pillemer and Finkelhor (1988) found equal numbers of victimized men and women. However, when estimates are corrected for the base rate probabilities of men and women in the population, Pillemer and Finkelhor found that men are twice as likely to be victimized as women.

Sociocultural Factors

Stress has been found to be associated with elder abuse (Boydston & McNairn, 1981). The relationship between abuse and stress seems to be stronger when the stressors are related to elder care than to more general, external stressors. More specifically, although Sengstock and Liang (1982) found some preliminary support for a relationship between external stress and abuse, Anetzberger (1987) found no relationship between the experience of recent life crises and abuse.

However, Anetzberger did find that perpetrators of elder abuse reported experiencing stress associated with close contact with the elder, including disturbing behaviors on the part of the elder, lack of time for personal interests, and absence of support from other family members. Furthermore, Levenberg, Milan, Dolan, and Carpenter (1983) found that frustration associated with life style changes made to meet the needs of the elder was frequently reported as a cause of abuse.

Several investigators have examined the role of social isolation in elder abuse. Phillips (1983) and Pillemer (1985c, 1986) found abused elderly persons had fewer social contacts than controls, and that families characterized by elder abuse had fewer social contacts and were less satisfied with these contacts than were controls. Furthermore, Anetzberger (1987) found that abusers reported feeling socially isolated. Thus, research findings suggest that stress and social isolation may place elders at increased risk for abuse.

Characteristics of Abusers

Mental illness, alcohol abuse, and dependency have been suggested as contributing factors to abuse of elderly persons (Lau & Kosberg, 1979). Studies conducted by Wolf et al. (1982) and Pillemer (1985a) found an association between the mental health of the perpetrator and elder abuse. Not only are abusers more likely to have a history of psychiatric hospitalization than nonabusive controls (Pillemer, 1985a), Wolf and Pillemer (1989) found abusers had recently experienced a decline in their mental health status. Pillemer (1985a, 1985b, 1986) found that many abusers were cognitively impaired and abused alcohol. Alcohol abuse by perpetrators of elder abuse was found by Wolf, Godkin, and Pillemer (1984) and Anetzberger (1987). Finally, research revealed abusers to be dependent on the abused for financial assistance (Wolf et al., 1984) and for housing (Pillemer, 1985a, 1985b).

Although a relationship between childhood abuse and the perpetration of abuse against one's own children and against one's spouse has received considerable support (cf. Straus et al., 1980), Pillemer (1986) found no relationship between childhood abuse and physical abuse of the elderly. However, Pillemer's (1986) results are based on the reports of elderly victims, who may not admit to the commission of violence against their children at an earlier time.

Characteristics of Abused Elders

In general, the characteristics of abused elders most often studied are impairment and dependency. Impairment has been conceptualized variously as chronic illness, severe disability, and psychological instability. Although many researchers have found that abused elders are cognitively and functionally impaired (Boydston & McNairn, 1981; Lau & Kosberg, 1979; Sengstock & Liang, 1982), others have not (Phillips, 1983; Wolf et al., 1984). Concerning dependency, a recent investigation by Wolf and Pillemer (1989) suggests that, in general, abused elders may be dependent on their abusers in some ways but not in others. For instance, Wolf and Pillemer (1989) found that abused elders were dependent on their families for daily needs, financial management, transportation, and companionship, but they had their own financial resources.

Relationship Factors

Relationship factors have not been extensively studied. However, there are a few findings worthy of note. First, Wolf, Godkin, and Pillemer (1984) found a long-standing history of relationship disturbance between abusers and the elders they abused. Second, Wolf and Pillemer (1989) found the recent behavior of the abuser to be more aversive than it had been in the past. Similar to other forms of abuse, this finding suggests an escalation of negativity over time in abusive relationships. Third, Wolf and Pillemer found that victimization differs, depending on the relationship between the abuser and the abused. That is, elders abused by their spouses are more likely to experience physical abuse than other forms of maltreatment and are more likely to be dependent on their abuser for companionship and financial support, whereas elders mistreated by their children are more likely to experience psychological abuse and neglect and to have their abusers depend on them financially. Furthermore, spouse abusers were more likely to have had medical problems and to have experienced a recent deterioration in physical health status, whereas children who abused an elderly parent were more likely to have a history of mental illness and alcohol abuse.

Consequences of Abuse

The consequences of maltreatment of elderly persons have not been studied extensively. However, it is reasonable to assume that a wide variety of physical and psychological symptoms may be associated with abuse, including stress associated with intervention on the part of medical personnel and social agencies (Marin & Morycz, 1990). Highlighting these possibilities, Wolf and Pillemer (1989) noted a variety of physical and psychological manifestations of abuse. Such manifestations include bruises, welts, malnutrition, sprains, dislocations, abrasions, lacerations, bone fractures, burns, wounds, cuts, punctures, social isolation, and humiliation. In addition to these, Johnson (1986) has suggested that dehydration, emaciation, drug addiction, sleep disturbances, fatigue, hypo/hyperthermia, rashes, internal injuries, and suicidal behavior may also be associated with abuse.

DEVELOPMENTAL CONSIDERATIONS

Longitudinal methodologies are crucial in documenting the developmental trajectory of abusers and their victims across the family life cycle. Family members' efforts to keep the family secret and their fear of retribution from perpetrators are likely to impede participation in longitudinal studies. Although this may be true for any study conducted on sensitive issues, it may be especially true when abusive individuals must be identified so that follow-up contact can be made. Identification as an abuser may put an individual at risk for criminal prosecution. Fear of prosecution upon being reported to the appropriate agencies may result, not only in unwillingness to participate in research, but also in a transient lifestyle. Abusive families may move frequently to avoid detection and subsequent criminal prosecution, thus making it difficult to locate them at a later time. Furthermore, when abuse is identified by social agencies and mental health workers, intervention efforts are likely to alter outcomes, confounding the data. Thus, any statements made about abuse across the life span are derived exclusively from cross-sectional data, and they must be considered tentative.

Abusers

As the literature reviewed in this chapter suggests, abusers have limited resources for handling stress. Abusers throughout the family life cycle have been found to be low in self-esteem, rigid and inflexible, and easily threatened. They generally have poor emotional control; they externalize difficulties; and they have communication problems. These communication problems include deficits in appropriate self-assertion and misinterpretation and distortion of others' communication; in addition, anecdotal data suggest that they may be low in interpersonal sensitivity. That is, abusers may not accurately identify problems or the feelings of others and, as a result, they may feel confused and distressed during interpersonal interactions. Thus, it seems that abusers may lack the characteristics and skills needed to establish and maintain healthy and secure relationships with others. This may be particularly problematic in family relationships, where appropriate attachment to others has long been thought important to healthy family functioning. Although numerous mechanisms may account for inability to form healthy attachments, for example, mental illness, mental deficiencies, or social and emotional deficits, childhood abuse may be particularly salient in explaining this phenomenon.

In general, research has found that abused children evidence many of the same socioemotional and cognitive deficits as abusers. As noted earlier, abused children have problems in self-regulation, establishing trust in others, identifying the problems and feelings of others, and deficiencies in social cognition, social competency, and communication skills. Furthermore, recent studies examining the relationship between attachment and abuse have suggested that abused infants and toddlers are more likely to be insecurely attached to their caregivers (Egeland & Sroufe, 1981; Lamb, Gaensbauer, Malkin, & Shultz, 1985). This may be especially true when the primary caregiver is also the person responsible for their mistreatment (Lamb et al.) Although not empirically established, socioemotional and cognitive deficits of abused children are conceptualized as consequences rather than causes of abuse. Therefore, it seems that abusive home environments may offer maximal opportunity for a variety of dysfunctional learning experiences that are likely to have a negative impact on future functioning. Tendencies toward family isolation may compound the problem, because isolation limits opportunities for corrective experiences that would promote adequate social functioning. Thus, in addition to its effects on intrapersonal development, childhood victimization may have important implications for future family functioning.

Victims

Some victim characteristics seem universal. First, victims are available targets. Victims of family abuse tend to be family members who come into regular and frequent contact with their abuser. Second, victims tend to be less powerful than abusers, where power is defined in terms of physical strength and stature. Third, victims tend to be invested in the relationship, and often they fail to report the occurrence of abuse. Fourth, victims may be a source of stress to the abuser. That is, when abusers have difficulty communicating with a family member or when caring for a family member interferes with personal goals and desires, family members are likely to be viewed as stressors rather than sources of pleasure or satisfaction.

Because no research to date has been conducted on the correlates of victimization across the life span, it is impossible to know what differences may exist between those victimized only in childhood, in childhood and adulthood, and in adulthood only. Research does suggest that abuse during important developmental periods in childhood has a negative impact on the development of adequate social, communication, and self-control skills. Such deficits are likely to increase the probability of aggressive behavior toward others that may extend into adulthood.

Life Cycle Stressors

Cross-sectional research suggests that there may be a relationship between abuse and stressful stages of the life cycle. Sociologists focusing on the family have identified common developmental stages that may be associated with increased stress. These stages include committing to a relationship and entering into marriage, beginning a family, and caring for elderly family members. Stress during these stages is likely to be associated with adaptation to new roles and responsibilities for which the individual has no prior experience. Furthermore, rapidly changing social structures and norms have rendered many of the rules and guides of previous generations obsolete. For some individuals, these developmental stages are associated with the occurrence of abuse. For instance, women report being hit as their relationships become more serious, young children are abused more frequently than other age groups, and parents are more likely to be abused when they become elderly.

Limitations in intrapersonal and interpersonal resources, as noted above, are likely to compromise an individual's ability to cope with a variety of stressors, including those associated with changes in the life cycle, and environmental variables, such as close proximity of family members, unemployment, and family isolation. Thus, the challenge to our understanding of physical abuse across the family life cycle may be in determining transitions and family life cycle changes that interact with individual characteristics and environmental contexts to trigger the development of physical abusive patterns of behavior within the family.

CONCLUSIONS

Physical abuse during childhood, young adulthood, adulthood, and late adulthood is alarmingly prevalent in our society, and attitudes toward such behavior, although negative, are surprisingly accepting. Characteristics and reactions of the families, perpetrators, and victims of physical abuse in each situation are very similar. In all cases, families that are financially and socially stressed and isolated are at higher risk for experiencing physical abuse. Young males, who are under- or unemployed, socially isolated, and psychologically stressed seem to be at greatest risk for physically abusing a child or adult member of their families. In turn, their victims are family members, typically females during young and full adulthood, who are financially, or otherwise, dependent and socially isolated. The physical and psychological effects in all cases are significantly destructive. Victims across the life cycle respond by accepting responsibility for the abuse and maintaining the relationship with the abusers. However, the most striking finding by intrafamily violence researchers is the relative stability or consistency in the occurrence of physical abuse across the life cycle. Children who are abused or witness spouse abuse in their families of origin are at risk for physically abusing a child or spouse in their families of procreation. In turn, their abused or witnessing children are at risk for growing up to abuse their own.

Researchers have not learned enough about intrafamily violence to break its cycle. A major impediment to breaking the cycle seems to be the tradition of conducting research on physical abuse at one stage of the life cycle without regard for the occurrence of physical abuse at other stages. That is, those interested in child abuse do not examine child abusers' behavior relative to the spouse or elderly parents. Likewise, those interested in wife abuse do not examine the behavior of abusers relative to their children or parents. Given the strong relationship between abusing one's children, spouse, and parents, and the similarities in the characteristics of individuals engaging in physical abuse at different stages of the life cycle, integrated and developmentally focused research seems prudent. In addition, longitudinal research documenting the development of abused children, spouses, and elders, and the development of their abusers is sorely lacking. We can determine what happens to abusers and the abused across the life cycle only by assessing developmental sequences empirically. The theoretical integration of empirical findings and the theoretical guidance that are currently lacking may become possible after we adopt a developmental perspective.

REFERENCES

Allen, R., & Wasserman, G. A. (1985). Origins of language delay in abused infants. *Child Abuse & Neglect, 9,* 335–340.

American Humane Association. (1985). *Highlights of official child neglect and abuse reporting (1983).* Denver, CO: Author.

Anderson, S. C., & Lauderdale, M. L. (1982). Characteristics of abusive parents: A look at self-esteem. *Child Abuse & Neglect, 6,* 285–293.

Andrews, B., & Brewin, C. R. (1990). Attributions of blame for marital violence: A study of antecedents and consequences. *Journal of Marriage and the Family, 52,* 757–767.

Anetzberger, G. J. (1987). *The etiology of elder abuse by adult offspring.* Springfield, IL: Thomas.

Appelbaum, A. S. (1977). Developmental retardation in infants as a concomitant of physical child abuse. *Journal of Abnormal Psychology, 5,* 417–423.

Arias, I., & Johnson, P. (1989). Evaluations of physical aggression among intimate dyads. *Journal of Interpersonal Violence, 4,* 298–307.

Arias, I., Samios, M., & O'Leary, K. D. (1987). Prevalence and correlates of physical aggression during courtship. *Journal of Interpersonal Violence, 2,* 82–90.

Barahal, R. M., Waterman, J., & Martin, H. P. (1981). The social cognitive development of abused children. *Journal of Consulting and Clinical Psychology, 49,* 508–516.

Benedict, M. I., White, R. B., & Cornely, D. A. (1985). Maternal perinatal risk factors and child abuse. *Child Abuse & Neglect, 9,* 217–224.

Berger, L. R. (1978). Abortions in America: The effects of restrictive funding. *New England Journal of Medicine, 298,* 1474–1477.

Bernard, M. L., & Bernard, J. L. (1983). Violent intimacy: The family as a model for love relationships. *Family Relations, 32,* 283–286.

Blumberg, M. (1964, Winter). When parents hit out. *Twentieth Century, 173,* 39–44.

Bograd, M. (1988). Feminists perspectives on wife abuse. In K. Yllo & M. Bograd (Eds.), *Feminist perspectives on wife abuse* (pp. 11–26). Newbury Park, CA: Sage.

Bousha, D. M., & Twentyman, C. T. (1984). Mother–child interactional style in abuse, neglect, and control groups: Naturalistic observations in the home. *Journal of Abnormal Psychology, 93,* 106–114.

Boydston, L. S., & McNairn, J. A. (1981). Elder abuse by adult caretakers: An exploratory study. In *Physical and financial abuse of the elderly* (pp. 135–136). Publication No. 97–297, United States House of Representative Select Committee on Aging, Washington, DC: U. S. Government Printing Office.

Buchanan, A., & Oliver, J. E. (1977). Abuse and neglect as a cause of mental retardation: A study of 140 children admitted to subnormality hospitals in Whiltshire. *British Journal of Psychiatry, 131,* 458–467.

Burgess, R. L., & Conger, R. D. (1978). Family interactions in abusive, neglectful, and normal families. *Child Development, 49,* 1163–1173.

Camras, L. A., Grow, J. G., & Ribordy, S. C. (1983). Recognition of emotional expression by abused children. *Journal of Clinical Child Psychology, 12,* 325–328.

Carmen, E. H., Reiker, P. P., & Mills, T. (1984). Victims of violence and psychiatric illness. *American Journal of Psychiatry, 141,* 378–383.

Cate, R. M., Henton, J. M., Koval, J., Christopher, F. S., & Lloyd, S. (1982). Premarital abuse. *Journal of Family Issues, 3,* 79–90.

Corey, E. J. B., Miller, C. L., & Widlak, R. W. (1975). Factors contributing to child abuse. *Nursing Research, 24,* 293–295.

Dietrich, K. N., Starr, R. H., Jr., & Weisfeld, F. E. (1983). Infant maltreatment: Caretaker-infant interaction and developmental consequences at different levels of parenting failure. *Pediatrics, 72,* 532–540.

Disbrow, M. A., Doerr, H., & Caufield, C. (1977). Measuring the components of parents' potential for child abuse and neglect. *Child Abuse & Neglect, 1,* 279–296.

Dobash, R. E., & Dobash, R. P. (1979). *Violence against wives: A case against the patriarchy.* New York: Free Press.

Egeland, B., & Sroufe, L. A. (1981). Developmental sequelae of maltreatment in infancy. *New Directions for Child Development, 11,* 77–92.

Elmer, E. (1967). *Children in jeopardy: A study of abused minors and their families.* Pittsburgh: University of Pittsburgh Press.

Fagan, J. A., Stewart, D. K., & Hansen, K. V. (1983). Violent men or violent husbands. In D. Finkelhor, R. J. Gelles, G. Hotaling, & M. A. Straus (Eds.), *The dark side of families: Current family violence research* (pp. 49–67). Newbury Park, CA: Sage.

Federal Bureau of Investigation. (1982). *Uniform crime reports.* Washington, DC: United States Department of Justice.

Ferraro, K. J., & Johnson, J. M. (1983). How women experience battering: The process of victimization. *Social Problems, 30,* 325–339.

Finkelhor, D. (1983). Common features of family abuse. In D. Finkelhor, R. J. Gelles, G. Hotaling, & M. A. Straus (Eds.), *The dark side of families: Current family violence research* (pp. 17–28). Newbury Park, CA: Sage.

Fitch, F. J., & Papantonio, M. A. (1983). Men who batter: Some pertinent characteristics. *Journal of Nervous and Mental Diseases, 171,* 190–192.

Friedrich, W. N., Einbender, A. J., & Luecke, W. J. (1983). Cognitive and behavioral characteristics of physically abused children. *Journal of Consulting and Clinical Psychology, 51,* 313–314.

Frodi, A. M., & Lamb, M. E. (1980). Child abusers' responses to infant smiles and cries. *Child Development, 51,* 238–241.

Gaines, R., Sandgrund, A., Green, A. H., & Power, E. (1978). Etiological factors in child maltreatment: A multivariate study of abusing, neglecting, and normal mothers. *Journal of Abnormal Psychology, 87,* 531–540.

Garbarino, J., & Sherman, D. (1980). High-risk neighborhoods and high-risk families: The human ecology of child maltreatment. *Child Development, 51,* 188–198.

Gelles, R. J. (1988). Violence and pregnancy: Are pregnant women at greater risk of abuse? *Journal of Marriage and the Family, 50,* 841–847.

Gelles, R. J., & Cornell, C. P. (1985). *Intimate violence in families.* Newbury Park, CA: Sage.

Gelles, R. J., & Cornell, C. P. (1987). Adolescent-to-parent violence. In R. J. Gelles (Ed.), *Family violence* (pp. 153–167). Newbury Park, CA: Sage.

Gelles, R. J., & Straus, M. A. (1979). Violence in the American family. *Journal of Social Issues, 35,* 15–39.

George, C., & Main, M. (1979). Social interactions of young abused children: Approach, avoidance, and aggression. *Child Development, 50,* 306–318.

Gil, D. (1971). Violence against children. *Journal of Marriage and the Family, 33,* 637–648.

Gil, D. (1979). *Child abuse and violence.* New York: AMS.

Goldberg, W., & Tomlanovich, M. C. (1984). Domestic violence victims in the emergency department. *Journal of the American Medical Association, 251,* 3259–3264.

Goldstein, D., & Rosenbaum, A. (1985). An evaluation of the self-esteem of maritally violent men. *Family Relations, 34,* 425–428.

Green, A. H. (1978). Self-destructive behavior in battered children. *American Journal of Psychiatry, 135,* 579–583.

Hampton, R. L., Gelles, R. J., & Harrop, J. W. (1989). Is violence in Black families increasing? A comparison of 1975 and 1985 national survey rates. *Journal of Marriage and the Family, 51,* 969–980.

Hargreaves, E. F. (1987). Maternal employment and violence toward children. In R. J. Gelles (Ed.), *Family violence* (pp. 89–105). Newbury, CA: Sage.

Helton, A. (1986). Battering during pregnancy. *American Journal of Nursing, 86,* 910–913.

Henton, J., Cate, R., Koval, J., Lloyd, S., & Christopher, S. (1983). Romance and violence in dating relationships. *Journal of Family Issues, 4,* 467–482.

Herrenkohl, E. C., & Herrenkohl, R. C. (1979). A comparison of abused children and their nonabused siblings. *Journal of the American Academy of Child Psychiatry, 18,* 260–269.

Herrenkohl, E. C., Herrenkohl, R. C., & Toedter, L. J. (1983). Perspectives of the intergenerational transmission of abuse. In D. Finkelhor, R. J. Gelles, G. T. Hotaling, & M. A. Straus (Eds.), *The dark side of families: Current family violence research* (pp. 305–316). Newbury Park, CA: Sage.

Herrenkohl, E. C., Herrenkohl, R. C., Toedter, L. J., & Yanushefiski, A. M. (1984). Parent–child interactions in abusive and nonabusive families. *Journal of the American Academy of Child and Adolescent Psychiatry Journal, 23,* 641–648.

Hilberman, E., & Munson, K. (1977–78). Sixty battered women. *Victimology; an international journal, 2,* 460–470.

Hoffman-Plotkin, D., & Twentyman, C. T. (1984). A multimodal assessment of behavioral and cognitive deficits in abused and neglected preschoolers. *Child Development, 55,* 794–802.

Holman, R. R., & Kanwar, S. (1975). Early life of the "battered child." *Archives of Diseases in Childhood, 50,* 78–80.

Hughes, H. M., & Barad, S. (1983). Psychological functioning of children in a battered women's shelter: A preliminary investigation. *American Journal of Orthopsychiatry, 53,* 525–531.

Hughes, H. M., & Rau, T. J. (1984, August). *Psychological adjustment of battered women in shelters.* Paper presented at the meeting of the American Psychological Association, Toronto.

Johnson, B., & Morse, H. (1968). *The battered child: A study of children with inflicted injuries.* Denver, CO: Department of Welfare.

Johnson, C. F., & Showers, J. (1985). Injury variables in child abuse. *Child Abuse & Neglect, 9,* 207–216.

Johnson, T. (1986). Critical issues in the definition of elder mistreatment. In K. Pillemer & R. S. Wolf (Eds.), *Elder abuse conflict in the family* (pp. 167–196). Dover, MA: Auburn House.

Johnson, T., O'Brien, J., & Hudson, M. (Eds.). (1985). *Elder neglect and abuse: An annotated bibliography.* Westport, CN: Greenwood.

Kalmuss, D. (1984). The intergenerational transmission of marital aggression. *Journal of Marriage and the Family, 46,* 11–19.

Kempe, C. H., Silverman, F. N., Steele, B. F., Droegmueller, W., & Silver, H. K. (1962). The battered-child syndrome. *Journal of the American Medical Association, 181,* 105–112.

Kent, J. T. (1976). A follow-up study of abused children. *Journal of Pediatric Psychology, 1,* 25–31.

Kinard, E. M. (1980). Emotional development in physically abused children. *American Journal of Orthopsychiatry, 50,* 686–696.

Koski, M. A., & Ingram, E. M. (1977). Child abuse and neglect: Effects on Bayley Scale scores. *Journal of Abnormal Child Psychology, 5,* 79–91.

Lahey, B. B., Conger, R. D., Atkeson, B. M., & Treiber, F. A. (1984). Parenting behavior and emotional status of physically abusive mothers. *Journal of Consulting and Clinical Psychology, 52,* 1062–1071.

Lamb, M. F., Gaensbauer, R. J., Malkin, C. M., & Schultz, L. A. (1985). The effects of child maltreatment on security of infant–adult attachment. *Infant Behavior and Development, 8,* 35–45.

Lau, E. E., & Kosberg, J. (1979). Abuse of the elderly by informal care providers. *Aging, 299,* 10–15.

La Violette, A. D., Barnett, O. W., & Miller, C. L. (1984, August). *A classification of wife abusers on the Bem Sex-Role Inventory.* Paper presented at the Second Annual Conference on Research on Domestic Violence, Durham, NH.

Levenberg, J., Milan, J., Dolan, M., & Carpenter, P. (1983). Elder abuse in West Virginia: Extent and nature of the problem. In L. G. Schultz (Ed.), *Elder abuse in West Virginia: A policy analysis of system response.* Boston, MA: John Wright, PSG.

Levinger, G. (1966). Sources of marital dissatisfaction among applicants for divorce. *American Journal of Orthopsychiatry, 36,* 803–807.

Light, R. J. (1973). Abused and neglected children in America: A study of alternative policies. *Harvard Educational Review, 43,* 556–598.

Lo, W. A., & Sporakowski, M. J. (1989, September). The continuation of violent dating relationships among college students. *Journal of College Student Development, 30,* 432–439.

Lynch, M. A. (1975). Ill-health and child abuse. *Lancet, 2,* 317–319.

Lynch, M. A., & Roberts, J. (1977). Predicting child abuse: Signs of bonding failure in the maternity hospital. *British Medical Journal, 1,* 624–626.

Main, M., & George, C. (1985). Response of abused and disadvantaged toddlers to distress in agemates: A study in the day care setting. *Developmental Psychology, 21,* 407–412.

Makepeace, J. M. (1981). Courtship violence among college students. *Family Relations, 30,* 97–102.

Makepeace, J. M. (1983). Life events stress and courtship violence. *Family Relations, 32,* 101–109.

Makepeace, J. M. (1986). Gender differences in courtship violence victimization. *Family Relations, 35,* 383–388.

Malone, J., Tyree, A., & O'Leary, K. D. (1989). Generalization and containment: Different effects of past aggression for wives and husbands. *Journal of Marriage and the Family, 51,* 687–697.

Margolin, G., John, J. S., & Gleberman, L. (1988). Affective responses to conflictual discussion in violent and nonviolent couples. *Journal of Consulting and Clinical Psychology, 56,* 24–33.

Marin, R. S., & Morycz, R. K. (1990). Victims of elder abuse. In R. T. Ammerman & M. Hersen (Eds.), *Treatment of family violence* (pp. 136–164). New York: Wiley.

Matthews, W. J. (1984). Violence in college couples. *College Student Journal, 18,* 150–158.

McCord, J. (1983). A forty-year perspective on effects of child abuse and neglect. *Child Abuse & Neglect, 7,* 265–270.

Miller, R. B., & Dodder, R. A. (1989). The abused: abuser dyad: Elder abuse in the state of Florida. In R. Filison & S. R. Ingman (Eds.), *Elder abuse: Practice and policy* (pp. 166–178). New York: Human Sciences.

Nakou, S., Adam, H., Stathacopoulou, M. A., & Agathonos, H. (1982). Health status of abused and neglected children and their siblings. *Child Abuse & Neglect, 6,* 279–284.

Oates, R. K., Davis, A. A., Ryan, M. G., & Stewart, L. F. (1979). Risk factors associated with child abuse. *Child Abuse & Neglect, 3,* 547–554.

O'Leary, K. D., & Curley, A. D. (1986). Assertion and family violence. *Journal of Marital and Family Therapy, 12,* 281–289.

Pagelow, M. D. (1981). *Woman-battering: Victims and their experiences.* Newbury Park, CA: Sage.

Phillips, L. (1983). Abuse and neglect of the frail elderly at home: An exploration of theoretical relationships. *Journal of Advanced Nursing, 8,* 379–392.

Pillemer, K. (1985a). *Domestic violence against the elderly: A case-control study.* Unpublished doctoral dissertation. Department of Sociology, Brandeis University, Waltham, MA.

Pillemer, K. (1985b). The dangers of dependency: New findings on domestic violence against the elderly. *Social Problems, 33,* 146–158.

Pillemer, K. (1985c). Social isolation and elder abuse. *Response to the victimization of women and children, 8,* 2–4.

Pillemer, K. (1986). Risk factors in elder abuse: Results from a case-control study. In K. A. Pillemer & R. S. Wolf (Eds.), *Elder abuse: Conflict in the family* (pp. 239–263). Dover, MA: Auburn House.

Pillemer, K., & Finkelhor, D. (1988). The prevalence of elder abuse: A random sample survey. *Gerontologist, 28,* 51–57.

Rosenbaum, A., & O'Leary, K. D. (1981). Marital violence: Characteristics of abusive couples. *Journal of Consulting and Clinical Psychology, 49,* 63–71.

Rosenberg, M. S., & Reppucci, N. D. (1983). Abusive mothers: Perception of their own and their children's behavior. *Journal of Consulting and Clinical Psychology, 51,* 674–682.

Rosenblatt, G. C. (1980). *Parental expectations and attitudes about childrearing in high vs. low risk child abusing families.* Saratoga, CA: Century Twenty One.

Rounsaville, B. J., & Lifton, N. (1983). A therapy group for battered women. In M. Rosenbaum (Ed.), *Handbook of short-term therapy groups* (pp. 155–179). New York: McGraw-Hill.

Sammons, L. N. (1981). Battered and pregnant. *MCN: American Journal of Maternal Child Nursing, 6,* 246–250.

Sandgrund, A., Gaines, R. W., & Green, A. H. (1974). Child abuse and mental retardation: A problem of cause and effect. *American Journal of Mental Deficiency, 79,* 327–330.

Sengstock, M., & Liang, J. (1982). *Identifying and characterizing elder abuse.* Unpublished manuscript. Detroit, MI: Wayne State University, Institute of Gerontology.

Sherrod, K. B., O'Connor, S., Vietze, P., & Altemeier, W. (1984). Child health and maltreatment. *Child Development, 55,* 1174–1183.

Silver, L. B., Dublin, C. C., & Lourie, R. S. (1969). Does violence breed violence? Contributions from a study of child abuse syndrome. *American Journal of Psychiatry, 126,* 152–155.

Smith, P., Bohnstedt, M., & Grove, K. (1982). *Long-term correlates of child victimization: Consequences of intervention.* Paper presented at the annual meeting of the Pacific Sociological Association, San Diego.

Spinetta, J. (1978). Parental personality factors in child abuse. *Journal of Consulting and Clinical Psychology, 46,* 1409–1414.

Spinetta, J., & Rigler, D. (1972). The child abusing parent: A psychological review. *Psychological Bulletin, 77,* 296–304.

Star, B., Clark, C. G., Goetz, K. M., & O'Malia, L. (1979). Psychosocial aspects of wife battering. *Social Casework: The Journal of Contemporary Social Work. 6,* 479–487.

Stark, E., Flitcraft, A., & Frazier, W. (1983). Medicine and patriarchal violence: The social construction of a "private" event. In V. Navaro (Ed.), *Women and health: The politics of sex in medicine,* (Vol. 4, pp. 177–209). New York: Baywood.

Starr, R. H., Jr. (1982). A research-based approach to the prediction of child abuse. In R. H. Starr, Jr. (Ed.), *Child abuse prediction: Policy implications* (pp. 105–134). Cambridge, MA: Ballinger.

Starr, R. H., Jr., Ceresnie, S. J., Dietrich, K. N., Fischhoff, J., Schumann, B., & Demorest, M. (1982, August). *Child abuse: A case-sibling assessment of child factors.* Paper presented at the meeting of the American Psychological Association, Washington, DC.

Steinmetz, S. (1981). Elder abuse. *Aging, 6,* 315–316.

Stern, L. (1979). The high risk infant and battering. In *Child abuse and developmental disabilities: Essays* (pp. 20–24). Publication No. OHDS 79-30266, United States Department of Health, Education, and Welfare, Washington, DC: U. S. Government Printing Office.

Steuer, J., & Austin, E. (1980). Family abuse of the elderly. *American Geriatrics Society Journal, 28,* 372–376.

Straus, M. A. (1980). Victims and aggressors in marital violence. *American Behavioral Scientist, 23,* 681–704.

Straus, M. A. (1986). Medical care costs of intra-family assault and homicide to society. *New York Academy of Medicine Bulletin, 62,* 556–561.

Straus, M. A. (1987, September). *Violence in Hispanic families in the United States: Some preliminary findings on incidence and etiology.* Paper presented at the Research Conference on Violence and Homicide in Hispanic Communities, Los Angeles, CA.

Straus, M. A., & Gelles, R. J. (1986). Societal change and change in family violence from 1975 to 1985 as revealed by two national surveys. *Journal of Marriage and the Family, 48,* 465–479.

Straus, M. A., Gelles, R. J., & Steinmetz, S. (1980). *Behind closed doors: Violence in the American family.* Landover Hills, MD: Anchor.

Telch, C. F., & Lindquist, C. V. (1984). Violent versus nonviolent couples: A comparison of patterns. *Psychotherapy, 21,* 242–248.

Walker, J. C. (1983). Protective services for the elderly: Connecticut's experience. In J. I. Kosberg (Ed.), *Abuse and maltreatment of the elderly: Causes and interventions* (pp. 292–301). Littleton, MA: John Wright PSG.

Walker, L. E. (1979). *The battered woman.* New York: Harper & Row.

Walker, L. E. (1984). *The battered woman syndrome.* New York: Springer.

Warren, C. (1978, April). *Parent batterers: Adolescent violence and the family.* Presented at the annual meeting of the Pacific Sociological Association, Anaheim, CA.

Weinstock, E., Tietze, C., Jaffe, F. S., & Dryfoos, J. G. (1976). Abortion need and services in the United States, 1974–1975. *Family Planning Perspectives, 8,* 58–69.

Wolf, R. S., & Pillemer, K. A. (1989). *Helping elderly victims: The reality of elder abuse.* New York: Columbia University Press.

Wolf, R., Godkin, M., & Pillemer, K. (1984). *Preliminary findings from three model projects on elderly abuse.* Worcester, MA: University of Massachusetts Medical Center, University Center on Aging.

Wolf, R., Strugnell, C., & Godkin, M. (1982). *Preliminary findings from three model projects on elderly abuse.* Worcester, MA: University of Massachusetts Medical Center.

Wolfe, D. A. (1985). Child-abusive parents: An empirical review and analysis. *Psychological Bulletin, 97,* 462–482.

Wolfe, D. A., Fairbank, J., Kelly, J. A., & Bradlyn, A. S. (1983). Child abusive parents' physiological responses to stressful and non-stressful behavior in children. *Behavioral Assessment, 5,* 363–371.

Wolfe, D. A., Jaffe, P., Wilson, S., & Zak, L. (1985). Children of battered women: The relation of child behavior to family violence and maternal stress. *Journal of Consulting and Clinical Psychology, 53,* 657–665.

Wolfe, D. A., & Mosk, M. D. (1983). Behavioral comparisons of children from abusive and distressed families. *Journal of Consulting and Clinical Psychology, 51,* 702–708.

Yllo, K., & Straus, M. A. (1981). Interpersonal violence among married and cohabiting couples. *Family Relations, 30,* 339–347.

CHAPTER 15

Sexual Abuse in Families

JEFFREY J. HAUGAARD

There has been a dramatic increase in the amount of attention focused on sexual abuse within families over the past three decades. In the 1960s, changes in societal beliefs about the preeminent value of family privacy were influenced by those advocating for women's and children's individual rights. As social scientists, physicians, and others began asking questions about the prevalence and consequences of sexual abuse within families, the extent of the problem became more evident. This, in turn, led to heightened societal concern, further research, and the development of various therapeutic, social service, and legal interventions for victims and perpetrators of family sexual abuse.

It is now clear that sexual abuse occurs in many families. Evidence suggests that some form of sexual abuse may be occurring in 10 to 20% of families. Millions of children and adults are victims of family sexual abuse, either by being the target of sexual abuse or by living in families where sexual abuse occurs. Some, or many, of these children and adults carry the scars caused by their victimization for many years.

Despite the plethora of books, journal and magazine articles, and presentations in the public media, basic issues in the study of family sexual abuse remain unresolved. Sexual abuse is difficult to define, and a generally accepted definition has yet to be developed. The process by which sexual abuse causes harm is unclear, as is the process by which sexual abuse develops in families. In this chapter, I review the research that has focused on sexual abuse within families, first looking at parent/child sexual abuse, then examining sexual abuse between siblings, and finally, exploring sexual abuse between spouses. Each section contains a discussion of the obstacles to defining sexual abuse clearly, information on prevalence and consequences, and a discussion of the factors influencing the development of sexual abuse.

SEXUAL ABUSE BETWEEN PARENTS AND CHILDREN

Parent/child sexual abuse has received some attention for many years, and has been the principal focus of those studying sexual abuse within families for the past 20 years. The potential harm of parent/child incest has been recognized for many years. However, it was not until the late 1970s and early 1980s that the prevalence of parent/child incest was understood.

Definitional Issues

Incest refers to sexual behaviors between individuals in a family (although the definition of family can vary). Because sexual behaviors between parents and children are prohibited legally, the terms parent/child incest and parent/child sexual abuse are similar. The presence of abuse can be defined solely by the act in some cases (e.g., those involving genital fondling or intercourse). However, many parent/child interactions cannot be defined easily based on the act alone—for example, a parent bathing a child, sleeping with a child, or appearing nude in front of a child. Factors such as the age of the child, intent of the parent, potential harm to the child, and context of the behavior must be considered when determining whether specific cases involving these types of interactions are abusive. However, these factors are often difficult to quantify and specify, making their use problematic. For example, it is difficult to determine when a parent should stop bathing a child, the intent of a parent who regularly allows a school-age child to sleep with him or her, and the conditions under which parent/child nudity is appropriate.

Atteberry-Bennet (cited in Haugaard & Reppucci, 1988) found that other factors may influence the definition of parent/child incest. She reported that potential sexual encounters occurring between a father and daughter were rated as more abusive than the same encounters occurring between mothers and sons. She also found that professional affiliation was associated with tendencies to rate behaviors as abusive—therapists were more likely to rate some acts as abusive than were lawyers.

The lack of a generally accepted definition of parent/child incest can lead to problems when comparing empirical studies and can make it difficult for clinicians, child protective service workers, and others to determine whether specific parent/child interactions are abusive. The necessity of considering many factors, each of which are difficult to quantify, when defining parent/child incest probably prohibits the development of a definition that will reliably discriminate cases that are abusive from those that are not. Thus, although some definitional guidelines can be presented, these must be used cautiously. It would be unwise to base decisions about particular cases on definitional guidelines dogmatically.

Prevalence and Consequences of Parent/Child Incest

Prevalence

Community-based studies of the prevalence of child sexual abuse have included probability samples of women from San Francisco (Russell, 1983) and Los Angeles (Wyatt, 1985), and men and women in Los Angeles (Siegel, Sorenson,

Golding, Burnam, & Stein, 1987). Participants were asked to describe any child sexual abuse experiences in face-to-face interviews. Each study used slightly different definitions of sexual abuse. Russell and Wyatt included children under the age of 18 and included encounters that involved physical contact and those that involved no contact (such as an encounter with an exhibitionist). Siegel et al. included only incidents that occurred before the child turned 16 and that involved physical coercion.

The reporting of the results makes it difficult to distinguish those abused within their immediate family, but some specific information is available. In Russell's (1983) sample of 930 women, 42 (4.5%) had been abused by a father or father figure and 1 by her mother. Approximately one third of those abused by a father or father figure had experienced vaginal, oral, or anal intercourse; one third had experienced genital fondling; and one third had experienced other sexual behaviors. The one incident with a mother involved genital fondling. In Wyatt's sample of 248 women, 4 (1%) had been abused by their fathers, 19 (7%) by a stepfather, foster father, or mother's boyfriend. None of the women had been abused by a mother. Among the 3,132 adults interviewed by Siegel et al. (1987), approximately 28 (1%) of the women and none of the men reported a sexual abuse experience with a parent.

Finkelhor (1979) and Haugaard and Emery (1989) were among researchers who investigated the prevalence of child sexual abuse among college undergraduates. Finkelhor included noncontact abuse experiences and experiences that were wanted or unwanted. Haugaard and Emery included only unwanted experiences that involved physical contact. Haugaard and Emery found that 6% of the undergraduates had experienced sexual abuse with a father or father figure. Finkelhor found that 8% had such an experience. No experiences with mothers were reported.

Reports from samples of children in therapy because of sexual abuse show a much higher prevalence of parent/child incest that do community- or college-based studies. Rimsza and Niggemann (1982) found that 20% of their sample were abused by a father. Reinhart (1987) found 27% of a sample of boys were abused by a father. Mian (1986) found that 38% of her sample had been abused by their fathers. The higher prevalence of father/child abuse in clinical samples suggests that these children may experience more detrimental effects, leading them to be referred for therapy more often.

Consequences

A variety of negative consequences of parent/child incest have been reported in empirical studies and clinical reports. Several factors may influence the development of these consequences. The first is the sexual activity itself. Various factors, such as the identity of the perpetrator, type of sexual activity, length of abuse, and amount of physical coercion involved, have been associated with differing outcomes in victims (see Browne & Finkelhor, 1986). Second is the reaction of meaningful adults in a child's life, if the abuse is revealed. For example, some studies have shown that a positive and supportive reaction by a child's mother reduces the negative impact of earlier abuse (e.g., Conte & Schuerman, 1987). In many cases, family disruption will result from disclosure of the abuse. If the father is removed from the home and this results in a loss of financial and social support for the family, the victim may experience guilt and may be the target of anger from other family members (Giarretto, 1982). The final factor is the influence of involvement with the child protective and legal systems. Poorly handled legal cases can increase the risk of negative consequences (Kirkwood & Mihaila, 1979).

A variety of negative emotional and behavior consequences have been associated with child sexual abuse in general, and with parent/child incest in particular. Emotional consequences include anxiety, anger, depression, and guilt (e.g., Fischer, 1983; Gelinas, 1983). Behavioral consequences include aggressive and sexualized behaviors as children (e.g., Kohan, Pothier, & Norbeck, 1987), and sexual problems as an adult (Fritz, Stoll, & Wagner, 1981). Parent/child incest has also been associated with higher rates of adolescent suicide and running away, interpersonal difficulties, and school failure (see Browne & Finkelhor, 1986; Haugaard & Reppucci, 1988 for reviews).

The specific consequences of parent/child incest can be difficult to determine. Incest is likely to occur in families that experience many other problems (Conte & Schuerman, 1987; Harter, Alexander, & Neimeyer, 1988), and these other problems also may contribute to behavioral or emotional problems. It is important, therefore, to consider other family characteristics when determining the influence of child sexual abuse. Both Conte and Schuerman and Harter et al. found some specific negative influence of parental incest on victims, but the apparent influence of the incest was reduced when other family characteristics were considered.

Clinical studies and community surveys of adults have shown that the consequences of parent/child incest can persist for many years. Wheeler and Walton (1987) found that female therapy patients who had experienced childhood incest scored higher on 9 of the 20 subscales of the Millon Clinical Multiaxial Inventory than therapy patients who had not experienced incest. Incest victims scored in the clinically significant range on the avoidant and borderline personality styles and on the anxiety and dysthymic clinical syndromes. Briere and Runtz (1988) found that college women who had experienced child sexual abuse had more dissociative, somatic, anxious, and depressive symptoms on the Hopkins Symptom Checklist than nonabused women. Abuse that was most predictive of symptoms was perpetrated by a parent, was accompanied by physical coercion, involved intercourse, and occurred over an extended period of time. As discussed later, sexually abused children seem to be at greater risk for sexual and physical abuse in adolescent and adult relationships (e.g., Russell, 1990). Briere, Evans, Runtz, and Wall (1988) found increased symptoms on the Trauma Symptom Checklist and increased suicide attempts among male and female adult crisis center clients who had been sexually abused as children. There were no differences in symptoms or suicide behavior between the men and women. Krug

(1989) found severe symptoms in several adult males who had been sexually abused by their mothers for an extended period.

Long-term consequences of incest can affect future generations. Childhood abuse may increase the chance of some adults abusing their children. The degree of this increase is not clearly understood. Kaufman and Zigler (1987) demonstrated that retrospective studies of the continuity of abuse across generations (those in which an abusive parent is asked about any abuse that he or she suffered as a child) showed much higher rates of continuity than prospective studies (in which an abused person is followed to see if he or she becomes an abusive parent). The problem with basing an estimate of the continuity of abuse on retrospective studies is that they do not measure the number of abused people who do not eventually abuse their own child. Thus, they can be misleading. Goodwin, McCarthy, and Divasto (1981) found that 38% of a group of abusive mothers had been sexually abused as children, and 24% of a group of nonabusive mothers had been sexually abused as children. This study suggests that sexual abuse increases the chance of becoming an abusive parent. However, it indicates also that a substantial number of abuse victims do not abuse their children.

Childhood abuse may impair an adult's ability to be a successful parent, even in families in which the adult is not abusive. As noted above, a variety of long-standing symptoms can result from child sexual abuse. Several studies have shown that parents with psychiatric disorders have a more difficult time parenting their children, and that these children often display increased symptoms and decreased prosocial behavior (e.g., Billings & Moos, 1983; Lee & Gotlib, 1989; Turner, Beidel, & Costello, 1987). Some of the parent disorders that are most commonly associated with problems in their children are those found among adult victims of incest (such as depression and anxiety). Thus, the consequences of parent/child incest may be handed to future generations through a variety of paths.

Little work has been done on the long-term consequences of parent/child incest on the family. Some descriptive studies have reported positive outcomes for families that engage in sustained and intensive treatment (e.g., Kroth, 1979). A variety of factors are likely to influence the outcome for the family. The extent to which the nonabusive parent can rally to the side of the children is an important consideration, as is the extent to which the nonabusive parent can lead the family without the presence of the perpetrator. Whether the perpetrator remains in or leaves the family can have important consequences, and these consequences will depend on the overall significance of the perpetrator in the family. In cases where there are positive ties between the perpetrator and the family, programs that require the perpetrator to continue financial support of the family and allow for the possibility that the perpetrator can rejoin the family after successful treatment, may facilitate the family's recovery from the abuse. In other situations, programs that aid the family to develop a life independent from the perpetrator may provide for the best hope for the family remaining viable.

Etiology of Parent/Child Incest

I have suggested that the explanations for the occurrence of parent/child incest can be grouped into four categories: the individual deviance explanation; the chaotic explanation; the male dominance explanation; and the functional explanation (Haugaard, 1988).

Individual Deviance Explanation

An early individual deviance explanation focused on a lack of internal controls by the perpetrator and victim. The perpetrator was often described as mentally retarded or psychotic, and the victim as mentally incapacitated (for a review, see Mieselman, 1978). The psychoanalytic perspective also focused on individual deviance, suggesting that poorly resolved Oedipal issues encouraged some men to seek sexual relations with their daughters, as a way to deal with their desire to be sexual with their young mother (Cormier, Kennedy, & Sangowicz, 1962).

This type of individual deviance explanation seems appropriate in only a small minority of cases. The view of the perpetrator as psychotic or mentally retarded is countered by research showing that he often functions well in society, shows few overt signs of individual disturbance, and has an average IQ (e.g., Finkelhor, 1979; Haywood, Grossman, & Cavanaugh, 1990). There is some empirical evidence for individual deviance in incestuous fathers. One study found incestuous fathers to be higher on the psychopathic deviate scale of the MMPI than nonincestuous fathers (Anderson & Shafer, 1979). Scott and Stone (1986) found MMPI scores among incestuous fathers that suggested covert antisocial tendencies that might lead them to take improper risks and be deficient in empathy.

Recent work on individual deviance in incestuous families focuses on the sexual orientation of the father. It is hypothesized that many incest perpetrators have a primary sexual arousal to children, although they also may have sexual relations with a spouse (Lanyon, 1986). Evidence supporting this comes from Abel, Becker, Cunningham-Rathner, Mittelman, and Rouleau (1988), who found that among 199 incarcerated men who had engaged in incest, 131 also had molested children outside their family.

Several studies have compared the sexual arousal of incest perpetrators and other child molesters. Abel, Becker, Murphy, and Flanagan (1981) found that 6 incest perpetrators had sexual arousal patterns similar to those of 10 pedophiles who had molested only nonrelatives. In contrast, Quinsey, Chaplin, and Carrigan (1979) found that 9 incest perpetrators had higher arousal to slides of nude adult women than nude female children, whereas 15 nonincestuous child molesters showed a more similar response to the women and children. Abel et al. (1981) found that one incest perpetrator had a much higher response to the child stimuli and a much lower response to the adult stimuli than the average of all six incest perpetrators. This suggests that some, but not all, incest perpetrators have a sexual arousal pattern primarily aimed at children.

Chaotic Explanation

The chaotic explanation focuses on a lack of external regulation. It suggests that the occurrence of incest rises because societal prohibitions of sex between family members have little influence on family members' behavior (Will, 1983). Such families are characterized as socially and physically isolated from the larger community. Sexual relations occur between nuclear and extended family members both within the same generation and across generations.

The lack of systematic study of chaotic families makes this explanation difficult to evaluate. A few historical studies have reported a higher level of incest in communities experiencing chaotic conditions (Bagley, 1969). However, the rate of incestuous behavior in chaotic communities has not been compared to the rate in less chaotic communities during the same period.

Functional Explanation

The functional explanation is based on the premise that behaviors within a family are interrelated. The analysis of incestuous behavior focuses on the ways in which it helps to maintain a set of behaviors within which the family system functions most effectively (for example, see Dell, 1989; Steinglass, 1987). In some cases, the family system may influence the onset of incest. In other cases, other factors may influence the onset, and the incest may then be maintained because it provides some stability for the family system (Minuchin et al., 1975).

One hypothesis for the function of incest is that it can reduce parental conflict (Lustig, Dresser, Spellman, & Murray, 1966; Machotka, Pittman, & Flomenhaft, 1967). This happens as the father's approach to the daughter allows conflicted parents to withdraw from each other physically or emotionally. The parental distancing reduces marital conflict that might have led to the breakup of the family. In some cases, the father will turn his sexual attention to the daughter, further reducing the need for contact between the parents. If the family is stabilized because of a reduction in parent conflict, there is pressure from the system for the incest to continue.

Clinical examples frequently show a marked power difference in the relationship between parents in an incestuous family. One pattern has been described as a "pathological exaggeration of generally accepted patriarchal norms" (Herman, 1983, p. 83). It involves a dominant father and a submissive mother (Browning & Boatman, 1977; Finkelhor, 1979; Herman, 1981). A second pattern involves an angry and dominant mother who treats a passive and dependent father like a child (Greene, 1977). The less-powerful parent in both patterns often is primarily associated with the child subsystem. The dominant parent may take a child into the parental subsystem, and this child may take on the sexual role of a spouse. The chance of incest between a child and submissive parent who functions in the child subsystem may be more likely because of the lower prohibition of sibling incest than parent/child incest (Meiselman, 1978).

Some empirical evidence supports the functional explanation. Among 586 female undergraduates, those who had experienced incest rated their family as having greater male/female power differences than those who had been abused by someone outside the family or those who had not been abused (Alexander & Lupfer, 1987). Other evidence shows that parental distancing is not always present in incestuous families. Herman (1983) found that the father still had regular sexual relations with his wife in many incestuous families. DeYoung (1982) noted that only 43% of her clinical sample of couples from incestuous families stated that they were sexually alienated from each other. Finally, emotional alienation between the parents was a primary factor in only 16% of the cases seen in an incest treatment program, and sexual alienation in only 15% (Kroth, 1979).

Male-Dominance Explanation

The male-dominance explanation provides a reinterpretation of many of the observations upon which the functional perspective is based. Primary objections to the functional explanation are that it fails to consider strong societal influences on sexual behavior in and outside of families, and that it reduces the responsibility of the perpetrator (e.g., Bograd, 1984). The occurrence of incest is seen as another demonstration of the inequality of power between men, women, and children, and of the extent to which society supports the desires of men (McIntyre, 1981; Wattenberg, 1985). It is argued that incestuous behavior does not occur because it stabilizes the family; rather, it begins because of the desire of the father and continues because of the untoward legal, financial, and emotional consequences to the mother and child if they took steps to have it halted.

From the male-dominance perspective, the functional explanation encourages the inappropriate belief that the mother and daughter share some of the responsibility for the development of incest (Taubman, 1984). It is also argued that the functional explanation encourages the belief that the mother knows about ongoing incest and chooses not to intervene. The male-dominance explanation suggests that the mother is often unaware of the incest because the father can coerce the daughter to keep the incest secret. Individual deviance explanations are faulted for failing to consider the societal context that supports incest by teaching men that they have the right to have their sexual urges satisfied and that it is the place of women to satisfy them (Waldby, Clancy, Emetchi, & Summerfield, 1989).

What research there is to support the male-dominance explanation centers on reports that mothers from incestuous families are often physically and emotionally abused by their male partners (Herman, 1981; Truesdell, McNeil, & Deschner, 1986). This suggests that some women in incestuous families are often powerless. Other evidence, however, indicates that physical abuse or other domineering behaviors by the father takes place in a minority of incestuous families (Kroth, 1979).

Combining Explanations

Although each of the four explanations has its champions, each seems inadequate to account for the occurrence of incest. It is more likely that incestuous behavior is stimulated by a combination of factors, making various combinations of explanations most effective for understanding incest. For example, the male-dominance explanation aids in understanding how incest might be more prevalent in one society than another, but fails to explain why incest occurs in only a minority of families in any society. The functional explanation points to types of families in which the chance of incest is increased, but fails to explain how incest develops in some conflicted families but not others. By combining explanations, a clearer understanding of the development of incest in a particular family can be achieved. This may lead to more effective interventions for the family.

SEXUAL ABUSE BY SIBLINGS

The study of sexual abuse between siblings has gained momentum during the past decade. Clinicians treating adult perpetrators of child sexual abuse began to discover that many of the adults had begun their abusive behaviors as an adolescent or a child. Treatment of adolescent sexual offenders revealed that many of their victims had been a sibling. Clinicians treating victims of sibling abuse reported on the extent to which the siblings had been traumatized by their experiences. The combination of the trauma experienced by victims of sibling abuse, the frequency with which the clinical reports suggested that it might be occurring, and the concern that abuse of siblings might promote the development of an abusive adolescent and adult, propelled the study of sibling abuse.

Definitional Issues

Defining Behaviors as Abusive

Defining sexual abuse by a sibling can be more difficult than defining parent/child sexual abuse. At issue is distinguishing abusive incidents from those that involve sexual exploration or other behaviors unlikely to have a negative influence on the development of the siblings.

As noted in a previous section, certain parent/child interactions can be defined as sexual abuse because the act itself is sexual and the child is assumed to be unable to consent because of the power differential between the parent and child. A similar combination of act and power differential can be used to define sibling abuse in cases when there is a clear difference in power between the children; for example, when a 17-year-old fondles a 5-year-old. However, a power differential may not be apparent in many cases, as when an 8-year-old fondles a 7-year-old. Also, it is unclear whether certain acts that are abusive when they occur between a parent and child are also abusive if they occur between siblings of any age (e.g., genital fondling).

Some researchers have used a specific age difference when defining sexual behaviors as abusive. For example, Finkelhor (1980) and DeJong (1989) used a 5-year age difference. This can provide a clear distinction for conducting research; however, applying age-difference standards in clinical practice can be problematic. There is no theoretical or empirical reason to believe, for instance, that a 4-year age difference results in nonabusive acts, while a 5-year difference results in abusive acts. DeJong suggested that sexual activity between siblings in different developmental stages is likely to be exploitive. Distinguishing developmental stages can be difficult, however, and age differences of one or two years may place children in different developmental stages sometimes and in the same stage other times.

Some researchers have used the act itself to define sibling sexual abuse. For example, DeJong (1989) defined sex between siblings that included attempted or completed penile–vaginal or penile–anal intercourse as abusive because it was "not typical of sexual exploratory behavior in childhood" (p. 276).

The use of coercion by one of the siblings can be a useful defining feature (DeJong, 1989; Finkelhor, 1980). However, detecting coercion can be difficult in some cases. For example, a child may feel obliged to engage in sexual activity that a sibling suggests, although there are no specific coercive acts. The extent to which one sibling feels victimized is an additional criterion (Wiehe, 1990). Sexual activity that results in one child verbalizing or displaying behaviors indicating displeasure with it may be considered abusive from that child's perspective.

The duration of the sexual activity also can be used to distinguish sexual exploration from abuse. Wiehe (1990), for example, suggested that sexual exploration involves only a few sexual contacts. After the child's curiosity has been satisfied, further sexual encounters are likely to involve some other motivation. DeJong (1989) suggested that exploitive sexuality may occur if both siblings do not have the same motivation (e.g., exploration, physical pleasure).

Only a few of these factors can be used to demarcate acts into those that are always abusive and those that are never abusive. In some cases, sibling abuse can be defined by using only one factor, as when one sibling physically forces another to be sexual. In many cases, however, several factors will need to be considered simultaneously. While this can result in a process of definition that is not always reliable, such a process is preferable to one where a certain age difference or a certain act is always considered a defining feature of abuse.

Labeling a Sibling as an Abuser

A child who sexually abuses another may be involved in legal and mental health interventions. Therefore, the issue of whether or not one of the siblings must be an abuser if sexual abuse has occurred is important. The competence of a sibling to understand that an act is abusive should be considered when determining whether the child is an abuser. It is possible that some children will not comprehend the abusive nature of their acts with another sibling. The extent to which a child attempts to keep the activity secret may provide some clues about his or her understanding about the acts, but the secrecy may be because of the apparent prohibition against the acts, rather than because of an understanding that the acts are abusive. Intervention with a child who understands the abusive nature of the interaction is likely to differ from intervention for a child who does not understand that it is abusive.

Prevalence and Consequences of Sibling Sexual Abuse

Prevalence

Surveys of undergraduates about sexual activity between siblings have shown prevalences of 15% for women and 10% for men (Finkelhor, 1980), and 7% for women and 4% for men (Haugaard & Tilly, 1988). Finkelhor (1980) reported that approximately 25% of the encounters in his study were exploitive, or approximately 4% of the women and 2.5% of the men. In studies involving probability samples of women, the prevalence of sibling sexual abuse was 2.5% (Russell, 1983) and 3% (Wyatt, 1985). Among the 29 cases in Russell's survey, 26 were perpetrated by a brother and 3 were perpetrated by a sister. Twenty-seven percent of the cases of abuse by a brother involved intercourse, 61% involved genital fondling or digital penetration, and 12% involved nongenital fondling. The three cases with a sister involved genital fondling or digital penetration.

DeJong (1989) studied 831 children under the age of 14 who were evaluated for suspected sexual abuse. Thirty-five children had been abused by a sibling—5% of the girls and 2% of the boys. Thirty-one children (89%) had experienced attempted or completed vaginal or anal penetration, and 10 children (29%) were injured during the abuse. The high prevalence of intercourse is similar to that found by O'Brien (1991) who studied adolescent sexual abusers. O'Brien reported that 46% of those who abused siblings engaged in completed vaginal or anal intercourse—compared to 28% of those who abused children outside the family.

In summary, nonclinical samples show that approximately 2%–4% of children experience sexual abuse perpetrated by a sibling. If the presence of coercion or an age difference of 5 years or more is used to differentiate abuse from other sexual interactions, about one quarter of sexual activity between siblings is abusive. Abuse by siblings is less common than abuse by fathers, stepfathers, or uncles (Finkelhor, 1979; Russell, 1983; Wyatt, 1985). Of concern is the high percentage of sibling abuse cases that involve intercourse and/or some type of injury. O'Brien (1991) found that the average number of separate sexual incidents between siblings was 18, which was considerably more than the number of incidents between adolescents and nonsiblings. O'Brien also found that the length of time over which the incidents occurred was longer for sibling abuse. This raises the possibly that sibling sexual abuse often can proceed from less intrusive forms of sexuality to intercourse, a pattern that has been noted in studies of adult/child sexual abuse.

Consequences

Several factors mentioned in the previous section have been associated with harmful outcomes in sexual abuse victims: repeated abuse, engaging in intercourse, presence of physical coercion, and the presence of injury (see Haugaard & Reppucci, 1988). Thus, the consequences of sibling abuse may be severe for many children.

There are several clinical reports documenting the negative effects of sibling abuse on some children (e.g., Laviola, 1989; Wiehe, 1990). These have shown that the consequences can be devastating for some children. The nature of these reports makes it impossible to estimate the percentage of victims of sibling abuse that suffer few, some, or many negative consequences. Little information is available about differences in the consequences experienced by children who are sexually abused by siblings and others. In his study of college students, Finkelhor (1980) found long-term consequences of sibling abuse. Those who had experienced sexual activity with a sibling 5 or more years older had lower levels of "sexual self-esteem" than those who had experiences with a sibling who was a peer, or those who had no sibling sexual experiences.

The long-term consequences to the abusive sibling are varied, and may depend on the motivation for the abuse, as well as the reaction of the family and community, once the abuse is revealed. Ongoing abuse that is not revealed may set a pattern of sexual excitement paired with exploitive behavior that can be repeated in the future relationships of the abuser. Abuse that is revealed, but not confronted, may set the stage for the expectation that future exploitive behavior will also go unchallenged.

Adolescents who are forced to accept a sexual-deviate label by legal or mental health agencies or by their families, without any consideration of the family or societal dynamics that influenced the abusive behavior, may feel ostracized and angry, and may get little benefit from any treatment that they receive. This may increase the chance of a repetition of their exploitive behaviors. Adolescents who receive treatment that takes family and social context into consideration may be able to confront and overcome the individual, family, and social factors that influenced their behavior.

Etiology of Sibling Sexual Abuse

Some research has been completed on the development of sexually abusive behaviors in children and adolescents (e.g., Becker, Cunningham-Rathner, & Kaplan, 1986; Fehrenbach & Monastersky, 1988). There is less information on the factors that influence a child or adolescent to aim his or her abusive behaviors at a sibling. Smith and Israel (1987) studied 25 families referred to a sexual assault treatment center because of sexual activity between siblings. They found three dynamics prevalent among the families: distant, inaccessible parents; parental stimulation of a sexual climate in the home; and the presence of many family secrets, particularly extramarital affairs. In eight families a daughter had been sexually abused by the father before being abused by a sibling. Smith and Israel suggested that the combination of a sexual climate in the home, a parent modeling prohibited sexual activity (the affairs or father/daughter incest), and lack of supervision created a climate where the development of sexual activity between siblings was enhanced. They did not discuss the development of coercive or exploitive sex between the children, and it is not clear what percentage of the sexual behavior was exploitive.

O'Brien (1991) compared adolescents who had sexually abused siblings and those who had abused children outside the family. The families of the adolescents who abused a sibling were more likely to have a parent who had been sexually abused as a child. Other incidents of incest were more likely to have occurred in these families as well. There was no difference in the percentage of families that had substance abuse problems. Both groups of adolescents had poor peer relationships and 40% of both groups of adolescents had been sexually abused when they were children.

These studies, along with studies of adolescent sexual abuse perpetrators, suggest that certain characteristics and experiences of the adolescent, combined with certain family characteristics, may increase the likelihood of sibling sexual abuse. Adolescents who have been abused and who have poor peer relationships seem to be at risk for engaging in coercive sex with others. Such an adolescent, living in a family in which there is a focus on sexuality and in which there is little parental control, may engage a sibling in abusive sexuality.

SEXUAL ABUSE BETWEEN SPOUSES

The study of sexual abuse between spouses has lagged behind the study of other forms of intrafamilial sexual abuse and the study of other forms of violence between spouses. Until recently, sexual abuse between spouses received little notice, except in isolated criminal cases. This is probably because of the long-held social and legal expectations that wives have an obligation to be sexual with their husbands on demand, and may have led to the assumption that sexual abuse between spouses rarely occurred. Just as the abuse of children gained more attention as societal beliefs about the rights of children changed, the issue of women being sexually assaulted by their husbands changed as new beliefs about sexual relations between husbands and wives began to emerge. Concern with the issue grew as the prevalence of sexual assault between spouses became better understood.

Definitional Issues

The process of defining marital sexual abuse can be problematic. Many of the objective factors that can be used to define parent/child or sibling sexual abuse are not applicable when defining marital abuse, such as type of act, or age or power differential. The only obvious defining characteristic of marital sexual assault is whether or not one partner engages in sexual activity without giving consent. The lack of consent of one partner is often clear, such as when a husband physically forces his wife to have sex with him or when he has sex with her when she is unconscious. However, there are a substantial number of situations in which the consent of one partner may not be clear. For example, one partner could dislike having sex very much, yet have sex in order to keep the other partner from becoming angry. Also, one partner could continue to request sex until the other partner reluctantly agrees. The point at which asking becomes badgering or threatening is unclear.

Rather than being a dichotomous variable (either present or not present) consent is best thought of as lying along a continuum. On one end is clear and active consent, and on the other is clear and active lack of consent. In the middle are varying degrees of the presence or absence of consent. The challenge with any continuous variable is dividing it into two or more discrete categories—in the case of marital sexual assault, where does consent end and lack of consent begin? One challenge for researchers in this area is to make the division in a place that can be reliably measured. The other challenge is to make the division so that the abused group includes those that have truly been assaulted, but is not so heterogeneous that the group ceases to have any meaning.

Marital Rape and Wife Rape

Pagelow (1988) and Russell (1990) propose that the term *wife rape* is preferable to *marital rape*. They state that the use of spouse rape hides the fact that the wife is invariably the victim of sexual assault. Furthermore, they suggest that the term *spouse rape* is often used for political purposes, because it is difficult to gather political support for women's issues.

The problem with this argument is that no research has been published that addresses the issue of husbands being sexually assaulted by their wives. Such an idea may sound incredible; however, it is reasonable to assume that the prevalence of other forms of domestic violence was considered incredible before such forms were studied. The use of the term *marital rape* is preferable until there is empirical evidence that wives only are the victims of marital rape.

Rape and Assault

The interview format used by Russell (1990) involved asking women early in an interview if they had ever been the victim of rape or attempted rape, and then later asking them if they had been sexually assaulted by their husbands. Only 7% of the women who said that they had been sexually assaulted by their husbands had stated earlier that they had been raped. Another 9% said that they had experienced something similar to rape. The small percentage of women who identified the sexual assault as a rape suggests that the definition of rape held by many women may include only sexual assault by nonfamily members. Consequently, using the term *rape* in family violence research may be problematic.

Definitions Used in Research

Russell (1990) defined *wife rape* as vaginal, anal, or oral intercourse or forced digital penetration when a husband physically forces his wife to have sex, when he threatens her with physical harm if she does not have sex, or when he has sex with her when she is asleep, unconscious, or in some other way helpless. She included women who experienced either completed rape or attempted rape; although she does not provide criteria for attempted rape. Russell noted that other forced sex acts, such as fondling of breasts or the husband's penis are not included in her definition of wife rape. This exclusion does not indicate an acceptance of these acts; rather, it is made to form a relatively circumscribed group of rape victims.

Finkelhor and Yllo (1985) asked women, "Has your spouse ever used physical force or threat to try to have sex with you," and considered all women who answered *yes* to have been raped. Thus, their definition is broader than Russell's, in that it includes any act that the respondent felt was sexual. It is narrower in one factor—not including sexual acts that occurred when the wife was asleep or unconscious, and thus might not have been considered *forced* by the respondents. Shields and Hanneke (1988) included sexual acts in which "moderate or severe" force was used. The sexual acts were diverse, including intercourse, fondling, posing for pictures, and watching others have sex. Frieze (1983) also included any sexual act that a wife stated she was coerced into participating in by her husband.

Prevalence of Marital Sexual Assault

Community Surveys

Russell (1990) conducted a large-scale study of the prevalence of wife rape (the term that she prefers) in 1978. She and her colleagues interviewed 930 women, randomly selected in San Francisco. Eighty-seven women (14%) of the 644 who had ever been married reported at least one experience of wife rape. Eighty-five percent had experienced penile–vaginal rape, 10% had experienced attempted penile–vaginal rape, and 5% had experienced completed or attempted anal or oral sex. Russell noted the conservative nature of the findings. Two groups of potential victims were not considered to have been raped: women who reported that they did not want to have sex with their husbands but did so from a sense of obligation, and women who refused to discuss the forced sex that they said they had experienced.

Finkelhor and Yllo (1985) surveyed a probability sample of 323 women in the Boston area, who had a child between 6 and 14 years. Ten percent of the women had experienced physical force or the threat of force to engage in sex with her husband or cohabiting partner. Women with less education and lower incomes at the time of the survey were more likely to have experienced forced sex. Women who had been sexually abused as children were three times as likely to have experienced forced sex by their husbands than those women who had not been sexually abused as children.

Surveys of Selected Groups of Women

Several studies have examined the co-occurrence of physical and sexual abuse of wives by their husbands. These studies cannot be used to understand sexual assault of wives in nonphysically abusive homes. However, they can shed light on the development of sexually assaultive behaviors in a marriage.

Shields and Hanneke (1988) questioned 92 married or previously married women referred from various social service agencies and self-help groups. They found that 48% of the women had experienced nonsexual violence, 41% had experienced sexual and nonsexual violence, and 11% had experienced no violence. None of the women had experienced sexual violence only. In a later study (Hanneke, Shields, & McCall, 1986), women were recruited through family planning agencies, a college campus, and a newspaper advertisement. Among the 307 married or previously married women, 1% had experienced rape only, 8% had experienced both rape and other forms of physical assault, and 22% had been battered only.

Frieze (1983) interviewed 137 self-selected battered women and a comparison group of 137 women. Within the battered group, 34% of the women had been raped by their partner. Among those who had never experienced physical assault by their partner, 3% reported being raped or being forced to have sex with their partners (the type of force was not specified). These findings can be compared with those of Russell's (1990) community sample. When she examined the percentage of women who had experienced physical or sexual violence, she found that 12% had experienced wife beating only, 10% had experienced wife rape only, and an additional 10% had experienced wife beating and wife rape. These and similar studies suggest that, for the majority of women, rape experiences are embedded in a marriage of general violence.

Consequences of Marital Sexual Assault

Determining the specific consequences of marital sexual assault may help to guide the treatment of the victims and their families; however, these consequences are difficult to isolate. As has been shown, most of those who experience wife rape have also experienced other forms of violence. Furthermore, Shields and Hanneke (1983) found that the nonsexual violence experienced by those who were also raped was more severe than the nonsexual violence experienced by the other women in their study. Women who have been raped by their partners also are more likely to have been sexually abused as a child. They may have had other detrimental experiences within their marriage relationship, outside their marriage, and before their marriage. The problems associated with isolating the specific influences of marital rape should not be used to suggest that there are minimal consequences associated with marital rape. Many of these women are traumatized by their experiences of repeated sexual and physical assault.

Many women blame themselves, at least in part, for their marital rape (Frieze, 1983). This may be due to many husbands' assertions that their aggressive behavior is due to the wife's sexual inadequacies. To the extent that the guilt and belief about personal sexual inadequacy is accepted, this may lead to many raped wives having difficulty establishing sexual intimacy in subsequent relationships (Russell, 1990). Bowker (1983) found that marriages in which wives had been raped were of lower overall quality than those in which physical, but not sexual, assault had occurred. Shields and Hanneke (1983) found that marital rape resulted in decreases in self-esteem and marital satisfaction, even after the consequences of other forms of marital violence were statistically controlled.

The consequences of marital rape on other family members have not been investigated. The consequences to children of being raised in violent homes have been well documented (Van Hasselt, Morrison, Bellack, & Hersen, 1988). Young children may be unable to distinguish sexual violence from other forms of violence, especially if it takes place outside their field of vision. Older children may be able to distinguish sexual violence between their parents by what they hear and see. This may have a specific influence on their emotions or behaviors and may influence their later sexual and relationship development. The form or extent of this influence is unknown at this time.

Etiology of Marital Sexual Assault

Pagelow (1988) suggests several causes of wife rape from a social and historical perspective: the belief that wives should obey their husbands in all respects, including their expectations to have sex; the legal exemption that prohibited husbands from being prosecuted for raping their wives; and the "rape culture" present in our society. These factors may account for the higher prevalence of wife rape in this society than in others. However, they do not help distinguish what leads particular men to be sexually aggressive with their wives.

Investigations into the factors that distinguish men who do and men who do not rape their wives have not appeared in the literature. Thus, it is difficult to hypothesize about the factors that contribute to specific cases of wife rape. However, literature on the etiology of rape has shown that a small percentage of men seem to be sexually aroused by violence or violent sexuality (e.g., Malamuth & Check, 1983; Malamuth, Check, & Briere, 1986). These men may be prone to sexual assault, and for many of them, their wives may be the most convenient and safe target for their violence.

More information must be gathered directly from the men who are sexually violent toward their wives. This information would be difficult to collect because these men are likely to be loath to talk about their behavior. However, researchers have gathered information from men who sexually assault children, and this has resulted in increased understanding about child sexual abuse. Information from husband-rapists also may be available to researchers willing to search for it.

CONCLUSION

A significant percentage of families in the United States experience some form of sexual abuse. Although there may be only a single incident in some families, the abuse in most of them occurs many times. There is a meaningful chance that those who are victims of ongoing sexual abuse in a family will suffer negative emotional and physical consequences. Sexual abuse in families is a clear public health problem.

Many of the characteristics associated with negative outcomes for victims of all forms of sexual abuse are likely to be present in cases of familial abuse. The abuser often is a meaningful person in the victim's life, either because of emotional ties or financial dependency. In most cases, the victim and perpetrator live together. Thus, a person to whom the victim may need to turn for support, and the place within which most of us gain some of our strengths, are also associated with feelings of helplessness, pain, and victimization. The family and family home have become sources of anxiety rather than support.

Different forms of sexual abuse occur together in many families. Several theories have been proposed to explain this, but none of them is generally accepted at this point. The co-occurrence of these different forms suggests the importance of looking for other forms of sexual abuse in a family in which one form has recently been revealed.

The etiology of family sexual abuse is unclear. It seems that many individual, familial, and societal factors place certain families at higher risk for the occurrence of sexual abuse. The complex picture presented by the combination of these risk factors points to the difficulty of identifying families in which sexual abuse is likely to occur. This complicates the task of the prevention and detection of sexual abuse in families.

The entire area of sexual abuse within families is complicated and filled with uncertainty. This is because the field has emerged relatively recently. Moreover, we are faced with complex individual, family, and social factors that must be considered in any investigation. This is not an area for those who need firm answers (or, I believe, for those that believe that they possess firm answers). Rather, it is an area for those with open minds, who are interested in struggling with the many complexities that the area of familial sexual abuse presents.

REFERENCES

Abel, G. G., Becker, J. V., Cunningham-Rathner, J., Mittelman, M., & Rouleau, J. (1988). Multiple paraphiliac diagnoses among sex offenders. *American Academy of Psychiatry and the Law. Bulletin., 16,* 153–168.

Abel, G. G., Becker, J. V., Murphy, W. D., & Flanagan, B. (1981). Identifying dangerous child molesters. In R. B. Stuart (Ed.), *Violent behaviors: Social learning approaches to prediction, management, and treatment.* New York: Brunner/Mazel.

Alexander, P. C., & Lupfer, S. L. (1987). Family characteristics and long-term consequences associated with sexual abuse. *Archives of Sexual Behavior, 16,* 235–245.

Anderson, L. M. & Shafer, G. (1979). The character disordered family: A community treatment model for family sexual abuse. *American Journal of Orthopsychiatry, 49,* 436–445.

Bagley, C. (1969). Incest behavior and incest taboo. *Social Problems, 16,* 505–519.

Becker, J. V., Cunningham-Rathner, J., & Kaplan, M. S. (1986): Adolescent sexual offenders. *Journal of Interpersonal Violence, 1,* 431–445.

Billings, A. G., & Moos, R. H. (1983). Comparisons of children of depressed and nondepressed parents. *Journal of Abnormal Child Psychology, 11,* 463–486.

Bograd, M. (1984). Family systems approaches to wife battering: A feminist critique. *American Journal of Orthopsychiatry, 54,* 558–568.

Bowker, L. H. (1983). Marital rape: A distinct syndrome? *Social Casework, 64,* 347–352.

Briere, J., Evans, D., Runtz, M., & Wall, T. (1988). Symptomatology in men who were molested as children. *American Journal of Orthopsychiatry, 58,* 457–461.

Briere, J., & Runtz, M. (1988). Symptomatology associated with childhood sexual victimization in a nonclinical adult sample. *Child Abuse & Neglect, 12,* 51–59.

Browne, A., & Finkelhor, D. (1986). The impact of child sexual abuse: A review of the research. *Psychological Bulletin, 99,* 66–77.

Browning, D. H., & Boatman, B. (1977). Incest: Children at risk. *American Journal of Psychiatry, 134,* 69–72.

Conte, J. R., & Schuerman, J. R. (1987). Factors associated with an increased impact of child sexual abuse. *Child Abuse & Neglect, 11,* 201–211.

Cormier, B. M., Kennedy, M., & Sangowicz, J. (1962). Psychodynamics of father daughter incest. *Canadian Psychiatric Association Journal, 7,* 203–217.

Dell, P. F. (1989). Violence and the systemic view: The problem of power. *Family Process, 28,* 1–14.

DeJong, A. R. (1989). Sexual interactions among siblings and cousins: Experimentation or exploitation? *Child Abuse & Neglect, 13,* 271–279.

DeYoung, M. (1982). *Sexual victimization of children.* Jefferson, NC: McFarland.

Fehrenbach, P. A., & Monastersky, C. (1988). Characteristics of female adolescent sexual offenders. *American Journal of Orthopsychiatry, 58,* 148–151.

Finkelhor, D. (1979). *Sexually abused children.* New York: Free Press.

Finkelhor, D. (1980). Sex among siblings: A survey on prevalence, variety, and effects. *Archives of Sexual Behavior, 9,* 171–194.

Finkelhor, D., & Yllo, K. (1985). *License to rape.* New York: Holt, Rinehart & Winston.

Fischer, M. (1983). Adolescent adjustment after incest. *School Psychology International, 4,* 217–222.

Frieze, I. H. (1983). Investigating the causes and consequences of marital rape. *Signs: Journal of Women and Culture in Society, 8,* 532–553.

Fritz, G. S., Stoll, K., & Wagner, N. N. (1981). A comparison of males and females who were sexually molested as children. *Journal of Sex & Marital Therapy, 7,* 54–59.

Gelinas, D. J. (1983). The persisting negative effects of incest. *Psychiatry, 46,* 312–332.

Giarretto, H. (1982). *Integrated treatment of child sexual abuse.* Palo Alto, CA: Science & Behavior Books.

Goodwin, J., McCarthy, T., & DiVasto, P. (1981). Prior incest in mothers of abused children, *Child Abuse & Neglect, 5,* 87–96.

Greene, N. B. (1977). A view of family pathology involving child molest: From a juvenile probation perspective. *Juvenile Justice Digest, 13,* 29–34.

Hanneke, C. R., Shields, N. M., & McCall, G. J. (1986). Assessing the prevalence of marital rape. *Journal of Interpersonal Violence, 1,* 350–362.

Harter, S., Alexander, P. C., & Neimeyer, R. A. (1988). Long-term effects of incestuous child abuse in college women: Social adjustment, social cognition, and family characteristics. *Journal of Consulting and Clinical Psychology, 56,* 5–8.

Haugaard, J. J. (1988). The use of theories about the etiology of incest as guidelines for legal and therapeutic interventions. *Behavioral Sciences and the Law Journal, 6,* 221–238.

Haugaard, J. J., & Emery, R. E. (1989). Methodological issues in child sexual abuse research. *Child Abuse & Neglect, 13,* 89–100.

Haugaard, J. J., & Reppucci, N. D. (1988). *The sexual abuse of children: A comprehensive guide to current knowledge and intervention strategies.* San Francisco: Jossey-Bass.

Haugaard, J. J., & Tilly, C. (1988). Characteristics predicting children's responses to sexual encounters with other children. *Child Abuse & Neglect, 12,* 209–218.

Haywood, T. W., Grossman, L. S., & Cavanaugh, J. L. (1990). Subjective versus objective measurements of deviant sexual arousal in clinical evaluations of alleged child molesters. *Psychological Assessment: A Journal of Consulting and Clinical Psychology, 2,* 269–275.

Herman, J. (1981). *Father–daughter incest.* Cambridge, MA: Harvard University Press.

Herman, J. (1983). Recognition and treatment in incestuous families. *International Journal of Family Therapy, 5,* 81–91.

Kaufman, J., & Zigler, E. (1987). Do abused children become abusive parents? *American Journal of Orthopsychiatry, 57,* 186–192.

Kirkwood, L. J., & Mihaila, M. E. (1979). Incest and the legal system: Inadequacies and alternatives. *University of California, Davis, Law Review, 12,* 673–669.

Kohan, M. J., Pothier, P., & Norback, J. S. (1987). Hospitalized children with a history of sexual abuse: Incidence and care issues. *American Journal of Orthopsychiatry, 57,* 258–264.

Kroth, J. A. (1979). *Child sexual abuse: Analysis of a family therapy approach.* Springfield, IL: Thomas.

Krug, R. S. (1989). Adult male report of childhood sexual abuse by mothers. *Child Abuse & Neglect, 13,* 111–119.

Lanyon, R. I. (1986). Theory and treatment in child molestation. *Journal of Consulting and Clinical Psychology, 54,* 176–182.

Laviola, M. (1989). Effects of older brother–younger sister incest: A review of four cases. *Journal of Family Violence, 4,* 259–274.

Lee, C. M., & Gotlib, I. H. (1989). Maternal depression and child adjustment: A longitudinal analysis. *Journal of Abnormal Psychology, 98,* 78–85.

Lustig, N., Dresser, J. W., Spellman, S. W., & Murray, T. B. (1966). Incest: A family group survival pattern. *Archives of General Psychology, 14,* 31–40.

Machotka, P., Pittman, F. S., & Flomenhaft, K. (1967). Incest as a family affair. *Family Process, 6,* 98–116.

Malamuth, N. M., & Check, J. V. (1983). Sexual arousal to rape depictions: Individual differences. *Journal of Abnormal Psychology, 92,* 55–67.

Malamuth, N. M., Check, J. V., & Briere, J. (1986). Sexual arousal in response to aggression: Ideological, aggressive, and sexual correlates. *Journal of Personality and Social Psychology, 50,* 330–340.

McIntyre, K. (1981). Role of mothers in father–daughter incest: A feminist analysis. *Social Work, 81,* 462–466.

Meiselman, K. C. (1978). *Incest: A psychological study of causes and effects with treatment recommendations.* San Francisco: Jossey-Bass.

Mian, M. (1986). Review of 125 children, six years of age and under, who were sexually abused. *Child Abuse & Neglect, 10,* 223–229.

Minuchin, S., Baker, L., Rosman, B. L., Leibman, R., Milman, L, & Todd, T. C. (1975). A conceptual model of psychosomatic illness in children. *Archives of General Psychiatry, 32,* 1031–1038.

O'Brien, M. J. (1991). Taking sibling incest seriously. In M. Patton (Ed.), *Family sexual abuse* (pp. 75–92). Newbury Park, CA: Sage.

Pagelow, M. D. (1988). Marital rape. In V. Van Hasselt, R. Morrison, A. Bellack, & M. Hersen (Eds.), *Handbook of family violence* (pp. 207–232). New York: Plenum.

Quinsey, V. L., Chaplin, T. C., & Carrigan, W. F. (1979). Sexual preferences among incestuous and nonincestuous child molesters. *Behavior Therapy, 10,* 562–565.

Reinhart, M. A. (1987). Sexually abused boys. *Child Abuse & Neglect, 11,* 229–235.

Rimsza, M. E., & Niggemann, E. H. (1982). Medical evaluation of sexually abused children: A review of 311 cases. *Pediatrics, 69,* 8–14.

Russell, D. E. (1983). The incidence and prevalence of intrafamilial and extrafamilial sexual abuse of female children. *Child Abuse & Neglect, 7,* 133–146.

Russell, D. E. (1990). *Rape in marriage.* Bloomington: University of Indiana Press.

Scott, R. L., & Stone, D. A. (1986). MMPI profile constellations in incest families. *Journal of Consulting and Clinical Psychology, 54,* 6–14.

Shields, N. M., & Hanneke, C. R. (1983). Battered wives' reactions to marital rape. In D. Finkelhor, R. Gelles, G. Hotaling, & M. Straus (Eds.), *The dark side of families* (pp. 119–130). Newbury Park, CA: Sage.

Siegel, J. M., Sorenson, S. B., Golding, J. M., Burnam, M. A., & Stein, J. A. (1987). The prevalence of childhood sexual assault. *American Journal of Epidemiology, 126,* 1141–1153.

Smith, H., & Israel, E. (1987). Sibling incest: A study of the dynamics of 25 cases. *Child Abuse & Neglect, 11,* 101–108.

Steinglass, P. (1987). A systems view of family interaction and psychopathology. In T. Jacob (Ed.), *Family interaction and psychopathology* (pp. 25–66). New York: Plenum.

Taubman, S. (1984). Incest in context. *Social Work, 29,* 35–40.

Truesdell, D. L., McNeil, J. S., & Deschner, J. P. (1986). Incidence of wife abuse in incestuous families. *Social Work, 86,* 138–140.

Turner, S. M., Beidel, D. C., & Costello, A. (1987). Psychopathology in the offspring of anxiety disorder patients. *Journal of Consulting and Clinical Psychology, 55,* 229–235.

Van Hasselt, V. B., Morrison, R. L., Bellack, A. S., & Hersen, M. (1988). *Handbook of family violence.* New York: Plenum.

Waldby, C., Clancy, A., Emetchi, J., & Summerfield, C. (1989). Theoretical perspectives on father–daughter incest. In E. Driver & A. Droesen (Eds.), *Child sexual abuse: A feminist reader* (pp. 88–107). New York: New York University Press.

Wattenberg, E. (1985). In a different light: A feminist perspective on the role of mothers in father–daughter incest. *Child Welfare, 64,* 203–211.

Wheeler, B. R., & Walton, E. (1987). Personality disturbances of adult incest victims. *Social Casework, 65,* 597–602.

Wiehe, V. R. (1990). *Sibling abuse.* Ashland, MA: Lexington.

Will, D. (1983). Approaching the incestuous and sexually abusive family. *Journal of Adolescence, 6,* 229–246.

Wyatt, G. E. (1985). The sexual abuse of Afro-American and White-American women in childhood. *Child Abuse & Neglect, 9,* 507–519.

CHAPTER 16

Psychological Abuse Between Adult Partners

Prevalence and Impact on Partners and Children

K. DANIEL O'LEARY and ERNEST N. JOURILES

Physical abuse of adult partners has attracted much national attention, both in the media and in research. In contrast, psychological abuse is seldom described in the media unless it is accompanied by some bizarre psychological manipulation and/or in the context of physical abuse, as was the case of Lisa and Joel Steinberg (Booth, McDowell, & Simpson, 1993). At some level, probably all adults have engaged in some forms of psychologically abusive behavior with their past or present partners, and defining psychological abuse is a key issue in this area. Indeed, because of the frequency of psychologically abusive behaviors in many families, such behavior is often downplayed. On the other hand, clinical observation of repeated hostile, belittling, and demeaning behaviors of a partner toward his or her spouse indicates that such actions have extremely negative effects on the recipient of such aggression, on the children who observe such aggression, and maybe even on the individual engaging in such psychological aggressive and/or abusive behaviors. According to Murphy and Cascardi (in press), there have been no integrative reviews of research in the area of psychological aggression and/or psychological abuse. In addition, although it is generally presumed that psychological abuse generally precedes physical abuse, there are almost no developmental or longitudinal studies of the transition from one form of abuse to the other. In this chapter, we review the effects of psychological aggression that are reported in physically abusive and nonphysically abusive relationships in order to get some notion of the relative impact of psychological and physical aggression in these relationships. We also review research in which physically abused women rated the impact of psychological and physical abuse.

NIMH grants MH 19107 and MH 35340 provided support to K. Daniel O'Leary during the writing of this chapter; the Hogg Foundation provided support to Ernest N. Jouriles. We thank Miriam Ehrensaft who provided helpful substantive comments on an earlier draft of this manuscript.

DEFINITION

Psychological abuse of an adult partner has been conceptualized with various categorical or subtyping schemes (cf., Marshall, 1992a, 1992b; Pence & Paymar, 1986; Walker, 1984). Interestingly, the subcategories of psychological aggression with adult partners have considerable overlap with the subtyping of psychological abuse and/or maltreatment of children (cf., Garbarino, Guttman, & Seeley, 1986; Hart, Germain, & Brassard, 1987). For example, schemes for both include: 1) rejection; 2) humiliation and degradation; 3) threats and/or terrorization; 4) exploitation and/or use of "male privilege" to obtain services; and 5) isolation. Some accounts also include threats to harm self, partner, and pets. Certain categories, such as jealousy, are primarily relevant, although not exclusively related to the psychological abuse of adult partners.

Tolman (1989) and Marshall (1992a, 1992b) have been attempting to map the varied domains of psychological abuse, and their work will help guide research that focuses on different ways in which partners abuse each other psychologically. Tolman's work suggests that psychological maltreatment of a female partner is comprised primarily of two factors: 1) verbal/emotional abuse; and 2) a dominance/isolation factor. Of all the forms of psychological aggression, overt verbal aggression and passive aggression have been studied most frequently, and our review focuses primarily on such aggression.

According to a number of authors (cf., Walker, 1979; Anderson, Boulette, & Schwartz, 1991), verbal abuse of a partner is an attempt to control or dominate a partner. Verbal abuse is generally seen as an extreme form of psychological aggression, just as physical abuse is seen as an extreme form of physical aggression, which may range from a push or slap to beating, choking, or use of a knife against a partner. Psychological aggression has been measured by several investigators who have attempted to provide an objective assessment of behaviors, largely verbal in nature, that are said by others to be psychologically aggressive. For example, in our own research, we have used both factor analytic measurement procedures as well as judgments by experienced clinicians to assess assertion and psychological aggression (O'Leary & Curley, 1986).

Verbal abuse is generally defined as recurring criticism and/or verbal aggression toward a partner. Such verbal behavior is a major component of psychological abuse of a partner, although verbal abuse is not synonymous with psychological abuse because psychological abuse can also take the form of neglect and ignoring of a partner, as well as a number of the forms of psychological abuse mentioned earlier. However, in contrast to the legal aspect of neglect as a form of abuse in children, neglect as a form of psychological abuse has been much less studied in intimate adult relationships. Consequently, neglect is not a central focus of this review. Instead, as noted earlier, the review focuses on verbal abuse of an adult partner. We focus on the prevalence and effects of psychological abuse. Moreover, we assess the effects of psychological abuse between adult partners on both children and adults. Finally, the effects and mechanisms of children observing psychological abuse between parents are reviewed.

PREVALENCE

The prevalence of psychological abuse has been summarized recently by Murphy and Cascardi (in press). They looked at the prevalence of specific acts of psychological aggression as depicted on the Conflict Tactics Scale (Straus, 1979) across different samples. Using data from Barling, O'Leary, Jouriles, Vivian and McEwen (1987) in which both men and women seeking marital treatment reported on their own behavior as well as that of their partners, they reported that over 90% of men and women engaged in the following acts across the last year: insulted or swore at partner; did or said something to spite partner; stomped out of the room, house, or yard; and sulked or refused to talk about an issue. Based on data from a young married sample in Barling et al., surprisingly, over 80% of both men and women engaged in each of the specific behaviors noted above. Given this information, as well as data from dating couples (Arias, Samios, & O'Leary, 1987), it can be unequivocally stated that psychological aggression, such as those behaviors noted above, is essentially normative.

In over 200 women who sought the services of shelters, Tolman (1989) found that three fourths of these women endorsed the majority of 58 separate items covering a wide range of abusive behaviors over the past six months. For example, Tolman indicated that the following percentages of women endorsed the items herein noted: swore at her (95%); insulted her in front of others (85%); ordered her around (89%), gave her the silent treatment (87%); monitored her time (85%), and restricted the use of car (54%).

The prevalence of children's exposure to interparent psychological abuse has not yet been investigated systematically. However, data from a number of sources suggest that children frequently witness such abuse. For example, a number of studies have assessed children's exposure to interpartner conflict with the O'Leary-Porter Scale (Porter & O'Leary, 1980), the Children's Perception Questionnaire (Emery & O'Leary, 1982), or a slightly modified version of one of these scales. These studies typically report means indicative of, at least, some exposure to conflict. Forehand and McCombs (1989), for example, found that both married and divorced mothers reported approximately 25% of their arguments with spouses or ex-spouses were witnessed by their adolescents (11–17 years). In a sample of families characterized by physical aggression in marriage (Jouriles, Barling, & O'Leary, 1987), 98% of the women reported that their husbands insulted or swore at them in front of their school-aged children (5–13 years), 95% of them indicated that their husbands did or said something to spite them in front of their children, and 90% indicated that their children were present when their husbands threatened to hit them or throw something at them. A significant number of children were reported to have witnessed these acts more than 20 times in the previous 12 months; 54% had witnessed the husband insult or swear at his wife; and 28% had seen the husband threaten to hit or throw something at his wife. Thus, the available evidence suggests that children frequently witness psychological abuse of a verbal nature between their parents.

In brief, psychological aggression is extremely common, even where physical abuse does not occur and where dating and/or marital satisfaction is quite high. In physically abusive couples, based on the clinical observations of many, the frequency of such actions is considerably higher and more extensive, although the exact nature of the differences in psychological aggression in physically abusive and nonphysically abusive couples is unclear. Given this state of affairs, it is not clear how to define psychological abuse specifically. Moreover, whereas there has been a clear move to have diagnoses that depict varied Partner Relational Problems in the Diagnostic and Statistical Manual for the DSM-IV, there is no proposed category of psychological abuse, although there is a category—Partner Relational Problems with Physical Abuse and Partner Relational Problems with Sexual Abuse (American Psychiatric Association, Task Force on DSM-IV, 1991, p. U.3). Given this state of affairs and the absence of a clear definition of psychological abuse, a reviewer in this area is left with varied measures of psychological aggression but no specific guides about when to consider such psychological aggression as abusive.

It is quite possible that the context of psychological abuse may be even more critical than the context of physical aggression. Contextual factors have been emphasized by many (cf., Brienes & Gordon, 1983; Murphy & Meyer, 1991) who argue that if we want to understand abuse issues, we must understand the social and economic climate in which men and women function. Although these arguments have generally been found in a feminist context, it is important to have an understanding of the context of psychological aggression, regardless of one's theoretical perspective.

Limitations in the literature on psychological abuse should be noted. First, the measures of psychological abuse of adult partners were quite limited until the appearance of measures by Straus (1979), Hudson and McIntosh (1981), O'Leary and Curley (1986), Tolman (1989), and Marshall (1992a; 1992b). The measures by Straus, O'Leary, and Curley focused primarily on verbal aggression, and the intent of the researchers was not to map the content domain of psychological aggression. Hudson and McIntosh, Tolman, and Marshall all sought to measure broader ranges of psychological abuse than had previous researchers, and their work clearly is valuable in this vein. Of interest, however, is the fact that the verbal/emotional abuse scale of the Tolman questionnaire discriminated battered women from nonbattered women better than did the dominance/isolation factor (Tolman, 1992). Whether the verbal abuse measure would distinguish men and/or women in maritally discordant, nonabusive relationships is the next relevant question for such research. Verbal aggression did not distinguish such groups in our own research (O'Leary & Curley). In short, measures of psychological aggression have only recently been developed, and we expect that a number of studies of physical violence will use measures such as those above, especially as investigators develop a greater appreciation of the impact of psychological abuse. Logically, it would be possible to use a host of marital measures, such as checklists of behaviors engaged in daily by partners, observational measures of negative problem-solving interactions, and even communication portions of general marital satisfaction inventories, as measures of psychological aggression. However, we argue against such a general approach, and urge the approaches used by those who have attempted to develop specific measures of psychological aggression (e.g., verbal aggression, threats of aggression, and dominance/isolation).

A limitation of the research of investigators who have provided broader maps of the content domain of psychological aggression (Hudson & McIntosh, 1981; Tolman, 1989; Marshall, 1992a) is that it does not provide any measure and/or data on psychological aggression by women toward men. As noted in the section on prevalence in this chapter, both men and women admit to engaging in frequent psychological abuse of their partners. It seems important to know something about how gender differences have an impact on psychological abuse, as well as to continue a broad mapping of the types of behaviors considered to be psychologically abusive by men and women. Marshall (1992b) has provided a measure of psychological violence against men by women to supplement the scale she developed to measure severity of violence against women. Moreover, she used these scales to provide ratings of severity and abusiveness of behaviors used by both men and women to help clarify gender differences in psychological aggression. Basically, the psychological aggressions measured were threats of mild violence, threats of moderate violence, and threats of serious violence. Although these behaviors are broader than some measures of psychological aggression, they clearly do not represent the full content domain of psychological aggression.

EFFECTS OF PSYCHOLOGICAL ABUSE ON ADULTS

In interviews with approximately 200 women, the majority of whom reported physical battering, Walker (1979) noted the following when commenting on the relative effects of psychological and physical abuse. "Most of the women in this project describe incidents involving psychological humiliation and verbal harassment as their worst battering experiences, whether or not they had been physically abused" (p. xv). Later in the book, Walker described various forms of reported psychological abuse. She noted that most of the batterers threatened to harm the families or close friends of the battered women. "Batterers repeatedly would frighten their women with terrorizing descriptions of how they would torture them. . . . Battered women all stated that they were aware that their partners could kill them" (p. 75). Given the severity of this psychological violence and the associated physical violence, any comparative statements about the impact of psychological and physical violence must be confined to this population. One could certainly imagine some forms of psychological abuse where no physical abuse has existed, which could have lesser effects than the psychological effects here depicted.

Folingstad, Rutledge, Berg, Hause, and Polek (1990) found that 72% of their sample of over 200 women with "long-term ongoing abusive relationships" rated psychological abuse as having a more severe impact on them than physical abuse. Despite the fact that the women indicated that the abusive relationships were ongoing, the vast majority of the women reported being out of the relationship. More specifically, 46% of the total sample of women rated emotional ridicule as the worst type of abuse. Fifteen percent of the total sample rated threats of abuse as the worst type of abuse, and 14% of the sample rated jealously as the worst type of abuse. Although this study is very informative about the importance of psychological abuse, the women in this sample had a wide variety of physically abusive incidents and "approximately one-fourth of the women had experienced only a small number of physically abusive incidents." Thus, it is unclear whether women in physically abusive relationships felt worse or more fearful than women in discordant, nonphysically abusive relationships. It is possible that a few incidents of physical abuse could be as important as many incidents of psychological abuse, but for most women frequent psychological abuse may be more damaging than an occasional physically abusive incident. At this point, the answer to this question is simply not known, but it is an important one to address.

In our own research on physical abuse, we examined whether fear of the partner was greater in physically abusive relationships than in maritally discordant, nonphysically abusive relationships or in self-defined satisfactory marriages (O'Leary & Curley, 1986). On average, the physically abused women reported physically abusive behavior several times per year. As expected, women in physically abusive relationships were more fearful of their husbands than women in discordant, nonphysically abusive relationships. Moreover, women in discordant, nonphysically abusive marriages were more fearful of their husbands than women in satisfactory marriages. Of special interest, given the Folingstad et al. (1990) results, was that our recent check on the specific behaviors wives feared most revealed that the nonphysically abused, maritally discordant women rated the partner's saying nasty things to them as the action they most feared. Moreover, the physically abused women rated fear of their partner hitting them as less severe than fear of their partner losing his temper or their partner saying nasty things to them (data taken from analyses of information from O'Leary & Curley). In brief, women in physically abusive relationships and women in discordant, nonphysically abusive relationships most fear their partner saying nasty things to them.

During the past few years, we have been evaluating a theoretical model of physical aggression against a spouse. The model we proposed was described in O'Leary and Vivian (1990) and in greater detail in O'Leary, Malone, and Tyree (in press). Our original intent was to examine the precursors of physical aggression in young married couples who were studied from one month prior to marriage until 30 months into marriage. The intent was foiled partially by the fact that approximately one third of both men and women reported that they engaged in physically aggressive behaviors against their partner. Given that physical aggression was so common in the young marriages selected to be generally representative of couples in Suffolk County, NY, a suburban county sixty miles from New York City, we were unable to examine the precursors of the first instances of physical aggression in a large segment of these couples. However, we were able to examine a number of factors that predicted physical aggression at 30 months into the marriage, although the physical aggression may also have occurred earlier. Indeed, physical aggression at premarriage was the best predictor of physical aggression at a later date. More specifically, physical aggression at one time period significantly correlated with physical aggression one year later, and the correlations were 0.48 for both men and women (O'Leary et al.). Because these correlations were so large, we decided to describe a model of the development of physical aggression without controlling for prior level of physical aggression. This methodology allowed us to examine those factors other than physical aggression that predicted physical aggression at a later time (O'Leary et al., in press).

We used a path model to evaluate the effects of the *premarriage* variables, such as personality styles (impulsivity, aggression, and defendence), violence in the family of origin, and physical aggression against parents and peers. We then measured psychological aggression directed at the marital partner and marital discord at 18 months after marriage in order to assess the impact of the premarriage variables on the relationship variables at 18 months. Finally, we measured physical aggression at 30 months after marriage to assess the direct and indirect effects of the variables at premarriage and at 18 months into marriage on physical aggression at 30 months after marriage. Before assessing the paths by which one variable influenced another, we first examined the first order correlations of each of the variables with the other variables. Psychological aggression was predicted by the following variables at premarriage for men: violence in the family of origin; physical aggression against peers; the three personality styles assessed, namely, impulsivity, aggression, and defendence; and relationship discord. For women, the following premarriage variables predicted psychological aggression at 18 months: physical aggression against parents and peers; the three personality styles assessed, namely, impulsivity, aggression, and defendence; and relationship discord. In predicting physical aggression for men at 30 months, all of the same variables were predictive for males except impulsivity. In addition, as predicted, psychological aggression at 18 months was predictive of physical aggression at 30 months. In predicting physical aggression for women at 30 months, violence in the family of origin was significant, as was psychological aggression and marital discord.

After assessing the first order correlations among the variables of interest, we then used a path analytic strategy to describe empirically our model with 272 couples assessed at premarriage, 18 months after marriage, and 30 months after marriage. This model for husbands is depicted in Figure 16.1. The model is too complex to describe in detail here, but we can say that it empirically

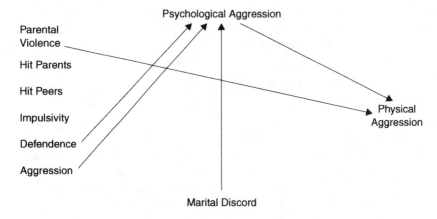

Figure 16.1. Path Model for Husbands

supported the hypothesis that psychological aggression at 18 months was the most potent predictor of physical aggression at 30 months for both men and women, and it had a direct effect on physical aggression. The other variable that had a direct effect on physical aggression for men was violence in the family of origin (parental violence). In addition, for men, as depicted in Figure 16.1, the personality variables, defendence and aggression, operated through psychological aggression, as did marital discord.

Disentangling Effects of Physical and Psychological Aggression

The effects of psychological aggression on relationships is often intertwined with the effects of physical aggression on those relationships. Indeed, as noted earlier, some women report that psychological aggression is more detrimental to them personally than is physical aggression. At first thought, this finding seems paradoxical when we consider the potential for serious physical injury from abusive behavior, such as punching, kicking, and beating. However, psychological aggression in highly discordant relationships or marriages is likely to occur on a daily basis, whereas physical aggression may occur several times per month.

The relative effects of psychological and physical aggression can be assessed in several ways. First, we can compare the reported negative impact of psychological aggression to the impact of physical aggression in men and women who report being the victims of *both* types of aggression. Second, we can compare the reports of men and women in psychologically abusive relationships without physical aggression to reports of men and women in relationships characterized by both psychological and physical aggression. In making comparisons of the latter type, some effort should be made to interpret or statistically control for the effects of marital discord when examining the effects of psychological aggression on an individual's functioning (e.g., on anxiety and depression).

Psychological Aggression and Co-Existing Physical Aggression

In relationships characterized by both physical and psychological aggression, the associations between psychological and marital satisfaction, depression, fear and anxiety can be examined. For example, O'Leary and Curley (1986) found that women's fear of their husbands was greater in a physically abusive relationship (where psychological aggression also existed) than in a group of women who were in a maritally discordant, nonphysically abusive relationship. This result was true even when the effects of marital discord were considered. Thus, fear of a male partner seems greater in women who are both psychologically and physically abused than in women who are in a discordant, but nonphysically abusive relationship. The above result may seem contradictory to the earlier mentioned finding that women in physically abusive relationships fear psychological aggression more than physical aggression (Folingstad et al., 1990; O'Leary & Curley, 1986). The finding can be reconciled by the fact that the comparisons are being made within and across groups of different women. Furthermore, women in a relationship characterized by both physical and psychological abuse may fear their husbands more than women in relationships characterized by only psychological abuse, who fear the psychological abuse more because of the repeated daily effect that it may have on their self-esteem.

Psychological Aggression Without Physical Aggression

In our research, we have examined the effects of psychological aggression on marital discord in young married men and women who had never engaged in physical aggression against their partners (Murphy & O'Leary, 1989). Psychological aggression at 18 months into the marriage predicted the first instances of physical aggression at 30 months. Moreover, when we examined the clinical utility of these findings, it was ascertained that those men and women who scored in the 90th percentile on the measure of psychological aggression at 18 months had a 30% to 50% chance of engaging in physically aggressive behavior against their partner within the next year. Of special interest was the fact that marital discord in these young couples did not predict first reports of physical aggression across time, although marital discord was significantly correlated with physical aggression at a particular point(s) in time. In couples who have not been physically aggressive, therefore, it seems that marital discord may be a negative side effect of the physical aggression.

Another way to look at the effects of psychological aggression is to examine the relationships of psychological aggression with other variables for men and women in physically abusive relationships versus those in relationships only characterized by psychological abuse. Stets (1990) followed this strategy and found different patterns of relationships for the two groups. These analyses led her to reason that physical and psychological aggression have different etiologies and effects.

In summary, psychological aggression is feared more than physical aggression by women in physically abusive relationships. However, women in physically abusive relationships report more fear of psychological aggression than women in nonphysically abusive relationships. These results may be largely a function of the frequency of psychologically abusive behaviors. In relationships characterized by both psychological and physical abuse, the frequency of psychological aggression is likely higher than in relationships without physical aggression.

MECHANISMS OF EFFECT OF PSYCHOLOGICAL ABUSE ON PARTNERS

The specific mechanisms of the effects of psychological abuse on adult partners have not been examined empirically, but there have been many clinical accounts of the ways in which psychological abuse adversely affects women. However, as mentioned by Pagelow (1984):

> Victims of all types of family violence share a common experience of denigration that results in diminished self-esteem. The shame and feelings of worthlessness so often expressed by battered wives is shared by maltreated children as well as maltreated elderly parents. . . . Wives who are battered by their husbands frequently report that the psychological abuse began first, followed by and then accompanying physical abuse. When a woman has been told that she is worthless, ugly, stupid, and sexually unsatisfactory by the man she married and loved, she begins to give the demeaning words credibility, and when she is isolated from others whose care might counterbalance this negative portrait, she comes to accept it as her self-image. (p. 80)

This depiction is meaningful, and it seems to make excellent clinical sense. Indeed, in a sample of 33 battered women who had sought counseling/support services from a community agency providing services for victims of domestic violence, 52% had Beck Depression Inventory Scores of 20 or greater, indicative of high levels of depressive symptomatology in at least half of that population of women. Moreover, the number, form, and subsequent consequences (injuries) were all significantly associated with extent of depressive symptomatology, as well as lower levels of self-esteem, as assessed on the Rosenberg Self-Esteem Scale. More specifically, both frequency and severity of physical aggression correlated at 0.54 or greater with self-esteem and depressive symptomatology. In an attempt to assess the role of physical abuse on self-esteem and depressive symptomatology, regression analyses indicated that self-esteem was more uniquely associated with physical aggression than depressive symptomatology. Given these results, continued and repeated physical abuse seems to have a more lasting and dramatic effect on the self-esteem of these women than on their reported depressive symptomatology. We do not know of any similar study with women who report psychological abuse alone (i.e., without physical aggression), but we believe that we can use the interpretation given above by Pagelow (1984) and our data that support her general position about the centrality of the self-esteem effect (Cascardi & O'Leary, 1992) to lead to the logical conclusion that psychological abuse operates in a similar function. Alternatively stated, the more frequent and severe the psychological aggression, the more likely a woman (or a man) will have lowered self-esteem.

For the past two decades, Expressed Emotion (EE) has attracted attention in research on relapse of schizophrenic patients following their hospital discharge, and some believe that this concept may be relevant to the treatment of other disorders. Expressed Emotion refers to the hostile and/or negative comments made by a parent or significant other about a patient. This concept has proved useful, given that schizophrenic patients whose family members have high EE, have higher relapse rates (Brown, Birley, & Wing, 1972; Hooley, 1985; Vaughn & Leff, 1976). The association between EE and psychological and physical abuse has not been evaluated empirically. However, conceptually, we would expect that EE would correlate both with psychological and physical abuse. If a parent or significant other makes overtly negative comments about a family member (patient) to an interviewer, one would expect that negative comments would be made directly to the patient at home. As such, high levels of EE may simply be summary statements about the level of negativity in the home. The high levels of EE could reflect psychological and/or physical abuse. However, it is very possible that parents who make many negative comments about the schizophrenic child in a clinical interview may not be physically abusive at home. Indeed, it would seem improbable that most schizophrenic patients are psychologically abused by high EE parents. Thus, the exact association between EE and psychological abuse remains to be demonstrated. Although they are certainly likely to be correlated, the relative predictive validity of the summary EE ratings and other measures of psychological aggression remains questionable.

EFFECTS OF INTERPARENTAL PSYCHOLOGICAL ABUSE ON CHILDREN

Broadly defined, interparent psychological abuse has not yet been examined empirically in terms of its impact on children's adjustment and competencies. However, one specific aspect of psychological abuse, that involving verbal conflict and aggression, has been researched extensively with respect to its relation to children's adjustment. In general, correlational research indicates that interparent verbal conflict and aggression predict a range of behavior problems and competencies in children. Levels of interparent conflict tend to correlate positively with externalizing behavior problems (e.g., aggression, delinquent behavior), internalizing behavior problems (e.g., depression, anxiety), and poor social and academic competence (see Grych & Fincham, 1990 for a review). These associations have been documented by researchers across the United States, Canada, and Europe, and in families of preschool-aged children, school-aged children, and adolescents. Moreover, such associations have been documented in both maritally intact and divorced families.

Dimensions of Conflict

Several dimensions of interparent verbal conflict and aggression, such as frequency, content, and intensity, seem to be important in the prediction of children's adjustment (Grych & Fincham, 1990). As we implied earlier, not all interparent verbal conflict can or should be classified as psychological abuse, but extremes on the dimensions of frequency, content, and intensity of verbal conflict are likely to meet most definitional criteria for psychological abuse.

Frequency

The most commonly used measures of interparent conflict and marital discord consist of items assessing the frequency of parents' disagreements. As indicated above, interparent conflict scores on these measures are found consistently to covary with children's adjustment problems (Grych & Fincham, 1990). Moreover, Cummings, Iannotti, and Zahn-Waxler (1985) found that preschool-aged children evidenced greater distress when exposed to two, rather than to one, "angry" conflict(s) between adult experimenters. Thus, it seems we can safely conclude that frequent interparent conflict increases risk for children's adjustment problems.

Content

The content of conflict is another dimension that seems to be important in predicting young children's adjustment. Specifically, interparent conflict regarding children (e.g., disputes about childrearing) may have a particularly negative effect on children's behavior. Several studies have shown that the frequency of parental childrearing disputes correlates positively with a variety of behavior problems in preschool and young school-aged children (Jouriles, Murphy, Farris, Smith, Richters, & Waters, 1991; Snyder, Klein, Gdowski, Faulstich, & LaCombe, 1988). In a sample of boys, the frequency of parental childrearing disputes has been found to correlate more positively with behavior problems than disputes about nonchild-related disagreements (e.g., handling family finances or how to spend holidays and free time; Jouriles, Murphy, Farris, Smith, Richters, & Waters, 1991). Moreover, these disputes about childrearing improve upon the prediction of boys' behavior problems after accounting for both nonchild disagreements and boys' exposure to general interparent conflict (Jouriles, Murphy, Farris, Smith, Richters, & Waters, 1991).

Intensity

Intensity is a third dimension of conflict that may be very important in under-standing how psychological abuse makes an impact upon children. One might define "intense" verbal conflict several different ways; for example, intensity can be defined along an affective dimension, ranging from calm, quiet discussion to yelling and screaming. It might also be defined along a process dimension, ranging from civil, problem-solving strategies to berating statements and name calling. Unfortunately, empirical work on interparent conflict and children's adjustment has typically conceptualized "intense" interparent conflict as that which involves physical aggression (Grych & Fincham, 1990). That is, intense conflict is equated with physical aggression, and less intense conflict is equated with verbal or psychological aggression. Thus, it difficult to draw conclusions from empirical work about the intensity of verbal conflict and its effects on children's adjustment. Psychological theory, however, suggests several ways in which "intense" interparent conflict may negatively influence children (see Mechanisms of Effect of Psychological Abuse on Children).

Actions of Parents and Children after Psychological Abuse

Another aspect of conflict that has received little research attention, but that may be very important in understanding the effects of conflict and psychological abuse on children, involves what parents do after the conflictual interaction. In one study, adult conflict resolved in front of the children resulted in less negative affect in children than adult conflict left unresolved (Cummings, Vogel, Cummings, & El-Sheikh, 1989). This study suggests that the resolution of interparent conflict in the children's presence may mitigate the negative impact of conflict on children. In another study, boys who interacted with their parents after a verbal marital conflict were less compliant with paternal commands, than were boys who interacted with their parents after a nonconflictual marital interaction (Jouriles & Farris, 1992). This latter study is particularly interesting because the boys did not witness their parents' marital conflict. The results of this study suggest that interparent conflict can affect children through indirect means, such as through parenting. These two studies, however, represent only a small aspect of what parents and children might do after interparent conflict. For example, it is common to hear mothers in abusive marital relationships indicate that they deserved to be yelled at and criticized because they did something wrong or are "no good." When children witness this, are they more likely to belittle or criticize themselves? Are these children more likely to dislike or abuse their own mothers because they believe her when she says she "deserves" such abuse? We believe that parent attributions about conflict *and* behaviors after conflictual interactions are a very promising area for understanding the impact of abuse and conflict on children.

˙erators and Confounds

˙onship between interparent conflict and children's adjustment seems
˙ated by certain demographic factors and sample characteristics.

For example, the association between marital conflict and children's behavior problems tends to be stronger in families of clinic-referred children as opposed to families of nonclinic children (Grych & Fincham, 1990; Jouriles, Bourg, & Farris, 1991; O'Leary & Emery, 1984). Parents' marital conflict also correlates more strongly with children's behavior problems in samples of low, relative to high, socioeconomic status (Jouriles, Bourg, & Farris, 1991). A number of studies have indicated that boys may be more strongly affected by general marital discord and interparent conflict than girls (e.g., Oltmanns, Broderick & O'Leary, 1977; Porter & O'Leary, 1980). Both boys and girls, however, seem to be affected by their parents' marital conflict. That is, marital conflict predicts behavior problems in both boys and girls (e.g., Emery & O'Leary, 1982; Grych & Fincham, 1990; Jouriles, Bourg, & Farris, 1991). Finally, it should be mentioned that a number of investigators have failed to obtain significant associations between these two problem areas (see Jouriles, Farris, & McDonald, 1991, for a review).

Earlier in this chapter, we noted that much of the research on effects of psychological abuse is confounded by other family problems, in particular, physical aggression. This is also true of most of the research examining relations between verbal parental conflict and childrens' behavior. Interesting findings have been obtained, however, in the handful of studies designed to isolate the effects of adult verbal conflict from those of physical aggression. In one such study, 3- to 6-year-old children in families characterized by verbal, but not physical, aggression exhibited externalizing problems at higher levels, than children in a comparison group characterized by the absence of both verbal and physical aggression (Fantuzzo, et al., 1991). In another study, parents' verbal aggression predicted both conduct and personality problems in school-aged children (5 to 12 years), after accounting for parents' general marital distress and physical marital aggression (Jouriles, 1992). Using an experimental design, Cummings and colleagues found preschool-aged children displayed increased emotional distress and aggression after witnessing a verbal confrontation between experimenters (Cummings, Iannotti, & Zahn-Waxler, 1985). Thus, the available evidence suggests that adult verbal conflict exerts a negative influence on children's behavior, even after accounting for conflict involving physical aggression between parents. Data indicate, however, that verbal conflict alone is not sufficient to explain the presence of clinical levels of child behavior problems (Emery & O'Leary, 1982; Fantuzzo et al., 1991; Jouriles, Murphy, & O'Leary, 1989; Rutter, 1979).

MECHANISMS OF EFFECT OF PSYCHOLOGICAL ABUSE BETWEEN ADULT PARTNERS ON CHILDREN

Psychological theory and clinical observations suggest several ways in which interparent conflict may negatively influence children. Bandura's (1969, 1986) social learning theory, for example, postulates that children's witnessing of frequent and intense interparent conflict (e.g., yelling, name calling, and insults) both allows children to add verbally aggressive conflict resolution strategies to their behavioral repertoire, and legitimizes their use. Thus, this observational learning increases the likelihood of children relying on these strategies in conflict situations. From a clinical standpoint, Bandura's theory is consistent with both informal observations in women's shelters and reports from women in abusive relationships about their children. For example, it is not uncommon in women's shelters to come across an obstreperous school-aged child who equates feeling angry with yelling and throwing things. That is, these children think that they are "supposed" to yell and throw things when they are angry. They can even be heard saying, "It's the way people know you're mad." Similarly, we have witnessed, on several occasions, children and adolescents engage in verbal tirades when they lash out at their mothers because they are upset about not getting their way. These tirades have included obscene names ("bitch" and "whore"), threats of violence ("I'm going to throw this at you if you don't get out of here," and berating statements ("You're no good" or "You're a terrible cook."). In almost every case, mothers explain that their children's verbally abusive behavior is imitation of the mothers' husbands or boyfriends.

Family systems theories (e.g., Kerr & Bowen, 1988; Minuchin, 1974) suggest that children sometimes act defiantly to deflect attention away from their parents' marital difficulties. Many women in physically violent relationships have described incidents to us in which their children attempted to prevent the escalation of conflict once yelling had begun by doing something to distract their parents. These distraction strategies, as labeled by the mothers, have included a variety of "behavior problems," such as yelling at their parents, hitting a sibling, dropping a glass or plate, or hurting a pet. Reports from women in maritally violent families about their children's behavior during conflict are consistent with data from community samples in which children intervene in their parents' marital conflicts (Jenkins, Smith, & Graham, 1989; Vuchinich, Emery, & Cassidy, 1988). In addition, the attributions made by mothers in violent families about their children's behavior (i.e., preventing the escalation of conflict, distracting the parents from conflict) are consistent with reports from children in community samples. Specifically, community children often indicate that they interrupt their parents' arguments in order to stop the conflict (Jenkins et al.). These mother and child reports are virtual textbook examples from family systems theories.

Other theories may also be called on to account for children's reactions to intense interparent conflict. For example, Zillman's (1983) theory of excitation transfer suggests that exposure to affectively intense conflict increases children's emotional and psychological arousal and, consequently, their irritability and proneness to aggression. From a learning theory perspective, intense interparent conflict may function as a cue or discriminative stimulus for children, alerting them to the presence of danger (e.g., physical violence) or stressful family events (e.g., prolonged verbal arguments). In sum, theory, clinical observations, and empirical data suggest that witnessing intense parental conflict can negatively affect children's behavior.

Most of the theoretical and empirical literature pertaining to interparent psychological abuse and children's functioning focuses on conflict and various moderators and dimensions of this conflict. As noted earlier in our section on definitional issues, not all psychological abuse involves verbal conflict. Another dimension of marital functioning, which might be defined in some cases as psychological abuse, is alienation or disengagement from one's spouse (McDonald, 1992). Effects of interparent disengagement on children have not yet been investigated empirically, but psychological theory suggests several potential mechanisms by which disengagement might adversely influence children. Family systems theory, for example, suggests that when parents become disengaged, children may misbehave in order to reengage their parents with one another (Kerr & Bowen, 1988). From a social learning theory perspective (Bandura, 1986), spouses who are alienated from one another may be less likely to model positive conflict resolution strategies for their children. We believe that interparent disengagement represents another important area of investigation for understanding the impact of psychological abuse on children.

SUMMARY

The effects of psychological aggression between adult partners can have devastating effects on both adults and children. However, we are just beginning to understand the ways in which psychological aggression has an impact on adult partners and their children. Clearly, some adults and children have a resilience that allows them to withstand a great deal of psychological abuse, but overall, the effects of psychological abuse are significant, and, on average, to many people's surprise, battered women report that they fear psychological abuse more than physical abuse.

The dimensions of psychological abuse between adults have not been fully mapped and categorized, but at least one study utilizing factor analytic strategies has yielded two overall factors—a verbal/emotional abuse factor and an isolation/neglect factor. Moreover, the verbal/emotional abuse factor has been the most studied factor by far in terms of its impact on both children and adults, and our review focused on this type of psychological aggression. With women, psychological abuse by a husband seems to operate by lowering self-esteem.

Psychological abuse of men by their wives has received so little attention that its effects on men are unclear. In longitudinal research, however, psychological abuse by both husbands and wives has been shown to lead to physical aggression across time. This finding has very important clinical findings because, unlike violence in the adults' family of origin over which they had no control, psychological aggression against a partner is something that has the potential to be changed through therapeutic means. Both psychological and physical aggression between adult partners have negative impacts on children, and psychological and physical aggression contribute independently to children's emotional problems.

The impact of psychological aggression on children seems to be mediated by factors that can be of special importance to marital and family therapists. For example, it has been shown that following a conflict, the way in which the differences are handled by the parents can minimize its negative effect. In addition, several experimental studies have shown that parental conflict not observed by the children can have negative effects on the children through parenting. The implication of both of these areas of research is clear: 1) parents can be helped to minimize the effects their psychological aggression toward one another has on their children: and 2) through insight, they can be helped to learn that their parenting can be affected adversely by their psychological aggression toward one another.

The therapeutic implications of research on psychological aggression toward adult partners are also quite clear. In young married couples, psychological aggression is the most potent predictor of physical aggression, and efforts to decrease psychological aggression should, in turn, decrease physical aggression. In relationships characterized by both physical and psychological aggression, because of concern for safety, therapeutic efforts by most practitioners often have been directed at the physical aggression in a relationship. Although this is reasonable from several vantage points, the fact that physically battered women report that the psychological aggression is worse than the physical aggression highlights the need to place greater importance on changing psychological aggression in *both* preventative and treatment endeavors.

REFERENCES

American Psychiatric Association. (1991). *DSM-IV options book: Work in progress. Task Force on DSM-IV* (p. U.3.). Washington, DC: American Psychiatric Association Press.

Andersen, S. M., Boulette, T. R., & Schwartz, A. (1991). Psychological maltreatment of spouses. In R. T. Ammerman & M. Hersen (Eds.), *Case studies in family violence* (293–327). New York: Plenum.

Arias, I., Samios, M., & O'Leary, K. D. (1987). Prevalence and correlates of physical aggression during courtship. *Journal of Interpersonal Violence, 2,* 82–90.

Bandura, A. (1969). *Principles of behavior modification.* New York: Holt, Rinehart & Winston.

Bandura, A. (1986). *Social foundation of thought and action: A social cognitive theory.* Englewood Cliffs, NJ: Prentice-Hall.

Barling, J., O'Leary, K. D., Jouriles, E. N., Vivian, D., & MacEwen, K. E. (1987). Factor similarity of the Conflict Tactics Scales across samples, spouses, and sites: Issues and implications. *Journal of Family Violence, 2,* 37–54.

Booth, C., McDowell, J., & Simpson, J. (1993, January 18). 'Til death do us part (cover story). *Time,* pp. 38–45.

Breines, W., & Gordon, L. (1983). The new scholarship on family violence. *Signs: Journal of Women in Culture and Society, 8,* 490–531.

Brown, G. W., Birley, J. T., & Wing, J. K. (1972). Influence of family life on the course of schizophrenic disorders: A replication. *British Journal of Psychiatry, 121,* 241–258.

Cascardi, M., & O'Leary, K. D. (1992). Depressive symptomatology, self-esteem and self-blame in battered women. *Journal of Family Violence, 7,* 249–259.

Cummings, E. M., Iannotti, R. J., & Zahn-Waxler, C. (1985). Influence of conflict between adults on the emotions and aggression of young children. *Developmental Psychology, 21,* 495–507.

Cummings, E. M., Vogel, D., Cummings, J. S., & El-Sheikh, M. (1989). Children's responses to different forms of expression of anger between adults. *Child Development, 60,* 1392–1404.

Emery, R. E., & O'Leary, K. D. (1982). Children's perceptions of marital discord and behavior problems of boys and girls. *Journal of Abnormal Child Psychology, 10,* 11–24.

Fantuzzo, J. W., Depaola, L. M., Lambert, L., Martino, T., Anderson, G., & Sutton, S. (1991). Effects of interparental violence on the psychological adjustment and competencies of young children. *Journal of Consulting and Clinical Psychology, 59,* 258–265.

Folingstad, D. R., Rutledge, L. L., Berg, B. J., Hause, E. S., & Polek, D. S. (1990). The role of emotional abuse in physically abusive relationships. *Journal of Family Violence, 5,* 107–120.

Forehand, R., & McCombs, A. (1989). The nature of interparental conflict of married and divorced parents: Implications for young adolescents. *Journal of Abnormal Child Psychology, 17,* 235–249.

Garbarino, J., Guttman, E., & Seeley, J. W. (1986). *The psychologically battered child.* San Francisco: Jossey-Bass.

Grych, J. H., & Fincham, F. D. (1990). Marital conflict and children's adjustment: A cognitive–contextual framework. *Psychological Bulletin, 108,* 267–290.

Hart, S. N., Germain, R., & Brassard, M. R. (1987). The challenge: To better understand and combat the psychological maltreatment of children and youth. In M. R. Brassard, R. Germain, & S. N. Hart (Eds.), *Psychological maltreatment of children and youth.* (pp. 3–24). Elmsford, NY: Pergamon.

Hooley, J. M. (1985). Expressed emotion: A review of the critical literature. *Clinical Psychology Review, 5,* 119–139.

Hudson, W. W., & McIntosh, S. R. (1981). The assessment of spouse abuse: Two quantifiable dimensions. *Journal of Marriage and the Family, 43,* 873–885.

Jenkins, J. M., Smith, M. A., & Graham, P. J. (1989). Coping with parental quarrels. *Journal of the American Academy of Child and Adolescent Psychiatry, 28,* 182–189.

Jouriles, E. N. (1992). *Verbal and physical marital aggression and child behavior problems.* Unpublished manuscript, University of Houston.

Jouriles, E. N., Barling, J., & O'Leary, K. D. (1987). Predicting child behavior problems in maritally violent families. *Journal of Abnormal Child Psychology, 15,* 165–173.

Jouriles, E. N., Bourg, W. J., & Farris, A. M. (1991). Marital adjustment and child conduct problems: A comparison of the correlation across subsamples. *Journal of Consulting and Clinical Psychology, 59,* 354–357.

Jouriles, E. N., & Farris, A. M. (1992). Effects of marital conflict on subsequent parent–son interactions. *Behavior Therapy, 23,* 355–374.

Jouriles, E. N., Farris, A. M., & McDonald, R. (1991). Marital functioning and child behavior: Measuring specific aspects of the marital relationship. In J. P. Vincent (Ed.), *Advances in family intervention, assessment, and theory.* (Vol. 5, pp. 25–46). London: Kingsley.

Jouriles, E. N., Murphy, C. M., & O'Leary, K. D. (1989). Interspousal aggression, marital discord, and child problems. *Journal of Consulting and Clinical Psychology, 57,* 453–455.

Jouriles, E. N., Murphy, C. M., Farris, A. M., Smith, D. A., Richters, J. E., & Waters, E. (1991). Marital adjustment, parental disagreements about child rearing, and behavior problems in boys: Increasing the specificity of the marital assessment. *Child Development, 62,* 1424–1433.

Kerr, M. E., & Bowen, M. (1988). *Family evaluation: An approach based on Bowen theory.* New York: Norton.

Marshall, L. L. (1992a). The Severity of Violence Against Women Scales. *Journal of Family Violence, 7,* 103–121.

Marshall, L. L. (1992b). The Severity of Violence Against Men Scales. *Journal of Family Violence, 7,* 189–203.

McDonald, R. (1992). *Marital conflict, alienation, and child conduct problems.* Unpublished doctoral dissertation, University of Houston.

Minuchin, S. (1974). *Families and family therapy.* Cambridge, MA: Harvard University Press.

Murphy, C. M., & Cascardi, M. (in press). Psychological aggression and abuse in marriage. In R. L. Hampton (Ed.), *Issues in children's and families' lives. (Vol. II): Family Violence.* Newbury Park, CA: Sage.

Murphy, C. M., & Meyer, S. L. (1991). Gender, power, and violence in marriage. *Behavior Therapist, 14,* 95–100.

Murphy, C. M., & O'Leary, K. D. (1989). Psychological aggression predicts physical aggression in early marriage. *Journal of Consulting and Clinical Psychology, 57,* 579–582.

O'Leary, K. D. & Curley, A. D. (1986). Assertion and family violence: Correlates of spouse abuse. *Journal of Marital and Family Therapy, 12,* 281–289.

O'Leary, K. D., & Emery, R. E. (1984). Marital discord and child behavior problems. In M. D. Levine & P. Satz (Eds.), *Developmental variation and dysfunction* (pp. 345–364). New York: Academic.

O'Leary, K. D., Malone, J., & Tyree, A. (in press). *Physical aggression in early marriage: Relationship and prerelationship effects. Journal of Consulting and Clinical Psychology.*

O'Leary, K. D., & Vivian, D. (1990). Physical aggression in marriage. In F. D. Fincham & T. N. Bradbury (Eds.), *The Psychology of marriage: Basic issues and applications.* New York: Guilford.

Oltmanns, T. F., Broderick, J. E., & O'Leary, K. D. (1977). Marital adjustment and the efficacy of behavior therapy with children. *Journal of Consulting and Clinical Psychology, 45,* 724–729.

Pagelow, M. D. (1984). *Journal of family violence.* New York: Praeger.

Pence, E., & Paymar, M. (1986). *Power and control: Tactics of men who batter.* Duluth: Minnesota Program Development.

Porter, B., & O'Leary, K. D. (1980). Marital discord and childhood behavior problems. *Journal of Abnormal Child Psychology, 8,* 287–295.

Snyder, D. K., Klein, M. A., Gdowski, C. L., Faulstich, D., & LaCombe, J. (1988). Generalized dysfunction in clinic and nonclinic families: A comparative analysis. *Journal of Abnormal Child Psychology, 16,* 97–109.

Stets, J. E. (1990). Verbal and physical aggression in marriage. *Journal of Marriage and the Family, 52,* 501–514.

Straus, M. A. (1979). Measuring intrafamily conflict and violence: The Conflict Tactics Scales. *Journal of Marriage and the Family, 41,* 75–88.

Tolman, R. M. (1989). The development of a measure of psychological maltreatment of women by their male partners. *Violence and Victims, 4,* 159–177.

Tolman, R. M. (1992). Psychological abuse of women. In J. Campbell (Ed.), *Assessing the risk of dangerousness* (pp. 290–310). Newbury Park, CA: Sage.

Vaughn, C. E., & Leff, J. P. (1976). The influence of family and social factors in the course of psychiatric illness. *British Journal of Psychiatry, 129,* 125–137.

Vuchinich, S., Emery, R. E., & Cassidy, J. (1988). Family members as third parties in dyadic family conflict: Strategies, alliances, and outcomes. *Child Development, 59,* 1293–1302.

Walker, L. E. (1979). *The battered woman.* New York: Harper & Row.

Walker, L. E. (1984). *The battered woman syndrome.* New York: Springer.

Zillman, D. (1983). Arousal and aggression. In R. G. Geen & E. I. Donnerstein (Eds.), *Aggression: Theoretical and empirical reviews* (Vol. 1). New York: Academic.

CHAPTER 17

Developmental Systems Theory and Substance Abuse

A Conceptual and Methodological Framework for Analyzing Patterns of Variation in Families

HIRAM E. FITZGERALD, W. HOBART DAVIES, ROBERT A. ZUCKER, and MICHAEL KLINGER

In this chapter we focus our discussion on developmental system approaches to the study of substance abuse. Although alcohol abuse/dependence is used as the prototype of substance abuse, other types of substance abuse are referred to throughout the chapter. Our use of alcoholism as prototypical should not be interpreted as indicating that we believe that the dynamics of etiology are the same for all forms of substance abuse. We do not. Nevertheless, there are a substantial number of common themes (Hawkins, Catalano, & Miller, 1992), and it is within the context of these themes that we use alcoholism as prototypical of substance abuse.

Alcoholism, and the lesser problem of alcohol abuse, are the most common forms of substance abuse in contemporary American society, involving over 16 million individuals, or approximately 9% of the adult population (Grant et al., 1991). Estimates of the number of children of alcoholics (COAs) in the United States range as high as 28 million, with approximately 7 million under the age of 18 (Russell, Henderson, & Blume, 1985). There is evidence to suggest that the prevalence of alcoholism has increased during the 20th century, especially among younger adults, and that the well-established sex difference in incidence is narrowing because of the increased prevalence among women (Reich, Cloninger, VanEerdewegh, Rice, & Mullancy, 1988). Moreover, the age of first initiation has steadily decreased to about age 12, and the time between first initiation and the onset of problem drinking seems to be narrowing (Tarter & Blackson, 1992). Although a family history of alcoholism is neither a necessary nor a sufficient

Preparation of this chapter was supported by grant 2RO1 AA07065 from the National Institute on Alcohol Abuse and Alcoholism. Portions of this chapter were presented as an invited address at the annual meeting of the Nebraska Psychological Association, April 27, 1991.

condition to set COAs on a developmental pathway leading to substance abuse, COAs are at 6 to 10 times greater risk for alcohol abuse than are children with no family history of alcoholism (Cotton, 1979). Elderly individuals, who account for nearly 30% of all prescription drug use, drink less than younger individuals, although the proportion of the elderly who drink seems to have increased slightly over the past 20 years (Gomberg, 1990), as has the proportion of elderly persons addicted to opioids.

COAs not only are at high risk for alcoholism and/or problem drinking, they also are at high risk for various other types of behavior disorders. In fact, there is some evidence that nonspecific alcohol factors may be as important or more important than alcohol-specific factors in setting COAs on a developmental pathway leading to maladaptive functioning (Zucker & Fitzgerald, 1991a, 1991b). COAs are more likely to be raised in highly stressful families (Roosa, Tein, Groppenbacher, & Michaels, 1991), characterized by substantially higher rates of divorce (Paolino & McCrady, 1977) and spousal violence (Gayford, 1975). Moreover, data from the National Institutes of Mental Health Epidemiologic Catchment Area (ECA) study of the United States adult population indicate that co-morbidities, excluding drug disorders, occur in 37% of the alcohol dependence/abuse population and in 55% of such patients visiting specialized treatment settings (Regier et al., 1990). Frequently observed co-morbidities include antisocial personality disorder, bipolar disorder, schizophrenia, panic disorder, obsessive-compulsive disorder, and major depression. Thus, having an alcoholic parent is only one of a variety of factors that must be taken into account in any systematic analysis of experiences that may induce, facilitate, or maintain a developmental pathway (Gottlieb, 1991) leading to substance abuse and/or psychopathological behavior.

SYSTEMS THEORY, DEVELOPMENT, AND SUBSTANCE ABUSE

Contemporary research on substance abuse rapidly is embracing a paradigmatic view that is developmental in focus, as investigators attempt to unravel the biologic and experiential factors at work that shape a life course leading to substance abuse (cf. Zucker, 1987; in press). A second theme emerging in the substance abuse literature, although currently far less visible than the developmental perspective, is the notion that the study of etiologic (developmental) questions is served better by system models (Levine & Fitzgerald, 1992; Zucker, in press) than by disease models (Jellinek, 1960). Although family system theory has been a part of the substance abuse literature for at least the past two decades, it has been used more to conceptualize qualitative aspects of family relationships, than it has been to generate quantitative research models related to system development. Orford (1990) notes that the systems view of alcohol and the family is confined predominately to the United States, Canada, Yugoslavia, Britain, and Germany. In most other countries, the stress–victim view dominates, although it fails to account for two key characteristics of many alcoholic families. First, in many alcoholic families there are two alcoholics; which is the victim? Second, in many alcoholic families, the nonalcoholic brings to the marriage relationship problems from his or her own family of origin, a phenomenon that behavior geneticists refer to as *assortative mating* (Orford, 1990).

From the developmental system perspective, substance abuse is conceptualized as a life span problem with roots reaching at the least to the preschool years (Zucker & Fitzgerald, 1991a, 1991b), and perhaps even to conception (McGivern & Barron, 1991). Finally, from the developmental system perspective, the search for causal determinants of substance abuse must take into account intraindividual (within the individual), interindividual (between individuals), contextual (social–historical–temporal events or situations), and organism–environment transactional (ecological, bidirectional) sources of variance, rather than relying on simple main effects models.

This multifactorial approach suggests five major levels of analysis relevant to investigation of the structure and function of any system. First, the subsystems or individual components of the system must be identified and described (e.g., assessing the presenting state characteristics of individual family members, including genetic differences that may ultimately trigger different behavioral propensities or sensitivities). Second, the structure and functional connections of subunits must be identified and described (e.g., assessing spousal, parent–child, and sibling relationships). Third, one must identify and describe the properties that emerge when this collection of components is joined together into a specific dynamic structure (e.g., assessing family traditions, values, beliefs, resources, and cohesiveness). Fourth, one must identify adjunctive systems that may have direct effects on the family unit or that affect the family indirectly via individual members (e.g., assessing the impact of adjunctive systems on individual and family functioning). This includes evaluating the permissiveness of the culture for heavy drinking, the availability of alcohol and other drugs, dealing with the economic well-being of the neighborhood, and the social–historical events (cohort effects) that contribute to cultural values. Finally, one must describe, and eventually test, predictive models of change in the individual, the family, and the ecosystem over time (e.g., assessing models of system organization, as well as bifurcations that lead to system disorganization and reorganization.)

Adaptive Functioning

Developmental systems theory asserts that adaptive functioning is understood best from a perspective that views organizational processes as dynamic (changing), and behavior as embedded within the context in which it occurs. Thus, causal factors related to substance abuse, whether involving licit or illicit drugs, cannot be revealed by theories grounded in genetic or cultural determinism, but instead, require models that reflect the ". . . fusion of genes and environment" (Lerner, 1991).

A system is a functional whole composed of a set of component parts (subsystems, units) that, when coupled together, generate a level of organization fundamentally different from the level of organization represented in any individual or subset of the component parts. Each individual's developmental and experiential history is unique (Gottlieb, 1991). Although two siblings with the same alcoholic father experience the same objective event (their father's alcoholism), their subjective experiences may differ markedly. Siblings may differ in sex, birth order, temperament, genetic vulnerability, sensitivity to particular drug actions, age at onset of paternal alcoholism, parent–child interaction, family SES, family structure, peer group, interests, and value systems (Hoffman, 1991). Thus, each child in the alcoholic family not only has access to multiple possible developmental pathways, but these pathways differ from those available to his or her sibling. Similarly, different families have different presenting state characteristics. The family with an antisocial, alcoholic father differs from the family with an alcoholic father who is not antisocial, or the family in which both father and mother are alcoholic.

Everyday life in the alcoholic family often is organized around drinking (Steinglass, 1981). Thus, an alcoholic family system that is organized and regulated by paternal alcoholism is thrust into a crisis if the father becomes an abstainer. Paternal abstinence may be associated with increased paternal intrusiveness in the established family routine, thereby threatening the autonomy individual family members may have had when he was drunk and "out of the way." Three or more options are available to resolve such a crisis. Members of the family may act to re-establish the family's structure by encouraging the abstainer to resume drinking. They may begin the process of redefining the dynamic structure of the family in order to facilitate change and growth. They may act to end the family through divorce or separation.

Systems Models and Development

During the past decade, investigators have made greater use of models in their efforts to describe the interrelatedness of factors that account for some outcome variable. Investigators have used models to assess the genetics of alcoholism (Cadoret, 1990), social determinants of adolescent drinking behavior (Barnes, 1990), adjustment of COAs to an alcoholic father (Clair & Genest, 1982), family stress and coping strategies (Cronkite, Finney, Nekich, & Moos, 1990), quality of family life and drug consumption (Grichtig & Barber, 1989), school behavior and achievement in COAs (Knop, Teasdale, Schulsinger, & Goodwin, 1985), parental consumption and child adjustment (Seilhamer & Jacob, 1990), and stage progression of substance use (Windle, Barnes, & Welte, 1989). System models also have been used to test the effects of illicit drugs on human performance (Brook, Brook, Gordon, Whiteman, & Cohen, 1990; Lester et al., 1991). Most of these studies have tested models using regression, path, or latent variable analyses to assess whether the hypothesized relationships among selected variables fit the data collected. Although all such attempts to describe the pattern of relationships among variables are systemic, they are not developmental, unless they attempt to predict changes in state variables over time.

The purpose of a model is to hypothesize a set of pathways that might explain the effect of an exogenous variable on some outcome variable. One might, for example, hypothesize that parental personality characteristics have a direct effect on adolescent drug use. Figure 17.1 shows the hypothesized model that Brook et al. (1990) used in their cross-sectional and longitudinal studies of adolescent marijuana use. Their family interaction approach was an integration of social learning theory, psychoanalytic theory, attachment theory, and deviant behavior proneness. The model hypothesizes two exogenous variables, parental introjection of societal values and maternal psychological adjustment, which have direct effects on the parent–adolescent relationship. Maternal control techniques also are hypothesized to mediate the relationship between maternal adjustment and parent–adolescent mutual attachment. The peer group is hypothesized to have a buffering effect on a wide range of adolescent presenting state characteristics, and a direct effect on the adolescent's use of marijuana. Brook and her colleagues found that unconventionality, poor control of emotions, and intrapsychic distress discriminated users from nonusers. Parental personality traits that predicted a harmonious parent–teen relationship and a decrease in substance abuse included intolerance of deviance, responsibility taking, self-control, and intrapsychic harmony.

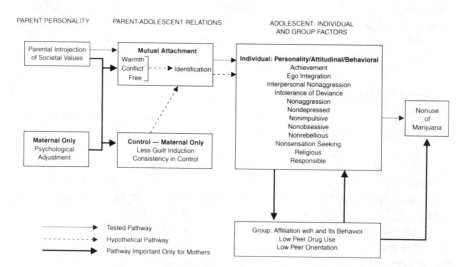

Figure 17.1. Hypothesized Developmental Model. (Note. From Brook, J. S., Brook, D. W., Gordon, A. S., Whiteman, M., & Cohen, P. The psychosocial etiology of adolescent drug use: A family interaction approach. *Genetic, Social, and Psychological Monographs, 116(2),* 111–267. Reprinted with permission of the Helen Dwight Reid Educational Foundation. Published by Heldref Publications, 1319 Eighteenth St., N. W., Washington, D.C. 20036-1802. Copyright © 1990.

Cross-sectional designs provide information about interfamily differences in organizational structure, but they cannot provide information about intrafamily change processes that affect the family's organization, deorganization, and reorganization. Only longitudinal designs allow one to assess change in individual or family functioning over time. Figure 17.2 is the schematic model that is guiding a major prospective longitudinal study of the etiology of alcoholism, other substance abuse, and coactive forms of psychopathology (Zucker, 1987; Zucker, in press; Zucker & Fitzgerald, 1991b; Zucker, Noll, & Fitzgerald, 1986). The grid depicts the developmental flow of risk factors over the lifetime of the individual (X axis) and the potential for continuity and discontinuity of sustaining risk across eight stages in the life cycle. The Y axis depicts five major domains of biopsychosocial functioning that generate the exogenous and endogenous variables that affect the presenting state characteristics of the system (cellular, organismic, family, nation) at various stages of development, as well as similar variables from adjunctive systems. Substantial evidence exists demonstrating the significant role that variables from each domain play in the developmental process. From such metamodels, we can generate research models to assess the influence of domain-specific and cross-domain variables that may induce or maintain vulnerability or may provide buffers that induce or maintain resilience. Moreover, the model allows us to assess the effects of alcohol-specific and alcohol-nonspecific factors on the individual's developmental trajectory over the life course. Note that throughout development, the individual is contextually embedded within a broader set of systems (biological, intraindividual, interindividual, social, and cultural) that may or may not have meaningful influences on developmental outcome.

From heuristic metamodels such as that presented in Figure 17.2, we can derive theoretic and/or research models to guide systematic investigation of the presenting state characteristics of individual members of the alcoholic family, relationships among members of the primary family system, and models of the dynamic structure (feedback loops) of the family system. The model in Figure 17.3 is derived from the schematic model shown in Figure 17.2. This is a baseline alcohol nonspecific model of child effects (Zucker, in press) that is being tested cross-sectionally and longitudinally in a study involving alcoholic and nonalcoholic families in which the target children are boys, initially 3 to 5 years old, and their female siblings (Zucker & Fitzgerald, 1991b). Eight domains are represented in the model: Parental family history of psychopathology and adaptive functioning (represented in the model as an exogenous variable); parental psychopathology and adaptive functioning; child cognitive and control functions; current family functioning; exogenous influences on family functioning, parental child rearing influences, child psychopathology, and adaptive behavior; and exogenous influences on the child's psychopathology and adaptive functioning. The hypothesized direction of effects is indicated by the arrowheads. (In dynamic system models, arrows with heads on each end often are used to represent variables that influence one another simultaneously. Simultaneity can be represented theoretically, but we do not yet have the techniques to assess it

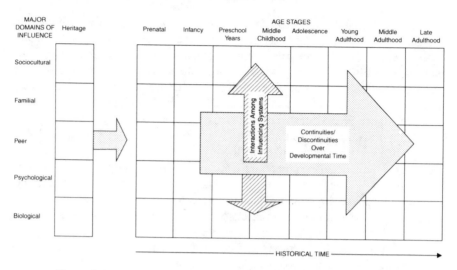

Figure 17.2. Schematic Model of Longitudinal Study of Etiology of Alcoholism

empirically. In structural equation models, arrows going in both directions represent covariances or, for standardized models, correlations. In Figure 17.3, the double headed arrows represent reciprocal or bidirectional influences, not simultaneous influences.) Within each domain, multiple research methods (self-report, other-report, direct observation) are used to assess presenting state characteristics

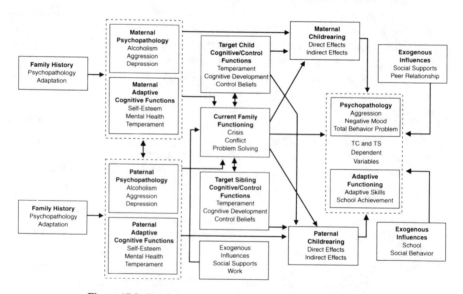

Figure 17.3. Baseline Alcohol Nonspecific Model of Child Effects

at various levels of systemic organization, using two or more data sources for each variable, using the same procedures or instruments over time, and assessing adaptive, as well as maladaptive, functioning. The use of multiple measures on each content area facilitates use of structural equation analysis techniques such as EQS, LISREL, and path analysis (McArdle, Hamagami, & Hulick, in press).

Heritability and Development

Although no specific genetic mechanism for alcoholism has yet been identified, the role of heredity in risk for some forms of alcohol dependence is nearly universally accepted. Alcoholics are more likely to have a family history of alcoholism than are nonalcoholics (Cotton, 1979), and COAs have greater tolerance for ethanol than do non-COAs (Schuckit, Risch & Gold, 1988). Evidence for the role of heredity is stronger for some types of alcoholics than others (Cloninger, 1987; McGue, in press; Zucker, 1987; Zucker et al., 1992). The more heritable form seems to be readily associated with antisociality, and with a strong family load of alcoholism. It is known to have onset early in life, and it is associated with high impulsivity and distractibility, and is usually reported to be more obviously detectable in males, although recent evidence (McGue, in press) suggests it may not be as sex specific as was previously thought. Although males are more at risk for alcoholism than females, data from the Swedish adoption studies suggest that daughters of alcoholic mothers are also at high risk, regardless of their fathers' drinking (Searles, 1990). Begleiter (1992) suggests that what seems to be heritable in COAs is a genotypic predisposition to nonspecific biological disregulation. Whether the genotype is expressed as alcoholism or some other form of psychopathology (hyperactivity, conduct disorder, aggression, depression), depends on the individual's particular developmental history. Moreover, experiential events may interact with genotypic predispositions differently at different times during development (Fillmore, 1987; Searles, 1990). Thus, there may be critical periods when individuals who are genotypically at risk for alcoholism are more vulnerable to environmental organizers than at other times. Johnson and Rolf (1990) suggest four possible developmental trajectories for the expression of biopsychosocial maladaptation, one of which illustrates continuity and three of which illustrate discontinuity in development. Maladaptive functioning may begin in childhood and continue through adulthood; may begin in adolescence and continue into adulthood; may appear for the first time in adulthood; or may begin in childhood, become masked through adolescence, and then reappear in adulthood. Interestingly enough, if an individual delays onset of drug use, he or she can reduce drug involvement substantially (Kandel & Yamaguchi, 1985).

Prenatal Exposure to Drugs

Fetal Alcohol Syndrome (FAS)

The teratogenic effects of maternal abuse of alcohol during pregnancy are well documented. FAS is the third leading cause of mental retardation in the United

States. FAS refers to a specific set of characteristics associated with prenatal exposure to high levels of ethanol, especially, although not exclusively, when exposure occurs during the first trimester (Barr, Streissguth, Darby, & Sampson, 1990). The specific characteristics required for a diagnosis of FAS generally fall into three areas (Cooper, 1987): 1) prenatal and/or postnatal growth retardation; 2) central nervous system involvement; 3) characteristic facial dysmorphology. Some investigators refer to Fetal Alcohol Effects (FAE) to distinguish the visible teratogenic effects associated with FAS from those that are both milder and also less visible during the immediate postnatal period. Such "sleeper" effects may appear later in development as learning disabilities, attentional deficits, hyperactivity, or perceptual-motor dysfunctions (Barr et al.). However, there is considerable controversy as to whether FAE may be present in COAs and whether the term FAE should be used in scientific publications at all because of the difficulty of operationally defining such effects (Sokol & Clarren, 1989). Nevertheless, evidence still exists that FAS as an organismic insult, has some short-term macrosystem impacts.

Exposure to Other Drugs

Opioid drugs readily cross the placental barrier and have been identified as teratogens. Women who consume opioids during pregnancy are at risk for toxemia, maternal syphilis, hepatitis, placental problems, and abnormal presentations (Hans, 1989). During the neonatal period and early infancy, drug-exposed infants are characterized by tremor, hypertonicity, hyperactive reflexes, high-pitched crying, poor sleep and feeding rhythms, fever, prematurity, intrauterine growth retardation, and rapid respiration (Chasnoff & Griffith, 1991; Hans, 1989). Research in this area is complicated by the fact that the average woman consumes as many as ten different drugs during her pregnancy (Brackbill, McManus, & Woodward, 1985), so it is difficult to separate out the effects of one type of drug over another. Hans (1989) compared 36 women (42 infants) who used opioid drugs throughout pregnancy with 43 women (47 infants) who did not use opioid drugs and who consumed no more than 1 drink per day of alcohol. The drug-using women also used alcohol, marijuana, heroin, cocaine, valium, and/or talwin, and all were involved in a low-dose methadone maintenance program. The drug-exposed infants had shorter head circumferences, poor psychomotor development scores, were more tense, and had poorer fine and gross motor coordination. At age two, however, there were few differences between groups that could be attributed exclusively to drug exposure. However, when drug exposure was combined with very low SES, differences between the groups were dramatic. Mothers of drug-exposed infants often have poor maternal resources, which when combined with poor SES, often leads to poor parent–child relationships (Chasnoff & Griffith, 1991).

In one of the few studies to use structural equation modeling (EQS) to study the effects of prenatal drug exposure on infant outcome, Lester et al. (1991) compared 80 cocaine-exposed infants with 80 control infants. Lester et al. present evidence based on infant cries to support the hypothesis that two neurobehavioral syndromes, excitable and depressed, are associated with cocaine-exposed infants. They attribute the excitable syndrome to the direct effects of cocaine exposure, via an excess buildup of the neurotransmitters norepipinephrine and dopamine at postsynaptic reception sites. The cries of the excitable infants were characterized by longer duration, higher fundamental frequency, and a higher and more variable first formant. The depressed syndrome (25% of the infants) reflected indirect effects that are mediated by intrauterine growth retardation. The cries of depressed infants were characterized by long-latency, fewer utterances, lower amplitude, and more dysphonation. Despite the clear evidence for teratogenic effects in the neonatal period and during early infancy, evidence demonstrating long-term effects of exposure to drugs prenatally has yet to be reported.

Childhood Through Adulthood

Antisocial Behavior/Aggression

Numerous studies have found that COAs are at higher risk to develop various behavioral problems—including aggression, antisocial behavior, delinquency, incompetent interpersonal relationships, emotional and personality problems, cognitive deficits, and school failure—than are children of nonalcoholics. However, with some exceptions (Jacob & Leonard, 1986), most studies treat alcoholics as a homogeneous group and do not distinguish children of less severe alcoholics from children of more severe alcoholics. Consequently, little is known about the effects of severity of parental alcoholism on children's outcomes. In addition, different criteria used to define alcoholism in various studies make it difficult to assess the effects of parental alcohol consumption level on children's behavior. White (1987) used LISREL to test four models of the ways in which investigators operationalize problem drinking: heavy intake, frequent intoxication, use of alcohol for escape, and experiencing negative consequences associated with drinking. A 2-factor solution, consisting of use intensity and alcohol-related problems, proved to be the best description of problem drinking. White suggested that the peak period for alcohol-related problems is more accurately represented as 15 to 24 years old than the current tendency to cite 20 to 24 years.

A number of studies have reported that parental aggression is one of the leading causes of antisocial and aggressive behavior during childhood, and of delinquency, crime, and alcoholism in adulthood (Robins, 1966). Rydelius's (1981) 20-year follow-up study in Sweden on social adjustment and health status of children of lower SES alcoholic fathers, found a pattern of functioning similar to that observed when the children were 4 to 12 years old. Compared with children of nonalcoholics, COAs engaged in more criminal activity and physical aggression. Gonzalez, Zucker, and Fitzgerald (1992) classified each of 192 men into one of five groups based on their degree of drug, as well as alcohol, involvement. Alcoholic men who also were drug dependent or abusers had the highest lifetime alcohol problem scores and the highest scores on a measure of antisocial behavior. In other words, level of drug involvement seems tied to level of antisociality, but the issue of what precedes what has not yet been settled. A longitudinal study of ego and cognitive functioning provides some evidence that personality correlates among teenage drug abusers, as summarized in Table 17.1, are in evidence as early as age 3 (Block, Block, & Keyes, 1988). The developmental picture includes rebelliousness, unconventionality, behavior problems, poor frustration tolerance, lack of motivation and goal directedness, lack of concern for others, and various types of antisocial behavior. In other words, the picture observed in 3-year-olds is not inconsistent with attributes leading to more drug involvement at age 14, and also more drug involvement among alcoholic men in their late 20s and early 30s.

Alcoholic parents of 3- to 5-year-old sons (at least the father, but in 44% of the families, also the mothers) scored higher than comparison parents on measures of antisocial behavior, depression, and lifetime alcohol problems (Fitzgerald et al., 1993). Antisocial behavior scores for alcoholic men, in particular, were more than double the mean for comparison men, suggesting that their 3-year-old sons may have been exposed to levels of antisocial behavior that correspond to levels found in district court arrestees and convicted felons (Zucker, et al., 1992). The level of spousal violence is high in alcoholic, antisocial families, particularly in instances where the husband has a history of antisocial behavior and a severe

TABLE 17.1. Personality Correlates of Marijuana and/or Hard Drug Use in 14-year-olds

Girls	Boys
Rebellious	Sensuousness
Rejection of conservative values	Interest in girls
Unconventional in thinking	Perception of different contexts in sexual terms
Unable to delay gratification	Self-indulgent
Absence of overcontrol	Regards self as physically attractive
Unambitious	Unconcern with application of moral standards
Limit stretching	Unconcern with rationality
Not likable	Less intelligent
Anti-intellective	Unproductive
Ruminative	Undependable
Unpredictable	Not submissive
Sensual	Directly hostile
Without charm	Not protective of others
Unarousing of nurturance in others	Not sympathetic to others
Overreactive to minor frustrations	Guileful
Unsympathetic to others	Ungiving
Not behaving in sex-typed manner	Unethical
	Unconventional
	Overreact to frustrations
	Lack of guilt
	Unpredictable

Source: Adapted from Block, J., Block, J. H., & Keyes, S. (1988). Longitudinally foretelling drug usage in adolescence: Early childhood personality and environmental precursors. *Child Development, 59,* 336–355.

drinking problem (Tarter, Hegedus, Goldstein, Shelly, & Alterman, 1984). We must be cautious, however, linking alcoholism and marital violence causally, for as Orford (1990) reminds us, violence is one of the leading factors cited by wives in their petitions for divorce throughout the world, and it is not always linked to alcoholism.

Depression

Depression is a frequent correlate of alcoholism. In the ECA investigation of co-morbidity of mental disorders with alcohol abuse (Regier et al., 1990), affective disorders were found in 13.4% of the subjects with an alcohol disorder, as compared with 7.5% among subjects without an alcohol disorder. Research that has addressed the effects of the relationship of alcohol and depression has focused mostly on child outcomes, rather than actual specific behaviors of mothers and fathers who are alcoholic or depressed or both. There is some indication that the relationship between parental alcoholism and depression and anxiety in children may be via parental depression and, indirectly, via alcoholism (Merikangas, Weissman, Prusoff, Pauls, & Leckman, 1985).

Hyperactivity

A number of investigators have reported an association between familial alcoholism and child hyperactivity (West & Prinz, 1987). Activity level is one of the dominant aspects of temperament that distinguishes COAs from non-COAs, and the differences are even more marked when we compare COAs with a family history of antisociality to COAs without such a history (Tarter & Blackson, 1992). In a 10–15-year follow-up study of sons of alcoholics, Knop et al. (1985), found consistently significant differences between high- and low-risk groups only for impulsivity, restlessness, and verbal deficiency. The sons of alcoholic fathers from this cohort exhibited higher rates of hyperactive behavior than did sons of nonalcoholic fathers.

Retrospective studies have reported that alcoholics tend to recall more hyperactive behavior in childhood than do nonalcoholics (Alterman, Petrarula, Tarter, & McGowan, 1982). In addition, other studies of hyperactive children tend to report higher incidence of childhood hyperactivity, alcoholism, and antisocial behavior in the parents of hyperactives (Earls, Reich, Jung, & Cloninger, 1988; Hetchman, Weiss, & Perlman, 1984).

Cognitive Functioning

In addition to social and emotional problems, children living with alcoholic parents are likely to have poor cognitive function and to experience school failure. Knop et al. (1985) conducted a prospective study on a large sample of young adult COAs (19–20 years) in Copenhagen. Sons of alcoholics were significantly more likely than sons of nonalcoholics to score lower on the WAIS vocabulary test, to fail examinations in school, to repeat a grade, and to be referred to a school psychologist, than were comparison children. Differences between COAs and non-COAs in cognitive and adaptive skills have been identified as early as the preschool years (Noll, Zucker, Fitzgerald, & Curtis, 1992). In the Noll et al. study, 25 intact families with an alcoholic father were matched with 25 intact families with no parental alcoholism. Three-to-five-year-old sons in these families differed in fine-motor and personal–social skills, and, to some degree, in language and adaptive skills, with COAs scoring lower than non-COAs. Because children in both groups scored above age norms, it is unlikely that prenatal exposure to alcohol contributed to the differences. Predictors of children's performance were related to poorer environmental stimulation at home, as well as the father's lifetime alcohol problems.

In addition to cognitive functioning as assessed by standardized instruments or school performance, there is another aspect of cognitive functioning that has captured the interest of alcoholism researchers. This aspect of cognition involves expectancy. At what age do COAs begin to construct a schema or expectancy for alcohol-related behavior? Although there is no definitive answer to this question, it is clear that such schema formation is well underway in the preschool years (Zucker & Fitzgerald, 1991a), and becomes more well defined by 8 to 9 years of age (Miller, Smith & Goldman, 1990). Expectancies of middle-school aged children are predictive of their drinking behavior in early to middle adolescence (Christiansen, Smith, Roehling, & Goldman, 1989), but the continuity of expectancies from earlier age periods has not yet been studied. Using structural equation modeling, Sher and Walitzer (1989) showed that alcohol expectancies mediate the relationship among paternal alcoholism, behavior undercontrol, and alcohol involvement.

INTRAFAMILIAL RELATIONSHIPS, FAMILY STRUCTURE, AND ADJUNCTIVE SYSTEMS

Longitudinal and cross-sectional studies of nonalcoholic clinically depressed mothers consistently find that such mothers report their children to have more behavior problems than do nondepressed mothers (Ferguson, Hans, Horwood, Gretton, & Shannon, 1985), fathers (Webster-Stratton, 1988), teachers (Ferguson et al.), or independent observers of mother–child interaction (Campbell & Ewing, 1991). Lahey, Conger, Atkenson, and Treiber (1984) suggest that depressed mothers may have a lower threshold for child misbehavior, which, in turn, biases their ratings of their children's behavior problems. Collectively, these findings suggest a direct effect of maternal depression on maternal perceptions of their children's deviant behavior. Our findings with alcoholic families and their 3-year-old sons (Fitzgerald et al., 1993) are consistent with this suggestion in that only maternal variables predicted children's behavior problems. Maternal depression, a pattern of behavior involving negative self-perceptions and lack of ability to relate to others, was positively related to children's total behavior problems, as well as to externalizing and internalizing problems.

There are several possible explanations for the stronger relationship between characteristics of mothers and COAs, than between fathers and COAs. The most parsimonious explanation is that mothers are more accurate reporters of their children's behavior than are fathers. Regardless of societal changes in the role of fathers in caregiving, such changes have not altered the fact that during the early years of development, mothers continue to be the primary socializing agents of their young children (Nyquist, Slivken, Spence, & Helmreich, 1985). We might expect, therefore, that their perceptions of their young children are crafted from a richer set of direct behavioral interactions than are those of the children's fathers. On the other hand, the differences found in the Fitzgerald et al. (1993) study were not between high-risk mothers' and fathers' ratings of their children's behavior problems, but in parental characteristics that predicted their children's ratings.

Regardless of the amount of time fathers spend interacting with their children, their interactions differ qualitatively from those of their wives and their children. Fathers treat their sons differently than their daughters, to the extent that fathers seem to play a major role in the sex-role differentiation of their children (Lytton & Romney, 1991). Fathers play more games than mothers during interactions with infants, and they show higher levels of affect. Several authors have suggested that the mother's biological connection to the child leads to her role as primary caregiver, thereby freeing fathers to focus on play and connections to the outside world. It is apparent that role expectations play a large part in the different quality of parenting by mothers and fathers (Clarke-Stewart, 1980). On the other hand, the long-term consequences of differential socialization have not been clearly identified. For example, in their review of paternal influences on child and adolescent psychopathology, Phares and Compas (1992) noted that, despite the fact that problems with high occurrence in men (alcoholism, antisociality) are associated with problems with high occurrence in boys (conduct disorder, delinquency), the evidence for specificity of risk is weak. In other words, both COAs and children of depressed fathers are at risk for various internalizing and externalizing behavior problems.

Studies linking maternal depression and child problem behaviors also provide support for the contention that maternal depression is affected by family stress and family conflict, which in turn affects a mother's perceptions of her children (Ferguson et al., 1985; Campbell & Ewing, 1991). For example, Downey and Coyne (1990) link the externalizing problems of children with depressed mothers to high levels of marital conflict. The level of spousal violence is high in alcoholic families (Gayford, 1975), particularly in instances where the husbands have a history of antisocial behavior and a severe drinking problem. Higher rates of physical abuse have also been found among alcoholic parents (Tarter et al., 1984). Although a direct causal link between level of alcohol involvement and child abuse has not yet been established, there is some indication that fathers of abused boys have higher rates of alcoholism.

Richman, Stevenson, and Graham (1982) report that continued family stress is directly related to the maintenance of behavior problems in children. Thus, in high-risk families it is possible that maternal lifetime alcohol problems and depression mediate the effects of paternal antisocial behavior on children's adaptive functioning. Yang, Fitzgerald, and Zucker (1992) designed a study that predicted that the level of psychosocial functioning of alcoholics and their spouses is negatively related to the degree of disrupted family functioning and the level of their offspring's adaptive functioning. Path models were constructed to explain causal relations among such parental variables as lifetime alcohol problems, antisocial behavior, ego functioning, social support, stress, current depression, and children's variables, including temperament and behavior problems. Figure 17.4A shows the path model involving alcoholic fathers' variables predicting spousal ratings of children's behavior problems. Figure 17.4B shows the path model for alcoholics' wives' variables predicting their own ratings of their children's behavior problems. The results of the path analyses and hierarchical multiple regression analyses indicated that parents' current depression significantly predicted their children's behavior problems. Parents' ego functioning, maternal social support, and stress mediated parental psychopathology, including lifetime alcohol problems, antisocial behavior, and current depression. An alcoholic family environment in which parents reported more alcohol-related problems, antisocial behavior, and depression was associated with elevated risk, especially risk for behavior problems in 3- to 5-year-old sons. Parents' lifetime alcohol problems and antisocial behavior were positively linked to increased level of stress and to lowered levels of ego resiliency. Within the confines of

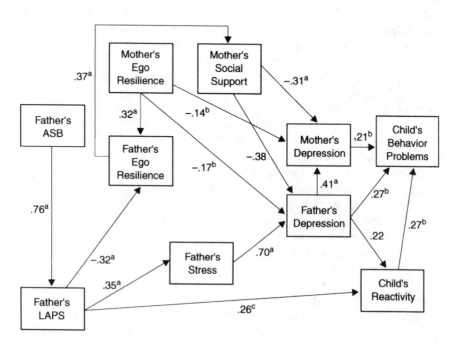

Figure 17.4A. Path Model: Alcoholic Fathers' Variables Predicting Spousal Ratings of Children's Behavior Problems. (Note: [a]=p <.05; [b] = p < .01; [c] = p < .001.)

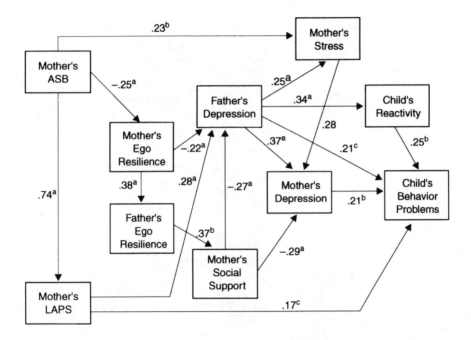

Figure 17.4B. Path Model: Alcoholic Wives' Variables Predicting Their Own Ratings of Children's Behavior Problems. (Note: [a]=$p < .05$; [b] = $p < .01$; [c] = $p < .001$.)

a currently cross-sectional, and in some cases retrospective, data base, this model indicates that stress increased parents' depression. Insofar as this is so, it is likely to be involved in exacerbating the child's vulnerability to behavior problems. Parents' ego resiliency and maternal social support was predictive of decreased parental depression. In such cases, parents seemed more likely to be involved in protective processes with regard to children's adaptive functioning. The path analysis also suggests there are indirect effects of alcoholic fathers through their spouses, as well as direct paternal effects on their children's behavior: Alcoholic fathers' support decreased mothers' current depression, whereas alcoholic fathers' current depression increased their spouses current depression. Both parents' current depression seemed causally linked to their children's behavior problems. Finally, children's temperament (reactivity) contributed significantly to their levels of behavior problems.

A study of over 2,000 14-year olds from over 40 schools in Ontario found less drug abuse among teenagers who had positive affective relationships with their parents, who participated in family decision making, who lived in families with strong cohesiveness, and whose parents were not drug abusers (Hundleby & Mercer, 1987). On the other hand, parental modeling, nonattendance at religious services, family conflict, low SES, and poor family sociability were all correlated with increased drug use and abuse. Equally important, however, this study found

TABLE 17.2.   Antecedents of Adolescent Substance Abuse and Level of System Influence

System Level	Antecedents
Intra- and Interindividual	Physiological characteristics Early and persistent behavior problems Aggressive behavior in boys Other conduct problems Hyperactivity in childhood and adolescence Difficult temperament Early initiation of drug use
Family	Family history of alcoholism Parental use of illegal drugs Poor family management practices Family conflict Traditions and values
Peer group	Early peer rejection Social influences to use drugs Peer modeling
School	Academic failure Lack of commitment to school
Culture	Laws and norms favorable toward drug use Availability of drugs Poverty Alienation and rebelliousness

Source: Antecedent conditions are taken from a variety of sources, including Hawkins, Catalano, & Miller (1992), Zucker (1987; in press), and Zucker & Fitzgerald (1991a).

that parental and family variables were less predictive of adolescent drug abuse than were peer variables. In fact, drug use by friends was the most predictive of all measures, followed by friends' delinquency, lack of achievement orientation, and lack of religiosity. In both their cross-sectional and longitudinal studies, Brook et al. (1990) also found that peers accounted for more variance associated with adolescents' marijuana use than any other set of variables, including parental variables. Other investigators also have drawn attention to the powerful role played by the peer group in influencing drug-using behavior, especially when family–child ties are weak (Bennett & Wolin, 1990; Braucht, 1982). For example, the teenager's closeness or estrangement from his or her parents will modulate the extent to which peers have a direct and lasting effect on his or her behavior, beliefs, values, and decision making (Radosevich, Lanza-Kaduce, Akers, & Krohn, 1980). In some instances, the family's ability to preserve its traditions seems to diminish the intergenerational transmission of alcoholism (Wolin, Bennett, Noonan, & Teitelbaum, 1980). Such factors as family size, family health, religiosity, rituals, workplace, ethnic origins, and traditions have seldom been studied in the alcoholism literature, other than as demographic descriptors of family presenting state characteristics. For example, rarely is the quality of the neighborhood considered when assessing "causal" factors related to alcohol and/or drug abuse. Nevertheless, the list of risk factors summarized in Table 17.2 clearly suggests that the search for causal antecedents of substance abuse must take into account variables at various levels of system organization.

SUMMARY

Historically, the substance abuse literature is noteworthy for its emphasis on disease models of addiction, its assumption that substance abuse is a problem rooted in adolescence and early adulthood, and its emphasis on intra-individual determinants of abuse, regardless of their presumed genetic or environmental origins. We suggest that developmental system models can be used to challenge each of these historical trends in alcoholism research, while at the same time providing both theoretical and methodological approaches that encourage multivariate analyses of substance abuse, that stress the analysis of alternative developmental pathways to substance abuse, and that promote the development and testing of models that attempt to predict the causal pathways that induce or maintain vulnerability or resilience in children reared in substance abusing families. Although family system theory has been influential in the substance abuse literature for several decades, only recently have investigators begun to use dynamic system models, structural equation analysis, and other multivariate techniques in an effort to identify the critical interrelationships among variables that lead to alternative developmental pathways for children reared in environments in which substance abuse and/or family psychopathology are critical factors affecting individual functioning, interpersonal relationships, and the dynamics of family life.

REFERENCES

Alterman, A. I., Petrarula, E., Tarter, R. E., & McGowan, J. (1982). Hyperactivity and alcoholism: Familial and behavioral correlates. *Addictive Behaviors, 7*, 413–421.

Barnes, G. M. (1990). Impact of the family on adolescent drinking patterns. In R. L. Collins, K. E. Leonard, & J. S. Searles (Eds.), *Alcohol and the family: Research and clinical perspectives* (pp. 3–38). New York: Guilford.

Barr, H. M., Streissguth, A. P., Darby, B. L., & Sampson, P. D. (1990). Prenatal exposure to alcohol, caffeine, tobacco, and aspirin: Effects on fine and gross motor performance in 4-year-old children. *Developmental Psychology, 26*, 339–348.

Begleiter, H. (1992). A potential phenotypic marker for the development of alcoholism. Distinguished Research Awardee Address, Annual meeting of the Research Society on Alcoholism, San Diego.

Bennett, L. A., & Wolin, S. J. (1990). Family culture and alcoholism transmission. In R. L. Collins, K. E. Leonard, & J. S. Searles (Eds.), *Alcohol and the family: research and clinical perspectives* (pp. 194–219). New York: Guilford.

Block, J., Block, J. H., & Keyes, S. (1988). Longitudinally foretelling drug usage in adolescence: Early childhood personality and environmental precursors. *Child Development,* 59, 336–355.

Brackbill, Y., McManus, K., & Woodward, L. (1985). *Medication in maternity: Infant exposure and maternal information.* Ann Arbor: University of Michigan Press.

Braucht, G. N. (1982). Problem drinking among adolescents: A review and analysis of psychosocial research. In *Alcohol and Health Monograph (No. 4): Special population issues* (pp. 143–164). Rockville, MD: National Institute on Alcohol Abuse and Alcoholism.

Brook, J. S., Brook, D. W., Gordon, A. S., Whiteman, M., & Cohen, P. (1990). The psychosocial etiology of adolescent drug use: A family interactional approach. *Genetic, Social, and General Psychological Monographs, 116,* 111–267.

Cadoret, R. J. (1990). Genetics of alcoholism. In R. L. Collins, K. E. Leonard, & J. S. Searles (Eds.), *Alcohol and the family: Research and clinical perspectives* (pp. 39–78). New York: Guilford.

Campbell, S., & Ewing, L. J. (1991). Follow-up of hard-to-manage preschoolers: Adjustment at age 9 and predictors of continuing symptoms. *Journal of Child Psychology & Psychiatry & Allied Disciplines, 31,* 871–889.

Chasnoff, I. J., & Griffith, D. R. (1991). Maternal cocaine use: Neonatal outcome. In H. E. Fitzgerald, B. M., Lester, & M. W. Yogman (Eds.), *Theory and research in behavioral pediatrics,* (Vol. 5, pp. 1–17). New York: Plenum.

Christiansen, B. A., Smith, G. T., Roehling, P. V., & Goldman, M. S. (1989). Using alcohol expectancies to predict adolescent drinking behavior after 1 year. *Journal of Consulting and Clinical Psychology, 57,* 93–99.

Clair, D., & Genest, M. (1987). Variables associated with the adjustment of offspring of alcoholic fathers. *Journal of Studies on Alcohol., 48,* 345–355.

Clarke-Stewart, A. (1980). The father's contribution to children's cognitive and social development in early childhood. In F. A. Pedersen (Ed.), *The father–infant relationship* (pp. 111–146). New York: Praeger.

Cloninger, R. (1987). Neurogenetic adaptive mechanisms in alcoholism. *Science, 236,* 410–416.

Cooper, S. (1987). The fetal alcohol syndrome. *Journal of Child Psychology & Psychiatry & Allied Disciplines, 28,* 223–227.

Cotton, N. S. (1979). The familial incidence of alcoholism: A review. *Journal of Studies on Alcohol, 40,* 89–116.

Cronkite, R. C., Finney, J. W., Nekich, J., & Moos, R. H. (1990). Remission among alcoholic patients and family adaptation to alcoholism: A stress and coping perspective. In R. L. Collins, K. E. Leonard, & J. S. Searles (Eds.), *Alcohol and the family: Research and clinical perspectives* (pp. 309–337). New York: Guilford.

Downey, G., & Coyne, J. C. (1990). Children of depressed parents: An integrative review. *Psychological Bulletin, 108,* 50–76.

Earls, F., Reich, W., Jung, K. G., & Cloninger, C. R. (1988). Psychopathology in children of alcoholic and antisocial parents. *Alcoholism: Clinical and Experimental Research, 12,* 481–487.

Ferguson, D. M., Hans, B. A., Horwood, L. J., Gretton, M. E., & Shannon, F. T. (1985). Family life events: Maternal depression, and maternal and teacher descriptions of child behavior. *Pediatrics, 75,* 30–35.

Fillmore, K. M. (1990). Critical explanations—biological, psychological, and social—of drinking patterns and problems from the alcohol-related longitudinal literature. In L. T. Kozlowski, H. M., Annis, H. D. Cappell, F. B. Glaser, M. S. Goodstadt, Y. Israel, H.

Kalant, E. M. Sellers, & E. R. Vingilis (Eds.), *Research advances in alcohol and drug problems* (Vol. 10, pp. 15–38). New York: Plenum.

Fitzgerald, H. E., Sullivan, L. A., Ham, H. P., Zucker, R. A., Bruckel, S., Schneider, A. M., & Noll, R. B. (1993). Predictors of behavior problems in three-year-old sons of alcoholics: Early evidence for the onset of risk. *Child Development. 64,* 110–123.

Gayford, J. J. (1975). Wife battering: A preliminary study of 100 cases. *British Medical Journal, 1,* 194–197.

Gomberg, E. S. L. (1990). Drugs, alcohol, and aging. In L. T. Kozlowski et al. (Eds.), *Research advances in alcohol and drug problems* (Vol. 10, pp. 171–213). New York: Plenum.

Gonzalez, F., Zucker, R. A., & Fitzgerald, H. E. (1992, August). Drug involvement among alcoholic men: Relationships to psychopathology and adaptation. Poster presented at the annual meeting of the American Psychological Association, Washington, DC.

Gottlieb, G. (1991). Experiential canalization of behavioral development: Theory. *Developmental Psychology, 27,* 4–13.

Grant, B. F., Harford, T. C., Chou, P., Pickering, R., Dawson, D. A., Stinson, F. S., & Noble, J. (1991). Prevalence of DSM-III-R alcohol abuse and dependence. *Alcohol Health & Research World, 15,* 91–96.

Grichtig, W. L. & Barber, J. G. (1989). The impact of quality of family life on drug consumption. *International Journal of the Addictions, 24,* 963–971.

Hans, S. L. (1989). Developmental consequences of prenatal exposure to methadone. *New York Academy of Sciences. Annals., 562,* 195–207.

Hawkins, J. D., Catalano, R. F., & Miller, J. Y. (1992). Risk and protective factors for alcohol and other drug problems in adolescence and early adulthood: Implications for substance abuse prevention. *Psychological Bulletin, 112,* 64–105.

Hetchman, L., Weiss, G., & Perlman, M. S. (1984). Hyperactives as young adults: Past and current substance abuse and antisocial behavior. *American Journal of Orthopsychiatry, 54,* 415–425.

Hoffman, L. W. (1991). The influence of the family environment on personality: Accounting for sibling differences. *Psychological Bulletin, 110,* 187–203.

Hundleby, J. D., & Mercer, G. W. (1987). Family and friends as social environments and their relationship to young adolescents' use of alcohol, tobacco, and marijuana. *Journal of Clinical Psychology, 44,* 125–134.

Jacob, T., & Leonard, K. (1986). Psychosocial functioning in children of alcoholic fathers, depressed fathers, and control fathers. *Journal of Studies on Alcohol, 47,* 373–380.

Jellinek, E. M. (1960). *The disease concept of alcoholism.* New Haven: Hillhouse.

Johnson, J. L., & Rolf, J. E. (1990). When children change: Research perspectives on children of alcoholics. In R. L. Collins, K. E., Leonard, & J. S. Searles (Eds.), *Alcohol and the family: Research and clinical perspectives* (pp. 162–193). New York: Guilford.

Kandel, D. B., & Yamaguchi, K. (1987). Job mobility and drug use: An event history analysis. *American Journal of Sociology, 92,* 836–878.

Knop, J., Teasdale, T. W., Schulsinger, F., & Goodwin, D. W. (1985). A prospective study of young men at high risk for alcoholism: School behavior and achievement. *Journal of Studies of Alcohol, 46,* 273–278.

Lahey, B. B., Conger, R. D., Atkenson, B. M., & Treiber, F. A. (1984). Parenting behavior and emotional stress of physically abusive mothers. *Journal of Consulting and Clinical Psychology, 52,* 1062–1071.

Lerner, R. M. (1991). Changing organism–context relations as the basic process of development: A developmental contextual perspective. *Developmental Psychology, 27,* 27–32.

Lester, B. M., Corwin, M. J., Sepkoski, C., Seifer, R., Peucker, M., McLaughlin, S., & Golub, H. L. (1991). Neurobehavioral syndromes in cocaine-exposed newborn infants. *Child Development, 62,* 694–705.

Levine, R. L., & Fitzgerald, H. E. (1992). Living systems, dynamical systems, and cybernetics: Historical overview and introduction to system dynamics. In R. L. Levine & H. E. Fitzgerald (Eds.), *Analysis of dynamic psychological systems: Basic approaches to general systems, dynamic systems, and cybernetics.* (Vol. 1, pp. 1–6). New York: Plenum.

Lytton, H. & Romney, D. M. (1991). Parents' differential socialization of boys and girls: A meta-analysis. *Psychological Bulletin, 109,* 267–296.

McArdle, J. J., Hamagami, F., & Hulick, P. (in press). Latent variable path models in alcohol use research. In R. A. Zucker, J. Howard, & G. M. Boyd (Eds.), *The development of alcohol problems: Exploring the biopsychosocial matrix of risk.* Rockville, MD: National Institute on Alcohol Abuse and Alcoholism.

McGivern, R. F., & Barron, S. (1991). Influence of prenatal alcohol exposure on the process of neurobehavioral sexual differentiation. *Alcohol Health & Research World, 15,* 115–125.

McGue, M. (in press). Evidence for causal mechanisms from human genetics data bases. In R. A. Zucker, J. Howard, & G. M. Boyd (Eds.), *The development of alcohol problems: Exploring the biopsychosocial matrix of risk.* Rockville, MD: National Institute on Alcohol Abuse and Alcoholism.

Merikangas, K. R., Weissman, M. M., Prusoff, B. A., Pauls, D. L., & Leckman, J. F. (1985). Depressives with secondary alcoholism: Psychiatric disorders in offspring. *Journal of Studies on Alcohol, 46,* 199–204.

Miller, P. M., Smith, G. T., & Goldman, M. S. (1990). Emergence of alcohol expectancies in childhood: A possible critical period. *Journal of Studies on Alcohol, 51,* 343–349.

Noll, R. B., Zucker, R. A., Fitzgerald, H. E., & Curtis, W. J. (1992). Cognitive and motor achievement of sons of alcoholic fathers and controls: The early childhood years. *Developmental Psychologist, 28,* 665–675.

Nyquist, L., Slivken, K., Spence, J., & Helmreich, R. (1985). Household responsibilities in middle-class couples: The contribution of demographic and personality variables. *Sex Roles: A Journal of Research, 12,* 15–34.

Orford, J. (1990). Alcohol and the family: An international review of the literature with implications for research and practice. In L. T. Kozlowski, H. M. Annis, H. D. Cappell, F. B. Glaser, M. S. Goodstadt, Y. Israel, H. Kalant, E. M. Sellers, & E. R. Vingilis (Eds.), *Research advances in alcohol and drug problems* (Vol. 10, pp. 81–155). New York: Plenum.

Paolino, T. J., & McGrady, B. S. (1977). *The alcoholic marriage: Alternative perspective.* New York: Grune & Stratton.

Phares, V., & Compas, B. E. (1992). The role of fathers in child and adolescent psychopathology: Make room for daddy. *Psychological Bulletin, 111,* 387–412.

Radosevich, M., Lanza-Kaduce, L., Akers, R. L., & Krohn, M. D. (1980). The sociology of adolescent drug and drinking behavior: A review of the state of the field: Part II. *Deviant Behavior, 1,* 145–169.

Regier, D. A., Farmer, M. E., Rae, D. S., Locke, B. Z., Keith, S. J., Judd, L. L., & Goodwin, F. K. (1990). Co-morbidity of mental disorders with alcohol and other drug abuse. *Journal of the American Medical Association, 264,* 2511–2518.

Reich, T., Cloninger, C. R., VanEerdewegh, P., Rice, J. P., & Mullancy, J. (1988). Secular trends in the familial transmission of alcoholism. *Alcoholism: Clinical and Experimental Research, 12,* 48–464.

Richman, N., Stevenson, J., & Graham, P. J. (1982). *Preschool to school: A behavioral study.* London: Academic.

Robins, L. (1966). *Deviant children grown up.* Baltimore: Williams & Wilkins.

Roosa, M. W., Tein, J-Y, Groppenbacher, N., & Michaels, M. (1991, November). Parenting and child health in alcoholic families. Paper presented at the National Council of Family Relations Annual Conference, Denver, CO.

Russell, M., Henderson, C., & Blume, S. (1985). *Children of alcoholics: A review of the literature.* New York: Children of Alcoholics Foundation.

Rydelius, P. (1981). Children of alcoholic fathers: Their social adjustment and their health status over 20 years. *Acta Paediatrica Scandinavica 286 (Suppl.),* 1–89.

Schuckit, M. A., Risch, S. C., & Gold, E. O. (1988). Alcohol consumption, ACTH level, and family history of alcoholism. *American Journal of Psychiatry, 145,* 1391–1395.

Searles, J. S. (1990). The contribution of genetic factors to the development of alcoholism: A critical review. In R. L. Collins, K. E. Leonard, & J. S. Searles (Eds.), *Alcohol and the family: Research and clinical perspectives* (pp. 3–38). New York: Guilford.

Seilhamer, R. A., & Jacob, T. (1990). Family factors and adjustment of children of alcoholics. In M. Windle & J. S. Searles (Eds.), *Children of alcoholics: Critical perspectives* (pp. 168–186). New York: Guilford.

Sher, K. J., & Walitzer, K. S. (1989, November). Children of alcoholics and the search for mediators of risk. Paper presented at the annual convention of the Association for the Advancement of Behavior Therapy. Washington, DC.

Sokol, R. J., & Clarren, S. K. (1989). Guidelines for use of terminology describing the impact of prenatal alcohol on the offspring. *Alcoholism: Clinical and Experimental Research, 13,* 597–598.

Steinglass, P. (1981). The alcoholic family at home: Patterns of interaction in dry, wet, and transitional stages of alcoholism. *Archives of General Psychiatry, 38,* 578–584.

Tarter, R. E., & Blackson, T. (1992). Objective measurement of behavioral activity in sons of substance abusers. Paper presented in symposium, "Childhood and familial characteristics and alcohol and substance abuse: Risk and etiology." Annual meeting of the American Psychological Association, Washington, DC.

Tarter, R. E., Hegedus, A. M., Goldstein, G., Shelly, C., & Alterman, A. I. (1984). Adolescent sons of alcoholics: Neuropsychological and personality characteristics. *Alcoholism: Clinical and Experimental Research, 8,* 216–222.

Webster-Stratton, C. (1988). Mothers' and fathers' perceptions of child deviance: Roles of parent and child behaviors and parent adjustment. *Journal of Consulting and Clinical Psychology, 56,* 909–915.

West, M. O., & Prinz, R. J. (1987). Parental alcoholism and childhood psychopathology. *Psychological Bulletin, 102,* 204–218.

White, H. R. (1987). Longitudinal stability and dimensional structure of problem drinking in adolescence. *Journal of Studies on Alcohol, 48,* 541–550.

Windle, M., Barnes, G. M., & Welte, J. (1989). Causal models of adolescent substance use: An examination of gender differences using distribution-free estimators. *Journal of Personality and Social Psychology, 56,* 132–142.

Wolin, S. J., Bennett, L. A., Noonan, D. L., & Teitelbaum, M. A., (1980). Disrupted family rituals: A factor in the intergenerational transmission of alcoholism. *Journal of Studies on Alcohol, 41,* 199–214.

Yang, H-Y., Fitzgerald, H. E., & Zucker, R. A. (1992). Causal models of alcoholic family environment predicting children's behavior problems. Unpublished manuscript, Michigan State University, Department of Psychology, East Lansing.

Zucker, R. A. (1987). The four alcoholisms: A developmental account of the etiologic process. In P. C. Rivers (Ed.), *Nebraska Symposium on Motivation: Alcohol & Addictive Behavior, 34,* 27–83.

Zucker, R. A. (in press). Pathways to alcohol problems and alcoholism: A developmental account of the evidence for multiple alcoholisms and for contextual contributions to risk. In R. A. Zucker, J. Howard, & G. M. Boyd (Eds.), *The development of alcohol problems: Exploring the biopsychosocial matrix of risk.* Rockville, MD: National Institute on Alcohol Abuse and Alcoholism.

Zucker, R. A., & Fitzgerald, H. E. (1991a). Early developmental factors and risk for alcohol problems. *Alcohol Health & Research World, 15,* 18–25.

Zucker, R. A., & Fitzgerald, H. E. (1991b). *Risk and coping in children of alcoholics: Years 6 to 10 of the Michigan State University Longitudinal Study.* (NIAAA Grant 2RO1 AA07065.) East Lansing: Department of Psychology, Michigan State University.

Zucker, R. A., Fitzgerald, H. E., Ham, H., Sullivan, L. S., Maguin, E., Jones, M-A., & Noll, R. B. (1992). Assessing antisocial behavior in alcoholic and nonalcoholic adults. Unpublished manuscript, East Lansing: Michigan State University, Department of Psychology.

Zucker, R. A., Noll, R. B., & Fitzgerald, H. E. (1986). *Risk and coping in children of alcoholics.* (NIAAA Grant 1RO1 AA07065). East Lansing: Michigan State University, Department of Psychology.

PART THREE

Implications

CHAPTER 18

Linking Societies, Families, and Individuals over Time

The Challenge of a Developmental Psychology of Families

ELIZABETH G. MENAGHAN

The authors in this volume have struggled to organize and synthesize what we know and what we need to know about individual and family processes from infancy to old age. That task is clearly enormous, and we are on very uneven terrain: some topics have well-developed streams of research, whereas others are still in their infancy. As several authors here note, the domain that "developmental family psychology" seeks to embrace has been carved up in many ways by differing research traditions. For example, with few exceptions, social gerontologists studying interaction between parents and children have not placed this work in the context of studies of parent–infant interaction, parent–adolescent interaction, or intergenerational relationships at midlife. Studies of sibling relationships among toddlers are independent of and isolated from discussions of sibling relationships among the aged, as Cicirelli (chapter 3) points out, and disconnected from debate about the startlingly high levels of sibling aggression reported by Arias and Pape (chapter 14); and studies of play in childhood are seldom linked to leisure patterns in adulthood (Orthner et al., chapter 9). Thus, similar behaviors, occurring at differing points in the life span, are examined by differing groups of researchers and theorists.

More fundamentally, as the organization of this volume itself echoes, studies of "normal development" and normative family sequences tend to be segregated from analyses of deadly struggle, cruel mistreatment, and assaultive verbal and physical interaction, as if we need differing theories and explanations for positive and negative outcomes. These deep divisions in our organization of knowledge are formidable obstacles to the accumulation of knowledge and to the generation of more encompassing theoretical arguments.

As if those obstacles are not enough, in this chapter I call attention to additional obstacles to progress. One major obstacle is the relative lack of attention to gender as a pervasive societal and family factor that profoundly conditions human development and family interaction patterns. Second, as difficult as it is to link individuals and families, I argue that we will not go far in understanding family functioning without paying greater attention to the economic and occupational contexts within which families reside. This issue also is linked inextricably with gender differences.

A third obstacle lies in the uneven attention to what Elder (1974) has called the forces for interpersonal and interactional continuity across individual life spans. I argue that these processes deserve greater attention, and that they are particularly crucial in discussions of marital interaction and marital continuity. Finally, there is tremendous diversity across the nation and across the globe in the sequencing of marital and childbearing activities, and in the fragility of spousal and parental—particularly paternal—bonds. This raises enormous obstacles to the study of families over time, but it also makes it essential that we expand our vision beyond normatively expected sequences and arrangements, and pay particular attention to family interactions across households, such as between children and noncustodial parents, and to families where childbearing precedes marital commitments. Having discussed these obstacles, I offer some suggestions about theoretical development and research design.

GENDER IN SOCIETY AND FAMILIES

At the core of family life is stratification by age and gender. Gender (like race and age) is a master status that powerfully affects perceptions, expectations, and behavior in individual interaction and may override or qualify the effects of other statuses. For example, indicators of higher SES are discounted or undercut by perceptions of minority racial status or female gender. The status groups formed by gender and race are stratified, with males and whites having an advantage relative to females and nonwhites in U.S. society. These hierarchies are internalized and become a standard by which individuals evaluate their own performance in work and family roles.

Internalization of such hierarchies influences the effects of work and family conditions, including unemployment, job loss, or low wage employment. The pervasive cultural demand that men should earn money through their labor (and that the primary way women should earn/obtain money is through alliances with individual men) ties self-worth much more closely to economic success for men than for women. Male economic failure reflects on individual self-worth so fundamentally, and male economic success is so nonsubstitutable a good that, throughout U.S. history, when hard times come men drift off, ride the rails, or become consumed by alcohol or drugs. In such situations, women certainly suffered economically, but their basic self-worth has been less profoundly shaken. Indeed, they have often expanded their own economic activities (Elder, 1974). Such expansion, despite time pressures, is likely to be positive precisely because wage earning is a basic male expectation: participating in activity that is *valued* for the more valued group has positive effects, whereas participation in activities less valued by the larger group (and therefore allocated to the less valued group) has more negative implications. Thus, for example, men's greater participation in housework and child care may be viewed as demeaning to men, (although not to women), whereas women's participation in earning is not considered demeaning, although it may engender subtle disapproval. These arguments suggest that events that signify failure at activities normatively expected for one's status group will have particularly negative effects.

Conditions of employment and specific occupations are also stratified by race and gender, with those jobs that are reserved for men, not women, being restricted further as for white men before other men (Reskin & Roos, 1990). Employment in a job that is *lower* than "appropriate" for one's race and gender has negative emotional consequences; and "invasion" of an occupation by members of "lower" groups is resisted and resented by members of "higher" groups. Wharton and Baron (1987) found that having to work with women distresses men (especially those men with strong beliefs in male privilege) independent of the actual, substantive demands or rewards of the job.

Thus, whereas men are privileged as a group, individual men are particularly vulnerable to feedback that threatens their economic success. The situation of men in "lower" ethnic groups is particularly entrapping: success as a man is judged by economic success, but opportunities for such success are profoundly limited by racial and ethnic exclusions.

If economic success is a non-substitutable goal for all men, making economic failure far more negative for them as a group, women seem to face similar dilemmas regarding family relationships. Responsibility for children is theirs, and no matter how adverse the circumstances, they are blamed for "failure" in child outcomes. Failed marital relationships also reflect badly on them. This suggests that mothers should be more negatively affected by marital problems, as well as by friction with children. Cusinato (chapter 5), in his review of the parenting literature, offers some support for the greater vulnerability of women to children's illnesses and troubles. In apparent contradiction to this is men's greater negative response to widowhood and divorce. One possible explanation is that women perceive problems sooner than their husbands, entertain the possibility of disruption for a longer period of time, and are more apt to take the initiative in finally dissolving the marriage (Furstenberg and Cherlin, 1991). Thus, they have more anticipatory rehearsal and preparation when disruption finally occurs.

The marital relationship is also more likely to be men's only intimate tie, whereas women's socially structured position as kin-keeper and relationship-maintainer afford them more social ties. She is also far more likely to maintain relationships with a couple's children, and, although in the first year or two after marital disruption, mothers' interaction with their children may be difficult, those patterns of interaction tend to return to baseline (Furstenberg & Cherlin, 1991). In contrast, former husbands may try to sustain relationships with their children in the period immediately following marital disruption, but interaction drops off sharply during the first few years, and it shows no recovery (Furstenberg & Nord, 1985).

Certainly, the gender role expectations for husbands and wives form a critical context for much of what happens over the marital life course. Sex stratification encourages and enforces the subordination of women to men, and gender-differentiated socialization encourages the development of differing interests, aspirations, and values between men and women. Thus, marriage brings together two people whose differences have been amplified by socialization, and who operate within a context of gender inequality. However, the ideal-normative script for a companionate marriage counsels the couple to treat each other as similar and equal. Similarly, leisure activities are developed along gender lines, making the joint leisure activities that Orthner and his colleagues (chapter 9) find so beneficial to marital commitment and satisfaction more difficult to achieve. Men's orientation toward sports participation (and vicarious participation as spectators) as a favored leisure activity collides with socialized female preferences, for example, and even settling on a jointly interesting movie may be difficult.

Adult roles are also strikingly different after the birth of children. Despite the upsurge in women's employment, primary responsibility for breadwinning remains the male's, and this responsibility carries privileges. The demands of husbands' jobs are generally accorded more importance, even when spouses are childless, and women's labor force attachment is more likely to be interrupted, part-time, or both. Both sex segregation of occupations and jobs, and fewer family-related interruptions mean that, even among dual-earner couples, husbands earn more money and work longer hours, and their greater economic contribution translates into greater power for them.

Thus, the typical marriage moves from a union of two people with differing interests and leisure choices, but similar levels of education and similar "entry level" earnings, to a partnership in which wives subordinate their own economic interests to their husbands and take on the greater responsibility for cleaning, purchasing, and children's care and supervision, and husbands concentrate more on their economic advancement. This background must to be taken into account as we study changes over time in the number of marital quarrels and in the growing distance between marital partners.

Gender division of responsibility for child rearing may also have pervasive effects on other male–female interaction patterns, including violence. As Cusinato (chapter 5) notes, U.S. societies assign primary responsibility for child care to individual biologic mothers. Coltrane (1988) argues that, when we take a global perspective, we can observe wide variation in the extent to which men assume responsibility for child rearing, especially after the child's first few years of life: some societies follow an "aloof father" pattern, with limited contact between children and adult men; whereas, others follow a "proximate father" pattern, with much informal father–child interaction and father nurturance. Coltrane uses data on 90 nonindustrial societies, and reviews a variety of socialization arguments advanced by Margaret Mead, Philip Slater, and Nancy Chodorow, which converge in predicting that men reared primarily by women, with little nurturance from fathers, will be "hypermasculine," will define themselves in opposition to women, will exaggerate differences between men and women, and will seek to reserve valued activities for men and to restrict female access to public activities. Using small societies as his unit of analysis, Coltrane obtained wide variation in his sample, both in how much fathers and other men participate in child socialization, and in the extent to which women participate in public or private community decisions, have access to positions of authority, and are revered in origin symbolism. He found that when there is high father–child proximity, women have higher status, and he concluded that societies with father-present patterns of child socialization produce men who are less hostile and aggressive toward women, and are less inclined to exclude women from public activities than are their counterparts in father-absent societies. Coltrane argues forcefully that ". . . we need to investigate gender differentiation in child-rearing practices to understand the social, psychological, and political processes that govern our everyday lives" (p. 1090). Such arguments and findings about how gender dynamics in child rearing affect gender dynamics and political arrangements in adulthood are certainly open to alternative explanations. Even if proved wrong, however, they have enormous value in widening the scope of the linkages we consider and in suggesting connections between the "normal functioning" we take for granted and the pathological patterns we abhor. They help to bridge the descriptive data Cusinato presents regarding usual patterns of parenting and the data regarding marital conflict (Heavey et al., chapter 11), physical and sexual violence (Arias & Pape, chapter 14), and sexual abuse (Haugaard, chapter 15).

ECONOMIC AND OCCUPATIONAL INFLUENCES ON FAMILY INTERACTION

Attention to gender highlights stratification *within* families. But family units are also stratified within the larger society. Quick et al. (chapter 8) provide a thoughtful account of the occupational and economic changes that have undermined employment security and wages for millions of adult wage earners, but such variables are almost completely absent from discussions in other chapters of the conflicts and distortions in interaction observed in families. I comment briefly on effects on marital relationships and parent–child relations in this chapter.

Much research on work and family stress has focused on employment status, with the general assumption that wives' employment, but husbands' *un*employment, are distressing both for adults and children. But, as I have argued elsewhere (Menaghan, 1991, in press), much depends on what employed people *do,* not merely whether or not they are employed. Three key occupational variables are the extent of self-direction and control permitted in the occupation, the wages earned, and the hours workers spend on the job. Gender differences in occupational experiences help to set the stage for discussion of how the effects of occupational experiences may also vary by gender.

The degree of self-direction a job affords is an aspect of work intimately tied to issues of control, challenge, and mastery. As Mirowsky and Ross (1986) have reported, low levels of such conditions produce senses of powerlessness and alienation, which color beliefs about the possibility of control in other aspects of life, and arouse psychological distress. The degree of self-direction exercised on the job also shapes more general attitudes and values (Schooler, 1987), including attitudes about the self, such as sense of self-worth and self-efficacy. Work by Karasek and others (Haynes & Feinleib, 1980; House, Strecher, Metzner, & Robbins, 1986; Karasek, 1979; Karasek, Baker, Marxer, Ahlbom, & Theorell, 1981) suggests that the combination of high job demands, but low decision latitude, is particularly lethal, generating high levels of emotional and physical distress.

Occupational and Economic Effects on Marriage

Men and women differ sharply in the average conditions they encounter at work because occupations, and jobs within occupations, remain segregated by sex, and much female employment tends to be in "female ghetto" occupations, such as secretarial and clerical, retail sales, cashiers, beauty/cosmetics, and young children's education (see Bielby & Baron, 1984; Reskin & Roos, 1990; and Jacobs, 1989). The combination of high job demands and low decision making that Karasek (1979) has identified as so negative is more characteristic of women's jobs than of men's jobs.

Even when wives are employed, their economic contribution tends to be downplayed and interpreted as secondary—by both husbands and wives, as well as by the larger society. Husbands remain responsible for providing for the family, and this recognized role of provider carries privileges. It legitimatizes greater attention to a husband's occupational requirements and to his career progress over his wife's, even when husbands and wives have similar earnings and potential earnings. Bielby and Bielby (1992) point out that the cultural assignment of "provider" roles to husbands, and the acceptance of this assignment as legitimate by both spouses, leads wives to subordinate their job interests to those of their husbands with little explicit bargaining (see also Ferree, 1990). As gender role beliefs change, however, husbands and wives may face greater overt conflict, as they struggle to work out jointly satisfying occupational and family arrangements. Ironically, "better" jobs—defined in terms of higher wages and greater occupational complexity—may have negative consequences for marital quality, despite their positive individual psychological consequences. Wives with good jobs may be less willing to subordinate their own preferences and to forgo occupational opportunities; their challenge to taken-for-granted patterns may increase marital problems. Husbands with good jobs may feel more entitled to claim breadwinner privileges, and may be less willing to jeopardize their own occupational progress by accommodating their wives. The challenges to family commitments and family satisfaction posed by greater occupational attachments of women have not been widely investigated, but this will be an increasingly important topic in the coming decade.

Occupational and Economic Consequences for Parent–Child Relationships

Occupational and economic conditions also affect interactions between parents and children. A large body of literature supports the expectations that low-quality interaction with socializing adults, and unstable, unpredictable social contexts compromise children's attachment and security, with attendant negative effects on learning (Crouter, Belsky, & Spanier, 1984; Estrada, Arsenio, Hess, & Holloway, 1987; Howes 1988). Occupational and economic conditions shape relations among adults in the household, as well as relations between parents and children. These include the adults' chosen strategies of child socialization, support, and control, the overall affective climate of the family, and the consistency and contingency of parental action.

Studies of the intergenerational transmission of economic position have established that the social and economic resources of parents affect their children's educational progress and their later adult occupational and economic status (Astone & McLanahan, 1991; Teachman, 1987). Higher levels of economic resources also reduce levels of parental distress that may affect parent–child interaction (Flanagan, 1990; Siegal, 1984). Both low overall economic levels and the experience of economic losses affect parental demoralization and depression, and disrupt skillful parenting (Conger et al., 1992).

Both social-psychological theory and empirical research suggest that the conditions adults experience at work, particularly their opportunities to exercise self-direction in substantively complex work, shape the values they hold for their children (Kohn & Schooler, 1983; Kohn, Slomczymski, & Schoenbach, 1986; Miller Schooler, Kohn, & Miller, 1979; Schooler, 1987; Siegal, 1984; Voydanoff, 1987). When parents' work is more substantively complex and offers greater opportunities for self-direction, parents place greater value on their children's developing self-direction, and they are less concerned with behavioral conformity per se (Kohn & Schooler, 1983; Spade, 1991). Such parents display more warmth and involvement, restrict their child's actions less frequently, and report less frequent spankings (Luster, Rhoades, & Haas 1989). Alternatively, working conditions that are routine, heavily supervised, and low in autonomy and substantive complexity erode the parents' intellectual flexibility, thus limiting a critical aspect of the child's intellectual environment. Recent findings that the complexity of current maternal occupation exerts a significant effect on a child's family environment lends further support to social structure and personality frameworks that argue that the working conditions parents face on the job influence parental values and behaviors relevant to parenting (Menaghan & Parcel, 1991).

Work stress research has shown that the work conditions more common to less desirable jobs—routinization, low autonomy, heavy supervision, and little demand or opportunity for substantively complex work—exacerbate psychological distress, and reduce self-esteem and personal control. To the extent that work experiences leave parents feeling uncertain about their own worth and emotionally distressed, they are less able to be available emotionally to their children or to provide them with responsive, stimulating environments (Belsky & Eggebean, 1991; Menaghan, 1991).

CONTRIBUTIONS OF INDIVIDUALS TO LIFE CHANCES AND CHANGES

One difficulty with research on the effects of specific experiences and contexts on an individual and a family life course is that we are unable (either practically or ethically) to make experience and initial characteristics independent in the way we can in an experimental situation. We cannot make random assignments of marital partners, occupations, or children. Some individuals marry young, while others delay, and some choose partners with seriously limited abilities to love, work, negotiate, or maintain commitments. The unobserved variables that lead to a premature marriage or an unfortunate partner choice may be the key variables that undermine family functioning, not the subsequent marital dissolution that we observe.

This is a particular problem in studies of marital trajectories, where assortative mating by education and social competence, while imperfect, is quite influential. In fact, sorting on such characteristics has increased even as sorting on other characteristics proxying for similarity in values has declined: Kalmijn's (1991) study of mate selection suggests that intermarriage across religious lines has increased dramatically since the 1920s, while marriages across educational lines have decreased. The process of assortative mating tends to pair individuals with compromised chances for satisfaction with other similar individuals, and individuals whose characteristics foreshadow more positive outcomes with other similar individuals. In assessing how interaction patterns shape individual outcomes, it is important to control for related differences in initial individuals' resources and vulnerabilities.

More generally, I argue that individuals are neither randomly nor fortuitously exposed to situations. As much as possible, individuals exert effort to select rewarding or compatible environments, as in mate selection or entry into specific occupations. Caspi and Bem (1990) refer to this as *pro active* interaction between persons and environments; this tends to produce stability, for better or worse, on individual trajectories. Individuals also elicit responses from others that tend to reinforce their initial behaviors and attitudes. Caspi and Bem refer to this as evocative interaction, and note as examples Clausen's (1991) finding that personal competence in late adolescence tends to "pull" affirmative responses from others, whereas personal irritability and explosiveness tend to evoke reciprocal hostility from others, reinforcing an individual's initial tendency to respond explosively to evidence of personal threat. Although they use somewhat different terms, Fitzgerald and his colleagues (chapter 17, this volume) raise some of these same concerns as they examine intergenerational effects of parental substance use.

NONNORMATIVE FAMILY SEQUENCES AND STRUCTURES

In his introductory chapter to this volume, L'Abate defines developmental family psychology as that part of psychology concerned with the life cycles of the various members of the same family. Discussing the life course, Elder (1991) similarly draws attention to the notion that lives are lived interdependently among family members and kinship units, and kinship and family are primary sources of variations and regulation in life trajectories. Lives are long, and kinship ties grow complex, especially as lifelong marital bonds become less likely. If we limit membership in "the same family" to those sharing the same household, or fall back on Census definitions of family households to define family memberships, we have an impoverished glimpse of the web of interconnections linking individuals across space and time. At any single time, many individuals are members of more than one family, and are linked biologically and emotionally to people who do not share their household.

Entwisle (chapter 7) provides a succinct and cogent summary of the diversity in American family patterns today. The challenge is for other scholars to include such families in their theories, as well as in their data.

Much public debate has focused on the "disappearing mother," as increasing numbers of women maintain stronger attachment to the labor force, even after having children. In contrast, the emergent father image sketched by Cusinato (chapter 5) suggests that fathers have increased their participation in child rearing. As several authors have pointed out, however, claims of increased paternal involvement seem premature, at best (see for example the excellent review of Thompson and Walker, 1989, or Furstenberg's 1988 discussion of good dads and bad dads). Close analyses tend to find little actual increase in the household work and child care undertaken by fathers living with their children. In any case, such discussions focus on temporal variations in activity among fathers who are living with their children. For better or for worse, this is a shrinking proportion of all fathers. Nonmarital pregnancies are increasingly resolved by elective abortion or by child rearing by unmarried mothers. Moreover, it is projected that approximately half the children born to married parents will experience the dissolution of their parents' marriage, and, in most cases, the departure of their fathers from their households. Such patterns are stronger for nonwhite ethnic groups, but they are occurring in virtually all groups in the society. As a result, to an unprecedented extent, U. S. fathers are detached from child rearing. As I note in my later discussion of cross-national research designs, this male withdrawal may not bode well for male–female relations or for women's social status.

The exaggeration of gender differences and uneven development of competencies, noted in the first section of this chapter, also have consequences for parent–child relationships when marriages end. Men have tended to be linked to their children in more indirect than direct ways, with their relationships with their children mediated by women. Furstenberg and Cherlin (1991) document the recurrent activities of wives in interpreting fathers and children to one another: mothers call attention to (even exaggerate, according to Thompson and Walker, 1989) men's domestic contributions; they explain men's absence because of work as *for* the family, and explain men's work-related moods similarly as suffering *for* us ("Daddy's had a hard day. Let's give him a little peace and quiet, help him cheer up"); they schedule and structure men's time with children; they bring men up to date with what the children have been doing; and they keep the household running smoothly by selectively enlisting the help of fathers and children.

Just as fish are unaware they are living in water, such background work may be almost invisible to fathers and children, unless it stops. Furstenburg and Cherlin (1991) call attention to newly divorced fathers' bewilderment at how badly visits with their children go, particularly visits in the fathers' new residences. Divorcing mothers now may become adept at emphasizing their former husbands' negative behaviors to their children; but even in the absence of active sabotage, the withdrawal of mothers from their mediating role undermines the previous foundation of father–child interaction. It is not surprising that men (and their children) begin to avoid such interaction, resent the deterioration of the good feelings these encounters seem to accomplish, and feel increasingly disconnected from their children, although they still love them. Baffled and hurt, they are likely to discover that they can, nevertheless, obtain some of the old pleasures of fatherhood by interacting with another woman's children. The same social structuring and support may be skillfully provided, and the interaction will go surprisingly smoothly.

Given this female negotiation of relationships between men and children, it is not surprising that children may report warm feelings and affection toward their stepfathers, along with feelings of estrangement from their own fathers (Cherlin, 1992; Furstenberg & Cherlin, 1991). It is also not surprising that stepmothers have more difficulty establishing comfortable relationships with stepchildren. Although fathers may be eager for everyone to get along, they are less likely to possess the skills to help that occur. Thus, basic gender differences make the addition of stepfathers less problematic than the addition of stepmothers.

Despite this relative difference, it is increasingly clear that neither addition "reconstitutes" the normative biologic two-parent family. When new marital commitments are added to ongoing parent–child families, relations between the new adult and the children do not generally resemble those between parents and children in intact families. Astone and McLanahan (1991) find differences in affection, interaction, supervision, and assistance. As they note, it is not clear whether stepparents are less willing to provide such supports or step-children are less willing to accept them. It is clear, however, that understanding the processes by which children and unrelated adults attempt to form a relationship is a task crucial to understanding contemporary family processes. These issues echo at the end of life, as we seek to understand the varying claims for care and assistance that aging parents make, and the varying acceptance or rejection of those claims by adult children. Do stepfathers receive the filial aid that is denied to biological fathers who did not reside with the child, for example? What grandparental connections are claimed or denied? Research on older adults and grandparents reviewed by Swensen (chapter 10) have not yet embraced the increased diversity of parental and grandparental links that characterize newer cohorts of the aging.

STRATEGIES FOR THEORETICAL DEVELOPMENT AND RESEARCH DESIGN

Cicirelli (chapter 2) argues eloquently that theory and research must be taken more seriously, and we must make more explicit the basic assumptions about human nature and human societies that underlie our theories. He contrasts organicist "unfolding" metamodels of individual development over the life span with both mechanist metamodels of virtually unlimited "molding" of individuals and social groups, and contextualist metamodels of bidirectional influences, with unpredictable outcomes for both individuals and societies. As Cicirelli notes, these metamodels may be partially compatible; in any case, greater self-conscious reflection on the direction of influence and the mutability of human behavior is likely to enhance theoretical development.

It is also important to be more explicit about the processes or mechanisms that connect societal structures and social changes, interaction among family members, and individual trajectories. Both Elder and Caspi (1988) and Patterson (1988) provide interesting exemplars for such theoretical work. It is no longer sufficient (indeed, it never was sufficient) to demonstrate empirical associations between, for example, family structure or economic hardship and individual and family outcomes. We must develop, and try to examine, the mediating "gears" transmitting effects from one set of conditions to outcomes. In addition to increasing our understanding, the explicit delineation of such gears provides one of the most promising ways to intervene if we hope to alter consequences.

If we take seriously the axiom that theoretical formulations should yield testable propositions that can lead to increased confidence in theoretical adequacy or theory-enhancing modifications, it is clear that many of the chapters rest on a fragile research base. As many authors acknowledge, in most cases they have provided descriptive summaries of available studies, attempting to order them in some fashion, and they have had to rely heavily on cross-sectional analyses with archival or self-report data. There are clear limits to what we can test when we are limited to cross-sectional studies. We can discern whether patterns of covariation are consistent with our theoretical arguments or expectations, but we are on shaky ground when we claim causal influences. For example, we may observe married couple families with early adolescent children, and find that the more conflicts parents report, the more behavior problems the child seems to have. Our arguments tend to suggest that the emotional turmoil of the parents disrupts their ability to be consistent, constructive, and engaged in interaction with their children. Having observed both marital conflict and child outcome simultaneously, however, we cannot rule out many alternative explanations. The obvious one is reverse causality: it is the child's difficulties that are prompting heated discussions and disagreement among the parents. In addition, both parental discord and child problems may share common causes without being causally linked themselves: rumors of plant closings and layoffs may have everyone on edge; chronic economic pressures may create recurrent dilemmas regarding consumption that have eroded a sense of cooperation and connectedness among family members; or at least one parent may have a lifelong history of irritability and anger that pervades their interactions with spouse and child.

Prospective Longitudinal Studies

The recurrent recommendation/solution is to amass more prospective, longitudinal data sets, which follow individuals and families over time. Such studies are a definite improvement over static "snapshots" of current family characteristics and their associations with current outcomes, and they permit us to consider the cumulative *history* of experiences more fully. They also permit the researcher to control for outcome levels both prior to and following events or family changes that are treated as causal. The need for such controls for prior status has become increasingly clear. For example, some analyses of longitudinal data archives suggest that much of the "effects" of family disruption apparent in children actually predate the family disruption itself, suggesting that prior research may have misspecified causal linkages.

Longitudinal data sets also permit us to consider both immediate and lagged effects of family factors. An exclusively short-term view may exaggerate negative effects, whereas a longer follow-up would show that such problems seldom persist over time; conversely, a short-term absence of effects may prompt claims about children's resilience in the face of difficult circumstances— an assumption that may prove to be unwarranted on longer-term follow-up. With longitudinal data, we can avoid these errors. Finally, longitudinal designs give us a better grasp of the problem of possible selection effects by permitting controls for preexisting individual characteristics. In much nonexperimental research, observed associations between contemporaneously assessed school and family circumstances on the one hand, and children's cognitive and emotional outcomes on the other, for example, may reflect effects of such parental characteristics (see Zaslow, Rabinovich, & Suwalsky, 1991 for a thoughtful discussion of this issue). As I have reviewed in more detail elsewhere, however, longitudinal studies, too, have limitations (Menaghan & Godwin, 1993).

Approximating Social Experiments

A partial solution is to capitalize on naturally occurring experiments. For example, not everyone experienced economic decline during the Great Depression of the 1930s, and individual characteristics were poor predictors of who would lose income and who would not. Thus, Elder (1974) was able to discuss causal impacts of economic loss and subsequent adaptation efforts with greater confidence than if he had contrasted employed and unemployed fathers at a more prosperous time.

A second solution is to conduct intervention research that is designed to test specific causal claims. These may be social or psychotherapeutic interventions. For example, many cross-sectional surveys and short-term longitudinal studies have found that individuals with more extensive social support have better emotional and physical health, and that individuals who lose social support show some deterioration in functioning, whereas those who increase their available support show improvement. If change in social support causes changes in functioning, then intervention to alter levels of social support should also show changes in functioning. If experimental interventions aimed at testing this hypothesis produce the changes in outcome that are theoretically expected, our theory is supported.

Of course, many explanatory variables are not susceptible to manipulation. For example, being from a family in which one or both parents are heavy alcohol users, as Fitzgerald et al. (chapter 17, this volume) discuss, seems to predict more difficulties than being from a family that does not include alcohol-dependent parents. We cannot assign children randomly to these two conditions; our only recourse is to consider what else might co-vary with parental alcohol use and to measure and control statistically for as many plausible alternative causal agents as possible.

Cross-National and Comparative Studies

Another problem in testing our theories is the difficulty of observing sufficient variation in our explanatory variables. Sometimes this is due to a flawed design, as when a researcher, attempting to show that harsh physical punishment in childhood produces an adult more likely to assault his or her spouse and/or child, obtains a sample of adults who were all raised in extremely punitive households. If virtually all the individuals studied had similar childhood experiences, then the researcher is unable to investigate whether variations in experience are linked to variations in adult actions.

Such design flaws can be remedied; the more intractable problem is a theoretically important variable that has little variation in the population being studied. An example is implicit in Arias and Pape's (chapter 14) discussion of explanations for physical violence in families. The authors present arresting data on the prevalence and correlates of various assaultive behaviors between family members. If we focus on the correlates of such behaviors within a single society, we focus on individual stressors and deficiencies. Arias and Pape also consider arguments that societal patterns of male dominance and male control through tactics of intimidation may underlie much of this behavior. Haugaard (chapter 15) notes that one cause of male violence against women and children, as well as male violations of sexual taboos forbidding sexual approaches to daughters and step-daughters, is the culture of patriarchy and male dominance that pervades our society and legitimates male use of force to obtain compliance, respect, and sexual access. To the extent that such attitudes and beliefs truly *pervade* the society, we cannot investigate their causal force, because we cannot observe variation. If we restrict the scope of our review of the literature or our research sites to the United States, as most of the studies reviewed in earlier chapters have done, such arguments are not susceptible to empirical test, because we essentially hold constant the broad social context that influences all families and all individuals. Because this is a constant, its effects cannot be analyzed.

Here, however, strategic selection of subgroups or strategic comparison of nations may offer a partial test of the argument. Adequate investigation of this question demands that we observe variations in the extent of male privilege and female powerlessness across societies, and attempt to link them to variations in rates of assault and violence. Of course, such cross-national and cross-cultural comparisons are very difficult, and making causal linkages is problematic. Still, it is worth seeing whether the pattern of co-variation is actually what such arguments would predict. In a related study, Yllo (1983) uses variations across states within the U.S. to investigate whether indicators of a more oppressive climate for women are linked as expected to greater physical assaults on women. Somewhat surprisingly, Yllo reports that states in which women have made political and economic gains have higher rates of male assault on women than do other states. Yllo argues that very strong and homogenous norms of male authority and female deference make dyadic violence less *necessary* to control women; it is when these traditional, societal level controls begin to erode that individual men may fall back on coercion and intimidation in their intimate relationships. Such hypotheses would not have emerged if we did not build some variation in our explanatory variables into our actual investigations. An additional example of intriguing cross-national and cross-cultural work is Coltrane's (1988) study of links between male involvement in child rearing and child socialization and the extent of hostility and antagonism between adult men and women discussed above.

In addition to providing crucial variations in putative explanatory variables, comparative and cross-national research may help to free us from the blinders of our own culture. A recurring issue for many of the authors of these chapters is dependency between people; we have, we claim, clear norms for age-appropriate variations in dependence on others, independence from others, and interdependence with others. But what is culturally normative in a single culture may not be optimal. For example, our societal model of rugged independence seems particularly ill-matched for young parents, whose need for economic and emotional resources may be more than they are able to supply for themselves.

In summary, the emerging field of developmental family psychology claims as its domain a diverse set of research topics scattered across disciplines and specialties. In order for the field to progress, I have argued that it will be critical to bring gender inequalities more fully into the picture, to link economic and occupational activities more closely to family experiences, to incorporate the influence of relatively enduring individual resources and liabilities into our arguments, and to include family structures and activity sequences that vary from the normative "cooperative parenting within life-long marital bonds," which remains the unexamined background to many of our arguments. In addition, our theoretical arguments need to identify the linking mechanism between our concepts, and our research must be designed to test those links. This is likely to demand greater use of longitudinal data sets, natural and planned experiments, and cross-national and comparative data. It will be interesting to follow the development of this fledgling field.

REFERENCES

Astone, N., & McLanahan, S. (1991). Family structure, parental practices, and high school completion. *American Sociological Review, 56,* 309–320.

Belsky, J, & Eggebean, D. (1991). Early and extensive maternal employment and young children's socioemotional development: Children of the National Longitudinal Survey of Youth. *Journal of Marriage and the Family, 53,* 1083–1110.

Bielby, W. T., & Baron, J. N. (1984). A woman's place is with other women: Sex segregation within organizations. In B. F. Reskin (Ed.), *Sex segregation in the workplace: Trends, explanations, and remedies* (pp. 27–55). Washington, DC: National Academy Press.

Bielby, W. T., & Bielby, D. D. (1992). I will follow him: Family ties, gender role beliefs, and reluctance to relocate for a better job. *American Journal of Sociology, 97,* 1241–1294.

Caspi, A., & Bem, D. J. (1990). Personality continuity and change across the life course. In Lawrence A. Pervin (Ed.), *Handbook of personality: Theory and research.* New York: Guilford.

Cherlin, A. J. (1992). *Marriage, divorce, remarriage: Revised and enlarged edition.* Cambridge, MA: Harvard University Press.

Clausen, J. (1991). Adolescent competence and the shaping of the life course. *American Journal of Sociology, 96,* 805–842.

Coltrane, S. (1988). Father–child relationships and the status of women: A cross-cultural study. *American Journal of Sociology, 93,* 1060–1095.

Conger, R. D., Conger, K. J., Elder, G. H. Jr., Lorenz, F. O., Simons, R. L., & Whitbeck, L. B. (1992). A family process model of economic hardship and adjustment of early adolescent boys. *Child Development, 63,* 526–541.

Crouter, A., Belsky, J., & Spanier, G. (1984). The family context of child development: Divorce and maternal employment. *Annals of Child Development, 1,* 201–238.

Elder, G. H., Jr. (1974). *Children of the great depression.* Chicago: University of Chicago Press.

Elder, G. H., Jr., & Caspi, A. (1988). Human development and social change: An emerging perspective on the life course. In N. Bolger, A. Caspi, G. Downey, & M. Moorehouse (Eds.), *Persons in context: Developmental processes* (pp. 77–113). New York: Cambridge University Press.

Estrada, P., Arsenio, W. F., Hess, R. D., & Holloway, S. D. (1987). Affective quality of the mother–child relationship: Longitudinal consequences for children's school-relevant cognitive functioning. *Developmental Psychology, 23,* 210–215.

Ferree, M. M. (1990). Feminism and family research. *Journal of Marriage and the Family, 52,* 866–884.

Flanagan, C. A. (1990). Families and schools in hard times. *New Directions for Child Development, 46,* 7–26.

Furstenberg, F. F., Jr., (1988). Good dads, bad dads: Two faces of fatherhood. In A. J. Cherlin (Ed.), *The changing American family and public policy.* Washington DC: Urban Institute.

Furstenberg, F. F., Jr., & Cherlin, A. (1991). *Divided families: What happens to children when parents part.* Cambridge, MA: Harvard University Press.

Furstenburg, F. F., Jr., & Nord, C. W. (1985). Parenting apart: Patterns of childrearing after marital disruption. *Journal of Marriage and the Family, 50,* 893–904.

Haynes, S. G., & Feinleib, M. (1980). Women, work, and coronary heart disease: Prospective findings from the Framingham study. *American Journal of Public Health, 70,* 133–141.

House, J. S., Strecher, V., Metzner, H. L., & Robbins, C. A. (1986). Occupational stress and health among men and women in the Tecumseh community health study. *Journal of Health and Social Behavior, 27,* 62–77.

Howes, C. (1988). Relations between early child care and schooling. *Developmental Psychology, 24,* 53–57.

Jacobs, J. (1989). *Revolving doors: Sex segregation and women's careers.* Stanford, CA: Stanford University Press.

Kalmijn, M. (1991). Shifting boundaries: Trends in religious and educational homogamy. *American Sociological Review, 56,* 786–800.

Karasek, R. A. (1979). Job demands, job decision latitude, and mental strain: Implications for job redesign. *Administrative Science Quarterly, 24,* 285–308.

Karasek, R. A., Baker, D., Marxer, F., Ahlbom, A., & Theorell, T. (1981). Job decision latitude, job demands, and cardiovascular disease: A prospective study of Swedish men. *American Journal of Public Health, 71,* 694–705.

Kohn, M. L., & Schooler, C. (1982). Job conditions and personality: A longitudinal assessment of their reciprocal effects. *American Journal of Sociology, 87,* 1257–1286.

Kohn, M. L., & Schooler, C. (Eds.) with the collaboration of J. Miller, K. A. Miller, C. Schoenbach, and R. Schoenberg. (1983). *Work and personality.* Norwood, NJ: Ablex.

Kohn, M. L., Slomczynski, K. M., & Schoenbach, C. (1986). Social stratification in and the transmission of values in the family: A cross-national assessment. *Sociological Forum, 1,* 73–102.

Luster, T., Rhoades, K., & Haas, B. (1989). The relation between parental values and parenting behavior: A test of the Kohn hypothesis. *Journal of Marriage and the Family, 51,* 139–147.

Menaghan, E. G. (1991). Work experiences and family interaction processes: The long reach of the job? *Annual Review of Sociology, 17,* 419–444.

Menaghan, E. G. (in press). The daily grind: Work stressors, family patterns, and intergenerational outcomes. In W. Avison & I. Gotlib, *Stress and mental health: Contemporary Issues and Future Prospects.* New York: Plenum.

Menaghan, E. G., & Godwin, D. (1993). Longitudinal research methods and family theories. In P. Boss, W. Doherty, R. La Rossa, W. Schumm, & S. Steinmetz (Eds.), *Sourcebook of family theories and methods: A contextual approach* (pp. 259–273). New York: Plenum.

Menaghan, E. G., & Parcel, T. L. (1991). Determining children's home environments: The impact of maternal characteristics and current occupational and family conditions. *Journal of Marriage and the Family, 53,* 417–431.

Miller, J., Schooler, C., Kohn, M. L., & Miller, K. A. (1979). Women and work: The psychological effects of occupational conditions. *American Journal of Sociology, 85,* 66–94.

Mirowsky, J., & Ross, C. E. (1986). Social patterns of distress. *Annual Review of Sociology, 12,* 23–45.

Patterson, G. (1988). Family process: Loops, levels, and linkages. In N. Bolger, A. Caspi, G. Downey, & M. Moorehouse (Eds.), *Persons in context: Developmental processes* (pp. 114–151). New York: Cambridge University Press.

Reskin, B. F., & Roos, P. (1990). *Job queues, gender queues: Explaining women's inroads into male occupations.* Philadelphia: Temple University Press.

Schooler, C. (1987). Psychological effects of complex environments during the life span: A review and theory. In C. Schooler & K. W. Schaie (Eds.), *Cognitive functioning and social structure over the life course* (pp. 24–49). Norwood, NJ: Ablex.

Siegal, M. (1984). Economic deprivation and the quality of parent–child relations: A trickle-down framework. *Journal of Applied Developmental Psychology, 5,* 127–144.

Spade, J. Z. (1991). Occupational structure and men's and women's parental values. *Journal of Family Issues, 12,* 343–360.

Teachman, J. (1987). Family background, educational resources, and educational attainment. *American Sociological Review, 52,* 548–557.

Thompson, L., & Walker, A. J. (1989). Gender in families: Women and men in marriage, work, and parenthood. *Journal of Marriage and the Family, 51,* 845–871.

Voyandoff, P. (1987). *Work and family life.* Newbury Park, CA: Sage.

Wharton, A. S., & Baron, J. N. (1987). So happy together? The impact of gender segregation on men at work. *American Sociological Review, 52,* 574–587.

Yllo, K. (1983). Sexual equality and violence against wives in American states. *Journal of Comparative Family Studies, 14,* 67–86.

Zaslow, M., Rabinovich, B., & Suwalsky, J. T. (1991) From maternal employment to child outcomes: Preexisting group differences and moderating variables. In J. V. Lerner & N. Galambos (Eds.), *Employed mothers and their children* (pp. 237–282). New York: Garland.

CHAPTER 19

Implications of a Developmental Family Systems Model for Clinical Practice

PENNY B. JAMESON and JAMES F. ALEXANDER

The primary therapeutic implications of the material in the preceding chapters involve two basic dimensions: (1) the means by which the therapist understands a family system; and (2) the selection of techniques appropriate for producing change in pathological systems. The perspective of the therapist is used to identify pathogenic elements in the family system, and to determine the end goal, or the presumed healthy state for that family. Techniques are then selected that are most likely to facilitate the transition from pathogenic to healthy states.

The material in the preceding chapters does not suggest novel therapeutic techniques; instead it suggests ways of understanding the clinical phenomena we encounter. In this chapter, we highlight the common themes, and integrate some of the seemingly divergent perspectives of the previous chapters. This integrated perspective raises a number of questions about both pathogenic and healthy states, and provides a basis for selection of intervention techniques.

In this era of managed care, it is a challenge to convince therapists that gathering and considering more information will result in more efficient and more effective treatment, particularly when research does not yet conclusively demonstrate the efficacy of including the myriad variables proposed in this volume. However, the outcome research on marital and family therapy suggests we have reached the limits of our extant models and measures (Alexander, Holtzworth-Monroe, & Jameson, in press). In that context, this volume constitutes a potential guide to the next step; namely, that we include a multilevel systemic and developmental perspective in our understanding of family therapy.

The case for including multilevel family systems perspectives in clinical work is clearly spelled out in the preceding chapters; evidence continues to mount that indicates a strong relationship between mental health and the successful embeddedness of individuals in supportive contexts or systems (Kegan, 1982). For example, the availability of a supportive relational structure is a significant factor in mental and physical health, just as its absence is a significant factor in mental and physical illness. Furthermore, beyond the usual parent-child relational focus, this support structure has significant horizontal (e.g. sibling relationships) and vertical (e.g., intergenerational relationships) dimensions to it, as well as contextual (e.g., cultural, occupational) influences.

Adding a developmental perspective further focuses attention on the meaning of behavior (Sroufe, 1989), and on the process of adaptation, as seen across time, as well as the continuities and discontinuities in that adaptation process. Two major themes emerge from this perspective. First, the family is an evolving meaning system whose sometimes paradoxical function is preserving meaning while supporting adaptation. Second, the different developmental status of family members produces nonshared environmental variance; the same events will not have the same meaning for or influence on different family members. These foci are present in several of the preceding chapters. Several chapters implicitly suggest that systemic pathology occurs when a single theme dominates the system; when that single theme heavily influences the family meaning system and its related interactional/communication processes, it does so at the expense of adaptive and relational needs of system members. This, in turn, creates deviant developmental trajectories along with symptoms that reflect the adaptive limitations of such trajectories.

At the extreme, a system-dominating theme can be established by pathologies such as alcoholism, abuse, mental or physical illness (see Arias & Pape, chapter 14; Haugaard, chapter 15; O'Leary & Jouriles, chapter 16). Less extreme forms can be seen when parents are incapable of allowing the children any semblance of autonomy. Another common dominating theme is that of spousal conflict. Some conflicting parents cannot, or will not, merge the systems they inherited from their family of origin. As a result, choices made by the children in that context become, implicitly or explicitly, conflicted and potentially dangerous loyalty tests; children must second guess parental responses, rather than express their own needs and negotiate compromises. A similar theme can arise from cultural conflict or from differing cultural identifications among family members.

Domination by a single theme is likely to produce increasingly rigid, defensive interactional processes that block both adaptation and development of the system and of its members. For example, parental alcoholism is most likely to be associated with child pathology when the other spouse is depressed (Fitzgerald et al., chapter 17). This may be because the depressed spouse is less likely than a nondepressed spouse to be able to maintain or provide organizing relational processes that are alternatives to those provoked by the behavior of the alcoholic. When a single theme with no positive meaning for members of the system consistently overrides other needs in the system, conflicts and relationships may evoke escalating defensiveness, negativity, blaming, or withdrawal. The likely immediate end is, at best, a mistrusting standoff; in the long run, increasingly automatic, negative schemas may become easily activated by any behavior construed as suspicious. The result of the defensive, negative interpersonal processes is an increasingly psychopathological developmental trajectory in an individual or individuals who are vulnerable by virtue of their constitution or developmental status.

Thus, the developmental family systems perspective leads to an approach to diagnosis and treatment that is quite different from that of the DSM-III-R. Beyond the obvious assertion that pathology has systemic, not simply individual, causes, the developmental family systems perspective insists that pathology has understandable roots in the past, and predictable consequences in the future. Problems, even those that may have a clear biological diathesis, are not conceptualized in terms of an individual's discrete behavioral excesses or deficiencies that should simply be modified or treated with drug therapy; rather the adaptive history of the "symptomatic" individual and of the system(s) in which the individual is embedded becomes central. Pathology is seen as an understandable adaptation to situations in which stress, external or internal to the system, has exceeded the adaptive capacities of the family system and its individual members. This emphasis on the adaptative quality of developmental trajectories, on the processes that facilitate or hinder it, and on the meaning and function of behavior represents a shift from a more traditional approach that emphasizes relational forms and role structures in its effort to understand family systems and pathology (Fuller & Fincham, chapter 4).

There is presently no single well-developed "developmental family systems theory," although considerable work is underway (e.g., Ford & Lerner, 1992). In fact, because of the variety of family forms, cultures, and developmental trajectories it may be inappropriate for us to expect a single expression of a "developmental family systems theory." As a generic perspective, however, the different approaches to a developmental perspective in the previous chapters represent an important new way to understand, and approach clinically, various expressions of dysfunction. In the following sections, we attempt to weave together the strands found in previous chapters to create a context for the clinical implications we propose. Our central focus is on the family as a meaning system whose resulting processes, when they are working adaptively, are characterized by culturally defined (and constrained) variations in warmth, expressiveness, and closeness, along with respect for individual identity—again, culturally defined. These processes are coupled with predictability or organization to promote the positive adaptation of all the members of the family.

WHAT DOES IT MEAN TO HAVE A SYSTEMIC, DEVELOPMENTAL PERSPECTIVE ON FAMILIES AND ON FAMILY DEVELOPMENT?

Tolstoy (1876) asserted in *Anna Karenina* that "Happy families resemble one another; each unhappy family is unhappy in its own way" (pt. I, ch. 1). Rather than presuming to understand pathologies as categories of similarity, we might use a thorough understanding of the permutations of normal family functioning as the most appropriate background for understanding the particularity of pathology. Such an approach presumes pathology to exist on a continuum with "normality," as opposed to being a discrete entity. In this section, we take this continuum notion as our basis, and use material from the preceding chapters, from developmental psychology, and from developmental psychopathology to elaborate on each aspect of the systemic, developmental perspective, and to raise some issues relevant for therapy.

Family Systems

A systemic approach conceptualizes the individual as being part of, as well as consisting of, a series of hierarchically arranged systems; the individual is nested hierarchically in a family system, which in turn is nested hierarchically within larger sociocultural units (Bronfenbrenner, 1977). Many theorists seem to be moving beyond the old individual focus versus systemic perspective dichotomy, and accept that we must study all levels and their interactions. However, most frameworks artificially examine the influence of one subsystem (e.g., an individual) on another subsystem (e.g., another individual). We still tend to separate conceptually the individual and the family system as if each were a discrete entity influencing the other. Instead, these are more like interdependent systems existing in a state of continuous mutual influence (Fogel, 1993). Considering them as separate systems is problematic, analogous to identifying the circulatory and respiratory systems of the human body as independent but interactive. In these two subsystems of the human body, there is a point, a semipermeable membrane, where there is no true boundary between the two. Instead, there is a process of transport (e.g., plasma, waste products, gases) across the membrane that seems to define the boundary of each system, but that, in actuality, is where parts of one subsystem truly become parts of the other.

The view of the family system as a meaning/value system mediating the behavior and relationships of individuals in that system has that same quality. It exists at the interface of two structures, is semipermeable to select information, and contains active transport systems for particularly significant content. Such a transactional emphasis differs from the more common interactional approach (Altman & Rogoff, 1987; Bronfenbrenner, 1977). The *mutuality* of influence such a perspective incorporates is new, and is, as yet, difficult to conceptualize methodologically. A one-way version is more familiar: Psychodynamic concepts such as introject and identification refer to a "taking in," or absorption of parental values and characteristics. Laing (1972) posed a more global distinction when he differentiated between the family and "the family," in which "the family" is the individual's internalization, often unconscious, of the spoken and unspoken rules governing interactions in one's family of origin. In contrast, contemporary dynamic systems theorists (Fogel, 1993) emphasize contemporary co-creation, coordination, and exchange; the individual and the immediate social context coexist in a process of continuous mutual influence. Development *emerges* from this context of coordinated exchange. Internal representations can exist, but they do not replace the exchange process. Instead, they modulate attentional processes and emotional responses, much in the way the permeability of the membrane influences the nature of what exchanges occur between the respiratory and circulatory subsystems. At the same time, ongoing interpersonal processes influence the internal representation of the family system; this somewhat fluid transaction between structure and processes makes this system more complicated than the biological one we used as an illustrative parallel.

Thus, family systems can be thought of as an organizing dynamic existing *in* and *between* individuals. The system exists "in individuals" as a shared way of organizing and evaluating experience. It exists "between individuals" in that ongoing shared experience alters what is "in" the individuals comprising the system. The family system grows out of shared history, and mediates between the family members, however family is defined, and the context in which the family is embedded. It is a paradoxical dynamic because it preserves tradition—sometimes several traditions—yet is constantly changing or developing. If it is a healthy system, the development is in the direction of increasingly inclusive, increasingly organized, and increasingly similar (in terms of developmental level of cognitive complexity) ways of processing experience. Generally, many basic values stay the same across time, but the rules about the expression of those values, along with more peripheral values, do and should change in order to reflect developmental mandates.

When a family presents for therapy, there is generally one individual who is identified as "the problem." The initial task of the therapist is to reconceptualize the problem within the system. Identifying points of stress and patterns of coping is important, and the function of the presenting symptoms is often a beginning point. However, it is often difficult to determine what is symptom and what is point of stress, let alone the difference between function and coping; linear cause-effect models are often not useful. For example, hyperactivity in children and distress in their families often go together, just as alcoholism in a parent and familial distress often go together. When a hyperactive child is appropriately treated, the family functioning often improves (Sroufe, 1989). However, when an alcoholic stops drinking, family processes often deteriorate (Fitzgerald et al., chapter 17). Symptoms must be understood in relation to the processes of the particular system in which they exist. Parental depression often (temporarily) decreases the aggressive expressions targeted at the depressed person; thus, a function of depression can be coping with aggression in the family (Coyne et al., 1987). It may be more efficient initially to look for the global organizing theme than to try to untangle the complex relationships among the component parts. The therapist can then use the novelty of his or her presence in the family to work toward construction of an alternative theme while trying to understand the particularity of the individual relationships to the pathological theme.

An alternative way of proceeding is to look at the family in terms of its response to the various forces acting in and on it. "Centrifugal" forces (Combrinck-Graham, 1985) are exerted on the family system, particularly relational processes, as individual members become involved in and committed to such extrafamilial systems as occupations, religious organizations, schools, and friendships. These contextual systems introduce selective opportunities for change, growth, and conflict through the family members involved. "Centripetal" forces are exerted by biological and emotional dependencies, as well as by the shared meaning system. The capacity of the system's relational processes to establish meaningful recalibrations in response to these forces determines whether the processes are functional or dysfunctional. Understanding the underlying meaning system, particularly the processes that defends it, can sometimes point the way toward the most significant source of blockage—both in the family's response to the stress and in the resistance they present in treatment. Affect provides a significant clue that can be used to bring to the surface those aspects of the family belief system producing blockage.

We suggest that the well-functioning family system protects and supports the adaptive development—differentiation and re-integration—of all its members, respecting the organic or genetic strengths and limitations of each, while preserving a family identity that is often rooted in historical traditions. This system selects aspects of the context and of the range of individuals' possible behaviors and endows them with meaning and value; from the myriad possibilities, the system defines what ought to be. This system alters the probability that a particular aspect of experience will be attended to and a particular behavior will occur. How the individuals are cared for, what is expected of them, and what, in the larger environment, is worth attention and energy is defined at this interactive interface between internal/historical forces and present and future needs. This view of the family system, particularly the definition of relational processes, emphasizes the scaffolding defining the adaptive behavioral repertoire. The nature of the scaffolding, however, can change in varying contexts. When the social context is relatively stable and homogeneous, the scaffolding is provided by clear role definitions, certain aspects of which have continuity both across time (e.g., "children respect parents") and in the larger social context (e.g., "authority is to be respected"). These roles define right relations between people, as well as valued behaviors; expectations are known implicitly.

However, when the social context is changing rapidly and the value context is diverse, relationships (rather than relatively inflexible role definitions) may provide the scaffolding; roles become too rigid for situations demanding more flexible adaptation, and the context cannot provide the reinforcement that would maintain the roles as functional. In such circumstances it falls upon communication processes within trusted relationships to lead to the discernment of right relationships and to support principled efforts of individuals. In contexts where change and diversity are significant, neither systems nor individuals can be structurally defined; rather than deriving primary identity from roles, people see themselves as having roles, often a variety of roles (Kegan, 1982), which may or may not be appropriate in particular contexts. The self is then construed, explicitly or implicitly, in terms of beliefs and values that shape one's relationship to others; roles are seen as contextually organized forms that can be utilized as convenient—a relationship that can be chosen.

Several of the chapters noted a fairly recent change in the values underpinning evaluation of satisfaction with one's family. This change is consistent with the proposed switch from role to relational definition, and it suggests that, although family functioning is still a major variable affecting physical and mental health, the way in which it functions has changed. This change has been described as a shift from the "institutional family" to the "companionate family" (see, for example, Orthner et al., chapter 9). Communication and relational processes and the activities supporting those (e.g., leisure activities as suggested by Orthner et al.) are now seen as central to the family's sense of well-being, whereas the earlier basis of satisfaction was adherence to shared role definitions.

Furthermore, these processes must be considered in relationship to the family's historical, as well as immediate, context. In the case of some ethnic minorities, maintaining any connection with cultural or familial traditions in a context that is hostile toward those traditions or toward that ethnic group puts both the family system and its members in a precarious and vulnerable position, one often intensified by poverty (see Entwistle, chapter 7).

Evidence of the adaptive function of family systems was presented in earlier chapters; for example, Lee and Gotlib (chapter 12) cited research suggesting that marital status may be the most powerful demographic predictor of mental health. Although the converse may be true, that mental health is the most powerful predictor of marital status, the relationship suggests the importance of working with family systems, or with whatever meaningful social units are available to clients. There is abundant evidence that contextual/systemic variables contribute to the etiology and maintenance (or exacerbation) of "individual" pathologies, such as depression, alcoholism, and agoraphobia, as well as to relapses and caregiver burden (see Hurtig, chapter 13; Lee & Gotlib, chapter 12; Swenson, chapter 10). Conversely, there are numerous suggestions that it is not the mere presence of pathology in the family that creates a pathological system or perpetuates pathology; rather, the long-term course of the pathology and its effect on family processes, such as closeness, expressiveness, and warmth, disrupts the developmental trajectories of the system and of the individuals in the system (see Fitzgerald et al., chapter 17; Lee & Gotlib, chapter 12). This disruption, in turn, affects the relationship of the family system to the larger context, the relationship of the individual to the family system, and the development of the individuals and the system. Pathology is likely to produce social isolation, thus decreasing the number of social outlets for all members of the family, and creating a closed system. The family may become organized—and blocked developmentally—by the pathology, by the resulting defensive relational processes, and by the corresponding meaning systems; the historically evolving shared meaning system is profoundly altered. In the functional family, the adaptive evolution of the system is guided by the real needs and characteristics of the individuals in the system. In the dysfunctional family, the adaptation is a defensive reaction to the pathology. One route to pathology occurs when the history and traditions of that system no longer maintain creative connections with family members in their current context.

Family System Development

Family systems approaches attempt to describe developmental changes in the form and processes of the family across time and transitional events such as the birth of a child. Olson and Lavee (1989) integrate a number of models from the interpersonal, family, and marital literature (e.g., Benjamin, 1977; Gottman, 1979; L'Abate, 1987; Leary, 1957; Parsons & Bales, 1955; Reiss, 1981) to propose a circumplex model in which families can be identified along axes of distance/closeness and organization/chaos. Three central process characteristics relate to the resulting family mapping: cohesion, adaptability, and communication. Families show considerable variability on the circumplex dimensions, both across families at similar points of development and within any given family across time. Olson and Lavee suggest that this variation may be "normal," and that problems occur only when familial processes are located at the extremes on either dimension; in these regions the cohesion and communication processes result in low adaptability.

Combrinck-Graham (1985) provides another view of family development, which focuses on the balance between extrafamilial and intrafamilial pressures. From this perspective, family development proceeds through periods in which family energies are spent primarily on internal events, generally meeting the needs of highly dependent members; for example, when there are newborns, toddlers, and elderly parents. These periods are balanced by others in which most members invest more energy on relatively autonomous pursuits; for example, when the children are school age, adolescents, or grown and gone from the home. Normative balances can be described across the family life span. One of the advantages of such multidimensional conceptualizations is their capacity to differentiate changes in organizational characteristics and processes from changes in relational characteristics and processes of a system. For example, a parent may grant more autonomy to an adolescent (thus less familial organization), but the adolescent and parent may still perceive their relationship as very close.

These fluctuations may correspond to common patterns of distress and unhappiness, which seem to be greatest at those periods when meeting familial dependency needs requires more energy. Conversely, happiness and satisfaction are greatest during those periods of minimal maintenance requirements, generally when the children are between 6 and 12 years or when they are adults no longer living in the home. (Fuller & Fincham [chapter 4] suggest the studies on which this widely cited pattern are based may have some serious problems, so this pattern should be regarded with caution.) Thus, we might expect the circumplex description of the family and its processes to move primarily along the organization/chaos axis, with more organizational requirements, thus more opportunities for conflict, in those periods of more intense caregiving, or "centripetal" emphasis. However, this generality must be looked at in the context of the specific family system. During times of increased organizational requirements, the accompanying reduction in freedom of choice and movement may require behaviors that violate certain individuals' needs for autonomous functioning. Increased maintenance and organizational demands also make explicit the power relationships in the family. In those periods we might expect to see less coping capacity, more distress, and possible exacerbation of pathology. Similarly, when the person's developmental history leaves them uncomfortable with or anxious about their dependency and relational needs, the period of intense caregiving to biologically constrained dependents will be problematic. On the other hand, in the person whose history has left him or her uncomfortable with his or her own autonomy or separateness, that same period of organizational connectedness may be the most satisfying; encouraging independence might be difficult and anxiety laden.

Pulls from the outside, "centrifugal" forces, affect both dimensions and introduce periods high in disruptive potential at points of transition. Starting school, dating, and new jobs all disrupt the equilibrium of the family system. At each point, parent–child relationships must be renegotiated in ways that accept the new commitments while maintaining open, expressive relationships (Kegan, 1982). Although those relationships may not change in terms of closeness, they will change in form, and that form carries different meanings for different individuals in the system. It is important for the clinician to understand both form and meaning of relational processes before and after such points of transition.

With respect to an individual's developmentally rooted interpersonal balance of autonomy and relatedness needs, there are also transitions or developmental epochs wherein specific individuals within a system seem to be particularly vulnerable to specific events. For example, an infant is particularly vulnerable to attachment disruptions, while preschoolers are vulnerable to loss of a parent.

The circumplex and centrifugal/centripetal perspectives on family development, similar to the "life tasks" approach seen in many of the chapters (e.g., McGreal, chapter 6; Swensen, chapter 10) describe families from the outside in terms of statistical norms. This approach might best be termed a "sociological" description. In contrast, other chapters (e.g., Fuller & Fincham, chapter 4) include a "phenomenological" approach, which attempts to describe family functioning as it appears to those inside the family. Ultimately, both perspectives are necessary for understanding adaptation and identifying points of blockage, especially when the family is culturally or organizationally "different" (Montalvo & Gutierrez, 1983).

For example, a recent study (Kreppner, 1989) documented the initial decrease in relational time available to the spouse and the first child following the birth of a second child; the first child and father are often in independent orbits around the new dyad. In most families, time with the mother, time in triadic and tetradic constellations increases markedly within the first 10 months. In some families, possibly those that are more flexible, the father and the first child increase their relational time during the period of the mother's unavailability. The general pattern of social initiatives adds another dimension; the mother's initiatives to the father are more frequent than vice versa (Kreppner, 1990). This perspective from the outside observer provides some clarity about the sources of stress introduced by the new baby, and about coping styles. However, such perspectives must be complemented in practice and in research by an understanding of the subjective reality of family members. In one family, the new infant may provide its mother a meaningful escape from pressures of a distressed marriage and a negativistic, demanding toddler. The relational patterns across time in this family are likely to be deviant and increasingly negative, increasing the father's and toddler's resentment. Thus, it is ultimately the interaction of the event and the meaning of the event in the system that establishes new processes and trajectories.

This emphasis on subjective reality, or a "phenomenological approach" attempts to describe the experience of change in family processes. How do family members understand changes in ways in which other family members experience, understand, and communicate about what is going on? How is their behavior functional in that context? The emphasis is on the familial meaning system as understood by the various individuals in the system. Such an approach assumes that these processes will change over the life span in rather predictable ways, so it often includes a "sociological" frame as a starting point (e.g., substance abuse, chapter 16). It also presumes that the same events will be understood differently by different members of the family, depending on the individual's capacity for including reasonably accurate understandings of the perspectives and motives of others in the system. This, in turn, is affected by characteristics of particular relational constellations.

For the clinician, understanding the family phenomenologically is essential when deciding on techniques and focus. When does a therapist initiate parent training instead of a more bidirectional parent–child communication process? When does she or he reframe family members' behaviors using emotion-based terms consistent with high relatedness needs, instead of using conceptual meta-phors that are more likely to be accepted by a family member whose autonomy needs are more phenomenologically available? How does a therapist know *not* to initiate traditional parent training with a mother when that process will structurally "trap" her in a highly interconnected parent role that ignores her autonomy needs, as opposed to initiating parent training with a mother or father (or both) when that parent's relational needs are consistent with such a role demand? Without attention to such questions that require both a sociological and phenomenological perspective, clinicians will find themselves applying various "one size fits all" technologies to families and experiencing the "ceiling effect" of therapeutic effectiveness.

The sociological perspective may have seemed sufficient when there was more (or we believed there was more) stability in family life and the surrounding culture. Much of the evidence now suggests the family's phenomenology must be understood and consciously examined for its fit with the external demands (Montalvo & Gutierrez, 1983). Both must be understood in terms of the develop-mental and social history of the family, so that decisions can be made about what can be changed and what is important to maintain. In spite of adversity or difficulty in adapting to the givens of their context, the family may decide to hang on to significant values, "keeping the faith" (Walsh, 1983). Other dearly held values must be scrutinized for the possibility that they are being used as a maladaptive defense. Thus, the therapist can help the family to know itself consciously from the inside, see itself from the outside, and use these perspectives to decide on meaningful adjustments.

Developmental Family Systems and Pathology

Within this hierarchically organized set of systems (person–(process)–family–(process)–context), the developmental psychopathology perspective asserts that pathology, or a developmental trajectory deviating from the norm, results when the stressors exceed a system's capacity to cope. Of particular interest is identification of the way in which an event or process alters "normal" developmental trajectories. The mediating/intervening systems may function as a sort of wall of defense, or immune system, when operating well, diffusing, deflecting, or encapsulating stressors and focusing adaptation. When a system or subsystem (family or individual) does not work, it can add stress to the individuals or to the system itself. The stressor may ultimately overcome normal family processes, comes to dominate systemic processes and meaning as described earlier. Stressors can be external, for example, discrimination or job loss. Or they may be internal, as in the case of an individual who is organically compromised, for example, by chronic illness, autism, or dementia (see chapters 12 and 13). Either may deplete the energy of the family and compromise the family system's ability to deal with more routine stress. The therapeutic difficulty is finding out what the relationship is between individual and systemic pathology, what and where the stressors are, and what the processes are that augment or diminish either stressors or the capacity of a system, including the individuals, to adapt.

Developmental psychology also adds a specialized focus on change that complements a systemic perspective; it adds a recognition that the earlier emphasis on systemic homeostasis may need to be balanced by a thorough understanding of change and adaptive processes (Speer, 1970). Developmental psychopathology, a relatively new hybrid combining developmental psychology with child and adult psychopathology, describes individuals as moving between periods of pathology and nonpathology (Zigler, 1989), affected by intrinsic and extrinsic factors. Furthermore, at any given time, some behaviors within a distressed individual's repertoire will be adaptive, while others will be maladaptive. Thus, when attempting to understand a family system, we must locate those periods in which things went well. We should also identify those aspects within a present episode that are functional both on an individual and a systemic level. As stated earlier, there are many ways to define and understand change; for therapeutic purposes, approaches emphasizing organizational and process change seem most appropriate (Cicirelli, chapter 2). Since therapy purports to be a change process, the developmental perspective may provide an important level of refinement, as well as insight into why only some interventions produce change.

An interesting example of the developmental psychopathology perspective comes from research on the effects of maternal depression on infant development. Researchers in this area (e.g., Cohn, Cambell, Matias, & Hopkins, 1991; Field et al., 1985; Gelfand & Teti, 1990; Hammen, Burge, & Stansbury, 1990; Lyons-Ruth, Connell, Grunebaum, & Botein, 1990; Radke-Yarrow, Belmont, Nottelmann, & Bottomly, 1992; Tronik & Gianino, 1986) are tracking depressed mothers and their infants, describing the interactional processes that seem to fail to organize the infant's developing adaptive capacity emotionally, socially, and cognitively. Ultimately, these researchers hope to describe the formation of developmental trajectories that, by middle childhood and adolescence, frequently are characterized by defensive and negative interpersonal processes, anger, sadness, and/or withdrawal. These patterns are categorized as oppositional/defiant disorder, conduct disorder, and depression. This work ultimately must be put into a larger context because it is clear that variables other than depression play an important role. Marital discord is likely related both to maternal depression and development of child pathology; without intervention, all three may interact in a progressively disruptive and destructive cycle. The results of this work should help us to refine interventions, as well as to move toward earlier intervention and, perhaps, prevention.

Developmental approaches add at least two other important perspectives that have not been integrated into family systems perspectives. The first is the focus on the nonshared aspects of the family system. Nonshared environmental variance is an empirically based claim that family members are likely to have different subjective experiences of the same phenomenon, depending on age, sex, perceived similarities to other family members, triangulated relationships, and sibling relationships (Reiss, Plomin, & Hetherington, 1991). For example, a 5-year-old generally has a much more difficult time coping with parental divorce than does a teenager. Part of the difference results from the attributional differences at those two ages. The 5-year-old may think his father left in disgust over some aspect of the child's behavior, such as nose picking; the child will assume unwarranted responsibility. The teenager is generally more likely to include his or her understanding of the parental perspective in forming an explanation of the event. Part of the difference probably results from the expanded relational resources and experiences of the teenager, but the specific understanding ultimately will depend on the developmental trajectory established prior to the divorce event.

The second addition from developmental psychology is a useful ordering of the predictable developmental differences in understanding self-other behavioral relationships. This is fully developed in the work of Kegan (1982), a discussion of which is beyond the scope of this chapter. For purposes of specifying clinical interventions, this ordering is covered only briefly and only in an individual focus, although Kegan consistently focuses on the interaction between the individual and his/her "culture of embeddedness."

In Kegan's (1982) developmental framework, each of the developmental "stages" involves the emergence of a qualitatively different way of understanding self in relationship to the system(s) in which one is embedded; each stage requires different environmental supports, as well as a different kind of challenge if the individual is to continue developing. Each stage involves a kind of egocentricity peculiar to it, a decentration from an earlier way of relating, and each new extrafamilial commitment produces a transition that carries a particular vulnerability.

For example, the transition from the "average" school-age child to the "average" teenager involves a shift from asymmetrical interpersonal processes structured largely by adults to symmetrical processes structured more by peers. The child must shift from relating in terms of roles and their implicit rules to relating in terms of an understanding of the needs of others. This change to a more intimate psychological relationship is particularly problematic for those whose history predisposes them to be uncomfortable with closeness, and/or whose self-esteem makes self-disclosure difficult. A common temptation is to use alcohol or drugs to dull the anxiety and to create the illusion of self-confident relationship with peers—a practice that can easily become generalized and habitual. Other problems result when the developing youngster has been discouraged from differentiating from the family, either because of parental needs or illness (e.g., diabetes, Hurtig, chapter 13). The particular egocentricity of the teenager is that he or she sees himself or herself as defined by relationships; moral value is understood in relational terms. A contextual challenge comes when different relationships (e.g., parents and peers) pose conflicting demands, forcing the young person to develop a conscious belief system that can provide a metaview of these conflicts. It is important to separate stage from age, however, because stage results from the interaction of the individual and the context. From Kegan's perspective, pathology has its origins in blocked development, so one would expect to find self- and other-concepts as well as relational processes characterized by immaturity.

Thus, one of the earliest organized social forms is created by role definitions, which in turn require some level of systemic organization. Identity is derived from roles, and self-esteem from one's ability to perform those roles in ways that are contextually approved. This role-based form of self-identification is developmentally appropriate for a school-age child, but it may be maladaptive in the child's parent. If the parent *is* rigidly *Mother* or *Father,* not a person who mothers or fathers, then the child is understood and reacted to emotionally in terms of the ways she or he complements the Mother or Father role definition. When the child is forced into a rigidly complementary role, his or her individual needs may not be recognized. The parent acts upon the child rather than interacting with him or her. If there are no familial or cultural rituals for relaxing this rigidity, adolescent peer emphasis on relationships built on some understanding of the needs of others may result in the adolescent's feeling blocked developmentally by the parentally defined role. Rebellion becomes a necessary transforming process. This rebellion, in turn, threatens the parent's self-definition, and may stimulate reciprocating negative interchanges that move the young person off an adaptive pathway.

APPLICATION OF A DEVELOPMENTAL FAMILY SYSTEMS PERSPECTIVE

An application of these principles can be seen in a common practice in family therapy—reframing (L'Abate, Ganahl, & Hansen, 1986). This technique generally involves the therapist's describing (referring to, explaining, interpreting) an individual's "negative" behavior, or a "negative" family process, in such a way that asserts or implies a different and more positive meaning than that initially held by the family (Alexander & Parsons, 1982; Morris, Alexander, & Waldron, 1988). Most reframes suggest that negative behaviors are relationally motivated; they also often normalize a behavior and/or imply a "misguided" positive motive rather than fundamental malevolence. Note that reframes do not simply "explain away" negative behaviors and disregard their sometimes painful nature. However, they do suggest that their meaning may not be what it appears to be. For example, with the family of a sexually reactive young male adolescent who previously was abused by a neighbor, the therapist might "wonder out loud" to the parents that the adolescent's current sexual acting out "couldn't maybe be a cry for help, a cry for control, and at the same time a way of letting you know how abandoned he felt. You [to the parents] didn't know at the time that he was being molested, but kids kind of want their parents to be magical . . . to protect them, even when it isn't realistic for the parents to be able to. So you [to the adolescent] might even be mad at them, and none of you know how to talk about all that pain."

Reframes such as this have the capacity to decrease negativity, defensiveness, and resistance in family members. They can represent an organizing systemic theme that has the power to counter the family's dominant pathological theme, and, as in the example just cited, they can integrate all the important perspectives and realities we've discussed—sociological, phenomenological, and developmental. When done well, they can become emotionally congruent reinterpretations of the inferred motivation behind problematic behaviors, reinterpretations that include developmental and interpersonal information in ways that help make sense of relational behavior and accompanying motivations. The resulting theme growing out of such reframes should be one that includes the perspectives and needs of all the family members. Well-chosen reframes and themes should have the potential to produce changes in ways of thinking that could free the obstacles to change, or alter the negative valence of communications that would be likely to produce a deviant developmental pathway in at least one child. This then sets the stage for family members to be more open to learning new, more appropriate ways of experiencing themselves and each other, and for learning new ways of behaving as therapy progresses.

As a specific example, take the hypothetical case of the Common family. This blended family consists of mother, father, a 13-year-old male and 10-year-old female from the father's first marriage and a 9-year-old male from the mother's first marriage, and a 3-year-old male from the Common's marriage. The father's first wife died a year before this marriage. The mother had been a primary care professional who became involved with the family through the illness and death of the first wife. She subsequently divorced her husband to marry the widower. They have now been married for 6 years, and describe their adjustment as good prior to an automobile accident in which the father, the identified "problem," suffered a "mild" closed head injury. He lost his civil engineering position 12 months earlier because of skill deficits resulting from his injury. He has been unable to find another job. The mother recently re-established her career as a physician's assistant, so the father stays home to care for the children. He has progressed from depression to alcohol abuse and has been very harsh on the children. Neighbors have called Protective Services, and although investigators found no clear evidence of child abuse, the internal climate of the family was such that they were referred for treatment.

The traditional approach would target the father and place him in a substance-abuse program; however, he says he does not have a problem. According to him, the noncompliant children, particularly the 13-year-old, are the problem. His wife identifies the father's disability as the problem; he requires more care than do the children combined. Moreover, she is responsible for all the housework plus all the relational work with the children, on top of a demanding and stressful, but very rewarding, job in a busy public health clinic.

Drawing on material from previous chapters, we can see that the therapist is dealing with a family whose developmental trajectory has been multiply interrupted by death, divorce, "blending," an accident leading to chronic disability, and job loss. The first task is to understand the individual and cumulative effects of those interruptions, to discover the organizing principle behind the family's relational processes. Sources of support in the various families of origin or other sources of social support are not, at this point, known. We have been alerted to the possible caregiver burden issues (chapters 12; 13). Our attention has been focused on the sibling subsystem as a potential source of strength (chapter 3). With this "sociological" framework we can more efficiently identify entry points and a beginning topography of the terrain. This system seems to be dominated by the unmet dependency needs of all family members. The father's disability is identified as the common hook on which family members hang their unhappiness.

This family should be just emerging from a period in which the care of young children and the reforming of a marital relationship have focused many of the energies inward, creating a period of high dependence/interdependence needs (Combrinck-Graham, 1985). At the point of the accident in "normative" developmental forces would be centrifugal, or movement toward increasing emphasis on processes supporting and encouraging autonomy of family members as each becomes increasingly involved with extrafamilial activities. However, this transition is being resisted by the two older children.

The therapist can begin by accepting the family structure and roles as they are and identifying the basic "homeostatic" function for each family member on the closeness/distance axis. This construct is related to the developmental notion of attachment. It could also be thought of in terms of an individual's learned balance between autonomy and dependency needs. Each individual is presumed to operate from one of three learned interpersonal positions: a need for contact closeness (an emphasis on dependence), a need for protective distance (an emphasis on autonomy), or a need for limited closeness balanced by distance (an emphasis on the balance between autonomy and dependence, or interdependence). Interpersonal communication/behavior, including pathology, serves to maintain or create the baseline interpersonal position. An initial assessment includes understanding how the behaviors of each family member can be understood as maintaining those positions.

As the Common family members described what the family was like before the accident, what were their daily routines, it became clear that the father was very uncomfortable with dependency needs, his or those of the other family members. The older children (his children) expressed many dependent behaviors and bids for attention that suggested they needed more relational closeness. The father said they learned this from his first wife. The current mother enjoyed some closeness with the children, but also found great relief from the closeness demands of the children in her career. Her child was very independent, while the mutual child, although quite young, seemed to have a capacity for independence that alternated with a great need for emotional and physical closeness. Thus, the "normative" developmental trajectory they were on met the needs of the parents, but not the children. In fact, the older children were doing some acting out even before the accident, behavior that the parents attributed to the disruption of the divorce and remarriage. Whatever the reasons were behind their interpersonal patterns, they were consistent in drawing the closeness or distance each needed.

The father's accident probably disrupted those patterns and redirected the family focus inward, forcing a kind of "homeostatic" adjustment that blocked development. It also affected the behaviors supporting the individual functions. The father was pushed into a position of closeness, first because he needed physical care, then because he became the primary caregiver. His new, harsh behavior likely served to keep the children at a distance. Similarly, the various child "misbehaviors" may have been maladaptive attempts to achieve their preferred degree of closeness or distance.

For example, the oldest son kept breaking his curfews. The consequence was that he would be grounded. This pattern not only served to aggravate the father, but also contributed to the "stuckness" of both the son and the family. This sensitive 13-year-old experienced the normal discomfort in his peer society, and his intimacy needs left him particularly vulnerable in that group. Breaking curfew and getting grounded freed him from having to deal with that culture and allowed him to stay close to his father. Thus, what seemed to be defiance was, in fact, an attempt to stay close and avoid the discomfort of the peer society. Ambivalence about who one is, how one can be oneself in the family and in the world, is what drove the behaviors of father and son, not mutual hate. These interpersonal style preferences will become even more significant when change technologies are introduced. Reframes can stress this reinterpretation, as well as point out the similarities between father and son.

Developmental theory generates a rich variety of hypotheses to be tested through reframes, while emphasizing the internal understandings of experience. As hypotheses receive support, this information can be used to revise the family's theme. For example, the father's relational self-definition is determined by commitment to social institutions such as work and family. His self-evaluation, as well as the understanding of his experience, is based on success within those contexts; the positive regard from those contexts become the supportive medium for his very existence, as he defines it. Paradoxically, autonomy is a central focus in his means of self-definition. It is likely that he sees the son's acting out as evidence of his (the father's) failure as a family leader. The related emotion will likely be anger at the son, primarily because the son's behavior threatens the father's self-esteem. Thus, his self-protective response is to distance himself from the son while trying to control him. This is further complicated by his job loss. To the extent to which his self-definition was invested in his career (and for many men, this is *the* central focus of self-definition), he is going to feel he is out of control. The drinking may well be self-medication for the resultant depression—his experience of having lost himself. Following a developmental projection, the challenge is to revise the father's self-understanding to emphasize his familial relational commitments, but in ways that acknowledge his need for distance. He is not only a worker and a father whose children are successful, rather he is a person who works—and relates to others. His understanding of the loss of autonomy needs to be revised in terms that are meaningful to him, as well as to his family. The risk is that he will remain stuck, or regress to a position where he defines himself in terms of the kind of care others provide for him. In this stance, he sees himself as worthwhile only to the extent to which others are willing to "put out" for him. He has given up on his own potential for autonomy.

The son, on the other hand, may be at a transition point between stages. In the former stage, self-understanding and evaluation are understood in terms of the roles he plays, while the implicit rules regulate interpersonal relationships. He is a son, a student, and a brother. In the emerging stage, the capacity for friendship is the central focus of his understanding of himself and his experience—he *is* his relationships. The movement is from a position of a differentiation defined by roles to one permitting interpersonal dependence and vulnerability. However, this youngster lost his mother at age 6, so this movement is complicated by residual ambivalence; just as he was becoming capable of increasing self-regulation, leaving to go to school, she left him. His father is already injured. What might happen were he to shift his loyalties or attentions to pleasing a peer culture? How might he be hurt if he depends on others? Furthermore, his relational needs lean toward an emphasis on closeness, a position not supported by cultural definitions of maleness. Like his father, his developmental push is toward a greater emphasis on relationship, and he risks getting stuck where he is, or regressing to dependency restricted to the immediate family, or moderating his anxiety through the use of alcohol or drugs. His anxiety needs to be acknowledged by someone in his family while he is confidently supported in moving on.

Space does not permit working this example through completely, nor does it permit discussion of how transference and countertransference issues might affect the system. But we hope the example makes more concrete some of the abstractions we have discussed. The therapist enters the system to create an alternative theme capable of supporting nondefensive interpersonal processes. That theme must be developed in reframes for each family member, based on his or her interpersonal style and subjective experience of the family, which, in turn, is heavily influenced by developmental level. Then, specific technical adjustments consistent with the significant baseline needs of family members can be worked out.

GENERAL RECOMMENDATIONS FOR THERAPISTS

A developmental family systems perspective calls for a particular set of clinical foci and techniques. Merely to call for "family therapy" is not enough. The therapist enters, temporarily, the system of each family in treatment, and thus becomes part of the developmental process of that family at that point in time. Some significant ways in which that process potential can be used include:

1. Organization of a theme and related processes that provide structure alternative to that imposed by a pathological theme and its related processes.
2. Selection of change techniques appropriate to each family in its particular circumstances and characteristics as seen from both a sociological and phenomenological perspective.
3. Anticipation of future developmental needs of each particular family, since clinical intervention at this time is only part of a process, with a history and a future.

To do this efficiently, we suggest the perspective of the family therapist must be informed by:

1. A developmental/phenomenological flavor that places the family's "reality" (cultural, etc.) at the forefront.
2. An assessment that includes, but is not biased toward, individual-level phenomena (e.g., processing distortions, developmental characteristics of attributions), but places this in a framework placing heavy emphasis on interpersonal processes (which can be defined by a circumplex model, or a systemic model based on interpersonal processes); and an awareness of the developmental variations among family members.
3. An assessment of the developmental trajectories for both individuals and the family system as a whole.
4. Sensitivity to the relational process with the therapist, since she or he represents, especially "phenomenologically," something very important to each family member. This is a two-way street, therefore, it has the potential for eliciting all kinds of "countertransference" issues for the therapist.

In this context, therapeutic techniques such as reframing, behavioral programs, communication training, and parent training can be used. Whether or not the addition of developmental perspectives improves our ability to help families remains a question for research and a sense of accountability on the part of therapists.

REFERENCES

Alexander, J., Holtzworth-Monroe, A., and Jameson, P. (in press). Research on the process and outcome of marriage and family therapy. In A. E. Bergin & S. L. Garfield (Eds), *Handbook of psychotherapy and behavior change.* New York: Wiley.

Alexander, J. F., & Parsons, B. V. (1982). *Functional family therapy.* Monterey, CA: Brooks/Cole.

Altman, I. & Rogoff, B. (1987). World views in psychology: Trait, interactional, organismic, and transactional perspectives. In D. Stokols & I. Altman, *Handbook of environmental psychology.* New York: Wiley

Arias, I., & Pape, K. (in press). In L. L'Abate (Ed.), *Handbook of developmental family psychology and psychopathology.* New York: Wiley.

Benjamin, L. S. (1977). Structural analysis of a family in therapy. *Journal of Counseling and Clinical Psychology, 45,* 391–406.

Bronfenbrenner, U. (1977). Toward an experimental ecology of human development. *American Psychologist,* 513–530

Cohn, J. F., Cambell, S. B., Matias, R., & Hopkins, J. (1991). Face-to-face interactions of postpartum depressed and nondepressed mother-infant pairs at 2 months. *Developmental Psychology, 26,* 15–23.

Combrinck-Graham, L. (1985). A developmental model for family systems. *Family Process, 24,* 139–150.

Coyne, J., Kessler, R., Tal, M., Turnbull, J., Wortman, C., & Greden, J. (1987). Living with a depressed person. *Journal of Consulting and Clinical Psychology, 55,* 347–352.

Field, T., Sandburg, D., Garcia, R., Vega-Lahr, N., Goldstein, S., & Guy, L. (1985). Prenatal problems, postpartum depression, and early mother-infant interactions. *Developmental Psychology, 12,* 1152–1156.

Fogel, A. (1993). *Developing through relationships: Communication, self, and culture in early infancy.* New York: Harvester Wheatsheaf.

Ford, D. H., & Lerner, R. M. (1992). *Developmental systems theory.* Newbury Park, CA: Sage.

Gelfand, D., & Teti, D. (1990). The effects of maternal depression on children. *Clinical Psychology Review, 10,* 329–353.

Gottman, J. M. (1979). *Marital interaction.* New York: Basic Books.

Hammen, C., Burge, D., & Stansbury, K. (1990). Relationship of mother and child variables in a high risk sample: A causal modeling analysis. *Developmental Psychology, 26,* 24–30.

Kegan, R. (1982). *The evolving self: Problem and process in human development.* Cambridge, MA: Harvard University Press.

Kreppner, K. (1990). Linking infant development-in-context research to the investigation of life-span family development. In K. Kreppner & R. Lerner (Eds.), *Family systems and life-span development.* Hillsdale, NJ: Erlbaum.

L'Abate, L. (in press). What is developmental family psychology? In L. L'Abate (Ed.), *Handbook of developmental family psychology and psychopathology.* New York: Wiley.

L'Abate, L., Ganahl, G., & Hansen, J. C. (1986). *Methods of family therapy.* Englewood Cliffs, NJ: Prentice-Hall.

Laing, R. D. (1972). *Politics of the family.* New York: Vintage.

Leary, T. (1957). *Interpersonal diagnosis of personality.* New York: Ronald Press.

Lyons-Ruth, K., Connell, D. B., Grunebaum, H., & Botein, S. (1990). Infants at social risk: Maternal depression and family support services as mediators of infant development and security of attachment. *Child Development, 61,* 85–98.

Montalvo, B., & Gutierrez, M. (1983). A perspective for the use of the cultural dimension in family therapy. In J. Hansen & C. Falicov (Eds.), *Cultural perspectives in family therapy* (pp. 15–32). Gaithersberg, MD: Aspen.

Morris, S. B., Alexander, J. F., & Waldron, H. (1988). Functional family therapy: Issues in clinical practice. In I. A. H. Falloon (Ed.), *Handbook of behavioral family therapy.* New York: Guilford.

Olson, D., & Lavee, Y. (1989). Family systems and family stress: A family life cycle perspective. In K. Kreppner & R. Lerner (Eds.), *Family systems and life-span development* (pp. 145–196). Hillsdale, NJ: Erlbaum.

Parsons, T., & Bales, R. F. (1955). *Family socialization and interaction process.* Glencoe, IL: Free Press.

Radke-Yarrow, M., Belmont, B., Nottlelmann, E., & Bottomly, L. (1992). Young children's self-conceptions: Origins in the natural discourse of depressed and normal mothers and their children. In D. Cicchetti & M. Beeghly (Eds.), *The self in transition.* Chicago: University of Chicago Press.

Reiss, D. (1981). *The family's construction of reality.* Cambridge, MA: Harvard University Press.

Reiss, D., Plomin, R., & Hetherington, E. M. (1991). Genetics and psychiatry: An unheralded window on the environment. *American Journal of Psychiatry, 148,* 283–291.

Speer, D. (1970). Family systems: Morphostasis and morphogenesis, or "Is homeostasis enough?" *Family Process, 9,* 259–277.

Sroufe, L. A. (1989). Pathways to adaptation and maladaptation: Psychopathology as developmental deviation. In D. Cicchetti (Ed.), *The emergence of a discipline: Rochester symposium on developmental psychopathology* (Vol. 1, pp. 13–40). Hillsdale, NJ: Erlbaum.

Tolstoy, L. (1876). *Anna Karenina.*

Tronick, E., & Gianino, A. (1986). The transmission of maternal disturbance to the infant. In E. Tronick & T. Field (Eds.), *Maternal depression and infant disturbance.* San Francisco: Jossey-Bass.

Walsh, F. (1983). Normal family ideologies: Myths and realities. In J. Hansen & C. Falicov (Eds.), *Cultural perspectives in family therapy* (pp. 1–14). Gaithersberg, MD: Aspen.

Zigler, E. (1989). Forward. In D. Cicchetti (Ed.), *The emergence of a discipline: Rochester symposium on developmental psychopathology,* (Vol. 1, pp. ix–xi). Hillsdale, NJ: Erlbaum.

Conclusion

CHAPTER 20

Looking to the Future

Diversity in Family Experience and Developmental Paths

ANN C. CROUTER and BRENDA SEERY

As the chapters in this book illustrate, the field of developmental family psychology encompasses a broad domain of study and draws from several disciplines and perspectives. At its most ambitious, this framework attempts to integrate life span developmental psychology, with its emphasis on the developing individual as an active producer of his or her own development, with perspectives from family studies and close relationships that emphasize the dynamic nature of interpersonal relationships. In order to make the field coherent and widely understood and recognized, scholars in this area must identify the most promising issues before them, issues that, if explored creatively, will define this emergent framework. Development of individuals and relationships across time, social and historical contexts as influences on development, and intrafamilial variability in the experience and perception of family life are recurrent themes in contemporary developmental research that deserve greater attention by developmental family researchers. We focus on these three issues in the belief that they represent the promise of developmental family psychology.

Farber's (1961) depiction of the family as "a set of mutually contingent careers" is a useful starting point. The choice of the word "career" infuses the notion of family with a temporal dimension. Because individuals change over time, family relationships must be examined from a temporal perspective. The term "mutually contingent" indicates that the developmental trajectories of family members are interrelated and, to some extent, interdependent. In studies of both marital (Gottman, 1979; Jacobson & Margolin, 1979) and parent–child relationships (Patterson, 1982, 1988), researchers have persuasively documented that, through interaction, individuals in a family develop a relationship history that, in turn, influences how they will treat one another in the future. Family members also come to share certain expectations about family roles (Peplau, 1983; Turner, 1970). These expectations do not evolve in a vacuum, but they are shaped, in part, by the prevailing attitudes and norms in society at large, which are themselves dynamic. Thus, in a time of rapid social change, family members are forced to reconsider, and, sometimes, to renegotiate family roles.

In so doing, family relationships develop and change. Thus, it is difficult, if not impossible, to understand the developmental course of family relations without reference to changing social and historical circumstances.

Interrelatedness, however, need not imply congruity. By emphasizing that families are composed of individuals, each of whom has embarked on developmental career or journey, Farber avoids the tendency to refer to the family as a "unitary family . . . anthropomorphically treated as if it were a single actor with a single class position, standard of living, and set of interests" (Ferree, 1990, p. 867). Farber's depiction of the family leaves open the possibility that, within a family, individuals may have quite different—even competing—perspectives and interests (Ferree, 1990; Hartmann, 1981). Gender, age, and generational station are often associated with these intrafamilial differences because they are linked to access to resources. The combination of common history, closeness, interrelatedness, and divergent perspectives and interests gives family relationships a unique emotional power that sets families apart from other social institutions.

Developmental family psychology as a domain of study is made particularly complex by the fact that it is concerned with at least two levels of analysis: 1) the development of individuals as they are influenced by close relationships; and, 2) the development of those close relationships themselves. Research at either of these levels is germane to this evolving field. Research at both levels, however, would be considerably improved by greater attention to the three themes implicit in Farber's brief definition of the family: time, social and historical context, and the diversity of experiences and perspectives of individuals within the same family.

TIME: A CENTRAL DIMENSION IN DEVELOPMENTAL STUDIES

In recent years, scholars in the fields of developmental psychology and family studies have become increasingly critical of cross-sectional research that attempts to address the issue of individual or family change. The major criticism leveled against cross-sectional research is that it confounds cohort and age effects. In the field of cognitive psychology, for example, longitudinal research by Schaie and his colleagues (Schaie, 1965; Schaie, Labouvie, & Buech, 1973; Schaie & Strother, 1968) has cast doubt on previous cross-sectional findings pointing to a "decline" in cognitive functioning from early to middle and late adulthood. Longitudinal research has revealed that these age differences do not reflect a true decline, but rather, result from historical changes in educational attainment across birth cohorts, findings that underscore the importance of following individuals across time.

Even careful longitudinal research faces methodological challenges. Whereas cross-sectional research confounds cohort and age effects, longitudinal research confounds age and time effects. Most longitudinal studies follow one cohort across time. Such studies map patterns of change or constancy, but often fail to explain the underlying processes of development. We are left wondering whether the observed changes are the result of age-related factors or of historical events that influenced subjects. To understand the processes underlying patterns of individual and family change, it is important to distinguish between age, cohort, and time effects.

Schaie & Strother (1968) have proposed a general developmental model that involves a series of sequential designs to deal with the inherent confounding problems of cross-sectional and longitudinal designs. By combining features of cross-sectional and longitudinal designs, it is possible to partition out the relative contributions of age, cohort, and time. Although these sequential designs have been most frequently used in life span research on cognitive functioning (see Schaie, 1965; Schaie, Labouvie, & Buech, 1973; Schaie & Strother, 1968), they certainly are appropriate for research in the field of developmental family psychology.

Schaie's (1965) three sequential designs are cohort-sequential, cross-sequential, and time-sequential (see Fig. 20.1). Whereas cohort-sequential and cross-

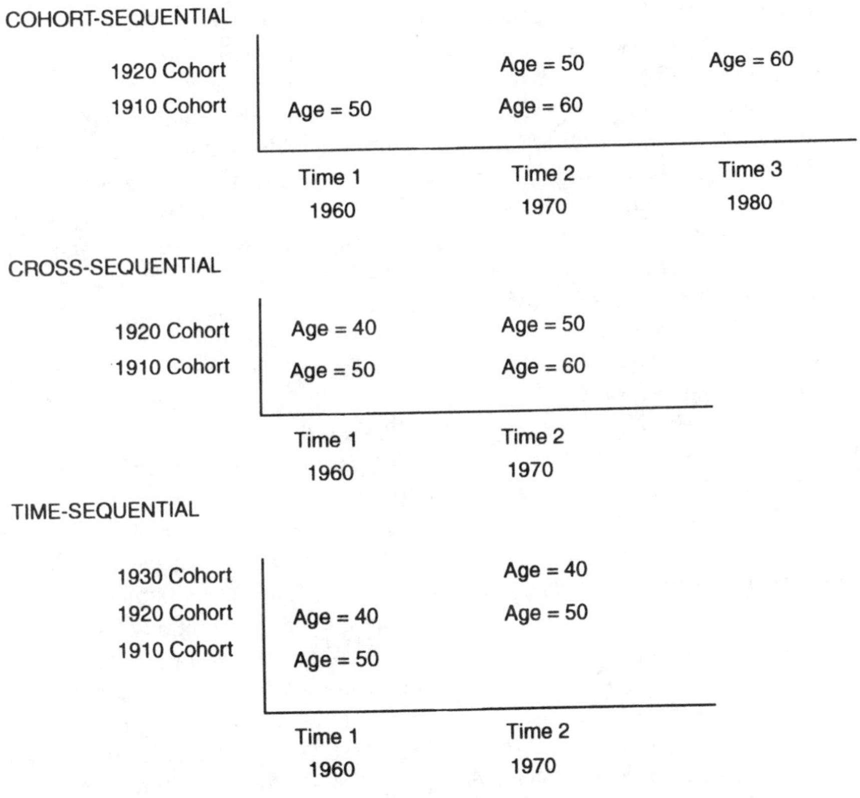

COHORT-SEQUENTIAL

	Time 1 1960	Time 2 1970	Time 3 1980
1920 Cohort		Age = 50	Age = 60
1910 Cohort	Age = 50	Age = 60	

CROSS-SEQUENTIAL

	Time 1 1960	Time 2 1970
1920 Cohort	Age = 40	Age = 50
1910 Cohort	Age = 50	Age = 60

TIME-SEQUENTIAL

	Time 1 1960	Time 2 1970
1930 Cohort		Age = 40
1920 Cohort	Age = 40	Age = 50
1910 Cohort	Age = 50	

Figure 20.1. Sequential Designs

sequential designs are employed with either dependent or independent samples at each time of measurement, the time-sequential design requires independent samples. The cohort-sequential design disentangles cohort and age effects and assumes that secular trends, or time of measurement effects, either are not important or do not exist. As such, it is an important design in studies of older adults. In its simplest form, this design measures two cohorts at the same ages at three different points in time. The cross-sequential design distinguishes cohort and time of measurement effects, and assumes age effects are constant or insignificant. Hence, it is particularly appropriate in studies of young and middle adulthood. In its most basic form, the cross-sequential design compares two cohorts at two measurement times, and, therefore, it involves three ages. Finally, the time-sequential model teases apart age and time of measurement effects, while assuming cohort effects are unimportant or not present. Schaie (1965) suggests that it is more suitable for studies of children. Again in its simplest form, the time-sequential design tests independent samples of two different age groups at two times of measurement, and, therefore, it involves a minimum of three cohorts.

These sequential designs are not without limitations, particularly with regard to the understanding of historical/social effects. Elder and Caspi (1990) have argued that, although these sequential models allow for the teasing apart of age, cohort, and period effects, the meaning of historical effects—cohort or period—remains ambiguous, with the exact nature of historical influences left to speculation. Furthermore, sequential designs ignore intracohort variability in the experience of historical change. For example, Elder and Caspi noted that Americans in the same cohort were not uniformly affected by the economic hardship of the Great Depression or World War II. In addition, analytic approaches to longitudinal data often focus on central tendencies of either change or constancy, an approach that masks the diversity of individual and family developmental trajectories. A promising direction involves combining sequential designs with approaches that identify developmental pathways and explore their antecedents and consequences. Examples of approaches that focus on these issues come from several fields.

Cognitive psychologists interested in individual differences in learning have become increasingly interested in *variability* in individuals' learning curves (Nesselroade, 1990). One approach to mapping variation in individual learning patterns has involved decomposing individuals' repeated scores on a given measure into two components: 1) intraindividual change patterns; and 2) clusters of change patterns representing interindividual differences or similarities in developmental trajectories. Although this technique has been more widely used in cognitive psychology (see Nesselroade, 1990, for a discussion), it is gaining acceptance in other areas of developmental psychology and family studies.

Belsky and Rovine (1990) used this general approach to describe patterns of marital change across the transition to parenthood. Using data collected at four points in time—the last trimester of pregnancy, and when children were 3, 9, and 36 months old—Belsky and Rovine noted an overall decline in marital quality for husbands and wives across the 3-year period. This central tendency, however, masked variability in marital change patterns. Further analyses revealed four distinct trajectories of marital change for wives and husbands: accelerating decline, linear decline, no change, and modest positive increase. Furthermore, these patterns of decline or increase in marital satisfaction were successfully predicted using prenatal information about spouses' backgrounds, personalities, and the quality of the marital relationship; indices of infant temperament at 3 and 9 months postpartum; and the accumulation of life events and income changes experienced during this 3-year period. Multiple variables were necessary to determine patterns of marital change. Although information about the prenatal period was sufficient to predict fathers' patterns of marital change, data on children's temperament at 3 months were necessary to correctly classify *mothers'* patterns.

In an example from yet another domain of research, Gustafson and Magnusson (1991) have used pattern analysis to describe the diversity of academic and occupational "developmental streams" in a sample of Swedish girls, as they moved from early adolescence (age 13), to middle adolescence (age 16), and into early adulthood (age 26). The pattern analysis approach involved constructing a single "variable pattern or profile" from a number of related variables (i.e., academic achievement as adolescents or occupational attainment as adults) for each subject at each point in time. These individual profiles were then aggregated into academic or occupational pattern subgroups, separately at each point in time. Movement of subjects in the same pattern subgroup at one age into several different pattern subgroups at another age indicated different developmental paths. Gustafson and Magnusson mapped 14 statistically significant "developmental streams," which reflected both change and constancy in adolescent girls' academic achievement from early to middle adolescence. For example, girls in the pattern subgroup characterized at age 13 by high intelligence, high achievement, high self-perceived academic ability, and high school adaptation were conspicuously overrepresented in the subgroup characterized by the same qualities as 16-year-olds. For the subgroup of girls characterized by high intelligence, high achievement, and moderately low school adaptation at age 13, however, *two* patterns of overrepresentation emerged by age 16: school adaptation dropped noticeably for some girls, while it increased considerably for others.

The emphasis on longitudinal patterns or pathways can also be applied to research on several generations. Furstenberg, Brooks-Gunn, and Morgan (1987) have described the separate and interwoven life courses of predominantly African American adolescent mothers and their children in a longitudinal study that spanned 17 years. Considerable diversity in mothers' and children's life course trajectories was found. Moreover, certain aspects of mothers' unfolding life courses—their economic, marital, educational, and fertility status—were associated with various child outcomes. For instance, mothers' lower economic status (i.e., welfare recipient), both as children themselves and during the first 5 years of their children's lives, was related to children's lower academic performance as preschoolers. In addition, mothers' lower economic status during their children's elementary and high school years was related to children's poorer academic achievement as adolescents. While mothers' welfare experience, both as children themselves and during the first 5 years of their children's lives, was associated with children's problem behavior as preschoolers, no relationship was found between mothers' lower economic status during children's elementary and high school years and problem behaviors during adolescence. In a different pattern of association, mothers' marital and educational status during the early years of children's lives were not associated with children's preschool academic and psychological outcomes. By children's adolescence, however, mothers' marital status and educational attainment were linked to children's high school standing, but not to behavioral and psychological outcomes.

Once two or more generations are included in longitudinal research, the issue of intergenerational transmission (for example, of values, parenting skills, or problems) and its underlying processes cannot be ignored. Caspi and Elder (1988) have explored the intergenerational transmission of problem behavior and conflictual family relationships across four generations of women. Using data from the Berkeley Guidance Study, they found that difficult or unstable personality characteristics were associated with marital difficulties and poor parenting practices. Additional analyses indicated that the causal process between unstable personalities and poor family relationships was unidirectional, from personality to relationships. Furthermore, across the four generations, unstable personalities, marital conflict, and nonoptimal parenting were significantly related to problem behaviors and unstable personalities of children in the subsequent generation. These children, in turn, created family environments characterized by marital conflict and arbitrary parenting.

Attention to longitudinal patterns can also reveal intriguing examples of discontinuity. Researchers interested in vulnerable populations, for example, have become increasingly interested in those characteristics of individuals or their contexts that seem to make these individuals more resilient than others facing similar challenges. Rutter and Quinton (1984), for example, conducted a longitudinal follow-up study of a sample of women from inner London who, due to difficult family circumstances, had spent their childhoods in residential children's homes. Rutter and Quinton emphasize that, despite the fact that these women had all experienced considerable hardship as children, they were surprisingly diverse in terms of psychological functioning as adults. Those women who functioned best had longitudinal pathways characterized by a "chain" of positive experiences: positive experiences in school had increased their "planfulness" with regard to marriage, which, in turn, had increased the likelihood that they would achieve a "harmonious marital relationship with a non-deviant spouse" (p. 203), which reduced the likelihood of poor social functioning in adulthood. This study exemplifies two themes we have emphasized: the value of following lives over time, and the importance of going beyond descriptions of central tendencies to delineating longitudinal pathways and patterns.

INFLUENCES OF CHANGING SOCIAL
AND HISTORICAL CONTEXTS

We have argued that longitudinal research is essential in developmental research on families. Without tracing individual or relationship trajectories over time, we cannot understand patterns of change or begin to piece together antecedents of these patterns into causal explanations. Development is played out, not only on a temporal canvas, but in a specific social and historical context that also undergoes change. Thus, attention to the role of social and historical context in the development of individuals and families is essential for scholars interested in developmental family psychology.

Scholars have thought about context in a variety of ways. Sensitized to the rich interplay of approach and avoidance behaviors in close relationships, family therapists and family systems theorists have emphasized the notion of "space" as a central dimension of individual and family experience (L'Abate, 1976). The concept of space connotes territoriality, interaction, and personal space, features of family environments that can be assessed through careful attention to nonverbal behavior. L'Abate points out that these dimensions of space vary systematically as a function of age, gender, social class, and culture. Thus, at some level, space can be thought of as an underlying feature of family ecology embedded within the social and historical context.

The focus on social and historical contexts is implicit in the concern among life span developmental psychologists with "cohort and period effects," as we have outlined above. Often, however, these effects are viewed as methodological obstacles to overcome, rather than as substantively interesting sources of variability in the process of individual and relationship development. We argue for an ecological orientation that views changing social and historical contexts as an opportunity for researchers to understand better the complexity of individual and relationship developmental processes (Bronfenbrenner, 1979, 1989; Elder, 1981).

The ecological perspective holds that development is the product of the interaction of person, process, and context (Bronfenbrenner & Crouter, 1983; Bronfenbrenner, 1989). Person characteristics include such characteristics as gender, personality, temperament, and developmental level, aspects of individuality that affect how people are treated by others, as well as how they interpret their experiences. Processes are the key activities that individuals engage in or the interactions that take place between them and the key people in their social environment. Parental involvement in joint activities, parental monitoring of children's after-school activities, children's exploratory play, sibling conflict, and the way in which husbands and wives divide housework and child care are family processes that play an important role in the socialization of children. The effects of such processes depend in part, however, on context. Important contextual dimensions include family structure, parents' occupational positions, neighborhood opportunities and constraints, the quality of key settings such as schools and daycare, and, at the broadest level, the cultural and subcultural variations revealed in comparative, cross-cultural studies. Individuals play an active role in shaping their developmental trajectories in the ways that they interpret and make sense of their experiences, and in the choices that they make about relationships, activities, and roles. A hallmark of the ecological perspective is the tenet that development cannot be understood without reference to the social contexts within which individuals are embedded.

Perhaps the most straightforward way in which the social and historical context has a direct bearing on the lives of families and family members has to do with the structuring of constraints and opportunities. For example, Elder (1974) has shown that economic deprivation during the Great Depression years often led to a decline in men's economic options and, hence, their influence inside the family. Women, however, often coped with income loss by entering the labor force or taking on income-producing activities at home, which increased their power inside the family.

Familial response to economic deprivation had important consequences for the development of children and adolescents, consequences that vary depending upon the child's gender, social class, and developmental level (Elder, 1974; Elder, 1984). Middle-class adolescent boys, for example, often fared quite well in hard times because they took on part-time jobs and household responsibilities that made important contributions to the family's welfare. Adolescent girls fared less well, however, because they were pulled into the domestic life of the family, and, thus, into the orbit of fathers, who sometimes took their anger and frustration out on them (Elder, Caspi, & Van Nguyen, 1986; Elder, Van Nguyen, & Caspi, 1985). While the life trajectories of economically deprived adolescent boys were characterized by high educational and occupational achievement, their female counterparts tended to marry early and experience somewhat constricted life options.

Flanagan's (1989) research on contemporary income loss for families in the Detroit area reveals similar themes. Focusing on families with adolescent offspring living in twelve communities hit hard by the recession of the early 1980s, Flanagan noted that income loss was related to more modest educational expectations for daughters, but not for sons. This finding is echoed in research on a large sample of German families with adolescents (Galambos & Silbereisen, 1987) in which family income loss was associated with paternal pessimism about the future for daughters, but not for sons. Thus, social and historical context, exemplified here by the income loss resulting from downturns in the economy, not only shapes contemporaneous opportunities (and constraints), but influences family members' expectations about the future, expectations which in turn may lead to certain choices (e.g., forgoing or delaying higher education). These choices, in turn, set the stage for the next set of decisions and experiences (Crouter & McHale, 1993).

The role of social and historical context is also evident in studies of "social issues," the definition of which shifts with changing social circumstances. The phenomenon of maternal employment, for example, has changed dramatically over the last five or six decades (Bronfenbrenner & Crouter, 1982; Hoffman, 1984). When the first empirical studies of the effects of maternal employment on children were conducted in the 1930s, it was relatively rare for married women with children, especially in the middle class, to work outside the home. From a methodological point of view, this represents a selection effect; the small group of mothers in that era who elected to work outside the home, for whatever reason, undoubtedly differed from the majority of mothers who were full-time homemakers on a host of psychological and social characteristics other than employment status. As mothers entered the labor force in increasing numbers across the next decades, the nature of these selection effects changed because educational and employment opportunities for women opened up, and norms and attitudes about maternal employment shifted.

The dynamic nature of social phenomena, such as maternal employment, poses a challenge to researchers interested in contextual influences. In the case of maternal employment, for example, findings with regard to the effects on children have shifted over time (Bronfenbrenner & Crouter, 1982). Contemporary research generally has not revealed the pattern of negative effects suggested by earlier studies, in large part because maternal employment is simply not the same social phenomenon today that it was 60 years ago.

Changing social norms and attitudes also have important implications for how individuals within families structure their relationships. As social, economic, and political institutions undergo change, family members are exposed to new ways of thinking, ideas that influence how they interact with one another. Married couples, for example, have been profoundly affected by changes in socially defined prescriptions for behavior. It has become increasingly acceptable, for example, for wives and mothers to work outside the home. Initially, family scholars anticipated that as women entered the paid labor force, their spouses would become more involved in household chores and childrearing. A number of studies, however, have revealed that the division of labor is still inequitable, with wives bearing the major share of the load (Berk, 1985; Pleck, 1983).

Much of the research that describes the division of labor simply reports averages or central tendencies. Ferree (1988), however, emphasized the considerable heterogeneity that exists in how couples divide housework. Her research reveals that men take on a greater share of domestic work when their wives contribute a relatively large portion of the household's income, endorse feminist attitudes, and indicate that they are willing to lower their standards for what constitutes satisfactory performance in household work (Ferree, 1988).

Other studies suggest that household tasks and child care are domains of domestic life that generate considerable marital tension, tension that may not be explicitly acknowledged or even discussed by spouses (Hochschild, 1989; Komter, 1989). There is surprisingly little explicit conflict over housework, in part because spouses, particularly husbands, tend to "emphasize the inevitability of the present situation by perceiving it as natural, necessary, and unchangeable" (Komter, p. 210). There are hints, however, that individuals are less satisfied with their marriages when their own attitudes are at odds with the status quo in their household. For example, McHale and Crouter (1992) found that husbands who performed a relatively high proportion of household tasks, yet held relatively conventional attitudes about gender roles, were less satisfied with their marriages, in comparison both to other husbands and to their own wives. Wives who held liberal attitudes about gender roles, but were shouldering the major share of housework were also dissatisfied, both in comparison to other wives and to their own husbands.

These issues become more challenging and complex when put in a temporal context because individuals' attitudes develop and change over time. The challenge for future research is to chart how attitudes develop in response to changing social and historical circumstances, and then to study how changing attitudes, in turn, influence behavior inside the family. Using the example of gender role attitudes and the division of household work, we might expect to see wives become more invested in an egalitarian division of housework, as they take on greater responsibility for providing for the family's economic needs (Ferree, 1988; Hood, 1986), a process that has yet to be mapped longitudinally. Ideally, such a study would attend, not only to attitudes and "behavioral outcomes" (e.g., actual division of labor), but would also monitor intermediate processes, such as marital conflict, negotiation, and experimentation with new role arrangements (Komter, 1989).

As the studies described above indicate, there is considerable "intracohort variability" in how individuals experience the changing social and historical context. Gender, age, and social class are structural determinants of individual reactions to contextual influences, but individual differences in temperament, personality, health, physical attractiveness, and competence must play an important role in this regard, too. Few scholars, however, have attempted to take advantage of intracohort variability in the effect of social and historical change to build a more comprehensive understanding of developmental processes.

One exception is a recent essay by Stewart and Healy (1989) in which they propose that the extent to which "cohort-defining events" make their mark on individuals is related to the extent to which those individuals are influenced by other socialization agents, including parents. Cohort-defining events are historical events that are sudden and defined enough to make their mark, usually on the adolescents and young adults in a society. Robert Wohl (1979) described the effect of World War I on the cohort of youth coming of age in Europe in his monograph aptly titled *The Generation of 1914*. In recent years, it could be argued that the Vietnam War, the Civil Rights Movement, and the Women's Movement have made their mark on young people making the transition from adolescence to adulthood.

Summarizing results of research on a sample of women, all of whom had graduated from college in 1964 (see Stewart, 1978, 1980), Stewart and Healy (1989) reported strikingly different patterns of association between mothers' employment and their daughters' work orientation, depending upon whether daughters reported having been strongly influenced by the Women's Movement. For those daughters who reported that the Women's Movement had had a major impact on them, there was virtually no relationship between their mothers' employment history and their own orientation toward employment. For those relatively unaffected by the Women's Movement, however, there was a strong, positive correlation between maternal employment history and daughters' orientations toward work. Stewart and Healy (1989) propose that "parental models are especially powerful when cohort experiences around the transition to adulthood are not very powerful for either individual or social historical reasons" (p. 40). This potentially powerful hypothesis is especially useful because it recognizes—indeed exploits—intracohort variability in the impact of historical circumstances on individuals.

WITHIN-FAMILY VARIABILITY

The central theme of this chapter is that developmental family researchers would be well served by focusing on the diversity of human experience. In our discussion of longitudinal research, we emphasized the importance of identifying developmental trajectories, an approach that reveals the diversity of paths individuals take through time. Similarly, the ever-changing social context introduces diversity, as individuals within cohorts confront contextual constraints and opportunities, and respond to changing attitudes and norms. In this third and final section, we move inside the family to focus on within-family variability in the experiences and perceptions of family members, a third promising direction for developmental family psychology.

Traditional depictions of family development referred to the family as a unit, a global entity that moves through time. Early studies of family relationships, such as the classic research by Blood and Wolfe (1960), reflected a global conceptualization of the family in their methodologies. Often data were collected from only one family member, usually the mother. The implication was that one family member could convey an accurate picture of "family life."

One of the first scholars to challenge this portrayal of the family was Bernard, who argued in *The Future of Marriage* (1972) that every marriage contains two marriages, his and hers, and that the two perspectives are often dramatically different. The theme of divergent experiences and perspectives within the family has been elaborated by contemporary feminist scholars (Ferree, 1990; Hartmann, 1981; Thompson & Walker, 1989; Thorne, 1982). In their view, referring to the family as a global unit masks the presence of power differentials, conflict, and inequality that exist between many husbands and wives. Pahl's (1980) research among working class British couples, for example, reveals that the "family budget" means something quite different to husbands and wives. Similarly, husbands and wives often have quite divergent views on such supposedly shared experiences as housework, sex, and parenting (Komter, 1989).

Few studies to date, however, have deliberately sought out multiple perspectives within the family and made an effort to understand the differences in points of view. In one study that took this approach, McHale, Crouter, and Bartko (1992) found that, although women tended to be happier than their husbands in families in which parenting and housework were divided in a more egalitarian way, the reverse was true in families with a more traditional division of labor. In this study, the discrepancy in spouses' income and work hours were significant correlates of the division of labor. The more men earned and worked relative to their wives, the less they contributed to domestic work. Indeed, discrepancies in resources and constraints proved to be stronger correlates of the division of labor than separate indices of resources and constraints for each spouse, a pattern consistent with social exchange theory (Huston & Burgess, 1979).

The parent–child relationship offers another angle on within-family variability (see Paikoff, 1991). Researchers studying adolescence, for example, have begun to focus on divergent perceptions of parents and adolescents, finding that the consequences of divergent viewpoints depend upon the substantive issue in question, as well as the characteristics of the individuals involved. Carlson, Cooper, and Spradling (1991), for example, reported that, in a sample of middle-class families with children in early adolescence, boys were more likely to experience divergent parent–child perspectives across a number of domains than were girls. Both boys and girls were more likely to diverge in viewpoint with their mothers than with their fathers. When examined in relation to adolescents' perceived competence, however, divergent father–child views in such domains as control and values were positively associated with perceived competence, whereas children reported higher perceived competence when their viewpoints converged with those of their mothers. Collins (1991) proposes that "discrepancies in perceptions may provide a stimulus for the adaptation of families to increasing physical, cognitive, and social changes in their adolescents" (p. 107). Attending to the shared and nonshared realities of adolescents and their parents will provide important insights about how parent–adolescent relationships develop. Again, such research is likely to emphasize individual differences in patterns across adolescence, consistent with our emphasis on diverse developmental pathways.

Within-family variability is a contemporary theme in research in child development as well. Interest in this issue has been stimulated by studies in behavioral genetics that have revealed how surprisingly different siblings in the same family are (Dunn & Plomin, 1990; Plomin & Daniels, 1987). Behavioral geneticists use research designs, such as adoption studies and twin studies, that capitalize on differences in genetic relatedness between siblings (or between parents and children). This body of research has shown that, for such important psychological characteristics as IQ and various dimensions of personality, as well as for various physical characteristics, such as vulnerability to disease, there is a strong genetic component, a strong "nonshared environment" component, and a surprisingly weak "shared environment" component (Dunn & Plomin). Thus, sibling similarity seems to be largely caused by genetic influences. Shared aspects of the family environment apparently contribute relatively little to individual development. The critical question then becomes, "Why are siblings in the same family so different?" (Dunn & Plomin; Plomin & Daniels).

Dunn and Plomin (1990) describe several aspects of the nonshared family environment: parental differential treatment, sibling influences, timing effects, and extrafamilial influences. We briefly touch on each to convey a flavor of this research area. First, parents may treat children differently. Even if parents are consistent in their treatment of children (e.g., equally permissive to 3-year-olds; see Dunn, Plomin, & Daniels, 1986), because of age spacing and individual differences, children may perceive that they are being treated quite differently. The perception of differential treatment is likely to be as important as differential treatment in an objective sense (McHale & Pawletko, 1992). Second, siblings influence one another. Dealing with a brother who is 3 years older is quite a different undertaking than dealing with a sister who is 3 years younger; there are two perspectives in this "shared" sibling relationship. Timing is another source of difference. Because siblings are usually of different ages, they experience family events, such as moves, divorce, parental illness, and mother's entry into the labor force, at different developmental points with quite different developmental effects (Hoffman, 1991). Finally, siblings are exposed to experiences outside the family that contribute to the development of differences. Two children in the same family may have quite different experiences in their peer groups, at school, in extracurricular activities, and with members of their extended family—experiences that contribute to sibling differences.

Many traditional topics in developmental psychology promise to be transformed by a more complete appraisal of the experiences and perspectives of multiple family members. Take, for example, research on parenting styles. Developmental researchers have identified three patterns of parental behavior that are associated with differential behavior patterns or psychological outcomes in children: authoritarian, permissive, and authoritative (Baumrind, 1967, 1971; Dornbusch, Ritter, Leiderman, Roberts, & Fraleigh, 1987). These associations between parenting styles and child outcomes are usually discussed in terms of "parent effects." A within-family approach with a focus on two siblings might reveal a quite different picture. Such a study might indicate that parenting style is not a traitlike phenomenon exhibited in all situations with all children. Indeed, some parents might treat two siblings quite differently. Data from two siblings would enable researchers to explore the possibility of "child effects," individual differences in children that might elicit different parenting responses in their mothers and fathers, as well as to compare the contributions of objectively experienced similarities and differences in sibling–parent interaction versus the effects of siblings' separate social constructions of reality.

In summary, virtually any topic in this handbook would benefit from new studies that exploit the multiple perspectives and experiences of members of the same family. They promise to make us rethink traditional notions about the family as a unit, to reconsider ingrained assumptions about causal directionality, and to pay more attention to the ways in which individuals construct their own understanding of their experience.

DISCUSSION

Over a decade ago, Elder (1981) noted that new historical research on families had "produced a greater sense of complexity and differentiation in the course of social change" (p. 489). In the same spirit, we believe that research in the field of developmental family psychology would benefit from research approaches that focus on, and, indeed, exploit diversity in family experience and perspectives as family members' "careers" take shape over time.

The themes we have emphasized in this chapter all point to the importance of going beyond "central tendencies" to consider variability in the experiences of individuals as family members. As we have shown, a number of contemporary longitudinal studies focus on identifying the antecedents and consequences of various developmental pathways. Similarly, an exciting direction for research on the impact of social and historical contexts involves recognizing that social change does not affect individuals within a cohort uniformly; a focus on intracohort variability in contextual effects offers the opportunity for generating new hypotheses that will strengthen the theoretical underpinnings of developmental family psychology. Finally, it is clear that families are composed of individuals with different resources and needs, who construct and interpret even "shared" experiences quite differently. Research that takes advantage of the diverse perspectives of individuals within the same family promises to make us rethink many traditional topics in developmental family psychology.

The three foci we have outlined represent promising directions for the field. Researchers will not realize the potential of these approaches, however, unless they apply them to samples that are far more heterogeneous than the white, middle-class, two-parent families that have been the focus of so much research to date. Hagen, Paul, Gibb, and Wolters (1990) randomly sampled articles published in *Child Development* over the past 50 years and found that, of those studies that even bothered to describe the demographic characteristics of the children in the sample, most were white, middle-class, school-aged, and American; most of the articles, however, failed to report the race or socioeconomic status of the children, an omission that reveals how frequently we fail to place the individuals and families that we study into any sociocultural context.

Other scholars (Harrison, Wilson, Pine, Chan, & Buriel, 1990; McLoyd, 1990; Spencer, 1990) have noted that conceptual models and empirical studies of "normative" child development often have excluded minority children from their samples. When minority children and youth have been included in comparative studies they are often cast as "deviant" or "deficient." These charges are strikingly similar to those leveled by Gilligan (1982) about women's position in "normative" models of adult development. In two recent *Child Development* review articles (Harrison et al.; McLoyd), the authors emphasized the varied contextual ecologies—family, economic, neighborhood—in which minority children develop, as compared to majority children. By emphasizing the contextual conditions associated with race and ethnicity, Harrison et al. and McLoyd cautioned researchers against attributing racial and ethnic differences to essential, stable characteristics of these groups, instead urging researchers to explore the contextual, cultural, and historical differences that most likely account for these racial and ethnic variations. Certainly, the same approach is necessary when researchers ponder gender differences in developmental processes and outcomes.

The importance of studying individuals and families from different class and ethnic backgrounds goes beyond fashionable notions of what is "politically correct" and beyond pragmatic concerns over the generalizability of research findings. In overlooking variability in the "ecology of human development" we run the risk of defining our field in such narrow terms that our research enterprise becomes narrow and uninformative. Consider the possibility, for example, that family processes may have quite different impacts on individuals and families from different ethnic, socioeconomic, and familial backgrounds. In a study of an ethnically diverse sample of high school students (Asian American, African American, Hispanic American, and anglo-American), for example, Dornbusch et al. (1987) explored the relationship between mothers' and fathers' parenting styles (authoritarian, permissive, and authoritative) and adolescents' academic performance. Although, generally, authoritarian and permissive parenting styles were associated with poorer academic achievement and authoritative parenting was linked to higher school performance, important ethnic and gender group variations in this pattern emerged. For Asian Americans, the correlations between authoritative and permissive parenting styles and academic performance were near zero. In the case of Hispanic Americans, the hypothesized negative association between authoritarian parenting and academic performance was found for girls, but not for boys. These ethnic group and gender variations illustrate the limitations of a universalistic approach to the study of family relationships, and underscore the importance of studying families from more diverse sociocultural backgrounds.

The directions that we have outlined in this chapter set an ambitious agenda for the field of developmental family psychology. No one study can do it all. We suspect, however, that, in conducting longitudinal family research on more heterogeneous samples, researchers will naturally begin to consider variability in the effects of social contexts, as well as the diversity of viewpoints within the same family. Thus, we would urge family researchers to study family relationships over time. Embarking upon even a modest, short-term longitudinal study provides a powerful lesson in the importance of coming to terms with the diversity of human experience.

REFERENCES

Baumrind, D. (1967). Child care practices anteceding three patterns of preschool behavior. *Genetic Psychology Monographs, 75*, 43–88.

Baumrind, D. (1971). Current patterns of parental authority. *Developmental Psychology Monographs, 4*(1, Pt.2).

Belsky, J., & Rovine, M. (1990). Patterns of marital change across the transition to parenthood: Pregnancy to three years postpartum. *Journal of Marriage and the Family, 52*, 5–19.

Berk, S. F. (1985). *The gender factory: The apportionment of work in American households.* New York: Plenum.

Bernard, J. (1972). *The future of marriage.* New York: World.

Blood, R. O., Jr., & Wolfe, D. M. (1960). *Husbands and wives.* New York: Free Press.

Bronfenbrenner, U. (1979). *The ecology of human development: Experiments by nature and design.* Cambridge, MA: Harvard University Press.

Bronfenbrenner, U. (1989). Ecology systems theory. In G. J. Whitehurst (Ed.), *Annals of child development* (Vol. 6, pp. 185–246). Greenwich CT: JAI.

Bronfenbrenner, U., & Crouter, A. C. (1982). Work and family through time and space. In S. Kamerman & C. Hayes (Eds.), *Families that work: Children in a changing world.* Washington, DC: National Academy Press.

Bronfenbrenner, U., & Crouter, A. C. (1983). The evolution of environmental models in developmental research. In P. Mussen (Ed.), *Handbook of child psychology.* New York: Wiley.

Carlson, C. I., Cooper, C. R., & Spradling, V. Y. (1991). Developmental implications of shared versus distinct perceptions of the family in early adolescence. In R. L. Paikoff (Ed.), *Shared views in the family during adolescence.* San Francisco: Jossey-Bass.

Caspi, A., & Elder, G. H., Jr. (1988). Emergent family patterns: The intergenerational construction of problem behaviour and relationships. In R. A. Hinde & J. Stevenson-Hinde (Eds.), *Relationships within families: Mutual influences* (pp. 218–240). Oxford, UK: Clarendon Press.

Collins, W. A. (1991). Shared views and parent–adolescent relationships. In R. L. Paikoff (Ed.), *Shared views in the family in adolescence.* San Francisco: Jossey-Bass.

Crouter, A. C., & McHale, S. M. (1993). Familial economic circumstances: Implications for adjustment and development in early adolescence. In R. M. Lerner (Ed.), *Early adolescence: Perspectives on research, policy, and intervention.* Hillsdale, NJ: Erlbaum.

Dornbusch, S. M., Ritter, R. L., Leiderman, P. H., Roberts, D. F., & Fraleigh, M. J. (1987). The relation of parenting style to adolescent school performance. *Child Development, 58,* 1244–1257.

Dunn, J., & Plomin, R. (1990). *Separate lives: Why siblings are so different.* New York: Basic Books.

Dunn, J. F., Plomin, R., & Daniels, D. (1986). Consistency and change in mothers' behavior toward young siblings. *Child Development, 37,* 348–356.

Elder, G. H., Jr. (1974). *Children of the great depression.* Chicago: University of Chicago Press.

Elder, G. H., Jr. (1981). History and the family: The discovery of complexity. *Journal of Marriage and the Family, 43,* 489–519.

Elder, G. H., Jr. (1984). Families, kin, and the life course: A sociological perspective. In R. D. Parke (Ed.), *The family: Review of child development research* (Vol. 7, pp. 80–135). Chicago: University of Chicago Press.

Elder, G. H., Jr., & Caspi, A. (1990). Studying lives in a changing society: Sociological and personological explanations. In A. I. Rabin, R. A. Zucker, R. A. Emmons, & S. Frank (Eds.), *Studying persons and lives* (pp. 201–247). New York: Springer.

Elder, G. H., Jr., Caspi, A., & Van Nguyen, T. (1986). Resourceful and vulnerable children: Family influences in hard times. In R. Silbereisen & R. H. Eyferth (Eds.), *Development as action in context: Problem behavior and normal youth development* (pp. 167–186). New York: Springer.

Elder, G. H., Van Ngugen, T., & Caspi, A. (1985). Linking family hardship to children's lives. *Child Development, 56,* 361–375.

Farber, B. (1961). The family as a set of mutually contingent careers. In N. N. Foote (Ed.), *Household decision-making.* New York: New York University Press.

Ferree, M. M. (1988). *Negotiating household roles and responsibilities: Resistance, conflict, and change.* Paper presented at the annual meeting of the National Council on Family Relations, Philadelphia.

Ferree, M. M. (1990). Beyond separate spheres: Feminism and family research. *Journal of Marriage and the Family, 52,* 866–884.

Flanagan, C. (1989). Economic stress in the family: Do the effects for daughters and sons differ? Paper presented at the biennial meeting of the Society for Research on Child Development, Kansas City, MO.

Furstenberg, J. F., Jr., Brooks-Gunn, J., & Morgan, S. P. (1987). *Adolescent mothers in later life.* New York: Cambridge University Press.

Galambos, N., & Silbereisen, R. (1987). Income change, parental outlook, and adolescent expectations for job success. *Journal of Marriage and the Family, 49,* 141–149.

Gilligan, C. (1982). *In a different voice.* Cambridge, MA: Harvard University Press.

Gottman, J. M. (1979). *Marital interaction: Experimental investigations.* New York: Academic.

Gustafson, S. B., & Magnusson, D. (1991). *Female life careers: A pattern approach.* Hillsdale, NJ: Erlbaum.

Hagen, J. W., Paul, B., Gibb, S., & Wolters, C. (1990, March). Trends in research on children as reflected by publications in *Child Development:* 1930–1989. Paper presented at the biennial meeting of the Society for Research on Adolescence, Atlanta, GA.

Harrison, A. O., Wilson, M. N., Pine, C. J., Chan, S. Q., & Buriel, R. (1990). Family ecologies of ethnic minority children. *Child Development, 61,* 347–362.

Hartmann, H. (1981). The family as the locus of gender, class, and political struggle: The example of housework. *Signs: Journal of Women and Culture in Society, 6,* 366–394.

Hochschild, A. (1989). *The second shift: Working parents and the revolution at home.* New York: Viking.

Hoffman, L. W. (1984). Work, family, and the socialization of the child. In R. D. Parke (Ed.), *Review of child development research: Vol. 7. The family.* Chicago: University of Chicago Press.

Hoffman, L. W. (1991). The influence of the family environment on personality: Accounting for sibling differences. *Psychological Bulletin, 110,* 187–203.

Hood, J. C. (1986). The provider role: Its meaning and measurement. *Journal of Marriage and the Family, 48,* 349–359.

Huston, T. L., & Burgess, R. L. (1979). Social exchange in developing relationships: An overview. In R. L. Burgess & T. L. Huston (Eds.), *Social exchange in developing relationships* (pp. 3–28). New York: Academic.

Jacobson, N. S., & Margolin, G. (1979). *Marital therapy.* New York: Brunner/Mazel.

Komter, A. (1989). Hidden power in marriage. *Gender and Society, 3,* 187–216.

L'Abate, L. (1976). *Understanding and helping the individual in the family.* New York: Grune & Stratton.

McHale, S. M., & Crouter, A. C. (1992). You can't always get what you want: Incongruence between sex role attitudes and family work roles and its implications for marriage. *Journal of Marriage and the Family, 54,* 537–547.

McHale, S. M., Crouter, A. C., & Bartko, W. T. (1992). Traditional and egalitarian patterns of parental involvement: Antecedents, consequences, and temporal rhythms. In D. Featherman, R. Lerner, & M. Perlmutter (Eds.), *Life-span and development and behavior* (Vol. II). Hillsdale, NJ: Erlbaum.

McHale, S. M., & Pawletko, T. M. (1992). Differential treatment of siblings in two family contexts. *Child Development, 63,* 68–81.

McLoyd, V. (1990). The impact of economic hardship on Black families and children: Psychological distress, parenting, and socioemotional development. *Child Development, 61,* 311–346.

Nesselroade, J. R. (1990). Adult personality development: Issues in assessing constancy and change. In A. I. Rabin, R. A. Zucker, R. A. Emmons, & S. Frank (Eds.), *Studying persons and lives* (pp. 41–85). New York: Springer.

Pahl, J. (1980). Patterns of money management within marriage. *Journal of Social Policy, 9,* 313–335.

Paikoff, R. L. (1991). *Shared views in the family during adolescence.* San Francisco: Jossey-Bass.

Patterson, G. R. (1982). *Coercive family process.* Eugene, OR: Castalia Press.

Patterson, G. R. (1988). Family process: Loops, levels, and linkages. In N. Bolger, A. Caspi, G. Downey, & M. Moorehouse (Eds.), *Persons in context: Developmental processes.* New York: Cambridge University Press.

Peplau, L. A. (1983). Roles and gender. In H. H. Kelley, E. Berscheid, A. Christensen, J. H. Harvey, T. L. Huston, G. Levinger, E. McClintock, L. A. Peplau, & D. R. Peterson (Eds.), *Close relationships.* New York: Freeman.

Pleck, J. H. (1983). *Working wives/working husbands.* Newbury Park, CA: Sage.

Plomin, R., & Daniels, D. (1987). Why are children in the same family so different from each other? *Behavioral and Brain Sciences, 10,* 1–16.

Rutter, M., & Quinton, D. (1984). Long-term follow-up of women institutionalized in childhood: Factors promoting good functioning in adult life. *British Journal of Developmental Psychology, 2,* 191–204.

Schaie, K. W. (1965). A general model for the study of developmental problems. *Psychological Bulletin, 64,* 92–107.

Schaie, K. W., Labouvie, G. V., & Buech, B. V. (1973). Generational and cohort specific difference in adult cognitive functioning: A fourteen-year study of independent samples. *Developmental Psychology, 9,* 151–166.

Schaie, K. W., & Strother, C. R. (1968). A cross-sequential study of age changes in cognitive behavior. *Psychological Bulletin, 70,* 671–680.

Spencer, M. B. (1990). Development of minority children: An introduction. *Child Development, 61,* 267–269.

Stewart, A. J. (1978). A longitudinal study of coping styles in self-defining and socially defined women. *Journal of Consulting and Clinical Psychology, 46,* 1079–1084.

Stewart, A. J. (1980). Personality and situation in the prediction of women's life patterns. *Psychology of Women Quarterly, 5,* 195–206.

Stewart, A. J., & Healy, J. M. (1989). Linking individual development and social changes. *American Psychologist, 44,* 30–42.

Thompson, L., & Walker, A. (1989). Gender in families: Women and men in marriage, work, and parenthood. *Journal of Marriage and the Family, 51,* 845–871.

Thorne, B. (1982). Feminist rethinking of the family: An overview. In B. Thorne & M. Yalom (Eds.), *Rethinking the family: Some feminist questions* (pp. 1–24). New York: Longman.

Turner, R. H. (1970). *Family interaction.* New York: Wiley.

Wohl, R. (1979). *The generation of 1914.* Cambridge, MA: Harvard University Press.

Author Index

Note. Numbers in italics indicate reference pages.

Festinger, L., 11, 14, *20*
Fetting, J., 243, 256, *260*, *263*
Fewell, R. R., 120, 121, *131*
Field, T., 402, *410*
Figley, C. R., 91, *112*
Fillmore, K. M., 357, *368*
Filsinger, E. E., 61, *89*, 228, *239*
Fincham, F. D., 60, 63, 64, 76, 77, 79, *80*, 221, *239*, 340, 342, 343, *347*
Finkelhor, D., 296, *303*, *306*, 311, 312, 314, 315, 317, 318, 319, 320 323, *327*
Finley, N. J., 207, *214*
Finney, J. W., 247, *262*, 353, *368*
Fischer, J. L., 102, *111*
Fischer, L. R., 210, 211, *214*
Fischer, M., 250, *260*, 312, *327*
Fischman, S. E., 275, *282*
Fitch, F. J., 293, *303*
Fitting, M. D., 243, 256, *262*, *263*
Fitzgerald, H. E., 351, 352, 355, 357, 359, 360, 362, 364, 366, *369*, *370*, *372*
Fitzgerald, R., 223, *239*
Flaherty, J. F., 100, *109*
Flaherty, M. J., 118, *129*
Flanagan, B., 314, *326*
Flanagan, C., 422, *431*
Flanagan, C. A., 381, *390*
Fleming, A., 68, *81*
Flitcraft, A., 295, *307*
Flomenhaft, K., 315, *328*
Floyd, F. J., 61, *81*, 226, 229, *240*
Foa, E. B., 11, 13, *20*
Foa, U. G., 11, 13, *20*
Fochtman, D., 268, *282*
Fodor, I., 246, *260*
Fogel, A. 395, *410*
Folingstad, D. R., 335, 338, *347*
Folkman, S., 72, 74, *80*
Folkrod, A. W., 122, *130*, 210, *216*
Foner, A., 106, *113*
Ford, D. H., 28, 29, 32, 33, 34, 35, 36, 38, 41, *42*, 394, *410*
Forehand, R., 332, *347*
Foster, H. H. Jr., 127, *129*
Foxman, R., 68, *81*
Fraley, M. S., 427, 429, *430*
Framo, J. L., 231, *239*
Franken, M. L., 202, *216*
Frankenstein, W., 246, *260*
Frazier, W., 295, *307*
Friedman, D. E., 164, *174*
Friedman, L. S., 245, *259*
Friedrich, W. N., 288, *303*
Frieze, I. H., 323, 325, *327*

Fritz, G. S., 312, *327*
Frodi, A., 180, *198*
Frodi, A. M., 287, *303*
Fromm, E., 163, *174*
Fuller, S., 205, *215*
Fuller, S. R., 205, *215*
Furman, W., 45, 47, *57*
Furstenberg, F., 193, *198*
Furstenberg, F. F., 45, 47, *56*, 101, *110*, 134, 146, 148, 150, *154*
Furstenberg, F. F. Jr., 117, 124, 126, *129*, 133, 146, 148, 149, 150, *153*, *154*, 210, 211, *214*, 377, 378, 383, 384, *390*, 419, *431*
Futterman, A., 206, *217*

Gabel, H., 121, *129*
Gaensbauer, R. J., 299, *305*
Gaensbauer, T., 180, *198*
Gaines, R., 287, 288, *303*, *306*
Galkowska, M., 223, *242*
Gallagher, D., 243, 245, 255, *260*
Gallagher–Thompson, D., 206, *217*
Gallambos, N., 422, *431*
Gallant, D. H., 253, *259*
Galub, H. L., 353, *369*
Gamble, W., 247, *262*
Gammon, G. D., 254, *264*
Ganahl, G., 404, *411*
Gander, A. M., 231, 232, *239*
Garbarino, J., 90, *108*, 287, *303*, 331, *347*
Garcia, R., 402, *410*
Garcia–Coll, C. T., 150, *154*
Garduque, L., 181, *198*
Garrett, B., 68, *79*
Garrett, E., 93, *109*
Gaudin, J. M., 148, *154*
Gayford, J. J., 351, 363, *369*
Gdowski, C. L., 341, *348*
Gegas, V., 90, 102, *110*
Geiss, S. K., 221, *239*
Gelfand, D. E., 119, *129*, 402, *410*
Gelinas, D. J., 312, *327*
Gelles, R. J., 187, *201*, 284, 285, 286, 287, 289, 290, 292, 294, 297, *303*, *304*, *307*
Genest, M., 353, *368*
George, C., 288, 289, *303*
George, J., 121, 127, *129*
George, L., 91, *110*
George, L. K., 46, *57*, 255, 256, *259*
Germain, R., 331, *347*
Geyer, S., 104, *109*
Giacobbe, J., 166, *174*
Gianino, A., 402, *411*

Subject Index

454